Glenda Kaufman Kantor
Jana L. Jasinski

Editors

OUT OF THE DARKNESS

Contemporary Perspectives on Family Violence

SAGE Publications
International Educational and Professional Publisher
Thousand Oaks   London   New Delhi

For information:

SAGE Publications, Inc.
2455 Teller Road
Thousand Oaks, California 91320
E-mail: order@sagepub.com

SAGE Publications Ltd.
6 Bonhill Street
London EC2A 4PU
United Kingdom

SAGE Publications India Pvt. Ltd.
M-32 Market
Greater Kailash I
New Delhi 110 048 India

Printed in the United States of America

Library of Congress Cataloging-in-Publication Data

 Out of the darkness : Contemporary research perspectives on family
 violence / edited by Glenda Kaufman Kantor, Jana L. Jasinski.
   p. cm.
  "A collection of 23 articles, a majority of which were first
 presented at the 4th International Family Violence Research
 Conference, at the University of New Hampshire in Durham, New
 Hampshire"—Introd.
  Includes bibliographical references and index.
  ISBN 0-7619-0775-0 (cloth : acid-free paper). — ISBN
 0-7619-0776-9 (pbk. : acid-free paper)
   1. Family violence—Congresses. 2. Family violence—Research-
 -Methodology—Congresses. I. Kantor, Glenda Kaufman.
 II. Jasinski, Jana. L. III. International Family Violence Research
 Conference (4th : University of New Hampshire)
 HV6626.O87 1997
 362.82'92—dc21   97-21053

Acquiring Editor:	C. Terry Hendrix
Editorial Assistant:	Dale Grenfell
Production Editor:	Sanford Robinson
Production Assistant:	Karen Wiley
Typesetter/Designer:	Danielle Dillahunt
Indexer:	Janet Perlman
Cover Designer:	Candice Harman

Contents

Introduction   vii
Glenda Kaufman Kantor and Jana L. Jasinski

PART I: THE PREVALENCE OF FAMILY VIOLENCE

1. Change in Cultural Norms Approving Marital Violence
   From 1968 to 1994   3
   Murray A. Straus, Glenda Kaufman Kantor,
   and David W. Moore

2. The Homicides of Children and Youth:
   A Developmental Perspective   17
   David Finkelhor

3. An Examination of Physical Assault and
   Childhood Victimization Histories Within a
   National Probability Sample of Women   35
   Terri L. Weaver, Dean G. Kilpatrick, Heidi S. Resnick,
   Connie L. Best, and Benjamin E. Saunders

PART II: CHILD ABUSE AND NEGLECT

4. Pandemic Outcomes: The Intimacy Variable   49
   Evvie Becker-Lausen and Sharon Mallon-Kraft

5. Pornography and the Organization of Intra- and
   Extrafamilial Child Sexual Abuse: A Conceptual Model   58
   Catherine Itzin

6. Black Mothers' Emotional and Behavioral Responses
   to the Sexual Abuse of Their Children   80
   Claudia Bernard

7. Children's Exposure to Marital Aggression:
   Direct and Mediated Effects   90
   Gayla Margolin and Richard S. John

8. The Effects of Neglect on Academic Achievement
   and Disciplinary Problems: A Developmental Perspective   105
   Kathleen A. Kendall-Tackett and John Eckenrode

9. The Traumatic Events Screening Inventory:
   Assessing Trauma in Children   113
   Jason H. Edwards and Karen C. Rogers

10. Measuring Physical and Psychological Maltreatment
    of Children With the Conflict Tactics Scales   119
    Murray A. Straus and Sherry L. Hamby

11. Methodological Issues in Classifying Maltreatment:
    An Examination of "Protective Issue" Children   136
    Heather N. Taussig and Alan J. Litrownik

PART III: WIFE ABUSE

12. Attitudes as Explanations for Aggression Against Family Members   151
    Sharon D. Herzberger and Quentin H. Rueckert

13. Woman Battering: A Comparative Analysis of Black and White Women   161
    Janice Joseph

14. Surviving Abusive Dating Relationships:
    Processes of Leaving, Healing, and Moving On   170
    Karen H. Rosen and Sandra M. Stith

15. Social Predictors of Wife Assault Cessation   183
    Etiony Aldarondo and Glenda Kaufman Kantor

16. Wife Abuse in Intact Couples:
    A Review of Couples Treatment Programs   194
    Pamela D. Brown and K. Daniel O'Leary

17. Expanding Batterer Program Evaluation   208
    Edward W. Gondolf

18. Feminist Therapy for Battered Women: An Assessment   219
    Maryse Rinfret-Raynor and Solange Cantin

19. Controlling Domestic Violence:
    Victim Resources and Police Intervention   235
    JoAnn L. Miller and Amy C. Krull

20. Collaboration Between Researchers and Advocates 255
        Edward W. Gondolf, Kersti Yllö,
        and Jacquelyn Campbell

PART IV: ETHICAL AND CULTURAL ISSUES IN FAMILY VIOLENCE

21. Ethical Issues in Trauma Research:
    The Evolution of an Empirical Model for Decision Making 271
        Elana Newman, Danny G. Kaloupek,
        Terence M. Keane, and Susan F. Folstein

22. Ethical Dimensions of Intervention With Violent Partners:
    Priorities in the Values and Beliefs of Practitioners 282
        Gilles Rondeau, Jocelyn Lindsay, Ginette Beaudoin,
        and Normand Brodeur

23. Conducting Ethical Cross-Cultural Research on Family Violence 296
        Lisa Aronson Fontes

    Name Index 313

    Subject Index 321

    About the Editors 325

    About the Contributors 327

Introduction

Most of the 23 chapters in *Out of the Dark-ness* were first presented at the 4th International Family Violence Research Conference at the University of New Hampshire in Durham, New Hampshire. The chapters exemplify the progress that has occurred in the field since the publication of the first proceedings, *The Dark Side of Families,* edited by our colleagues from the Family Research Laboratory: David Finkel-hor, Richard J. Gelles, Gerald T. Hotaling, and Murray A. Straus. We are greatly indebted to our colleagues for their mentorship, for their contributions to the field of research on family violence, and for helping to lead research on family violence out of the darkness.

The research reported in this book has been conducted by some of the leading researchers in the field from a variety of disciplines, and also represents a new generation of investigation and theoretical inquiry. The chapters address controversial issues, include international studies, and make important contributions to theory, methodology, assessment, interventions, and ethical approaches related to child abuse and wife abuse.

Resolving Controversies and Expanding Our Knowledge Base in Family Violence

Using child protective services caseloads or battered women's shelter occupancy as yardsticks of change suggests a continuing high level of serious abusive family patterns. Recent developments in the field of family violence include new pressures on child welfare, and on mental health and criminal justice professionals, to effectively assess, diagnose, substantiate, and treat or prevent wife abuse and child abuse. However, despite the pressures experienced by practitioners in the field, researchers and practitioners continue to debate the extent of family violence, how concepts should be measured, what treatment and evaluation strategies are best, and whether ethically and culturally sensitive research can be conducted. The chapters in this volume address new developments in knowledge and propose new solutions to some of the most complex questions related to the field of family violence.

Part I: The Prevalence of Family Violence

Is Wife Abuse Declining? Previous research findings by Straus and Gelles that assaults on marital partners were declining led to disbelief and criticism about the survey results by some segments of the research and practitioner community. In Chapter 1, Straus, Kaufman Kantor, and Moore analyze four national surveys conducted from 1968 through 1994. Their results suggest that approval for a husband slapping his wife has declined significantly over the years and indicates an important change in the culture. The authors conclude that efforts to combat family violence have been successful and that such efforts are part of the reason for reported declines.

Are Child Homicides Increasing? Increasing media attention has been given to the problem of child homicide. In Chapter 2, Finkelhor suggests that although global statistics do show an increase in homicides of children and youth, this is not a singular phenomenon. For example, although teen homicides have been increasing among minority youth, the seeming increase in infanticide and child abuse homicide probably reflect improved scrutiny given to the deaths of young children. Finkelhor concludes that the homicides in middle childhood, which occur at a rather low rate and include a mixture of child abuse, sexual violence, family murder-suicides, and other causes, have actually been decreasing.

What Characterizes the Victims of Intimate Assault? In Chapter 3, Weaver, Kilpatrick, Resnick, Best, and Saunders expand our knowledge of victim characteristics, and the nature of the assaults that women experience, by using data from a new national study and a sample of help-seeking women. Their findings are important because they document the multiple forms of victimizations that women experience including sexual assault, and because they document the psychological injuries experienced by these women.

Part II: Child Abuse and Neglect

Methodological and Theoretical Contributions

Almost all evaluations of services and research on family violence stress the need for improved measurement of family violence concepts. Diagnosis and detection of child maltreatment has also been hindered by lack of a universal definition of child abuse. Research on concepts central to child maltreatment also suffers from a lack of consensus over valid definitions of abusive parenting, and whether abuse should be defined by parental behaviors or by child outcomes such as endangerment or demonstrable harm or injury. Several chapters in this section draw our attention to theoretical constructs and also illuminate a wide range of both sources and consequences of child maltreatment. In Chapter 4, Becker-Lausen and Mallon-Kraft propose a unifying theoretical construct for the maladaptive outcomes experienced by abuse survivors. Their construct of impaired "intimacy" captures the wide-ranging problems experienced by abuse survivors in the realm of parent-child relations, friendships, teen pregnancy, and romantic and sexual bonds. In Chapter 5, Itzin uses a disturbing case study of child sexual abuse in the United Kingdom to elaborate the phenomenology of child sexual victimization by pornography, and she conceptualizes the organization of child sexual abuse as a continuum in which pornography is a part of all forms of intra- and extrafamilial child sexual abuse. Bernard's (Chapter 6) U.K.-based study goes beyond previous work in the field of child sexual victimization by suggesting that the areas of race, class, and gender are central to developing paradigms of child sexual victimization, and our responses to that experience. She demonstrates how Black mothers' reactions to the processes of discovery of child sexual abuse, and intervention of social welfare agencies, are shaped by mothers' racialized and gendered identities. Margolin and John (Chapter 7) shift our focus to the area of children's exposure to marital violence. They inform the debate on whether the consequences of children's exposure are a direct effect of witnessing or an indirect effect of the parent-child relationship, and whether children are differentially affected according to gender. Kendall-Tackett and Eckenrode (Chapter 8) examine one of the lesser studied sources of child maltreatment, child neglect, finding that neglect alone and in combination with abuse effects a decline in school performance among children entering middle school.

New or improved methodologies are detailed by authors in several of the chapters. Edwards and Rogers (Chapter 9) present information on a new assessment measure of children's exposure to a large number of potentially traumatic events; the Traumatic Events Screening Inventory improves on previous instrumentation by including both a child and parent version of their instrument. Straus and Hamby (Chapter 10) provide extensive new information on an old instrument (the Parent-to-Child CTS) regarding construct validity, reliability, normative data, and suggestions on when the Parent-to-Child CTS can be appropriately used.

Taussig and Litrownik (Chapter 11) carefully review the classification schema for abused children and propose and test a new schema reflecting a more refined hierarchy of child maltreatment, including the categories of nonabused, protective issue (children at risk but not substantiated for abuse), and substantiated cases of abuse. Their results indicate, for example, that protective issue children are more likely to be younger, male, and perceived as more competent than children with substantiated maltreatment.

Part III: Wife Abuse

■ Herzberger and Rueckert (Chapter 12) build on previous cognitive research, their own as well as that of others, to develop and test a new attitudinal measure of violence, assessing justifications for violence, assignment of blame, and tendencies to punish, in situations regarding intimate relationships. Their analysis of the association between attitudes and behavior raises important questions about the predictive power of attitudes in determining violent behavior.

The ability of any one variable to explain intimate violence is limited, and the experience of victimization may not be uniform across different cultural groups. Moreover, little attention has been paid to the victimization experiences of minority women. Joseph's cultural analysis of woman battering (Chapter 13) enriches our understanding of the patterns and responses to violence experienced by White and Black women. For example, Joseph finds that despite their more severe abuse-related injuries, Black women are less willing than White women to use social services agencies, including the police; Black women are more likely than White women to use defensive violence and to return to the relationship after a separation. Rosen and Stith (Chapter 14) also explore the dynamics of remaining and disentangling from abusive relationships. They find that women are propelled into leaving by a pile-up of negative events, or because they, much like those who initiate the process of recovery from chemical dependency, reach their personal bottoming-out point.

Three chapters provide new insights into changes in men's assaultive behavior toward partners, and interventions designed to effect changes in male batterer behavior. Aldarondo and Kaufman Kantor's (Chapter 15) analysis of data from a recent national survey of families explores the social factors that predict the continuity of abuse. Their results are important because they add to the literature demonstrating different types of batterers. For example, men engaging in more severe and repeated violence were found to be more likely to persist in violence toward their wives. Brown and O'Leary (Chapter 16) take on a controversial question in considering whether couples treatment works in violent marriages. Because treatment programs that use a couples therapy approach to end assaults on wives have been widely regarded as unsafe, few studies have examined them. Brown and O'Leary take an initial step in considering the merits of these programs by reviewing the available, albeit sparse, studies on this type of treatment, and they make recommendations for future evaluations while cautioning about the need for comprehensive assessments of aggression. Gondolf (Chapter 17) breaks new ground in the area of methodologies for assessing the effectiveness of batterer treatment. He proposes a broader evaluation process including consumer-based assessment, community or systems analysis, social impact assessment, and ethical decision making. These alternative evaluative strategies are suggested as means to better measure the process of social change in reducing women battering.

Interventions to reduce and control wife abuse must also consider the importance of providing support to victims. Rinfret-Raynor and Cantin (Chapter 18) discuss and evaluate a feminist therapy model for battered women and compare the effectiveness of three models of treatment. These authors show that a "woman-centered" approach with an emphasis on restoring self-esteem, growth, and independence and supplying concrete assistance can reduce the level of violence experienced. In Chapter 19, Miller and Krull's study begins where the domestic violence arrest experiments ended. This study examines how domestic violence victims from Milwaukee, Wisconsin, Colorado Springs, Colorado, and Omaha, Nebraska use personal and police resources to control the violence directed against them by their partners. The authors concluded that the victim's marital status, her employment, and her family influence her ability to control revictimization and that social structural explanations of domestic violence account for differences observed across cities.

Gondolf, Yllö, and Campbell (Chapter 20) call for collaboration between researchers and advocates in domestic violence. They illustrate the potential sources of misunderstanding and conflict inherent in collaborative models, as well as the efforts needed to achieve and maintain advocacy research. For example, the authors note that the agenda and concerns of advocates may seem lost or trivialized by researcher concerns with experimental designs and complex statistical analyses. Advocates fear that researchers may lack sufficient sensitivity to the ethical and safety concerns of victims. The result of successful collaborations, however, should be a more grounded, practical, relevant, and influential knowledge about domestic violence.

Part IV: Ethical and Cultural Issues in Family Violence

■ Family violence research entails a multitude of ethical considerations. The central issue is to balance the need for good science with the need for the safety of human research participants. Increasingly, researchers feel encumbered by human participants' concerns, and even federal agencies are at sea about appropriate handling of ethical issues in research. As noted above, practitioners are concerned about the sensitivity of researchers to the vulnerability of victims as well. A significant contribution of this volume is a strong section with three chapters addressing the leading ethical dilemmas of the day. Newman, Kaloupek, Keane, and Folstein (Chapter 21) make a major contribution to the field with their examination of ethical decision making in research. They direct our attention to ethical concerns about the vulnerability of trauma survivors in situations of research investigation, and they assess the risks and benefits of asking individuals about their traumatic histories and the research ethics of current consent procedures. They also argue that researchers need to develop empirical evidence on the effect of research on participants. Similarly, Rondeau, Lindsay, Beaudoin, and Brodeur (Chapter 22) argue for the importance of investigating the beliefs, values, and ethical dilemmas faced by practitioners. This chapter supplements the theoretical literature with field research conducted by the investigators, thus advancing our knowledge base in this important area. In the final chapter, Fontes exhorts us to conduct ethical cross-cultural research and cautions us against the abuse of power by research investigators, an overemphasis on differences and neglecting similarities between groups, and denial of diversity within groups (ethnic lumping) and of ignoring wider structural contexts.

The contents of this volume show that although some basic questions remain to be elaborated regarding who, how many, and why, there is also a new sophistication in the field of family violence research. This new sophistication is underscored by recognition of the complexity of family violence, and consequently the need for multidisciplinary and collaborative approaches in assessment, intervention, and evaluation. A major part of emerging out of the darkness is in seeing that we need to support and effect changes in both victim and batterer behavior, in seeing that there are wide variations in the forms, types, and consequences of abuse, and in bringing to bear a wide array of expertise, with greater sensitivity to affected populations.

GLENDA KAUFMAN KANTOR
JANA L. JASINSKI

PART I

THE PREVALENCE OF FAMILY VIOLENCE

CHAPTER 1

Change in Cultural Norms Approving Marital Violence From 1968 to 1994

Murray A. Straus
Glenda Kaufman Kantor
David W. Moore

Research on change in rates of assault on marital partners found a decrease from 1975 to 1985 (Straus & Gelles, 1986), and a further decrease from 1985 to 1992 (Straus & Kaufman Kantor, 1994). These studies have raised many questions. One of the questions is the validity of Straus and Gelles's argument that part of the decrease resulted from a change in the cultural norms that had made the marriage license an implicit hitting license. Although existence of these norms has been well documented (Dobash & Dobash, 1979; Straus, 1976), there is no direct evidence showing change in cultural norms.

The Battered Women's Movement and Cultural Change

■ Straus, Gelles, and Kaufman Kantor argue that the efforts by women's advocacy groups and service providers to reduce violence by hus-

AUTHORS' NOTE: An earlier version of this chapter was presented at the annual meetings of the American Sociological Association, Los Angeles, August 1994. Glenda Kaufman Kantor's research reported here was supported by Research Grant RO1AA09070 from the National Institute on Alcohol Abuse and Alcoholism. This chapter has benefited from helpful comments and suggestions by the members of the Family Research Laboratory seminar and from assistance with manuscript preparation by Doreen Cole.

bands are themselves a reflection of change in the culture and are also part of the process that produces further change (Straus & Gelles, 1986; Straus & Kaufman Kantor, 1994). These efforts included both educational campaigns and new social institutions such as shelters for battered women (Schecter, 1982), and new legal and criminal justice reforms promoting greater sensitivity to rape victims (Bachman, 1993; Spohn & Horney, 1991). Battered women's advocates also promoted changes in the criminal justice and legal systems including replacement of the policy of avoiding arrest in "domestic disturbance" cases with policies recommending or requiring arrest of men who assault their wives, court-ordered treatment for violent husbands, and procedural changes to facilitate obtaining an order of protection to forbid the offender from having contact with his former victim (Sherman, 1992). These legal changes are a continuation of a long-term trend. For example, in the 1870s U.S. courts stopped recognizing the common law rule that gave husbands the right to "physically chastise an errant wife" (Calvert, 1974). The legal norms have clearly changed. However, it is not clear to what extent the informal norms of American society have changed, and that question was the primary objective of the research reported in this chapter. Specifically, we tested the hypothesis that the rate of approval of slapping a spouse decreased from 1968 to 1994.

Group Differences in Norms Approving Marital Violence

■ A second objective was to investigate differences in the degree to which approval of marital violence is part of the social norms of different segments of American society, and whether there has been differential change in these norms. The "subculture of violence" theory (Amir, 1971; Wolfgang, 1958), for example, assumes that the higher rate of homicide in the American South, and among the lowest socioeconomic strata of society, is partly a reflection of norms approving violence in these segments of society.

There is no doubt about class differences in the rate of violent crime (Blau & Blau, 1982; Hindelang, 1978) including marital violence (Straus, Gelles, & Steinmetz, 1980). However, without independent data on cultural norms, ascribing the higher rates to differences in culture is only an inference that needs to be tested empirically (Baron & Straus, 1989; Loftin & Hill, 1974). In fact, the results of empirical research on regional and class differences in acceptance of violence have produced mixed results (Kaufman Kantor & Straus, 1987; Reed, 1971; Stark & McEvoy, 1970), and regional differences in overall violence rates have been found to vary over time (Nelson, Corzine, & Huff-Corzine, 1994; Parker, 1991). Consequently, the most appropriate hypotheses are that there are no significant differences between regions, between ethnic groups, or between educational and income groups in approval of marital violence and that each of these groups underwent parallel changes from 1968 to 1994.

Although the empirical evidence just cited on regional and class differences is mixed, the evidence on gender and age is clear. It shows that more men approve of violence in marriage than women (Straus et al., 1980) and that with age, approval of violence decreases (Stets & Straus, 1990; Suitor, Pillemer, & Straus, 1990). However, these differences do not preclude parallel patterns of change over the 26-year period covered by this research. We tested the hypothesis that approval of marital violence decreased for both men and women and among younger persons as well as older persons.

Method

■ A survey conducted for the National Commission on the Causes and Prevention of Violence in 1968 is the starting point for this research because it included questions on approval of slapping a spouse. The responses to these questions, when aggregated for the United States or for specific groups, provide information on the extent of adherence to cultural norms approving marital violence. Since then, four surveys conducted in 1985, 1992, and 1994 have used the identical questions and provide an opportunity to examine trends. The surveys asked nationally representative samples of American adults, "Are there any situations that you can imagine in which you would approve of a husband slapping his wife's face?" and " . . . a wife slapping her husband's face?"

Sample

Data from four surveys were combined for this study. Although the questions on approval of slapping a spouse were identical, before they could be merged into a single data file, each of the four files had to be edited to make the variable names and labels identical. In addition, some recoding of other variables and case selection had to be done to make the files comparable. For example, the studies used different categories for age, income, and education. To make them comparable, the three variables were transformed to stanine scores (Kaiser, 1958) before merging the four files. The studies used different categories for ethnic groups, but all four differentiated African Americans and Hispanic Americans. Consequently, it was possible to collapse the categories for all four into three groups: African American, Hispanic American, and Other. The Other category is overwhelmingly Whites of European ancestry. The combined data file included 9,672 cases. Deletion of cases that do not have information on one or more of the variables resulted in a sample for this chapter of 8,514.

1968 National Violence Survey. This survey was designed by Rodney Stark and James McEvoy III. The survey was conducted by Louis Harris Associates using face-to-face interviews with a national probability sample of persons age 18 and over ($N = 1,176$). Further information on the survey may be found in the National Commission on the Causes and Prevention of Violence (1969), Owens and Straus (1975), and Stark and McEvoy (1970). The data file used for this chapter was obtained from the Interuniversity Consortium for Political and Social Research at the University of Michigan.

1985 National Family Violence Survey. This survey was designed by Richard J. Gelles and Murray A. Straus and carried out by Louis Harris Associates using telephone interviews ($N = 6,002$). The sample consisted of two parts: a national probability sample of persons age 18 and over who were married or cohabiting with a person of the opposite sex, and oversamples of married or cohabiting African Americans, Hispanic Americans, and residents of smaller states. Further information on the survey may be found in Straus and Gelles (1986, 1990). The data tape and documentation are available from the Interuniversity Consortium for Political and Social Research at the University of Michigan, and on CD-ROM from Sociometrics Inc., Palo Alto, California.

1992 National Alcohol and Family Violence Survey. This survey was designed by Glenda Kaufman Kantor. The survey was conducted by the Institute for Survey Research of Temple University, using face-to-face interviews ($N = 1,970$). Hispanic American respondents had the choice of being interviewed in Spanish or English. The sample consisted of two parts: a national probability sample of persons age 18 and over who were married or cohabiting with a person of the opposite sex, and an oversample of 846 married or cohabiting Hispanic Americans. Further information on the survey may be found in Kaufman Kantor, Jasinski, and Aldarondo (1994).

1994 Gallup Survey. This survey was designed by David Moore and Murray A. Straus. The survey was conducted January 6-8, 1994 by the Gallup Organization using telephone interviews. It used random-digit dialing to select a national probability sample of persons age 18 and over. A "split ballot" design was used. The sample for this study consisted of the half of the sample who were asked the questions on approval of violence exactly as in the other three surveys ($N = 524$). Further information on the survey may be obtained from the Gallup Organization.

Comparability of Surveys. The four surveys differ in respect to several characteristics: size of the sample (from 524 to 6,002), universe sampled (all persons age 18 and over vs. married or cohabiting persons age 18 and over), method of interviewing (face-to-face vs. telephone), monolingual versus choice of English or Spanish, the organization conducting the survey, and the context in which the approval of violence questions were asked (a survey on violence, a survey on family problems, and a political opinion survey). These differences raise questions about the appropriateness of analyzing them as a single data set. For example, the Hispanic American sample interviewed in 1992 is likely to be less acculturated than the sample interviewed in 1985 because bilingual face-to-face interviews were conducted in 1992, and telephone interviews were conducted in the earlier, 1985 survey. However, as will be shown below, the findings follow uniform patterns over time, and this suggests that the trend findings are unlikely to be the result of confounding with one or more of the differences just listed.

Measures

Approval of Marital Violence. All four surveys asked: "Are there any situations that you can imagine in which you would approve of a husband slapping his wife's face?" and "Are there any situations that you can imagine in which you would approve of a wife slapping her husband's face?" Respondents could answer yes or no. These questions are direct measures of approval of marital violence. Moreover, they are probably more appropriate for measuring approval of marital violence than would be questions that asked about more severe forms of violence such as punching or kicking. This is because even persons who approve of punching and kicking are likely to be reluctant to admit that. However, there are also some potential problems. One is that the wording does not rule out self-defense. Fortunately, that possibility did not materialize. As will be shown below, when those who said yes were asked about the situation, none mentioned self-defense. However, the questions

themselves do not specify the situation under which the respondent might approve of slapping. Research by Greenblat (1983) and Arias and Johnson (1989) suggests that this affects the percentage who agreed. Greenblat, for example, found a much higher percentage approving if the question specified infidelity compared to other problems. Another limitation of the questions is that they are very obvious and direct and are not embedded in a justifying context phrase such as, "No matter how much a person may love his wife, there may be times when . . . ." The latter two problems suggest that the rates of approval of marital violence reported below should be regarded as lower-bound estimates.

Independent Variables. In addition to the year in which the survey was conducted, the following characteristics were used to test the hypotheses concerning group differences in norms approving marital violence: age, gender, education, income, ethnic group (African American, Euro-American, and Hispanic American), and region (Northeast, North Central, South, and West).

Statistical Analysis

The hypotheses were tested using logistic regression (logit) because the dependent variable is a dichotomy. The eight independent variables provide information on whether each is associated with approval of violence. In addition, they are important as controls for changes in the demographic composition of American society during the 26-year period of the study. For example, if fewer older persons approve of violence, there might be a decrease in approval of violence because of the aging of the population even if there is no difference in approval of violence by persons of the same age in 1968 and 1994. The same possibility applies to changes in the average education of the population, income, ethnic composition, and regional shifts in population. With these demographic sources of variation controlled, the decrease in the rate of approval of violence probably represents a change in the culture rather than change in the population composition.

Findings

Correlations

We first examined the zero-order correlations between the independent variables, covariates, and dependent variables (see Table 1.1). This allowed for a preliminary inspection of potential multicollinearity problems. It also provided a means to examine bivariate associations. The results of this analysis do not suggest that any potential problems with multicollinearity exist. The strong and significant correlation between approval for slapping by a husband or approval for slapping by a wife suggests that the underlying variable is approval of violence rather than anything specific to the role of husband or wife.

The correlations for approval of a husband slapping his wife's face indicate that approval of slapping by men declined over time, and was less often approved of by women, the poor, or older members of the population. The correlations for approval of slapping by wives showed that there is less approval for slapping by a wife in the South, and among men, older Americans, African Americans, and Hispanic Americans. The positive correlations between education, income, and approval of a wife slapping her husband's face suggest that higher education and income increase approval of slapping by women.

Trends

Figure 1.1 shows that the percentage of the U.S. population who approve of a husband slapping his wife's face (lower line) decreased steadily from the high of just over 20% in 1968 to half that rate in 1994.[1]

The decrease is statistically significant (see the row for year in Table 1.2, part A). Because the analysis controlled for changes in eight demographic variables, the significant decrease in the percentage approving a husband slapping his wife's face is more likely to indicate a change in the culture rather than a change in demographics.

Although approval of husband-to-wife violence decreased sharply from 1968 to 1994, that is not the case for wife-to-husband violence. The upper line in Figure 1.1 and the nonsignificant logit coefficient in part B of Table 1.2 show that the percentage of the U.S. population who approve of a wife slapping her husband's face remained almost identical over the 26 years.

What sort of situations did those who said that there are situations where they would approve of a husband slapping his wife or a wife slapping her husband have in mind? The 1968 survey asked those who approved to indicate the situation in which they would do so. None mentioned self-defense or altruistic situations such as to defend a child or to revive a spouse from a trance or seizure. The most frequently mentioned situation was if the partner was sexually unfaithful: 72% of those who approved of a husband slapping a wife had this in mind, as did 75% of those who approved of a wife slapping her husband.

Group Differences

Gender. Combining the four surveys, 16.1% of the men compared to 11.6% of the women approved of a husband slapping a wife, and 26.4% of the men compared to 18.4% of the women approved of slapping by a wife. Both differences are significant at the .001 level (see the rows for gender in Table 1.2). Thus, more men than women approve of marital violence, regardless of whether it is a husband slapping his wife or a wife slapping her husband.

The trend lines plotted in Figure 1.2 show that the percentage who approved of a husband slapping his wife decreased for both men and women during the 26-year period. However, the trends are not identical. At the start of the period more men than women approved a husband slapping. By 1992, the approval rates had converged. However, in 1994 the old differences reemerged because approval by women continued down, whereas approval by men increased. Despite this, approval by both men and women of a husband slapping his wife decreased substantially from 1968 to 1994.

Figure 1.3, on the other hand, shows that approval of a wife slapping her husband by either men or women did not change much during these 26 years. However, the small changes were in the direction of greater approval by men and

TABLE 1.1 Zero-Order Correlations Among Variables

	APPROVE.H SLAP	APPROVE.W SLAP	YEAR	GENDER	NORTHEAST	SOUTH	WEST	AFR.AMER	HISP.AMER	EDUC	INCOME	AGE
APPROVE.H SLAP	1.00											
APPROVE.W SLAP	.65***	1.00										
YEAR	-.06***	.01	1.00									
GENDER	-.07***	-.10***	-.03**	1.00								
NORTHEAST	.00	-.02	-.02	-.01	1.00							
SOUTH	.01	-.02*	.01	.02*	-.37***	1.00						
WEST	.01	-.00	.03**	.00	-.25***	-.38***	1.00					
AFR.AMER	-.02	-.02	-.13***	.04***	-.00	.13***	-.10***	1.00				
HISP.AMER	-.02	-.04***	.22***	.03**	-.05***	.07***	.16***	-.17***	1.00			
EDUC	.01	.06***	.03**	-.09***	.05***	-.10***	.02	-.04***	-.27***	1.00		
INCOME	.02*	.04***	.02	-.11***	.07***	-.11***	.00	-.12***	-.22***	.48***	1.00	
AGE	-.05***	-.08***	.00	-.06***	.00	.02	-.04***	-.04***	-.09***	-.10***	.04***	1.00
$\bar{X}$	13.35	21.49	2.19	.57	.20	.36	.21	.12	.17	.01	.01	.00
SD	34.02	41.07	.71	.49	.40	.48	.40	.33	.38	1.00	1.00	1.00

*p < .05; **p < .01; ***p < .001.

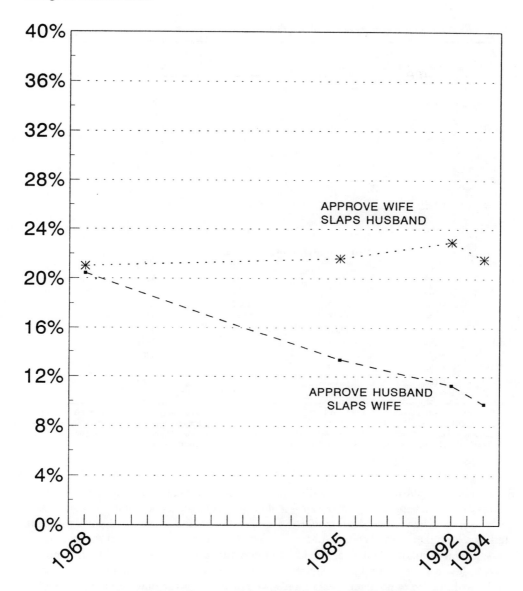

Figure 1.1. Approval of Slapping Spouse (adjusted for covariates and independent variables)

less approval by women. As a result, in 1994 the percentage of men who approved of a wife slapping her husband was double the percentage of women who approved (31% of men, 16% of women), whereas at the start of this period, men were only 30% more likely to approve slapping by a wife. The findings of greater approval of violence by women than by men are consistent with other research as well (Eagly & Steffen, 1986; Greenblat, 1983).

Region. Regional differences were investigated by creating dummy variables for three of the four census regions (Northeast, South, and West) and using the Midwest as the referent region. Part A of Table 1.2 shows that Southerners were significantly more likely to approve a husband slapping his wife, net of other demographic variables. This is consistent with the fact that the South has typically had the highest homicide rate of any region.

TABLE 1.2 Logistic Regression of Approval of Slapping a Spouse

Independent Variable	Logit Coefficient	SE	Significance	Odds Ratio
A. Approval of husband slaps wife				
YEAR	−.2973	.0480	.0001	.7428
GENDER	−.3946	.0642	.0001	.6740
NORTHEAST	.0676	.0995	.4971	1.0699
SOUTH	.1679	.0869	.0533	1.1829
WEST	.1736	.0982	.0772	1.1895
AFR.AMER	−.2041	.1043	.0504	.8154
HISP.AMER	−.1046	.0979	.2852	.9007
AGE	−.0705	.0172	.0001	.9320
EDUCATION	−.0201	.0191	.2924	.9801
INCOME	.0324	.0196	.0991	1.0329
Constant	−.7899	.1803	.0001	
B. Approval of wife slaps husband				
YEAR	.0337	.0375	.3683	1.0343
GENDER	−.4634	.0535	.0001	.6292
NORTHEAST	.0564	.0801	.4813	1.0580
SOUTH	−.0367	.0715	.6072	.9639
WEST	.0244	.0808	.7624	1.0247
AFR.AMER	−.1310	.0860	.1278	.8773
HISP.AMER	−.2836	.0821	.0005	.7531
AGE	−.1090	.0144	.0001	.8967
EDUCATION	.0394	.0159	.0133	1.0402
INCOME	.0162	.0164	.3231	1.0163
Constant	−.7923	.1506	.0001	

NOTE: YEAR = year of the study: 1968, 1985, 1992, 1994; GENDER = gender of respondent: female = 1, male = 0; NORTHEAST = lives in the Northeast = 1, other = 0; SOUTH = lives in the South = 1, other = 0; WEST = lives in the West = 1, other = 0; AFR.AMER = African American respondent = 1, other = 0; HISP.AMER= Hispanic American respondent = 1, other = 0; AGE = age of respondent (stanine score); EDUCATION = education of respondent (stanine score); INCOME = income of respondent (stanine score).

Part B of Table 1.2 shows that no parallel relationship exists for approving a wife slapping her husband when other demographic characteristics are taken into account. As for trends in approval of marital violence, graphs not shown follow a pattern similar to Figure 1.1. That is, within each region, approval of a husband slapping his wife decreased, whereas approval of a wife slapping her husband stayed about the same.

Ethnic Minorities. The data available permitted comparisons of African Americans and Hispanic Americans with other ethnic groups (which in these samples meant primarily Caucasians of European ancestry). The significant odds ratio of .81 for African Americans in part A of Table 1.2 shows that being African American is associated with a 20% reduction in the odds of approving a husband slapping his wife. Hispanic Americans also had a lower odds ratio, but the difference is not significant. Part B of Table 1.2 shows that the odds of approving a wife slapping her husband are lower for African Americans and Hispanic Americans than for other ethnic groups, but the odds ratio is significant only for Hispanic Americans.

In respect to trends, the percentage who approved of a husband slapping his wife decreased from 1968 to 1994 for all three ethnic groups. The percentage who approved of a wife slapping her husband also decreased for both African Americans and Hispanic Americans, but did not decrease for Euro-Americans.

Age. The significant odds ratio of .93 in part A of Table 1.2 indicates that each additional

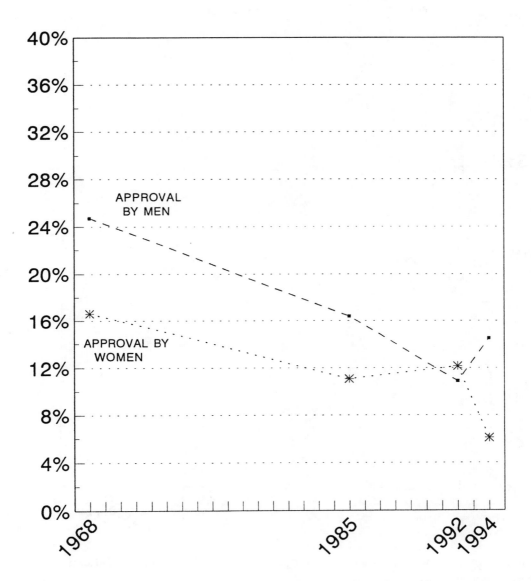

Figure 1.2. Approval of Husband Slapping Wife by Gender of Respondent (adjusted for covariates and independent variables)

year of age of the respondent is associated with a 7% reduction in the odds of approving a husband slapping his wife. Similarly, the odds ratio of .89 in part B indicates that each additional year of age is associated with an 11% reduction in the odds of approving a wife slapping her husband. Although fewer older respondents approved slapping a spouse, the

pattern of change from 1968 to 1994 shown in Figure 1.1 was found regardless of the age of the respondent.

Education. Part A of Table 1.2 shows that education is not significantly related to approving violence by husbands. However, the significant odds ratio of 1.04 for education in

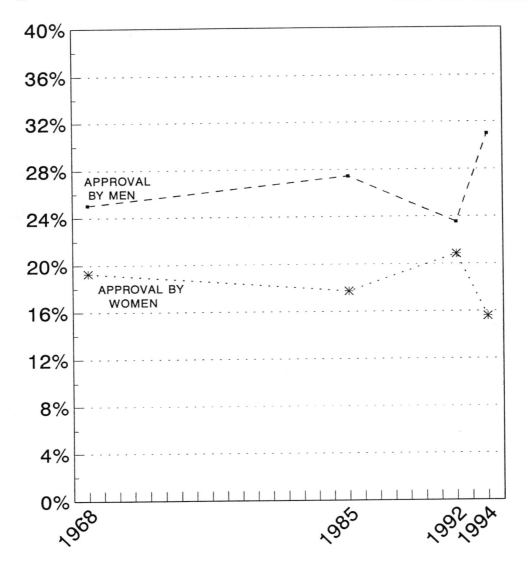

Figure 1.3. Approval of Wife Slapping Husband by Gender of Respondent (adjusted for covariates and independent variables)

part B shows each increase of one stanine score in education is associated with a 4% *increase* in the odds of approving a wife slapping her husband.

Income. Income was not found to be related to approving a husband slapping his wife, or a wife slapping her husband, nor did income alter the pattern of change from 1968 to 1994 shown in Figure 1.1.

Summary and Discussion

■ Approval of slapping by husbands decreased from 20% in 1968 to 13% in 1985, 12% in 1992, and 10% in 1994. Approval of slapping by wives, which was 22% in 1968, has not changed significantly.

Although a larger percentage of both men and women approved of a wife slapping her husband than a husband slapping his wife, fewer women than men approved of such violence by either husbands or wives.

Tests of the hypothesis that adherence to cultural norms approving or tolerating marital violence decreased from 1968 to 1994 produced mixed results. The percentage of the U.S. population who approved of a husband slapping his wife went down steadily during the 26-year period studied. We suggest that the efforts by women's advocacy groups and service providers to condemn male violence and aid battered women are part of the explanation of the large decrease in approval of slapping by husbands. We also believe that these efforts are part of the reason for the decrease in actual rates of assaults on wives from 1975 to 1992 (Straus & Gelles, 1986; Straus & Kaufman Kantor, 1994).

Unfortunately, approval of a wife slapping her husband did not decrease. All four surveys found a larger percentage of the population approved of a wife slapping a husband than of a husband slapping a wife, and the gap increased over the time period studied. Approval of wife-to-husband violence exceeded approval of husband-to-wife violence by only a small amount in 1968. Since then, the gap grew steadily until by 1994, the percentage who approved of a wife slapping a husband was more than double the percentage who approved of a husband slapping a wife. We suggest that one of the reasons that approval of a wife slapping a husband did not decrease, and one of the reasons that reports by women of actual assaults on their spouses did not decrease (Straus, 1993; Straus & Kaufman Kantor, 1994), is the absence of efforts to condemn violence by women.

The greater public acceptance of violence by wives than by husbands may occur because of a tendency to assume that a wife slapping a husband is primarily a symbolic act that is physically harmless (Eagly & Steffen, 1986; Greenblat, 1983). The fact that approval of a wife slapping her husband has not decreased since 1968 may be an unfortunate side effect of the gains women have made toward achieving equality with men. The status and behavior of women and the image of women may have become more like that of men, not only in socially

desirable characteristics but also in respect to violence and other crime. This may be one of the reasons for a recent tendency to glorify violence by women in novels, television, and films (e.g., *Thelma and Louise*). However, there are no signs that a female crime wave is imminent, and although arrest rates for simple assaults by women have risen, female participation in crimes of homicide remains exceedingly low (Steffensmeir & Allan, 1991).

If one assumes that education is associated with gender equality, the above interpretation is consistent with the finding that more education is associated with greater approval of a wife slapping her husband, but not with greater approval of slapping by a husband. Finally, some women may misinterpret the advice not to tolerate physical, verbal, or sexual abuse as advice to be violent themselves, especially because, in contrast to the legal norms, the informal norms of American society favor retaliation and do not usually distinguish between retaliation and self-defense. This interpretation is consistent with the finding that women initiate physical attacks on their spouses at about the same rate as men (Straus, 1993). However, men's and women's acts of violence are often not comparable. For example, aggression by women is rarely characterized as terroristic, as is sometimes the case with abusive men (Johnson, 1995).

Possible Limitations

A number of potential problems and limitations need to be kept in mind. For one thing, this study refers to a relatively minor act of violence—slapping a spouse—and does not stipulate the conditions under which approval exists. The findings may not apply to more severe assaults such as punching or kicking. However, there would be little point to doing a study of approval of punching, kicking, stabbing, or shooting a spouse because, at least in principle, everyone is against it. More important, severe violence tends to develop out of minor violence (Feld & Straus, 1989). Perhaps most important of all, even minor violence is an act that is a crime that would not be tolerated outside the family. Even if there were no risk of escalation, it is a serious social problem. It undermines the mental health of victims (Stets & Straus, 1990) and the stability of the family, and it harms millions of children who witness violence between their parents (Jaffe, Wolfe, & Wilson, 1990; Straus, 1992).

A related problem is that a behavior approved of by 20% of the population is not a broad enough consensus to be considered a cultural norm. As noted earlier, we think the rates reported in this chapter are lower-bound estimates. If the questions had been more adequately specified, much higher percentages approving violence are almost certain. When some situations are specified, for example, sexual infidelity, Arias and Johnson (1989) found that 44% of men approved of the husband slapping and 42% approved of the wife slapping. Similarly, when Greenblat (1983) asked about hitting a spouse for sexually related causes, 40% of men and 50% of women approved of a husband hitting his wife under such circumstances. For wives hitting their husbands for sexually related causes, 33% of the men approved of the wife hitting the husband, and 23% of the women approved of the wife hitting the husband. We think even these figures are lower-bound estimates. If so, a majority of Americans subscribe to the principle that it is legitimate to assault a spouse in certain situations.

Finally, there is the possibility that the decrease from 1968 to 1985 in the percentage who approved of a husband slapping his wife reflects only a change in what is politically correct to tell an interviewer and that the underlying norms continue to approve or tolerate marital violence. We agree that this probably is part of the explanation. However, even if it were the entire explanation, that would still be a significant change because the increased sensitivity is a reflection of the process of changing cultural norms.

Policy Implications

If our explanations of the findings are correct, there are important implications for policies that might reduce marital violence. For one thing, the findings suggest that social movements condemning violence against women, legal and institutional reforms, and systematic antiviolence educational efforts can produce major changes in public attitudes about violence and should therefore be expanded.

The continuing high rate of approval of violence by women also needs to be addressed because, like violence by men against their partners, it is a criminal act, and because it increases the risk of violence against women. Straus (1993) argued that the prevalence of seemingly harmless and justified "minor violence" by women helps perpetuate norms that make it legitimate to hit a spouse who persists in an objectionable behavior and "won't listen to reason." This is because sooner or later, she is likely to engage in behavior that her husband thinks is intolerable. When that happens, her previous use of violence to deal with his intolerable behavior will provide the justification for the husband to be violent also (see also Kaufman Kantor and Asdigian, in press). Consequently, one of the many steps needed to reduce assaults by men on their partners is a campaign to end what on the surface may seem to be harmless violence by women. The steps might include public service announcements directed at violence by women similar to those directed at male violence, and also school-based programs that explicitly recognize and condemn violence by girls as well as boys.

Important as such programs are for primary prevention of marital violence, it must not obscure the fact that women are the main victims of marital violence. They are physically injured to the point of needing medical attention 7 times as often as are husbands, they suffer psychological injury at much higher rates because of their concern with family well-being (Stets & Straus, 1990), and they are much more often locked into violent marriages because of the economic inequities of American society (Straus, 1976, 1992). Prevention of all forms of violence should continue to be a national priority and should make zero tolerance of violence by both men and women the major message to be communicated.

Note

1. Because adjusted rates are given in the graphs, they differ slightly from those previously reported in Stark and McEvoy (1971). The unadjusted rates of approval found in the present study are available from the authors.

References

Amir, M. (1971). *Patterns in forcible rape.* Chicago: University of Chicago Press.

Arias, I., & Johnson, P. (1989). Evaluations of physical aggression among intimate dyads. *Journal of Interpersonal Violence, 4,* 298-307.

Bachman, R. (1993). Predicting the reporting of rape victimizations: Have rape reforms made a difference? *Criminal Justice and Behavior, 30,* 371-379.

Baron, L., & Straus, M. A. (1989). *Four theories of rape in American society: A state-level analysis.* New Haven, CT: Yale University Press.

Blau, J. R., & Blau, P. M. (1982). The cost of inequality: Metropolitan structure and violent crime. *American Sociological Review, 35,* 114-129.

Calvert, R. (1974). Criminal and civil liability in husband-wife assaults. In S. K. Steinmetz & M. A. Straus (Eds.), *Violence in the family* (pp. 88-91). New York: Harper & Row.

Dobash, R. E., & Dobash, R. (1979). *Violence against women.* New York: Free Press.

Eagly, A. H., & Steffen, V. J. (1986). Gender and aggressive behavior: A meta-analytic review of the social psychological literature. *Psychological Bulletin, 100,* 309-330.

Feld, S. L., & Straus, M. A. (1989). Escalation and desistance of wife-assault in marriage. *Criminology, 27,* 141-161.

Greenblat, C. S. (1983). A hit is a hit is a hit . . . or is it? Approval and tolerance of the use of physical force by spouses. In D. Finkelhor, R. J. Gelles, G. T. Hotaling, & M. A. Straus (Eds.), *The dark side of families,* pp. 235-260. Beverly Hills, CA: Sage.

Hindelang, M. J. (1978). Race and involvement in common law/personal crimes. *American Sociological Review, 43,* 93-109.

Jaffe, P. G., Wolfe, D. A., & Wilson, S. K. (1990). *Children of battered women.* Newbury Park, CA: Sage.

Johnson, M. P. (1995). Patriarchal terrorism and common couple violence: Two forms of violence against women. *Journal of Marriage and the Family, 57,* 283-294.

Kaiser, H. F. (1958). A modified stanine scale. *Journal of Experimental Education, 26,* 261.

Kaufman Kantor, G., & Asdigian, N. L. (in press). Gender differences in alcohol-related spousal aggression. In R. W. Wilsnack & S. C. Wilsnack (Eds.), *Gender and alcohol.* New Brunswick, NJ: Rutgers University Press.

Kaufman Kantor, G., Jasinski, J. L., & Aldarondo, E. (1994). Sociocultural status and incidence of marital violence in Hispanic families. *Violence and Victims, 9,* 207-222.

Kaufman Kantor, G., & Straus, M. A. (1987). The drunken bum theory of wife beating. *Social Problems, 34,* 213-230.

Loftin, C., & Hill, R. H. (1974). Regional subculture and homicide: An examination of the Gastil-Hackney thesis. *American Sociological Review, 39,* 714-724.

National Commission on the Causes and Prevention of Violence. (1969). *Report of the Media Task Force.* Washington, DC: Government Printing Office.

Nelson, C., Corzine, J., & Huff-Corzine, L. (1994). The violent West reexamined: A research note on regional homicide. *Criminology, 32,* 149-161.

Owens, D., & Straus, M. A. (1975). The social structure of violence in childhood and approval of violence as an adult. *Aggressive Behavior, 1,* 193-211.

Parker, R. N. (1991). Violent crime. In J. F. Sheley (Ed.), *Criminology: A contemporary handbook* (pp. 143-160). Belmont, CA: Wadsworth.

Reed, J. S. (1971). To live-and-die-in-Dixie: A contribution to the study of Southern violence. *Political Science Quarterly, 86,* 429-443.

Schecter, S. (1982). *Women and male violence.* Boston: South End.

Sherman, L. (1992). *Policing domestic violence: Experiments and dilemmas.* New York: Free Press.

Spohn, C., & Horney, J. (1991). "The law's the law, but fair is fair": Rape shield laws and officials' assessments of sexual history evidence. *Criminology, 29,* 137-161.

Stark, R., & McEvoy, J., III. (1970). Middle class violence. *Psychology Today, 4,* 52-65.

Steffensmeir, D., & Allan, E. (1991). Gender, age, and crime. In J. F. Sheley (Ed.), *Criminology: A contemporary handbook* (pp. 67-93). Belmont, CA: Wadsworth.

Stets, J. E., & Straus, M. A. (1990). The marriage license as a hitting license: A comparison of assaults in dating, cohabiting, and married couples. In M. A. Straus & R. J. Gelles (Eds.), *Physical violence in American families: Risk factors and adaptations to violence in 8,145 families* (pp. 227-244). New Brunswick, NJ: Transaction.

Straus, M. A. (1976, Spring). Sexual inequality, cultural norms, and wife-beating. *Victimology, 1,* 54-76.

Straus, M. A. (1992). Children as witness to marital violence: A risk factor for lifelong problems among a nationally representative sample of American men and women. In D. F. Schwarz (Ed.), *Children and violence: Report of the 23rd Ross Roundtable on critical approaches to common pediatric problems* (pp. 98-104). Columbus, OH: Ross Laboratories.

Straus, M. A. (1993). Physical assaults by wives: A major social problem. In R. J. Gelles & D. R. Loseke (Eds.), *Current controversies on family violence.* Newbury Park, CA: Sage.

Straus, M. A., & Gelles, R. J. (1986). Societal change and change in family violence from 1975 to 1985 as revealed by two national surveys. *Journal of Marriage and the Family, 48,* 465-480.

Straus, M. A., & Gelles, R. J. (Eds.). (1990). *Physical violence in American families: Risk factors and adaptations to violence in 8,145 families.* New Brunswick, NJ: Transaction.

Straus, M. A., & Kaufman Kantor, G. (1994, July). *Change in spouse assault rates from 1975 to 1992: A comparison of three national surveys in the United States.* Paper presented at the World Congress of Sociology, Bielefeld, Germany.

Straus, M. A., Gelles, R. J., & Steinmetz, S. K. (1980). *Behind closed doors: Violence in the American family.* New York: Doubleday/Anchor.

Suitor, J. J., Pillemer, K., & Straus, M. A. (1990). Marital violence in a life-course perspective. In M. A. Straus & R. J. Gelles (Eds.), *Physical violence in American families: Risk factors and adaptations to violence in 8,145 families.* New Brunswick, NJ: Transaction.

Wolfgang, M. E. (1958). *Patterns of criminal homicide.* Philadelphia: University of Pennsylvania Press.

CHAPTER 2

The Homicides of Children and Youth

A Developmental Perspective

David Finkelhor

Murders of children, the ultimate form of child victimization, have received a great deal of deserved public notoriety in recent years, whether in the form of homicides by strangers, as in the death of Polly Klaas, kidnapped from her home in Petaluma, California, or homicides by relatives, such as Susan Smith, the South Carolina mother who drowned two sons, or Joel Steinberg, the New York lawyer who battered his daughter to death. Indeed, the statistics on child murder in the United States are grim and alarming. In 1994, according to Federal Bureau of Investigation data, 2,521 persons under 18 were victims of homicides.[1] That rate of 3.8 per 100,000 (over six children per day) makes the United States first among developed countries in juvenile homicide. In fact, the U.S. rate is dramatically out of line with other places in the world, really double even the next most murderous country for all ages of children except infants. (Table 2.1 illustrates this, albeit somewhat piecemeal because World Health Organization data do not have a consolidated category for ages 0-17.) Of course, the U.S. "gold medal" in child homicide is not unrelated to the generalized American prowess in lethal violence: The homi-

AUTHOR'S NOTE: I would like to thank Kathy Christoffel, Lauren Duncan, Michael Durfee, Sherry Hamby, Anne Keith, Milling Kinard, Murray Straus, and Carolyn West for helpful comments. Nancy Asdigian and Janis Wolak provided assistance with data analysis, and Kelly Foster helped with manuscript preparation. This research was supported by a grant from the Boy Scouts of America.

TABLE 2.1 Child and Youth Homicide Rates for 22 Developed Nations With Populations Greater Than 1 Million (by age, per 100,000)

Country	<1 Year Old	Country	1-4 Years Old	Country	5-14 Years Old	Country	15-24 Years Old
United States	8.0	United States	2.5	United States	1.5	United States	19.3
Denmark	7.3	Switzerland	1.2	Sweden	0.8	UK N. Ireland	7.9
UK Scotland	6.0	Canada	1.1	Canada	0.7	UK Scotland	5.8
Austria	5.1	Japan	1.1	Japan	0.5	Finland	4.2
New Zealand	5.1	Netherlands	0.9	Switzerland	0.5	Canada	3.1
Switzerland	4.6	New Zealand	0.9	New Zealand	0.4	Italy	2.7
Portugal	4.4	Norway	0.9	Australia	0.3	New Zealand	2.3
Japan	3.9	Sweden	0.9	Austria	0.3	Australia	2.1
Germany	3.5	Finland	0.8	Belgium	0.3	Israel	2.1
Norway	3.2	Germany	0.8	Finland	0.3	Portugal	1.7
Canada	2.9	UK Scotland	0.8	France	0.3	Austria	1.6
France	2.3	Australia	0.7	Germany	0.3	Belgium	1.5
Belgium	1.7	Belgium	0.7	Italy	0.3	Switzerland	1.5
Sweden	1.7	France	0.5	Netherlands	0.3	Netherlands	1.3
UK Wales, England	1.7	Portugal	0.5	Portugal	0.3	Sweden	1.3
Finland	1.5	UK Wales, England	0.5	Denmark	0.2	Denmark	1.2
Italy	0.9	Denmark	0.4	Norway	0.2	Germany	1.2
Netherlands	0.5	Italy	0.3	UK Wales, England	0.1	France	0.7
Australia	0.4	Austria	—	UK Scotland	0.1	UK Wales, England	0.7
Ireland	—	Ireland	—	Ireland	—	Norway	0.6
Israel	—	Israel	—	UK N. Ireland	—	Ireland	0.5
UK N. Ireland	—	UK N. Ireland	—	Israel	—	Japan	0.4

SOURCE: Figures are from World Health Organization (1995).

cide rate for all persons in the United States is 10.1 per 100,000, 3 times higher than any other developed country.

Murder is actually one of the few crimes in which children are *not* more victimized than adults. But the homicides of children have been increasing quite dramatically in recent years. They rose 53% from 1976 to 1992 according to FBI data, most of the jump coming since 1987 (Figure 2.1). Importantly, homicide is the only major cause of childhood death to have increased in incidence in the past 30 years. While deaths due to accidents, congenital defects, and infectious diseases were falling, growing numbers of children were being murdered. Homicide is now among the five leading causes of childhood mortality, accounting for 1 out of 20 deaths for those under age 18. More children now die from homicides than from cancer or infectious disease (Table 2.2).

Overall, juvenile homicides are among the most unequally distributed form of child victimization, with certain groups and certain lo-

calities experiencing the brunt of the problem. Minority children are particularly affected, making up 69% of all child homicide victims. Overall rates for Black children (8.4 per 100,000) and Hispanic children (4.7 per 100,000) dwarf the rate for Whites (1.7 per 100,000). The maldistribution is geographic, too. The difference between the states with the highest rates (California and Illinois) and those with the lowest rates (Maine, Montana, South Dakota, and Iowa) is a factor of about 25 (Table 2.3). Large cities have exposures that greatly exceed that of rural areas. Washington, D.C., which is entirely urban and heavily African American, has 10 times more child murders than the national average. On a regional basis, the West has the most child homicide. And boys are substantially more likely to be victims than girls.

However, a global summary like this of statistics on juvenile homicide is misleading and masks the multifaceted nature of the problem. There are really several different forms of the child homicide problem that are only revealed

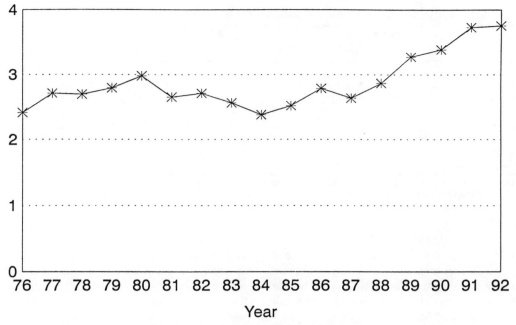

Figure 2.1. Child Homicide Rates, 1976-1992 (rate per 100,000 U.S. children, ages 0-17)
SOURCE: Uniform Crime Report.

by taking a developmental perspective. Not all of them are increasing. They have different sources, and ultimately different strategies for preventing them. This chapter tries to look at them individually.

From a developmental perspective, juvenile homicides should be broken down into at least three distinct segments, each of which has its own reality: young children, including infanticide and child abuse homicide; school-aged children; and teenagers. This chapter will discuss each in order of decreasing frequency, starting with teens, then young children, and finally, school-aged children. It will conclude with some general principles about development and violent victimization.

Teen Homicides

■ The murder of teenagers has received substantial publicity in recent years in part because it has been the most rapidly increasing form of homicide. Whereas the overall homicide rate was growing 44% from the early 1980s to the early 1990s, teen homicides were increasing 80%. Teens (ages 13-17) now are killed at a rate that is 50% higher than the average rate for all persons. Age 13 is clearly the line of demarcation for this phenomenon: That is the age at which rates begin to rise dramatically (Figure 2.2) and the age above which the recent historical increase has occurred (Figure 2.3).

The murder of teenagers is the type of juvenile homicide that most resembles and appears to be an extension of the adult homicide problem. Like adult homicides, teen homicides overwhelmingly involve male victims (83%), killed by other males (96%), using firearms (86%) and knives (10%). In contrast to other juvenile homicides, relatively few of these teen homicides are committed by family members. Also in contrast to other juvenile homicides, a much larger percentage are committed by other youth. But in spite of the stereotype that most teens are killed by other teens, in fact, almost two thirds of these teens (62%) were killed by an adult offender. Although teen murderers are predominantly youthful, they are primarily young adults, not juveniles themselves.

TABLE 2.2 Causes of Death for 0- to 17-Year-Olds in the United States

Cause	Total	Rate Per 100,000	<1	1-4	5-14	15-17
Congenital/perinatal condition	27,005	41.9	25,452	963	448	142
Motor vehicle accidents	6,679	10.3	190	783	1,975	3,731
Other accidents	5,339	8.3	740	1,783	1,675	1,141
Homicide	2,449	5.3	332	377	512	1,228
Cancer	2,243	3.5	90	513	1,094	546
Heart/circulatory disease	2,145	3.3	1,019	342	409	378
Suicide	1,725	2.7	—	—	264	1,461
Infectious diseases	1,329	2.1	734	294	188	113

NOTE: Figures are for 1990 and are from World Health Organization (1995). Figures for 15- to 17-year-olds were calculated by taking 30% of the number of deaths for 15- to 24-year-olds.

The big jump in teenage homicides in recent years has been popularly attributed to the rise of gangs, the spread of drugs, and increasing availability of handguns. The statistics clearly bear this out. In assigning a circumstance to the homicide, over half (56%) the teen killings for which a circumstance was listed were labeled by police as gang related. Drug-related homicides made up another 15%. There has been an enormous proliferation of handguns in the youth population, instigated by youth in the drug trade who needed to protect valuable drugs and money, but accelerated as other youth acquired guns to protect themselves from other armed youth (Sheley & Wright, 1995; Simonetti Rosen, 1995).

But sinister as this arms race is, this ecology of teenage homicide suggests also that it is somewhat limited in scope demographically and geographically, primarily to communities with gang and drug problems. Available data do bear out that in spite of the widespread publicity about the jump in teen homicides, the increase has not affected all segments of the population equally. Most dramatic has been disproportionate rise in risk for minority group teens. Teen homicide rates for Whites have been almost flat (up only 9% since the early 1980s), whereas they have skyrocketed for minorities, doubling in the same period. The rate for Blacks is up 132% and Hispanics up 93%. Most disturbing is the astronomic rise of rates for Asian teens, up 343%. Rural areas seem also to have been relatively unaffected. Rates barely rose between the early 1980s and 1990s in towns with populations under 25,000 while teen homicides were more than doubling in cities over 250,000.

The particular risk of homicide victimization among minority teens has led criminologists to look there for possible underlying explanations. For example, Sampson (1987) analyzed the social correlates of specifically Black teen homi-

TABLE 2.3 Child Homicide Rates by State, 1991-1992, per 100,000

State	1991-1992 Rate Per 100,000 U.S. Children	State	1991-1992 Rate Per 100,000 U.S. Children
Washington, D.C.	36.71	Ohio	2.72
California	6.60	Connecticut	2.67
Illinois	5.83	Tennessee	2.64
Missouri	5.25	Mississippi	2.55
New York	5.16	Hawaii	2.50
Texas	5.12	Delaware	2.45
Maryland	5.08	Indiana	2.33
Arkansas	4.35	Utah	2.23
Nevada	4.04	Vermont	2.10
Louisiana	4.00	New Mexico	2.01
Michigan	3.94	Kentucky	1.99
Virginia	3.92	Massachusetts	1.85
North Carolina	3.74	Rhode Island	1.77
Arizona	3.66	Florida	1.71
Colorado	3.61	Alabama	1.70
Oregon	3.59	Minnesota	1.63
Georgia	3.47	Nebraska	1.63
Oklahoma	3.35	South Carolina	1.41
Kansas	3.17	West Virginia	1.35
Wisconsin	3.10	Idaho	1.30
Wyoming	2.95	New Hampshire	1.08
New Jersey	2.94	North Dakota	.85
Alaska	2.90	Iowa	.28
Pennsylvania	2.79	South Dakota	.25
Washington	2.78	Montana	.23
		Maine	0

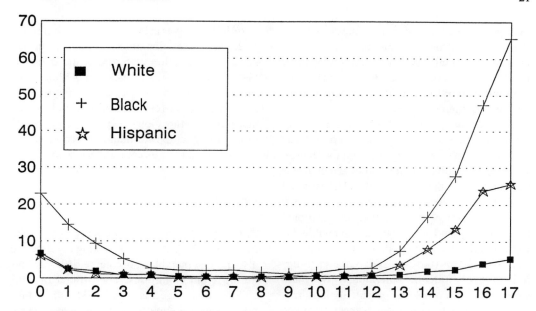

Figure 2.2. Race of Child Homicide Victims by Victim Age (rate per 100,000 U.S. children)
SOURCE: Uniform Crime Report, 1991-1992.

cide using 1980 data (that is prior to the big re-cent uptick in rates). Whereas communities with high levels of Black teen homicide had more economic adversity (higher unemployment, lower income, and lower welfare payments), the even more highly associated factor was the per-centage of Black households headed by a woman. Sampson speculated that Black family

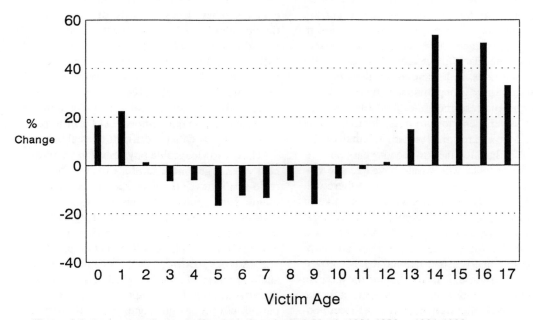

Figure 2.3. Percentage Change in Homicide Rate for U.S. Youth, 1981-1982 to 1991-1992
SOURCE: Uniform Crime Report, 1991-1992.

disruption meant among other things less effective social control over children, less involvement in community activities, and less general neighborhood surveillance, all of which permitted more delinquent activity and more vulnerability to homicidal violence.

Beyond the question of why homicide victimization rates may be high for minority teens is the question of why they are high for teens in general. Certainly, a major part of the explanation has to do with the marginal and transitional status of youth. As a group with relatively weak ties to and a lower stake in many conventional roles (family and job), they are available for risky and dangerous activities. The powerlessness of the status (less access to money, prestigious work, or influential individuals) gives them a motivation for quick but potentially high-risk avenues to money, power, and respect. But even the many teens who are not prone to risk taking themselves may be made vulnerable because they have relatively frequent and involuntary contact with others who are.

Although the increase in the teen homicide rate is serious in its own right, Fox (1995) has added to the alarm, arguing that it is just a harbinger of a future escalation in adult homicides as today's violent teens age and carry forward their violent habits. Moreover, the current demographic trends project a 28% increase in Black teens and a 50% increase in Hispanic teens by the year 2005, potentially more fuel for homicide rates, if the sources of alienation for these minority groups remain unchanged. Although Fox describes one plausible development, other scenarios are possible, too. It may be that the age for involvement in lethally risky activities has declined in recent years but primarily for those who would have become violent as adults anyway, meaning that there will not necessarily be an increase in the number of such individuals overall compared to historical rates. It may also be that such individuals kill one another off, perhaps earlier than later now, so some homeostasis is maintained. Moreover, some of the etiologic factors behind the increase in youth homicides such as competition for the drug market may have been a short-term phenomenon and may abate. In 1995, to the surprise

of many, there was a decline in overall homicide rates, demographics notwithstanding. In any case, the prediction of future crime rates has been a notoriously risky endeavor. Although the problem of teen homicides is a tragic problem requiring urgent remedies, it is not clear that alarm about future violent explosions will create more policy willpower than concern about the explosion we have already experienced.

Homicides of Young Children

■ Often eclipsed by the concern about teen murders is the fact that very young children are also quite vulnerable to homicide, although under different conditions. The official rate for children under age 5 is 3.6 per 100,000, and for many years was equal to the rate for teens, before the latter's recent rise. In fact, the rate of homicide for White children under age 5 is still nearly as high as the rate for White teens.

Moreover, there are strong hints that the actual homicide rate for young children is substantially higher than official statistics suggest. The homicides of young children are among the most difficult to document, because their presentation so often resembles deaths due to accidents and other causes. Thus, it is difficult to distinguish children who are suffocated from those who die from sudden infant death syndrome (SIDS). It is difficult to distinguish young children who are dropped, pushed, or thrown from those who die from falls. Even in many so-called accidental deaths, such as falls or auto fatalities, there may be a major component of willful parental negligence that is difficult to establish.

Thus, knowledgeable physicians have in recent years urged more careful examinations of child fatalities (Christoffel, Zieserl, & Chiaramonte, 1985), and most states have established child death review teams to ferret out child abuse fatalities that may have been previously overlooked (Durfee, Gellert, & Tilton Durfee, 1992; U.S. Advisory Board, 1995). When a team of such experts in Missouri carefully examined all the fatalities for children age 0-4 over a 4-year period, they found a great underestimation of the true extent of child maltreatment deaths using any individual record source, such as coroners' death certificates or police reports. In particular, only 39% of definite maltreatment fatalities and 18% of the combined definite/possible maltreatment fatalities got reported as homicides for purposes of the FBI Uniform Crime Report (UCR) (Ewigman, Kivlahan, & Land, 1993). This highlights how many actual homicides the official homicide data may miss.

This underestimation of young children's inflicted deaths has several distinguishable sources. One part is the definition of homicide that does not include many deaths that may have a large component of child maltreatment. So, for example, deaths due to gross negligence (a child left unsupervised on a window ledge falls to his death) may not meet a criminal standard of homicide or even manslaughter, so they are not counted. A second problem is the ambiguity of evidence in many child deaths and the lack of well-trained and systematic investigators. Finally, many states do not list a child fatality as a homicide unless charges are actually filed. Charges may not be filed for a variety of reasons.

All this means that some analysts have estimated the actual rate of homicides for young children to be double the official rate (see also Christoffel, 1990; McClain, Sacks, Froehlke, & Ewigman, 1993). The Centers for Disease Control and Prevention (CDC) believes the true rate of deaths due to child abuse and neglect is between 5.4 and 11.6 per 100,000 (U.S. Advisory Board, 1995). If child abuse deaths can all be equated with homicide, the upper bound of the CDC estimate would mean that young children have homicide rates higher than the rest of the population.

Moreover, the homicide rates for young children have been on the rise over the past 10 years. This is true whether one looks at the UCR data or at national child abuse fatality statistics, which, for example, show a rise between 1985 to 1992 from 1.30 to 1.94 per 100,000 (McCurdy & Daro, 1993; Weise & Daro, 1995). However, most of that increase has been among the youngest children, those age 0-1, and there are reasons to think that it could be artifactual. Because of the potentially large quantity of undiagnosed or unlabeled child homicide, particu-

larly among these very young children, better efforts to screen for it in ambiguous cases of child death could easily pump the numbers. As we indicated, many states have established child death review teams in recent years and it is very possible that this greater scrutiny has pushed up rates without any true underlying increase. Others, though, noting the growth of births to unmarried young mothers in very disorganized, drug- and crime-ridden environments, have believed that the rise was real.

Infanticides

■ Most of the homicides of very young children are committed by parents and caretakers and thus fall into what would be defined as child abuse. But within this group there appears to be justification for distinguishing a special category called "infanticide," although the boundaries of this distinction are sometimes unclear. A definition of infanticide suggested by the legal tradition in Britain and Canada is the killing of a recently born child by a relative in situations where the relative does not want the child, is ill-equipped to care for him or her, or is suffering from a childbirth-related psychiatric disturbance such as postpartum depression or psychosis. A prototypical situation is a mother who smothers, strangles, or drowns an unwanted child shortly after the birth. It is characterized by an actual intent to destroy the child, unlike much other child abuse, which tends to be an expression of frustration, anger, or extremely reckless or negligent behavior that goes too far. Unfortunately, instead of following some such definition, many studies of infanticide simply define it as murders by parents of children under the age of 6 or 12 months (Christoffel, Anzinger, & Amari, 1983; Jason, Carpenter, & Tyler, 1983). This is probably overly broad. In Canada, which has a special crime of infanticide similar to our proposed definition, more than 40% of the homicides by mothers of children under age 6 months did not qualify for this crime category (Silverman & Kennedy, 1988). Moreover, 13% of the homicides of children between ages 6 and 12 months did qualify. Thus, generalizations about infanticide from statistical profiles based on age, as most are, are possibly misleading.

If infanticides are defined by motive, and not age, it would appear that mothers are the predominant perpetrators. Studies suggest that these women tend to be teenage, single mothers, who receive very little or no prenatal care, some of whose births occur outside the hospital and involve low-birth-weight children (Emerick, Foster, & Campbell, 1986). This suggests a clearly defined group of young women, who do not wish to be pregnant, are very ambivalent about it or are psychiatrically disturbed, and who kill their children because they do not want them, are overburdened, or see them as a threat to themselves.

But men can be the perpetrators of infanticide, too. Fathers and boyfriends may assist mothers in killing unwanted children. Grandfathers and other relatives may participate in killing children whose out-of-wedlock birth brings shame on the family. Fathers may kill new babies when they disagree over the decision to have the child or feel resentful over the competition for the mother's attention. And boyfriends may kill children of girlfriends when they know or suspect that the child is not their own. It is significant to note that according to FBI homicide statistics, men predominate overall as the murderers of children under age 1.

One curious sociological fact about infant homicides, however, is that they show much less international variation than other homicide. Thus, although the United States has twice as much child homicide as even the next highest developed country, there is only a marginal difference for infant homicide (Table 2.1).

One possibility is that infant homicide is more related than other homicides to biological factors that have less variation across populations and socioeconomic strata. So, for example, if postpartum depression and colicky, difficult babies are significant contributors to the infant homicide and such conditions occur at similar rates across most groups of women and children, regardless of environment or nation, then we might expect that this form of child murder to be less related to social indicators or to vary less from country to country.

Child Abuse Homicides

■ Child abuse homicides are homicides of children by persons who are charged with their care, which would include parents, family members, baby-sitters, and friends who were taking responsibility for the children. The vast majority of child abuse deaths (92%) are to children age 5 and under (McClain et al., 1993), and a majority of what get recorded as homicides for children under age 5 are due to child abuse. Most statistics or studies on child abuse homicide do not segregate out the special group of "infanticides" that we have described above, so that generalizations from those statistics include the infanticide group. Moreover, statistics on child abuse *fatalities,* as opposed to *homicides,* which is how many studies are organized (Ewigman et al., 1993; U.S. Advisory Board, 1995), often encompass more than what gets recorded as homicide per se, counting also deaths due to neglect or negligence. Neglect deaths generally include situations in which a child dies because parents fail to feed the child or get obviously needed medical attention, and deaths due to negligence involve parents who fail to provide such basic supervision or precaution that the child dies in some obviously preventable accident, for example, a child left unattended on an open windowsill. About 42% of what are counted by child protection authorities as child abuse fatalities are classified as due to neglect, 54% to abuse, and 5% to both abuse and neglect (Weise & Daro, 1995).

Fatal outcomes in child abuse result most often among the youngest children, with 40% occurring to children under age 1, 18% to children between ages 1 and 2, and 13% to children ages 2 to 3 (McClain et al., 1993; see also Weise & Daro, 1995). The figures for children under 1, however, certainly include a large number of the homicides that we have termed infanticide (i.e., a recently born child killed because the parent does not want the child, is incapable of caring for him or her, or is suffering a childbirth-related psychiatric disturbance). But even excluding an estimated one third of the caretaker-inflicted deaths to children under 1 that might be classified as infanticides, child abuse homicides are still heavily concentrated among very young children.

Three factors account for the unusual vulnerability of this particular group of young children. First, of course, is the large burden and responsibility that such children impose on caretakers. The complete dependence and constant attention required by young children who are needy, impulsive, and not amenable to verbal control can readily overwhelm vulnerable parents. Not surprisingly, two of the most common triggers for fatal child abuse are crying that will not cease and toileting accidents (Krugman, 1985). Second, and perhaps most important, children of this age are small and physically vulnerable. This has several implications. They can still be picked up and shaken or thrown. Moreover, a limited amount of physical force is able to cause serious damage, and the immaturity of certain anatomical features (such as the relatively large size of the head and weakness of the neck) means that they are more likely to suffer fatal traumas than older children. As an indication of this, fatal child abuse is more concentrated among very young children than nonfatal child abuse. The major cause of death is cerebral trauma (Copeland, 1985), especially for the youngest victims. Third, there is often a delay in help-seeking that accompanies violence against young children. When such children are injured, but not fatally, they may not be able to communicate the seriousness of their injuries, and they are isolated in the care of those who may have hurt them, who also are reluctant to seek help. Thus, nonfatal injuries may turn fatal in the absence of care.

Child abuse homicides are more common in conditions of poverty, in families marked by paternal absence or divorce, and perhaps as a result, also among African Americans (2 to 3 times that of other racial groups). Drug use is implicated in 29%. Several studies show that boys and girls are at roughly equal risk for fatal abuse, but boys are at slightly higher risk for fatal neglect (Levine, Freeman, & Compaan, 1994). A possible explanation may be that young boys, more active and aggressive on average, may be more difficult to supervise, or treated as needing less care and supervision (Margolin, 1990). Interest-

ingly, male caretakers account for a disproportionate share of the child abuse homicides, whereas females, who spend more time caring for young children, are responsible for a greater portion of the child neglect fatalities (Levine et al., 1994). The inadequate preparation men receive for assuming the caretaking role with young children may result in lower levels of tolerance for crying, soiling, and disobedience.

A tragic fact about child abuse fatalities is that a large minority, ranging from 24% to 45% (Alfaro, 1988; Levine et al., 1994; Weise & Daro, 1995), occur in families that are already known to child protective authorities because of some family or child care problem they had been having. In as many as one in eight, the case was currently active (Levine et al., 1994). This clearly raises the hope that many deaths could, with proper intervention, somehow be prevented. Unfortunately, the 2,000 child abuse fatalities need to be placed in the context of over 1 million cases of child abuse and neglect that are substantiated by child welfare authorities every year. Some observers have doubted that the homicidal subgroup could ever be reliably detected from that larger pool, in part because the fatalities are so comparatively rare, and in part because so many of the factors that contribute to an actual death may be unpredictable (U.S. Advisory Board, 1995). Others, however, have noted that an important subgroup of child abuse homicides occurs in families with a long and serious history of child maltreatment and parental incompetence and that better research and more aggressive child welfare intervention might save a substantial number of lives (Kaufman Kantor, Williams, & Jasinski, 1995).

Interestingly, there is quite a bit of evidence that the homicides of young children are a very distinct social phenomenon. Unlike homicides for other age groups, the rate for young children does not appear to vary in close correlation with the overall murder rate. This has been found in state-to-state analyses (Straus, 1987) and in international comparisons (Christoffel & Liu, 1983; Fiala & LaFree, 1988). Some countries like Japan that have very low overall homicide rates have relatively high levels of young child homicide. The United States, which has an overall homicide rate 3 times higher than any other developed countries is only modestly higher when it comes to infants (Table 2.1). Straus has found that the sociodemographic variables that predict overall homicide levels in states have no predictive power when it comes to infant homicides, and reduced power for children ages 1 to 4.

If general violence levels do not predict young child homicide, what does? Fiala and La-Free (1988), analyzing the international data, find that levels of child homicide for young children are most closely related to conditions that affect the lives of women and mothers. When women have high labor force participation in the absence of access to education and generous social welfare spending, child homicide rates tend to be higher. Thus, in countries where females were less likely to work like Ireland and Italy (the data were for the 1960s and 1970s), the young children appeared to be more protected from homicide. When women worked but had substantial social welfare supports and education like in Sweden and Denmark, young children had low murder rates. By contrast, the United States has high female labor force participation but comparatively low social welfare spending, and this tended to account for the higher rates.

Baron (1993), analyzing U.S. state data, found gender inequality also a factor that predicted young children's homicide rates, possibly because it increases stress on women and undercuts their ability to protect children. Interestingly, Baron also found the percentage of households headed by females and the level of alcoholism (as measured by deaths due to cirrhosis) to be correlated with young child murders.

Thus, the implication from several comparative studies is that the homicides of young children are a quite distinct social problem from homicide in general and may be most closely related to the conditions of life for women and mothers.

Homicides of Middle Childhood

■ Middle childhood, the period from age 5 to age 12, marks a time of relative immunity from the risks of homicide. Although children of this age face substantial violence, in the form of both parental assaults at home and peer aggression at school, relatively little of it is lethal. The overall rate of 1.5 per 1,000 is far smaller than that for any other age, and the rate is even low among some of the population subgroups in which there are high overall child murder rates, such as Blacks. It is a rate lower than any other segment of the population including elderly persons.

This is a period of transition, which probably accounts for the low rate (Holinger, Holinger, & Sandlow, 1985). Children in middle childhood have outgrown some of the characteristics that create vulnerability for the very young, but have not begun to engage in the activities that make the rate so high for adolescents. Thus, they are less dependent, require less continual care, and have a certain self-sufficiency and socialization and verbal skills. This makes them less of a burden and less potentially frustrating for their parents and other adult caregivers, who are the primary perpetrators of early childhood homicide. They are also bigger and better able to hide, dodge blows, and get away from angry parents. It also takes more force and more energy to inflict a lethal injury on them. By the same token, children of middle childhood still are protected from some of the dangers that affect adolescents. They are under adult supervision and protection most of the time. They have yet to get access to weapons, drugs, and cars. Gang activity, although starting for some of them, is yet to become highly dangerous. Other criminally minded older children and adults are less likely to consider these children as threats or as candidates for involvement in criminal enterprises.

Yet children still do get murdered in this period, and the murders appear to be from a mixture of causes, some related to the homicides of early childhood and some to those of adolescence. Related to their still dependent status, children of middle childhood, like younger children, tend primarily to get murdered by family members (52% of the perpetrators). But unlike the case of younger children, these are not murders committed by hand. Over half are actually committed with firearms. Moreover, reflecting their greater independence, children in middle childhood begin to be prey for stranger homicides. One out of seven children killed in this period is killed by a stranger, more than 3 times the percentage for younger children. Children in this age group, especially the older ones, begin to be touched by the ravages of gang-type violence. About a quarter of these homicides for which police listed a cause were listed as gang related.

The homicides of middle childhood appear to stem from a wide variety of motives. For example, in addition to gang murders, children in this period begin to be vulnerable to sexual homicides. Pedophiles are attracted to children in this age range, and sometimes murder to hide their crimes. There are a significant number of negligent gun homicides for these children. Youth and other family members wield or misuse firearms that they believe to be harmless or unloaded. Some children in this period are killed in the course of other crimes, like robberies or car-jackings, in which children happen to be innocent participants. When family members murder children of this age, sometimes it is in the course of whole-family suicide-homicides (Resnick, 1970). The perpetrators of these crimes are typically fathers who shoot their wives and children before turning their weapons on themselves. Family members also play a role in arson murders, when youth or alienated parents start fires to a family household, and other children are caught in the blaze.

One of the most interesting and unrecognized facts about homicides in middle childhood, however, is that they appear to be on the decline, according to FBI data analyzed for this chapter. This decline may have been missed because overall rates for childhood, influenced by big rises for teen homicide, have been on the increase. But when changes in rates are examined by individual ages (Figure 2.3), using the FBI's supplementary homicide data file, one notes a marked decline for the ages of middle childhood from the 1980s to the 1990s. The decline has occurred for most nonteenage children down to age 2. In fact, it is quite possible that the decline has even affected the infants and 1-year-olds and that the appearance of a statistical increase is due, as suggested earlier, to the recent effect of child death review committees and the more intensive scrutiny being given to the deaths of very young children in ambiguous situations such as

accidents and SIDS. But if we exclude these infants, for whom the increase may have been an artifact, homicide rates for 2- to 12-year-olds have dropped 19% over the decade, a fact all the more impressive in that the rate for teens was rising 80% during the same period.

A look at some of the subcategories of homicide for this age group over this time period shows that the decrease has not been uniform (Figures 2.4 and 2.5). It occurred for Whites and Hispanics, but barely at all for Blacks. It occurred in all regions but the West and all city sizes except for the large ones. It applied to family and acquaintance homicides but not those committed by strangers. And all forms of homicide went down except for those by firearms. It would appear that there has been a decline except for the same kinds of homicides that result in the increase in the rate among teens, that is, African American or Asian victims, involving gangs, drugs, and firearms.

What kinds of factors could be responsible for this apparent decrease in child homicide among nonteenagers? A variety of considerations may be at work. The decade of the 1980s, for example, saw a much intensified effort to identify and report child abuse and neglect and some expansion of treatment programs in this area. This may have protected some children from family homicides who had not previously been protected. The decade has also seen a dramatic development and dissemination of medical technology and emergency medical care. It may be that many more children are surviving inflicted wounds and injuries than have in the past. The decade has certainly *not* seen a drop in firearm availability, as families from all walks of life have become concerned about crime, but it may be that due to publicity about the problem they are being better safeguarded against misuse. The drop in the 1981-1991 rate for negligent gun homicide was particularly marked. There was also a marked drop in the number of children killed as a result of arson: The 1980s saw a great expansion in the use of smoke detectors. A host of other factors may be at work in explaining the decline. This drop is not entirely isolated in that it corresponds to a drop that has also occurred for middle-age Americans (MacKellar & Yanagishita, 1995), and may

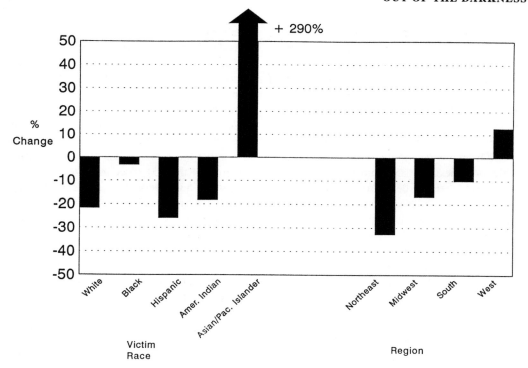

Figure 2.4. Percentage Change in Homicide Rate for 2- to 12-Year-Olds, 1981-1982 to 1991-1992, by Race and Region

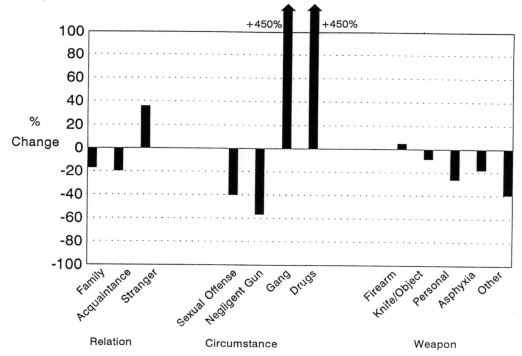

Figure 2.5. Percentage Change in Homicide Rate for 2- to 12-Year-Olds, 1981-1982 to 1991-1992, by Relation, Circumstance, and Weapon

share common roots. But because apparent successes in the fight against crime seem so infrequent, this is a phenomenon that warrants further study.

Child Homicide:
The Developmental Perspective

■ The preceding sections, breaking down juvenile homicide into three different subcategories, was organized in a largely developmental framework. The analysis could have, alternatively, organized the discussion in other ways, for example, emphasizing the perpetrator-victim relationship or the weapon choice, regardless of the children's age. However, the developmental framework has been particularly compelling in the analysis of child homicide (see also Christoffel et al., 1983; Crittenden & Craig, 1990) because it helps make sense of much of the other information about the crime. Elsewhere we have coined the term *developmental victimology* to describe this approach, one that asserts that the nature of crime victimization (and its effects) vary in certain patterned ways as children pass through the life cycle (Finkelhor, 1995; Finkelhor & Dziuba-Leatherman, 1994).

Juvenile homicide is particularly amenable to this kind of developmental analysis for a number of reasons. First, the definition of homicide is relatively clear and uniform across most of childhood. This is not true for other kinds of victimization. For example, in dealing with assault victimization, one is faced with the problem of how to categorize corporal punishment by parents, or in dealing with sexual assault, one is faced with the fact that the crime definition may differ for adolescents compared to prepubertal children. Second, because it is so serious, better and more complete data are available for homicide than for other kinds of crime and victimization. Most homicides are reported to authorities, even if they do not all get counted as homicides, which minimizes the problems of reporting biases. Third, homicide data are available across the whole age spectrum. Much other crime victimization data, like the National Crime Survey, only covers youth ages 12-17 or like the UCR, is not broken down by age at all.

A goal of developmental victimology is to demarcate developmental patterns that can be formulated as general principles regarding crime victimization. Three such principles are relatively easy to observe in the case of homicide and are worth articulating in the possibility that they might in fact be applicable to other kinds of crimes.

Principle 1: As children get older, family perpetrators make up a smaller portion of all perpetrators. With increasing age, children interact with a larger and larger circle of other individuals. They also spend less time with family members. So family-perpetrated homicides should decline as a proportion of the total. The data on homicide clearly bear this out (Figure 2.6), as the percentage of homicides declines with age, with three particular drops, after infancy, after age 7 and then again after age 12.

Principle 2: As children get older, their victimizations come to resemble those of adults. Thus, as children engage in more and more adult activities and take on adult responsibilities and characteristics, their crime victimization patterns should become more like adults. Indeed, the data on homicide show that in addition to more acquaintance homicides, as children age, more of the homicides involve firearms (Figure 2.7), one of the hallmark distinctions between child homicide and adult homicide.

Principle 3: As children get older, gender patterns become more specific. Among younger children, there is less differentiation between the sexes, so presumably gender would be less of a factor in differentiating the patterns or rates of victimization. As children age and activities and physical characteristics are more differentiated by gender, patterns of victimization should become more gender specific. In the case of homicide, we do see that there is a marked divergence of rates for boys and girls as they age (Figure 2.8). Prior to age 12, the male and female rates are extremely similar. After age 12, rates for males rise much more rapidly, so that they are nearly

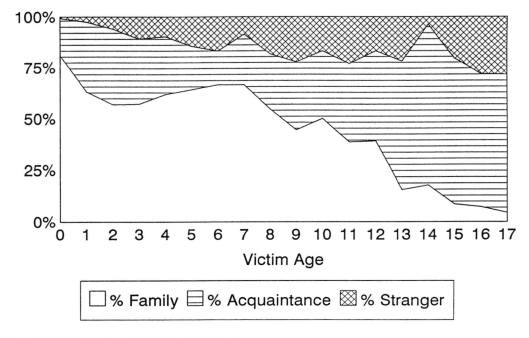

Figure 2.6. Relationship of Child Homicide Victims to Perpetrators
SOURCE: Based on 1991-1992 homicide data.

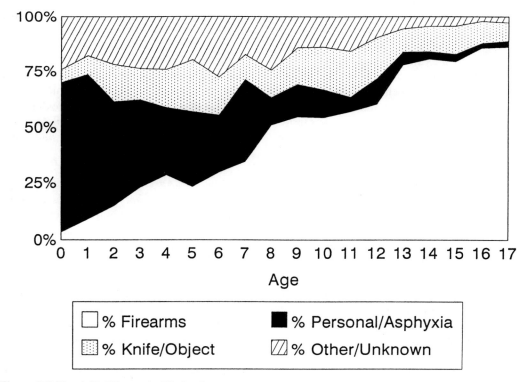

Figure 2.7. Homicide Weapon by Victim Age
SOURCE: Based on 1991-1992 homicide data.

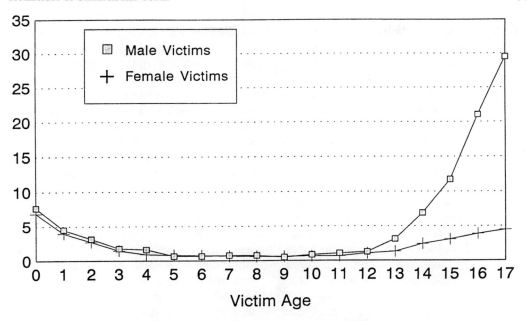

Figure 2.8. Gender of Child Homicide Victims by Victim Age (rate per 100,000 U.S. children)
NOTE: Average rate for 1991-1992.

7 times that of girls by age 17. Interestingly, unlike the previously indicated patterns, this is not a change that occurs gradually or in several steps over childhood, but undergoes a single, marked shift with the onset of adolescence.

One additional principle seems plausible from the prior principles, but we do not have data to explore it so clearly.

Principle 4: As children get older, their risk for victimization is decreasingly determined by family-related factors and increasingly related to more general social factors. Because families and parents govern the lives of younger children much more directly, factors such as maternal well-being, family composition, and quality of parenting should have a correspondingly greater effect on their risk of victimization. As children age and begin to interact with community institutions like schools and other individuals outside the family, general social and community factors such as race, community violence levels, and so forth should play a greater role in their risk for victimization. Some of the studies reviewed earlier provide support for this kind of propo-

sition, for example, Fiala and LaFree's (1988) findings that maternal conditions affect the homicide rate for young children internationally and Straus's (1987) findings that general sociological variables do better at predicting the homicides of older children. But Sampson's (1987) research finds that family factors are important in predicting teen homicide rates as well. It may be that in spite of its logic, such a proposition will not withstand careful empirical scrutiny.

Nonetheless, we present these propositions as examples of the kinds of empirical issues that might be part of the domain of a more formal field of developmental victimology.

Child Homicide Statistics

■ As illustrated by these examples, homicide statistics have a utility and credibility that other crime and abuse statistics often do not. Because of the seriousness of the crime, and other factors such as the common performance of a criminal investigation or an autopsy, there is often a substantial amount of information about the crime on which the statistics are based. Assault and abuse statistics may be based on a single self-report, as in the case of the National Crime Survey, or on a professional decision that is not subject to much review, as in the UCR or child abuse reports. Moreover, national homicide statistics are available for the whole universe of homicides over an extended period of time, rather than being based on a sample or on the aggregation of possibly incompatible state data.

Because homicide statistics exist when other data do not exist or are seen as inferior, analysts often want to use them to answer more general questions, such as trends in nonlethal violence against youth or level of child abuse. So, for example, people have been eager to read success (Besharov, 1990; Pritchard, 1992) or failure (Weise & Daro, 1995) in the fight against child abuse in general from decreases (in the United Kingdom) or increases (in the United States) in the child homicide rate.

But there are good arguments against trying to use homicide statistics and particularly child homicide statistics as indicators for other, more general kinds of crime, violence and maltreatment of children (Trocme & Lindsey, 1995). For one thing, homicides generally constitute only an extremely tiny fraction of the universe of violence and abuse suffered by children. Compared to estimates of child abuse homicides (1,200 to 2,000 per year) estimates of nonfatal child abuse run from 500,000 to 4 million per year, making the homicides far less than even 1% of the total. The ratio of homicides to assaults is equally lopsided. It is risky to make generalizations from such a tiny portion of the problem to something so much bigger and potentially more diverse.

One of the risks of making such generalizations is that small factors can affect the small problem but have little relevance for the larger problem. Thus, if improvements in emergency medicine result in saving the lives of a few dozen more severely assaulted children every year, it could make a dramatic change in the child homicide rate, but have no bearing on the overall issue of child assault or child abuse in general.

In addition, there is good evidence that homicide is a problem very distinct from the general problems of child abuse or violence against children in general. Studies of homicide suggest that

it is not distributed in the same way or predicted by the same characteristics as the more general problems (Gelles, 1991; Trocme & Lindsey, 1995). For example, older teens are much more likely to be murdered than younger teens, but the two groups have generally equivalent risks for being assaulted. Teen homicides seem to be much more disproportionately distributed geographically than assault. Similarly, child abuse homicides are much more heavily concentrated among very young children than child abuse in general.

Thus, much as we would like to be able to use child homicide data to interpret general trends in youth victimization, it is risky to do so. Child homicide needs to be considered a distinct phenomenon from other child victimization, and child homicide statistics primarily tell us about child homicide.

Another more general problem in using homicide statistics is that, even if better than other crime data, they have themselves many serious imperfections, particularly in regard to children. This was illustrated by a study in Missouri that scrutinized all deaths of children ages 0-4 in Missouri between 1983 and 1986 (Ewigman et al., 1993) and found many cases of homicide and child abuse deaths, even some of the obvious ones, being missed by the data-gathering systems. The three major sources of information—the FBI's UCR, child protective services agencies (CPS), and the death certificates that get reported as vital statistics—all had large areas where they failed to overlap. Of all the cases identified as definite child maltreatment deaths by one of the systems, the UCR failed to record 61%, vital statistics failed to identify 52%, and the CPS system failed to identify 21%. Part of the issue for the UCR data is that not all child maltreatment deaths can be classified as "homicides." But, remarkably, the UCR data failed to identify fully one third of the cases in which there was a *criminal* conviction as a result of the death. The death certificates missed many cases of child homicide for a number of additional reasons including a restrictive definition of homicide and the practice of filling out the certificates before criminal and child welfare investigations are complete. The CPS system misses homicide cases especially when the perpetrator is not a caretaker or when the case goes directly to the police and there are no additional children in the household who need to be protected.

In addition to these obvious missed cases, the systems almost certainly miss a great deal of homicide and child abuse that is more subtle and hidden. It is frequently hard to distinguish between intentional injuries and those due to accidents or natural causes or SIDS. Crimes against children are also relatively easy to conceal. Thus, the careful review of child deaths in Missouri determined that in addition to the definite maltreatment cases, there were an equal number of possible or probable maltreatment cases, most of which had been classified on death certificates as accidents. It would seem that a great deal of child homicide is being overlooked. Taking into account the lack of overlap among known cases and the hidden portion of the problem, some analysts have estimated that the actual rate of child homicide or child maltreatment fatality may be about double the numbers officially reported (U.S. Advisory Board, 1995).

Statistics on the homicides of older children have not been subject to the same scrutiny as those on younger children. But because accidents and intentional killings for this group may be more easily distinguished, the data may be more accurate for this group.

The existence of a large number of potentially uncounted homicides of young children has a number of important implications. One is simply that the problem may be much more serious than previously thought, rivaling in size the problem of teenage homicide. Another implication is that trends in homicide statistics for young children risk being affected by social change artifacts. If police get more training in child abuse issues, if autopsies and coroners' reviews become more systematic, if child death review teams bring more professional points of view to bear on child deaths, the number of child homicides may rise without any true underlying increase. In Los Angeles, for example, the local child death review team took credit for increasing from 50% to 87% the percentage of child abuse and neglect deaths that were sent to the district attorney for prosecution from 1989 to 1992 (U.S. Advisory Board, 1995). It is not certain that this sending of cases to the DA increased the number of cases that were classified in the UCR system as child homicides, but it seems quite probable that this would be one effect. In short, homicide statistics for young children in particular have a substantial imprecision and need to be well understood by those who compile them as well as those who use them.

Note

1. This chapter is concerned about persons ages 17 and younger because that is the statutory age of dependency in most states for most purposes. As the time when secondary education ends for most young people in the United States, it is also the point of an important life stage transition.

References

Alfaro, J. D. (1988). What can we learn from child abuse fatalities? A synthesis of nine studies. In D. J. Besharov (Ed.), *Protecting children from abuse and neglect: Policy and practice* (pp. 219-264). Springfield, IL: Charles C Thomas.

Baron, L. (1993). Gender inequality and child homicide: A state-level analysis. In A. V. Wilson (Ed.), *Homicide: The victim/offender connection* (pp. 207-225). Cincinnati, OH: Anderson.

Besharov, D. (1990). Gaining control over child abuse reports. *Public Welfare, 48*(2), 34-40.

Christoffel, K. K. (1990). Violent death and injury in U.S. children and adolescents. *American Journal of Diseases of Children, 144*, 697-706.

Christoffel, K. K., Anzinger, N. K., & Amari, M. (1983). Homicide in childhood: Distinguishable pattern of risk related to developmental levels of victims. *American Journal of Forensic Medicine and Pathology, 4*(2), 129-137.

Christoffel, K. K., & Liu, K. (1983). Homicide death rates in childhood in 23 developed countries: U.S. rates atypically high. *Child Abuse & Neglect, 7*, 339-345.

Christoffel, K. K., Zieserl, E. J., & Chiaramonte, J. (1985). Should child abuse and neglect be considered when a child dies unexpectedly? *American Journal of Diseases of Children, 139*, 876-880.

Copeland, A. R. (1985). Homicide in childhood: The Metro-Dade County experience from 1956-1982. *American Journal of Forensic Medicine and Pathology, 6*(1), 21-24.

Crittenden, P. A., & Craig, S. E. (1990). Developmental trends in the nature of child homicide. *Journal of Interpersonal Violence, 5*, 202-216.

Durfee, M., Gellert, G., & Tilton Durfee, D. (1992). Origins and clinical relevance of child death review teams. *Jour-*

nal of the American Medical Association, 237, 3172-3175.

Emerick, S. J., Foster, L. R., & Campbell, D. T. (1986). Risk factors for traumatic infant death in Oregon, 1973 to 1982. *Pediatrics, 77*(4), 518-522.

Ewigman, B., Kivlahan, C., & Land, G. (1993). The Missouri child fatality study: Underreporting of maltreatment fatalities among children younger than five years of age, 1983 through 1986. *Pediatrics, 91*(2), 330-337.

Fiala, R., & LaFree, G. (1988). Cross-national determinants of child homicide. *American Sociological Review, 53,* 432-445.

Finkelhor, D. (1995). The victimization of children in a developmental perspective. *American Journal of Orthopsychiatry, 65*(2), 177-193.

Finkelhor, D., & Dziuba-Leatherman, J. (1994). Victimization of children. *American Psychologist, 49*(3), 173-183.

Fox, J. A. (1995, March). *Homicide offending patterns: A grim look ahead.* Paper presented at the annual meeting of the American Academy for the Advancement of Science, Atlanta, GA.

Gelles, R. J. (1991). Physical violence, child abuse, and child homicide: A continuum of violence, or distinct behaviors. *Human Nature, 2*(1), 59-72.

Holinger, P. C., Holinger, D. P., & Sandlow, J. (1985). Violent deaths among children in the United States, 1900-1980: An epidemiologic study of suicide, homicide and accidental deaths among 5- to 14-year olds. *Pediatrician, 12,* 11-19.

Jason, J., Carpenter, M. M., & Tyler, C. W. (1983). Underrecording of infant homicide in the United States. *American Journal of Public Health, 73*(2), 195-197.

Kaufman Kantor, G., Williams, L., & Jasinski, J. (1995, November). *Detection and prevention of fatal child abuse: Is prevention possible?* Paper presented at the annual meeting of the American Society of Criminology, Boston.

Krugman, R. D. (1985). Fatal child abuse: Analysis of 24 cases. *Pediatrician, 12,* 68-72.

Levine, M., Freeman, J., & Compaan, C. (1994). Maltreatment-related fatalities: Issues of policy and prevention. *Law & Policy, 16*(4), 449-471.

MacKellar, F. L., & Yanagishita, M. (1995). *Homicide in the United States: Who's at risk?* Washington, DC: Population Reference Bureau.

Margolin, L. (1990). Fatal child neglect. *Child Welfare, 69*(4), 309-319.

McClain, P. W., Sacks, J. J., Froehlke, R. G., & Ewigman, B. G. (1993). Estimates of fatal child abuse and neglect, United States, 1979 through 1988. *Pediatrics, 91,* 338-343.

McCurdy, K., & Daro, D. (1993). *Current trends in child abuse reporting and fatalities: The results of the 1992 annual fifty state survey* (Working Paper No. 808). Chicago: National Committee for Prevention of Child Abuse.

Pritchard, C. (1992). Children's homicide as an indicator of effective child protection: A comparative study of Western European statistics. *British Journal of Social Work, 22*(6), 663-684.

Resnick, P. J. (1970). Murder of the newborn: A psychiatric review of neonaticide. *American Journal of Psychiatry, 126*(10), 1414-1420.

Sampson, R. J. (1987). Urban Black violence: The effect of male joblessness and family disruption. *American Journal of Sociology, 93*(2), 348-382.

Sheley, J. F., & Wright, J. D. (1995). *In the line of fire: Youth, guns, and violence in urban America.* New York: Aldine de Gruyter.

Silverman, R. A., & Kennedy, L. W. (1988). Women who kill their children. *Violence and Victims, 3*(2), 113-127.

Simonetti Rosen, M. (1995, April 30). A *Law Enforcement News* interview with Prof. Alfred Blumstein of Carnegie Mellon University. *Law Enforcement News,* pp. 10-13.

Straus, M. A. (1987). State and regional differences in U.S. infant homicide rates in relation to sociocultural characteristics of the states. *Behavioral Sciences and the Law, 5*(1), 61-75.

Trocme, N., & Lindsey, D. (1995). What can homicide rates tell us about the effectiveness of child welfare services? *Child Abuse & Neglect, 20*(3), 171-184.

U.S. Advisory Board. (1995). *A nation's shame: Fatal child abuse and neglect in the United States* (Report of the U.S. Advisory Board on Child Abuse and Neglect). Washington, DC: U.S. Department of Health and Human Services.

Weise, D., & Daro, D. (1995). *Current trends in child abuse reporting and fatalities: The results of the 1994 annual fifty state survey* (Working Paper No. 808). Chicago: National Committee to Prevent Child Abuse.

World Health Organization. (1995). *World health statistics annual.* Switzerland: Author.

CHAPTER 3

An Examination of Physical Assault and Childhood Victimization Histories Within a National Probability Sample of Women

Terri L. Weaver
Dean G. Kilpatrick
Heidi S. Resnick
Connie L. Best
Benjamin E. Saunders

Women's exposure to physical assault has been a rapidly emerging area of study over the past 10 years. The majority of research has examined women following physical assault by a romantic partner (i.e., spouse or boyfriend) who are seeking help at a shelter (e.g., Astin, Ogland-Hand, Coleman, & Foy, 1995; Kemp, Rawlings, & Green, 1991; Weaver & Clum,

AUTHORS' NOTE: This research was partially supported by National Institute of Drug Abuse Grant DA 05220-01A2, Dean G. Kilpatrick, principal investigator. Points of view or opinions expressed within this chapter are those of the authors and do not necessarily represent the official position or policies of the National Institute of Drug Abuse. Correspondence concerning this chapter should be addressed to Terri L. Weaver, Ph.D., who is now at the University of Missouri–St. Louis, Department of Psychology, 8001 Natural Bridge Road, St. Louis, MO 63121.

1996), emergency room or health clinic (e.g., Bergman, Larsson, Brismar, & Klang, 1987), or outpatient clinic (e.g., Jouriles & O'Leary, 1985). Compared with nonvictimized comparison groups, these studies and others have documented wide-ranging psychological and physical health sequelae following exposure to physical assault.

However, overreliance on a sampling strategy limited to select or help-seeking samples may lead researchers to draw faulty or contradictory conclusions about unique factors associated with romantic partner assault. For example, national samples of physically assaulted women may be different demographically, may experience less severe forms of physical assault, and may have different victimization histories compared with help-seeking populations.

A second limitation of existing sampling strategies lies in the choice of the comparison group. Existing studies have relied on comparisons with nonvictimized women or women within maritally distressed (but not violent) relationships. However, studies have less frequently compared the experiences of victims of romantic partner assault with the experiences of those women who are physically assaulted by strangers. Society has generally viewed assault by persons known to victims to be less serious and less traumatic compared with assaults by strangers. In a review of the literature, Simon (1995) highlighted numerous findings in which the police and legal system have treated romantic partner assault (domestic violence) as a family matter rather than a criminal act, resulting in decreased aggressiveness in prosecution, decreased convictions, and less severe sanctions.

Taken together, to examine the unique aspects of romantic partner assault, sampling strategies must be expanded to examine a broader (less select) sample of victims and findings must be compared not only with nonvictims but also with stranger assault victims. The present study addressed these issues by examining individual and assault characteristics within a national probability sample of romantic partner assault victims and comparing these characteristics with two comparison groups: a national probability sample of nonvictims of physical assault and victims of stranger assault. Use of a national probability sample in conjunction with the designated comparison groups provided us the opportunity to examine potentially distinguishing historical and current factors associated with romantic partner assault. Existing research examining individual and assault characteristics of romantic partner assault is briefly reviewed to provide a context for the choice of variables.

Individual Characteristics

Demographic Variables. Within a representative sample of women, age and income were found to be negatively associated with domestic assault (Straus, Gelles, & Steinmetz, 1980). In addition, in a large sample of Caucasian army men ($N = 11,870$), Pan, Neidig, and O'Leary (1994) found that more severe physical assaults were perpetrated by men who earned lower income, reported an alcohol or a drug problem, and had more marital discord and depressive symptomatology compared with men who perpetrated less severe forms of assaults. Findings from these two large studies suggest that demographic factors, substance use, and marital discord may serve as risk factors for physical assault or risk factors for more severe assaults. Within this study, income, education, age, marital status, race, employment, and substance use were assessed for their relationship to romantic partner and stranger violence.

Childhood Victimization Histories. Within help-seeking samples, women assaulted by romantic partners frequently report histories of multiple victimizations. For example, within a shelter sample of 43 battered women, one study found that 53% of women reported a history of childhood sexual abuse and 71% reported a history of childhood physical abuse (Weaver & Clum, 1996). This "cycle of victimization" may play an etiological role in precipitating later victimization at the hands of assaultive partners. Interestingly, when battered women were compared with nonbattered but maritally distressed women, rates of childhood physical and sexual abuse were similar. Specifically, 34% of battered women and

24.3% of maritally distressed women reported childhood physical abuse, whereas 42% of battered women and 48.6% of maritally distressed women reported childhood sexual abuse (Astin et al., 1995). By using an appropriate comparison group, these findings suggest that childhood abuse is not a unique predictor of romantic partner assault. To examine the relationship between childhood history and adult assault, childhood physical and sexual abuse was assessed within the national sample.

Assault Characteristics. A woman's relationship to her perpetrator has a number of implications for the type of assault she experiences. Because of the intimate relationship of the victim to the perpetrator, these experiences can be chronic, and periods of acute assault often alternate with periods in which women are under constant threat of harm (Follingstad, Neckerman, & Vormbrock, 1988). In this way, romantic partner assaults are typified by series or multiple experiences of physical violence, rather than a single incident. One study compared crime experiences (physical and sexual assault) of women by categorizing their relationship to their perpetrator (husband vs. stranger) (Riggs, Kilpatrick, & Resnick, 1992). Based on retrospective reports averaging 13 years postcrime, authors found that women attacked by their husbands (physically or sexually) were more likely to experience a series of attacks rather than a single incident compared to women attacked by strangers. Limitations of this study include the retrospective nature of the data and the very small sample sizes (approximately 10-14 women per group).

Within groups of romantic partner assault victims, research has examined a number of physical and psychological injuries. Physical injury includes cuts, burns, bruises, sprains, black eyes, lost teeth, and so on (Dutton, 1992). Posttraumatic stress disorder (PTSD) has been noted within a number of shelter samples at rates ranging from 45% to 84%, with the lower estimate associated with assessment by interview and the higher estimate associated with assessment by self-report (Astin et al., 1995; Houskamp & Foy, 1991; Kemp et al., 1991). Similar to the findings

in the sexual assault literature (e.g., Kilpatrick, Saunders, et al., 1989), experiences of life threat and severe physical injury increase the likelihood of PTSD (Houskamp & Foy, 1991). In addition, frequency of abuse has been found to predict number of and severity of psychological symptoms (Follingstad, Brennan, Hause, Polek, & Rutledge, 1991). Frequency of assault may also be related to severity of physical injury, given the generally escalating nature of domestic violence. Given these findings, series versus single assault, physical injury, perceived life threat, and PTSD were compared within the two assault victim groups.

In summary, this study examined the individual characteristics of a national probability sample of victims of romantic partner assault and compared these findings with a national probability sample of victims of stranger physical assault and nonvictims. In addition, assault characteristics were compared within the two assault groups. We had two a priori hypotheses: (a) It was expected that both physical assault groups (romantic partner and stranger) would have significantly higher rates of PTSD compared with nonvictims of assault, and (b) it was expected that the national sample of victims of romantic partner assault would report significantly more experiences of series assaults compared with victims of stranger assault. Following univariate analyses, logistic regressions were conducted to examine multivariate relationships between variables predicting series assaults and between variables predicting stranger/romantic partner assault.

Method

Participants

National Probability Sample From the National Women's Study

The sample consisted of 4,008 women, of whom 2,008 were a national probability household sample of U.S. adult women (age 18 or older), and the remaining 2,000 women were an oversample of women aged 18-34 years. To correct for the effects of oversampling, the data were weighted by age and race to 1989 estimates of the distribution of these characteristics in the U.S. population of adult women. All analyses were conducted with the weighted sample data. Additional details about the National Women's Study methodology are provided elsewhere (Resnick, Kilpatrick, Dansky, Saunders, & Best, 1993).

This study surveyed women in three waves, with Wave 1 being the initial contact and Waves 2 and 3 comprising the 2-year follow-up period. Only women who completed at least one of the two follow-up waves were used in this study ($N = 3,358$). Across Waves 2 and 3, 43 women reported a physical assault at the hands of a romantic partner, 62 women reported a physical assault at the hands of a stranger, and the remaining women did not report a history of physical assault ($N = 3,253$).

Procedure

Representative Sample

Multistage geographic sampling was used. Stratified samples of counties in areas defined as central city, standard metropolitan statistical areas (SMSAs) and as non-SMSAs within four major regions of the country were generated as primary sampling units (PSUs) during the first stage of a two-stage sampling procedure. The second stage involved systematic selection of residential telephone exchanges in the PSUs. Random-digit dialing was used to identify households within each strata. The sampling, interviewing, and monitoring procedures were conducted by the survey research firm of Schulman, Ronca, and Bucuvalas, Inc. (SRBI). Only well-trained, experienced, female SRBI interviewers were used.

Measures

The interview consisted of six sections administered in the following sequence: (a) introductory questions, (b) depressive disorders screening, (c) victimization screening, (d) drug and alcohol screening, (e) PTSD interview schedule, and (f) demographics. Information from the demographics, victimization screen-

ing, and PTSD sections were of interest in this study.

Victimization Screening

Childhood victimization screening included retrospective reports of completed and attempted rape, contact sexual molestation, and physical assault, occurring before the age of 18. These assessments were conducted at the initial contact with participants (Wave 1). Completed rape was operationalized as affirmative responses to detailed behavioral descriptions of unwanted sexual advances using force or threat of harm resulting in vaginal, oral, anal, or digital penetration. Attempted rape was defined as an attempt by someone to force unwanted sexual contact as described above. Sexual molestation was operationalized as someone touching your breasts or pubic area (other than the rape) involving force or threat of force. Physical assault was defined as a physical attack with a weapon (gun, knife, or other weapon) or a physical attack without a weapon with the intent to kill or seriously injure. For the purposes of analyses within this study, the category of sexual molestation included both sexual molestation experiences and experiences of attempted rape.

Participants were asked to report up to three completed rape incidents (first, most recent, and worst) and about one type of each of the remaining forms of assault (completed molestation, attempted sexual assault, and physical assault).

The most serious or only incident of physical assault in adulthood was assessed prospectively during Waves 2 and 3. Characteristics of the physical assault were assessed including relationship to the perpetrator, fear of death or serious physical injury, the extent of physical injury sustained during the assault, whether the perpetrator and/or victim was under the influence of any substances, and whether the assault was a series or a single assault.

PTSD Screening

PTSD was assessed using the National Women's Study (NWS) PTSD module (Kilpatrick, Resnick, Saunders, & Best, 1989; Resnick et al., 1993). A positive current PTSD diagnosis was assigned if the respondent reported the occurrence of *DSM-III-R* criteria B (one reexperiencing), C (three avoidance), and D (two increased arousal) symptoms within the 6 months before the interview. Kappa coefficients were calculated between NWS PTSD module and the PTSD assessment of the Structured Clinical Interview for *DSM-III-R* (Spitzer, Williams, & Gibbon, 1987). Coefficients of agreement (kappa) were .77 for lifetime PTSD and .71 for current PTSD (Kilpatrick et al., in press).

Results

Demographic Comparisons and Rates of PTSD

Overall comparisons between the three national probability groups were conducted on demographic variables and rates of current PTSD. Chi-square analyses yielded significant differences for groups on variables of employment, χ^2 (2, $N = 3,358$) = 7.52, $p < .05$; marital status, χ^2 (6, $N = 3,358$) = 21.05, $p < .01$; race, χ^2 (2, $N = 3,358$) = 31.54, $p < .001$; and rates of current PTSD, χ^2 (2, $N = 3,358$) = 10.53, $p < .01$. The three groups were not significantly different on income and education. A one-way ANOVA yielded significant differences between groups on age, $F(2, 3346) = 9.85$, $p < .001$.

Follow-up analyses were conducted to determine which groups accounted for the significant findings in the overall group analyses. These comparisons are listed in Table 3.1.

Victims of romantic partner assault were significantly younger than victims of stranger assault and nonvictims of assault. Racially, a higher percentage of victims of romantic partner assault were White than was the case for victims of stranger assault. A significantly higher percentage of victims of stranger assault were non-White compared with the nonvictims. Victims of romantic partner assault were more likely to be married and more likely to be employed compared with victims of stranger assault. Last, victims of romantic partner and stranger assault had significantly higher rates of current PTSD compared with nonvictims of assault.

Childhood Victimization History

Overall comparisons between the three groups were made on rates of childhood victimization, including three frequency scores: frequency of childhood physical abuse, childhood rape, and sexual molestation; and two combined scores: total childhood sexual abuse (rape and/or sexual molestation) and total childhood abuse (physical abuse and/or rape and/or sexual molestation). Overall analyses yielded significant findings for four of the five types of childhood victimization. Significant findings included childhood physical abuse, χ^2 (2, $N = 3,358$) = 19.66, $p < .0001$; childhood rape, χ^2 (2, $N = 3,358$) = 14.2, $p < .001$; total sexual abuse, χ^2 (2, $N = 3,358$) = 12.86, $p < .01$; and total childhood abuse, χ^2 (2, $N = 3,358$) = 18.46, $p < .001$. Follow-up comparisons were examined between groups to determine which comparisons accounted for the significant findings. The findings are listed in Table 3.2.

Compared with nonvictims of assault, victims of romantic partner assault were significantly more likely to report sexual molestation in childhood, childhood rape, any form of childhood sexual abuse, and any childhood abuse. Compared with nonvictims of assault, victims of stranger assault were significantly more likely to report experiences of physical abuse, childhood rape, any form of childhood sexual abuse, and any childhood abuse. Interestingly, when victims of romantic partner assault were compared with victims of stranger assault, there were no significant differences on childhood victimization history.

Assault Characteristics

Assault characteristics were examined to determine whether the relationship to the perpetrator systematically affects the nature of the physical assault. Comparisons between the two physical assault groups are listed in Table 3.3. Women assaulted by romantic partners were significantly more likely than women assaulted by strangers to have minor or serious injuries, to be assaulted by perpetrators under the influence of alcohol, and to have multiple or series assaults. No significant differences occurred

TABLE 3.1 Demographic Characteristics and PTSD Rates for Victims of Romantic Partner (Husband/Boyfriend) Physical Assault ($N = 43$), Victims of Stranger Physical Assault ($N = 62$), and Nonvictims of Physical Assault ($N = 3,253$)

Characteristic	Stranger Perpetrator	Romantic Partner Perpetrator	Nonvictims
Age in years[a1]			
Mean (SD)	46.38 (21.52)	32.80 (10.71)	44.67 (17.79)
Race[2][*1] N (%)			
White	34 (54.9)	33 (77.2)	2,680 (82.4)
Non-White	28 (45.1)	10 (22.8)	573 (17.6)
Marital status[3] N (%)			
Married	34 (54.9)	31 (70.9)	2,126 (65.4)
Separated	5 (8.7)	8 (17.7)	329 (10.1)
Widowed	4 (6.0)	0 (0)	340 (10.5)
Single	19 (30.4)	5 (11.4)	457 (14.0)
Income N (%)			
$10,000-$15,000	24 (41)	9 (21.0)	836 (27.7)
$25,000-$35,000	25 (43)	18 (41.5)	1,210 (40.1)
$35,000-$50,000	9 (16.0)	16 (37.5)	969 (32.1)
Education N (%)			
Some high school	11 (18.2)	5 (11.2)	523 (16.1)
High school graduate	50 (80.2)	38 (88.8)	2,727 (83.9)
Employment[b4] N (%)			
Employed	29 (46.4)	31 (72.6)	1,748 (54)
Unemployed	33 (53.6)	12 (27.4)	1,506 (46)
Current PTSD[c][*2] N (%)	15 (24.5)	12 (27.2)	238 (7.3)

NOTE: Superscript letters indicate a significant difference between victims of romantic partner assault and nonvictims of assault. Superscript numbers indicate a significant difference between victims of romantic partner assault and victims of stranger assault. Asterisks and superscript numbers indicate a significant difference between victims of stranger assault and nonvictims of assault.

a. $F(1, 3285) = 19.20, p < .001$.
b. $\chi^2 (1, N = 3,296) = 6.14, p < .05$.
c. $\chi^2 (1, N = 3,296) = 24.26, p < .0001$.
1. $F(1, 102) = 14.61, p < .001$.
2. $\chi^2 (1, N = 105) = 5.49, p < .05$.
3. $\chi^2 (3, N = 105) = 9.38, p < .05$.
4. $\chi^2 (1, N = 105) = 7.14, p < .01$.
*1. $\chi^2 (1, N = 3,315) = 29.26, p < .0001$.
*2. $\chi^2 (1, N = 3,315) = 25.08, p < .0001$.

with respect to perceived life threat and victims using substances.

Multivariate Logistic Regression Predicting Series Assault

A multivariate logistic regression was used to examine which variables significantly predicted whether a romantic partner assault would be a single or series form of assault. To choose the most parsimonious set of predictors, individual and assault characteristics that were significantly associated with series assault in the univariate analyses were retained within the multivariate model. Age and the composite score for childhood abuse were significantly associated with multiple assaults, $F(1, 41) = 3.99, p = .05$, for age, and $\chi^2 (1, N = 43) = 6.49, p < .05$, for composite score for childhood abuse. None of the assault characteristics was significantly associated with series assault. However, level of injury was correlated at the trend level, $\chi^2 (2, N = 43) = 4.64, p = .097$, and we elected to include it in the model as a predictor. Therefore, the three predictors in the model were age, composite childhood abuse, and level of injury.

TABLE 3.2 Childhood Victimization Histories of Victims of Romantic Partner (Husband/Boyfriend) Perpetrators of Physical Assault ($N = 43$), Victims of Stranger Assault ($N = 62$), and Nonvictims of Physical Assault ($N = 3,253$)

Victimization	Romantic Partner Perpetrator N (%)	Stranger Perpetrator N (%)	Nonvictims N (%)
Physical abuse[*1]	3 (7.0)	7 (10.9)	80 (2.5)
Rape[a *2]	8 (19.0)	12 (19.0)	274 (8.4)
Molestation[b]	8 (17.6)	8 (13.1)	294 (9.0)
Any childhood sexual abuse[c *3]	13 (29.5)	17 (28.0)	509 (15.6)
Any childhood abuse[d *4]	14 (32.5)	21 (33.4)	550 (16.9)

NOTE: Superscript letters indicate a significant difference between victims of romantic partner assault and nonvictims of assault. Superscript numbers indicate a significant difference between victims of romantic partner assault and victims of stranger assault. Asterisks and superscript numbers indicate a significant difference between victims of stranger assault and nonvictims of assault.

a. χ^2 (1, $N = 3,296$) = 6.14, $p = .01$.
b. χ^2 (1, $N = 3,296$) = 3.81, $p = .05$.
c. χ^2 (1, $N = 3,296$) = 6.21, $p = .01$.
d. χ^2 (1, $N = 3,296$) = 7.36, $p = .01$.
*1. χ^2 (1, $N = 3,315$) = 15.27, $p < .01$.
*2. χ^2 (1, $N = 3,315$) = 7.89, $p < .01$.
*3. χ^2 (1, $N = 3,315$) = 5.46, $p < .05$.
*4. χ^2 (1, $N = 3,315$) = 11.12, $p < .01$.

These variables were entered in a single block. Findings are listed in Table 3.4.

The logistic regression revealed that the composite score of childhood abuse was the only significant predictor of series assault. Specifically, experiencing some form of childhood victimization increased the odds of series assault fivefold (odds ratio = 5.33) (95% confidence interval = 1.15; 24.53).

Multivariate Logistic Regression Predicting Romantic Partner Versus Stranger Assault

A second series of logistic regressions was run with romantic partner versus stranger assault as the criterion measure. Three assault characteristics were used within the model: severity of injury, perpetrator under the influence (specifically perpetrator using alcohol), and series

TABLE 3.3 Assault Characteristics of Victims of Romantic Partner Physical Assault ($N = 43$) and Victims of Stranger Physical Assault ($N = 62$)

Characteristic	Romantic Partner Perpetrator N (%)	Stranger Perpetrator N (%)	χ^2	p
Injury				
None	4 (9.7)	22 (34.7)	8.65	.01
Minor	24 (55.6)	24 (39.3)		
Serious	15 (34.7)	16 (26.0)		
Life threat	29 (67.8)	36 (70.1)	.05	.81
Victim using substances				
Alcohol	3 (8)	1 (1.8)	5.96	.20
Drugs	0 (0)	4 (6.7)		
Both	1 (1.5)	1 (.8)		
Neither	39 (89.4)	56 (90.7)		
Perpetrator using substances				
Alcohol	13 (30.1)	3 (4.7)	15.03	.005
Drugs	0 (0)	8 (13.2)		
Both	6 (13.6)	9 (13.9)		
Neither	18 (40.7)	33 (53.2)		
Not sure	6 (13.0)	9 (15)		
Series assault	16 (36.4)	8 (12.8)	8.11	.004

TABLE 3.4 Logistic Regressions Predicting Single Versus Series Physical Assaults and Romantic
Partner/Stranger Perpetrator of Physical Assaults

Predictors	Odds Ratio	p	B	95% Confidence Interval	−2 Log Likelihood	Model Chi-Square
First logistic regression, predicting series/ nonseries assault					46.120	$\chi^2(3) = 10.68\, p < .05$
Age	.96	.33	−.04	(.89, 1.04)		
Any child abuse	5.33	.03	1.67	(1.15, 24.53)		
Injury	.13	.39	−.94	(.12, 1.31)		
Second logistic regression, predicting romantic partner/ stranger assault					98.459	$\chi^2(5) = 43.11\, p < .001$
Age	.95	.002	−.05	(.92, .99)		
Injury	5.06	.02	1.62	(1.23, 20.70)		
Perpetrator using alcohol	6.81	.01	1.92	(1.51, 30.88)		
Series assault	2.94	.07	1.08	(.91, 9.30)		
Race	4.77	.006	1.56	(1.55, 14.59)		

assault (see Table 3.3). Demographic variables included age, employment status, and race. Marital status was not used in the model because it was confounded with the definition of the romantic partner assailant.

A multivariate logistic regression analysis was run first entering the three demographic variables: age, employment, and race as a block. Age and race remained significant predictors and employment status was nonsignificant. Next the regression was rerun, with age, race, severity of injury, series assault, and perpetrator using alcohol as predictors. Nearly all variables within the model significantly predicted romantic partner assault, creating a "profile" of victims of intimate acquaintance assault (see Table 3.4): Romantic partner assault victims were more likely to be attacked by perpetrators using alcohol, to be White, younger, and to experience serious injury. Experiencing a series assault was significant at the trend level ($p < .10$).

Discussion

Demographic Characteristics

There were a number of significant demographic differences between groups. Victims as-

saulted by romantic partners were significantly younger than both other groups (stranger-assault and nonvictim groups), which parallels Straus et al.'s (1980) finding that age was negatively associated with domestic assault within a representative sample. Because younger men are also more likely to assault their romantic partners (O'Leary, 1993), this finding may represent a cohort effect in which romantic partner violence is simply more common in younger groups.

Victims of assault by romantic partners within the national probability sample were more likely to be married and employed compared with nonvictims and victims of stranger assault. Because romantic partner assault by definition occurs with a intimate partner, being with a partner in and of itself is a risk factor for this type of assault. However, this finding must be interpreted with caution because the romantic partner assault victims were not significantly more likely to be married compared with the nonvictims. The increased rate of employment within the romantic partner assault group suggests that this group is functioning better vocationally than the other two national probability groups.

In terms of racial composition, victims of stranger assault had the highest proportion of non-Whites, differing significantly from the victims of romantic partner assault and nonvictims. This finding contrasts with the review by O'Leary (1993), who reported that non-White groups were more likely to commit severe domestic assaults in referred or select samples (e.g., military personnel). All of the physical assaults within the current study were aggravated assaults, thus meeting the definition of "serious assaults." Therefore, the increased proportion of minorities in victims of romantic partner assault from previous studies may actually reflect a sampling bias associated with the use of select samples of assault victims. In the present study, the greater proportion of minority victims of stranger assault may partially result from the fact that more minorities live in urban settings, where "street crime" (i.e., stranger assault) is more likely (Bachman, 1994). However, it is also possible that this finding is associated with the methodology of assessment of physical assault in adulthood. That is, participants were asked about their only or worst physical assault experience. Therefore, non-Whites could have additional incidents of romantic partner assaults that were not assessed.

Analyses were conducted to compare the demographic composition of the national sample with a shelter (help-seeking) sample of battered women (Weaver, Kilpatrick, Resnick, Best, & Saunders, 1995). These analyses revealed that compared with the help-seeking sample, victims of romantic partner assault and nonvictims within the national probability sample were significantly more likely to be married and more likely to be employed. The help-seeking sample and victims of stranger assault were comparable on these two variables. Being legally married and having a job suggests that victims of romantic partner assault and nonvictims within the national sample had greater access to economic resources, compared to help-seeking victims and victims of stranger assault. This finding suggests that diminished economic resources may be associated with vulnerability to experiencing a particular type of assault (e.g., stranger physical assault) and, in addition, may increase the likelihood of pursuing a particular type of help-seeking (e.g., shelter services) following romantic partner assault.

Childhood Victimization Experiences

Victims of romantic partner and stranger assault were distinctive for nearly every form of childhood victimization compared with nonvictims of assault. For *any* form of childhood abuse, both groups of victims were nearly twice as likely to experience abuse in childhood compared with nonvictims. Interestingly, all of these differences washed out when the two groups of assault victims in this sample were compared. Although it is likely that there are multiple pathways to experiencing physical assault in adulthood, a history of victimization in childhood may be one *general* risk factor for later assault, regardless of the relationship to the perpetrator in these later assaults.

Interestingly, within the group of victims of romantic partner assault, logistic regression analyses found that childhood victimization significantly predicted series assaults. Therefore, besides being a general risk factor for later victimization, childhood assault may play an important role in coping *after* an assault occurs. Specifically, women with a history of childhood abuse may be less able to extricate themselves from abusive relationships after the onset of an attack. This difficulty may be due in part to complications resulting from abuse-related psychological sequelae. That is, long-term consequences of childhood physical and sexual abuse have many overlapping sequelae, including substance abuse, self-injurious behavior, general psychological distress, interpersonal problems, and functional (academic and vocational) difficulties (Malinosky-Rummell & Hansen, 1993). It is possible that these psychological outcomes associated with childhood abuse make women more vulnerable to revictimization within the same relationship by interfering with active attempts to escape or to terminate the relationship. Based on their extensive clinical experience with battered women, Goodman and Fallon (1995) also note that childhood victimization experiences may make a woman particularly vulnerable to experiences of chronic abuse in adulthood.

One limitation is worth mentioning. Although childhood victimization significantly predicted series assault, we do not know about the initial assault characteristics within this group of women. It is possible that women with series victimization histories experienced more severe initial assaults with their partners compared with women with single incidents, suggesting that they had less of a "window of opportunity to escape." To answer this question we would need to get more information about the temporal emergence of assault characteristics.

It is interesting to note that the rates of childhood abuse reported by the two assault groups within the national sample (roughly 7%-10% for physical abuse and 28% for childhood sexual abuse) were significantly lower than the rates of 30%-70% of women reporting childhood abuse within shelter samples (Astin et al., 1995; Weaver & Clum, 1996). This discrepancy may result from differing definitions of childhood abuse across studies. However, it is also possible that women reporting to shelter services do have more complex histories of abuse and are in need of more intensive services compared with women within the larger community.

Assault Characteristics and Posttraumatic Stress Disorder

Approximately one fourth of the two assault groups met diagnostic criteria for current PTSD. As predicted, this rate was significantly higher for the two assault groups compared with nonvictims. Because a significant proportion of women in these groups reported subjectively feeling as if their life was in danger, and life threat is associated with the development of PTSD, this relationship is not surprising and suggests that life threat is likely to occur during physical assault regardless of whether the perpetrator is a romantic partner or is unknown.

Rates of PTSD within the national study were somewhat less than rates reported by the shelter sample of Weaver and Clum (1996, 30% reported current PTSD) and substantially lower than rates reported by the shelter sample of Astin et al. (1995, 58% reported current PTSD). Rates of PTSD may differ across shelters depending on the current and historical victimization histories of the shelter's members.

Within the national sample, there were differences in severity of physical injuries by type of assailant; over one third of the romantic partner assault victims experienced serious injury, compared with victims of stranger assault (26%). Part of the reason for this finding could be explained by the fact that victims of romantic partner assault, as predicted, were more likely to experience series assaults. Repeated assaults, compared with a single assault, are more likely to escalate in severity, resulting in an increased likelihood of more serious injuries. These findings dispel the myth that assault by someone "known" is somehow less serious than assault by a stranger and mirror the findings of Riggs et al. (1992). In addition, logistic regression analyses revealed that injury continues to be a significant predictor of romantic partner assault after controlling for series assault, indicating that such assaults may be more violent in addition to being *repeated* assaults. Considering that offense seriousness is one of the most important variables used to determine sentencing (cited in Simon, 1995), it is even more surprising that crimes in which the offender is known to the victim consistently receive shorter sentences. Given the seriousness of these crimes, these data provide empirical support for stiffening prosecution practices and sentencing for these crimes.

Perpetrators of romantic partner assault were more likely to be using alcohol. This finding is consistent with domestic violence and alcohol use in nonrepresentative samples (O'Leary, 1993). Perpetrators under the influence of alcohol were nearly 7 times more likely to be perpetrators of romantic partner assault. Given that childhood physical and childhood sexual assault is associated with adult substance use (Malinosky-Rummell & Hansen, 1993), alcohol dependence may reflect another mechanism through which the cycle of violence is perpetuated in adulthood. This finding also suggests that treatment programs for adult male alcoholics may benefit from screening for assault of romantic partners. These programs could then dovetail the treatment of the substance problem with compensatory violence management techniques, specifically targeting domestic violence. In addition, Fagan (1993) has commented on alcohol's role in providing a "context" for the perpetration of violence against intimates. Further research is needed to examine the temporal, situational, attitudinal, and other individual factors that combine to create this context.

Summary and Conclusions

■ The present study has a number of limitations, including a critique of the definition of physical assault. Women assaulted by romantic partners may be less likely to ascribe life-threatening intent to "known" assailants. Therefore, rates of adult and childhood physical assault may be underestimates of the actual rates. In addition, decision rules within the study required that there be a cap on the number of events of physical assault that were assessed. Therefore, because of the study's design, women with multiple victimization histories may not have had the opportunity to report all of their experiences of physical assault. It is suggested that future studies use assessments of physical assault that focus on the *actions* rather than the *intent* of the perpetrator. However, a strength of the study is that women's reports of physical assault were assessed within a year of their occurrence, making it less likely that reports were affected by memory distortion.

In summary, this study examined physical assault by romantic partners within a national sample and compared the findings with victims of stranger assault and nonvictims of assault. This study found that several factors appear to be distinctive for physical assault by romantic partners. These factors include younger victims, increased likelihood of employment, more series assaults, increased injury, and perpetrator under the influence of alcohol. Increased rates of childhood victimization, PTSD, and life threat appear to be more generally related to physical assault rather than to relationship with the perpetrator.

References

Astin, M. C., Ogland-Hand, S. M., Coleman, E. M., & Foy, D. W. (1995). Posttraumatic stress disorder and childhood abuse in battered women: Comparisons with mari-

tally distressed women. *Journal of Consulting and Clinical Psychology, 63,* 308-312.

Bachman, R. (1994). *Violence against women. A national crime victimization survey report.* Washington, DC: U.S. Department of Justice, Office of Justice Programs, Bureau of Justice Statistics.

Bergman, B., Larsson, G., Brismar, B., & Klang, M. (1987). Psychiatric morbidity and personality characteristics of battered women. *Acta Psychiatrica Scandinavica, 76,* 678-683.

Dutton, M. (1992). *Empowering and healing the battered woman: A model for assessment and intervention.* New York: Springer.

Fagan, J. (1993, Winter). Interactions among drugs, alcohol, and violence. *Health Affairs, 12*(4), 65-79.

Follingstad, D., Brennan, A., Hause, E., Polek, D., & Rutledge, L. (1991). Factors moderating physical and psychological symptoms of battered women. *Journal of Family Violence, 6*(1), 81-95.

Follingstad, D., Neckerman, A., & Vormbrock, J. (1988). Reactions to victimization and coping strategies of battered women: The ties that bind. *Clinical Psychology Review, 8,* 373-390.

Goodman, M. S., & Fallon, B. C. (1995). *Pattern changing for abused women.* Thousand Oaks, CA: Sage.

Houskamp, B., & Foy, D. (1991). The assessment of posttraumatic stress disorder in battered women. *Journal of Interpersonal Violence, 6,* 367-375.

Jouriles, E., & O'Leary, K. D. (1985). Interspousal reliability of reports of marital violence. *Journal of Consulting and Clinical Psychology, 53,* 419-421.

Kemp, A., Rawlings, E., & Green, B. (1991). Posttraumatic stress disorder (PTSD) in battered women: A shelter sample. *Journal of Traumatic Stress, 4,* 137-148.

Kilpatrick, D., Resnick, H., Freedy, J., Pelcovitz, D., Resick, P., Roth, S., & Van der Kolk, B. (in press). The posttraumatic stress disorder field trial: Emphasis on Criterion A and overall PTSD diagnosis. In *DSM-IV sourcebook.* Washington, DC: American Psychiatric Press.

Kilpatrick, D., Resnick, H., Saunders, B., & Best, C. (1989). *The National Women's Study PTSD module.* Unpublished instrument. Charleston: Medical University of South Carolina, Department of Psychiatry and Behavioral Sciences, Crime Victims Research and Treatment Center.

Kilpatrick, D., Saunders, B., Amick-McMullan, A., Best, C., Veronen, L., & Resnick, H. (1989). Victims and crime factors associated with development of crime-related post-traumatic stress disorder. *Behavior Therapy, 20,* 199-214.

Malinosky-Rummell, R., & Hansen, D. J. (1993). Long-term consequences of childhood physical abuse. *Psychological Bulletin, 114*(1), 68-79.

O'Leary, K. D. (1993). Through a psychological lens: Personality traits, personality disorders, and levels of violence. In R. J. Gelles & D. R. Loseke (Eds.), *Current controversies on family violence* (pp. 7-30). Newbury Park, CA: Sage.

Pan, H. S., Neidig, P. H., & O'Leary, K. D. (1994). Predicting mild and severe husband-to-wife physical aggression. *Journal of Consulting and Clinical Psychology, 62,* 975-981.

Resnick, H., Kilpatrick, D., Dansky, B., Saunders, B., & Best, C. (1993). Prevalence of civilian trauma and posttraumatic stress disorder in a representative national sample of women. *Journal of Consulting and Clinical Psychology, 61,* 984-991.

Riggs, D., Kilpatrick, D., & Resnick, H. (1992). Long-term psychological distress associated with marital rape and aggravated assault: A comparison to other crime victims. *Journal of Family Violence, 7,* 283-296.

Simon, L. M. J. (1995). A therapeutic jurisprudence approach to the legal processing of domestic violence cases. *Psychology, Public Policy, and Law, 1,*(1), 43-79.

Spitzer, R., Williams, J., & Gibbon, M. (1986). *Structured Clinical Interview for DSM-III-R nonpatient version.*

New York: New York State Psychiatric Institute, Biometrics Research Department.

Straus, M. A., Gelles, R. J., & Steinmetz, S. K. (1980) *Behind closed doors: Violence in the American family.* Garden City, NY: Anchor/Doubleday.

Weaver, T. L., & Clum, G. A. (1996). Interpersonal violence: Expanding the search for long-term sequelae within a sample of battered women. *Journal of Traumatic Stress, 9,* 797-817.

Weaver, T. L., Kilpatrick, D. G., Resnick, H. S., Best, C. L., & Saunders, B. E. (1995, July). *An examination of physical assault and childhood victimization histories within two samples: A national sample and a help-seeking sample of women.* Paper presented at the 4th International Family Violence Research Conference, Durham, NH.

PART II

CHILD ABUSE AND NEGLECT

CHAPTER 4

Pandemic Outcomes

The Intimacy Variable

Evvie Becker-Lausen
Sharon Mallon-Kraft

Researchers have suggested that about a third of abuse survivors grow up to abuse their own children (Gelles, 1987; Kaufman & Zigler, 1987). Yet developmental and prevention research, studies of intergenerational transmission of abuse, and clinical practice with families suggest that problematic parent-child relationships are a much more common outcome (Becker-Lausen & Rickel, 1995; Rickel & Becker-Lausen, 1995).

Many studies have linked child sexual abuse to interpersonal difficulties (Browne & Finkelhor, 1986; Courtois, 1988). For example, Elliott and Gabrielsen (1990) surveyed 2,963 adult professional women, 32% of whom reported sexual molestation prior to age 16. Compared with the professional women who were not molested, the sexually abused women reported significantly greater impairment in and dissatisfaction with interpersonal relationships. This impairment and dissatisfaction pervaded their personal lives. Finkelhor and his colleagues (Finkelhor, Hotaling, Lewis, & Smith, 1989) reported similar findings from a survey of 2,626 adult males and females: Those reporting childhood sexual abuse were more likely to report difficulties in intimate and sexual relationships.

Child Maltreatment and Interpersonal Difficulties: Mediator Variables

To test the hypothesis that broader forms of maltreatment would also be related to interper-

AUTHORS' NOTE: This chapter was originally presented as a paper at the 4th International Family Violence Research Conference, Durham, New Hampshire, July 1995. Direct correspondence to Dr. Evvie Becker-Lausen, Department of Psychology, Box U-20, University of Connecticut, Storrs, CT 06269.

sonal difficulties, Becker-Lausen, Sanders, and Chinsky (1995) employed a newly developed measure of childhood maltreatment, the Child Abuse and Trauma (CAT) scale (Sanders & Becker-Lausen, 1995). The CAT scale factors into three subscales: (a) Neglect/Negative Home Environment, (b) Punishment, and (c) Sexual Abuse. In normative samples, the three are highly intercorrelated.

Becker-Lausen and associates (1995) also tested whether depression and dissociation were mediator variables between childhood maltreatment and later negative life experiences, including interpersonal difficulties. Results showed the broader maltreatment experiences were related to later interpersonal difficulties, and depression was the primary mediator between them, although dissociation also showed mediating effects.

The direction of the relationships among in childhood maltreatment, depression, and interpersonal difficulties may be questioned on the grounds that depressed individuals may report events more negatively than others do. However, in addition to work demonstrating that depressed people actually view the world more realistically than nondepressed people (Alloy & Abramson, 1979; Layne, 1983), other studies, both prospective and retrospective, have supported the direction of the paths proposed by Becker-Lausen and associates (1995) for childhood maltreatment, depression, and interpersonal difficulties (Briere & Runtz, 1988; Browne & Finkelhor, 1986; Fichman, Koestner, & Zuroff, 1994; Webster-Stratton & Hammond, 1988; Widom, 1989).

For example, Dodge, Bates, and Pettit (1990), in a study of physical abuse and aggression in 309 kindergarten children found that those who had been physically harmed by parents had significantly higher levels of aggression than nonharmed children. This finding held across teacher, peer, and observer ratings and was equally true for girls and boys. Furthermore, Dodge and associates found no correlation between abuse and child temperament or the child's health problems, concluding, "There is no evidence in our data for blaming the victim of abuse" (p. 1682).

Vissing, Straus, Gelles, and Harrop (1991) reported similar findings for a national sample: Children who experienced frequent verbal abuse from parents had higher rates of physical abuse, delinquency, and other interpersonal problems compared to those who did not experience verbal abuse. These findings held for all age levels, for both boys and girls, and regardless of whether physical abuse was also present. Those children who experienced both verbal and physical abuse had the highest levels of aggression, delinquency, and interpersonal problems, (underscoring the importance of investigating the aggregated effects of different forms of abuse).

However, Dodge and associates (1990), who used the Child Behavior Checklist (CBCL; Achenbach & Edelbrock, 1986), had teacher ratings of the child's "internalizing" behaviors (the tendency to withdraw or isolate from others), as well as the "externalizing" aggressive behaviors. When the researchers looked at the ratings of internalizing behaviors, they found that these behaviors were 19% higher in harmed boys and a full 87% higher in harmed girls, both of which represented statistically significant differences from the nonharmed children.

"Even though our study focused on aggression, our findings indicate that abused children, particularly girls, are also at risk for the development of internalizing problems, such as withdrawal and isolation, that have been hypothesized to be precursors of depression," the authors noted (Dodge et al., 1990, p. 1682).

The investigators speculated that the cognitive developmental pathways for externalizing and for internalizing behaviors are quite different. Harmed children who were aggressive were likely to develop "biased and deficient patterns of processing social information, including a failure to attend to relevant cues, a bias to attribute hostile intentions to others, and a lack of competent behavioral strategies to solve interpersonal problems" (Dodge et al., 1990, p. 1682).

Although the results supported the authors' hypothesis that the path between physical harm and externalizing behavior was mediated by the development of this particular cognitive style, these results did not hold as a mediator for internalizing behaviors. Dodge and associates (1990) concluded that internalizing outcomes may be mediated by the development of a different set of patterns (e.g., self-blame): "Why some children follow a path of hostile attributions and aggression and other children a path of self-blame and depression awaits further inquiry" (p. 1682).

Assessing Pandemic Outcomes

■ Finkelhor and Dziuba-Leatherman (1994) have suggested that we address "pandemic" child victimization, such as corporal punishment. In concurring with this suggestion, we recommend the simultaneous investigation of pandemic outcomes of maltreatment. For whether maltreatment leads to depression, aggression, or other negative behaviors and emotions (Dodge et al., 1990; Widom, 1989), problematic relationships with romantic and/or sexual partners, with friends, and with children and/or stepchildren often are the result (Becker-Lausen et al., 1995; Elliott & Gabrielsen, 1990).

To begin to assess these outcomes, we suggest that the term *intimacy* conveys a range of experiences that are problematic for survivors of abuse and neglect (Briere, 1992). The dictionary definition, "a close, familiar and affectionate personal relationship" (*Random House Webster's College Dictionary,* 1992, p. 707), provides a broad construct that includes parent-child relations and friendships, as well as the romantic or sexual bonds commonly associated with the term.

Focus on this construct may help unify research into such wide-ranging outcomes as sexual promiscuity (the avoidance of intimacy), teen pregnancy (an intimacy fantasy often shattered by the realities of parenting demands), and problematic parenting (e.g., intrusive, restrictive, or insensitive caregiving), as well as research into partner relationships (e.g., power and control dynamics, violent reactions to conflict).

The broad term we are proposing need not be bound by any narrow theoretical interpreta-

tions, making it particularly appealing for multidisciplinary research and interventions.

Building an Intimacy Model

■ A useful explication of the construct "intimacy" comes from the literature on chemical dependency. Chemically dependent individuals are a clinical population that commonly has great difficulty with intimate relationships, according to Coleman (1987a). He suggests that a healthy intimate relationship is characterized by the capacity for constructive, respectful expression of positive and negative emotions. These expressions should be mutually acceptable and promote the psychological well-being of the individuals involved; their function is primarily to define boundaries, to communicate concern and commitment, to negotiate roles, and to resolve conflicts. Other researchers have suggested that intimacy is a human need that varies for individuals depending on their temperament and on the reinforcement value of interpersonal interaction (Marshall, 1989).

Studies have indicated that the capacity for healthy intimate relationships is associated with fewer negative responses to stress, better physical health, a strong sense of well-being, resistance to depression, a greater sense of meaning in life, and less use of psychiatric services (see review by Marshall, 1989).

Many intimacy theorists have tended to view intimacy as an all-or-none phenomenon, with the absence or avoidance of intimacy at one end of a continuum and the capacity for deep intimacy at the other. For instance, Perlman and Fehr (1987, cited in Marshall, 1989) proposed that intimacy involves the relative presence or absence of three factors (represented as continua) conceptualized as the capacity for (a) closeness and interdependence, (b) mutual self-disclosure, and (c) warmth and affection.

However, if problems with intimacy are conceptualized as arising from childhood maltreatment, we may consider intimacy *dysfunction,* or what Briere (1992) has termed "intimacy disturbance" (p. 50), to be the result of such factors as a lack of healthy role models, boundaries between family members that are too weak or too firm, and low self-esteem (Coleman, 1987a). The boundary difficulties resulting from these factors may lead to two distinct problems with intimacy: The individual may be needy, intrusive, enmeshed, or controlling, resulting from a lack of clear boundaries between self and others, or the person may be avoidant and distancing, the result of boundaries too tightly drawn.

These differing styles lead to variable outcomes for the individual and must, therefore, be incorporated into any model. Considering again the three dimensions proposed by Perlman and Fehr (1987, cited in Marshall, 1989) as necessary for the development of intimacy (closeness and interdependence, mutual self-disclosure, and warmth and affection), we suggest that dysfunction may occur at either end of these continua, rather than only at the avoidant end. Furthermore, these three dimensions are likely to be highly intercorrelated. Therefore, a single continuum may represent capacity for intimacy, where either extreme is unhealthy, with healthy relationships occurring in the middle range.

Those who are low on interdependence, self-disclosure, and warmth may be most easily recognized as having interpersonal disturbances, because their avoidance behaviors lead them to have fewer interpersonal ties. Those at the other extreme, who have extremely high needs for closeness, engage in excessive self-disclosure, are smotheringly warm, and may be more likely than avoidant individuals to be involved in intimate relationships. However, they may be viewed by significant others as intrusive and overly demanding or controlling, creating intimacy difficulties that lead others to pull away emotionally. Ironically, these intrusive individuals may feel as lonely as those who avoid interaction, because their behavior prevents the effective communication characteristic of true intimacy, described above by Coleman (1987a).

Coleman and other writers, particularly in the chemical dependency literature (Beattie, 1987; Schaef, 1986), use the term *codependency* to refer to the intrusive end of the continuum, as we are conceptualizing it. However, as Briere (1992) has delineated, a number of differences exist between those who postulate a "codepen-

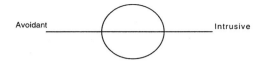

Figure 4.1. Avoidant Versus Intrusive Continuum (circle is "healthy middle")

dency" model and those who view the behavior as an outcome of childhood trauma.

Trauma theorists see the etiology and developmental mechanisms as quite different from those of codependency theory, Briere (1992) suggests. Specifically, in trauma models, the behavior is considered a "logical extension" of the coping behaviors learned in childhood in response to particular traumatic experiences (p. 71). Furthermore, in trauma theory, the behavior is seen as inextricably linked to the individual's survival instincts and, thus, not a matter of choice. Codependency writers too often appear to be suggesting that the individual is electing to behave in this manner, Briere notes.

In the continuum for intimacy proposed here, dysfunction is represented at either extreme and postulated as an outcome of traumatic childhood experiences, particularly with caretakers. In this model, the "healthy middle" ground represents firm yet flexible boundaries, as illustrated in Figure 4.1.

Coleman (1987b) provides two clinical examples that illustrate the two extremes proposed here. The epitome of the avoidant style is expressed by a client as an expectancy that intimacy is a painful and dangerous experience: "If I don't get close to anyone, I can't get hurt. I won't lose myself and get confused" (p. 40). At the other extreme is a quote from the partner of an excessively needy man who constantly seeks affection and approval: "I can never seem to convince John that I love him. He needs to be constantly touched and reassured. I have to tell him twenty times a day. He doesn't want to go anywhere without me. I am his only true friend" (p. 40).

These quotations illustrate the conceptualization of the two opposite poles of the continuum. Intimacy dysfunction, then, may be defined as a generalized expectancy that a close, familiar personal relationship will not bring satisfaction. (Expectancies for any specific situation are the result of learning that has occurred not only in the same situation but also in any situation the individual has *perceived* as similar. Generalizations often are the result of failure to make the appropriate differentiations between the current situation and past situations [Rotter, 1982].) At one extreme, this lack of satisfaction results from the anticipation of pain associated with relating to others (avoidant). At the other extreme, it results from the anticipation of disappointment or frustration in relationships, which the individual may often describe as a feeling of being "let down" by others (intrusive).

We suggest that these are powerful expectancies, learned in childhood from long-standing interactions with significant others (often more than one person). Learning experiences interact with individual variations in affiliational needs so that the value of interpersonal ties to the individual may, in part, determine at which end of the continuum they fall. As suggested above, loneliness may exist at both ends of the spectrum, because neither style allows for the healthy communication of positive and negative emotions that Coleman (1987a) described as necessary for true intimacy.

It is useful to point out the distinction made by Weiss (1973) between "social loneliness," a sense of isolation resulting from few social contacts (e.g., when one moves to a new city), and "emotional loneliness," the feeling of emptiness resulting from the absence of intimate and emotional bonds in relationships.

Emotional loneliness, the more severe condition, is at the heart of intimacy dysfunction, and it has been associated with the highest rates of emotional distress and with externalizing behavior problems, including aggression, anger toward others, and paranoia (Check, Perlman, & Malamuth, 1985; Marshall, 1989; Mikulincer & Segal, 1990).

Mikulincer and Segal (1990) found that emotional loneliness was also associated with self-concerns, including self-doubt, shame, anxiety, and anger toward self, as well as with depressive feelings, all of which might be classified as internalizing styles.

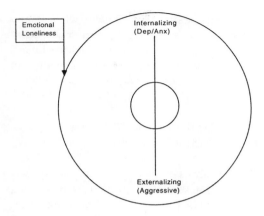

Figure 4.2. Internalizing/Externalizing Continuum

Thus, intimacy dysfunction, and the emotional loneliness that accompanies it, may be conceptualized as existing at the behavioral extremes of a continuum representing internalizing and externalizing behaviors, as shown in Figure 4.2. Again, the middle ground is the locus of health. By superimposing Figure 4.2 on Figure 4.1, we now have a graphic representation of intimacy dysfunction, as shown in Figure 4.3.

Recall that Dodge and associates (1990) found physically harmed children more likely than nonharmed children to be identified as externalizing and/or as internalizing. Here we are beginning to construct a framework to examine the etiology and intergenerational transmission

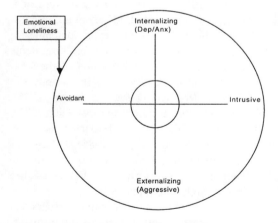

Figure 4.3. Intimacy Dysfunction Model 1

of intimacy dysfunction. Children who grow up in homes where they are rejected or abused by their parents often develop emotional loneliness, and they compensate for this loneliness in a variety of unhealthy ways (Marshall, 1989).

Interpersonal Discomfort Versus Interpersonal Sensitivity

■ An analysis of data on 301 college students (Becker-Lausen, 1992; Becker-Lausen et al., 1995) provided some limited support for the dimension of avoidance versus intrusion, for the relationship of these constructs to child maltreatment, and on some potential outcomes of these patterns.

Participants were given a measure of interpersonal difficulties, namely, the Object Relations Scale (ORS; Hargrove, 1985; Hower, 1987). Factor analysis of the ORS by Elliott and Gabrielsen (1990) suggested a six-factor solution. However, the two factors most relevant here are those representing the constructs labeled interpersonal discomfort (ID) and interpersonal sensitivity (IS). The most global factor, ID, is described as the degree to which an individual engages in emotionally distancing behaviors, or what we have termed avoidance; for example, "I feel most comfortable with more distant, cool relationships," and "It is hard for me to get close to other people emotionally." Elliott and Gabrielsen found scores on these factor items were significantly different for professional women who reported child sexual abuse compared to those who did not report such abuse.

In our sample, higher scores on these items were associated with higher scores on the measure of general childhood maltreatment, the CAT scale (Sanders & Becker-Lausen, 1995), on the Beck Depression Inventory (Beck, 1972), and on the Dissociative Experiences Scale (DES: Bernstein & Putnam, 1986). These emotionally distancing participants also reported experiencing a greater number of stressful life events in high school and college.

Few questions in this particular interpersonal measure were designed to assess the intrusive, needy end of the continuum we are proposing. Thus, only a few inferences may be drawn from

the data that at least suggest further research into intrusiveness as a construct, based on the IS factor identified by Elliott and Gabrielsen (1990). Two questions with slightly different wording asked respondents to indicate how likely they were to be hurt by others. Individuals in our sample endorsing these items scored higher on depression and on the CAT scale. Within the CAT, however, the items were most strongly associated with the Neglect/Negative Home Environment subscale.

Interestingly, in Elliott and Gabrielsen's (1990) sample of nearly 3,000 women, scores on the questions noted above were significantly higher for sexually abused women than for those who did not report abuse, just as they were for ID. However, comparisons of the two factors, ID and IS, revealed nearly identical means for nonabused women (ID, mean = 2.33; IS, mean = 2.31), whereas for the abused women, the distancing factor mean was notably higher than the sensitivity factor (ID, mean = 3.47; IS, mean = 2.52). The authors do not report whether the differences in the means of the two factors are significant within the sexually abused group. Perhaps the strong association with Neglect/Negative Home Environment in our sample points to differences in the relationship between types of maltreatment and types of interpersonal difficulties.

Consequently, we have support for a relationship between child maltreatment history and emotional distancing, with very limited support for a relationship between child maltreatment history and oversensitivity. It appears that individuals who are more depressed than their peers and who experience more than their share of stressful life events comprise both groups. Clearly, this is an area that requires further study. The strong findings for the Neglect/Negative Home Environment subscale of the CAT scale are especially interesting, and other studies being conducted currently also suggest the robustness of this factor of the CAT (Julien, Chinsky, Becker-Lausen, & Sanders, 1996).

The Importance of Trust

■ Another key element in intimate relationships is that of interpersonal trust, an often identified problem in the treatment of survivors of childhood trauma (Briere, 1992; Herman, 1992). Unfortunately, trust is rarely operationalized or measured adequately in the trauma literature.

Rotter (1971) attempted to operationalize interpersonal trust, designing an instrument for the purpose of testing theories about the effect of trust on interpersonal behavior. He defined interpersonal trust as "a generalized expectancy held by an individual that the word, promise, oral or written statement of another individual or group can be relied on" (Rotter, 1982, p. 288). Years of research with this measure have supported the utility of this definition, Rotter (1982) reports.

A number of studies have found those scoring high on trust are better adjusted, better liked by others, and more trustworthy than low trusters (Rotter, 1982). The findings on trustworthiness indicate high trusters are less likely to lie, cheat, or steal (i.e., engage in externalizing behaviors) and are also less likely to be unhappy, maladjusted, or without friends (i.e., internalizing and/or lonely).

Returning to the intimacy construct, it seems evident that one's level of trust would influence one's ability for interdependence. The ability to give and accept constructive feedback, as well as positive and negative emotional expression, are dependent on the ability to believe others will be honest with us and will keep our confidences.

Thus, in the model, high trust falls into the healthy middle, with low trusters either avoidant of intimacy or overly demanding of affection, and engaging in either internalizing or externalizing behaviors. Therefore, we propose that intimacy dysfunction, the generalized expectancy that interpersonal relationships will be painful or disappointing (as described above), is interwoven with trust, as defined by Rotter (1982). That is, intrusive individuals expect that the word of others cannot be relied on to be constant from one moment to the next; avoidant individuals believe that communications from others cannot be relied on to be positive or encouraging. Internalizing individuals expect feedback from others to be critical, often anticipating such feedback with harsh, internal evaluations of their own behavior. Finally, externalizing per-

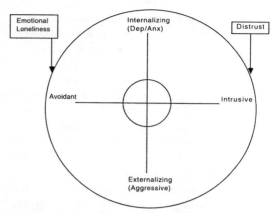

Figure 4.4. Intimacy Dysfunction Model 2

sons assume a hostile intent in communications from others (Dodge et al., 1990).

The final model is provided in Figure 4.4, with the addition of trust at the outer perimeter.

Summary

■ We have proposed that the construct intimacy—"a close, familiar and affectionate personal relationship" (*Random House Webster's College Dictionary*, 1992, p. 707)—provides a useful umbrella for understanding a variety of negative consequences for survivors of child maltreatment.

Intimacy dysfunction (Coleman, 1987a) is a frequent outcome of child maltreatment. We define intimacy dysfunction as a generalized expectancy that relationships will not be satisfying. This lack of faith in others, learned primarily through childhood experiences (often with multiple significant others), occurs in different ways for different individuals: They may become overly intrusive in relationships or avoidant; they may engage in externalizing or internalizing behavior.

At all of the extremes, individuals are distrustful of others and emotionally lonely. Emotional loneliness is a result of the interaction of these forces within the individual, whereas trust—a generalized expectancy that the communications of others can be relied on (Rotter, 1982)—is key to understanding intimacy dysfunction. However, depending on where the individual falls on the continua, the nature of this lack of faith in others' communications may involve subtle differences in expectancies.

Finally, healthy intimacy, including high trust, firm but flexible boundary distinctions, and the capacity for affection and nurturance, can be conceptualized as lying in the middle ranges of the variables, or what we have termed the healthy middle ground.

We believe these definitions will be useful for further research, particularly for identifying mediators and moderators of child maltreatment outcomes. We invite others to join us in articulating these definitions and testing the assumptions underlying them.

References

Achenbach, T. M., & Edelbrock, C. (1986). *Manual for the Teacher's Report Form and teacher version of the Child Behavior Profile.* Burlington: University of Vermont.

Alloy, L. B., & Abramson, L. Y. (1979). Judgment of contingency in depressed and nondepressed students: Sadder but wiser? *Journal of Experimental Psychology: General, 108,* 441-485.

Beattie, M. (1987). *Codependent no more.* New York: Harper/Hazelden.

Beck, A. T. (1972). *Depression: Causes and treatment.* Philadelphia: University of Pennsylvania Press.

Becker-Lausen, E. (1992). Child abuse and negative life experiences: An analysis of depression and dissociation as mediator variables (Doctoral dissertation, University of Connecticut, 1991). *Dissertation Abstracts International, 53*(1B), 557.

Becker-Lausen, E., & Rickel, A. U. (1995). Integrating research on child abuse and teen pregnancy: Identifying mediator variables for pregnancy outcome. *Journal of Primary Prevention, 16,* 39-53.

Becker-Lausen, E., Sanders, B., & Chinsky, J. M. (1995). The mediation of abusive childhood experiences: Depression, dissociation, and negative life outcomes *American Journal of Orthopsychiatry, 65,* 560-573.

Bernstein, E. M., & Putnam, F. W. (1986). Development, reliability, and validity of a dissociation scale. *Journal of Nervous and Mental Disease, 174,* 727-735.

Briere, J. (1992). *Child abuse trauma: Theory and treatment of lasting effects.* Newbury Park, CA: Sage.

Briere, J., & Runtz, M. (1988). Symptomatology associated with childhood sexual victimization in a nonclinical adult sample. *Child Abuse & Neglect, 12,* 51-59.

Browne, A., & Finkelhor, D. (1986). Impact of child sexual abuse: A review of the research. *Psychological Bulletin, 99*(1), 66-77.

Check, J. V. P., Perlman, D., & Malamuth, N. M. (1985). Loneliness and aggressive behavior. *Journal of Social and Personal Relationships, 2,* 243-252.

Coleman, E. (1987a). Chemical dependency and intimacy dysfunction: Inextricably bound. *Journal of Chemical Dependency Treatment, 1*(1), 13-26.

Coleman, E. (1987b). Marital and relationship problems among chemically dependent and codependent relationships. *Journal of Chemical Dependency Treatment, 1*(1), 39-59.

Courtois, C. A. (1988). *Healing the incest wound: Adult survivors in therapy.* New York: Norton.

Dodge, K. A., Bates, J. E., & Pettit, G. S. (1990). Mechanisms in the cycle of violence. *Science, 250,* 1678-1683.

Elliott, D. M., & Gabrielsen, D. L. (1990, August). *Impaired object relations in professional women molested as children.* Paper presented at the 98th annual convention of the American Psychological Association, Boston.

Fichman, L., Koestner, R., & Zuroff, D. C. (1994). Depressive styles in adolescence: Assessment, relation to social functioning, and developmental trends. *Journal of Youth and Adolescence, 23,* 315-330.

Finkelhor, D., & Dziuba-Leatherman, J. (1994). Victimization of children. *American Psychologist, 49,* 173-183.

Finkelhor, D., Hotaling, G. T., Lewis, I. A., & Smith, C. (1989). Sexual abuse and its relationship to later sexual satisfaction, marital status, religion, and attitudes. *Journal of Interpersonal Violence, 4,* 379-399.

Gelles, R. J. (1987). The family and its role in the abuse of children. *Psychiatric Annals, 17,* 229-232.

Hargrove, J. (1985). Replication and extension of Leopold Bellak's model of ego function assessment (Doctoral dissertation, Rosemead School of Psychology, 1985). *Dissertation Abstracts International, 46,* 641B.

Herman, J. L. (1992). *Trauma and recovery.* New York: Basic Books.

Hower, M. G. (1987). A revision of the Ego Function Assessment Questionnaire (Doctoral dissertation, Rosemead School of Psychology, 1987). *Dissertation Abstracts International, 48,* 1515B.

Julien, P., Chinsky, J. M., Becker-Lausen, E., & Sanders, B. (1996, August). *Childhood maltreatment, dissociation, and eating disorder symptomatology in college females.* Paper presented at the 104th annual convention of the American Psychological Association, Toronto, Canada.

Kaufman, J., & Zigler, E. (1987). Do abused children become abusive parents? *American Journal of Orthopsychiatry, 57,* 186-192.

Layne, C. (1983). Painful truths about depressives' cognitions. *Journal of Clinical Psychology, 39,* 848-853.

Marshall, W. L. (1989). Intimacy, loneliness, and sexual offenders. *Behavioral Research and Therapy, 27,* 491-503.

Mikulincer, M., & Segal, J. (1990). A multidimensional analysis of the experience of loneliness. *Journal of Social and Personal Relationships, 7,* 209-230.

Random House Webster's College Dictionary. (1992). New York: Random House.

Rickel, A. U., & Becker-Lausen, E. (1995). Intergenerational influences on child outcomes: Implications for prevention and intervention. In B. A. Ryan, G. R. Adams, T. P. Gullotta, R. P. Weissberg, & R. L. Hampton (Eds.), *The family-school connection: Theory, research, and practice* (pp. 315-340). Thousand Oaks, CA: Sage.

Rotter, J. B. (1971). Generalized expectancies for interpersonal trust. *American Psychologist, 26,* 443-452.

Rotter, J. B. (1982). *The development and application of social learning theory.* New York: Praeger.

Sanders, B., & Becker-Lausen, E. (1995). The measurement of psychological maltreatment: Early data on the Child Abuse and Trauma scale. *Child Abuse & Neglect, 19,* 315-323.

Schaef, A. W. (1986). *Co-dependence: Misunderstood—Mistreated.* San Francisco: Harper & Row.

Vissing, Y. M., Straus, M. A., Gelles, R. J., & Harrop, J. W. (1991). Verbal aggression by parents and psychosocial problems of children. *Child Abuse & Neglect, 15,* 223-238.

Webster-Stratton, C., & Hammond, M. (1988). Maternal depression and its relationship to life stress, perceptions of child behavior problems, parenting behaviors, and child conduct problems. *Journal of Abnormal Child Psychology, 16,* 299-315.

Weiss, R. S. (1973). *Loneliness: The experience of emotional and social isolation.* Cambridge: MIT Press.

Widom, C. S. (1989). The cycle of violence. *Science, 244,* 160-166.

CHAPTER 5

Pornography and the Organization of Intra- and Extrafamilial Child Sexual Abuse

A Conceptual Model

Catherine Itzin

This chapter reviews the research and clinical literature on the nature and extent of pornography and organized abuse, drawing on existing data on the incidence and prevalence of child sexual abuse; child pornography; prostitution; and the international traffic in women and children. It uses a case study to explore the phenomenology of being used in and abused by pornography as a child. From this perspective, it is possible to see the processes by which child sexual abuse is organized inside and outside of the family and the role of adult and child pornography in it. This approach highlights some of the limitations of current definitions and categories of child sexual abuse based on pedophile typologies and sex offender classifications. It

also provides the basis for developing a model, based on the experience of the child, that conceptualizes the relationship between pornography and the organization of child sexual abuse as one in which pornography is a part of all forms of intrafamilial and extrafamilial abuse and is itself a form of organized abuse. The chapter includes a discussion of some characteristics of pornography and child sexual abuse extrapolated from the case study, including gender, intra- and intergenerational patterns of victimization, coercion and compliance, pornography and prostitution, and the function of incest as a form of "pimping" for the perpetrator(s) within the family and as grooming for extrafamilial abuse.

The Nature and Extent of Pornography and Organized Abuse

Current Knowledge About Pornography and Child Sexual Abuse

A review of the research and the clinical literature indicates a general lack of consistency in the terminology used to define and categorize *child sexual abuse,* and specifically in definitions of *organized child sexual abuse.* The term *child sexual abuse,* for example, has been used interchangeably and synonymously with *sexual victimization, sexual exploitation, sexual assault, sexual misuse, child molestation, sexual mistreatment,* and *child rape* (Russell, 1983, p. 133).

Another definitional category is *pedophilia.* Some research has used the clinical diagnostic criteria of the American Psychiatric Association (1980, cited in Langevin & Lang, 1985) to define pedophilia as "the act or fantasy of engaging in sexual activity with prepubertal children as a repeatedly preferred or exclusive method of achieving sexual excitement" (Langevin & Lang, 1985, p. 404). Finkelhor (1986) has defined pedophilia as "adult sexual contact with a child or adult masturbation to sexual fantasies involving children" (p. 90). Kelly's (1988) review of the research identified the three most common distinctions as being made between pedophiles (men whose sexual interest is restricted to children), child molesters (men whose sexual interest includes both children and adult women), and incest offenders (p. 54). Kelly categorized incest as a subcategory of child sexual abuse. Russell (1983) has categorized child sexual abuse as either extrafamilial: defined as one or more unwanted sexual experiences with persons unrelated by blood or marriage, ranging from petting (touching of breasts or genitals or attempts at such touching) to rape, before the victim turned 14 years, and completed or attempted forcible rape experienced from the ages of 14 to 17 years; or intrafamilial: defined as "any kind of exploitative sexual contact that occurred between relatives no matter how distant the relationship before the victim turned 18 years old" (pp. 135-136).

Seng (1986) categorized child sexual abuse as a subcategory of child abuse, in which he includes "intrafamilial child sexual abuse or incest"; child molestation, defined as sexual abuse involving "an adult and child who are not related by blood or marriage" (p. 51); and pedophilia, defined as "psychosexual perversion in which children are the preferred sexual object" (p. 52). Seng's typology makes a distinction between incestuous fathers (most of whom are not pedophiles) and child molesters (most of whom are pedophiles) and considers "multiple victim behaviour" as characteristic of child molestation but not incest. Seng categorizes *sex ring activity* as child molestation that occurs in groups with multiple victims and/or multiple offenders. *Sexual exploitation* is another category of child sexual abuse, involving "a subtle shift from use of children for personal gratification to the use of children as objects" (p. 56). One form of sexual exploitation in Seng's typology is prostitution, in which he includes the "exchange of children among syndicated sex rings" (p. 59). The most common form of sexual exploitation, however, according to Seng, is "the use of children in the production of pornographic photography" (p. 56).

Quite a lot is known now, based on research in the United States and the United Kingdom, about the incidence and prevalence of child sexual abuse. Kelly (1988) cites abuse prevalence findings in different studies ranging from 12% to 38% with variations explained by differences in methodology, age, and definition of abuse. The research has tended to make conceptual and definitional distinctions between intrafamilial and extrafamilial abuse (Russell, 1983) or between familial and nonfamilial abuse (Waterhouse, Dobash, & Carnie, 1994). A survey of over 4,000 readers of *Cosmopolitan* magazine in the United Kingdom in 1989 found that 13% of women reported having been sexually abused as children (Itzin & Sweet, 1990). In the United States, Russell (1983) found, in a probability sample of 930 women in San Francisco, a prevalence of 16% for intrafamilial abuse before the age of 18, and 31% for extrafamilial abuse.

Much less in known about the ways in which pornography is implicated in child sexual abuse. A recent report on child sexual exploitation commissioned by five U.K. children's charities acknowledges the dearth of research in this field (Kelly, Wingfield, Burton, & Regan, 1996). What is known has to be extrapolated from existing information from various sources: from child pornography, from prostitution, from the international traffic in women and children, from some of the research on child sexual abuse generally, and specifically the child sexual abuse that has been defined as "organized."

Respondents in the *Cosmopolitan* survey described a range of circumstances in which they had been abused with pornography as children by different family members—fathers, grandfathers, uncles, brothers—and by their friends (Itzin & Sweet, 1990). In another study, women reported being used to pose for child pornography and then living into adulthood in dread of finding the photographs published; pornography being used to initiate and legitimize their sexual abuse ("if she can, you can"); and the devastating effects of "simply" finding their father's pornography ("shock, confusion, disgust, guilt, fear and utter hopelessness about sex"). "I feel," said one woman, "as if my whole life has been poisoned by it" (Itzin, in press). A review of the notes of 78 children who contacted the U.K. charity telephone helpline for children who are experiencing abuse (Childline) over a 6-month period revealed that for 32 of them their sexual abuse was "linked to either being shown pornography magazines or videos or becoming involved in the making of abusive videos" (Kelly et al., 1996, p. 2). In Germany, police have estimated that "130,000 children are forced by parents or other close acquaintances to participate in the production of pornography" (Groner, 1992, cited in Kelly et al., 1996, p. 40).

The most obvious source of information on child sexual abuse and pornography is child pornography itself, which is now generally regarded as the evidence—recorded on film or videotape—of serious sexual assaults on children (Hames, 1993; Kelly, 1992; Tate, 1992). This kind of material ranges from "posed photographs of naked and semi-naked children, through more explicit shots of their genitalia

thumbed apart to still, film and video recording of oral, vaginal and anal sex" (Tate, 1992, p. 203). Among the material seized by Scotland Yard's Obscene Publications Branch have been items showing

> a boy of about eleven being forced to sit on top of an erect penis, in visible discomfort and pain as he is positioned to show as much of the genitals as possible to the camera and penetrated anally; a woman placing a female child (aged about eight) on top of a man's erect penis; Portuguese boys masturbating and performing oral sex; a female child (aged about four or five) being forced to perform fellatio on an adult male; several children of both sexes lying together being urinated on by an adult male. (Itzin, 1992, p. 51)

Ennew (1986) records the contents of a booklet of child pornography obtained by mail order from an address in Denmark, described as "photographs imported from the USA," including children as young as 2 with genitals exposed to the camera, penetrated vaginally and orally, presented precociously, posed provocatively, and "inviting" sexual abuse (pp. 121-123).

Police in the United States and the United Kingdom have identified as a characteristic of pedophile behavior the recording of their abuse of children and its collection as a record of the abuse for purposes of masturbation and to share and exchange with other pedophiles (Tate, 1992). Records of child sexual abuse in photographs and films are also used to blackmail abused children to prevent them from disclosing the abuse, and to seduce other children (Burgess & Hartman, 1987). In some cases, the abuse is organized to meet the immediate sexual needs of the perpetrator, but it is also recorded for explicitly commercial purposes "as an item of trade" (Hames, 1993). John Bulloch, for example, convicted in 1985 on 13 counts of the abuse of two 12-year-old girls, described "the child pornography business he built up as a by-product of his paedophilia" (Tate, 1992). The trade in child pornography is part of the multi-million-pound international pornography industry (Baxter, 1990).

Further evidence of the relationship between child sexual abuse and pornography is available from research and clinical work with sex offenders. In Canada, Marshall (1988) found, in a study of nonincarcerated sex offenders, that over a third reported being incited by pornography to commit an offense, and over half of those who committed child sexual abuse said they deliberately used pornography in preparing to commit the offense. In the United Kingdom, clinical work with sex offenders has shown that for a substantial proportion of offenders, pornography is implicated at every stage: in fantasy arousal to abuse, in predisposing men to commit abuse, in legitimizing and normalizing abuse, in creating and reinforcing false belief-systems about victims of abuse, in reducing and overcoming internal and external inhibitions to abuse, in targeting victims and overcoming victim resistance, in initiating and carrying out abuse, and in reinterpreting victim behavior to support further abuse (Wyre, 1992). In the United States, Carter, Prentky, Knight, Vanderveer, and Boucher (1987) found, among sex offenders at a treatment center, that child molesters were likely to use pornography prior to and during their offense.

Another source of information on pornography and child sexual abuse is prostitution. Research has shown that the median age for entry into prostitution is 14 (Weisberg, 1985, cited in Baldwin, 1992, p. 101). Silbert and Pines found that 70% of the 200 street prostitutes they surveyed in San Francisco were under 21 years of age. Of these, 60% were under 16, and many of those who were over 16 had started to work as prostitutes under the age of 16. Some were only 10, 11, or 12 years old (Silbert & Pines, 1984, p. 862, cited in Russell, 1993, p. 114). Allen (1981) found that the average age at which the child prostitutes in his study had first experienced sexual intercourse was 12 years old, the youngest being 9. Of a sample of prostitutes in New York, 82% had had sexual intercourse before the age of 13 (Janus & Heid Bracey, 1980, cited in Ennew, 1986). In these cases, the prostitution is evidence of commercialized child sexual abuse.

Silbert and Pines (1984) found that 38% of their sample of prostitutes described having been "involved in the taking of sexually explicit photographs of themselves when they were children for commercial purposes, and/or the per-

sonal gratification of the photographer" (p. 866). Ten percent of their respondents had been used as children in pornographic films and magazines, all of them under the age of 13 when they were victimized. Twenty-two percent of the 178 cases of juvenile sexual exploitation mentioned the use of pornographic materials by the adult prior to the sexual act: This included both adult and child subjects for purposes of their own and the child's sexual arousal, to legitimize their action and to persuade the child to participate. This corroborates, from the experience of the victims, what is known about the use of pornography from the perpetrators of child abuse. (The information on pornography in this study was unsolicited and was volunteered incidentally: it almost certainly, therefore, represents an underreporting of the incidence of pornography-related abuse.)

In evidence to public hearings held by the Minneapolis City Council in 1983, Barry (1988) described how

> pornography is used by pimps as part of the illegal action of procuring and attempting to induce young girls and women into prostitution by presenting young women and girls with pornography which fraudulently represents actually painful sexual practices and acts as pleasing and gratifying to the female represented in pornography. . . . Many pimps "season" or break down their victims through sessions of rape and other forms of sexual abuse. Sometimes these sessions are photographed or filmed and used in a variety of ways which include the personal pleasure of the pimp and his friends, blackmailing the victim by threatening to send them to her family, and selling them to the pornographers for mass production. (pp. 29-30)

In Barry's view, "Pornography is a form of prostitution and consequently pornographers are pimps" (pp. 29-30).

Prostitutes giving evidence to the hearings said:

> One of the very first commonalities we discovered as a group, we were all introduced to prostitution through pornography, there were no exceptions in our group, and we were all under 18. Pornography was our textbook, we learned the tricks of the trade by men exposing us to pornography and us trying

to mimic what we saw. I cannot stress enough what a huge influence we feel this was. (p. 71)

Another source of information on pornography and child sexual abuse is the international traffic in women and children for prostitution and pornography (Ennew, 1986; Sariola, 1986). This trade has seen a major development in the form of "sex tourism" (Ireland, 1993), a business that "involves the use and abuse of Third World women [and children] as part of the sexual recreation of Western men, including paedophiles" as a "planned item of state national income" involving "the interlocking interests of air carriers, tour operators and hotel companies" (Barry, 1992, p. 3). There was evidence in 1991 that "several hundreds of thousands of young children between the ages of six years and fifteen years had been forced or sold into prostitution" (European Forum on Child Welfare, 1993). It has been estimated that 60% of all tourism in Thailand and 50% of tourism in Kenya, the Philippines, and South Korea is sex tourism (Groner, 1992). Many of these prostitutes will be children who are poor and Black and who, like women who are poor and Black, are "disproportionately targeted for prostitution" (Baldwin, 1993, p. 77). The United Nations recognizes "child prostitution and pornography . . . as a vast national and transnational problem"; that "child pornography is often interrelated with child prostitution"; . . . that "there are major child pornography markets in North America and Europe . . . [and] Eastern Europe has emerged as a new market"; and that Asia is a key area of concern in regard to "transnational trafficking of children for sexual purposes" (Muntarbhorn, 1995, pp. 60-61).

Current Knowledge About Pornography and Organized Child Sexual Abuse

■ There are very little empirical data on the incidence and prevalence of organized abuse or the role of pornography in it, and, like child sexual abuse, *organized abuse* has been defined differently in various studies. Research in the United States has shown that child pornography

is a core activity in most abuse where an individual or group of adults abuse large numbers of children (Burgess, 1984). In one study, Burgess and Hartman (1987) distinguished between three kinds of sex rings:

1. A solo ring consisting of one adult who is sexually involved with small groups of children, [which] has no transfer of children or photographs to other adults;

2. A syndicated ring including several adults who form a well-structured organization for the recruitment of children, the production of pornography and the establishment of an extensive network of customers; and

3. A transitional ring [where] there may be more than one adult involved with several children [and] pornographic photographs may be sold. (p. 248)

All of these forms of organized abuse involved pornography.

In another American study, the multidisciplinary team of clinicians in the Sexual Information and Trauma Team in a family development center identified a subgroup, from their population of sexual abuse victims, of children who had been sexually abused by a ring (defined as "a group of adults, male and/or female, who gather for the express purpose of sexual exploitation of children"), all of which had involved child pornography (Hunt & Baird, 1990, p. 196).

In the United Kingdom, a survey of 71 National Society for the Prevention of Cruelty to Children (NSPCC) child protection teams identified child pornography as a form of organized abuse, in addition to network and ritual abuse, and found child pornography to be involved in 16% of cases (Creighton, 1993). A study of the prevalence of sex rings in Leeds (Wild, 1989) found 31 sex rings identified by police over a 2-year period within a geographically defined population of 710,000. A total of 47 male perpetrators aged 16-82 and 334 children aged 4-15 were involved. In this study, adult pornography was found to have been shown to a third of the children. Child pornography was produced in two rings, and in one ring, "socially deprived boys . . . were sometimes blackmailed into participating after videotapes of them engaged in sexual activities had been made" (Wild, 1989, p. 556).

A survey of police forces, social services departments, and the NSPCC in England and Wales covering the 4-year period from January 1988 to December 1991 produced an estimated national incidence rate for organized abuse of 967 cases over 4 years, or an average of 242 cases per year, but no data on pornography (Gallagher, Hughes, & Parker, 1994, 1996). La Fontaine (1993) defined organized abuse as "abuse by multiple perpetrators, some of whom are outside the immediate household and who act together to abuse the child/ren" (p. 230). La Fontaine's (1994) report for the Department of Health on the extent and nature of organized and ritual abuse in the United Kingdom defined organized abuse as "multiple abuse, involving more than one adult and, usually, more than one child" (p. 3). It considered four categories of organized abuse: ritual abuse, pedophile networks, family-based abuse, and institutional abuse. Child prostitution was considered to be possibly another "distinct type of organized abuse," but it was not discussed and the study did not consider the links between pornography and organized abuse.

In the absence of a body of research on pornography and child sexual abuse or common definitions of what constitutes organized abuse, it is possible to draw on a range of knowledge and research from different perspectives to build up a picture of the relationship between pornography and child sexual abuse. It is also possible to see, through this process, that much of this abuse is "organized" in significant ways. In child pornography, for example, some of the child sexual abuse recorded will have been perpetrated by individual adults on individual children, but it will also have involved more than one child and more than one adult. All of it will have been organized for purposes of publication and for sale or exchange in the form of child pornography. Prostitution is itself frequently a form of organized abuse of women and children insofar as most prostitution is organized and controlled by pimps, and it is a major business and source of income for organized

crime internationally (Baldwin, 1992; Baxter, 1990).

The process of looking at a wide range of child sexual abuse and how it is organized suggests that there is a problem in the use of the concept "organized abuse" as including some forms of abuse that are organized, but not others, and in obscuring the ways in which all child sexual abuse is organized. Nor are the existing definitions of organized abuse fully or sufficiently inclusive of all the abuse that is organized. There is also a need to recognize the limits of knowledge based on incidence and prevalence data and the potential for developing knowledge, understanding, and theory by exploring the phenomenology of being used in and sexually abused with pornography as a child, focusing on (in the words of one of those victims) "what is done to the person or persons involved" (Kroon, 1980). The purpose of this chapter is to consider the ways in which all forms of child sexual abuse are organized and the roles of adult and child pornography in this: looking at what, how, where, by whom, for what purpose, with what characteristics, and with what effects.

Pornography and the Organization of Child Sexual Abuse: A Case Study

Methodology

There are, from various sources, personal accounts from survivors of their experience of pornography and child sexual abuse (Danica, 1988; Davies, 1994; DeCamp, 1992; Kroon, 1980; Minneapolis Hearings, 1988). These accounts have often been published with a view to providing evidence that the abuse exists and that it involves the making and use of pornography, and with a view to overcoming the disbelief and denial that is a common response to accounts of both intra- and extrafamilial abuse and to research showing a high level of incidence and prevalence. The case study in this chapter uses autobiography for a different purpose: to developing a more complex and sophisticated conceptual understanding of organized abuse that captures the way in which abuse is organized in and across different contexts, and the different ways in which pornography can be—and often is—implicated.

The subject in this study was selected from a sample of 132 women who, in response to a television documentary in the United Kingdom on pornography in 1992, contacted a helpline for people who felt they had been harmed by pornography, a number of whom agreed to participate in a pilot study researching their experience of pornography-related harm (Itzin, in press). The data in this study were obtained, retrospectively, by the author, from one of the respondents from that research sample, using a semistructured, life-history interview schedule. Aged 53 at the time of the interview, Alice (a pseudonym) described her experience as a child and adolescent: of incest, of abuse organized within her family, of abuse organized outside her family, of being prostituted, and of being used in and abused with pornography. The interview is presented in the next section of this chapter in the form of a narrative that describes the nature of the abuse and the role of pornography in it at different stages in her childhood. It is followed by a final section that extrapolates some of the characteristics of pornography and the organization of child sexual abuse from this case material and discusses it in relation to other autobiographical accounts.

Incest as Grooming for Organized Abuse

My first conscious memories are from when my sister was born when I was 2½, I was sent to my grandparents and stayed with them. My abuse started there. I have a memory then of my grandfather holding me, putting his fingers into me, touching me and watching me naked, especially wanting to see me naked. I also remember sleeping in a bed with an aunt, who also wanted me in the bed naked. They all lived in the same house.

I've always had these memories. I've never forgotten them. I remember it—and the time—because it was the first time that I was sent away from my mother. It was at the birth of my sister, and she was born on Boxing Day. I don't know how long I was there, but it felt a long time. I did go back to visit my mother with the baby, but I didn't stay back at home. My brother, who was in [the] hospital with pneumonia, was a year

younger than me. There were three of us in 2½ years.

I was born illegitimately, early: a premature, illegitimate baby. My mother was sent away by her family to another town, as it was a disgrace. She knew of a man she'd met at a cinema who offered to marry her, and she accepted that in order to not go back to her own family. They were married and lived in this very damp rented house. My mother used to go out to the local pub to play cards and to drink, and her brothers and her sisters used to come and baby-sit whilst my stepfather was working. My stepfather always used to work until about 9 or 10 o'clock at night, in order to fund my mother's drinking and spending. We were very poor, and my stepfather often went to the soup kitchen to feed us because it was wartime.

My mum was one of 11 children: six girls and five boys. She was the third-eldest child. My mother would never profess to be an alcoholic, but she drank daily, quite a lot daily. I remember her often drunk. She smoked continually. She was very unemotional, very cold, very distant. And she was obsessively linked to her mother: she could never be apart from her mother. But she didn't return home after she had me. I think she wanted to be away from that environment. I think she thought I'd be at risk from my grandfather.

One of my aunts, who is now dead, told me that my grandfather was my father. My mother would never tell me who my father was, she told me it would "never do me any good to know." Those were her words. But I believe that I was probably the child of incest between my mother and her father. My mother's eldest sister told me this when I was in my twenties, after I'd had an illegitimate child of my own when I was 19, and my mother was furious with me. My aunt was reassuring me that my mother had no need to be cross because, in her words: "history was repeating itself except that the fathers were different."

I think my mother's leaving home was quite an act of love. It took me a long time in my adult life to realise that she had actually tried to protect me from them, because then she went on to abuse me, so it became very contradictory.

My mum's abuse of me was physical and emotional and it had long-lasting effects. I've since been reliably told that my mother also sexually abused me, but I don't remember it. I was told by a man my mother had an affair with that my mother had sexually abused me too. She told him she'd been abusing me from infancy and it had turned her on, that she'd been sexually aroused. I think this is likely to be true, but I don't remember it.

My grandfather had his own business. He used to have a workshop near to where we lived, and we (my sister and brother and I) used to have to go down and see him at the workshop. We were abused at his workshop. Separately, not together. We would be told to go down and see grandad, take him something down or give him a message. We were actually sent—by my grandmother, by my mother. Once I took a school friend down, and she wouldn't come with me again after that. He abused both of us. He sexually assaulted us. He made us take our knickers off and touched us and orally abused us.

My stepfather did not abuse me. He was never there. He used to be up first in the morning, and he'd come in last at night. If we were still awake, once the baby-sitters had gone, he'd read us a story. He was fabulous, he still is. He didn't know that all of this was happening.

Abuse Organized Within the Family

My mother didn't acknowledge that she knew what was going on, but I know that she knew, because she saw it and turned and walked away. On one occasion when I was 8 and my grandfather was abusing me, I heard footsteps coming up the stairs. I was in a position to see my mother standing in the doorway. She stood for a while, and then turned and went away. That memory was very destructive for a long time. It was probably worse than the abuse itself, watching while my mother turned away.

I told my stepfather once, because one time when he came home from work, I was crying because I'd been hurt. My uncle had abused me and hurt me. My stepfather wanted to know why I was crying, and I told him what had happened. He told my mother. She came and got me out of bed. I told her, and she took me to my grandparents. I was 8, I think, 8 or 9. She took me in to confront my grandparents and my uncle because he lived with them, with his parents. I was told I was fabricating, it was a lie. I stood and said to my grandfather, "You know it's true, you know this is happening." He told me I'd got an overactive imagination. My mother hit me, and put me in the back room for telling lies, and making her look stupid. But she knew it was true, be-

cause she had seen us. So the whole thing was totally confusing. I got punished for talking, so I never did it again.

I was abused by my mother's younger brothers—my uncles—when they were baby-sitting, and also by the older aunt. They told me that they'd been taught by their father, my grandfather. I also know that my mother and her brothers were abused by their father. . . .

The sexual abuse I experienced from my uncles when they were baby-sitting would be intercourse, oral sex, anal sex, and at times both. The physical abuse included needles put under my toenails and fingernails, being tied up, being frightened. The psychological abuse was always threats, the unknown. . . . The emotional abuse was one moment to do things that indicated they cared about me, and then the next moment to hurt me. They'd tell me I was really nice and they cared about me, and they'd offer to give me a sweet and then take it away. They'd say they wouldn't hurt me, and then they would. They threatened to make up stories to my mother to get me into trouble. They said they'd tell my teachers things about me that weren't true.

They terrorised me until I did what they wanted me to do. . . . Like they said they would catch me coming home from school and would take me away and hang me unless I did what they told me to do, which could be the sexual abuse, or it could be the photography.

Pornography and Intrafamilial Abuse

My uncle would make me look at pornographic literature and then take photographs of me doing it naked when he was baby-sitting. This is age 4 to 11 that I remember. He'd show me photographs of adults, men and women with whips and leather and children and animals. It would be photographs of oral sex, penetrative sex, both vaginally and anally. Somebody must have given him these, because he was only a teenager. Then he would make me act out some of them. If we were alone, this would be putting things inside myself, or he would put them in and then take the photographs. Sitting in provocative positions, masturbating; in sexually provocative poses and smiling. That was always the big criterion of photographs: smiling.

I don't know where his camera came from, so it's quite possible that someone had given him the money and a camera to take the pictures with. He knew ways of making money, and later he used to sell me to his friends anyway. He used to charge them to have sex with me, so it is quite possible that someone had paid him to take photographs.

One of the friends' fathers was a contact of my grandfather's. He was a photographer, and his shop was only yards away from the school. If we were at his friend's house—the photographer's house—then often, his father would be involved and he would take photographs of the boys, the teenagers, with me and with their dog. This was just filming at home by individuals. . . . Pornography was the filming later in the groups. At home it was just still photographs.

Pornography and Extrafamilial Abuse

This was from the age of 4 to 11 or 12, when we moved. We left that house when I was 12, and went to live next door to my grandmother and grandfather, and aunts and uncles. I think it was my 12th birthday we left. I can only remember up to 11, and then I have a complete blank from 11 to 13. I still have a complete blank of two years, I can't remember any of it. But we did move, and I know at 13 my memory returns and I'm at the other house. By 13 we had moved, and then the sexual abuse accelerated with other uncles, with uncles' friends and my grandfather's friends. Prior to that, it had just been family and family connections, then it just seemed like it was everybody.

And pornography started. One of the forms of organized abuse would be to make pornography. Me on my own, and in groups and with other children I didn't know. At 13, my younger uncles were older than me, ranging from five years upwards. They were in the senior level of the same school. By this time, they were making money by selling me to their friends. So when I was supposed to be at school playing netball, I was being sold for sex to my uncles' friends and to their friends' fathers, including the photographer.

I didn't know who this man was when I first met him. But when my uncle wanted me to go back with him and his friend to the friend's house, I realised I'd been there before, that I'd met this photographer before when I was younger. This man had a studio at the back of his house, it was like a townhouse, terraced, but at the back they had a long garden with a big studio. He had cameras, and white umbrellas set up in there with lots of big lights, chairs and some

tables. He took children's portraits. That was his job, taking photographs of children. He would have a [movie] camera in there as well as a still camera. I'd be taken there in order to be photographed. And there'd be other children and other adults there, and my uncle and his friend, the photographer's son. At this point, I knew that he was a friend of my grandfather's, but I didn't know in what context. But later, I knew my grandfather was involved in the pornography, because I saw him paying him for the pictures.

There were groups there, and group sex. It would all be organised before I got there. When I'd be taken there, the people were already there, the extra children were already there. I would then be made to be a perpetrator, and I would have to be involved in sexual abuse with younger children. Oral sex or penetrating their vagina or rectum. And that included abusing my brother. I would also be abused by other older children and by male and female adults. There were babies involved too. They would be naked. . . . Any scenario you could think of happened, virtually. The babies weren't being penetrated, so you couldn't prove sexual abuse. But fingers would be in vaginas, rectums. I don't know about new babies, or tiny babies, but certainly toddlers would be penetrated. Sometimes we would be involved in going in big bathrooms, and photographs would be taken of children playing in the bath and then the adults joining in, and that could involve all of the things that I've said before. Afterwards, we'd be given sweets.

For me, my greatest fear was I'd suffocate. As a small child I was terrified I would die by suffocation, and ever since being a small child, whenever I vomit I swallow it, and I still do it. After coming round from theatre when I've been for surgery, I wake up vomiting and swallowing. Because we had to swallow semen. The penis in our mouths would make us gag and retch, and we had to swallow before anything came up. If we didn't swallow it and made a mess, we had to lick it up.

In the pornography, there was also violence— tying up, restraint. There was pushing things inside us: instruments, bottles, rods, in our vaginas and rectums. Fruit, bananas, cucumbers, things like that, ice cubes. Being hung upside down, being tethered with a dog collar round our necks and on all fours. Animals mounting us in that position. There was also [tape] recording. Not just photographs, there were recorders going.

Child Prostitution

Another form of organised abuse was to be prostituted. In my early childhood, in addition to what was going on at home—the incest as I later learned it was—I'd be taken to places for group sex, group pornography and group prostitution. It had already been mapped out before I actually got there. We were taken out to places where it was already planned out. This is what I mean by "organised abuse," and the organised abuse included pornography. We were taken out where we met strangers and other children. Me and my brother and sister were taken there. I have memories of going, my sister has some memories, but my brother doesn't want to talk about it. I was taken by an aunt, by uncles, by my grandfather.

It was after one of these sessions—where we'd be in group sex, but without the cameras—that I saw my grandfather buy the pictures, and I knew that he must have been involved in the pornography too. In the making of pornography, prostitution is taking place. They go together, and I was prostituted to make the pornography. But also I was just prostituted, sold for sex. Sometimes, there was a combination of prostitution and filming. Whereas the pornography was set up for pornography, prostitution was set up so you could be sold for sex, but sometimes filmed. This film wasn't necessarily sold, it was for the individuals that were there, as distinct from the pornography which was to make pornography for sale.

The prostitution could be with just one person, or two or three, or a group, but on those occasions, there wasn't just an emphasis, like there is in pornography, on the image—the emphasis was on sexual satisfaction, and on sexual gratification, and everybody there got it. In the prostitution, I had to sexually meet everyone's needs. That wasn't always so with the pornography, where the main point was to take photographs or make film.

Perpetrator Networks

Where there was prostitution with photographs, money was flying around, you know, not only for the photographs, but also for the sex that was happening at the same time. I became aware of this when I saw money being exchanged between my grandfather and the father of my uncle's friend. I couldn't separate what the money was for:

whether it was for the photographs, when they were handed over, or whether it was for the sex. But I knew there was some kind of networking between my grandfather and other people. . . .

There was a network of people whose paths crossed for these purposes. It could be to do with their work or socially, their paths crossed: not just related to the abuse. . . . One of our local policemen was part of the group that was into the pornography, and also one of the local doctors was a part of it. And two of the local teachers were part of this abuse network. My grandfather was a freemason, and a lot of the abusing people were in high places. We knew that by the cars they used to come in, and in those days there were very few cars, it's not like now, and by the kind of clothes they wore.

No one ever told me not to say anything, not ever, but I knew I shouldn't. That came from my mother saying to me once . . that it was none of my business to know what other people did in their house, and it was none of their business to know what we did in ours.

Coercion: The Obedient Smile

My fear has always been that the photographs of me will turn up. An ongoing concern all my life is that the pornography that was taken is going to turn up somewhere, and if it doesn't, I'd like to know who has it, where has it gone to? When I was in my twenties, I saw some of it: my uncle showed me some that he still had. It was me at age 9. It was photographs taken in the shed, this sort of shed place at the back of the pornographer's house, with younger children and men and women. He had about six of these photographs. And then, when my mother died, this was 11 years ago when I was in my forties, he came to the funeral and he said to me, "Are you still as good as you always were?" He put his arms round me, and then he said he'd still got the photographs, did I want to see them again, would I like more sessions?

My response when I saw the photographs was total horror. And the thing that struck me more than anything else was how small I was. I'd always felt I'd been a big girl, but I just looked so small. And the other thing that struck me was that my eyes were dead, but I was smiling. I couldn't believe that I was hurting so much and smiling. But they asked me, they told me to smile. I'd learnt from a very early age obedience was the name of the game. This was about total obedience, it wasn't about questioning anything. From babyhood, I'd been taught to be obedient, not just in the smiling but in everything. Don't vomit, be quiet, do this, do that, and I did it. I was like a human robot, that when someone clicked, I jumped. And when they let me go and finished with me, I used to say thank you. The reward was being a good girl.

Consent: The Sexualized Child

The biggest thing for me was being told that I was a good girl, patted on the head. That was the only affection I ever got, and I'd do anything for that. I'd go out to the park and not actually look for people to abuse me, but I'd be very friendly with someone, and if they abused me, I'd do anything if they'd tell me I was a good girl. They'd smile at me, they'd put their arm around me, they'd stroke my head, they'd just tell me, "Good girl" and it didn't matter how much they hurt me in between any of those things. That happened in the local bakery and in the park numerous times. So I was a willing accomplice to sexual abuse, having learned I could be told, "Good girl." It was the only positive feedback I had growing up.

At the bakery, for example, we were playing hide and seek one day. My brother and sister were hiding, and I was supposed to be finding them, and the man on the bread-cutting machine said they may go down in the basement, have a look down there. So I went into the basement, and he followed. He started to sexually touch me, and then he had intercourse with me. He told me I was a good girl, gave me a cake and told me to come back the next day without my knickers. I went back the next day without my knickers, and he did it again.

In the park, I was talking to this man who was really nice to me. My sister and I were on the see-saw, and I went down. After he'd finished with his hand in my knickers and his fingers in my vagina, I went back to play with her. She told me she'd seen me, and I told her she hadn't, she was lying. He was a complete stranger, I hadn't a clue who he was. What he did felt nice, and he was nice, and he told me I was a good girl, and he gave me a sweet.

I used to go swimming to get clean, because we hadn't got a bath in our house. On the way home from the swimming baths, almost daily for a long, long time, seven years or so, there was a man in the local rec, where I had to go through

to get home, and he was one of the men that was nice and made me feel nice who I ended up having intercourse with. I'd be 10 or 11 then. At about this time, sexual activities had become the norm. I didn't even know it was wrong.

It just felt like this is what you do to please people, and if you don't get hurt, you're lucky, and if you feel nice, it's great, and sometimes you get a sweet, sometimes you don't, sometimes you get a pat on the head. Both were good: in fact, a pat on the head was better than the sweet. And I knew how to be nice, I knew how to smile, and by this time I was an expert in knowing what to do to sexually arouse. I'd been taught a whole lot by the time I was 11. My grandad used to say: "Alice, when you've been taught all that I need to teach you, the world will be your oyster."

I knew what I had to do, I never questioned it. I'd learned what was expected of me. The feedback was that I was doing well, that I was pleasing, and as long as I did what I was told, I'd continue to be pleasing. I didn't think it was wrong. It was a place that I fit into, I used to say it's the place I belong to best, it's the thing I'm best at. It's what I knew best, and I always felt confident in being able to do well by the time I got to 11. The rewards were affection and praise. I was desperately seeking approval, and this gave it.

Normalizing Child Sexual Abuse

I didn't know I was doing anything wrong until I went [into] nursing at 17. I went to a lecture on sexually transmitted diseases, and it was there that I first heard all about incest, not only that it was wrong, but that it was illegal. It was like being absolutely hit over the head, and I was more terrified of being put in prison for doing something illegal all of my childhood than what had actually happened to me. Although I could easily have died from what was done to me as a child, the thought of being incarcerated in prison for what I'd done frightened me so much that I took an overdose.

From the moment that I heard about incest being illegal, then I had to look at what the rest of it meant, the sex with strangers, what did that mean, and the pornography. The whole lot of it just felt devastating. Everything that I'd done and felt I'd had to do I discovered at the age of 17 that I didn't have to do, that most people don't have to do it, but I had. I was then to discover the enormity of the damage that had been done to me. But that's another story.

Some Characteristics of Pornography and the Organization of Child Sexual Abuse

Gender

Most incest is perpetrated by men: most often by fathers on daughters, or by uncles, grandfathers, and brothers—by male members of the immediate or extended family. It is always an abuse of power: both adult and male power. Alice was abused from the age of 2 by her grandfather, and then by her uncles. They told her they'd been taught by their father, her grandfather, whom Alice later came to learn was probably also her father.

Women may also, in a minority of cases, be the sexual abusers of children. La Fontaine (1994) found women more commonly implicated in family-based abuse, and that "nearly two thirds of the cases of 'paedophile networks' involved no women at all" (p. 12). She found that the majority of alleged perpetrators were men, but women were also represented amongst alleged perpetrators as "implicated jointly with a partner, as knowing of the abuse, not protecting the child or assisting a male abuser" (p. 12).

This is also reflected in other survivor accounts. Danica (1988), for example, describes how her father sexually abused her from the age of 4, and how, on the first occasion, her mother had listened from the bottom of the stairs, much as Alice recalls her mother doing. She describes how her father began his "training" of her from the age of 11, with her mother as an accomplice, instructing her in what to wear, waking her in the night to send or to take her to her father, sometimes watching while the abuse was perpetrated. A woman interviewed by Davies (1994) said her mother allowed, even encouraged, her father to abuse her and her two young brothers and sometimes joined in the abuse. Alice's mother was actively a perpetrator of physical, emotional, and psychological abuse. With respect to the sexual abuse, her role was more passive—in failing to protect her child, in permitting and enabling the abuse to take place, and in failing to prevent it or to stop it happening.

Incest as Grooming for Organized Abuse

Baldwin (1992) has described incest "as a form of seasoning, a practice of a father pimping his daughter to himself" (p. 113). This was Alice's experience: her grandfather's incest was for his own sexual purposes, and also part of a process of grooming her for abuse organized within the family and outside the family for purposes of child prostitution and child pornography. This has also been reported in other autobiographical accounts. Davies (1994) interviewed a woman who described "being conditioned" from the age of 4 or before, so much so that she thought it was "the normal condition of all children to receive almost daily sexual attention from an adult" (p. 14). Danica (1988) describes how, at the age of 9, her father had taken her to the stock car races, and how he and his brother (her uncle) had sold her through the afternoon to a steady stream of customers in the back of the car in the field where the cars were parked. Alice's grandfather and uncles sold her to their friends. This form of family-based abuse is child prostitution, and in these cases, the extrafamilial abuse is organized by the family for people outside the family and may then involve both family members and non-family members.

Pornography and Prostitution

Like Alice, one of the women interviewed by Davies (1994) was filmed: "more than 15 years of it, hundreds of scenes, thousands of feet of film." Like Alice, she said that although she didn't understand it at the time, she now thinks "they used to plan it all in advance, map it out." A typical event would involve adults (which sometimes included her mother and father), and children as young as 2 or 3 through to teen age. The abuse would include anal, oral, and vaginal penetration of the children by the adults and by each other, with objects as well as fingers, hands and penises, tying up, gagging, blindfolding, and whipping. The men who filmed were also perpetrators, and she was beaten if she was not compliant, or if, like Alice, she gagged and choked on semen.

The case material used by Davies (1994) illustrates the symbiotic relationship between pornography and prostitution, and how even the women and girls who claim to consent to their participation can be seen to have been induced by poverty and drug addiction and "predisposed" to participate by their own previous experiences of child sexual abuse. Davies, for example, quotes a woman who described herself as "happy to make pornography," including "sadistic stuff if the money was right." She was a drug addict and a prostitute who "could make £20 opening her mouth for some stranger's penis on the streets of Kings Cross or £250 for doing the same thing in the tatty temporary studio in the front room of someone's flat." Davies also cites the example of the man who "persuaded a 13-year-old girl to make pornographic videos for him simply by offering her an escape from her thoroughly deprived background" (p. 17).

Networks of Perpetrators

One of the women interviewed by Davies (1994) said friends of her parents took part, and she described "a network of adults who shared a secret and obsessive interest and who used each other's children, sometimes separately and sometimes in grotesque gatherings devoted to abuse without limit, endless rape and whippings and [how] always there were cameras" (p. 14). Danica (1988) describes her father building "what he called a studio" in their basement, and parties that her parents organized that ended up in the basement. She describes on one occasion being raped by three "very important men," a judge, a lawyer, a doctor, and then by her own father. The filmed record of this gang rape was subsequently sold by her father (pimp and pornographer) to the participants. Alice also describes the involvement of eminent men in the community in her abuse, and a network likely connected to her grandfather being a freemason.

Coercion and "Consent"

The compliance of children in child sexual abuse, prostitution, and pornography is sometimes achieved through the use of violence and threats of violence. This was the experience of Danica, who was beaten into submission. Alice's submission was achieved through sys-

tematic emotional and physical abuse and neglect, such that the sexual abuse itself was perceived less as abuse than an opportunity to win favour and approval.

The "smile" of the victim (child or woman) in pornography is often cited as the evidence of her consent. Davies (1994) describes a video of a "girl with her wrists and ankles chained to an iron bar in the ceiling and a grotesque dildo hanging out of her." The pornographer who was showing the video pointed to the girl's smile as evidence of her consent. Davies acknowledges the "tired kind of smile" on the girl's face, but also describes "the mark in her make up where a tear had rolled down to her jaw" (p. 17).

Danica (1988) recalls how, at the age of 11, her father called her to the basement and showed her some photographs of her mother: "naked. smiling that smile I know. The smile I have learned to make for the camera too. The smile I make when he says, wet your lips, lift your head, smile. The clenched teeth. The eyes of the hunted facing the camera. Caught. Powerless" (p. 41). She didn't believe her mother would do this, but her father had said: "She does whatever I tell her to do. Just as you'll learn to do what I tell you to do." Alice always smiled, however much she was being hurt. She was happy to smile. This pleased people. They told her she was a good girl. They gave her sweets. These were her only pleasures and happiness in an otherwise miserable, emotionally deprived, and abusive childhood.

Denial and the Silencing of Victims

One of the most extreme examples of child sexual abuse organized for the purposes of making pornography is quoted by DeCamp in his book on the coverup of a pedophile network in Lincoln, Nebraska. DeCamp was a U.S. state senator and the attorney representing one of the victims of a pedophile network, who testified under oath to his part in the making of pornography in which one of the victims was sexually murdered (called "snuff pornography"). In response to their testimony, the boy and a young woman victim of the same organized abuse network were convicted of perjury and given prison sentences. But, wrote DeCamp (1992), "I have not a shadow of a doubt that her story [like his] is true" (p. 225).

It is another characteristic of organized abuse that the victims, when they do tell their stories, are not believed, particularly when the alleged perpetrators are men of power and influence in the community or in government. But the evidence of the truth of the accounts—and the evidence of the organized child sexual abuse—is to be found in the pornography itself. The corroboration, as Davies (1994) has described it, is the "widely distributed, easily available, for sale to anyone who would like to look, images of pornography in Britain in 1994" (p. 14).

Pornography and Intra- and Intergenerational Patterns of Victimization

Perpetrators

Abuse within the family, that is, incest, may be intra- as well as intergenerational. In Alice's family, her mother's brothers as well as her mother had been victims of incest perpetrated by their father. Although it is neither predetermined nor inevitable for the abused in one generation to become the abusers of and within the next generation, the experience of having been abused does appear to be a factor in creating a predisposition toward the same or similar forms of subsequent victimizing and revictimization.

The view that "today's child molester may well be yesterday's incest victim" (Seng, 1986, p. 49) is supported by empirical data. Fagan and Wexler (1988) found that "sex offenders more often came from families with spousal violence, child abuse and child sexual molestation according to both official and self reports" (p. 363). Seghorn, Prentky, and Boucher (1987) found that the "incidence of sexual assault in childhood among child molesters was higher than the incidence of such abuse reported in the literature" (p. 262). Carter et al. (1987) found that 57% of the child molesters in their study were themselves molested as children, and "of the sizeable proportion of child molesters who were molested, 77% were assaulted by strangers or casual acquaintances" (p. 200). Burgess (1985) reported on the "increasing frequency of a history of childhood sexual victimisation in sex of-

fenders." She explains this as a process of "identification with the exploiter," whereby "the child has already introjected some characteristics of the adult and has transformed himself from the person threatened into the person who made the threat" (p. 123), or alternatively where the child "maintains a victim rather than a survivor position, and is at risk for future victimization" (p. 119).

Briere and Runtz (1989) found among the most "significant predictors of self-reported sexual response to children among university males" to be masturbating to pornography, together with "negative early sexual experiences" and "self-reported likelihood of raping a woman" (p. 71) and that "the 'bad experiences' item was one of the most powerful predictors of sexual interest in children" (p. 73). Carter et al. (1987) found that the childhood sexual assaults on the men who later became child molesters "often involved pornographic materials" (p. 206) and that their subsequent sexual assaults on children frequently involved the use of pornography "prior to and during their offenses" (p. 205).

The precise nature of the relationship between having been abused as a child and then going on to abuse, or to being abused again and the role of pornography in this, is something that needs further consideration both conceptually and empirically, but there is the potential, based on this case material, to begin to conceptualize the relationships between pornography and the organization of intra- and extrafamilial child sexual abuse.

Victims

The effects of childhood sexual abuse and pornography on the subsequent behavior of victims is also reflected in research on prostitution and pornography. Allen (1981, cited in Ennew, 1986) found that 90% of girls and boys who were exploited as prostitutes reported having been physically abused by parents, and 50% claimed to have been sexually abused. Weisberg (1985, cited in Baldwin, 1992) reported 66% of prostituted girls and women having been sexually abused by fathers or stepfathers. The Silbert and Pines (1984) study found that 60% of the 200 prostitutes they interviewed reported having been sexually abused as children, and 73%

reported having been raped; 10% of the sample had been used, as children, in pornographic films and magazines, and 38% had had sexual photographs taken of them as children.

This case study shows how the sexual abuse of children sexualizes them and makes them vulnerable to stranger abuse. Alice describes how as a result of being sexualized as a child by her abuse, she became "naturally" seductive and sexually active as a child with strange men, routinely and regularly: how she prostituted herself in the playground, on the streets to and from school, and in the local shops, anywhere anytime. To her this was "normal" behavior, and it was not until she was 17, attending a lecture on sexually transmitted diseases, that she realized that her sexual abuse was not "normal." Burgess, Groth, and McCausland (1981) found that child victims of organized abuse often went on to become prostitutes and pimps and to repeat sexual acts on younger children. Wild and Wynne (1986) illustrated "how abnormal and sexualised the behaviour of children involved in a sex ring may become" with the example of girls who had been victimized subsequently deliberately seeking out a replacement perpetrator when "their" perpetrator had been apprehended, including trying to recruit men in their homes with sexually provocative behavior (p. 184).

Sexualized behavior in children is recognized clinically as a symptom of their having been sexually abused. It is also interpreted by men who sexually abuse children, and in particular those categorized as pedophiles, as evidence of children's sexual maturity and precociousness, and used by them to rationalize their sexual abuse of children.

Effects on Victims of Child Sexual Abuse Involving Pornography

The rest of Alice's story—and the subject of another paper—tells of living with the trauma and trying to recover from the effects of having been sexually abused as a child: of the "traumatic sexualization, betrayal, powerlessness and stigmatization" described by Finkelhor and Browne (1985), and in the words of the woman herself, the "torture and its legacy of self-injury,

self-abuse, attempted suicide and life-long depression." Her belief that being abused in and through pornography aggravated the trauma of the child sexual abuse she experienced is supported by the clinical observations of Hunt and Baird (1990) that "being photographed while being sexually abused exacerbates the shame, humiliation, and powerlessness that sexual abuse victims typically experience" and that "denial of the abuse becomes even more important . . . and is achieved at greater cost" (p. 202). Hunt and Baird found the effects on children of being photographed in the act of being abused to be "devastating." The record of their sexual abuse is "then used to reinforce the children's sense of responsibility for the abuse and to ensure their silence" and the children "become the instrument of their own torture" (p. 201). Burgess et al. (1981) found that having been used in pornography was a poor prognosis factor for victims of child sex rings.

Conclusion

Conceptualizing Child Sexual Abuse to Include Pedophilia and Pornography

Typologies that classify child sexual abusers by particular characteristics for purposes of treatment, risk assessment, and policing typically distinguish between incest offenders and pedophiles, who are then further subcategorized. Waterhouse et al. (1994) classify their Scottish sample of convicted child sexual offenders as "random abusers, paedophiles, incest offenders and deniers" (the latter somewhat confusingly, as denial is widely acknowledged to be a characteristic of all child sexual abusers). They then subclassify the pedophiles as "professional, committed and latent" (p. vii). From his clinical work with sex offenders, Wyre (1993, 1996) has categorized child sexual abusers within a pedophile typology as "fixated," "inadequate," "inadequate fixated," "regressed," "professional," and "parapaedophiles." In addition, he includes the categories of "sadistic" and "aggressive sadistic" in his typology: Incest is an altogether separate category. This is consistent with pedophile classifications based on the American Psychiatric Association's diagnostic criteria used in the United States for research and clinical purposes (see Knight, 1988, 1992; Knight, Carter, & Prentky, 1989). Of these typologies, only Wyre's includes the use of adult and child pornography by each type of offender. With respect to policing, in the United Kingdom, Scotland Yard has now established a Paedophile and Child Pornography Unit.

From a clinical or a policing perspective, typologies that categorize child sexual abusers by predictable patterns of beliefs, sexual preferences, and behaviors may be useful in assisting in their arrest and treatment. But conceptualizing pedophilia as separate from incest and organized abuse, and pornography and child prostitution as further separate categories, also obscures the fact that one and the same perpetrator can appear in any or all categories. Seng (1986) acknowledges that the distinctions between sexual exploitation (including child pornography), incest, and child molestation can become blurred by the fact that the offenders may very well be the same; "that is, an incestuous father may involve his daughter as a participant in child pornography and child molesters are indeed very apt to involve their victims in pornography" (p. 56). This was certainly the case for Alice. Even the diagnostic definition of pedophilia as "the act or fantasy of engaging in sexual activity with prepubertal children as a repeatedly preferred or exclusive method of achieving sexual excitement" is not supported by research. Langevin and Lang (1985) found that 66% of heterosexual pedophiles were married at some time, 91% had vaginal intercourse with an adult female, and even 50% of homosexual pedophiles had done so. They found that "empirical controlled studies" did not support the view that pedophiles were "shy, unassertive, sexually ignorant" and have "an aversion to adult females" (p. 405).

Eldridge (in press) cites research with 99 sex offenders by Weinrott and Saylor (1991) showing that, by their own account, one third of the convicted rapists admitted child sexual abuse, one third of extrafamilial abusers were also incest offenders, and half of the incest offenders

had also abused children who were not their own. Becker and Coleman (1988, cited in Salter, 1995) found that 44% of the men in their sample who had molested female children in the home had also molested female children outside the home. In addition, 11% had also molested male children outside the home and 18% had committed rape. Abel, Becker, Cunningham-Rathner, Mittelman, and Rouleau (1988) found that 49% of the incest offenders who molested girls within the family also molested girls outside the family and 19% were also rapists. In their research on "child abuse which involves kin and family friends," Cleaver and Freeman (1996) found "considerable overlap" between the "men who establish connections between families, and the commerce of child pornography and prostitution." They also cite the case of a member of a pedophile ring whose sexual interest and sexual abuse of his own children had been "kept a secret from his family." All of this, they believe, raises issues about "current police and social services practices which deal with these . . . as if they were discrete phenomena" (pp. 233, 243).

Academics who act as advocates for pedophiles are concerned about the "failure to differentiate between *paedophilia* and what is called *man-boy love*," which "leaves all adult-child relationships overshadowed by the psychiatric term 'paedophilia,' with its connotations of pathology" (Howitt, 1995, p. 26). They seek to separate this "true pedophilia" (i.e., man-boy love, which they wish to regard as "normative") from adult male homosexuality, from the sexual abuse of girls by men who are not true pedophiles, and from incest and to argue that "the child may exploit the adult rather than being a victim" (Howitt, 1995, p. 241, citing Brongersma, 1984, 1990).

There are feminist concerns, however, about the use of the term and the category of pedophilia. Kelly et al. (1996) describe it as "dangerous to create classifications of sexual abuse which are constructed as mutually exclusive categories" (p. 14) because this pathologizes some men and shifts attention from the "recognition of abusers as 'ordinary men'—fathers, brothers, uncles, colleagues" and from the "centrality of power and control to notions of sexual deviance"; because it constructs pedophilia as a

74 OUT OF THE DARKNESS

"specific, and minority, 'sexual orientation,' " distracting attention from "the widespread sexualisation of children," and focusing "attention on a kind of person rather than kinds of behaviour"; because it distracts attention from the similarities between pedophiles and other men who sexually abuse children with respect to "how they entrap and control children" and their "production and consumption of child pornography"; and because, as pedophiles themselves want it to do, it puts an "emphasis on boys rather than girls as victims" (p. 19). It leads to the presumption that all or most "sex tourists" are pedophiles, which is not necessarily the case (Kelly, 1996). Nor is it the case that most of the men who are the customers of children and young people involved in prostitution in the United Kingdom are pedophiles. On the contrary, most of them are likely to be "normal" heterosexual males—just "ordinary men."

But the strongest argument against this "privileging" of pedophilia and the mutually exclusive categorizing of pedophilia and incest is that phenomenologically it doesn't happen that way. Alice's and other survivors' accounts of their abuse suggest that the existing definitions of child sexual abuse that ignore pornography and isolate pedophilia from incest, incest from extrafamilial abuse, and all of these from something called "organized abuse" are misleading. In the United States, Finkelhor (1979) found that fathers and stepfathers were implicated in up to half of the cases of child sexual abuse among a sample of 530 female and 266 male university students. In their Scottish study, Waterhouse and associates (1994) categorized 48% of their sample of 500 convicted sex offenders as familial (where the perpetrator was related to and/or responsible for the victim) and 52% as nonfamilial (where the perpetrator was not related to or responsible for the victim). According to Kelly et al. (1996), children are more likely to be abused by a man they know than by a stranger (p. 10). In her representative sample of 930 women, Russell (1983) found a greater prevalence of extrafamilial abuse than intrafamilial abuse, but only 15% of Russell's sample were abused by strangers. A U.K. study found that child sexual abusers were unknown to the child victim or to the child's family in only about 25% of cases

(Mrazek, Lynch, & Bentovim, 1983). Waterhouse et al. also found that only 10% of offenders were strangers to the child victims but that 61% of the offenses were committed in the home of the child victim and that "the majority of the perpetrators were not strangers to the child and indeed usually lived in the home of the victim at the time that the abuse occurred" (p. iii). Although there are variations in definition between studies of what constitutes familial and nonfamilial or intrafamilial and extrafamilial abuse, the very clear message is that most child sexual abuse is not perpetrated by "pedophiles" (Russell, 1984). Wyre's view, notwithstanding his use of pedophile classifications for treatment and policing purposes, is that incest and pedophilia should not be regarded as separate and different phenomena: They are "inextricably linked" (Wyre, in Howitt, 1995, p. 137).

Typologies based on offender classifications or on whether the abuse occurred inside or outside the family and judgments about its seriousness, usually defined in terms of penetration and/or use of force, have real limitations and provide "little insight into the nature of the trauma experienced by the child" (Finkelhor & Browne, 1985, p. 537). On the assumption that "intrafamilial abuse was expected to be generally more upsetting and traumatic than extrafamilial abuse," Russell (1983, p. 135) used a broader definition of what constitutes intrafamilial abuse, but then found that "children who are sexually abused outside the family are abused in a significantly more serious manner" (p. 142). This suggests that there may not be significant, qualitative differences in the degree of damage experienced by children abused within or outside the family, but Russell (1986) also found that incest can be more traumatic because of the betrayal. This kind of typology of abuse does not reflect the complex and cross-cutting factors that characterize the experience of having been sexually abused as a child, such as the relationship between the abuser and the victim, the length of time over which the abuse takes place, the number of different abusers over time, the nature of the abuse and the level of violence and/or intimidation, the role of pornography in the abuse, and the short- and long-term effects of the abuse on the victims.

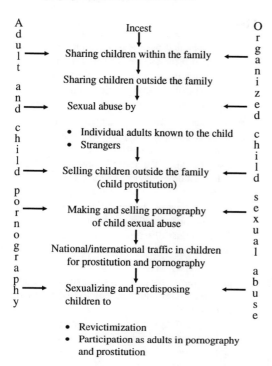

Figure 5.1. Pornography and the Organization of Child Sexual Abuse

Conceptualizing the Relationships Between Pornography and the Organization of Child Sexual Abuse

Kelly (1988) conceptualizes sexual violence as a continuum to reflect the extent and the range of sexual violence reported in a study of 60 women. This concept of continuum was developed to capture the "basic common character underlying the many different forms of violence" reported (of the "abuse, intimidation, coercion, intrusion, threat and force men use to control women") and because sexual violence is "a continuous series of elements or events that pass into one another" (p. 76). Kelly et al. (1996) found that the sexual exploitation of children for commercial purposes is "not easily separable from other forms of sexual abuse in childhood" (p. 14). The case study in this chapter shows how intrafamilial child sexual abuse is related to extrafamilial child sexual abuse and to child sexual exploitation. Figure 5.1 illustrates this diagram-

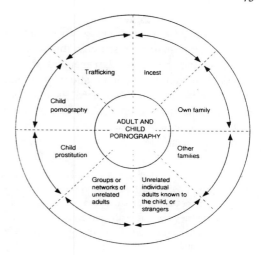

Figure 5.2. How Child Sexual Abuse Is Organized

matically. All of the abuse in Alice's childhood was organized, and making pornography was one of the forms of abuse that was organized. Pornography was also part of the organization of all the other forms of abuse.

Figure 5.2 conceptualizes these interrelationships in the form of concentric circles. The outer circle is the boundary of child sexual exploitation and includes all those who have sex with children for their own personal gratification or for profit. Within this boundary there are the variety of different ways in which abuse may be organized: incest; sharing children within and between families; abuse by adults outside the family, individually and among groups of unrelated adults; and child prostitution and the making of child pornography. These are overlapping rather than discrete categories, which may involve the same perpetrators, the same victims, the same or similar activities, and the same locations. Figure 5.2 also shows how, in addition to abuse that is organized for the purpose of making child pornography, all the other forms of abuse can, and do, involve the use of adult and child pornography.

It seems to be conceptually useful, therefore, to define all adult sex with children as child sexual abuse within which there are categories of activity defined by characteristics common to different kinds of child sexual abuse in different circumstances. Where classifications are used, there is a need for common definitions shared within the international research community, by clinicians and child protection agencies, and for purposes of national and international policing. Whatever classifications are used, they need to take account of the range of characteristics of child sexual abuse identified in this and other studies, for example:

- All child sexual abuse is carried out by people who choose to have sex with children either because they think it is acceptable to do so, or because they choose to allow their desire to override any inhibitions they may have, and they may rationalize this in various ways.

- Sometimes it is carried out by fathers (biological or step-) or cohabiting males in a parental role, or by grandfathers or uncles or brothers who are heterosexual in their adult relationships and have sex with female partners, but who may also sexually abuse either male or female children.

- Sometimes it is carried out by unrelated or noncustodial males who may be strangers, but are more likely to be known to the child as "trusted" adults, who may be either heterosexual or homosexual and who may or may not also have adult sexual relationships.

- Sometimes it is carried out by men who are primarily interested in "having sex with children" and not with other adults (the so-called pedophiles), who may be homosexual or heterosexual in terms of sexual preference, but who may have sex with women to get access to children, and who may sexually abuse either male or female children, but who may be fixated on certain age and/or gender and/or physical characteristics.

- Sometimes, when carried out by any of the above, it may involve more than one adult and/or more than one child (i.e., the multiple abuse usually called organized abuse).

- Whatever the relationship of the perpetrator to the victim, and whatever the sexual preference of the abuser, the majority of abuse occurs in the home of the child by known adults, and only a small proportion (from 10% to 25% in different studies) is perpetrated by strangers.

- Coercion and/or violence may occur in various forms ranging from the manipulative to the brutal in all of these circumstances.

- All of this abuse is organized, in the sense of being planned or engineered in the form of a desire or a fantasy that is acted on, including that which is explained as "impulse," or an intention that is put into practice in circumstances that have been either created or presented.

- However the abuse is organized, it really just represents different ways of initiating and carrying out the sexual abuse of children. This is also true when the abuse is organized around or to include elements of ritual. There may be differences that are useful for purposes of police investigations or perpetrator treatment, but they are not significant phenomenologically: They are just different ways of being a child sexual abuser.

- Pornography, in the form of adult and/or child pornography used to season/groom/initiate/coerce children into agreeing to be abused, or the production of child pornography (the records of children being sexually abused), may be implicated in every form of child sexual abuse, however it is organized.

- Commercial child sexual exploitation in prostitution and pornography may also be an aspect of any form of child sexual abuse, however it is organized.

Summary

■ From case studies and the range of sources cited in this chapter, a picture begins to emerge of the nature and extent and the characteristics of pornography and child sexual abuse, which suggests that both adult and child pornography can be instrumental to the abuse of individual children by individual adults and that the use of and the making of pornography may very well be a characteristic of the abuse of more than one child by one or more adults. It would also appear to be the case that there is considerable overlap in the experience of the victims between incest, organized family-based abuse, and extrafamilial abuse. The value of a phenomenological approach is its ability to generate theory and conceptual models. From this model of the organization of intra- and intergenerational incest, of intra- and extrafamilial child sexual abuse, of child sexual exploitation, and the role of adult and child pornography in it, it is possible to extrapolate some implications for the protection of children.

First is the need to remain aware that adult pornography is commercially available in newsagents, local shops in every neighborhood in the United Kingdom that sell cigarettes, newspapers, sweets, soft drinks, and millions of copies of more than 70 different pornography titles every month (Baxter, 1990). This includes pseudo child pornography in the form of young and childlike-looking women, shown with their pubic hair shaved, genitals exposed, and posed to look like little girls, stimulating male sexual arousal to children's bodies (Itzin & Sweet, 1989). All of this adult pornography is socially legitimated and normalized within "the family" and the wider culture. At the same time is the need to recognize that adult pornography can, and may often, be implicated in child sexual abuse in the ways that have been evidenced in this chapter. In addition, children are now trafficked, and child pornography traded, on the Internet on a substantial scale worldwide (Hughes, 1996).

The focus in child protection training and practice on abuse in a familial context needs to broaden to include the existing knowledge base on the relationship between pornography and the organization of child sexual abuse, the fact that there may be overlap of both perpetrators and victims and location in a substantial minority of cases, and that there may also be an additional dimension of commercial child sexual exploitation. Police and social workers should be advised that where there is child sexual abuse, they should look for both adult and child pornography; where there is child pornography to assume that child sexual abuse is taking place; and in either event, to make a record of the presence and/or use of adult or child pornography in cases of child sexual abuse. The role of pornography in the organization of child sexual abuse is an underresearched area. Not every case will bear all of the characteristics modeled from this case study, but it is likely that each case will bear some of these characteristics and that pornography may be instrumental to the abuse.

References

Abel, G. G., Becker, J. V., Cunningham-Rathner, J., Mittelman, M., & Rouleau, J. L. (1988). Multiple paraphilic diagnoses among sex offenders. *Bulletin of the American Academy of Psychiatry and the Law, 16*, 153-168.

Allen, E. E. (1981). Testimony before the Committee on the Judiciary United States Senate 1981 by the chairman of Jefferson County Task Force on Child Prostitution and Pornography.

Baldwin, M. (1992). Split at the root: Prostitution and feminist discourses of law reform. *Yale Journal of Law and Feminism, 5*, 47-120.

Baldwin, M. A. (1993). Strategies of connection: Prostitution and feminist politics. *Michigan Journal of Gender and Law, 1*, 65-79.

Barry, K. (1988). Evidence to Minneapolis Public Hearings 1983. In *Pornography and sexual violence: Evidence of the links* (pp. 29-30). London: Everywoman.

Barry, K. (1992). *The Penn State Report—International meeting of experts on sexual exploitation, violence and prostitution.* State College, PA: UNESCO and Coalition Against Trafficking in Women.

Baxter, M. (1990, May 5). Flesh and blood: Does pornography lead to sexual violence? *New Scientist*, pp. 37-41.

Becker, J. V., & Coleman, E. M. (1988). Incest. In V. B. van Hasselt, R. L. Morrison, A. S. Bellack, & M. Hersen (Eds.), *Handbook of family violence* (pp. 187-205). New York: Plenum.

Briere, J., & Runtz, M. (1989). University males' sexual interest in children: Predicting potential indices of "pedophilia" in a nonforensic sample. *Child Abuse & Neglect, 13*, 65-75.

Brongersma, E. (1984). Aggression against pedophiles. *International Journal of Law and Psychiatry, 7*, 79-87.

Brongersma, E. (1990). Boy-lovers and their influence on boys: Distorted research and anecdotal observation. *Journal of Homosexuality, 20*, 145-173.

Burgess, A. W. (1984). *Child pornography and sex rings.* Lexington, MA: Lexington Books.

Burgess, A. W. (1985). Dangerous sexual offenders: Commentary. *Medical Aspects of Human Sexuality, 19*, 119-123.

Burgess, A. W., Groth, A. N., & McCausland, M. P. (1981). Child sex initiation rings. *American Journal of Orthopsychiatry, 51*, 110-119.

Burgess, A. W., & Hartman, C. R. (1987). Child abuse aspects of child pornography. *Psychiatric Annals, 7*, 248-253.

Carter, D. L., Prentky, R. A., Knight, R., Vanderveer, P. L., & Boucher, R. J. (1987). Pornography in the criminal and developmental histories of sexual offenders. *Journal of Interpersonal Violence, 2*, 196-211.

Cleaver, H., & Freeman, P. (1996). Child abuse which involves wider kin and family friends. In P. Bibby (Ed.), *Organised abuse: The current debate* (pp. 231-245). Aldershot, UK: Ashgate.

Creighton, S. J. (1993, December). Organized abuse: NSPCC experience. *Child Abuse Review, 2*, 232-243.

Danica, E. (1988). *Don't: A woman's word.* Dublin: Attic.

Davies, N. (1994, November 26). Dirty business. *Guardian*, pp. 12-17.

DeCamp, J. W. (1992). *The Franklin cover-up: Child abuse, satanism and murder in Nebraska.* Lincoln, NE: AWT.

Eldridge, H. J. (in press). Adult male perpetrators of child sexual abuse: Patterns of offending and strategies for effective assessment and intervention. In C. Itzin, J. Hammer, & S. Quaid (Eds.), *Home truths: Responses to family-based violence and abuse.* London: Routledge.

Ennew, J. (1986). *The sexual exploitation of children.* Cambridge, UK: Polity.

European Forum on Child Welfare (EFCW). (1993). *Child pornography and sexual exploitation* (EFCW Position Statement). London: Barnardos.

Fagan, J., & Wexler, S. (1988). Explanations of sexual assault among violent delinquents. *Journal of Adolescent Research, 3*, 363-385.

Finkelhor, D. (1979). *Sexually victimized children.* New York: Free Press.

Finkelhor, D. (1986). *A sourcebook on child sexual abuse.* Beverly Hills, CA: Sage.

Finkelhor, D., & Browne, A. (1985). The traumatic impact of child sexual abuse: A conceptualization. *American Journal of Orthopsychiatry, 55*, 530-541.

Gallagher, B., Hughes, B., & Parker, H. (1994). *Organised and ritual child sexual abuse, research report to the Department of Health.* Manchester: Department of Social Policy and Social Work.

Gallagher, B., Hughes, B., & Parker, H. (1996). The nature and extent of known cases of organised child sexual abuse in England and Wales. In P. Bibby (Ed.), *Organised abuse: The current debate* (pp. 215-231). Aldershot, UK: Ashgate.

Groner, L. (1992). *The opinion of the Committee on Culture, Youth, Education and the Media.* Committee on Civil Liberties and Internal Affairs on Pornography, B3-0420/92.

Hames, M. (1993, December). Child pornography: A secret web of exploitation. *Child Abuse Review, 2*, 276-281.

Howitt, D. (1995). *Paedophiles and sexual offenses against children.* Chichester, UK: Wiley.

Hunt, P., & Baird, M. (1990, May/June). Children of sex rings. *Child Welfare, 69*, 195-207.

Hughes, D. (1996). Sex tours via the Internet. *Agenda: Empowering Women for Equality*, No. 28, pp. 71-76.

Ireland, K. (1993, December). Sexual exploitation of children and international travel and tourism. *Child Abuse Review, 2*, 263-271.

Itzin, C. (1992). "Entertainment for men": What it is and what it means. In C. Itzin (Ed.), *Pornography: Women, violence and civil liberties* (pp. 27-55). Oxford: Oxford University Press.

Itzin, C. (1996). Pornography and the organisation of child sexual abuse. In P. Bibby (Ed.), *Organised abuse: The current debate* (pp. 167-197). Aldershot, UK: Ashgate.

Itzin, C. (in press). *Women's experience of pornography-related harm* (Violence, Abuse and Gender Relations Research Report No. 12). University of Bradford Violence, Abuse and Gender Relations Research Unit.

Itzin, C., & Sweet, C. (1989, April 27). Tackling the monsters on the top shelf. *The Independent*, p. 16.

Itzin, C., & Sweet, C. (1990, March). What you feel about pornography. *Cosmopolitan*, pp. 8-12.

Kelly, L. (1988). *Surviving sexual violence.* Cambridge, UK: Polity.

Kelly, L. (1992). Pornography and child sexual abuse. In C. Itzin (Ed.), *Pornography: Women, violence and civil liberties* (pp. 113-124). Oxford: Oxford University Press.

Kelly, L. (1996, Summer). Weasel words: Paedophiles and the cycle of abuse. *Trouble & Strife, 33*, 44-49.

Kelly, L., Wingfield, R., Burton, S., & Regan, L. (1996). *Splintered lives: Sexual exploitation of children in the context of children's rights and child protection.* Essex, UK: Barnardos.

Knight, R. A. (1988). A taxonomic analysis of child molesters. In R. A. Prentky & V. L. Quinsey (Eds.), *Annals of the New York Academy of Science: Vol. 528. Human sexual aggression: Current perspectives* (pp. 2-20). New York: New York Academy of Science.

Knight, R. A. (1992). The generation and corroboration of a taxonomic model for child molesters. In W. O'Donohue & J. H. Geer (Eds.), *The sexual abuse of children: Clinical issues* (Vol. 2, pp. 24-70). Hillsdale, NJ: Lawrence Erlbaum.

Knight, R. A., Carter, D. L., & Prentky, R. A. (1989). A system for the classification of child molesters: Reliability and application. *Journal of Interpersonal Violence, 4*, 3-23.

Kroon, L. (1980). Personal experiences in the pornography industry. *Newspage, 4*,(8). (Women Against Violence in Pornography and Media)

La Fontaine, J. S. (1993). Defining organised sexual abuse. *Child Abuse Review, 2*, 223-231.

La Fontaine, J. S. (1994). *The extent and nature of organised and ritual abuse: Research findings.* London: HMSO.

Langevin, R., & Lang, R. A. (1985). Psychological treatment of paedophiles. *Behavioural Sciences and the Law, 3*, 403-419.

Marshall, W. L. (1988). The use of sexually explicit stimuli by rapists, child molesters, and non offenders. *Journal of Sex Research, 26*, 267-288.

Minneapolis Hearings. (1988). The complete transcripts of public hearings on ordinances to add pornography as discrimination against women: Minneapolis City Council, Government Operations Committee, December 12 and 13, 1983. In *Pornography and sexual violence: Evidence of the links.* London: Everywoman.

Mrazek, P., Lynch, M. A., & Bentovim, A. (1983). Sexual abuse of children in the United Kingdom. *Child Abuse & Neglect, 7*, 147-154.

Muntarbhorn, V. (1995). Violence against children: The sale of children, child prostitution, and child pornography. In *Children in trouble* (Proceedings of the United Nations Expert Group Meeting on Children and Juveniles in Detention: Application of Human Rights Standards, pp. 54-56). Vienna: Austrian Federal Ministry for Youth and Family.

Russell, D. E. H. (1983). The incidence and prevalence of intrafamilial and extrafamilial sexual abuse of female children. *Child Abuse & Neglect, 7,* 133-146.

Russell, D. E. H. (1984). *Sexual exploitation: Rape, child sexual abuse, and workplace harassment.* Beverly Hills, CA: Sage.

Russell, D. E. H. (1986). *The secret trauma: Incest in the lives of girls and women.* New York: Basic Books.

Russell, D. E. H. (1993). *Making violence sexy: Feminist views on pornography.* Milton Keynes, UK: Open University Press.

Salter, A. C. (1995). *Transforming trauma: A guide to understanding and treating adult survivors of child sexual abuse.* Thousand Oaks, CA: Sage.

Sariola, H. (1986). *Child prostitution, trafficking and pornography* (Report). Finland: Defence for Children International and Central Union for Child Welfare.

Seghorn, T. K., Prentky, R. A., & Boucher, R. J. (1987). Childhood sexual abuse in the lives of sexually aggressive offenders. *Journal of the American Academy of Child and Adolescent Psychiatry, 26,* 262-267.

Seng, M. J. (1986). Sexual behaviour between adults and children: Some issues of definition. *Journal of Offender Counselling, Services and Rehabilitation, 11*(1), 47-61.

Silbert, M., & Pines, A. (1984). Pornography and sexual abuse of women. *Sex Roles, 11/12,* 857-868.

Tate, T. (1990). *Child pornography.* London: Methuen.

Tate, T. (1992). The child pornography industry: International trade in child sexual abuse. In C. Itzin (Ed.), *Pornography: Women, violence and civil liberties* (pp. 203-217). Oxford: Oxford University Press.

Waterhouse, L., Dobash, R., & Carnie, J. (1994). *Child sexual abusers.* Edinburgh: Scottish Office Central Research Unit.

Weinrott, M. R., & Saylor, M. (1991). Self-report of crimes committed by sex offenders. *Journal of Interpersonal Violence, 6,* 286-300.

Wild, N. J. (1989). Prevalence of child sex rings. *Paediatrics, 83,* 553-558.

Wild, N. J., & Wynne, J. M. (1986, July 19). Child sex rings. *British Medical Journal, 293,* 183-185.

Wyre, R. (1992). Pornography and sexual violence: Working with sex offenders. In C. Itzin (Ed.), *Pornography: Women, violence and civil liberties* (pp. 236-248). Oxford: Oxford University Press.

Wyre, R. (1993). *Working with sex abuse: Understanding sex offending.* Birmingham, UK: Gracewell Clinic.

Wyre, R. (1996). The mind of the paedophile. In P. Bibby (Ed.), *Organised abuse: The current debate* (pp. 87-105). Aldershot, UK: Ashgate.

CHAPTER 6

Black Mothers' Emotional and Behavioral Responses to the Sexual Abuse of Their Children

Claudia Bernard

Little research has been initiated in Britain that looks specifically at the accounts of Black mothers whose children have been sexually abused. It has been well documented that the discourse on childhood sexual abuse has seldom addressed the dynamics of race, class, and gender in the analysis of mothers' responses to the abuse of their children (Abney & Priest, 1995; Mtezuka, 1996; Wilson, 1993). As a consequence, there is a paucity of reliable research highlighting the ways Black mothers' responses are shaped by their racial and gender experiences.

This chapter offers an examination of the responses of Black mothers when their children have been sexually abused and the problems these mothers face. Special attention will be given to the intersection of race, gender, and class. I intend to demonstrate that the concerns of Black mothers are shaped by racism and gender oppression. Although childhood sexual abuse transcends class and race boundaries, an examination of the issues affecting Black families must include research that addresses the specificity of their experiences. In arguing for the importance of developing paradigms that put race, gender, and class at center stage, this chapter will focus on key factors that affect Black mothers' help-seeking and protective strategies.

The research on which this chapter is based is an exploratory study of Black mothers' reactions and responses to the sexual abuse of their children. The study is still in progress and is primarily concerned with examining how Black mothers experience the processes of disclosure and discovery, and the intervention of child protection services.

The Role of Mothers in Childhood Sexual Abuse: Existing Research

The questions most frequently asked of mothers are, "How could she not have known?" and "Why did she not do something about it?" Existing research has shown that explorations of sexual abuse within families must relate to fundamental questions of how we understand the role of mothers, who in the majority of cases are the nonabusing parents (see, e.g., Deblinger, Russell Hathaway, Lippmann, & Steer, 1993; Dempster, 1993; Finkelhor, 1986; Hooper, 1992; MacLeod & Saraga, 1988; Print & Dey, 1992; Russell, 1986; Smith, 1994, 1995; Wyatt & Mickey, 1988). The scholars noted above contend that professional perceptions of mothers are often very negative, and much controversy generally surrounds the debate about mothers' responses to the sexual abuse of their children. This body of research conveys the message that mothers of children who have been sexually abused are typically depicted as "colluding" or "failing to protect" their children, and several studies have revealed that professional perceptions of nonabusing mothers are often pejorative and blaming. Most notable is the argument that the mother's absence or unavailability may lead to inadequate supervision and unmet emotional needs, increasing the child's vulnerability (Strand, 1990). In particular, Hooper (1992) argues that beliefs about mothers have been based on clinical hypotheses, the accounts of survivors of childhood sexual abuse, and the abstract formulations of theoreticians, but very little on mothers' own stories.

A common theme emerging from the approaches that have analyzed mothers' accounts is the suggestion that when children have been sexually abused, the responsibility falls predominantly on their mothers to engage with child protection services and to protect their children from further abuse (Deblinger, Lippmann, Stauffer, & Finkel, 1994; Print & Dey, 1992; Russell, 1986; Salt, Myer, Coleman, & Sauzier, 1990; Wyatt & Mickey, 1988). Such work has raised some significant questions that are important for understanding the psychological impact on mothers and the ways this may

influence their reactions and responses (Deblinger et al., 1994; Gomes-Schwartz, Horowitz, & Cardarelli, 1990; Hooper, 1992; Jacobs, 1990; Johnson, 1992). Child protection intervention often places the responsibility for the abuse on mothers. Mothers are typically seen as being responsible for the care and well-being of their children, and when something goes wrong it is the mother who is blamed (Milner, 1993).

Additionally, mothers are frequently left alone to cope with assumptions of collusion, their own feelings of self-blame, and the problems of helping their children deal with the consequences of the abuse. A number of authors have also suggested that being believed and supported by mothers on the discovery of the abuse can play a crucial role in children's recovery (Deblinger et al., 1994; Erooga & Masson, 1989; Hooper, 1992; Saraga, 1994; Sirles & Lofberg, 1990).

Hooper (1992) contends that mothers' responses will be determined by the extent of power relations within the family and are augmented by the emotional, social, and financial stresses that mothers face. Hooper's central contention is the need to understand the effect abuse has on mothers and how this can influence their emotional and behavioral responses. Her analysis emphasizes that sensitive input from child protection professionals during abuse investigations may positively affect mothers' coping responses and, in turn, aid their abused children's recovery.

Gaps in the Research

Arguably, the scholars noted above have made a considerable contribution to the body of research by critiquing many of the mother-blaming theories that predominate in the literature on childhood sexual abuse. However, their analyses do have some major limitations. Most notably, more attention could usefully have been paid to the complex interaction of race and gender oppression and their influences on Black mothers' help-seeking strategies. The prevailing tendency in much of the existing research is for Black mothers' experiences to be either ignored or "added on" to an analysis of gender (Bernard,

1994c). Consequently, discussion is often framed in terms of "mothers" as if they are a unitary category while overlooking the cultural, structural, and material forces that shape Black mothers' lives. A further limitation in the existing research is that it generally reflects the experiences of White mothers, and inappropriate generalizations are then applied to Black mothers (Mtezuka, 1996; Phillips, 1995; Wilson, 1993).

Not surprisingly, this absence of research on the significance of race and racism often affects the choices that may be open to Black mothers. Clearly, what is needed is an exploration of the particular issues facing Black mothers for us to understand the multifaceted nature of their experiences and to help child protection professionals gain more effective practice with Black families.

Childhood Sexual Abuse
and Black Families:
Key Concerns

It could be argued that when childhood sexual abuse is suspected in Black families, there are additional problems for Black mothers in talking about the abuse outside the family that White mothers are not faced with. One difference for Black mothers is the relevance of racism to their daily lives. Speaking out about childhood sexual abuse is a taboo for most mothers. However, this may have broader implications for Black mothers who have to deal with multiple layers of racism in predominantly White societies. Perhaps most important, Black mothers face the double jeopardy of dealing with a child protection service they may see as hostile and, at best, culturally insensitive to their needs (MacLeod & Saraga, 1988; Phillips, 1995; Wilson, 1993).

Black mothers in Britain may have to consider the consequences of the abuse not only for their children and themselves but also for their families and communities (Mtezuka, 1996): For Black people, the fear of feeding racist myths and cultural stereotypes is ever present (Abney, 1996; Droisen, 1989; Wilson, 1993). For example, Droisen (1989) writes about the role of racism and anti-Semitism in Black and Jewish children's experiences of sexual abuse: "If a white man abuses his child, the situation is looked at in terms of his individual problem. But if a Black man abuses a child, racist stereotyping will point the finger at Black culture" (p. 162).

This example illustrates one way racism may affect the experiences of Black children who have been sexually abused. According to Droisen, by internalizing the negative stereotypes from outside, Black children may wrongly connect sexual abuse exclusively to the Black community. Especially damaging to Black children who have been abused is the internalization of Blackness being associated with badness (MacLeod & Saraga, 1988). These factors may intersect to influence Black children's capacity to tell their mothers of the abuse. For instance, some Black children may feel that they are betraying their mothers if they speak of abuse (Driver & Droisen, 1989). Thus, research suggests that Black children may not be able to talk to their mothers about the abuse because of feelings of poor self-worth.

Additionally, the social status of Black mothers is central to how they experience their roles and identities, not only in their families and communities but in society as a whole. If we are to understand the choices Black mothers make, we must have some understanding of the complex set of power relationships they have to negotiate in their daily lives.

The family is seen as a major source of empowerment for Black women. In a society that is hostile and racist, Black women's families and communities are supposedly their safe havens. It is here that cushioning the effects of racism is usually undertaken. However, when violence and abuse takes place within the family, the illusion of the family as a safe haven is shattered, and the effects on Black mothers can be especially traumatic (Bernard, 1994a). Here it could be argued that Black mothers are in the contradictory position where they have to extol the virtues of the family and community and at the same time expect little in the way of support and protection from the violence and abuse they experience at the hands of men in the family.

Wilson (1993) has suggested that the position of Black women in the family can have a crucial part to play in influencing mothers' responses to their children's abuse. She demonstrated quite clearly in her analysis the way the gender and power imbalances in Black families can circumscribe Black mothers' roles. These factors will influence how they interpret their children's experience of abuse, and also how they respond to the abuse. Phillips (1995) contends: "The negative view of African Caribbean culture is sometimes juxtaposed with an over-idealised view about the strength and resilience of African Caribbean women, resulting in an unrealistic and unhelpful approach to working with African Caribbean families" (p. 120).

Although it is necessary to challenge harmful stereotypes surrounding perceptions of Black families, it is also important not to present Black families as harmonious and conflict free, because this not only colludes with abusers but also serves to silence children and their mothers in talking about the violence and abuse they experience. Analyses in relation to sexual abuse and Black families must therefore not only be grounded in an understanding of the gendered power relations between Black men and women, but they must also be located within wider debates of racism. Essentially, although all mothers of abused children may have some common experiences, differences involving race and social class can lead to very different ways of responding to their children's abuse.

A central implication of the omission of Black mothers' accounts in research is that assumptions will be made about their protective strategies without examining the additional complexities that have an effect on their responses (Wilson, 1993). I argue that interventions that are underpinned by research based on the experiences of White mothers are limited in offering an explanation of Black mothers' responses.

Method

■ The research used a qualitative design drawing on in-depth interviews with 30 Black[1] mothers living in Britain whose children had been sexually abused. Participation in the study was voluntary. Respondents were recruited through a number of social services departments, voluntary agencies, and community groups and through publicity material distributed in medical and health centers. To be eligible for the study, the mothers had to have acknowledged that the sexual abuse had occurred, and discovery of the abuse had to have taken place at least 6 months before the interview (see Bernard, 1994b, for a more detailed discussion on conceptual and methodological issues).

The study involved asking the mothers about their experiences of the discovery and intervention processes. Essentially, I wanted to explore what the concerns and priorities for Black mothers were when they discovered the abuse. I also wanted to find out from mothers their own feelings about the abuse, their understanding of their own responses, and their understanding of the consequences for their children and themselves. The study involved mothers who had not spoken about the abuse outside of their families before my interview and whose children had experienced intrafamilial and/or extrafamilial abuse.

Research Findings

■ For the purposes of this chapter, I have chosen to focus on three broad themes that emerged as dominant factors for all the mothers interviewed: shame, isolation, and perceived powerlessness in their dealings with child protection agencies. These themes should be understood not as separate entities but as inextricably linked within the complex set of relationships that Black women have to negotiate.

Why are some Black mothers reluctant to report their suspicions of sexual abuse to child protection services? For the mothers in my study, a number of factors had an effect on their decisions whether to involve the child protection services. Among the most significant concerns the mothers expressed were the following:

- Perceptions that child protection services would take a blaming attitude toward them
- Fear of the possible consequences for them and their families
- Lack of proof of the identity of the abuser (particularly when the suspicion was of someone

outside the family and in a position of authority)

- Feeling that they ought to have known about
  the abuse, or that their children should have
  been able to tell them sooner
- Fear that because they are Black, their concerns
  would not be taken seriously by child protection services
- Fear that the authorities would take a more
  heavy-handed approach with them because
  they are Black
- Feeling torn about going outside their families
  and communities to report the abuse
- Feelings of shame, stigma, isolation, and powerlessness

Although some of these issues are common to
all mothers, certain issues are more particular to
Black mothers. One crucial difference for Black
mothers is the combination of race and gender
oppression: The negative construction of Black
people in society and oppressive power relations
within Black families have an effect on Black
mothers' perception of the choices they believe
are open to them.

Shame and the Societal Perception
of Black Families

A major issue for all the mothers in my study
was the feeling of shame. If the abuse was intrafamilial, this had resonance for the mothers
because of existing racist assumptions about
Black males in particular, and the negative social
construction of the Black family in general. Let
us consider some of the issues that are at stake
here for Black mothers. For those in the Black
community, the possibility of Black men's involvement in sexual abuse toward their children
opens up painful and difficult issues. The per-
vasive images of Black males in British society
present them as "feckless," "oversexed," and
"violent" and as "criminals," "drug pushers,"
"absent fathers," and so on (Milner, 1993). The
mothers in my study were acutely aware of these
stereotypes, and their loyalty to partners in the
face of racism sometimes influenced their help-
seeking. Black mothers may not want to show
White society that things are failing in their
families, and powerful internal and external

pressures act to discourage them from seeking
outside help. Additionally, for Black mothers,
to raise the issue in public can invite a racist
backlash and incur marginalization and even exclusion from their communities.

Not surprisingly, the discovery of sexual
abuse creates a climate of insecurity and anger,
and the mothers in my study found it difficult to
know whom to trust. In confronting the truth
about sexual abuse, some mothers experienced
confusing emotions of sadness, anger, and conflict. A number of the mothers in my study indicated that the anger and betrayal they felt
caused them a good deal of uncertainty and confusion. Therefore, what may be interpreted as a
failure to take immediate action and report the
abuse to child protection agencies may in fact
be a mother processing the knowledge of the
abuse and weighing the consequences for her
and her family that might result from reporting
it. This combination of issues interacted in very
powerful ways to add to mothers' feelings of
shame and stigma and manifested themselves in
such ways that some mothers in my study felt
immobilized when it came to seeking help outside their immediate family.

Powerlessness in the Face
of Child Protection Services

In my study, when women did involve the
child protection services, they were left feeling
disempowered and devalued. Again, racism had
complex repercussions on the interaction between Black mothers and child protection agencies. For many mothers, enlisting the help of
child protective services is like grasping the
point of a double-edge sword. Not only do they
have to challenge the oppression within their
own family and community, but they must also
confront antagonistic professionals in many
child protection agencies. Some salient points
are illustrated in the following examples.

Maureen's Story

Maureen, a mother of Caribbean origin, suspected
that her 12-year-old daughter was being sexually
abused. Her daughter has learning and communication disabilities and was attending a special

needs school. Maureen became suspicious when she began to notice drastic changes in her daughter's behavior: Her daughter had become very distressed, cried often, and masturbated constantly. Maureen reported her concerns to the school, social services, and the police, but the behavior was attributed to the child's disabilities and the matter was not investigated further. Maureen's response was described as obsessive, and she was labeled by professionals as suffering from Munchausen syndrome by proxy. In desperation, she took her daughter to the hospital and threatened to leave her there until she was examined. When medically examined, the child was found to have a vaginal discharge, her hymen was damaged, and there were tears on her hymen that were at least 2 years old. It took Maureen nearly 2 years of persistence before professionals would consent to have her daughter medically examined.

Mary's Story

Mary is the single parent of a 14-year-old girl with learning disabilities. Her daughter resided with foster care parents during the week and spent every weekend with Mary. Some months after the start of this arrangement, Mary began to notice changes in her daughter's behavior: She became aggressive, became very distressed when it was time to return to the foster parents, and indicated strongly that she did not want to go back to them. She then began running away from the foster parents, soiling herself, and stealing. Mary's attempts to bring this to the attention of the child protection services were not taken seriously and her daughter's behavior was attributed to her disabilities. It took Mary months of persistence before the matter was investigated and her daughter was removed from the foster parents.

What emerges from the above examples is that the interventions with these families were coercive rather than supportive. Of particular importance is that the mothers' attempts to report their suspicions were met with resistance and even hostility from professionals. Their overriding impressions were that their daughters' statuses as Black children with disabilities deemed them not worthy of serious consideration. Here we can see the complex interaction of race, gender, and disability in shaping the experiences of these Black children and their

mothers. Research suggests there is a lack of willingness to investigate childhood sexual abuse when the victims are children or young people with learning disabilities. The argument usually put forward is that children with learning disabilities are not credible witnesses (Gunn, 1989).

Additionally, these mothers inferred that a determining factor of the responses they received from the child protection services was that their allegations were being made against White professional workers and foster care parents. Both these mothers were left feeling that their interactions with professionals served only to compound their feelings of isolation and betrayal. What is clearly highlighted by the above examples is the way that professionals' responses can serve to deny and minimize the seriousness of Black mothers' concerns, leaving them feeling devalued and disempowered, and ultimately leaving their children exposed to further risk.

For Black mothers, enlisting the help of law enforcement agencies may also exacerbate the problems of reporting. Doing so means using an agency that is typically known for its oppressive policing of the Black community. Additionally, Black women may wish to protect Black men from potentially racist police intervention or surveillance and may thus be reluctant to seek their help (Mama, 1989). The Black community in Britain has seen too much police intervention of a particular kind, and it does not experience the police force as protectors in the same way that the White community may (Mama, 1993). Moreover, if a mother does take action and go to the police, she may be condemned by her own community for betrayal (Wilson, 1993). Although some mothers in my study talked about feeling betrayed and angry about the abuse, some still wished to protect Black men and so were reluctant to seek the help of the police. Black mothers clearly have to weigh these issues when they seek help because they are afraid not only of further stigmatization but also betrayal of their communities. For some mothers, the consequence of involving the police could be marginalization or exclusion from the community. Issues of race and gender oppression are intricately interwoven here to trap Black mothers in a web of contradictions. The mothers in my study felt a strong sense of responsibility not only toward their partners but to the Black community as a whole. At the same time, they expressed a tremendous amount of anger at the double-bind situation in which they found themselves.

Isolation

The presence or absence of support networks in the community was a significant factor for a number of mothers in determining whether they approached child protection services. Factors of isolation are key concerns here. Most mothers in my study initially sought help from extended family members or close friends, and although some mothers felt supported, others related feeling blamed and unsupported.

An important factor for a number of mothers was the pressure from family members not to report the abuse to child protection services. Some mothers felt there was a denial that the abuse could have occurred. Among the mothers that I interviewed, a number did not involve child protection services and had not previously discussed the matter outside of the family. One mother described how with the help of extended family members the abuser was confronted and "dealt with"; therefore, she felt no further need to involve child protection services. It is possible, however, that mothers who had not involved child protection services were still angered by the pressures that were put on them by family members.

This example illustrates a point made by Wilson (1993) that the subject of sexual abuse is surrounded by a wall of silence in Black communities. This has a powerful impact on the way Black women and children are able to talk about their experiences of violence in the family to outside agencies. Racism is a factor in contributing to the denial that sexual abuse happens in Black communities or conversely adds to the pressure to hush up the matter. The denial from the people to whom they turn for help can add to mothers' feelings of isolation. A major point is that all of these elements interact to control how sexual abuse is talked about, understood, and explained in Black communities. These elements will work to create feelings of isolation and heighten already existing feelings of stigmatization. Some knowledge of how these factors can affect mothers' thought processes, explanations, and possible actions are important if we are to understand their protective strategies.

A common theme running through most of the mothers' stories was the fear of the removal of the child and the breakup of the family. This is a very real fear for all families, but it is particularly salient for Black families. This factor strongly influenced some mothers' decisions not to involve the child protective services. The mothers in this study felt vulnerable to implied criticisms of their parenting and their capacity to protect their children from abuse. There is evidence to show the overrepresentation of African Caribbean children in the public care system, and also by what happens to Black children once they are in the care system (Barn, 1993; Bebbington & Miles, 1989; Johnson, 1991). Such research shows that Black mothers' perceived fears of overreactions by professionals are not necessarily unwarranted.

Balancing the Needs of Mothers and the Needs of Their Children: Assessing Risk Factors

Given the tensions and complexities involved in Black mothers' circumstances, great challenges will be faced by child protection workers in identifying risk factors to Black children. Hooper (1992) stresses the significance of empowering mothers as one of the best ways to help abused children. That said, what are the issues involved in protecting Black children and at the same time giving support to their mothers? As Channer and Parton (1988) so succinctly put it: "Attempts to reduce racism . . . [have] to recognise that protecting the interests of Black children may well involve intensive supervision of their parents" (p. 105).

For child protection professionals to work effectively with Black mothers, the mothers' fears and uncertainties must be recognized and validated. However, although child protection workers must guard against taking a blaming attitude toward mothers, they must be able to assess accurately what the risk factors are for

Black children. This position presents a formidable challenge to professionals whose central focus is the children's welfare. A major problem in attempting to empower Black mothers is the danger that the needs of mothers and their children will be conflated. Clearly, it is necessary to understand some of the reasons why some mothers may be reluctant to involve child protection services. However, practitioners must also be open to the possibility that there will be some mothers who are not willing to accept the abuse of their children. Working in a supportive and sensitive way with mothers should not get in the way of assessing the needs of Black children. It is imperative that child protection workers have a good understanding of the complex issues involved so that they can recognize when children's needs may be in conflict with their mothers. A key concern here is whether some mothers' reluctance to involve child protection services could be seen by child protection workers as protecting abusers and further endangering their children. The implications of avoiding confronting these difficult issues could mean that some Black children will be left in abusive situations. As I indicated earlier, a number of the mothers in my study did not involve child protection services. This certainly poses questions about the long-term safety needs of some of these children.

In assessing risk factors, child protection workers have to be able to assess whether a mother has the capacity to empathize with her child and protect him or her from further abuse. They must be able to examine behavior to understand what reactions may stem from coping strategies developed for survival in a racist society, and what behaviors may ultimately be dangerous for Black children. Child protection professionals must be aware that when they examine behaviors, there are many potential pitfalls. One such danger is that they may draw on oversimplified cultural explanations that may unwittingly lead to the acceptance of a lower threshold for intervention with Black children (Jones, 1994; Phillips & Dutt, 1990). Some commentators suggest that where White practitioners may fear being labeled racist, they may fail to intervene, and their inaction could leave Black children exposed to further abuse (Jones,

1994). Conversely, without some examination of the ideas and assumptions they may hold about Black mothers and Black families, some professionals may intervene in ways that are insensitive and reinforce mother-blaming.

Conclusion

■ In this chapter, I have argued for the need to explore the way race and gender intersect to shape Black mothers' experiences of the help-seeking and intervention processes when their children have been sexually abused. The preliminary results of this study indicate some important points for consideration. Most important, the results suggest that a greater awareness of the importance of race and power dynamics is necessary to identify what individual risk factors exist for Black children. If child protection professionals fail to explore the race and gender dimensions of Black mothers' experiences, their interventions may undermine the contributions Black mothers can make to their children's protection and recovery. Several key themes have emerged from analysis of selected findings in my research. These themes indicate how assumptions can be made about Black mothers' protective strategies without a thorough examination of the complex web of issues that influence their responses.

Clearly, the numbers of women interviewed for this study are not sufficiently representative of all Black mothers, and neither do I want to imply that Black women are a homogeneous group. In focusing on Black mothers I also recognize that there are important diversities between Black mothers themselves. Indeed, Black women's experiences are shaped by racial origin, ethnicity, class, religion, and other cultural factors that influence what choices they feel are open to them and their children. Nevertheless, it is still important that Black mothers' common experiences are acknowledged.

This study has highlighted that there is a need for more research on the complex interrelationship of race and gender oppression and how this may shape Black mothers' reactions and responses. We should be able to draw on frameworks that enable us to understand what Black mothers' particular experiences are so that we can begin to comprehend their protective strategies. Interventions that do not critically engage with issues of race, gender, and class are limited in offering an explanation of Black mothers' responses. Because the experiences of Black mothers are qualitatively different from those of White mothers, these differences must be examined when intervention strategies are being formulated. Whereas all mothers have to deal with a number of common issues, race and gender intersect to shape not only the way that Black mothers may react to their children's experiences but also how professionals respond to them. Sensitive intervention strategies that are underpinned by an analysis of race, gender, and class will be more likely to result in interventions that do not vilify Black mothers. Ultimately, providing the right support for mothers will indirectly help their children in the recovery process.

Note

1. *Black* is used here to define people who suffer racism because of their skin color. In the context of British society, it refers to those of African, Caribbean, and South Asian origin.

References

Abney, V. D. (1996). Cultural competency in the field of child maltreatment. In J. Briere, L. Berliner, J. A. Bulkley, C. Jenny, & T. Reid (Eds.), *The APSAC handbook on child maltreatment* (pp. 409-417). Thousand Oaks, CA: Sage.

Abney, V. D., & Priest, R. (1995). African Americans and sexual child abuse. In L. A. Fontes (Ed.), *Sexual abuse in nine North American cultures: Treatment and prevention* (pp. 11-30). Thousand Oaks, CA: Sage.

Barn, R. (1993). *Black children in the public care system.* London: Batsford.

Bebbington, A., & Miles, J. (1989). The background of children who enter local authority care. *British Journal of Social Work, 19,* 349-368.

Bernard, C. (1994a, October). *Black women and domestic violence.* Paper presented at the Criminology in the 1990s Conference: Black Women, the Law, and Mental Health, London.

Bernard, C. (1994b). The research process: Dynamics of race, gender and class. *Research Policy and Planning: The Journal of Social Services Research Group, 12*(2), 20-22.

Bernard, C. (1994c). Social work with mothers whose children have been sexually abused. In C. Lupton & T. Gillespie (Eds.), *Working with violence* (pp. 96-112). London: Macmillan.

Channer, Y., & Parton, N. (1988). Racism, cultural relativism and child protection. In Violence Against Children Study Group (Ed.), *Taking child abuse seriously* (pp. 105-120). London: Unwin Hyman.

Deblinger, E., Lippmann, J., Stauffer, L., & Finkel, M. (1994). Personal versus professional responses to child sexual abuse allegations. *Child Abuse & Neglect, 18,* 679-682.

Deblinger, E., Russell Hathaway, C., Lippmann, J., & Steer, R. (1993). Psychosocial characteristics and correlates of symptom distress in non-offending mothers of sexually abused children. *Journal of Interpersonal Violence, 8,* 155-168.

Dempster, H. (1993). The aftermath of child sexual abuse: Women's perspectives. In L. Waterhouse (Ed.), *Child abuse and child abusers* (pp. 58-72). London: Jessica Kingsley.

Driver, E., & Droisen, A. (Eds.). (1989). *Child sexual abuse: Feminist perspectives.* London: Macmillan.

Droisen, A. (1989). Racism and anti-Semitism. In E. Driver & A. Droisen (Eds.), *Child sexual abuse: Feminist perspectives* (pp. 158-167). London: Macmillan.

Erooga, M., & Masson, H. (1989). The silent volcano: Groupwork with mothers of sexually abused children. *Practice, 1,* 24-41.

Finkelhor, D. (1986). *A sourcebook on child sexual abuse.* Beverly Hills, CA: Sage.

Gomes-Schwartz, B., Horowitz, J. M., & Cardarelli, A. P. (1990). *Child sexual abuse: The initial effects.* London: Sage.

Gunn, M. (1989). Sexual abuse and adults with mental handicap: Can the law help? In H. Brown & A. Craft (Eds.), *Thinking the unthinkable: Papers on sexual abuse and people with learning difficulties* (pp. 51-64). London: Family Planning Association.

Hooper, C. A. (1992). *Mothers surviving sexual abuse.* London: Routledge.

Jacobs, J. L. (1990, Spring). Reassessing mothers' place in incest. *Signs,* pp. 500-514.

Johnson, J. T. (1992). *Mothers of incest survivors: Another side of the story.* Indianapolis: Indiana University Press.

Johnson, M. R. D. (1991). Race, social work and child care. In P. Carter, T. Jeffs, & M. K. Smith (Eds.), *Social work and social welfare* (pp. 95-107). Milton Keynes, UK: Open University Press.

Jones, A. (1994). Anti-racist child protection. In T. David (Ed.), *Protecting children from abuse* (pp. 25-37). Staffordshire, UK: Trentham.

MacLeod, M., & Saraga, E. (1988). Challenging the orthodoxy: Towards a feminist theory and practice. Family secrets: Child sexual abuse [Special issue]. *Feminist Review, 28,* 15-65.

Mama, A. (1989). *The hidden struggle: Statutory and voluntary responses to violence against Black women in the home.* London: London Housing Unit.

Mama, A. (1993). Black women and the police: A place where the law is not upheld. In W. James & C. Harris (Eds.), *Inside Babylon: The Caribbean diaspora in Britain* (pp. 135-151). London: Verso.

Milner, J. (1993). A disappearing act: The differing career paths of fathers and mothers in child protection investigations. *Critical Social Policy, 38,* 48-63.

Mtezuka, M. (1996). Issues of race and culture in child abuse. In B. Fawcett, B. Featherstone, J. Hearn, & C. Toft (Eds.), *Violence and gender relations: Theories and interventions* (pp. 171-177). London: Sage.

Phillips, M. (1995). Issues of ethnicity and culture. In K. Wilson & A. James (Eds.), *The child protection handbook* (pp. 108-125). London: Bailliere Tindall.

Phillips, M., & Dutt, R. (1990). *Towards a Black perspective in child protection.* London: Race Equality Unit.

Print, B., & Dey, C. (1992). Empowering mothers of sexually abused children—A positive framework. In A. Bannister (Ed.), *From hearing to healing: Working with the aftermath of child sexual abuse* (pp. 57-81). London: Longman.

Russell, D. E. H. (1986). *The secret trauma: Incest in the lives of girls and women.* New York: Basic Books.

Salt, P., Myer, M., Coleman, L., & Sauzier, M. (1990). The myth of the mother as "accomplice" to child sexual abuse. In B. Gomes-Schwartz, J. M. Horowitz, & A. P. Cardarelli (Eds.), *Child sexual abuse: The initial effects* (pp. 109-131). London: Sage.

Saraga, E. (1994). Living with uncertainty. In T. David (Ed.), *Protecting children from abuse* (pp. 107-119). Staffordshire, UK: Trentham.

Sirles, E. A., & Lofberg, C. E. (1990). Factors associated with divorce in intrafamily child sexual abuse cases. *Child Abuse & Neglect, 14,* 165-170.

Smith, G. (1994). Parent, partner, protector: Conflicting role demands for mothers of sexually abused children. In M. Morrison & R. C. Beckett (Eds.), *Sexual offending against children* (pp. 179-202). London: Routledge.

Smith, G. (1995). Hierarchy in families where sexual abuse is an issue. In C. Burck & B. Speed (Eds.), *Gender, power and relationships* (pp. 86-99). London: Routledge.

Strand, V. C. (1990). Treatment of the mother in the incest family: The beginning phase. *Clinical Social Work Journal, 18,* 353-366.

Wilson, M. (1993). *Crossing the boundaries: Black women and incest.* London: Virago.

Wyatt, G. E., & Mickey, M. R. (1988). The support by parents and others as it mediates the effects of child sexual abuse. In G. E. Wyatt & G. Johnson Powell (Eds.), *The lasting effects of child sexual abuse* (pp. 211-225). Newbury Park, CA: Sage.

CHAPTER 7

Children's Exposure to Marital Aggression

Direct and Mediated Effects

Gayla Margolin
Richard S. John

Although exposure to aggression between one's parents has been shown to serve as a risk factor or risk marker for child adjustment problems (Holden & Ritchie, 1991; Margolin, in press; Sternberg et al. 1993), research on this connection now needs to address the processes or mechanisms that account for negative outcomes in children. Research conducted thus far has focused on dimensions of the violence as well as on characteristics of the children to determine whether one form of violence exposure is more detrimental than another or whether boys versus girls or younger versus older children are more vulnerable to the effects of vio-

lence. Missing from these data, however, is a conceptual understanding as to how marital violence affects children. Are children frightened when they witness interparental violence? Do children feel caught in a conflict of loyalties? Do parents who are embroiled in abusive marriages exhibit overly controlling, punitive forms of parental discipline or insufficient warmth and nurturance?

There are two competing theories as to the source of impact when children live with interparental violence. The first theory points to the direct trauma of the exposure. Hearing about or directly witnessing violence can be, at the least,

AUTHORS' NOTE: Preparation of this study was supported by National Institute of Mental Health Grant RO1 36595. Correspondence can be directed to Gayla Margolin, Department of Psychology, University of Southern California, Los Angeles, CA 90089-1061.

unsettling, or, at the other extreme, terrifying for a youngster. The impact of such exposure is believed to be more powerful, however, the closer the child is in emotional connection to the victim and in physical proximity to the violence (Bell & Jenkins, 1993; Garbarino, Dubrow, Kostelny, & Pardo, 1992; Martinez & Richters, 1993). Thus, violence that occurs at the hands of one parent and that victimizes the other parent may create a world for children that is frightening, confusing, and lacking security and safety. Interparental violence transforms the home into a dangerous and unpredictable environment. As concluded by Janoff-Bulmann (1992), "The most devastating negative life events on children are likely to be those that involve victimization by the very people who are looked to for protection and safety." (p. 86).

The second theory concerns the nature of the parent-child relationship in families with interparental violence. There is evidence that marital conflict, even when it does not involve violence, is associated with impaired parenting (Erel & Burman, 1995). Specifically, parents experiencing marital conflict experience greater disagreements over child rearing (Block, Block, & Morrison, 1981), are more emotionally unavailable or withdrawn from their children (Dickstein & Parke, 1988; Howes & Markman, 1989), and provide more inconsistent and punitive discipline (Fauber, Forehand, Thomas, & Wierson, 1990; Jouriles, Pfiffner, & O'Leary, 1988).

Similar patterns are found in research on linkages between marital violence and parenting as those found in research on nonviolent marital conflict and parenting. Men who abuse their wives have been found to be physically aggressive with their children (O'Keefe, 1994) and in particular toward their sons (Jouriles & LeCompte, 1991). Holden and Ritchie's (1991) assessment of parenting in abusive couples portrays batterers, compared to nonbatterers, as more irritable, less involved in child rearing, less physically affectionate, and more likely to use physical punishment and power assertive responses. Abused wives, although reporting high levels of parenting stress, did not report different discipline strategies than did control wives. Based on direct observation, Margolin, John,

Ghosh, and Gordis (1996) found that aggression in the marriage was associated with specific patterns in the parent-child communication. Husbands' physical aggression in the marriage was associated with fathers' exhibiting more authoritarian behaviors, fewer authoritative behaviors, more negative affect, and more controlling behaviors.

For the most part, theoretical models attempting to identify mechanisms accounting for the negative reactions exhibited by child witnesses to marital aggression contain either direct paths between marital aggression and child outcomes, or indirect paths through parenting. Despite considerable debate in the marital conflict literature regarding the respective merits of these two models (Emery, Fincham, & Cummings, 1992; Fauber & Long, 1991), there have been no studies directly comparing these two models within the same sample. Moreover, despite widespread acknowledgment that both the marital relationship and the parenting relationship have significant effects on children, there has been little attempt to examine the joint or combined effects of direct and indirect paths.

The present study seeks to examine whether (a) marital aggression has direct effects on child outcomes, (b) marital aggression has effects that are mediated through the parent-child relationship, and (c) the combination of direct and mediated effects accounts for more variance in children's adjustment than do the separate effect models. According to Baron and Kenney (1986), demonstration of a mediated model requires three steps: that marital aggression is related to child outcomes, that marital aggression is related to the parent-child relationship, and that the relationship between marital conflict and child outcomes is significantly reduced once parenting is accounted for in the equation. Support for a combined model would be found if both marital aggression and parenting contribute unique variance to child outcomes.

The basic model to be tested in this study is presented in Figure 7.1. As can be seen in this figure, five constructs are examined: marital aggression, positive parenting, power assertive parenting, children's hostility, and children's depression and anxiety. Both the positive and

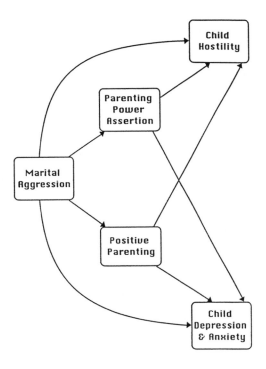

Figure 7.1. Latent Variables (rounded boxes) With Eight Paths (arrows) in Proposed Model of Direct and Mediated Effects of Marital Aggression on Children's Adjustment

negative dimensions of parenting are represented because even though these dimensions tend to be inversely related, they represent separate theoretical pathways as to how parenting may be disrupted. Positive parenting and power assertive parenting are two of the most frequently studied parenting variables and are represented in most all theories of parent-child socialization (Maccoby & Martin, 1983). Positive parenting or warmth, as examined here, reflects a number of aspects of parents' emotional supportiveness, such as parents' admiration, praise, shared decision making, nurturance, and companionship. These characteristics may mitigate the effects of exposure to abusive or frightening experiences. Power assertive parenting refers to the presence of negativistic, controlling, punitive parent-to-child interactions, which have been associated with a number of childhood problems (Farrington, 1978; Patterson, 1982;

Patterson & Stouthamer-Loeber, 1984). A recent meta-analysis based on nonclinical samples shows both positive parenting and the absence of power assertive parenting to be negatively associated with child externalizing behavior (Rothbaum & Weisz, 1994).

Two dimensions of child outcomes are included in this model to examine specific indexes of children's distress. Whereas depression and anxiety are representative of an internalizing childhood disorder, hostility is representative of an externalizing disorder. Based on modeling and social interactional theories, it has been hypothesized that the most direct risk of exposure to aggression by others is aggression by the child witness (e.g., Parke & Slaby, 1983; Patterson, 1982; Widom, 1989). The data on exposure to marital aggression, however, have revealed a broader range of outcomes, including internalizing as well as externalizing behaviors (Margolin, in press). There is, in fact, tremendous variability across studies as to whether the child witnesses versus nonwitnesses differ on internalizing only, externalizing only, or both internalizing and externalizing dimensions. The variability in findings is confusing due to the different measures and reporters for assessing child outcomes, and the different comparison groups that are used. Overall, however, the data point to multiple pathways of effects, with children appearing to be vulnerable to a variety of developmental problems due to the stress of witnessing interparental violence.

Two other important dimensions not evident in the figure are that this entire model is being examined from the child's perspective, that is, using measures derived from direct assessments of the child, and that the model is tested separately for boys and girls. Studies using multiple reporters have produced a fairly consistent picture that parents, particularly mothers, report more distress in child witnesses than do the children themselves (Hughes, Parkinson, & Vargo, 1989; McCloskey, Figueredo, & Koss, 1995; Sternberg et al., 1993). McCloskey et al. (1995), for example, reports that total family violence (both experiencing violence from either of the parents and witnessing interparental violence) accounts for about 12% of the variance in child psychopathology in children's reports as compared to 56% of the variance in the mothers' reports. Thus, running this model strictly from the perspective of the children presents a stringent test of the effects of interparental aggression on children.

The data on child outcomes related to witnessing interparental aggression and violence have been quite mixed with respect to gender, with some studies showing greater vulnerability in boys than girls (Doumas, Margolin, & John, 1994; Jaffe, Wolfe, Wilson, & Zak, 1986; Wolfe, Jaffe, Wilson, & Zak, 1985), others, particularly several community studies, showing greater vulnerability in girls than boys (O'Keefe, 1994; Spaccarelli, Sandler, & Roosa, 1994), and still others failing to find gender differences altogether (Fantuzzo et al., 1991). The notion that boys are more likely to exhibit problems of an aggressive nature whereas girls are more likely to exhibit internalizing problems has not been borne out. Despite the lack of consistency in the nature and direction of the gender effects, the number of studies reporting differences for boys and girls dictates that models should be run separately for boys and girls. Moreover, even if there are not differences in the overall amount of problems exhibited, the pathways explaining those problems may differ for girls and boys.

Thus, the purpose in testing these models is to go beyond documenting the effect of marital aggression on children and, instead, to explore the pathways of effects of both marital aggression and parenting. It is hypothesized that children's adjustment will be affected by both direct and mediated effects. As can been seen in Figure 7.1, all the arrows point from left to right suggesting the sequence we are predicting—marital abuse to parenting to child outcomes. Because this a cross-sectional model, we cannot rule out bidirectional relationships, particularly between parenting and child outcomes. Our intent here, however, is to focus on the parenting relationship as a intervening variable between marital aggression and child outcomes, with a possibility that the parent-child relationship can either exacerbate or mitigate the effects of marital aggression.

Procedures

Participants

Participants in this study were a sample of 180 children and their families recruited from the community through public announcements and direct mailings (see Margolin, John, & Foo, 1997, for additional description of the sample). One girl and one boy were not included due to difficulty with the forms, resulting in a total N of 178 (90 girls and 88 boys). The following criteria were used to determine eligibility for the study: (a) One child in the family needed to be between ages 8 and 11 inclusive, (b) both parents needed to be residing in the family home so that there was ongoing marital interaction, (c) both parents either were the biological parents of the child or else had been living with the child since age 2 to avoid any additional parenting influences, (d) both parents and the child had to read and speak English, and (e) both parents and the child had to be willing to participate in at least one laboratory session. The parents were not prescreened for marital conflict. The questionnaires that children completed for this study were included as part of a larger study, and families received $60.00 for their participation.

Children in this sample ranged from 8 years, 0 months to 11 years, 11 months ($M = 10.12$, $SD = 1.15$ for boys; $M = 9.84$, $SD = 1.10$ for girls). Ninety-five percent of the children were in Grades 2 through 6 (median = Grade 4 for boys and girls). Ninety-one percent of the boys and 87% of the girls had at least one sibling (one sibling = 45.5% of boys and 38.9% of girls; two siblings = 29.5% and 22.2%, respectively; and three or more siblings = 15.9% and 25.6%, respectively). There were two Caucasian parents in 53.4% of families with boys and 52.2% of families with girls, two African American parents in 28.4% and 26.7%, and parents of other or mixed ethnicities in 18.2% of boy and 21.1% of girl families. T tests on child's age, and chi-square analysis on grade, number of siblings, and parents' ethnicity, indicated no differences in the girl versus boy samples.

Parents of the children in this sample had been living together for 4 to 28 years ($M = 14.5$,

$SD = 4.4$ for parents of boys; $M = 13.5$, $SD = 3.7$ for parents of girls). This was the first marriage for 80.7% of boys' mothers and 85.6% of girls' mothers, and 78.4% of boys' fathers and 73.3% of girls' fathers. Mothers' age ranged from 24 to 51 years ($M = 38.3$, $SD = 5.6$ for boys; $M = 36.6$, $SD = 5.1$ for girls), and fathers' age ranged from 24 to 59 ($M = 40.7$, $SD = 6.6$ for boys; $M = 39.0$, $SD = 5.7$ for girls). Years of education ranged from 10 to 20 for both mothers and fathers (for mothers, $M = 14.4$, $SD = 2.2$ for boys; $M = 14.3$, $SD = 2.1$ for girls; for fathers, $M = 14.9$, $SD = 2.6$ for boys; $M = 14.9$, $SD = 2.5$ for girls). T-test comparisons between boys and girls on parent characteristics revealed only one difference: Boys' mothers were somewhat older than were girls' mothers, $t(176) = 2.14$, $p < .05$.

Procedures

These data were collected during a laboratory visit. To obtain data from the children, graduate-level laboratory assistants met alone with the child and read each item of each questionnaire aloud to standardize administration and to obviate problems certain children might have reading the forms.

Measures

To conduct the analyses, we created a path model with five latent variables (theoretical constructs), from 22 manifest variables (measured or observed data). We selected manifest variables based on our determination that they relate conceptually to the theoretical constructs. Table 7.1 lists each latent variable, the manifest variables comprising each latent variable, and the component loadings on the manifest variables. As recommended (Falk & Miller, 1992), three or more manifest variables were used to created each composite variable with the exception of power assertive parenting, which was derived from two manifest variables. As indicated by the component loadings for each manifest variable, we can conclude that the manifest variables are adequate indicators of the latent constructs.

Marital Aggression. Marital aggression is represented by four manifest variables, all ob-

TABLE 7.1 Measurement Model Component Loadings of Manifest Variables Full (eight-path) Latent Variable Model

Variable	Girls (n = 90)	Boys (n = 88)
Parents' marital aggression (Conflict Tactics Scales— modified child version)		
Mother's physical	.73	.80
Father's physical	.82	.80
Mother's verbal symbolic	.85	.88
Father's verbal symbolic	.86	.82
Positive parenting (Parent-Child Relationship Questionnaire— brief child version)		
Mother's warmth	.80	.80
Mother's personal relationships	.85	.83
Mother's disciplinary warmth	.78	.83
Father's warmth	.64	.82
Father's personal relationships	.76	.86
Father's disciplinary warmth	.80	.85
Parenting power assertion (Parent-Child Relationship Questionnaire— brief child version)		
Mother's power assertion	.90	.95
Father's power assertion	.89	.78
Child hostility (Children's Hostility Inventory— child version)		
Assaultiveness	.73	.46
Verbal hostility	.42	.73
Resentment	.47	.66
Irritability	.79	.67
Child depression and anxiety (Children's Depression Inventory [CDI] and How-I-Feel-Questionnaire)		
Negative mood (CDI)	.59	.66
Interpersonal problems (CDI)	.71	.78
Ineffectiveness (CDI)	.67	.65
Anhedonia (CDI)	.82	.69
Negative self-esteem (CDI)	.47	.60
Anxiety (SAS)	.60	.55

tained from the child's report on the Conflict Tactics Scales (CTS; Straus, 1979): Wife's Verbal/Symbolic Aggression, Husband's Verbal/Symbolic Aggression, Husband's Physical Aggression, and Wife's Physical Aggression. Verbal/Symbolic Aggression was represented by six items: (a) insulted or swore at the other one, (b) sulked and/or refused to talk about it, (c) stomped out of the room or house (or yard),

(d) did or said something to spite the other one, (e) threatened to hit or throw something at the other one, and (f) threw or smashed or hit or kicked something. Physical Aggression was represented by five items: (a) threw something at the other one; (b) pushed, grabbed, or shoved the other one; (c) slapped the other one; (d) kicked, bit, or hit with a fist; and (e) hit or tried to hit with something.[1] For each item, the child indicated how often (*never, once, a few times,* or *lots of times*) each parent exhibited the behavior described in the particular item.

Although we included both wives' and husbands' aggression, we are not implying that aggression from the male and female partner are of equal significance in terms of dangerousness or consequences. The objective here, however, was limited to evaluating the overall amount of aggression as perceived and reported by the child. Seriousness of the aggressive act goes beyond what we asked the child to report.

Parenting Relationship. Both parenting constructs were obtained from the child's report on the 40-item short version of the Parent-Child Relationship Questionnaire (PCRQ; Furman, Adler, & Buhrmester, 1984). The child goes through the entire questionnaire twice, one time responding with respect to her or his mother and the other time responding with respect to her or his father. Positive parenting is the composite of child's separate reports for mother and father on warmth (six items, e.g., "How much do you and this parent care about each other?"), personal relationship (10 items, e.g., "How much do you and this parent do nice things for each other?"), and disciplinary warmth (six items, e.g., "How much does this parent ask you for your opinion on things?"). Power assertive parenting reflects mothers' and fathers' separate scores on an 11-item Power Assertion dimension, which involves physical punishment, verbal punishment, dominance, guilt induction, deprivation of privileges, and quarreling (e.g., "How much does this parent order you around?" "How much does this parent yell at you for being bad?").[2] Children state their response to each item using a 5-point scale (*hardly at all, not*

too much, somewhat, very much, or *extremely much*).

Children's Psychological Adjustment. Children's hostility was assessed through self-reports on the 38-item Children's Hostility Inventory (CHI; Kazdin, Rodgers, Colbus, & Siegel, 1987), an instrument derived from the Buss-Durkee Hostility Inventory for adults. Four of the seven available subscales were used, including Assaultiveness (six items, e.g., "I only hit back once in a while, even if someone hits me first"), Verbal Hostility (six items, e.g., "I can't help getting into arguments when others don't agree with me"), Irritability (six items, e.g., "I can remember getting so mad that I picked up the nearest thing and broke it"), and Resentment (four items, e.g., "Almost every week I see someone I dislike"). Children respond to each item using a true-false format.

Children's depression and anxiety were assessed from children's self-reports reflecting six indicators, including five subscales from the Children's Depression Inventory (CDI; Kovacs, 1992) and the total score from the How-I-Feel Questionnaire (Spielberger, 1973). The 26-item CDI[3] contains the following subscales: Negative Mood (six items), Interpersonal Problems (four items), Ineffectiveness (four items), Anhedonia (eight items), and Negative Self-Esteem (four items). For each item, the child selects one of three statements to describe how she or he has been in the past 2 weeks. For example, for Item 1, which loads on Negative Mood (Weiss et al., 1991), the choices are: "I am sad once in a while," "I am sad many times," or "I am sad all the time." In addition, the total score from the How-I-Feel Questionnaire (Staic Form C-2, 20 items) was used. Using a three-choice response format (*hardly ever, sometimes,* or *often*), children indicate how often they experience symptoms reflecting anxiety (e.g., "I worry about making mistakes," "I feel like crying").

Structural Modeling

The relationships among these variables were examined through latent variable path analysis using partial least squares (LVPLS) estimation procedures (Falk & Miller, 1992), also called "soft modeling." In this procedure, latent or composite variables are created from the manifest variables. In creating the composite variable, the new variables are iteratively calculated to create optimal linear correlations, somewhat resembling canonical correlational procedures. Three restrictions are placed on each new variable: (a) The new variable has maximum variance given the manifest variables, (b) the composite variable is standardized so that its variance equals one, and (c) the composite variables are calculated to optimize the linear correlations among them (Falk & Miller, 1991, 1992).

There are several advantages to this approach. First, based on the assumption that multiple measures are better than single measures for estimating any one construct, this procedure combines several manifest variables to create each latent variable. As noted by Miller, Cowan, Cowan, Hetherington, and Clingempeel (1993), "This method of data reduction creates a smaller set of theoretical variables whose relationship can be investigated without sacrificing the information available from a larger group of manifest variables" (p. 6). Second, this method also allows for the simultaneous examination of multiple predicted variables, in this case, both childhood depression and hostility. Third, the method indicates how much variance of each predictor is accounted for by previously entered predictors. As compared to other, more commonly used structural equation models that require very large numbers of participants, the LVPLS model can be used with relatively modest sample sizes, such as that presented here.

Results

■ A set of three nested path models was estimated for both the girl and boy samples using data from the child reporters. First, a four-path model was estimated, including only direct effects from marital aggression to each of the two parenting latent variables and each of the two child adjustment latent variables. Next, a six-path model was estimated to represent only indirect effects of marital aggression on child ad-

justment, including paths from marital aggression to each of the parenting latent variables and from each of the parenting latent variables to each of the child adjustment latent variables. Finally, a full eight-path model was estimated, including both direct effects of marital aggression on child adjustment and indirect effects (via parenting) on child adjustment latent variables.

For girls, all three models demonstrated adequate fits with root mean square, or RMS, cov(E, U) ranging from .076 to .088, indicating little difference among the three in terms of the correlations among the variables not explained by the paths specified in the model. (Specifically, RMS cov[E, U] is the average correlation between the residuals on the composite and the manifest variables.)

As indicated in the top panel in Figure 7.2, the direct effects of marital aggression on girl outcomes are strong and approximately equivalent (.37 for hostility and .40 for depression/anxiety). Marital aggression also shows a direct effect on parenting, albeit a somewhat stronger effect for positive parenting (−.32) than for power assertion (.18). The six-path indirect model, displayed in the middle of Figure 7.2, shows comparable paths from power assertion (.24 and .27) and from positive parenting (−.32 and −.24) to the child outcomes.

In the full model (bottom panel), the effect of aggression on girls' adjustment is split between direct effects and indirect effects through parenting. Once indirect effects through parenting are included, the path coefficients for direct effects of marital aggression on girls' hostility and depression/anxiety are somewhat attenuated but still greater than .10. In predicting girls' hostility, the path coefficients are .16 from marital aggression, .23 from power assertion, and −.28 from positive parenting. The indirect effect of marital aggression through positive parenting to child hostility is notable given the relationship between marital aggression and positive parenting (−.32). For girls' depression and anxiety, the three inputs are quite comparable, .18 from marital aggression, −.19 through positive parenting, and .22 through power assertion.

Figure 7.3 presents the three panels of direct, indirect, and combined effects for boys. The overall fit for the boy models is somewhat better

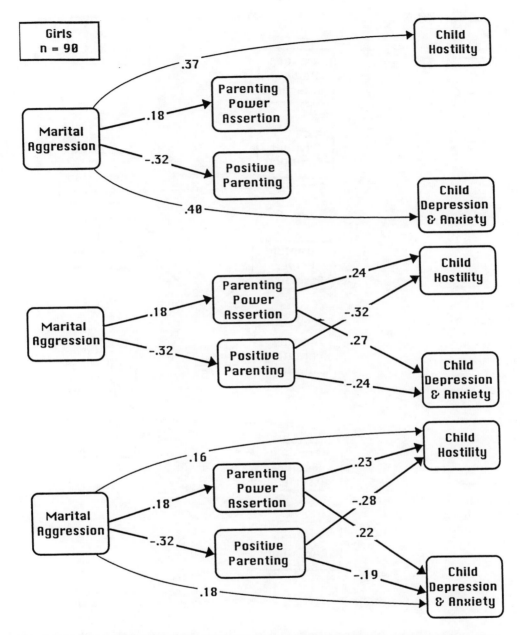

Figure 7.2. Path Coefficients for Direct Only (top), Mediated Only (middle), and Combined (bottom) Models of Marital Aggression on Girls' Hostility and Depression/Anxiety

than that for the girls, ranging from RMS cov(E, U) of .087 for the four-path model to .063 for both the six- and eight-path models. As displayed in the top panel of Figure 7.3, there is a somewhat stronger direct effect from marital aggression to child hostility (.35) than to child de-

pression and anxiety (.26). Marital aggression shows a significant effect on parenting power assertion (.26) but a negligible effect on positive parenting (−.09).

The middle panel shows that the effect of parenting power assertion is stronger than the effect

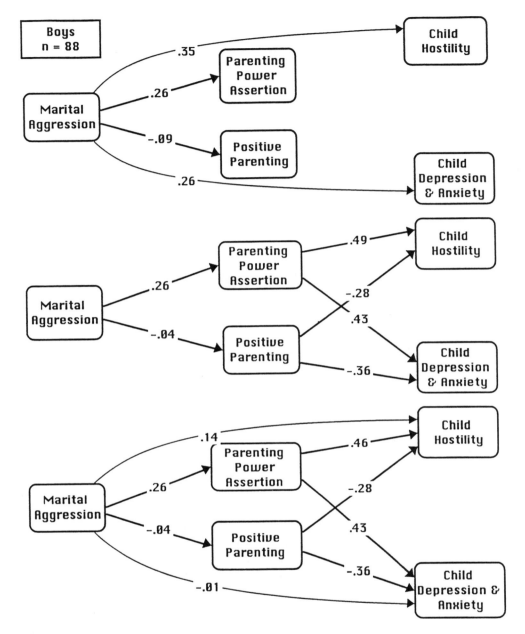

Figure 7.3. Path Coefficients for Direct Only (top), Mediated Only (middle), and Combined (bottom) Models of Marital Aggression on Boys' Hostility and Depression/Anxiety

of positive parenting on boys' hostility (.49 vs. −.28) and on boys' depression and anxiety (.43 vs. −.36). In the full eight-path model (bottom panel), the direct paths from marital aggression to boys' adjustment latent variables are negligible, and the indirect effect path coefficients are

virtually identical to those estimated in the six-path indirect effects only model (middle panel).

The primary indirect effect of marital aggression on boys' adjustment is via parenting power assertion, which is affected by marital aggression and has robust effects on both boys' hostil-

TABLE 7.2 Variance Accounted for in Boys' and Girls' Hostility and Depression for Nested Cross-Sectional Models

Model Tested	R^2	F	(df)	ΔR^2	F_{diff}	(df)
Girls						
Hostility						
Direct effects	.14	14.33*	(1, 88)			
Mediated effects	.19	10.20*	(2, 87)			
Combined effects	.22	8.18*	(3, 86)			
Combined vs. direct				.08	4.35*	(2, 85)
Combined vs. mediated				.03	3.31	(1, 86)
Depression						
Direct effects	.16	16.76*	(1, 88)			
Mediated effects	.16	8.29*	(2, 87)			
Combined effects	.17	5.87*	(3, 86)			
Combined vs. direct				.01	<1	(2, 85)
Combined vs. mediated				.01	<1	(1, 86)
Boys						
Hostility						
Direct effects	.12	11.73*	(1, 86)			
Mediated effects	.35	22.88*	(2, 85)			
Combined effects	.36	15.75*	(3, 84)			
Combined vs. direct				.24	15.56*	(2, 83)
Combined vs. mediated				.01	1.31	(1, 84)
Depression						
Direct effects	.07	6.47*	(1, 86)			
Mediated effects	.34	21.89*	(2, 85)			
Combined effects	.34	14.42*	(3, 84)			
Combined vs. direct				.27	16.97*	(2, 83)
Combined vs. mediated				.00	<1	(1, 84)

$*p < .05.$

ity and depression/anxiety. Boys' hostility and depression/anxiety are predicted to a somewhat lesser degree by positive parenting, but there is little evidence that positive parenting mediates the effects of marital aggression. For boys, there are no direct effects on depression/anxiety once the indirect effects of parenting power assertion and positive parenting are taken into account. The direct effect of marital aggression on boys' hostility, although still present, also is greatly attenuated once indirect parenting effects are accounted for.

Table 7.2 presents a summary of the overall variance accounted for in predicting boys' and girls' hostility and depression by the direct, mediated, and combined models. For both boys' and girls' hostility and depression/anxiety, all three models (direct effects only, mediated effects only, and combined effects) produce significant tests of total R^2, as indicated in Table 7.2. For girls' hostility, the combined effects model accounts for significantly more variance than the direct effects only model, indicating that the mediated effects (through positive parenting and power assertion) contribute in a unique way to predicting girls' hostility. However, the direct effects of marital aggression do not contribute to predicting girls' hostility over and above the variance accounted for by the mediated pathway, through the two parenting latent variables. For girls' depression, the direct and mediating effects only models are almost totally overlapping. The combined effects model accounts for barely more variance than either of the other two nested models, and the change in R^2 is not significant.

As evidenced in the bottom panel of Table 7.2, boys' hostility and depression/anxiety are predicted approximately equally well by the mediated effects and combined effects models. As indicated, the combined effects model accounts for significantly more variance in boys' hostility and in boys' depression than the corresponding direct effects only models. The relatively small amount of variance accounted for by the direct effects only model is completely overlapping with that accounted for by the mediated effects only model. Hence the combined effects models for hostility and depression do not yield significantly greater R^2 than the mediated effects only models.

Discussion

■ The data presented here offer a window into how marital aggression affects children's adjustment, as seen through children's own eyes. There are three main findings from these data. First, marital aggression directly influences parenting, with notable effects between marital aggression and parenting power assertion for boys and between marital aggression and positive parenting for girls. Second, marital aggression has some direct effects on children's adjustment, but to a large extent, those effects are mediated through parenting. Third, overall, the marital aggression and parenting constructs examined here explain considerably more variance in boys', relative to girls', self-reported adjustment.

It has long been recognized in the family systems literature that tension and conflict in one family subsystem are likely to spill over into other family subsystems (Hinde & Stevenson-Hinde, 1988; Margolin, 1981; Margolin, Christensen, & John, 1996). As seen in these data, marital aggression spills over into the parent-child relationship. For boys, the spillover is found in the association between marital aggression and parenting power assertion, supporting previous research that men who abuse their wives are more aggressive toward their children, particularly their sons (e.g., Jouriles & LeCompte, 1991). The present study potentially broadens this conclusion in that distinctions are not made between power assertion emanating from the fathers versus the mothers, or between power assertion reflecting physical dominance versus

verbal dominance of the child. Moreover, the finding is not limited to boys in that there also is a relationship, albeit not quite as strong, between marital aggression and parenting power assertion in families with girls. One explanation of these data is that the hostile, coercive behaviors exhibited in both the marital and the parent-child relationships are due to a generalized interpersonal style of the parents. Engfer (1988) posits a "common factor" hypothesis that a parent's interpersonal style may be a common determinant of both the marital and the parent-child relationships. That is, certain parents may possess an aggressive, demanding interpersonal style that is exhibited indiscriminantly in close family relationships, and perhaps nonfamily relationships as well.

The effects of marital aggression on parenting, however, are more generalized in that there also is an inverse relationship on positive parenting in families with girls. This connection to positive parenting indicates that the experience of a highly conflictual and aggressive marital relationship may detract from the child's perception of the parents' warmth, nurturance, and involvement. It is not difficult to imagine how the security of the parent-child relationship is violated for child witnesses to marital aggression. In watching one caretaker verbally or physically attack the other, both caretakers become less emotionally available to the child (Margolin, in press). The perpetrator may be viewed by the child as dangerous and frightening whereas the victim may be perceived as overwhelmed and requiring caretaking herself. If marital aggression increases the child's need for emotional support and neither of the parents is available to provide that support, the child may rate the parents as low on positive parenting.

Issues of gender specificity are raised because the relationship between marital aggression and positive parenting applies only to parents of girls. According to Jaffe, Wolfe, and Wilson (1990), exposure to marital aggression tends to lead girls, in particular, to conclude that victimization is inevitable and that no one can change that pattern. Thus, perhaps marital aggression leaves girls, more than boys, feeling unprotected, vulnerable, and mistrusting of the parents, which would be reflected in their reports on positive dimensions of the parent-child relationship. Moreover, with reports of parents' warmth and supportiveness coming only from child reporters, it is unclear whether the effect on positive parenting would be observed in the parents' actual behavior or is a function of the daughter being less inclined to seek out the parents for emotional support, thereby setting into motion a cycle of distance and uninvolvement.

Comparing the full eight-path model to the four- and six-path models provides evidence that parenting indeed is a mediator of marital aggression for three out of the four dependent variables. For boys, parenting power assertion mediates the relationship from marital aggression to both children's hostility and children's depression/anxiety. For girls, parenting dimensions mediate the effects of marital aggression on hostility, but not on depression/anxiety. With respect to boys, despite the fact that both power assertion and positive parenting predict to the child outcomes, only power assertion meets the three criteria to be a mediator: (a) Marital aggression accounts for variation in child adjustment; (b) parents' power assertion accounts for variation in children's adjustment; and (c) when parents' power assertion is entered simultaneously to marital aggression, the path from marital aggression to children's hostility and depression is significantly reduced. The strongest demonstration of a mediator is evidenced when the path from marital aggression to child outcomes is reduced to zero, as is the case with the path coefficient from marital aggression to boys' depression/anxiety (.26 in the direct model and −.01 in the combined model). The change in the path coefficients for boys' hostility, in contrast, from .35 in the direct model to .14 in the combined model, indicates a partial mediation. R^2 change data indicate that both marital aggression and parenting power assertion make independent contributions to boys' hostility. For girls' adjustment, the path from marital aggression to girls' hostility is partially mediated once both parenting dimensions have been introduced (.37 to .16 for girls' hostility and .40 to .18 for girls' depression/anxiety). Parenting contributes unique variance to girls' hostility whereas marital aggression does not.

The search for mediators offers theoretical clarity as to why there is a connection between marital aggression and children's outcomes. It is quite common when examining social-psychological phenomena to look for associations between pairs of variables. In this spirit, a large literature has developed examining connections between marital conflict and children's outcomes (e.g., Emery, 1982; Fincham & Osborne, 1993). These connections can help identify an at-risk population, in this case children who witness interparental conflict and abuse. The data, however, often fail to speak to how or why such effects occur (Baron & Kenney, 1986). Moreover, we know that the associations between marital conflict and children's adjustment are, for the most part, quite modest (Fincham, 1984; Jouriles, Farris, & McDonald, 1991; Reid & Crisafulli, 1990). Thus, even though the literature points to marital conflict as a risk factor for children, there is tremendous variability in children's reactions. By identifying mediators, we may be better able to explain why some children are greatly affected by exposure to marital conflict whereas others are not.

Although we know from these data that the effects of marital adjustment on boys' adjustment are transmitted, in part, via parents' power assertion, there still are a number of possible mechanisms underlying this process. It has been suggested that one benefit of quality marital relations is enabling the parents to establish healthy parent-child relations (Belsky, 1984; Fincham, Grych, & Osborne, 1994). Thus, in addition to the possibility of parents' generalized tendencies to become aggressive in conflictual situations, it may be that lack of support between spouses causes the parents to use less effective parenting practices, resorting, for example, to harsh, punitive discipline styles. On the other side, it also has been suggested that children exposed to marital aggression may become sensitized to conflict processes such that parent-child conflicts assume additional qualities of threat (Davies & Cummings, 1994). Even fairly typical discipline strategies on the part of parents may take on a different meaning in the context of a family in which there is marital aggression. In other words, children's ratings of the parents' power assertion may reflect children's readily accessible perceptions of hostility, negativity, and control. To sort out these competing albeit not mutually exclusive processes, it would be useful to obtain data from additional reporters, for example, parents as well as the child, and to obtain direct observations of parent-child interactions.

Understanding the mediating effects of parenting also must take into consideration bidirectional effects. Although only unidirectional arrows are examined in this model, we know that children are not simply passive recipients of marital and parenting influences (Bell & Harper, 1977). Children's hostility, for example, may elicit harsh, punitive discipline without much parental warmth. Likewise, children's depression and anxiety create challenges for parents and can detract from mutually enjoyable parent-child relations. Less is known about how children's problems or poor parenting directly affect the marriage. It is generally recognized, however, that conflicts surrounding child rearing can activate conflict in the marital system and that there may be reciprocal influences among marital, parent-child, and child subsystems (Margolin et al., 1996). To understand these linkages across systems more fully requires taking account of bidirectional influences and recognizing that with each subsystem influencing the others, the overall family system is undergoing frequent change and realignment.

Overall the combined direct and mediated models account for greater variance in the adjustment of boys than of girls. From a developmental psychopathology perspective, the overriding objective of studying the effects of marital aggression on children is to identify the extent to which we can attribute children's symptomatology to familial variables. We learn from these data that these specific family variables account for a significant portion of the variance in boys' hostility and depression/anxiety. Yet, even for boys, there is approximately 65% of variance unaccounted for, due perhaps to intrapersonal variables characterizing the boys themselves or to variables external to the family system. For girls' adjustment, there is even more unexplained variance (78% for hostility and 83% for depression/anxiety). Perhaps girls at this developmental stage are more receptive to the influ-

ences of peers and other nonfamily members. Social support has been identified as a nonfamily variable serving an important protective function for children exposed to stressors in general (e.g., Garmezy, 1983) and marital conflict in particular (Jenkins & Smith, 1990). In line with these findings, it is possible that girls', more than boys', overall adjustment is associated with social relations external to the family. An important future direction would be to test expanded models, including both familial and nonfamilial variables, toward the objective of obtaining greater understanding of what variables, either singly or in combination, contribute to children's adjustment.

Finally, in addition to understanding the relationship between family violence factors and child adjustment, an important reason for testing such models is to inform clinical interventions. In light of the important role of parenting in understanding how marital aggression affects children's adjustment, it becomes obvious that interventions directed toward adults who are perpetrators or victims of marital abuse should incorporate parent education programs (Bilinkoff, 1995; Margolin, 1995; Mathews, 1995). The relatively small variance due to direct effects alone suggest that even if a clinical intervention is effective in eliminating the marital aggression, that may not be sufficient to improve children's adjustment. Given that children's adjustment is, for the most part, affected via parenting variables, the more direct route toward improved child outcomes may derive from interventions aimed at parenting. Moreover, improving parenting skills for the benefit of the child may be a more acceptable and readily obtainable goal to the parents than altering aggressive patterns in the marriage.

Notes

1. Although the child version of the CTS includes eight physical aggression items, we omitted the three most severe items (beat each other up, threatened each other with a knife or gun, and actually used a knife or gun against each other). The decision not to administer these three items was based on the fact that we were using a nonclinical population and did not want to stress children who may not have witnessed

severe violence between their parents by introducing the idea that some parents engage in these behaviors.

2. The one item of the Power Assertion Scale that questions directly about the use of physical punishment was eliminated from this study due to our decision not to obtain any evidence of physical child abuse in this nonreferred sample.

3. The full CDI contains 27 items but, as sometimes done in previous research studies using the CDI (Weiss et al., 1991), this study excluded Item 9, which pertains to suicide.

References

Baron, R. M., & Kenney, D. A. (1986). The moderator-mediator variable distinction in social psychological research: Conceptual, strategic, and statistical considerations. *Journal of Personality and Social Psychology, 51,* 1173-1183.

Bell, C. C., & Jenkins, E. J. (1993). Community violence and children on Chicago's southside. In D. Reiss, J. E. Richters, M. Radke-Yarrow, & D. Scharff (Eds.), *Children and violence* (pp. 46-54). New York: Guilford.

Bell, R. Q., & Harper, L. V. (1977). *Child effects on adults.* Hillsdale, NJ: Laurence Erlbaum.

Belsky, J. (1984). The determinants of parenting: A process model. *Child Development, 55,* 83-96.

Bilinkoff, J. (1995). Empowering battered women as mothers. In E. Peled, P. G. Jaffe, & J. L. Edleson (Eds.), *Ending the cycle of violence: Community responses to children of battered women* (pp. 97-105). Thousand Oaks, CA: Sage.

Block, J. H., Block, J., & Morrison, A. (1981). Parental agreement-disagreement in child-rearing orientations and gender-related personality correlates in children. *Child Development, 49,* 1163-1173.

Davies, P. T., & Cummings, E. M. (1994). Marital conflict and child adjustment: An emotional security hypothesis. *Psychological Bulletin, 116,* 387-412.

Dickstein, S., & Parke, R. (1988). Social referencing in infancy: A glance at fathers and marriage. *Child Development, 59,* 506-511.

Doumas, D., Margolin, G., & John, R. S. (1994). The intergenerational transmission of aggression across three generations. *Journal of Family Violence, 9,* 157-175.

Emery, R. E. (1982). Interparental conflict and the children of discord and divorce. *Psychological Bulletin, 92,* 310-330.

Emery, R. E., Fincham, F. D., & Cummings, E. M. (1992). Parenting in context: Systemic thinking about parental conflict and its influence on children. *Journal of Consulting and Clinical Psychology, 60,* 909-912.

Engfer, A. (1988). The interrelatedness of marriage and the mother-child relationship. In R. A. Hinde & J. Stevenson-Hinde (Eds.), *Relationships within families: Mutual influences.* (pp. 104-118). Oxford: Clarendon.

Erel, O., & Burman, B. (1995). Interrelatedness of marital relations and parent-child relations: A meta-analytic review. *Psychological Bulletin, 118,* 108-132.

Falk, R. F., & Miller, N. B. (1991). A soft models approach to family transitions. In P. A. Cowan & E. M. Hetherington (Eds.), *Family transitions* (pp. 273-301). Hillsdale, NJ: Lawrence Erlbaum.

Falk, R. F., & Miller, N. B. (1992). *A primer for soft modeling.* Akron, OH: University of Akron Press.

Fantuzzo, J. W., DePaola, L. M., Lambert, L., Martino, T., Anderson, G., & Sutton, S. (1991). Effects of interparental violence on the psychological adjustment and competencies of young children. *Journal of Consulting and Clinical Psychology, 59,* 258-265.

Farrington, D. P. (1978). The family backgrounds of aggressive youth. In L. A. Hersov & M. Bergor (Eds.), *Aggression and antisocial behavior in childhood and adolescence* (pp. 73-93). London: Pergamon.

Fauber, R., Forehand, R., Thomas, A. M., & Wierson, M. (1990). A mediational model of the impact of marital conflict on adolescent adjustment in intact and divorced families: The role of disrupted parenting. *Child Development, 61,* 1112-1123.

Fauber, R., & Long, N. (1991). Children in context: The role of the family in child psychotherapy. *Journal of Consulting and Clinical Psychology, 59,* 813-820.

Fincham, F. D. (1984). Understanding the association between marital conflict and child adjustment: Overview. *Journal of Family Psychology, 8,* 123-127.

Fincham, F. D., Grych, J. H., & Osborne, L. N. (1994). Does marital conflict cause child maladjustment? Directions and challenges for longitudinal research. *Journal of Family Psychology, 8,* 128-140.

Fincham, F. D., & Osborne, L. N. (1993). Marital conflict and children: Retrospect and prospect. *Clinical Psychology Review, 13,* 75-88.

Furman, W., Adler, T., & Buhrmester, D. (1984, July). *Structural aspects of relationships: A search for a common framework.* Paper presented at the Second International Conference of Personal Relationships, Madison, WI.

Garbarino, J., Dubrow, N., Kostelny, K., & Pardo, C. (1992). *Children in danger.* New York: Jossey-Bass.

Garmezy, N. (1983). Stressors of childhood. In N. Garmezy & M. Rutter (Eds.), *Stress, coping, and development in children* (pp. 43-84). New York: McGraw-Hill.

Hinde, R. A., & Stevenson-Hinde, J. (1988). *Relationships within families: Mutual influences.* Oxford: Clarendon.

Holden, G. W., & Ritchie, K. L. (1991). Linking extreme marital discord, child rearing, and child behavior problems: Evidence from battered women. *Child Development, 62,* 311-327.

Howes, P., & Markman, J. J. (1989). Marital quality and child functioning: A longitudinal investigation. *Child Development, 60,* 1044-1051.

Hughes, H. M., Parkinson, D., & Vargo, M. (1989). Witnessing spouse abuse and experiencing physical abuse: A "double whammy"? *Journal of Family Violence, 4,* 197-210.

Jaffe, P. G., Wolfe, D. A., & Wilson, S. K. (1990). *Children of battered women.* Newbury Park, CA: Sage.

Jaffe, P. G., Wolfe, D. A., Wilson, S. K., & Zak, L. (1986). Family violence and child adjustment: A comparative analysis of girls' and boys' behavioral symptoms. *American Journal of Psychiatry, 143,* 74-76.

Janoff-Bulmann, R. (1992). *Shattered assumptions: Towards a new psychology of trauma.* New York: Free Press.

Jenkins, J. M., & Smith, M. A. (1990). Factors protecting children living in disharmonious homes: Maternal reports. *Journal of the American Academy of Child and Adolescent Psychiatry, 29,* 60-69.

Jouriles, E. N., Farris, A. M., & McDonald, R. (1991). Marital functioning and child behavior: Measuring specific aspects of the marital relationship. In J. P. Vincent (Ed.), *Advances in family intervention, assessment and theory* (Vol. 5, pp. 25-46). London: Jessica Kingsley.

Jouriles, E. N., & LeCompte, S. H. (1991). Husbands' aggression toward wives and mothers' and fathers' aggression toward children: Moderating effects of child gender. *Journal of Consulting and Clinical Psychology, 39,* 190-192.

Jouriles, E. N., Pfiffner, L. J., & O'Leary, K. D. (1988). Marital conflict, parenting, and toddler conduct problems. *Journal of Abnormal Child Psychology, 16,* 197-206.

Kazdin, A. E., Rodgers, A., Colbus, D., & Siegel, T. (1987). Children's Hostility Inventory: Measurement of aggression and hostility in psychiatric inpatient children. *Journal of Clinical Child Psychology, 16,* 320-328.

Kovacs, M. (1992). *Children's Depression Inventory manual.* North Tonawanda, NY: Multi-Health Systems.

Maccoby, E. E., & Martin, J. A. (1983). Socialization in the context of the family: Parent-child interaction. In P. H. Mussen (Ed.), *Handbook of child psychology: Socialization, personality, and social development* (Vol. 4, pp. 1-101). New York: John Wiley.

Margolin, G. (1981). The reciprocal relationship between marital and child problems. In J. P. Vincent (Ed.), *Advances in family intervention, assessment, and theory: An annual compilation of research* (Vol. 2, pp. 131-182). Greenwich, CT: JAI.

Margolin, G. (1995). Witnessing domestic violence. In R. Gelles (Ed.), *Vision 2010: Families and violence, abuse, and neglect* (pp. 24-25, 38-39). Minneapolis, MN: National Council on Family Relations.

Margolin, G. (in press). The effects of domestic violence on children. In P. K. Trickett & C. Schellenbach (Eds.), *Violence against children in the family and community.* Washington, DC: APA Press.

Margolin, G., Christensen, A., & John, R. S. (1997). The continuance and spill-over of everyday tensions in distressed and nondistressed families. *Journal of Family Psychology, 10,* 304-321.

Margolin, G., John, R. S., & Foo, L. (1996). *Interactive and unique risk factors for husbands' emotional and physical abuse of their wives.* Manuscript submitted for review.

Margolin, G., John, R. S., Ghosh, C., & Gordis, E. (1997). Family interaction process: An essential tool for exploring abusive relations. In D. D. Cahn & S. A. Lloyd (Eds.), *Family abuse: A communication perspective* (pp. 37-58). Thousand Oaks, CA: Sage.

Martinez, P., & Richters, J. E. (1993). The NIMH Community Violence Project: II. Children's distress symptoms associated with violence exposure. In D. Reiss, J. E. Richters, M. Radke-Yarrow, & K. Scharff (Eds.), *Children and violence* (pp. 22-35). New York: Guilford.

Mathews, D. J. (1995). Parenting groups for men who batter. In E. Peled, P. G. Jaffe, & J. L. Edleson (Eds.), *Ending the cycle of violence: Community responses to children of battered women* (pp. 106-120). Thousand Oaks, CA: Sage.

McCloskey, L. A., Figueredo, A. S., & Koss, M. P. (1995). The effects of systemic family violence on children's mental health. *Child Development, 66,* 1239-1261.

Miller, N. B., Cowan, P. A., Cowan, C. P., Hetherington, E. M., & Clingempeel, W. G. (1993). Externalizing in preschoolers and early adolescents: A cross-study replication of a family model. *Developmental Psychology, 29,* 3-18.

O'Keefe, M. (1994). Linking marital violence, mother-child/father-child aggression, and child behavior problems. *Journal of Family Violence, 9,* 63-78.

Parke, R. D., & Slaby, R. G. (1983). The development of aggression. In E. M. Hetherington (Ed.), *Socialization, personality and social development: Handbook of child psychology* (pp. 548-641). New York: John Wiley.

Patterson, G. R. (1982). *Coercive family process.* Eugene, OR: Castalia.

Patterson, G. R., & Stouthamer-Loeber, M. (1984). The correlation of family management practices and development. *Child Development, 55,* 1299-1307.

Reid, W. J., & Crisafulli, A. (1990). Marital discord and child behavior problems: A meta-analysis. *Journal of Abnormal Child Psychology, 18,* 105-117.

Rothbaum, F., & Weisz, J. R. (1994). Parental caregiving and child externalizing behavior in nonclinical samples: A meta-analysis. *Psychological Bulletin, 116,* 55-74.

Spaccarelli, S., Sandler, I. N., & Roosa, M. (1994). History of spouse violence against mother: Correlated risks and unique effects in child mental health. *Journal of Family Violence, 9,* 79-98.

Spielberger, C. (1973). *State-Trait Anxiety Inventory for children: Preliminary manual.* Palo Alto, CA: Consulting Psychologists Press.

Sternberg, K. J., Lamb, M. E., Greenbaum, C., Cicchetti, D., Dawud, S., Cortes, R. M., Krispin, O., & Lorey, R. (1993). Effects of domestic violence on children's behavior problems and depression. *Developmental Psychology, 29,* 44-52.

Straus, M. A. (1979). Measuring intrafamily conflict and violence: The Conflict Tactics (CT) Scales. *Journal of Marriage and the Family, 41,* 75-88.

Weiss, B., Weisz, J. R., Politano, M., Carey, M., Nelson, W. M., & Finch, A. J. (1991). Developmental differences in the factor structure of the Children's Depression Inventory. *Psychological Assessment: A Journal of Consulting and Clinical Psychology, 3,* 38-45.

Widom, C. S. (1989). The cycle of violence. *Science, 244,* 160-166.

Wolfe, D. A., Jaffe, P., Wilson, S. K., & Zak, L. (1985). Children of battered women: The relation of child behavior to family violence and maternal stress. *Journal of Consulting and Clinical Psychology, 53,* 657-665.

CHAPTER 8

The Effects of Neglect on Academic Achievement and Disciplinary Problems

A Developmental Perspective

Kathleen A. Kendall-Tackett
John Eckenrode

Child neglect is the most prevalent type of all child maltreatment, yet we seem to know less about its effects than we do for either physical or sexual abuse (Dubowitz & Black, 1994). Our lack of attention to this form of mal-treatment is often referred to as the "neglect of neglect." Although neglect has not commanded as much attention as physical and sexual abuse, previous research has revealed that neglect can have serious consequences. For example, in

AUTHORS' NOTE: An earlier version of this chapter was presented at the 4th International Family Violence Research Conference, Durham, New Hampshire, July 1995. This chapter is reprinted from *Child Abuse & Neglect, 20,* K. A. Kendall-Tackett and J. Eckenrode, pp. 161-169, 1996, with kind permission from Elsevier Science Ltd., The Boulevard, Langford Lane, Kidlington 0X5 1GB, UK. We gratefully acknowledge the use of the Maltreatment and the Academic and Social Adjustment of School Children data set. This data set has been given to the National Data Archive on Child Abuse and Neglect for public distribution by John Eckenrode, Ph.D., Department of Human Development and Family Studies, Cornell University. Funding to prepare the data for public use was provided by a grant from the National Center on Child Abuse and Neglect (90-CA-1305). We wish to thank Patrick Collins, Elizabeth Rowe, and Edward Frongillo of Cornell University for their many helpful comments and suggestions. Correspondence regarding this chapter may be sent to Kathleen A. Kendall-Tackett, Ph.D., Perinatal Education Group, 34 Western Ave., Henniker, NH 03242; phone and fax: (603) 428-8716; e-mail: kkendallt@aol.com.

their longitudinal study of 267 high-risk mother-infant pairs, Egeland, Sroufe, and Erickson (1983) found that the neglected children had more difficulty performing tasks at both 42 and 56 months than either the control group or other maltreated children. The researchers concluded that neglected children in their sample had low self-esteem, "had the most difficulty pulling themselves together to deal with various tasks . . . and lacked the agency necessary to cope with their environments" (p. 459). By the time these children were early school age, they had deficits in cognitive performance, academic achievement, behavior in the classroom, and social interactions. By second grade, all of the neglected children were in special education programs (Egeland, 1991). Overall, the neglected children demonstrated more developmental problems than any other maltreated group of children (Erickson, Egeland, & Pianta, 1989).

In two more recent studies (Eckenrode, Laird, & Doris, 1993; Leiter & Johnsen, 1994), researchers found that neglected children had the poorest school performance of all maltreated children for Grades K-12. The performance of the neglected children was compared with physically abused, sexually abused, and a group of nonabused children matched for age, sex, and family income. Leiter and Johnsen (1994) hypothesized that neglect led to learning deficits because neglectful parents would be less likely to provide a stimulating environment for the child, read to the child, supervise homework, and be involved in their child's academic life.

Adequate school performance is an important developmental milestone, and poor school performance can have serious long-term effects. For example, Zingraff, Leiter, Johnsen, and Myers (1994) found that good grades and low rates of behavior problems during elementary school reduced the risk that maltreated children will become delinquent as they mature.

A developmental approach is needed to fully understand the long-range effects of child neglect. Egeland, Sroufe, and colleagues (Egeland & Sroufe, 1981; Egeland et al., 1983; Erickson et al., 1989) have already applied a developmental approach to infancy and early childhood, and they noted a pattern of declining functioning in the neglected children. These researchers also noted differing patterns of problems for children who experienced neglect alone and those who experienced neglect in combination with abuse. The results of Eckenrode and associates (1993) and Leiter and Johnsen (1994) highlight the plight of neglected children in school—the next major developmental period—and have found that these children continue to do poorly. From a developmental standpoint, however, the age range covered by these samples (ages approximately 6-18) is quite broad. Furthermore, although Eckenrode and associates examined the results of neglect alone versus neglect in combination with abuse, the results were reported with no differentiation by age.

The present study will examine school performance of neglected children using secondary data analysis of the Eckenrode and associates (1993) data. School performance was measured by average grades in math and English, number of grade repetitions, number of discipline referrals, and number of suspensions and was examined for elementary, junior high, and senior high school students. Two key questions were considered: What is the developmental course for neglected children in school? and What are the developmental effects of neglect alone versus neglect in combination with abuse?

Method

Sample

Subjects were drawn from a population of 8,569 children attending public school in a small city in New York State, Grades K-12, in 1987-1988. The maltreated children were located from records of the New York State Child Abuse and Maltreatment Register. From a group of 1,239 children who had at least one substantiated incident of maltreatment at some point in their lives, a sample of 420 maltreated children was drawn. All children who had been either sexually or physically abused were included in the sample, but only one out of every four neglected children were included because of their high numbers on the Child Abuse Register. A comparison group of 420 nonmaltreated children was drawn from the general population of school children. The comparison group was matched with the maltreated group on gender, grade in school, school, residential location, and classroom when possible. All students in both groups were in regular classrooms.

The present study focuses on neglected children ($N = 324$ of the 420 maltreated children). The entire group ($N = 420$) of nonmaltreated children served as the comparison group. The neglected group was further divided into two groups. The "neglected only" group included only children for whom neglect without any other type of maltreatment was recorded ($N = 217$). The "neglect with abuse" group ($N = 107$) included those who had experienced neglect in combination with either physical abuse ($N = 56$) or sexual abuse ($N = 51$).

In addition to being divided into maltreatment categories, the subjects were classified as elementary ($N = 481$), junior high ($N = 115$), or senior high ($N = 148$) school students based on the school they were *currently* attending.

Measures

Data on school performance and disciplinary problems were collected using school records, which provided information on academic performance, grade repetitions, school transfers, home moves, and disciplinary actions. Four dependent measures were used in the present study.

1. *Current grades in math and English.* This variable was an average of each student's current math and English grades, where $0 = F$ and $4 = A$.
2. *Number of grade repetitions.* This variable indicates the total number of grade levels that subjects repeated during their entire academic career to date.
3. *Discipline referrals.* This variable was the total number of discipline referrals recorded during the entire academic career to date.
4. *Suspensions.* This variable included the total number of suspensions the subject ever received.

Analyses

The primary analyses were 3 (grade level of subject) × 3 (neglect status) analyses of covari-

ance for each of the four dependent measures, with sex of child and socioeconomic status (SES) as covariates. SES was a dichotomous variable indicating whether the family was receiving public assistance at the time data were collected.

On performing the primary analyses, we unexpectedly observed that the senior high students had lower cumulative scores on measures such as grade repetitions, suspensions, and disciplinary referrals than did their younger counterparts. There are two possible explanations for this. First, there may be cohort effects, that is, seniors may have had different experiences as younger children than did children now in elementary or junior high school. Second, there may be selective attrition of seniors due to dropping out of school. To address these issues, we undertook a second set of analyses dividing seniors into two age groups. The first group was 14- to 15-year-olds, to account for the possibility that the students with the poorest academic performance may have dropped out at age 16 (the legal age for leaving school in New York State). The second group consisted of the rest of the seniors (i.e., ages 16 to 20).

Results

■ For each of our four dependent measures there were main effects for both age and neglect status. In general, there were no interaction effects between age and neglect status; the performance of the neglected students paralleled that of the nonmaltreated students but at a lower level. Specific findings are presented below. In each section, age main effects are presented first, followed by findings for neglect status, and finally the analyses for the split senior high groups.

Grades

The average grade was 2.19 ($N = 609$) for combined current grades in math and English. There was a significant main effect for age of student, $F(2, 608) = 63.92, p < .0001$. Grades were highest among elementary school students, regardless of neglect status ($M = 2.51$),

TABLE 8.1 Mean Comparison of Neglected and Nonmaltreated Children on Average Grades
in Math and English

| Neglect Type | Age of Student | | | | |
	Elementary	Junior High	All Seniors	Senior High Ages 14-15	Ages 16-20
Nonmaltreated	2.67 ($N = 202$)	1.96 ($N = 62$)	1.89 ($N = 85$)	2.10 ($N = 33$)	1.71 ($N = 52$)
Neglect only	2.32 ($N = 97$)	1.37 ($N = 35$)	1.65 ($N = 43$)	1.92 ($N = 12$)	1.50 ($N = 31$)
Neglect and abuse	2.26 ($N = 54$)	1.34 ($N = 16$)	1.77 ($N = 15$)	1.75 ($N = 5$)	1.75 ($N = 10$)

and were significantly lower for junior high school students ($M = 1.69$), $t(465) = 23.02$, $p < .0001$, or senior high school students ($M = 1.80$), $t(434) = 19.99$, $p < .0001$. The grades for junior and senior high students also differed significantly, $t(255) = 2.29$, $p < .02$. The means are found in Table 8.1.

Similarly, the grades were lower for neglected and abused/neglected students than they were for their nonneglected counterparts, $F(2, 608) = 5.56$, $p < .004$. The grades of neglected students ($M = 1.97$) differed significantly from those of nonmaltreated students ($M = 2.35$), $t(523) = 11.31$, $p < .0001$, as did those of abused/neglected students ($M = 2.00$), $t(434) = 9.49$, $p < .0001$. The grades of neglected and abused/neglected students did not differ significantly from each other, however. Interestingly, the neglected subjects' grades made a drop in junior high school that paralleled that of their nonmaltreated counterparts. However, in most cases, the average grades were several tenths of a point lower for the neglected subjects at each age range. The age of subject by neglect status interaction was not significant.

We repeated the analysis restricting the senior high group to 14- to 15-year-olds, and found a significant main effect for age, $F(2, 505) = 33.53$, $p < .0001$, and a marginally significant effect for neglect status, $F(2, 505) = 2.79$, $p < .063$, but no significant age by neglect status interaction. These same main effects were also found when the senior group was restricted to the 16- to 20-year-olds: main effects for age, $F(2, 555) = 44.36$, $p < .0001$, and neglect status, $F(2, 555) = 4.12$, $p < .017$. For both groups of neglected students, grades improved between junior and senior high school, whereas a similar rebound was not evident among the nonmaltreated students.

Number of Grade Repetitions

The total number of grades repeated ranged from 0 to 2, with a grand mean of .30 ($N = 698$).

There was a significant age of subject main effect, $F(2, 696) = 10.96$, $p < .0001$. In general, junior high school students had the highest number of grade repetitions ($M = .44$) and were significantly higher than either elementary school students ($M = .24$), $t(588) = 22.47$, $p < .0001$, or senior high students ($M = .39$), $t(235) = 3.56$, $p < .0001$. The means are found in Table 8.2.

There was also a significant main effect for neglect status, $F(2, 696) = 9.17$, $p < .0001$. The highest number of grade repetitions was for abused/neglected students ($M = .48$). This number was significantly higher than for nonmaltreated ($M = .20$), $t(494) = 28.84$, $p < .0001$, and neglected only ($M = .41$), $t(303) = 5.65$, $p < .0001$, students. The number of grade repetitions for neglected students also differed significantly from the nonmaltreated students, $t(596) = 23.75$, $p < .0001$.

Similarly, when the senior high group was restricted to 14- to 15-year-olds, there were main effects for both age, $F(2, 612) = 8.93$, $p < .0001$, and neglect status, $F(2, 612) = 3.65$, $p < .026$ and a marginally significant interaction, $F(4, 612) = 2.28$, $p < .059$. This appeared mainly due to there being no repetitions among the small group of 14- to 15-year-old students who were both abused and neglected. Similarly, for the 16- to 20-year-olds, there were age, $F(2, 640) = 17.08$, $p < .0001$, and neglect, $F(2, 640) = 11.07$, $p < .0001$, but no interaction.

Number of Disciplinary Referrals

The number of disciplinary referrals for subjects' entire academic career ranged from 0 to

TABLE 8.2 Mean Comparison of Neglected and Nonmaltreated Children on Number of Grade Repetitions

| Neglect Type | Age of Student | | | | |
| | Elementary | Junior High | Senior High | | |
			All Seniors	Ages 14-15	Ages 16-20
Nonmaltreated	.14 (N = 258)	.32 (N = 59)	.29 (N = 77)	.17 (N = 30)	.36 (N = 47)
Neglect only	.35 (N = 132)	.49 (N = 35)	.58 (N = 36)	.40 (N = 10)	.65 (N = 26)
Neglect and abuse	.42 (N = 72)	.80 (N = 15)	.43 (N = 14)	.00 (N = 6)	.75 (N = 8)

46, with a mean of 1.40 ($N = 744$). There was a significant main effect of age of subject, $F(2, 742) = 25.15$, $p < .0001$, with junior high students receiving significantly more disciplinary referrals ($M = 2.89$) than elementary students ($M = .68$), $t(595) = 3.19$, $p < .002$. Senior high students also received significantly more referrals than did elementary school students ($M = 2.55$), $t(628) = 2.77$, $p < .006$, but the number of referrals for junior and senior high students did not differ significantly from each other. The means for these analyses are found in Table 8.3.

There was also a significant main effect for neglect status, $F(2, 742) = 7.84$, $p < .0001$. Subjects who were neglected ($M = 1.71$) or abused/neglected ($M = 2.21$) had more disciplinary referrals than their nonmaltreated counterparts ($M = 1.03$). None of these pairwise comparisons was significant, however, possibly due to a high mean square error. There was a marginally significant age of subject by neglect status interaction, $F(4, 742) = 2.08$, $p < .082$, which appears to reflect the larger increase in referrals between elementary school and junior high for the two neglected groups in comparison to the nonmaltreated students.

When the senior high group was restricted to the 14- to 15-year-olds, there was a main effect for age, $F(2, 644) = 22.92$, $p < .0001$, and a marginally significant effect for neglect status, $F(2, 644) = 1.98$, $p < .14$. There was no significant interaction. In contrast, when the senior high

group was restricted to the 16- to 20-year-olds, there was a main effect for both age, $F(2, 689) = 28.03$, $p < .0001$, and neglect status, $F(2, 689) = 9.59$, $p < .0001$, and a significant age by neglect status interaction, $F(4, 689) = 2.74$, $p < .028$. For nonmaltreated students, the number of disciplinary referrals leveled off after junior high, but for neglected and abused/neglected students, the number continued to increase through senior high.

Number of Suspensions

The total number of suspensions students had ranged from 0 to 28, with a mean number of .27 ($N = 737$). A significant age main effect, $F(2, 735) = 32.36$, $p < .0001$, revealed the highest number was for the junior high school students ($M = 1.06$). This number was significantly higher than the number of suspensions for elementary ($M = .02$), $t(591) = 11.66$, $p < .0001$, and senior high ($M = .45$), $t(259) = 4.53$, $p < .0001$, students. The number of suspensions for senior high students was also significantly higher than for elementary school students, $t(621) = 4.94$, $p < .0001$. The means are found in Table 8.4.

A main effect for neglect status, $F(2, 735) = 8.35$, $p < .0001$, indicated a significant difference in the number of suspensions for neglected ($M = .38$), $t(631) = 2.78$, $p < .0006$, and abused/neglected ($M = .52$), $t(533) = 4.05$, $p <$

TABLE 8.3 Mean Comparison of Neglected and Nonmaltreated Children on Total Discipline Referrals

| Neglect Type | Age of Student | | | | |
| | Elementary | Junior High | Senior High | | |
			All Seniors	Ages 14-15	Ages 16-20
Nonmaltreated	.57 (N = 271)	1.95 (N = 62)	1.78 (N = 87)	1.53 (N = 34)	1.94 (N = 53)
Neglect only	.72 (N = 137)	3.56 (N = 36)	3.27 (N = 44)	2.15 (N = 13)	3.74 (N = 31)
Neglect and abuse	1.01 (N = 73)	4.88 (N = 17)	4.65 (N = 17)	1.33 (N = 6)	6.45 (N = 11)

TABLE 8.4 Mean Comparison of Neglected and Nonmaltreated Children on Total Number of Suspensions

Neglect Type	Age of Student				
				Senior High	
	Elementary	Junior High	All Seniors	Ages 14-15	Ages 16-20
Nonmaltreated	.02 ($N = 270$)	.45 ($N = 62$)	.30 ($N = 87$)	.24 ($N = 33$)	.33 ($N = 54$)
Neglect only	.01 ($N = 135$)	1.67 ($N = 36$)	.50 ($N = 42$)	.17 ($N = 11$)	.61 ($N = 31$)
Abuse and neglect	.04 ($N = 72$)	2.00 ($N = 17$)	1.13 ($N = 16$)	1.00 ($N = 5$)	1.09 ($N = 11$)

.0001, students compared to their nonmaltreated counterparts ($M = .14$). There was no significant difference in number of suspensions between neglected and abused/neglected students, however.

A significant age of subject by neglect status interaction, $F(4, 735) = 5.0, p < .001$, revealed that neglected students in junior or senior high had many more suspensions than their nonmaltreated counterparts, whereas in elementary school the number was equally low in all groups. This pattern was similar to that observed for disciplinary referrals.

The analysis with the 14- to 15-year-olds revealed significant main effects for age, $F(2, 639) = 30.86, p < .0001$, and for neglect status, $F(2, 639) = 4.42, p < .012$, and a significant age by neglect status interaction, $F(4, 639) = 5.12, p < .0001$. The analysis for the 16- to 20-year-olds also revealed main effects for age, $F(2, 683) = 32.10, p < .0001$, and neglect status, $F(2, 683) = 7.29, p < .001$, and a significant age by neglect status interaction, $F(4, 683) = 4.96, p < .001$.

Discussion

■ The results revealed that neglected children did indeed fare more poorly in school than did their nonmaltreated counterparts and that performance markedly decreased in the transition from elementary school to junior high. These were robust effects and held true even when controlling for the effects of gender and SES. Neglect alone was equally detrimental to grades and number of suspensions as was neglect in combination with physical or sexual abuse. The combination of abuse and neglect was detrimen-

tal in terms of number of disciplinary referrals and grade repetitions.

Math and English grades dropped for all subjects in junior high, but even more so for neglected and abused/neglected students than for nonmaltreated students. These findings are consistent with those of Leiter and Johnsen (1994) that neglected children are more likely to show deficits in school performance. The drop in grades that occurred for all students in junior high has also been noted in previous research on adolescence. For example, Sroufe, Cooper, and DeHart (1992) note that grades typically drop when students enter middle school. Some of the explanations for this phenomenon include more difficult classes and grading, the process of changing from one school to another, and in many cases, the onset of puberty (Entwisle, 1990). The presence of neglect appears to exacerbate the potential stressfulness of these changes. The neglected students may have cognitive deficits, but also difficulty "pulling themselves together" and coping with new situations, as researchers have found with young children (Egeland et al., 1983).

The results for grade repetitions and disciplinary referrals presented a more complicated picture. With cumulative measures such as these, we would expect that the oldest students would have the highest frequencies. We would not expect that the senior high students would *lose* numbers of these events. To determine whether the lower numbers of grade repetitions and disciplinary referrals were due to selective attrition from the sample, we first analyzed the data for seniors less than age 16. Because students can drop out of school at age 16, we assumed we would have a broader band of student performance with the younger students (presumably, the students with the poorest performance would drop out at age 16, leaving behind only the "better" students). We found the opposite of what we expected—the younger seniors had fewer repetitions, discipline referrals, and suspensions than the older seniors. These findings suggest a cohort effect for the 14- to 15-year-olds, possibly due to a change in policy that might have resulted in a lower total number of both disciplinary referrals and grade repetitions.

Our findings on number of suspensions remain our most difficult to explain. Even with the divided senior high age group, the junior high students still had substantially more suspensions than did their senior high counterparts. To consider a possible cohort effect, we examined the number of suspensions the current junior high and senior high students received in both elementary school and junior high. Both groups had a low number of suspensions in elementary school. However, there was a substantial difference between the groups in the number each had in *junior* high. Among the current seniors, only 2% had more than two suspensions while in junior high, with the highest number being 8. Among the current junior high students, however, a full 8% had more than 2 suspensions and 6% had more than 4. Among this top 6% ($N = 7$), the number of suspensions ranged from 5 to 28. This particular group of junior high students may indeed be different in an unknown way, or may reflect a change in district policy with regard to suspensions.

Another goal of the present study was to determine if there was an additive effect of maltreatment in combination with neglect. The combination of abuse and neglect seemed to have the most deleterious impact on disciplinary referrals and grade repetitions. However, our analysis had some limitations because of the nature of the data. Because of the relatively small numbers of subjects who had experienced neglect in combination with either sexual abuse or physical abuse, we combined them, which gave a crude measure of whether there was an additive effect. In doing so, we lost information on the differential effects of physical abuse and sexual abuse in combination with neglect. The impact of abuse combined with neglect should be

addressed in future studies with larger samples of children who have experienced either sexual abuse and neglect, or physical abuse and neglect.

The results of the present study have implications for timing of interventions. Junior high appears to be a particularly problematic time for neglected and abused/neglected children. To be most effective, these problems should be anticipated and primary prevention programs should be implemented in elementary school. Along these same lines, school personnel at junior high schools should be alerted to the fact that a drastic increase in behavior problems and a decline in grades may be a sign not only of abuse but also of a history of neglect that had not previously been identified.

In conclusion, child neglect is often ignored because it is more commonplace and does not seem as "serious" as other types of maltreatment. The present study, however, demonstrated that neglect does have a serious impact on children's abilities to perform in school, whether it occurs alone or in combination with other forms of maltreatment—and these effects are too serious to ignore.

References

Dubowitz, H., & Black, M. (1994). Child neglect. In R. M. Reece (Ed.), *Child abuse: Medical diagnosis and management* (pp. 279-297). Philadelphia: Lea & Febiger.

Eckenrode, J., Laird, M., & Doris, J. (1993). School performance and disciplinary problems among abused and neglected children. *Developmental Psychology, 29,* 53-62.

Egeland, B. (1991). A longitudinal study of high-risk families: Issues and findings. In R. H. Starr & D. A. Wolfe (Eds.), *The effects of child abuse and neglect: Issues and research* (pp. 33-56). New York: Guilford.

Egeland, B., & Sroufe, A. (1981). Developmental sequelae of maltreatment in infancy. In R. Rizley & D. Cicchetti (Eds.), *New directions for child development: Developmental perspectives in child maltreatment.* San Francisco: Jossey-Bass.

Egeland, B., Sroufe, L. A., & Erickson, M. (1983). The developmental consequence of different patterns of maltreatment. *Child Abuse & Neglect, 7,* 459-469.

Entwisle, D. (1990). Schools and the adolescent. In S. Feldman & G. Elliot (Eds.), *At the threshold: The developing adolescent* (pp. 197-224). Cambridge, MA: Harvard University Press.

Erickson, M. F., Egeland, B., & Pianta, R. (1989). The effects of maltreatment on the development of young children. In D. Cicchetti & V. Carlson (Eds.), *Child maltreatment*. Cambridge: Cambridge University Press.

Leiter, J., & Johnsen, M. C. (1994). Child maltreatment and school performance. *American Journal of Education, 102,* 154-189.

Sroufe, L. A., Cooper, R. G., & DeHart, G. B. (1992). *Child development: Its nature and course.* New York: McGraw-Hill.

Zingraff, M. T., Leiter, J., Johnsen, M. C., & Myers, K. A. (1994). The mediating effect of good school performance on the maltreatment-delinquency relationship. *Journal of Research in Crime and Delinquency, 31,* 62-91.

CHAPTER 9

The Traumatic Events Screening Inventory

Assessing Trauma in Children

Jason H. Edwards
Karen C. Rogers

The assessment of trauma in children appears to be in its infancy. However, the need for and interest in accurately assessing trauma has grown dramatically. Increasing interest in the study of trauma in general, and childhood trauma in particular, is suggested by the relatively recent formation of the International Society for Traumatic Stress Studies and the *Journal of Traumatic Stress*. Terr (1979, 1981) conducted early groundbreaking work in studying childhood trauma. In 1980, the conceptualization of some traumatic stress reactions as posttraumatic stress disorder (PTSD) was included for the first time in the *Diagnostic and Statistical Manual of Mental Disorders*

(*DSM-III*; American Psychiatric Association, 1980). Changes were made to the initial conceptualization of PTSD in more recent editions of *DSM*. Yet the concept of exposure to a traumatic event remains central to the conceptualization. However, recent studies suggest that exposure to a traumatic event does not necessarily mean that a child will develop symptoms consistent with PTSD (Kendall-Tackett, Williams, & Finkelhor, 1993; McNally, 1993).

A central issue in the development of reliable and valid child trauma assessment instruments is the operational definition of the phenomenon. Similar to research on stress, different perspectives on defining trauma have developed includ-

AUTHORS' NOTE: The authors contributed equally to this chapter.

ing a particular event to which a child has been exposed, the child's appraisal of an event, the child's reaction to an event, symptoms of psychopathology, or a combination of the aforementioned perspectives. Hence there are a number of research approaches to identifying trauma and studying the impact of trauma on children. For instance, one approach is to identify children exposed to one specific event (McFarlane, 1987). Other studies identify a class of trauma such as sexual abuse or physical abuse and may not clearly define the traumatic event (McLeer, Callaghan, Henry, & Wallen, 1994; Pelcovitz et al., 1994). From an event-based perspective, characteristics such as frequency, intensity, and predictability may be very relevant (Lonigan, Shannon, Finch, Daugherty, & Taylor, 1991; Pynoos et al., 1987). Moreover, the child's appraisal of the event can be quite important as reflected in the incorporation of this factor in DSM-IV (American Psychiatric Association, 1994) criteria for PTSD.

Child Trauma Inventories

■ There appears to be a dearth of systematic research on children's exposure to potentially traumatic events. There is some suggestion that exposure to traumatic events may be relatively common (Elmer, 1977; Sedlak, 1990). The existent scales measure exposure and/or impact of exposure, especially in terms of PTSD symptoms. The majority of the scales focus on the latter area with measurement of PTSD being of primary interest. For many of the scales, the basic psychometric properties have not been established. Several of the scales are briefly reviewed below. The reader is directed to Stamm (1996) for a more in-depth review of child trauma instruments.

The PTSD-focused scales tend to use structured or semistructured interviews with questions pertaining to an identified traumatic event. The Children's Impact of Traumatic Events Scale (Wolfe, Gentile, Michienzi, Sas, & Wolfe, 1991) measures PTSD symptoms resulting from sexual abuse. Other PTSD scales concentrate on an identified traumatic event, which can include sexual abuse. These instruments include the

Child Post-Traumatic Stress Reaction Index (Frederick & Pynoos, 1988), Clinician-Administered PTSD Scale for Children (Nader, Kriegler, Blake, & Pynoos, 1994), My Worst School Experience Scale (Hyman, 1996), and When Bad Things Happen Scale (Fletcher, 1996). Furthermore, there are a number of structured interviews for assessing children's emotional/behavioral functioning often in terms of DSM criteria that incorporate evaluation of PTSD symptomatology. These interviews include the Diagnostic Interview for Children and Adolescents (Welner, Reich, Herjanic, Jung, & Amado, 1987), the Child and Adolescent Psychiatric Assessment (Angold, Cox, Prendergast, Rutter, & Simonoff, 1987), the Diagnostic Interview Schedule for Children (Costello, Edelbrock, & Costello, 1985), and the Child Assessment Schedule (Hodges, Cools, & McKnew, 1989).

Some scales focus on the impact of a traumatic event without an emphasis on assessing DSM symptoms. The Dimensions of Stressful Events Rating Scale (Fletcher, 1996) assesses dimensions of a stressful event that may contribute to increasing the traumatic impact on a child. The Schillace Trauma Scale (Schillace, 1996) measures the impact of a traumatic event on older adolescents.

Few trauma inventories screen for exposure to a variety of potentially traumatic events. Fletcher (1996) developed the Tough Times Checklist (children age 8-12 years), Teen Times Checklist (adolescents), and Child's Upsetting Times Checklist (parents of child) to assess exposure to 68 stressful life events. The Brief Assessment of Traumatic Events (Lipovsky & Hanson, 1993) involves a semistructured interview of 10 stressful events with 30% of the items addressing sexual abuse.

The Traumatic Events Screening Inventory (TESI; Ribbe, 1996; Ribbe et al., 1995a, 1995b) provides a lifetime screening for exposure in children to a wide variety of potentially traumatic events by assessing both the child's and parent's perspective. It is partly based on the Brief Assessment of Traumatic Events. The TESI differs from other trauma assessment instruments by incorporating a combination of beneficial features. Namely, the TESI (a) functions as a screening instrument for a broad array of potentially traumatic events with follow-up questions for each endorsed traumatic event, (b) assesses both the child/adolescent's and parent's perspective, (c) requires relatively little time to administer yet is comprehensive, (d) can be used with other inventories and approaches (e.g., PTSD-focused evaluations), and (e) has clinical and clinical research applications. The TESI operationalizes trauma in terms of exposure to potentially traumatic events as a first step and can be combined with other approaches in assessing child trauma. It is the purpose of this chapter to discuss the TESI in more detail and present preliminary child trauma clinical research using this instrument.

Traumatic Events Screening Inventory

Development of the TESI

The TESI was developed by the Child Trauma Research Group as a means of screening for trauma in a child psychiatric outpatient population. There was interest in developing an easy to use yet comprehensive clinical scale to assess exposure to potentially traumatic events. It was thought that this type of inventory would be helpful not only in cases where trauma was already identified but particularly when an identified traumatic event was not ostensibly part of the presenting problem. Clinical research was also of interest, and the TESI was developed as a preliminary means to help distinguish between children who were exposed to sexual abuse, physical abuse, nonabuse trauma, or no trauma. The items used in the inventory were based on the types of trauma exposure reported in the literature to ensure broad coverage of potentially traumatic events. The TESI was designed to assess exposure to severe accidents, disasters, illness or painful medical procedures, family conflict or violence, community conflict or violence, and sexual molestation. The TESI has been revised periodically.

Description of the TESI

The TESI is an 18-item questionnaire concerning potentially traumatic events to which a child may have been exposed. Follow-up questions are included for each of the 18 traumatic events to determine the characteristics of the exposure. There is a child (TESI-C) and a parent (TESI-P) version of the inventory. The TESI-C is administered to children and adolescents in a structured interview format. The child's responses to each traumatic event question are coded as *yes, no, not sure,* or *refused.* The interviewer may also code the response as of questionable validity. If a traumatic event is endorsed, then follow-up questions are asked. An example of one of the questions is "Have you ever been in a really bad storm, like a tornado or a hurricane, a flood or an earthquake?" If a child answered affirmatively to this particular question, the examiner would find out what happened, the age of the child at the time, who was with the child, whether the child was afraid someone would be hurt or killed, and other relevant information. The screening inventory is appropriate for ages 6-18 although it has been used with children as young as 5 years of age. The wording of the questions reflects research on children's responses to linguistic cues (Saywitz, Geiselman, & Bornstein, 1990). The interview duration is approximately 15-30 minutes depending on the number of traumatic events endorsed.

The TESI-P is completed by parents as a paper-and-pencil measure. It includes the same 18 traumatic events in the same order as the child version of the instrument with similar follow-up questions if an event is endorsed. An example of one of the questions is "Has your child ever been in a really bad storm, like a tornado or a hurricane, a flood or an earthquake?" It usually takes approximately 15 minutes for parents to complete the TESI-P depending on the number of traumatic events endorsed.

Preliminary Research

■ As part of an ongoing pilot study testing the use of the TESI, an investigation of exposure to traumatic events in children was conducted.

TABLE 9.1   Number of Traumatic Events
Reported by Children and Mothers

	Children	Mothers
M	5.79	4.31
SD	2.20	2.66
Minimum	2.00	0
Maximum	12.00	10.00

TABLE 9.2   Children and Mothers Reporting
Child Exposure to Traumatic Events

No. of Traumatic Events	Children (%)	Mothers (%)
1	100	96
>3	90	50
>6	32	37

Method

Procedure

The questionnaire was administered to a subset of consecutively seen intakes in a child psychiatric outpatient clinic in the New England area. During the first appointment, children were administered the TESI-C and mothers completed the TESI-P. The clinicians administering the TESI-C included psychiatrists, psychologists, postdoctoral fellows, and psychiatry residents. The TESI is one of a number of assessment measures used in the clinic as part of the initial evaluation of children.

Participants

Preliminary data are available on 26 children (10 females and 16 males). The age range was from 7 to 18 years of age. The number of one-parent and two-parent households was approximately evenly divided. Ten of the mothers were college educated, and another 13 mothers were high school educated.

Results

■ Table 9.1 shows the number of traumatic events endorsed by children and mothers regarding their child. The mean number of traumatic events reported by children is higher than mothers reported concerning their child's exposure to traumatic events.

Table 9.2 shows the percentage of children and mothers reporting child exposure to traumatic events by number of traumatic events. Every child in the sample endorsed at least two different types of potentially traumatic events, with 90% of the children reporting more than three traumatic events and approximately 33%

reporting more than six traumatic events. For mothers, 50% reported that their children had been exposed to more than three traumatic events and 37% reported exposure to more than six traumatic events.

Table 9.3 shows the five most frequently endorsed traumatic events by children and three of the same five traumatic events that were frequently endorsed by mothers concerning their children. A higher percentage of children compared to mothers reported exposure to four of the five traumatic events. The traumatic events most frequently endorsed by children and mothers included "Have you ever had a pet that was killed?" (over 74% of children and 48% of parents endorsed this statement); "Has a person who was very important to you ever gotten really sick or hurt?" (72% of children and 56% of parents); and "Have you seen people in your family

TABLE 9.3   Frequently Reported Traumatic
Events by Children and Mothers

Traumatic Event	Children (%)	Mothers (%)
Have you ever been in a really bad accident, like a car accident or a fall?	47	32
Have there been some other times when something happened that really scared you?	50	22
Have you seen people in your family really yelling or screaming at each other a lot?	53	53
Has a person who was very important to you ever gotten really sick or hurt?	72	56
Have you ever had a pet that was killed?	74	48

really yelling or screaming at each other a lot?" (53% of children and mothers).

Discussion

■ Preliminary research suggests high levels of endorsement by both children and parents of child exposure to potentially traumatic events. In fact, approximately one third of children and parents endorsed child exposure to more than six potentially traumatic events. It is possible that the high rates of exposure to traumatic events are reflective of children who reach clinical status. Children not referred for mental health services may have much lower rates of exposure to traumatic events.

Another interesting finding concerns the apparent discrepancy between children and parents on some of the more commonly reported traumatic events. Children appeared to be more likely to report exposure to these traumatic events than mothers. Unfortunately, the small sample size did not allow for empirical assessment of agreement between children and their mothers or for preliminary investigations of the relationship between the TESI and other instruments such as the Child Behavior Checklist (Achenbach, 1991). Yet there is some suggestion that adults may significantly underestimate the degree to which a child experiences a specific event as traumatic (Yamamoto, 1979). Furthermore, differences between child and parent reports concerning the child's functioning are not uncommon (Edelbrock, Costello, Dulcan, Conover, & Kalas, 1986; Hodges, 1993; Kinard, 1996; Mulhern, Fairclough, Smith, & Douglas, 1992; Thompson, Merritt, Keith, Murphy, & Johndrow, 1993). However, the results from this preliminary investigation must be viewed with caution in light of the very small sample size.

The TESI appears to show promise as a useful and efficient screening inventory to assess child exposure to potentially traumatic events. Identification of traumatic event exposure allows the clinician to comprehensively assess and understand a child's functioning and thereby assist in treatment. As noted previously, the scale seems to have a number of advantages over other inventories. In addition to its clinical utility, the TESI appears to be of potential benefit for clinical research purposes. Furthermore, this approach to assessing trauma can be integrated with other methods. A current limitation is the level of psychometric maturity. Yet this limitation presently does not appear to interfere significantly with the clinical benefits of using this inventory. Research on the psychometric properties of the TESI is planned to evaluate the reliability and validity of the scale. Ongoing revisions will be made based on the research findings. Moreover, future research will involve investigating the relationship between the TESI and other child psychological instruments, and with treatment outcome. There is much to be learned about the scope of traumatic exposure in children and resulting developmental outcomes. The TESI seems to be of potential benefit in helping to answer these and many other questions concerning childhood trauma.

References

Achenbach, T. M. (1991). *Manual for the Child Behavior Checklist/4-18 and 1991 profile.* Burlington: University of Vermont, Department of Psychiatry.

American Psychiatric Association. (1980). *Diagnostic and statistical manual of mental disorders* (3rd ed.). Washington, DC: Author.

American Psychiatric Association. (1994). *Diagnostic and statistical manual of mental disorders* (4th ed.). Washington, DC: Author.

Angold, A., Cox, A., Prendergast, M., Rutter, M., & Simonoff, E. (1987). *The Child and Adolescent Psychiatric Assessment (CAPA).* Unpublished manuscript.

Costello, E. J., Edelbrock, C. S., & Costello, A. J. (1985). Validity of the NIMH Diagnostic Interview Schedule for Children: A comparison between psychiatric and pediatric referrals. *Journal of Abnormal Child Psychology, 13,* 579-595.

Edelbrock, C., Costello, A. J., Dulcan, M. K., Conover, N. C., & Kalas, K. (1986). Parent-child agreement on child psychiatric symptoms assessed via structured interview. *Journal of Child Psychology and Psychiatry, 27,* 181-190.

Elmer, R. (1977). A follow-up study of traumatized children. *Pediatrics, 59,* 273-279.

Fletcher, K. E. (1996). Psychometric review of the When Bad Things Happen Scale. In B. H. Stamm (Ed.), *Measurement of stress, trauma, and adaptation* (pp. 435-437). Lutherville, MD: Sidran.

Frederick, C., & Pynoos, R. S. (1988). *Child Post-Traumatic Stress Reaction Index.* Unpublished manuscript.

Hodges, K. (1993). Structured interviews for assessing children. *Journal of Child Psychology and Psychiatry, 34,* 46-68.

Hodges, K., Cools, J., & McKnew, D. (1989). Test-retest reliability of a clinical research interview for children: The Child Assessment Schedule (CAS). *Psychological Assessment: Journal of Consulting and Clinical Psychology, 1,* 317-322.

Hyman, I. A. (1996). Psychometric review of My Worst Experience and My Worst School Experience Scale. In B. H. Stamm (Ed.), *Measurement of stress, trauma, and adaptation* (pp. 212-213). Lutherville, MD: Sidran.

Kendall-Tackett, K. A., Williams, L. M., & Finkelhor, D. (1993). Impact of sexual abuse on children: A review and synthesis of recent empirical studies. *Psychological Bulletin, 113,* 164-180.

Kinard, M. E. (1996, July). *Depressive symptoms in maltreated children: Comparing mother, teacher, and self-reports.* Paper presented at the Trauma and Memory International Research Conference, Durham, NH.

Lipovsky, J. A., & Hanson, R. (1993). *The Brief Assessment of Traumatic Events.* Unpublished manuscript.

Lonigan, C. J., Shannon, M. P., Finch, A. J., Daugherty, T. K., & Taylor, C. M. (1991). Children's reactions to a natural disaster: Symptom severity and degree of exposure. *Advances in Behavior Research and Therapy, 13,* 135-154.

McFarlane, A. C. (1987). Posttraumatic phenomena in a longitudinal study of children following a natural disaster. *Journal of the American Academy of Child and Adolescent Psychiatry, 26,* 764-769.

McLeer, S., Callaghan, M., Henry, D., & Wallen, J. A. (1994). Psychiatric disorders in sexually abused children. *Journal of the American Academy of Child and Adolescent Psychiatry, 33,* 313-319.

McNally, R. J. (1993). Stressors that produce posttraumatic stress disorder in children. In J. R. T. Davidson & E. B. Foa (Eds.), *Posttraumatic stress disorder: DSM-IV and beyond* (pp. 57-74). Washington, DC: American Psychiatric Press.

Mulhern, R. K., Fairclough, D. L., Smith, B., & Douglas, S. M. (1992). Maternal depression, assessment methods, and physical symptoms affect estimates of depressive symptomatology among children with cancer. *Journal of Pediatric Psychology, 17,* 313-326.

Nader, K., Kriegler, J., Blake, D. D., & Pynoos, R. S. (1994). *Clinician-Administered PTSD Scale for Children.* Unpublished manuscript.

Pelcovitz, D., Kaplan, S., Goldenberg, B., Mandel, F., Lehane, J., & Guarrera, J. (1994). Post-traumatic stress disorder in physically abused adolescents. *Journal of the American Academy of Child and Adolescent Psychiatry, 33,* 305-312.

Pynoos, R. S., Frederick, C., Nadar, K., Arroyo, W., Steinber, A., Eth, S., Nunex, F., & Fairbanks, L. (1987). Life threat

and posttraumatic stress in school-age children. *Archives of General Psychiatry, 44,* 1057-1063.

Ribbe, D. (1996). Psychometric review of the Traumatic Events Screening Instrument for Children (TESI-C). In B. H. Stamm (Ed.), *Measurement of stress, trauma, and adaptation* (pp. 386-387). Lutherville, MD: Sidran.

Ribbe, D., Cone, P., Lukovits, M., Racusin, R., Rogers, K., Edwards, J. H., & National Center for PTSD and Dartmouth Child Trauma Research Group. (1995a). *The Traumatic Events Screening Inventory-Child (TESI-C).* Unpublished manuscript, Dartmouth Medical School.

Ribbe, D., Cone, P., Lukovits, M., Racusin, R., Rogers, K., Edwards, J. H., & National Center for PTSD and Dartmouth Child Trauma Research Group. (1995b). *The Traumatic Events Screening Inventory-Parent (TESI-P).* Unpublished manuscript, Dartmouth Medical School.

Saywitz, K. J., Geiselman, R. E., & Bornstein, G. (1990). Enhancing children's eyewitness memory: A test of the cognitive interview with children. *Journal of Applied Psychology, 77,* 744-756.

Schillace, R. (1996). *Psychometric review of the Trauma Scale.* In B. H. Stamm (Ed.), *Measurement of stress, trauma, and adaptation* (pp. 273-275). Lutherville, MD: Sidran.

Sedlak, A. J. (1990). *Technical amendment to the study findings—National incidence and prevalence of child abuse and neglect: 1988.* Washington, DC: National Center for Child Abuse and Neglect.

Stamm, B. H. (Ed.). (1996). *Measurement of stress, trauma, and adaptation.* Lutherville, MD: Sidran.

Terr, L. C. (1979). Children of Chowchilla: A study of psychic trauma. *Psychoanalytic Study of the Child, 34,* 547-623.

Terr, L .C. (1981). Psychic trauma in children: Observations following the Chowchilla school-bus kidnapping. *American Journal of Psychiatry, 138,* 14-19.

Thompson, R. J., Jr., Merritt, K. A., Keith, B. R., Murphy, L. B., & Johndrow, D. A. (1993). The role of maternal stress and family functioning in maternal distress and mother-reported and child-reported psychological adjustment of non-referred children. *Journal of Clinical Child Psychology, 22,* 78-84.

Welner, Z., Reich, W., Herjanic, B., Jung, K. G., & Amado, H. (1987). Reliability and validity in parent-child agreement studies of the Diagnostic Interview for Children and Adolescents. *Journal of the American Academy of Child Psychiatry, 26,* 649-653.

Wolfe, V. V., Gentile, C., Michienzi, T., Sas, L., & Wolfe, D. (1991). The Children's Impact of Traumatic Events Scale: A measure of post-sexual abuse PTSD symptoms. *Behavioral Assessment, 13,* 359-383.

Yamamoto, K. (1979). Children's ratings of the stressfulness of experiences. *Developmental Psychology, 15,* 581-582.

CHAPTER 10

Measuring Physical and Psychological Maltreatment of Children With the Conflict Tactics Scales

Murray A. Straus
Sherry L. Hamby

The Conflict Tactics Scales or CTS (Straus, 1979b, 1990a) is intended to measure use of nonviolent discipline (previously called reasoning), psychological aggression, and physical assault in parent-child and other family relationships. The Psychological Aggression and Physical Assault scales provide a basis for identifying psychological and physical maltreatment. The purpose of this chapter is to facilitate the use of the CTS by pre-senting information based on 20 years of experience and over 100 papers and articles that have used the CTS to measure child maltreatment.

Two revisions of the CTS became available in 1996. One of them, the CTS2 (Straus, Hamby, Boney-McCoy, & Sugarman, 1996), is designed to measure relationships between partners in a marital, cohabiting, or dating relationship. The second new version is for measuring parent-child relationships and is called the CTSPC. In

AUTHORS' NOTE: This research is a project of the Family Violence Research Program of the Family Research Laboratory, University of New Hampshire, Durham, NH 03824. A publications list will be sent on request. We are indebted to David Finkelhor, David Moore, Christine Smith, and Barbara Wauchope for valuable comments and suggestions and to Dianne Cyr Carmody and Barbara A. Wauchope for locating research using the CTS to measure child maltreatment. The research was supported by the University of New Hampshire and by National Institute of Mental Health Grant T32 MH15161 for Family Violence Research Training.

this chapter, "CTS" will be used to identify material that applies to both the original CTS (called CTS1 from here on) and the CTSPC. CTSPC and CTS1 will be used for material that applies only to those specific instruments.

The CTSPC has so far been used in only one empirical study. However, the considerable body of experience with the CTS1 is likely to be applicable to the CTSPC because the CTSPC is based on the same theoretical and measurement strategy as the CTS1. This chapter therefore makes available information based on both the CTS1 and the CTSPC to facilitate understanding and appropriate use of these instruments. The specific objectives of the chapter are to provide the following: (a) examples of applications of the CTS to research on child maltreatment that illustrate potential uses, (b) theoretical rationale underlying both the CTS and the CTSPC, (c) description of the subscales and scoring methods to measure different levels of maltreatment, (d) data on validity and reliability, and (e) assessment of the CTS both in absolute terms and relative to other measures of child maltreatment.

The CTS and Other Approaches to Measuring Maltreatment

■ Standardized self-report methods for measuring child maltreatment such as the CTS can, for some purposes, be a useful alternative to the present dependence on data describing cases reported to child protective services agencies (CPS). Because of this dependence on CPS cases, a large proportion of research on physical maltreatment of children does not directly measure maltreatment. Instead, as Knudsen (1988) and Fink and McCloskey (1990) note, these studies depend on the judgments of child protection workers. In principle, a careful clinical evaluation may provide the best data on child maltreatment. In practice, there are many problems with such data. The definitions of maltreatment used by agencies are ambiguous and subject to various interpretations (see below and Knudsen, 1988). Moreover, as Knudsen shows, these definitions tend to change over time. Even when the formal definitions remain constant, the

staff changes and policies for interpreting the definitions change. To compound all of this, only a small proportion of CPS staff have a degree in a clinically relevant field. Moreover, they are burdened with caseloads that almost preclude the type of in-depth assessment that, in principle, would provide the best data. There are also many studies comparing clinical judgments with assessments based on quantitative instruments such as the CTS. To the surprise and chagrin of most of the authors, these studies have generally found the quantitative assessment to be more accurate both in diagnosis and prognosis (Dawes, Faust, & Meehl, 1989).

The parent-child part of the CTS1 (see Appendix A and Straus, 1996) can be administered in about 3 minutes, and the equivalent parts of the CTSPC (in Straus, Hamby, Finkelhor, Moore, & Runyan, 1996) in about 5 minutes. Both can be administered by interviewers who are not clinically trained or as a self-administered questionnaire. Despite its brevity, the CTS provides data on the prevalence and chronicity of physical and psychological maltreatment. It can be used in house-to-house random sample epidemiological studies, for screening and preliminary diagnosis in clinical settings, and to evaluate the extent to which a treatment or prevention program has reduced the rate of child maltreatment.

Research on Child Maltreatment Using the CTS

■ Since the first use of the CTS in the early 1970s (Straus, 1973), it has become the most widely used instrument for research on spouse abuse (Morash, 1987). Although fewer studies have used the CTS to measure child maltreatment, the contributions of these studies to knowledge of child maltreatment include

■ National rates of physical maltreatment (Gelles, 1978; Straus, 1990b; Straus, Gelles, & Steinmetz, 1980; Wauchope & Straus, 1990)

■ Trends and cross-national comparison of the incidence of maltreatment (Gelles & Edfeldt, 1986; Hampton, Gelles, & Harrop, 1989;

Straus & Gelles, 1986; Straus & Kaufman Kantor, 1995)

- Risk factors for physical maltreatment (e.g., Cantrell, Carrico, Franklin, & Grubb, 1990; Eblen, 1987; Giles-Sims, 1985; Jouriles & Norwood, 1995; Meredith, Abbott, & Adams, 1986; Rollins & Ohenaba-Sakyi, 1990; Straus, 1979a; Straus & Kaufman Kantor, 1987)
- Effects of physical maltreatment (Dembo et al., 1989; Downs, Miller, & Panek, 1993; Gelles & Straus, 1987; Hotaling, Straus, & Lincoln, 1989; Jouriles & Norwood, 1995; O'Keefe, 1994)
- Effects of psychological maltreatment on children (Vissing, Straus, Gelles, & Harrop, 1991)

Description and Theoretical Rationale of the CTS

Description

The CTS is intended to measure the tactics or behaviors used by parents when there is conflict or hostility toward a child. It is not intended to measure the existence of or the amount of conflict or hostility, although one can assume that conflict or hostility exists when there is psychological or physical aggression against a child (see Straus, 1979b, for the theoretical distinctions between conflict, hostility, and conflict tactics).

The CTS begins with the statement "Parents and children use many different ways of trying to settle differences between them. I'm going to read a list of some things that you and ... (name of child) ... might have done *when you had a problem with this child.* I would like you to tell me how often you did it with ... (him/her) ... in the past year."

Following this is a list that begins with the items from the Nonviolent Discipline scale, such as "Discussed an issue calmly," and then goes on to the items in the Psychological Aggression scale, such as "Insulted or swore at him/her," and ends with the Physical Assault or "violence" items, such as "Slapped or spanked him/her" and "Kicked, bit, or hit with fist."

There have been four versions of the CTS (see the test manual, Straus, 1996). Because there is

rarely a need to use previous versions, this chapter refers entirely to the most recent versions. All versions of the CTS can be used in face-to-face interviews, telephone interviews, or with minor alterations, as a self-administered questionnaire.

Rationale for Focus on Acts of Maltreatment

The CTS was designed on the premise that physical and verbal attacks on children are inherently acts of maltreatment, regardless of whether an injury occurs. For this reason, with certain exceptions, the CTS scales are identified in this chapter as measures of maltreatment. Of course, information on injuries resulting from acts of maltreatment is also important, and for some purposes, essential. Nevertheless, for the reasons given below, it is important to measure acts of maltreatment and injury separately.

The conceptual issue that is most relevant for understanding the CTS is the difference between a measure of maltreatment based on an *injury* as compared to a measure based on *acts of maltreatment.* Legal and administrative definitions recognize both aspects but put primary reliance on injury. For example, the definition in the federal Child Abuse Act of 1974 (Public Law 93-247) begins, "The physical or mental *injury* . . . " (emphasis added), and then adds, " . . . or maltreatment [that threatens a child's health or welfare]." Similarly, the National Committee for Prevention of Child Abuse (1985) defines physical abuse as "non-accidental *injury*" (emphasis added). However, sexual abuse is always defined in terms of acts, regardless of whether there is any evidence of injury. The CTS applies this principle to all types of maltreatment for the reasons listed below.

Consistent With Legal Usage. It is not generally realized that the law of assault *in respect to adults* makes an assault a crime regardless of whether it results in injury. As Marcus (1983) puts it: "Physical contact is not an element of the crime . . . [assault]." Or as the FBI's Uniform Crime Reports puts it: "Attempts are included [in the tabulation of aggravated assault] because it is not necessary that an injury results" (U.S. Department of Justice,

1985, p. 21). However, in the United States and most other countries, the assault statutes contain an exception from prosecution for parents who assault a child for purposes of discipline and control. The severity of the assault that parents are permitted varies tremendously between societies and between historical eras (Korbin, 1987; Radbill, 1987) and between groups within a society (Gelles & Straus, 1979; Giovannoni & Becerra, 1979). At some point, however, all societies and groups draw a line.

Injury and Assault Loosely Linked. A second reason for making acts the criterion for child maltreatment is that the connection between assaults and injury is far from direct. In most instances, a child who is kicked or thrown against a wall will not be injured enough to require medical care. Only a small proportion of confirmed cases of physical abuse involve injury that requires medical care (Garbarino, 1986). Similarly, only a small proportion of battered women suffer injuries that need medical care (Stets & Straus, 1990). Conversely, a child who is "only" slapped might fall and hit his or her head on an object and be seriously injured. This chance aspect of injury may be one of the reasons why the legal definition of assault is based on the act carried out rather than whether an injury was produced.

More Realistic Estimate of Prevalence. Because most instances of physical maltreatment do not result in an injury that needs medical attention, statistics based on injury underestimate the extent of child maltreatment by a huge amount. Consequently, injury-based statistics can give a misleading picture of the need for treatment and prevention programs.

Permits Investigation of the Link Between Maltreatment and Injury. By measuring assaultive acts (both physical and psychological) separately from injuries, it is possible to investigate such issues as the circumstances under which injury does and does not result, and the type of acts that are most likely to result in injury. For example, Vissing and associates (1991) found that verbal aggression

by parents is associated with a higher rate of psychological injury than is severe physical aggression. If the measure of maltreatment had required an injury, that issue could not have been investigated because all children in both groups would have been injured.

Ignores Psychological Consequences of Physical Assaults. Another reason for the focus on acts is that some of the most serious consequences of physical maltreatment are likely to be psychological, and therefore not easily observed. For children this can include low self-esteem, aggressiveness, and delinquency (Hotaling et al., 1989).

Reflects Humane Values. A final reason for focusing on acts, despite the great importance of injuries, is a moral or humane values criterion. It should not be necessary for a child to be injured to classify certain parental behavior as abusive. From the perspective of this value orientation, punching or kicking a child is *inherently* wrong, even though no injury occurs.

Despite these arguments, the distinction between acts and injuries is not that clear. In the long run, it is doubtful if a society would define an act as abusive if it did not tend to result in injury. In addition, for certain immediate purposes, such as estimating the need for medical or psychological services, data on injuries are the most appropriate measure. It is also important to recognize that use of acts of maltreatment, rather than injuries, can cause misunderstanding by those who think of child abuse as indicating an injured child.

The CTS Physical and Psychological Maltreatment Measures

Prevalence and Chronicity Measures

Each of the CTS scales and subscales can be used to estimate *prevalence* rates, such as a rate per 1,000 children, or a percentage, that is, a rate per 100 children. The scales can also be used to measure the *chronicity* of maltreatment, that is, among those known to have physically or psychologically mistreated a child, how often it occurred. Finally, the CTS scales can be used to classify cases into types, such as no violence, minor assaults only (i.e., ordinary corporal punishment, but nothing more severe), severe assault, and very severe assault.

Criteria for Maltreatment

Normative Criteria. As suggested earlier, the acts that constitute maltreatment are, to a considerable extent, a matter of social norms and administrative practice. Spanking or slapping a child, or even hitting a child with an object such as a stick, hairbrush, or belt, is not maltreatment provided no injury occurs, according to either the legal or informal norms of American society, although it is in Sweden and several other countries (Straus, 1994). The CTS attempts to take such normative factors into consideration by giving users a choice of measures that draw the line between discipline and maltreatment at different points.

Severity and Chronicity Criteria. Operationalization of maltreatment is further complicated by the need to consider the chronicity of assaults, or combinations of severity and chronicity. For physical maltreatment, the line has usually been drawn on the basis of the severity of the assault. For psychological maltreatment, the line has been drawn on the basis of chronicity. However, research is needed on the efficacy of these and alternative procedures, including combinations of chronicity and severity (as in *DSM-IV*; American Psychiatric Association, 1994).

Physical Maltreatment Measures

Several physical maltreatment subscales can be constructed from the CTS Physical Assault items.

Very Severe Assault (also called Severe Physical Abuse). This subscale consists of assaultive acts such as kicking, punching, burning, and attacks with weapons that are almost universally regarded as indicators of abuse. The Very Severe Assault subscale is probably the closest approximation to the behavior that is

likely to produce a report of abuse to CPS in each of the states.

Severe Assault (also called Physical Abuse). Although the Very Severe Assault subscale may be the most suitable measure for purposes of estimating the number of children in need of official intervention, it underestimates the number of children who are being severely assaulted because it excludes the item on hitting a child with an object. This item was omitted from the Severe Assault subscale because the object is often a traditionally established object such as a hairbrush or belt. Although the percentage of the population who follow that tradition is declining, it is still legally permissible (see, e.g., *New Hampshire v. Johnson,* 1992). However, if an adult were to be hit with a hairbrush or belt, it would be considered a serious assault, and one can argue that the same standard should apply to children. The Severe Assault subscale does that. The rate of physically maltreated children, when measured by the CTS1 Severe Assault subscale, is almost 5 times times greater than when the Very Severe Assault subscale is used because the Very Severe Assault subscale includes only attacks that are more dangerous than hitting with an object.

Frequency Times Severity Weighted (FS) Scale. The FS scale method of scoring the physical assault items takes into account both the chronicity and the severity of assaults on children by their parents. Severity (in the sense of injury-producing potential) is indicated by weighting the CTS1 items as follows: Items K, L, and M (the minor assault acts) are unweighted, that is, they have a weight of 1; Item N, kick, bit, punch = 2; Item O, hit with object = 3; Item P, beat up = 4; Item Q, burned, scalded = 5; Item R, threatened with a knife or gun = 6; Item S, used knife or gun = 8.

The FS scale is computed by multiplying the severity weight for each item by the frequency ("chronicity") with which it occurred, and summing the products. This procedure assigns a much higher score to children who are attacked with a weapon than to those who are slapped or spanked, and at the same time allows for the fact that chronic slapping or spanking is abusive.

Because the FS scale is a continuous variable, it would be helpful to establish a threshold to demarcate a level of assault that is considered as requiring intervention. There is an obvious need for research on this issue. One approach would be a logistic regression analysis using injury as the dependent variable. Such an analysis could determine if there is a threshold beyond which the probability of injury increases sharply.

Parental Assault Types. This procedure uses the physical assault items to classify parents into one of the following four types:

1. Nonviolent: Parents who did not use of any of the CTS assault items.
2. Minor assault: Parents whose physical assaults are confined to items in the Minor Assault subscale, roughly corresponding to legal corporal punishment.
3. Severe assault: Parents who hit the child with an object (CTS1 Item O) but did not use any of the acts judged to be more dangerous (CTS1 Items N, P, Q, R, S).
4. Very severe assault: CTS1 Items N, P, Q, R, or S.

A similar typology can be constructed using the CTSPC physical assault items.

Severity and Chronicity. The above procedures, with the exception of the FS scale, do not allow for the fact that chronic use of spanking and slapping is a form of physical abuse even though it may pose little danger of injury. Hotaling et al. (1989) therefore used two criteria to identify cases of child maltreatment: Either the parent engaged in one or more of the acts in the Severe Assault subscale or the parent engaged in a very high frequency (the 90th percentile) of minor assaults such as slapping or spanking.

Corporal Punishment. The Minor Assault subscale has been used to measure legally permissible corporal punishment (Straus, 1994). However, there is wide disagreement about the boundary of legitimate corporal pun-

ishment. One of the items in dispute is hitting with an object such as a hairbrush or belt. There is also disagreement about including throwing something at the child.

Just as certain types of objects are traditionally legitimate for hitting a child, there are also types of objects that can be thrown. For example, one can throw a bucket of water, but not a pot of hot water. In general, American cultural norms permit parents to throw objects that carry a small risk of injury.

If both hitting with an object and throwing things are culturally permissible, why was hitting with an object included in the Severe Assault (physical abuse) subscale and throwing something included in the Minor Assault (corporal punishment) subscale? The reason is our judgment that hitting a child with a stick, belt, hairbrush, and so on carries a higher risk of injury to the child than does throwing things at a child because the object thrown is typically something having low risk of injury.

There might also be an objection to including pushing, shoving, and grabbing as indicators of corporal punishment. They are included because these acts are among the most frequently used methods of corporal punishment. But this is often not realized by parents who grab and shove because it is usually embedded in getting a child to go somewhere or come from somewhere. An example is a child who will not get out of the car and is grabbed roughly by the angry parent and jerked out of the car with far more force than is necessary. The rough handling part of grabbing and moving the child is a type of corporal punishment and, as noted above, a type that is believed to be extremely frequent.

The most important limitation of the CTS as a measure of corporal punishment, however, is that the CTS asks about what happened in the previous 12 months. Spanking, hand slapping, and other modes of corporal punishment, however, occur on average 2 or 3 times a week with preschool children (Straus, 1994). Corporal punishment is such an everyday, taken-for-granted part of child rearing that parents do not realize how often they have done it during the previous 12 months. The rate based on asking about the previous week is several times greater than asking about what happened in the past year, but is also an underestimate. For this reason the CTSPC includes supplemental questions about corporal punishment in the previous week.

Psychological Maltreatment Measures

Conceptualization. The Psychological Aggression scale of the CTS measures verbal and symbolic communications that are intended to cause psychological pain or fear on the part of the child. The scale covers only a limited aspect of the many forms of maltreatment to which labels such as psychological maltreatment has been applied (see Vissing et al., 1991, for a conceptual analysis). Psychological aggression as just defined may be inflicted as a means to some other end, for example, a parent who attempts to end some objectionable behavior by exclaiming, "Stop it, you dummy." This is what Gelles and Straus (1979) identify as "instrumental" aggression. Or the psychological aggression may be an end in itself, for example, a parent is angry with a child and expresses the anger by a deprecating remark such as, "You're stupid." Gelles and Straus label this "expressive" aggression.

Psychological Aggression Scale. As in the case of physical assault, contemporary social norms seem to tolerate a certain amount of psychological aggression by parents. Just as an occasional spanking does not constitute "physical maltreatment," occasional psychological aggression does not constitute "psychological maltreatment." It is difficult to know at what point psychological aggression by parents becomes psychological maltreatment according to contemporary American norms, just as it is difficult to draw the line between corporal punishment and physical abuse. In the case of physical assaults, the CTS relies mainly on the dangerousness of the assault because there is agreement that the items in the Severe Assault subscale, such as kicking a child, are more dangerous than slapping a child's hand. However, there is no similar consensus on which psychologically aggressive acts are more dangerous. Consequently, we used the chronicity of psychological ag-

gression as the criterion. In the absence of established standards, the results of applying three thresholds to the parents in the 1985 National Family Violence Survey are presented below.

Annual Chronicity Threshold	Rate Per 1,000	Estimated No. of Children
10 or more instances	257	16,190,000
20 or more instances	138	870,000
25 or more instances	113	712,000

Even using 25 or more instances of psychological aggression as the criterion produces a rate of psychological maltreatment that is 113 times greater than the rate of 1 per 1,000 confirmed cases of emotional maltreatment reported to state CPS (National Center on Child Abuse and Neglect, 1996).

Reliability, Validity, and Norms

Reliability

Internal consistency reliability, as measured by coefficient alpha, of the CTS1 Physical Assault scale has ranged from .42 to .71 with an average of .58 across eight samples or subsamples (Amato, 1991; Kaufman Kantor, Jasinski, & Aldarondo, 1994; Straus & Gelles, 1986; Straus et al., 1980; Straus, Hamby, Finkelhor, et al., 1996). The internal consistency of the Psychological Aggression scale has ranged from .62 to .77 with an average of .68 (Kaufman Kantor et al., 1994; Straus & Gelles, 1986; Straus et al., 1980; Straus, Hamby, Finkelhor, et al., 1996).

Amato (1991) found a test-retest reliability for reports of physical assault (over a 14-week period) of .80. Although this is a good test-retest reliability, the internal consistency of these scales is lower than would be desired. It indicates that parents who engage in one of the acts of maltreatment in each scale typically do not engage in the others. The discussion section of the paper on the CTSPC (Straus, Hamby, Finkelhor, et al., 1996) analyzes possible reasons for the low reliability. Despite the lack of internal consistency reliability, there is considerable evidence indicating the validity of the CTS.

Validity

Interfamily Agreement. Some studies have compared parents' and children's responses to the Physical Assault scale. McCloskey and Figueredo (1995) found that mother's and child's reports of father's aggressive behavior were significantly related. Jouriles and Norwood (1995) reported correlations ranging from .30 to .46 for mother's and child's reports of both maternal and paternal aggression. Richters and Martinez (1993) report a high correlation among violent families (.67) between parents' reports of spousal assault (CTS) and child's report of witnessing assault in the family. Kruttschnitt and Dornfeld (1992) reported high agreement between mothers and children for aggression toward children (average 87%), but the high agreement was largely due to agreement on rates of nonoccurrence. Of the violent events that were reported by at least five mothers, the average kappa was .42. Other studies have included two or more informants (e.g., Kolko, Kazdin, Thomas, & Day, 1993; O'Keefe, 1994) but have not reported intrafamily agreement. More research in this area is needed, especially for samples that include high enough rates of assault to calculate stable estimates of the agreement for the *occurrence* of assault.

Nonzero Prevalence Rates. Contrary to concerns that a random sample of parents interviewed by a stranger would not divulge abusive behavior, the rates of maltreatment revealed by the CTS and the CTSPC (reported in Straus & Gelles, 1988, 1990, and in Straus, Hamby, Finkelhor, et al., 1996) are many times higher than the rate for abuse cases known to CPS. This is consistent with the long-standing belief of case workers that there are many times more cases than are referred to them.

Another bit of evidence confirming the ability of the CTS to obtain data on assault is the consistency of the National Family Violence Survey rates with the rate obtained by the randomized response technique, which is widely assumed to be able to elicit more complete reporting of deviant behavior. Zdep and Rhodes (1976) used this technique, which guarantees the anonymity of the respondent, to estimate the prevalence of child maltreatment. Their estimate of 15% is almost identical to the rate obtained that year by the National Family Violence Survey using the CTS.

Not Confounded With Social Desirability Response Sets. A major threat to the validity of all self-report data is confounding with "social desirability response sets." It is almost certain that many parents who respond to the CTS questions do not reveal incidents that actually occurred. Because this is the case, differences in the maltreatment rate between groups of respondents, such as those with low and high education, may reflect a greater concern of one group to present itself in a favorable light. Several studies have investigated this possibility for reports of assault on a spouse or dating partner (e.g., Arias & Beach, 1987; Saunders, 1986; Saunders & Hanusa, 1986). Surprisingly, all found weak or nonsignificant correlations with standard measures of social desirability response sets. A meta-analytic review of these studies (Sugarman & Hotaling, in press) found an average effect of −.18. Some studies have used a response set score as a statistical control, but it did not change the findings. Although social desirability seems to have been measured in only one child maltreatment study (Newberger & White, 1987), the findings are similar to those just summarized for spouse maltreatment.

"Lower Bound" Estimates. Despite the ability of the CTS to elicit information from parents on physical maltreatment, and despite the evidence that the CTS is not confounded with social desirability response sets, it is best to regard the results of using the CTS as "lower bound" estimates. This is because, even with the best designed instrument, not every parent will be willing or able to divulge such information. Consequently, although the CTS rates of physical maltreatment are several times higher than the rate based on cases known to

CPS, the actual prevalence rate is probably even higher.

Construct Validity. The construct validity of the CTS can be assessed by the degree to which use of the CTS results in findings that are consistent with theoretical or empirical propositions about the aspect of maltreatment that the instrument purports to measure. Some examples of such findings are listed below.

- There is a broad consensus that stress increases the risk of child maltreatment, and the results of two studies using the CTS are consistent with that theory (Eblen, 1987; Straus & Kaufman Kantor, 1987).
- Studies using the CTS show that parents who were victims of assault as children have a higher rate of maltreatment toward their own children (Straus, 1990b; Straus et al., 1980); these findings are consistent with social learning theory and with many empirical studies (see meta-analysis by Hotaling & Sugarman, 1986).
- Children who were victims of severe physical assault have much higher rates of psychological problems, vandalism, theft, and drug use (Dembo et al., 1989; Downs et al., 1993; Gelles & Straus, 1988, 1990; Hotaling et al., 1989; Jouriles & Norwood, 1995; O'Keefe, 1994).
- Vissing et al. (1991) found that the more psychological aggression a child was exposed to, the higher the probability of delinquency, excessive aggression, and interpersonal problems.

All of the above findings are consistent with "strong" theories and previous empirical findings and therefore contribute to confidence in the construct validity of the CTS.

Norms

Normative tables for the CTS1 based on a 1985 nationally representative sample of 3,232 children are given in the appendix to Straus and Gelles (1990). Normative tables for the CTSPC based on a 1995 nationally representative sample are given in the manual for the CTS (Straus, 1996).

Evaluation of the CTS as a Measure of Child Maltreatment

Limitations of the CTS

Some of the shortcomings of the CTS as a measure of child maltreatment reflect the fact that it was originally developed for use in research on *physical* abuse of *spouses* and then modified slightly to apply to child maltreatment. The following indicates how the CTSPC deals with some of these shortcomings, but others remain.

1. *Some Physical Assault Items Are Not Well Suited To Infants.* For example, shaking a child of 6 is appropriately labeled as minor assault, but can be life threatening for an infant. The CTSPC includes an item on shaking and provides for differential scoring according to the age of the child.

2. *Some CTS1 Reasoning Scale Items Are Not Appropriate for Use With Young Children.* The Reasoning scale has been replaced by the Nonviolent Discipline scale in the CTSPC.

3. *Referent for CTS1 Item O Is Ambiguous.* This item, "Hit or tried to hit with something," does not indicate the type of object. The CTSPC omits this item.

4. *One-Year Referent Period.* The CTS asks respondents to recall what happened in the past year—something that is often unrealistic. The one-year referent period is used because it seemed to pose the lesser of two problems: the problem of accuracy of recall, and the problem of low rates and even more highly skewed distributions if a shorter referent period is used.

The one-year referent period is primarily a means of uncovering more cases of maltreatment than might occur with a shorter period, such as a month. A one-month referent period will omit cases where maltreatment did not occur in the previous months, but had occurred in a prior month that year. However, this is partly counteracted because, with a one-year referent period, incidents that occurred more than a month previously may be forgotten. Using a one-month referent period and multiplying by 12 to produce annual prevalence rates might yield a much higher rate. However, although that may be correct for producing aggregate estimates for a population, a one-month referent period would be less satisfactory as a screening tool because it is likely to omit many cases. Empirical research is needed to learn the consequences of using different referent periods.

In the case of corporal punishment of young children, for the reasons given previously, even a one-month recall period is unrealistic. Consequently, the CTSPC includes supplemental questions on corporal punishment and other disciplinary practices in the past week.

5. *Falsification of Responses.* Prevalence rates based on the CTS must be considered as lower-bound estimates. When the CTS is used for clinical screening the problem is more serious because lying is a characteristic of one type of abuser—those with antisocial personalities (cf. Holtzworth-Munroe & Stuart, 1994). Thus, the CTS is likely to miss one of the most dangerous types of parents. Repeated in-depth interviews, or "disguised" measures (Straus, 1964), probably have the best chance with this type of parent.

An additional possibility for detecting refusals and "faking good" is to examine the responses on the Reasoning and Psychological Aggression scales. Richters and Martinez (1993) reported that a small number of their respondents failed to endorse *any* item—even "discuss calmly." They concluded that these individuals had not accurately completed the questionnaire. This conclusion is supported by the fact that virtually all individuals receive nonzero scores on Reasoning in the major studies that have been conducted. Very few, in fact, score zero even on Psychological Aggression and we also recommend that such a protocol be interpreted cautiously.

6. *Low Internal Consistency Reliability.* The CTS was designed on the assumptions that it is not practical to include a truly comprehensive list of abusive acts and that a sample of abusive acts would be sufficient because abusive parents seldom limit their attacks to just one or two types of attack. Thus, parents who punch a child are also likely to engage in other types of severe attack. However, the low reliability coefficients reported earlier, and the even lower coefficients for the subscales reported in Straus, Hamby, Finkelhor, et al. (1996), indicate very low correlations between items. For this reason, additional items increase the number of cases detected (Straus, 1990a). Consequently, the CTSPC has been expanded from 18 to 22 items.

7. *No Empirical Data on Chronicity Thresholds for Psychological Maltreatment.* The thresholds for identifying cases of psychological maltreatment are not based on empirical evidence. Vissing and associates (1991) found a linear increase in the probability of a highly aggressive child with each increase in instances of psychological aggression, whereas for delinquency, there was a nonlinear relation: A rapid increase in delinquency did not begin until about 20 instances of psychological aggression. These findings suggest that it will not be easy to determine a specific threshold because adverse effects begin at different points depending on the outcome variable. Research on appropriate thresholds is needed.

8. *Insufficient Range of Severity in Psychological Aggression Items.* The psychological aggression items in the CTS have not been classified into more and less severe on the basis of their injury-producing potential. The CTSPC includes items that are intended to differ enough in severity to distinguish between minor and severe acts of psychological aggression.

Alternative Measures

The problems just summarized suggest that despite the evidence of construct validity presented earlier, there are grounds for caution. Consequently, a decision concerning whether to use the CTS will depend on the alternatives. This section therefore reviews some of the other methods that have been used in research on physical abuse of children.

Officially Reported Cases. Annual statistics are compiled on the number of child abuse cases reported to CPS under the mandatory reporting laws that are in effect in all the states (National Center on Child Abuse and Neglect, 1996). These are the most widely known and widely accepted statistics on child maltreatment in the United States. However, it is generally acknowledged that there are many more maltreated children than are officially reported. Thus, the 1984 rate for physical abuse cases known to CPS was estimated by Straus and Gelles (1988) to be 6.8 per 1,000 children. By contrast, the CTS rate using Very Severe Assault as the criterion is 23 per 1,000, and 110 per 1,000 when using Severe Assault. Thus, the CTS rate is from 3.4 to 16 times greater than the officially reported rate. Similar results have been found with the CTSPC (Straus, Hamby, Finkelhor, et al., 1996).

National Incidence Studies. These studies tabulated all cases of child abuse known to service providers in a sample of 26 counties (National Center on Child Abuse and Neglect, 1981; Sedlak & Broadhurst, 1996). The procedure went beyond the official reporting system described above by also collecting data on cases known to personnel of community institutions (schools, hospitals, police, courts), regardless of whether the cases had been officially reported. The 1980 study found a physical abuse rate of 3.4 per 1,000 children. This is 26% higher than the rate of officially reported cases of physical abuse in 1980. However, because the CTS1 rate was more than 300% greater than the CPS rate, it suggests that most cases of maltreatment are not known to any service provider. The Third National Incidence Study (Sedlak & Broadhurst, 1996) found a rate of 9.1 per 1,000, but even this much higher rate is only about a fifth of the Severe Assault rate of 49 per 1,000 based on a 1995 national survey of parents using the CTSPC (Straus, Hamby, Finkelhor, et al., 1996).

Intervention Rates and Prevalence Rates. The differences between the rates produced by the CTS and those produced by the two methods just described can be interpreted as showing that the latter methods result in a severe underestimate of the number of physically abused children in the United States. Although this may be correct, it is more useful to think of the CPS rate and the CTS rate as measures of different phenomena. The CPS rate is best thought of as an "intervention" rate because it consists entirely of cases in which there has been an intervention in the form of a report of abuse to CPS. The CTS rate is best thought of as an approximation to a period-specific prevalence rate. Intervention rates and prevalence rates are so different that under some circumstances, they can have a negative correlation. Thus, Straus and Gelles argue that the year-by-year steady increase in the intervention rate (CPS reports) between 1975 and 1985 is one of the reasons why the prevalence rate (as measured by the CTS) decreased during this period, and have continued to decrease (Straus & Kaufman Kantor, 1995).

Prediction Instruments. There instruments are intended to identify parents who have a higher than normal risk of abusing their children. The Adult-Adolescent Parenting Inventory (ASPI) of Bavolek (1984) focuses on the behavior of the parent toward the child and includes subscales for use of corporal punishment, inappropriate expectations, lack of empathy, and role reversal. The Child Abuse Potential (CAP) inventory of Milner (1986), on the other hand, focuses on the attitudes and personality of the parent and includes subscales for Distress, Rigidity, Unhappiness, Problems With Child and Self, Problems With Family, and Problems From Others. Other instruments are reviewed in Schneider, Helfer, and Hoffmeister (1980).

Despite occasional use of terminology that might suggest otherwise, these instruments do not measure the occurrence of acts of physical abuse. For example, Milner's CAP inventory results in an overall measure called the Abuse Scale. However, none of the items refers to physical assaults, nor should they. This is because the instrument is a tool for prevention work and is intended to identify parents at risk of being abusive before abuse actually occurs.

There is a certain irony in the fact that these instruments were developed for use in programs designed to provide services that can aid high-risk parents avoid having the risk become a reality. The irony is that these instruments may be more appropriate for research than for prevention programs. The problem is not deficiencies in the instruments per se. The CAP inventory, for example, exemplifies sound psychometric techniques, including validity studies presented with commendable clarity in the test manual. The problem is the high incidence of "false positives" inherent in predicting any phenomenon with a low incidence rate (Light, 1973). For example, Milner administered the CAP inventory to abusing parents and to a comparison group. The discriminant analysis correctly classified 93% of parents. Assuming 93% accuracy and an incidence of clinically identifiable child abuse of 2%, application of the CAP inventory to all parents in a community would correctly identify 2 out of every 100 parents as being at high risk of being abusive and incorrectly identify 7. Thus, 78% of the cases assessed would be falsely labeled (cf. Light, 1973, p. 571, for estimation procedures).

Medical Diagnosis. Kempe, Silverman, Steele, Droegemueller, and Silver's (1962) article, which helped mobilize medical and public attention on child abuse, described the use of medical diagnostic techniques to distinguish between children who are the victims of accidental injury and those who are the victims of inflicted injuries. Studies of children admitted to emergency departments of urban hospitals for accidental injury suggest that about 10% of such children are abuse victims. Other studies (reviewed in Pless, Sibald, Smith, & Russell, 1987) have produced far lower figures. Regardless of which rate is correct, protocols for evaluating children admitted to emergency rooms (such as the SCAN Sheet described in Pless et al., 1987) are extremely important because they can identify children who are in the greatest need for protective services.

Even if all hospitals were to use a child abuse detection protocol, it would still leave undetected more than 95% of physically abused children. This is because, as noted in the discussion of why the CTS is based on assaults rather than injuries, less than 5% of child abuse cases known to CPS involve an injury that is serious enough to need hospital care. Most physically maltreated children (in contrast to the cases that make front-page headlines) involve repeated severe beatings, but not injuries. These children and parents are in dire need of assistance, but not medical assistance. Consequently, hospital-based detection methods serve a different purpose than self-report instruments such as the CTS.

Conclusions

■ This chapter describes and evaluates the CTS and its revision, the CTSPC, as a means of identifying cases of physical and psychological maltreatment of children. The internal consistency reliability of the CTS is low because parents who engage in one type of maltreatment do not necessarily mistreat the child in other ways. Despite this, when the CTS has been used in epidemiological surveys, it reveals many times more cases than have been reported to CPS. Nevertheless, rates based on the CTS must be regarded as lower-bound estimates. Similarly, clinical screening with the CTS, although identifying many cases that would not otherwise be known, will still miss a large number of cases. Research on the etiology and consequences of maltreatment has provided a substantial body of evidence indicating construct validity. The brevity and minimal reading level of the CTS make it feasible for clinical screening, for epidemiological survey research, for tracking progress among families receiving services, and for obtaining data on the effectiveness prevention and treatment programs.

Appendix A:
Original Conflict Tactics Scales (CTS1)
and Parent-Child
Conflict Tactics Scales (CTSPC)
Items Arranged by Scale and Subscale

CTS1	*CTSPC*
Reasoning	**Nonviolent Discipline**
A. Discussed an issue calmly with (child name)	A. Explained why something was wrong
B. Got information to back up your side of things	B. Put him/her in "time out" (or sent to his/her room)
C. Brought in, or tried to bring in, someone to help settle things	Q. Took away privileges or grounded him/her
	E. Gave him/her something else to do instead of what he/she was doing wrong
Psychological Aggression	**Psychological Aggression**
D. Insulted or swore at him/her	N. Threatened to spank or hit him/her but did not actually do it
E. Sulked or refused to talk about an issue	F. Shouted, yelled, or screamed at him/her
F. Stomped out of the room or house or yard	J. Swore or cursed at him/her
G. Cried (this item is not scored)	U. Called him/her dumb or lazy or some other name like that
H. Did or said something to spite him/her	L. Said you would send him/her away or kick him/her out of the house
I. Threatened to hit or throw something at him/her	
J. Threw or smashed or hit or kicked something	
Physical Assault	**Physical Assault**
Minor Assault (Corporal Punishment)	*Minor Assault (Corporal Punishment)*
K. Threw something at him/her	H. Spanked him/her on the bottom with your bare hand
L. Pushed, grabbed, or shoved him/her	D. Hit him/her on the bottom with something like a belt, hairbrush, a stick, or some other hard object
M. Slapped or spanked him/her	P. Slapped him/her on the hand, arm, or leg
	R. Pinched him/her
	C. Shook him/her (this is scored for Very Severe if the child is <2 years)
Severe Assault (Physical Abuse)	*Severe Assault (Physical Abuse)*
N. Kicked, bit, or hit him/her with a fist	V. Slapped him/her on the face or head or ears
O. Hit or tried to hit him/her with something	O. Hit him/her on some other part of the body besides the bottom with something like a belt, hairbrush, a stick, or some other hard object
P. Beat him/her up	
Q. Burned or scalded him/her	T. Threw or knocked him/her down
R. Threatened him/her with a knife or gun	G. Hit him/her with a fist or kicked him/her hard
S. Used a knife or fired a gun	
	Very Severe Assault (Severe Physical Abuse)
	K. Beat him/her up, that is, you hit him/her over and over as hard as you could
	I. Grabbed him/her around the neck and choked him/her
	M. Burned or scalded him/her on purpose
	S. Threatened him/her with a knife or gun

Appendix B:
Prevalence Rates and Chronicity

Each CTS maltreatment scale can be expressed as a measure of the prevalence of maltreatment, or as a measure of the chronicity of maltreatment.

The *prevalence* version of a CTS scale identifies cases who reported one or more abusive acts. It can be used clinically to identify maltreatment cases, or can be used in research to measure the percentage of a population who engaged in maltreatment.

The *chronicity* version of a CTS scale measures *how often* maltreatment occurred in an identified maltreatment case, or among a group of known abusers, for example, among cases confirmed by CPS.

Why Separate Measures of Prevalence and Chronicity Are Needed

When the items in each CTS scale are summed, the resulting measure is extremely skewed. Applying the Very Severe Assault subscale to the 1985 National Family Violence Survey data, for example, resulted in a distribution in which 97.7 of the cases have a score of zero. No transformation can normalize a distribution that skewed. Consequently, the sum of the items in the CTS Physical Assault scales cannot be used with statistical techniques (such as ordinary least square regression) that assume at least an approximately normal distribution. Moreover, the problem becomes worse when one attempts to improve the sensitivity of the scale by weighting according to the severity of the assault because this extends the tail of the distribution even further. The chronicity version of the CTS Maltreatment scale will be much closer to a normal distribution because it omits all cases with a score of zero.

Prevalence

At the individual case level, the prevalence measure is a dichotomy that indicates whether one or more instance of a type of maltreatment occurred during the referent period. When the CTS is used in research, the dichotomized CTS scales are the basis for computing rates because the mean of 0-1 dichotomy is a proportion. One need only multiply this by 100 to obtain a percentage, or by 1,000 to obtain a rate per 1,000.

Period-Specific Prevalence Rates. The standard version of the CTS asks the respondent about events in the previous year. This results in an annual prevalence rate, such as the percentage of a population who committed or suffered maltreatment per year. It has the advantage of being relatively easy for the general public to understand. Moreover, because annual prevalence rates are frequently used in epidemiology and criminology, expressing child maltreatment as a rate per thousand or a percentage (rate per hundred) permits comparisons with other related phenomena. For this reason most all the statistics in Straus et al. (1980) and Straus and Gelles (1990) are in the form of annual rates. However, the CTS can be administered with instructions to describe what happened in the previous month, 6 months, etc., or since the onset of treatment, since treatment was completed, etc.

Lifetime Prevalence Rate. The CTS obtains data on both the preceding 12 months and on whether each act had *ever* occurred. These data can be used to identify lifetime prevalence by coding children who were assaulted either during the referent year of the survey or at some previous time as 1, and all other children as 0. However, the rate estimated on the basis of this variable must be used with considerable caution because recall errors are almost certain to be large.

Chronicity

If the case or cases under study are those who committed a certain type of maltreatment, the sum of the CTS scale is automatically a measure of chronicity because there are no cases with a score of zero. The following procedure is for use when the sample is not made up of parents known to have mistreated a child.

Illustration of SPSS Commands to Compute Severe Assault Scales.
Where

SA = variable name for the Severe Assault scale
SAP = variable name for Severe Assault Prevalence scale
SAC = variable name for Severe Assault Chronicity scale
ITEM1, ITEM2, etc. = variable names for the severe assault items in the scale

Note: The following example is for CTS1 items. For the CTSPC items, Category 7 (not in last year but in some previous year) must first be recoded to zero.

COMPUTE SA = ITEM1 + ITEM2 + ITEM3, etc.
VARIABLE LABELS SA "SEVERE ASSAULT SCALE"

COMPUTE SAP = SAP
VARIABLE LABELS SAP "SEVERE ASSAULT: PREVALENCE"
RECODE SAP (1 THROUGH HIGH = 1)

COMPUTE SAC = SA
VARIABLE LABELS SAC "SEVERE ASSAULT: PREVALENCE"
RECODE SA (0 = SYSMIS)

Additional information on scoring the CTS is in the appendix to Straus and Gelles (1990) and in Straus, Hamby, Finkelhor, et al. (1996).

References

Amato, P. R. (1991). Psychological distress and the recall of childhood family characteristics. *Journal of Marriage and the Family, 53*, 1011-1019.

American Psychiatric Association. (1994). *Diagnostic and statistical manual of mental disorders* (4th ed.). Washington, DC: Author.

Arias, I., & Beach, S. R. H. (1987). Validity of self-reports of marital violence. *Journal of Family Violence, 2*, 139-149.

Bavolek, S. J. (1984). *Handbook for the Adult-Adolescent Parenting Inventory (AAPI)*. Schaumburg, IL: Family Development Associates.

Cantrell, P. J., Carrico, M. F., Franklin, J. N., & Grubb, H. J. (1990). Violent tactics in family conflict relative to familial and economic factors. *Psychological Reports, 66*, 823-828.

Dawes, R. M., Faust, D., & Meehl, P. E. (1989). Clinical versus actuarial judgment. *Science, 243*, 1668-1674.

Dembo, R., Williams, W., Berry, E., Wish, E. D., La Voie, L., Getreu, A., Schmeidler, J., & Washburn, M. (1989). Physical abuse, sexual victimization and illicit drug use: Replication of a structural analysis among a new sample of high risk youths. *Violence and Victims, 4*, 121-138.

Downs, W. R., Miller, B. A., & Panek, D. D. (1993). Differential patterns of partner-to-woman violence: A comparison of samples of community, alcohol-abusing, and battered women. *Journal of Family Violence, 8*, 113-135.

Eblen, C. N. (1987). *The influence of stress and social support upon child abuse.* Unpublished doctoral dissertation, Arizona State University, Tempe.

Fink, A., & McCloskey, L. (1990). Moving child abuse and neglect prevention programs forward: Improving program evaluations. *Child Abuse & Neglect, 14*, 187-206.

Garbarino, J. (1986). Can we measure success in preventing child abuse? Issues in policy, programming and research. *Child Abuse & Neglect, 10*, 143-156.

Gelles, R. J. (1978). Violence toward children in the United States. *American Journal of Orthopsychiatry, 48*, 580-592.

Gelles, R. J., & Edfeldt, A. W. (1986). Violence towards children in the United States and Sweden. *Child Abuse & Neglect, 10*, 501-510.

Gelles, R. J., & Straus, M. A. (1979). Determinants of violence in the family: Toward a theoretical integration. In W. R. Burr, R. Hill, F. I. Nye, & I. L. Reiss (Eds.), *Contemporary theories about the family* (pp. 549-581). New York: Free Press.

Gelles, R. J., & Straus, M. A. (1987). Is violence toward children increasing? A comparison of 1975 and 1985 national survey rates. *Journal of Interpersonal Violence, 2*, 212-222.

Gelles, R. J., & Straus, M. A. (1988). *Intimate violence.* New York: Simon & Schuster.

Gelles, R. J., & Straus, M. A. (1990). The medical and psychological costs of family violence. In M. A. Straus & R. J. Gelles, *Physical violence in American families: Risk factors and adaptations to violence in 8,145 families.* New Brunswick, NJ: Transaction.

Giles-Sims, J. (1985). A longitudinal study of battered children of battered wives. *Family Relations, 34*, 205-210.

Giovannoni, J. M., & Becerra, R. M. (1979). *Defining child abuse.* New York: Free Press.

Hampton, R. L., Gelles, R. J., & Harrop, J. W. (1989). Is violence in Black families increasing? A comparison of 1975 and 1985 National Survey rates. *Journal of Marriage and the Family, 51*, 969-980.

Holtzworth-Munroe, A., & Stuart, G. L. (1994). Typologies of male batterers: Three subtypes and the differences among them. *Psychological Bulletin, 116*, 476-497.

Hotaling, G. T., Straus, M. A., & Lincoln, A. J. (1989). Intrafamily violence, and crime and violence outside the family. In L. Ohlin & M. Tonry (Eds.), *Family violence* (pp. 315-375). Chicago: University of Chicago Press.

Hotaling, G. T., & Sugarman, D. B. (1986). An analysis of risk markers in husband to wife violence: The current state of knowledge. *Violence and Victims, 1,* 101-124.

Jouriles, E. N., & Norwood, W. D. (1995). Physical aggression toward boys and girls in families characterized by the battering of women. *Journal of Family Psychology, 9,* 69-78.

Kaufman Kantor, G., Jasinski, J. L., & Aldarondo, E. (1994). Socioeconomic status and incidence of marital violence in Hispanic families. *Violence and Victims, 9,* 207-222.

Kempe, C. H., Silverman, F. N., Steele, B. F., Droegemueller, W., & Silver, H. K. (1962). The battered child syndrome. *Journal of the American Medical Association, 181,* 17-24.

Knudsen, D. D. (1988). *Child protective services: Discretion, decisions and dilemmas.* Springfield, IL: Charles C Thomas.

Kolko, D. J., Kazdin, A. E., Thomas, A. M., & Day, B. (1993). Heightened child physical abuse potential. *Journal of Interpersonal Violence, 8,* 169-192.

Korbin, J. E. (1987). Child abuse and neglect: The cultural context. In R. E. Helfer & R. S. Kempe (Eds.), *The battered child* (pp. 23-41). Chicago: University of Chicago Press.

Kruttschnitt, C., & Dornfeld, M. (1992). Will they tell? Assessing preadolescents reports of family violence. *Journal of Research in Crime and Delinquency, 29,* 136-147.

Light, R. J. (1973). Abused and neglected children in America: A study of alternative policies. *Harvard Educational Review, 43,* 556-598.

Marcus, P. (1983). Assault and battery. In S. H. Kadish (Ed.), *Encyclopedia of crime and justice* (pp. 88-90). New York: Free Press.

McCloskey, L., & Figueredo, A. J. (1995). *Socioeconomic and coercive power within the family: Correlates of wife and child abuse.* Unpublished manuscript, University of Arizona.

Meredith, W. H., Abbott, D. A., & Adams, S. L. (1986). Family violence: Its relation to marital and parental satisfaction and family strengths. *Journal of Family Violence, 1,* 299-305.

Milner, J. S. (1986). *The Child Abuse Potential inventory: Manual* (2nd ed.). Webster, NC: Psytec.

Morash, M. (1987). Wife battering. *Criminal Justice Abstracts, 18,* 252-271.

National Center on Child Abuse and Neglect. (1981). *Study findings: National study of incidence and severity of child abuse and neglect.* Washington, DC: Department of Health, Education, and Welfare.

National Center on Child Abuse and Neglect. (1996). *Child maltreatment 1994: Reports from the states to the National Center on Child Abuse and Neglect.* Washington, DC: Government Printing Office.

National Committee for Prevention of Child Abuse. (1985). *Long range plan: 1985-1990, executive summary.* Chicago: Author.

Newberger, C., & White, K. M. (1987, April). *Parental awareness and conflict tactics in relation to individual and environmental variables.* Paper presented at the biennial meeting of the Society for Research in Child Development, Baltimore.

New Hampshire v. Johnson, No. 90-533 (New Hampshire Supreme Court, June 25, 1992).

O'Keefe, M. (1994). Linking marital violence, mother-child/father-child aggression, and child behavior problems. *Journal of Family Violence, 9,* 63-78.

Pless, I. B., Sibald, A. D., Smith, M. A., & Russell, M. D. (1987). A reappraisal of the frequency of child abuse seen in pediatric emergency rooms. *Child Abuse & Neglect, 11,* 193-200.

Radbill, S. X. (1987). Children in a world of violence: A history of child abuse. In R. E. Helfer & R. S. Kempe (Eds.), *The battered child* (4th ed.). Chicago: University of Chicago Press.

Richters, J. E., & Martinez, P. (1993). The NIMH Community Violence Project: I. Children as victims of and witnesses to violence. *Psychiatry, 56,* 7-21.

Rollins, B. C., & Ohenaba-Sakyi, Y. (1990). Physical violence in Utah households. *Journal of Family Violence, 5,* 301-309.

Saunders, D. G. (1986). When battered women use violence: Husband-abuse or self-defense? *Violence and Victims, 1,* 47-60.

Saunders, D. G., & Hanusa, D. (1986). Cognitive-behavioral treatment of men who batter: The short-term effects of group therapy. *Journal of Family Violence, 1,* 357-372.

Schneider, C., Helfer, R. E., & Hoffmeister, J. K. (1980). Screening for the potential to abuse: A review. In C. H. Kempe & R. E. Helfer (Eds.), *The battered child* (3rd ed., pp. 420-430). Chicago: University of Chicago Press.

Sedlak, A. J., & Broadhurst, D. D. (1996). *The third national incidence study of child abuse and neglect (NIS-3).* Washington, DC: U.S. Department of Health and Human Services, National Center on Child Abuse and Neglect.

Stets, J. E., & Straus, M. A. (1990). Gender differences in reporting marital violence and its medical and psychological consequences. In M. A. Straus & R. J. Gelles (Eds.), *Physical violence in American families: Risk factors and adaptations to violence in 8,145 families* (pp. 151-165). New Brunswick, NJ: Transaction.

Straus, M. A. (1964). Measuring families. In H. T. Christenson (Ed.), *Handbook of marriage and the family* (pp. 335-400). Chicago: Rand McNally.

Straus, M. A. (1973). A general systems theory approach to a theory of violence between family members. *Social Science Information, 12,* 105-125.

Straus, M. A. (1979a). Family patterns and child abuse in a nationally representative American sample. *Child Abuse & Neglect, 3,* 213-225.

Straus, M. A. (1979b). Measuring intrafamily conflict and violence: The Conflict Tactics (CT) Scales. *Journal of Marriage and the Family, 41,* 75-88.

Straus, M. A. (1990a). The Conflict Tactics Scales and its critics: An evaluation and new data on validity and reliability. In M. A. Straus & R. J. Gelles (Eds.), *Physical violence in American families: Risk factors and adap-*

tations to violence in 8,145 families (pp. 49-73). New Brunswick, NJ: Transaction.

Straus, M. A. (1990b). Corporal punishment, child abuse and wife beating: What do they have in common? In M. A. Straus & R. J. Gelles (Eds.), *Physical violence in American families: Risk factors and adaptations to violence in 8,145 families* (pp. 403-424). New Brunswick, NJ: Transaction.

Straus, M. A. (1994). *Beating the devil out of them: Corporal punishment in American families.* San Francisco: Jossey-Bass/Lexington.

Straus, M. A. (1996). *Manual for the Conflict Tactics Scales.* Durham: University of New Hampshire, Family Research Laboratory.

Straus, M. A., & Gelles, R. J. (1986). Societal change and change in family violence from 1975 to 1985 as revealed by two national surveys. *Journal of Marriage and the Family, 48,* 465-479.

Straus, M. A., & Gelles, R. J. (1988). How violent are American families? Estimates from the National Family Violence Resurvey and other studies. In M. A. Straus & R. J. Gelles (Eds.), *Physical violence in American families: Risk factors and adaptations to violence in 8,145 families* (pp. 95-112). New Brunswick, NJ: Transaction.

Straus, M. A., & Gelles, R. J. (Eds.). (1990). *Physical violence in American families: Risk factors and adaptations to violence in 8,145 families.* New Brunswick, NJ: Transaction.

Straus, M. A., Gelles, R. J., & Steinmetz, S. K. (1980). *Behind closed doors: Violence in the American family.* New York: Doubleday/Anchor.

Straus, M. A., Hamby, S. L., Boney-McCoy, S., & Sugarman, D. B. (1996). The revised Conflict Tactics Scales (CTS2): Development and preliminary psychometric data. *Journal of Family Issues, 17,* 283-316.

Straus, M. A., Hamby, S. L., Finkelhor, D., Moore, D., & Runyan, D. (1996). *Identification of child maltreatment with CTSPC: Development and psychometric data for a national sample of American parents.* Durham: University of New Hampshire, Family Research Laboratory.

Straus, M. A., & Kaufman Kantor, G. (1987). Stress and child abuse. In R. E. Helfer & R. S. Kempe (Eds.), *The battered child* (pp. 75-88). Chicago: University of Chicago Press.

Straus, M. A., & Kaufman Kantor, G. (1995, November). *Trends in physical abuse by parents from 1975 to 1992: A comparison of three national surveys.* Paper presented at the annual meeting of the American Society of Criminology, Boston.

Sugarman, D. B., & Hotaling, G. T. (in press). Intimate violence and social desirability: A meta-analytic review. *Journal of Interpersonal Violence.*

U.S. Department of Justice. (1985). *Crime in the United States.* Washington, DC: Government Printing Office.

Vissing, Y. M., Straus, M. A., Gelles, R. J., & Harrop, J. W. (1991). Verbal aggression by parents and psycho-social problems of children. *Child Abuse & Neglect, 15,* 223-238.

Wauchope, B., & Straus, M. A. (1990). Physical punishment and physical abuse of American children: Incidence rates by age, gender, and occupational class. In M. A. Straus & R. J. Gelles (Eds.), *Physical violence in American families: Risk factors and adaptations to violence in 8,145 families* (pp. 133-150). New Brunswick, NJ: Transaction.

Zdep, S. M., & Rhodes, I. N. (1976). Making the randomized response technique work. *Public Opinion Quarterly, 40,* 531-537.

CHAPTER 11

Methodological Issues in Classifying Maltreatment

An Examination of "Protective Issue" Children

Heather N. Taussig
Alan J. Litrownik

Researchers continue to focus on detailing the consequences of maltreatment; however, operationalizing the independent variable (i.e., maltreatment) has only recently received attention (cf. Cicchetti & Barnett, 1991; McGee, Wolfe, Yuen, Wilson, & Carnochan, 1995). As researchers become more interested in comparing the effects of different types of maltreatment, clearly defined and operational-

ized classification procedures become critical. Although classification has always been an important issue in studies of maltreatment, the majority of earlier studies typically compared a group of children who experienced a particular type of maltreatment (e.g., sexual abuse) to a nonabused control group (cf. Kendall-Tackett, Williams, & Finkelhor, 1993), or compared heterogeneous groups of maltreated children to

AUTHORS' NOTE: The research reported herein was supported by grants from the National Institute of Mental Health ("Screening Impact on Services and Costs for Foster Children") and the National Center on Child Abuse and Neglect ("Psychological Impact of Child Maltreatment"). We would like to express our appreciation to the project staff, interviewers, San Diego Department of Social Services, foster parents, and children who made this work possible. All correspondence and reprint requests should be directed to Alan Litrownik, Child and Family Research Group, 9245 Sky Park Court, Suite 228, San Diego, CA 92123.

nonmaltreated control groups (e.g., Kaufman, Cook, Arny, Jones, & Pittinsky, 1994; Shields, Cicchetti, & Ryan, 1994). The problem with these earlier approaches is that neither of them permits the comparison of the effects of different types of maltreatment, either individually or in combination.

As more researchers begin to try to tease apart the distinct effects of different types of maltreatment, many have encountered difficulties in their classification of maltreatment. The simplest method of classification is to place children into mutually exclusive groups based on the type of maltreatment they have experienced (e.g., sexual, physical, neglect). The problem with this approach, of course, is that maltreatment does not fit neatly into discrete categories. The majority of children who are identified as maltreated have experienced multiple types of maltreatment. For example, Manly, Cicchetti, and Barnett (1994) and McGee et al. (1995) reported that over 80% of the populations that they studied had experienced more than one type of maltreatment.

Some have dealt with this dilemma by according greater relative salience to certain maltreatment categories. For example, Manly et al. (1994) classified children into one of three groups: (a) those with any reports of sexual abuse, with or without other subtypes of maltreatment; (b) those with any reports of physical abuse, without sexual abuse and with or without physical neglect; and (c) those with physical neglect without physical abuse or sexual abuse. This classification system assumes a hierarchy of maltreatment types (i.e., sexual abuse is accorded the greatest salience and neglect is accorded the lowest), although the authors gave no theoretical or empirical justification for this classification scheme. Whenever researchers classify children who have experienced multiple types of maltreatment into discrete categories, information is lost, and although alternative approaches continue to be developed, there are still basic definitional problems that plague this area of research (Ammerman & Hersen, 1990; Cicchetti & Barnett, 1991; Herrenkohl, 1990).

Most of these definitional problems surround the question of what constitutes a case of abuse or neglect. Definitional differences occur across disciplines (e.g., medical, legal, sociological), as well as within (Cicchetti & Barnett, 1991). From a research perspective, clear definitions and standard methods of data collection are critical because the lack of specificity in defining or measuring maltreatment may obscure real differences between maltreatment groups as well as contribute to inconsistent findings across studies (Manly et al., 1994).

In addition to the definitional problems surrounding the various types of maltreatment, another classification issue that has recently been raised concerns how to treat children who are deemed *at risk* for experiencing maltreatment. Investigators' criteria differ greatly regarding participant inclusion in studies of maltreatment, and rarely are they delineated. In some studies, maltreatment has to be *substantiated* for the individual to meet study inclusion criteria. In others, children who are referred to protective services (prior to any substantiation) are included, as well as children who are believed to be at risk for experiencing a particular type of maltreatment. This lack of specificity regarding individuals' maltreatment characteristics across various studies greatly limits comparability (Ammerman & Hersen, 1990).

Many researchers who study maltreated children obtain their samples from protective services agencies and thus classify their participants' maltreatment status based on a review of records from these agencies. There are several advantages to using protective services case records to obtain samples for studies of maltreatment. First, researchers obtain the information from protective services caseworkers who have experience and training in this area. Second, it has been argued that cases obtained from social service records reflect a fairly representative sample of children who are experiencing maltreatment. Finally, with the use of protective services records, an investigator can select cases that have been legally substantiated, and thus these cases typically represent the more severe instances of maltreatment (Cicchetti & Barnett, 1991).

Using case records, however, has its drawbacks, particularly when attempting to compare the results obtained from different samples. Different states have different definitional criteria for various types of maltreatment, making the comparability of samples difficult at best. The two national incidence surveys, NIS-1 and NIS-2 (National Center on Child Abuse and Neglect [NCCAN], 1981, 1988) are good examples of how definitional changes can dramatically affect incidence estimates. Both studies examined the incidence of six major types of maltreatment throughout the United States and across a number of countries. In the second study, however, there was a change in the "harm requirement." In the NIS-1 study, maltreatment was counted only if the child had suffered "demonstrable harm," whereas in NIS-2, the standard of demonstrable harm was replaced by the "endangerment standard." Under this revision, cases in which a child's health was endangered by maltreatment were also counted. Not surprisingly, this expanded definition led to much higher incidence rates.

Another methodological problem that is highlighted by both the NIS-1 and NIS-2 studies concerns *indicated* cases of maltreatment. Indicated cases were defined as those "for which the final CPS assessment had not yet been made at the time the study data form was required, but where the investigating CPS caseworker regarded the available evidence as sufficient to warrant continued investigation" (NCCAN, 1988, p. 6-6). Unfortunately, researchers did not separate incidence estimates for the substantiated and indicated groups, arguing in the NIS-2 study that they were classified together "to minimize the effects of time constraints on data collection and to conform with the approach taken in the NIS-1" (NCCAN, 1988, p. 6-6). It is impossible to know, therefore, what percentage of the indicated cases were eventually substantiated, but by combining them with the substantiated cases, the total incidence estimates may be somewhat inflated. Although this inflation may not have an extremely detrimental effect on overall incidence estimates, if maltreatment researchers combine substantiated and indicated cases prior to their examinations of the sequelae of maltreatment, the consequences may be more critical. By combining children who have a substantiated case of maltreatment (e.g., sexual abuse) with those children who are identified as having indicated cases, we may obfuscate differences between maltreatment types as well as differences between maltreated and nonmaltreated children.

In their most recent report, NCCAN (1995) redefined indicated maltreatment as "a type of investigation disposition that concluded that maltreatment could not be substantiated under State law or policy but there was reason to suspect that the child may have been maltreated or was at-risk of maltreatment" (p. B-4). In this report, NCCAN distinguished between states that used two-tier and three-tier classification systems. Whereas three-tier states considered indicated (or at-risk cases) to be a distinct type, it is difficult to know how these cases were classified in states that only had two categories for classification, *substantiated* and *unsubstantiated*. Thus, a dichotomous classification scheme has implications for researchers who are attempting to study the effects of different types of maltreatment. Depending on how the indicated cases are handled, it is possible that different outcomes will result.

Another issue that confronts maltreatment researchers is how various systems' responses affect both researchers' definitions and classifications. When a report is made to child protective services, the resulting involvement of various agencies typically follows a continuum from protective services' initial investigation to court-ordered removal of the child from the home. Again, most studies do not describe where their participants fall on this continuum at the time of their investigation. Furthermore, similar to the indicated cases in the NIS reports, the various systems involved in cases of maltreatment must also deal with children for whom there is no substantiated maltreatment but who are deemed to be at risk of experiencing maltreatment. These at-risk children, for whom intervention is warranted, are often referred to as *protective issue* cases. Not surprisingly, almost all of the maltreatment studies that used case records or legal outcomes for classification purposes did not mention whether children with protective issue were included in their samples, and if so, where they were included.

Another issue complicating the protective-issue classification is whether children who are classified as protective issue for a particular type of maltreatment have siblings with substantiated cases of that type of maltreatment. No research has examined whether protective-issue children who have siblings with substantiated maltreatment differ from protective-issue children who do not have siblings with substantiated cases of maltreatment. Some researchers (e.g., Manly, Cicchetti, and their colleagues) have argued that children without substantiated abuse but who live in maltreating families have the same experience and/or outcomes as their maltreated siblings. This has not, however, been empirically substantiated. Whereas studies have demonstrated that witnessing family violence is detrimental and can have some similar effects as being the target of physical abuse (e.g., Jaffe, Wolfe, Wilson, & Zak, 1986), a child who has a substantiated case of physical abuse may not have the same behavioral or emotional sequelae as a child who enters the child protective system because there is a protective issue related to physical abuse. The detriment may be qualitatively or quantitatively different for these children. Although protective-issue children deserve to be studied, their inclusion into groups of children who have substantiated maltreatment may obscure the unique effects of a particular type of maltreatment or the effects of maltreatment as a general phenomenon.

As stated above, Manly, Cicchetti, and their colleagues have argued for combining children with substantiated maltreatment experiences with their siblings who were not known to have experienced any direct maltreatment (Manly et al., 1994; Toth, Manly, & Cicchetti, 1992). In their 1992 study, Toth et al. examined the relationship between maltreatment and depression in groups of physically abused and physically neglected children. The investigators began with five groups of children, two of which were composed of children with no substantiated maltreatment but who had siblings who had substantiated cases of either physical abuse or neglect. Toth et al. (1992) argued:

> Because research reveals that the vast majority of children in families receiving protective services are maltreated and because children exposed to intrafamilial violence may manifest similar consequences to those who have experienced direct

abuse, we felt that all children present in a physically abusive family would be exposed to comparable levels of adversity. (p. 101)

The authors went on to report that statistical comparisons between the children with substantiated maltreatment and those with unsubstantiated maltreatment indicated no differences on any of the dependent measures. The sample sizes for these groups, however, were quite small (ranging from 6 to 29 children), and thus insufficient power to detect any true differences could account for the findings. The authors, however, felt that their explanation and statistical analyses justified combining siblings without substantiated maltreatment with their siblings who had substantiated maltreatment. This rationale was employed in a subsequent study (Manly et al., 1994), but no statistical analyses comparing the unsubstantiated cases to the substantiated cases were conducted. The authors argued in this study that "frequently one child may come to the attention of authorities for maltreatment concerns although siblings have had similar experiences" (Manley et al., 1994, p. 127).

In sum, a number of crucial methodological issues surrounding the operationalization and classification of maltreatment have been identified. These include issues related to (a) what constitutes different types of maltreatment, (b) if and how multiple maltreatment experiences should be classified, (c) how reports are substantiated or indicated, (d) how the systems' responses affect classifications and descriptions of samples, (e) how researchers have dealt with children who are at risk for maltreatment but have no substantiation, and (f) whether siblings' maltreatment experiences should play a role in how children are classified. Most researchers either have not explicitly dealt with these issues or have done so without sufficient theoretical and/or empirical justification. As Cicchetti and Barnett (1991) state, the lack of explicit classification schemes leads to confusion "surrounding how to interpret findings, thereby obscuring the detection of existing real differences in the causes, course, sequelae, prognosis, intergenerational transmission patterns, and treatment response for the different types of maltreatment" (pp. 359-360).

In an effort to begin to address some of these issues, the current study attempted to explore the methodological issue concerning whether protective-issue children should be classified as substantiated cases. A cohort of children who had been removed from their homes because of substantiated maltreatment or because there was a protective issue related to a specific type of maltreatment were classified, based on case records, as either substantiated, protective-issue, or unsubstantiated cases for each type of maltreatment. Differences (i.e., sociodemographic and global functioning) between these three classification groups for each of three types of maltreatment (i.e., sexual abuse, physical abuse, and neglect) were examined. We also examined the results obtained when two group comparisons were made: (a) combining protective-issue and substantiated children (as previous researchers have done) prior to contrasting them with unsubstantiated cases, and (b) examining only the substantiated cases as compared to the unsubstantiated cases.

Method

Participants

The participants in the study consisted of 544 children, ages 4 to 17. The mean age of the cohort was 8.85 years ($SD = 3.62$). There were roughly equal numbers of males ($n = 247$) and females ($n = 297$). The ethnic breakdown of the sample was as follows: 46.0% Caucasian, 31.6% African American, 18.4% Hispanic, and 4.0% other. The children were recruited for the study between May 1990 and October 1991, after they were removed from their homes and placed in a shelter facility operated by San Diego County Department of Social Services. Only those children who were placed in out-of-home care after becoming legal dependents of the court and who remained in placement for at least 5 months were recruited for the study. Of the 789 eligible children, we were able to obtain interviews with 544 (68.9%) children and caretakers. Primary reasons for not obtaining interview data included refusal to participate by the caretaker and inability to contact the caretaker.

Maltreatment Classification

The San Diego County Department of Social Services' records were accessed to determine the type of maltreatment classification for each child. Case record data were obtained for each of the participants, and maltreatment status was determined based on a review of the legal petitions and narratives that were filed leading to the child's current episode of out-of-home care. Based on this chart review by trained raters (i.e., trained to criterion of 90% agreement with periodic reliability checks all above 90%), each child received a code of *present, absent,* or *protective issue* for each of four types of maltreatment (sexual abuse, physical abuse, emotional abuse, and neglect), and a code of *present* or *absent* for caretaker absence. For the purposes of the current study, each child was classified on the variables of sexual abuse, physical abuse, and neglect, because they were the only three that had a sufficient number of participants (at least 30) in their protective-issue groups. Thus, we ended up with three maltreatment variables, and every child received one of three possible classifications (present, absent, or protective issue) for each of these three variables. A child could therefore receive a code of present on more than one type of maltreatment. This classification scheme allowed us to avoid placing children in discrete maltreatment groups and to capture the fact that a child may have been removed from his or her home for more than one reason.

Procedure

Children were interviewed with their caretakers an average of 7.7 months ($SD = 3.0$ months) following their entry into the foster care system, and the children had been living with their current caretakers an average of 6.5 months at the time of the interview. The procedure consisted of scheduling a $1\frac{1}{2}$ hour meeting/interview with the child and the child's current primary caretaker. Two interviewers then went to the home, and one interviewer talked with the caretaker while another spoke with the child. The interviewers administered a battery of measures to each informant. The measures in-

TABLE 11.1 Descriptive Information for the Sexual Abuse Variable

Sexual Abuse	Age	% Female	Total Competence	Internalizing Problems	Externalizing Problems	Total Behavior Problems
NO n = 411	8.6 (3.5)	48.9	13.7 (4.0)	9.7 (8.0)	16.3 (11.5)	42.1 (27.7)
YES n = 94	10.4 (3.7)	85.1	13.6 (3.6)	12.0 (9.3)	15.7 (11.7)	44.6 (29.7)
PI n = 35	8.2 (3.5)	37.1	13.7 (3.8)	10.5 (9.0)	14.6 (10.8)	41.1 (27.0)

NOTE: All values not in parentheses represent means or percentages where indicated. Values in parentheses are standard deviations. NO = sexual abuse absent group; YES = sexual abuse present group; PI = protective-issue group.

cluded in the current study were a demographics questionnaire (a project-designed measure) and the Child Behavior Checklist (CBCL; Achenbach, 1991). The CBCL consists of 118 items that "describe children and youth," and the respondent is asked to rate each item on a 3-point scale, where 0 indicates *not true,* 1 indicates *somewhat or sometimes true,* and 2 indicates *very true or often true.* The items consist of both behavior problems and competencies, and the scores on the items can be computed to create both behavior problem and competency scores. In the present study, the scales used included the Total Competence scale and the three broad-band behavior problem scales: Externalizing Problems, Internalizing Problems, and Total Behavior Problems. The scored CBCL results in a behavior profile that displays the items and distributions of raw scores for each scale, as well as percentiles and T scores based on normative samples of each sex in different age ranges. Both clinical and borderline clinical cutpoints are indicated. In the majority of analyses described below, participants' T scores were not used. Rather, in accordance with the recommendations of Achenbach (1991), raw scores were used in all analyses, except those describing the percentage of the sample that met clinical cutpoints on the various scales.

Results

Child Behavior Checklist Descriptive Data

Prior to any analyses using the CBCL raw scores, we wanted to examine how the sample scored relative to the normative populations used in Achenbach's (1991) study of validity and reliability. Using the participants' T scores, we calculated the percentage that met either clinical or borderline clinical cutpoint criteria for the four summary scales used in this study. In our sample, 68.4% of children met cutpoint criteria for Total Competence, 49.1% for Externalizing Problems, 38.2% for Internalizing Problems, and 51.3% for Total Behavior Problems.

Classification Comparisons Within Maltreatment Groups

To examine differences between protective-issue and substantiated groups within each type of maltreatment, we conducted a series of one-way and chi-square analyses, with the dependent variables consisting of age, gender, and the four scales from the CBCL. The analyses were conducted within each type of maltreatment to compare the present, absent, and protective-issue groups. The group means for each of the dependent variables are provided in Tables 11.1, 11.2, and 11.3. Table 11.1 gives the values for the sexual abuse group, Table 11.2, the physical abuse means, and finally, the neglect group information is presented in Table 11.3. When there was a significant main effect, two post hoc contrasts were conducted, one comparing the present (YES) group to the absent (NO) group, and one comparing the YES group to the protective-issue (PI) group.

The one-way ANOVA comparing the sexual abuse groups' mean ages was significant, $F(2, 537) = 10.3, p < .05$. Post hoc contrasts indicated that the YES group was older than both the NO

TABLE 11.2 Descriptive Information for the Physical Abuse Variable

Sexual Abuse	Age	% Female	Total Competence	Internalizing Problems	Externalizing Problems	Total Behavior Problems
NO	8.9	57.3	13.9	9.7	15.5	41.0
n = 330	(3.8)		(3.9)	(8.3)	(11.8)	(27.8)
YES	8.9	51.4	13.0	11.5	17.6	47.0
n = 146	(3.5)		(3.8)	(8.1)	(17.6)	(26.5)
PI	8.3	46.9	14.1	9.2	15.9	39.8
n = 64	(3.1)		(3.8)	(9.2)	(15.8)	(31.6)

NOTE: All values not in parentheses represent means or percentages where indicated. Values in parentheses are standard deviations.
NO = physical abuse absent group; YES = physical abuse present group; PI = protective-issue group.

group $(p < .05)$ and the PI group $(p < .05)$. When examining physical abuse, the three levels did not differ in their mean ages, and thus contrasts were not conducted. The ANOVA examining neglect was significant, $F(2, 537) = 3.3, p < .05$, as was the contrast comparing the YES group to the NO group $(p < .05)$, indicating that neglected children were significantly younger than children removed for other types of maltreatment.

The next set of analyses was conducted to determine whether there were any gender differences among the three groups within each type of maltreatment. First, a chi-square analysis was conducted to examine any sex differences between the three levels of the sexual abuse variable. The results of the analysis showed that, indeed, there were differences, $\chi^2 (2, N = 540) = 44.9, p < .05$, between the percentage of males and females in the three different groups. As shown in Table 11.1, there were roughly equal numbers of males and females in the NO group, a much greater number of females in the YES group, and the PI group contained many fewer

females (approximately one third). The chi-square gender analysis for the physical abuse group was nonsignificant. The differences in gender for the neglect group approached significance, $\chi^2 (2, N = 540) = 4.7, p < .10$, with roughly equal numbers of males and females in the YES and PI groups, and more females than males in the NO group.

In addition to examining the age and gender differences among the three groups that comprise each of the maltreatment variables, we also wanted to examine whether there were any differences in level of behavior problems and/or competencies among the different groups. Again, all of the means used in these comparisons are given in Tables 11.1, 11.2, and 11.3. We conducted a series of one-way analyses examining the differences within each maltreatment variable. For sexual abuse, the ANOVA for Internalizing Problems was significant, $F(2, 537) = 3.1, p < .05$. The contrast comparing the NO group to the YES group was also significant $(p < .05)$, indicating that those who had substan-

TABLE 11.3 Descriptive Information for the Neglect Variable

Sexual Abuse	Age	% Female	Total Competence	Internalizing Problems	Externalizing Problems	Total Behavior Problems
NO	9.4	61.5	12.8	11.5	16.8	46.5
n = 161	(3.7)		(3.6)	(9.2)	(11.8)	(30.5)
YES	8.6	51.7	14.1	9.7	15.8	41.1
n = 346	(3.6)		(4.0)	(7.9)	(11.4)	(26.7)
PI	8.5	48.5	13.5	7.7	15.5	36.7
n = 33	(3.2)		(3.3)	(7.9)	(10.9)	(27.7)

NOTE: All values not in parentheses represent means or percentages where indicated. Values in parentheses are standard deviations. NO = neglect absent group; YES = neglect present group; PI = protective-issue group.

tiated sexual abuse were rated by caretakers as having more Internalizing Problems than children who were removed for other types of maltreatment. None of the other one-way analyses within the sexual abuse variable was significant.

When examining physical abuse, a number of trends and significant differences among groups emerged. First, examining Total Competence, the one-way ANOVA approached statistical significance, $F(2, 391) = 2.5, p = .08$. The analysis of group differences on Internalizing Problems was significant, $F(2, 537) = 3.0, p < .05$, with contrasts indicating that the YES group had significantly higher scores than the NO group ($p < .05$) and that there was a trend ($p = .06$) for YES scores to be higher than PI scores. This set of analyses underscores the importance of power, as there was a greater difference between the PI group mean and the YES group mean than between the YES group and NO group means, yet the contrast between the PI and YES groups did not reach statistical significance. Finally, the differences among the three physical abuse groups on Total Behavior Problems also approached statistical significance, $F(2, 537) = 2.6, p = .07$.

In examining the neglect variable, several differences were also observed among the three groups. The one-way ANOVA for Total Competence reached statistical significance, $F(2, 391) = 4.6, p < .05$, with contrasts indicating that the YES group had higher mean Total Competence scores than did the NO group ($p < .05$). The three levels of the neglect variable also differed on Internalizing Problems scores, $F(2, 537) = 4.2, p < .05$. Contrasts indicated that the YES group had fewer Internalizing Problems than the NO group ($p < .05$). Finally, the analysis examining group differences on the Total Behavior Problems scale approached significance, $F(2, 537) = 2.9, p = .06$.

The results of the first set of analyses suggested that the three groups were indeed different, but again, we were particularly interested in examining how the PI group differed from the YES group within each type of maltreatment. We were concerned that because of the small n in the three PI groups, we may not have had enough power to detect true differences. This

was confirmed in analyses in which the difference between the YES and the PI groups was greater than the difference between the YES and NO groups, and yet only the latter comparison reached statistical significance.

Effect of Combining the Protective-Issue and Substantiated Groups

In an attempt to further explore what effect combining the YES and PI groups might have on the results of analyses, we conducted a series of t tests. The first set of analyses involved comparing the YES group to the NO group, and PI children were eliminated from the analyses. To then examine what effect combining the PI group with the YES group would have, we conducted a second set of analyses. In these analyses, the PI and YES groups were combined to form a new group (YES/PI), and then this group was compared to the NO group. This is how researchers (cf. Manly et al., 1994; Toth et al., 1992) have traditionally dealt with protective-issue children; that is, they have combined their at-risk or indicated groups with children who have substantiated maltreatment. Our two sets of analyses were conducted to evaluate empirically the effects of such a practice.

The means for the three groups as well as the results of the t tests are presented in Table 11.4. Examining the two rightmost columns, one can see where the addition of the PI children to the YES group had a significant impact on the results. In examining the sexual abuse and neglect groups, it is apparent that the combination of the PI and YES groups did not significantly affect the results. Sexually abused children showed more Internalizing Problems than children with other types of maltreatment both before and after combining the PI children with the YES children. Similarly, neglected children showed greater Total Competence and fewer Internalizing and Total Behavior Problems, even after including the PI children into the YES group. For physical abuse, however, the inclusion of PI children had an impact on the results of each analysis. When the NO group was compared to just the YES group, physically abused children were reported by caretakers to have a greater

TABLE 11.4 Means and Results of t Tests Examining the Effect of Combining YES and PI Groups

	Group Means			Results of t Tests	
	NO	YES	YES/PI	NO vs. YES	N vs. YES/PI
Sexual abuse					
Total Competence	13.7	13.6	13.6	ns	ns
	(4.0)	(3.6)	(3.6)		
Internalizing Problems	9.7	12.0	11.6	YES > NO	YES/PI > NO
	(8.0)	(9.3)	(9.2)		
Externalizing Problems	16.3	15.7	15.4	ns	ns
	(11.5)	(11.7)	(11.4)		
Total Behavior Problems	42.1	44.6	43.6	ns	ns
	(27.7)	(29.7)	(29.0)		
Physical abuse					
Total Competence	13.9	13.0	13.3	NO > YES	ns
	(3.9)	(3.8)	(3.8)		
Internalizing Problems	9.7	11.5	10.8	YES > NO	ns
	(8.3)	(8.1)	(8.5)		
Externalizing Problems	15.5	17.6	17.1	YES > NO	ns
	(11.8)	(17.6)	(10.8)		
Total Behavior Problems	41.0	47.0	44.8	YES > NO	ns
	(27.8)	(26.5)	(28.3)		
Neglect					
Total Competence	12.8	14.1	14.1	YES > NO	YES/PI > NO
	(3.6)	(4.0)	(4.0)		
Internalizing Problems	11.5	9.7	9.5	NO > YES	NO > YES/PI
	(9.2)	(7.9)	(7.9)		
Externalizing Problems	16.8	15.8	15.8	ns	ns
	(11.8)	(11.4)	(11.3)		
Total Behavior Problems	46.5	41.1	40.7	NO > YES	NO > YES/PI
	(30.5)	(26.7)	(26.8)		

NOTE: Standard deviations are in parentheses. NO = absent group; YES = present group; PI = protective-issue group; YES/PI = combined group.

number of problems on each of the four CBCL scales than children removed from the home for other types of maltreatment. When the PI and YES groups were combined, however, these effects were no longer apparent.

Discussion

◼ First, it should be noted that this sample of children who were removed from their homes due to maltreatment evidenced a number of behavior problems as well as deficits in social competence, relative to a normative group. That is, between 33% and 64% of the youth were identified on the four CBCL scales as reaching the borderline clinical cutpoint (i.e., above the 10th percentile). This is consistent with prior re-

ports of problem functioning in foster care populations (e.g., Hochstadt, Jaudes, Zimo, & Schacter, 1987). Additionally, children who were sexually abused were reported by their caretakers to have more Internalizing Problems than those who experienced other types of maltreatment, and those who were physically abused had more problems in all areas assessed (i.e., lack of Social Competence; Total, Internalizing, and Externalizing Problems) than those who experienced other types of maltreatment. In contrast, caretakers' ratings of neglected children indicated that they were perceived to have fewer problems than those who experienced other types of maltreatment. These findings deserve further discussion and investigation; however, the focus of the present chapter is on the methodological issue concerning protective-issue children.

Specifically, the results of our analyses suggest that protective-issue children differ from children with substantiated maltreatment in a number of significant ways. Within the sexual abuse variable, protective-issue children were significantly younger than children with substantiated maltreatment. Additionally, children removed for a protective issue for sexual abuse differed in their gender distribution from children who were removed for substantiated sexual abuse. There were many more females removed for substantiated sexual abuse, and more males removed as a protective issue for sexual abuse. It is not surprising that children removed for substantiated sexual abuse tended to be older and were more likely to be female, given what we know about the characteristics of sexual abuse (e.g., Kendall-Tackett et al., 1993). We can see, however, that combining protective-issue children with substantiated children has the potential to change the overall group characteristics, and this may affect outcome studies.

In examining behavior problems and competencies among our cohort, we again found some important differences between children who were removed for protective reasons and those removed for substantiated maltreatment. First, within the physical abuse variable, there was a trend for protective-issue children to have higher Total Competence scores than the substantiated group, indicating that protective-issue children were rated by caretakers as more competent than those children who had substantiated physical abuse. There was also a trend for the physical abuse protective-issue children to have lower Total Behavior Problems scores than children in the substantiated group.

Although several other one-way analyses were significant, the contrasts comparing the substantiated and protective-issue groups were mostly nonsignificant. This was likely a result of insufficient power to detect true differences. The mean differences, in some cases, were greatest between the substantiated and protective-issue groups, and yet these contrasts did not attain statistical significance. Despite the lack of significant differences, when examining the means one can see that across maltreatment types, the protective-issue children appear to be displaying fewer behavior problems than children with substantiated maltreatment.

A final method of examining the protective-issue groups' differences was to evaluate the result of combining them with their respective substantiated groups prior to the analyses of differences between the present and absent groups. The results of our analyses suggested that for the physical abuse variable, the combination of the substantiated and protective-issue groups affected the results. That is, differences between children who had experienced physical abuse and those who had not were apparent only prior to the inclusion of protective-issue children into the substantiated group. Once the two groups were combined, the differences were no longer statistically significant. These findings are critical, because previous researchers (Manly et al., 1994; Toth et al., 1992) have combined children who are at risk for maltreatment with children who have substantiated maltreatment. What these researchers may have done, in effect, is decrease their chances of finding true differences between groups.

Some limitations to the current study warrant mention. First, as previously indicated, there is the issue of power. Given the relatively small n in our protective-issue groups, we may not have been able to detect differences. Second, there are classification and procedural limitations. In terms of classification, reviewing and coding chart records limits conclusions about the specific maltreatment experiences of a child. Clearly, some of the protective-issue children may have actually been victims themselves. In no way can maltreatment classifications represent the total experiences of a child, or perhaps more important, their perception of these experiences. Additionally, although all of the children in our study were in out-of-home placement (important study control), this fact may limit the generalizability of our results. Perhaps children with maltreatment reports who remain in their homes have different characteristics than those who are removed. Only future studies will help disentangle some of these factors.

Despite the limitations of the current study, the results have important implications for maltreatment researchers. Given that protective-issue children differ from children with substantiated maltreatment on age, gender, and behavioral indexes, researchers must be wary of the fact that by placing protective-issue children into groups with substantiated children, they may be obscuring effects. Although it may not, in every case, be detrimental to combine these two groups, researchers should be cognizant of what they are doing, why they are doing it, and what effects it may have on their results. Furthermore, to aid in the comparability of studies, researchers should be explicit about the placement of protective-issue children in their studies.

This study represents an initial step in the process toward a more explicit and specific system for the classification of maltreatment. In terms of the issues surrounding protective-issue children, more research needs to be conducted with a greater number of participants and additional dependent measures. Research on similar classifications of maltreatment, such as indicated and at risk, should also be conducted to examine whether these children also differ in significant ways from children with substantiated cases of maltreatment. Studies focusing on how a sibling's maltreatment status may affect the protective-issue classification should also be conducted. Of the 544 children in the current sample, 371 (68.2%) had a sibling who was also included in our study. In examining those children who were removed from their homes solely due to one or more protective reasons ($n = 46$), all but 4 of them (91.3%) had a sibling who was also included in the current study. Such high percentages suggest that siblings are an important factor to consider in our studies of protective-issue children.

Our attempts to better define how we classify maltreated children require that we examine both theoretical and empirical results of the assumptions and decisions that are made. These decisions need to be specifically communicated with theoretical and empirical justification provided. As Cicchetti and Barnett (1991) observed, "The time has now come for researchers to begin to specify the inclusion and exclusion criteria characterizing their respective samples" (p. 360). It is hoped that with continued thought, discussion, and investigation, we will bring the issues surrounding the classification of maltreatment to the forefront—a critical step in advancing our understanding of causes and sequelae of maltreatment and in developing appropriate interventions to reduce both the risk and impact of maltreatment.

References

Achenbach, T. M. (1991). *Manual for the Child Behavior Checklist/4-18 and 1991 profile.* Burlington: University of Vermont, Department of Psychiatry.

Ammerman, R. T., & Hersen, M. (1990). Research in child abuse and neglect: Current status and an agenda for the future. In R. T. Ammerman & M. Hersen (Eds.), *Children at risk: An evaluation of factors contributing to child abuse and neglect* (pp. 3-19). New York: Plenum.

Cicchetti, D., & Barnett, D. (1991). Toward the development of a scientific nosology of child maltreatment. In D. Cicchetti & W. Grove (Eds.), *Thinking clearly about psychology: Essays in honor of Paul E. Meehl* (pp. 346-377). Minneapolis: University of Minnesota Press.

Herrenkohl, R. C. (1990). Research directions related to child abuse and neglect. In R. T. Ammerman & M. Hersen (Eds.), *Children at risk: An evaluation of factors contributing to child abuse and neglect* (pp. 85-108). New York: Plenum.

Hochstadt, N. J., Jaudes, P. K., Zimo, D. A., & Schacter, J. (1987). The medical and psychosocial needs of children entering foster care. *Child Abuse & Neglect, 11,* 53-62.

Jaffe, P., Wolfe, D., Wilson, S., & Zak, L. (1986). Similarities in behavioral and social maladjustment among child victims and witnesses to family violence. *American Journal of Orthopsychiatry, 56,* 142-146.

Kaufman, J., Cook, A., Arny, L., Jones, B., & Pittinsky, T. (1994). Problems defining resiliency: Illustrations from the study of maltreated children. *Development and Psychopathology, 6,* 215-229.

Kendall-Tackett, K. A., Williams, L. M., & Finkelhor, D. (1993). Impact of sexual abuse on children: A review and synthesis of recent empirical studies. *Psychological Bulletin, 113,* 164-180.

Manly, J. T., Cicchetti, D., & Barnett, D. (1994). The impact of subtype, frequency, chronicity, and severity of child maltreatment on social competence and behavior problems. *Development and Psychopathology, 6,* 121-143.

McGee, R. A., Wolfe, D. A., Yuen, S. A., Wilson, S. K., & Carnochan, J. (1995). The measurement of maltreatment: A comparison of approaches. *Child Abuse & Neglect, 19,* 233-249.

National Center on Child Abuse and Neglect. (1981). *Study findings: National study of the incidence and severity of child abuse and neglect* (DHHS Publication No. OHDS 81-30325). Washington, DC: Government Printing Office.

National Center on Child Abuse and Neglect. (1988). *Study findings: Study of national incidence and prevalence of child abuse and neglect: 1988.* Washington, DC: U.S. Department of Health and Human Services.

National Center on Child Abuse and Neglect. (1995). *Child maltreatment 1993: Reports from the states to the National Center on Child Abuse and Neglect.* Washington, DC: Government Printing Office.

Shields, A. M., Cicchetti, D., & Ryan, R. M. (1994). The development of emotional and behavioral self-regulation and social competence among maltreated school-age children. *Development and Psychopathology, 6,* 57-75.

Toth, S. L., Manly, J. T., & Cicchetti, D. (1992). Child maltreatment and vulnerability to depression. *Development and Psychopathology, 4,* 97-112.

PART III

WIFE ABUSE

CHAPTER 12

Attitudes as Explanations for Aggression Against Family Members

Sharon D. Herzberger
Quentin H. Rueckert

When called on to address questions about the causes of violence in the family, both researchers and practitioners increasingly turn to attitudinal and cognitive explanations. We say that men beat women because men hold patriarchal beliefs or because they believe that violence is a legitimate method of solving problems. We also establish treatment programs motivated by the belief that changes in attitudes will lead to behavior change (e.g., Jennings, 1987).

The fascination with attitudes stems from evidence of a frequent linkage between attitudes and behavior. Children who believe that aggression is wrong are less likely to aggress against a peer (Boldizar, Perry, & Perry, 1989). Adults who have been abused as children, except those who have been severely abused (Kelder, McNamara, Carlson, & Lynn, 1991), are less rejecting of the use of severe corporal punishment (Herzberger & Tennen, 1985). One well-known attitude scale, the Inventory of Beliefs about Wife Beating (IBWB; Saunders, Lynch, Grayson, & Linz, 1987), elicits dramatically different responses from batterers and advocates for battered women. The batterers are more likely to believe that wife beating is justifiable and that the offender should be held less responsible and should be punished less for the violent

AUTHORS' NOTE: Copies of this chapter may be obtained from Sharon Herzberger at sharon.herzberger@mail.trincoll.edu or at the Department of Psychology, Trinity College, Hartford, CT 06106. We want to thank members of the Psychological Assessment Seminar for their contributions to the initial development of the ATA and to thank Joe Thomas and Henry Price for their kind cooperation with this research.

act. Attitudes have thus been shown to relate to aggression against a variety of victims and may be implicated as both a precursor and a consequence of aggressive behavior.

This chapter presents a history of the evolution of two researchers' thoughts about the relationship between attitudes about violence and violent behavior. We, the researchers, began work some time ago on an attitudinal measure to complement that of Saunders and associates (1987). The measure passed standard tests of validity and internal consistency, but during our testing sessions we began to question the practical significance of our instrument. We thus widened our investigation to examine the utility of other measures, as well, and to assess the general magnitude of the relationship between aggression and aggressive attitudes. Our search, detailed in this chapter, has implications for research and clinical practice in this focused area, and it also provides lessons about the importance of a multivariate approach to research on family violence.

Development of the Attitudes Towards Aggression Scale

■ Because of the perceived need to have a variety of valid measures of attitudes about violence, we began work on a new instrument. The scale we developed is called the Attitudes Towards Aggression scale (ATA) and has 20 items, which cover verbal, sexual, and physical aggression. Respondents judge aggression that transpires in private and public settings, as well as when the offender or victim is described as sober or drunk. The items request judgments about the justification for violence, the assignment of blame, and the tendency to punish (see Table 12.1). Unlike the IBWB, this scale was designed to tap aggression toward both married or dating partners.

The items were selected following a series of pilot tests of an original set of 46 items. They were tested on a diverse sample, including students at a community college ranging in age from 17 to 74, residents from two Hartford area neighborhoods, and employees of a health care facility and a small business, also in the Hartford area.

Items that were regarded as vague or that were endorsed by fewer than 10% of the pilot sample were eliminated. The remaining 20 items demonstrate good internal consistency (Cronbach's alpha = .77 for men and .82 for women). The overall scale did not correlate with social desirability ($r = .04$), as measured by the Crowne-Marlowe Social Desirability Scale (Crowne & Marlowe, 1964).

Validation of the Attitudes Towards Aggression Scale

■ The 20 items were then used in a validation study, employing both criterion-groups and convergent validity methods. To obtain a diverse group of participants, the sample was drawn from three sources: adults from community college classes, adult criminals from a halfway house and treatment center, and adult criminals from an alternative-to-incarceration facility (see Table 12.2 for demographic information).

Before testing the validity of the scale, we again checked the endorsement frequencies (see Table 12.3). Both the control and criminal samples showed varied endorsements of the items, with only one item endorsed by more than 90% of a given subsample. Again, the total scale score was independent of a socially desirable response set and the scale showed good internal consistency both overall (Cronbach's alpha = .77 overall) and within each subsample (ranging from .67 to .79).

We then tested the scale's validity in a variety of ways. First, we tested the construct validity of the scale. Men are generally more approving of violence than women (Greenblat, 1985; Koski & Mangold, 1988) and are more likely than women to assign blame to the victim rather than to the perpetrator of the violence (Sugarman & Cohn, 1986). Therefore, we predicted that men would score higher on the ATA than women. This prediction was confirmed, $F(1) = 14.37$, $p < .0002$: The mean ATA score for men was 42.98 ($SD = 13.51$) and for women, 32.05 ($SD = 12.86$).

TABLE 12.1 Attitudes Towards Aggression Scale

Attitudes are important to study because they shape how a person reacts to other people and events. This survey is designed to look at people's attitudes about various ways of dealing with problems in dating or other intimate relationships.

In the list below you will find statements about situations that can occur in intimate relationships. As you think about the situation described, remember that pressures in relationships sometimes lead people to do things they wouldn't normally do. We want to know your honest reaction to each situation. Don't think about how you "should" answer the question or how a "perfect person" would answer it. Instead, answer the questions according to how you honestly feel. Use the following scale to note your answer. Circle:

SD	if you *strongly disagree* with the statement.
D	if you *disagree*
LD	if you *lean towards disagreement*
LA	if you *lean towards agreement*
A	if you *agree*
SA	if you *strongly agree*

1. A joke at another person's expense is basically harmless.   SD   D   LD   LA   A   SA

2. If my partner beat me up, I would call the police.   SD   D   LD   LA   A   SA

3. A sexually unfaithful partner deserves to be slapped.   SD   D   LD   LA   A   SA

4. Slapping your partner when you're drunk is unforgivable.   SD   D   LD   LA   A   SA

5. A person who tolerates being sworn at deserves to be sworn at.   SD   D   LD   LA   A   SA

6. If my partner slaps me, I am justified in slapping back.   SD   D   LD   LA   A   SA

7. It is hard to understand why someone would hit a partner who lied.   SD   D   LD   LA   A   SA

8. People should accept that yelling and screaming is just part of being in a relationship.   SD   D   LD   LA   A   SA

9. If a woman gets raped when she's drunk, she is partially to blame.   SD   D   LD   LA   A   SA

10. If people stay in physically abusive relationships, then they deserve the treatment they get.   SD   D   LD   LA   A   SA

11. A woman who flirts all evening is in no way responsible if she's raped.   SD   D   LD   LA   A   SA

12. I would consider ending the relationship if my partner slapped me.   SD   D   LD   LA   A   SA

13. It's worse for a man to slap a woman than it is for a woman to slap a man.   SD   D   LD   LA   A   SA

14. If you push your partner around when you're drunk, you should be forgiven because your judgment is impaired.   SD   D   LD   LA   A   SA

15. If a boyfriend forces his girlfriend to have sex, she should call the police.   SD   D   LD   LA   A   SA

16. It is okay to hit your partner jokingly.   SD   D   LD   LA   A   SA

17. If you're naked in bed with someone, you're agreeing to have sex.   SD   D   LD   LA   A   SA

18. Physical fighting between intimate partners is nobody's business but their own.   SD   D   LD   LA   A   SA

19. Being sexually aggressive makes men more attractive.   SD   D   LD   LA   A   SA

20. Cutting your partner down when you are angry is understandable.   SD   D   LD   LA   A   SA

TABLE 12.2 Demographic Information for Study Sample

Variable	Control n	Control %	Criminal n	Criminal %
Age[a]				
18-20	25	30.9	3	6
20-30	26	32.1	25	50
30-40	18	22.2	18	36
40-50	9	11.1	3	6
50-60	2	2.5	0	0
Race				
African American	8	9.9	28	56
Caucasian	65	80.2	17	34
Hispanic	3	3.7	4	8
Other	5	6.2	1	2
Gender				
Men	32	39.5	34	68
Women	49	60.5	16	32

a. Age categories do not add up to 100% because one respondent from each group chose not to identify his or her age.

We also predicted that known criminals, especially those convicted of violent offenses, would demonstrate more tolerance for aggression on the ATA than would people with no known history of crime and that this would be true for both men and women. As Figure 12.1 shows, criminal group members scored significantly higher than control group members on the ATA, $F(1) = 11.39$, $p < .001$. Figure 12.2 separates the relatively small number of criminals who reported being convicted of violent crime from nonviolent criminals and controls ($ns = 14$, 33, and 79, respectively). The figure shows that violent criminals scored highest on the ATA, with nonviolent criminals scoring in the middle and controls receiving the lowest scores, $F(1) = 8.36$, $p < .0004$. However, perhaps due to the small sample of self-confessed violent criminals, post hoc tests revealed no significant difference in the mean scores of the violent and nonviolent criminal groups. As predicted, no significant interactions between criminal history and gender were found on the ATA.

After these tests of the scale's construct validity, we turned to a convergent validity assessment by relating scores on the ATA with the verbal aggression and violence items on the Conflict Tactics Scales (CTS; Straus, 1989). Table 12.4 shows the standardized beta coefficients and the R^2 for the CTS regressed onto the

ATA. The top part of the table shows the ATA as the sole predictor of CTS violence. The next section shows ATA, gender, and criminal history as joint predictors. As shown, the ATA score significantly relates to CTS-assessed violence, even after controlling for gender and prior criminal behavior.

In summary, we appear to be developing a scale that is internally consistent, independent of social desirability response bias, and to which individuals respond as predicted given the nature of the instrument.

Doubts Emerge

■ This brings us, however, to the second part of this tale. You will recall that the ATA predicted CTS scores even when gender and criminal history were controlled. But if we look more carefully at the relationship among these variables, it is evident that violence against a partner, as measured by the CTS, is even more strongly related to gender and to other forms of violence

TABLE 12.3 Endorsement Frequency of Attitudes Towards Aggression Scale Items

Item	Men	Women	Controls	Criminals
1	28.8	13.8	21.0	22.0
2	65.2	18.5	28.4	64.0
3	33.3	44.6	38.3	40.0
4	47.0	42.4	38.8	54.0
5	27.3	18.8	20.0	28.0
6	47.0	42.2	45.7	42.9
7	54.5	50.8	46.9	62.0
8	37.9	26.2	29.6	36.0
9	21.5	4.6	8.8	20.0
10	27.8	21.5	21.0	30.0
11	59.1	43.1	39.5	70.0
12	69.7	23.1	35.8	64.0
13	59.1	39.1	48.8	50.0
14	27.3	20.3	18.5	32.7
15	36.9	23.1	23.8	40.0
16	62.1	52.3	53.1	64.0
17	58.5	47.7	48.1	61.2
18	45.5	24.6	25.9	50.0
19	22.2	20.3	23.1	18.4
20	25.8	15.4	18.5	24.0

NOTE: The figures represent the percentage of the sample that expressed tolerance for violence in its selection of a response option for that item.

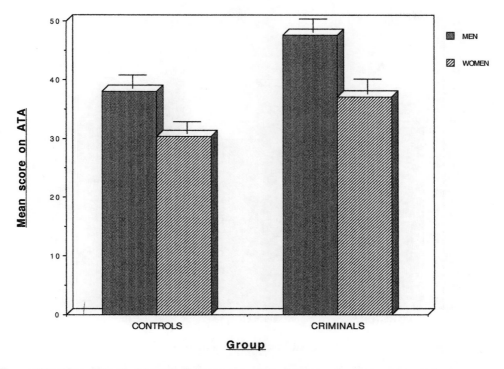

Figure 12.1. Mean Attitudes Towards Aggression Scale Score by Gender and Group Membership

or criminality than to one's attitudes about violence against a partner.

Furthermore, as shown in the bottom portion of Table 12.4, when we regress the CTS score on gender and criminal history, deleting ATA, and compare this regression model against the model including ATA, we see that attitudes about violence add approximately 4% of the variance in explaining CTS scores over that explained by gender and criminal history alone.

There are at least three ways to think about this small increment. First, the ATA is a scale under development. Perhaps the scale needs improvement before it can truly be said to be measuring stable attitudes about violence against intimates. For example, although the scale is internally consistent, we have not examined its reliability over time, and this must be done before we conclude that we are measuring a stable phenomenon.

Second, perhaps we are measuring the linkage between attitudes and behavior about as much as we would expect theoretically. We know that when specific, strong, and accessible

attitudes are measured along with a set of conceptually similar behaviors, a strong relationship may be found (Eagly & Chaiken, 1993). But attitude researchers (Eagly & Chaiken, 1993) also warn us that attitudes are often weakly tied to behavior, especially when the behavior and the attitudes are not linked temporally.

Third, we know that violence within the family is multiply determined (e.g., Kaufman & Zigler, 1989). Perhaps it should not be surprising, then, that attitudes about the use of violence compete with other factors to predict or explain in a post hoc fashion the actual use of violence.

A Widening Investigation

■ With these hypotheses in mind, we examined other studies of attitude-violent behavior relationships. Using published investigations cited in a new meta-analytic report by Sugarman and Frankel (1996), as well as other sources, we searched for studies that examined not only the univariate relationship between attitudes and

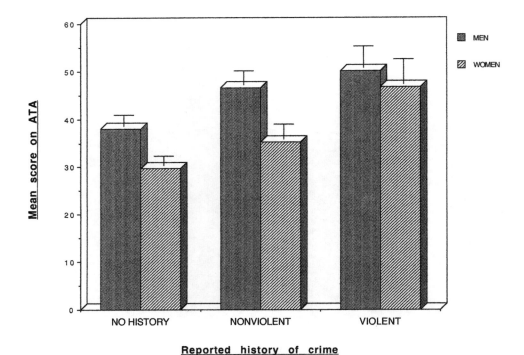

Figure 12.2. Mean Attitudes Towards Aggression Scale Score by Gender and History of Crime

TABLE 12.4 Standardized Estimates for Regression Analysis Predicting Conflict Tactics Scales Score

Variable	R^2	F	Beta
Model	.11	15.27***	
ATA[a]			.34***
Model	.36	23.06***	
ATA			.23**
Gender (male = 1, female = 2)			.24**
Group (criminal = 1, control = 2)			−.53***
Model	.32	29.09***	
Gender (male = 1, female = 2)			.17*
Group (criminal = 1, control = 2)			−.60***

a. Attitudes Towards Aggression scale.

*$p < .05$; **$p < .01$; ***$p < .001$.

aggressive behavior but the relationship between these factors controlling for other characteristics known to relate to violence.

Sugarman and Frankel's (1996) meta-analysis disclosed a strong relationship between attitudes and violent behavior. The authors found, in fact, that attitudes about violence were the only component of "patriarchal ideology" that consistently related to behavior.

Like Sugarman and Frankel, we found a fairly consistent, moderate relationship between attitudes and behavior across the studies we reviewed. The strongest correlation was found by Holden, Coleman, and Schmidt (1995). They found high correlations between attitudes toward spanking and mothers' reports of spanking, whether they collected reports via a questionnaire ($r = .73, p < .001$) or a daily telephone interview ($r = .54, p < .001$).

However, Holden and his colleagues did not report the contributions of attitudes isolated from other factors known to correlate with aggression. Neither did some of the other investigators of this topic (e.g., Saunders & Size, 1986;

Walker, 1984). Therefore, we cannot use these investigations to study how much attitudes independently contribute to our understanding of violent behavior.

Fortunately, we found five studies that did examine the relationship between attitudes and violent behavior in a multivariate way. The results of these studies are summarized in Table 12.5 and are discussed here.

Saunders and associates (1987), as we explained earlier, found that batterers, who were male, scored higher on all subscales of the IBWB than did female advocates for battered women, who presumably had not engaged in partner violence. This might be seen as strong evidence for an attitude-behavior link, particularly because the attitudes measured were directly tied to a pattern of conceptually similar behavior. However, when the authors compared the male batterers to male college students (thereby in a sense controlling for gender), many of the differences disappeared.

Stith and Farley (1993) found that approval of marital violence contributed significantly ($r = .35, p < .001$) to actual marital violence among both alcoholics and batterers, about the same contribution as a measure of sex-role egalitarianism ($r = -.33, p < .001$). When marital violence was regressed onto approval of marital violence and five other variables, the total R^2 equaled .19. The model was significant, but again approval of violence did not account for a major proportion of the variance.

A similar result was found by Smith (1990). He constructed attitudinal measures of patriarchal beliefs and of approval of violence against wives and found that both significantly related to wife beating as measured by the CTS ($rs = .32$ and $.37$, respectively). Together, they explained 18% of the variation in wife beating, as assessed through multiple regression. Unfortunately, Smith does not report the separate contribution of approval of violence. Four indexes of socioeconomic status (e.g., income, education) explained in total 14% of the variance in wife beating. When the two sets of measures were combined, the amount of variance explained rose to 20%.

Eisikovits, Edleson, Guttmann, and Sela-Amit (1991) studied the contributions of attitudes about violence and cognitive style (e.g., rational beliefs, self-control, locus of control) to explaining previous partner violence by men. Attitudes correlated significantly with the use of physical violence ($r = -.39, p < .01$). Multiple regression analysis with both attitudinal and cognitive style measures revealed that attitudes contributed 16% of the variance in predicting group membership; together, attitudes and cognitive style accounted for 25%.

Murphy, Coleman, and Haynes (1986) found a significant correlation between rape myth acceptance scores (Burt, 1980) and men's coercive sexual behaviors (e.g., touching a breast or genitals against the women's will, forced sexual activity). But when a regression analysis controlled for other factors, such as neuroticism and hostility, the attitude measure no longer contributed significantly to the prediction of coercive sexual behavior.

These studies suggest that our finding of a moderate attitude-behavior correlation on the ATA is not uncommon. It is also not uncommon to see the relationship dissipate when the contribution of attitudes is considered in the context of the contribution of other factors.

Discussion

Correlations of .30 to .40 are generally considered moderate (Wolf, 1986), and they can signify a useful association between two variables (Prentice & Miller, 1992). Relationships of that magnitude may aid researchers in predicting group membership or may foretell the possible effectiveness of a treatment.

As the studies reviewed here demonstrate, however, often a significant part of the contribution made by attitudes to understanding aggressive behavior stems from the correlation between the attitude and some third variable such as gender (as in our study and that of Saunders et al., 1987) or neuroticism (e.g., Murphy et al., 1986). Thus, the independent weight accorded attitudes as explanations for violence is mitigated, and we begin to wonder whether we should turn our attention to other factors (cf. Dibble & Straus, 1980; Eisikovits et al., 1991; Sugarman & Frankel, 1996).

TABLE 12.5 Summary of Studies

Saunders, Lynch, Grayson, and Linz (1987)		Means on IBWB subscales			
		Batterers	*Male Students*	*Female Students*	*Advocates*
	WJ	2.42^{ac}	2.17^c	1.53	1.26^a
	WG	2.70^a	2.50	2.02	1.34^a
	HG	5.48^a	5.61	6.16	6.67^a
	OR	3.83^{ab}	4.45^b	4.50	5.24^a
	OP	3.20^{ab}	3.73^b	4.08	4.25^a

NOTE: Pairs of means marked with a or b differ significantly at $p < .01$. WJ means marked with c differ at $p < .04$.

Stith and Farley (1993)	Model: Severe marital violence, $R^2 = .19$, $F = 3.26**$
Variable	*Standardized Coefficient*
Approval of marital violence	.25*
Marital stress	−.06
Level of alcoholism	.03
Sex-role egalitarianism	−.24*
Self-esteem	−.16
Observation of marital violence	−.10

*$p < .05$, **$p < .01$.

Smith (1990)	Model: Wife beating, $R^2 = .20$
Variable	*Logit Coefficient (unstandardized)*
Patriarchal beliefs index	.42**
Approval of violence index	.41**
Income	−.03
Education	−.19*
Occupational status	−.13
Employment status	−.20

*$p < .05$; **$p < .01$.

Eisikovits, Edleson, Guttmann, and Sela-Amit (1991)	Model: Physical violence	
Variable	*Beta*	R^2
Attitudes	−.39	.16*
Rational cognitions	−.31	.25*

*$p < .01$.

Murphy, Coleman, and Haynes (1986)	Model: Coercive sexual behavior, $R^2 = .17$, $F = 2.73*$
Variable	*Standardized Coefficient*
Hostility index	−.235*
Extroversion	.170*
Neuroeroticism	.144
Rape likelihood index	.134
Rape myth acceptance	.066
Adversarial sexual beliefs	.008
Sex-role stereotyping	.006

*$p < .01$.

Unfortunately, we do not have the capability of addressing this concern due to the nature of most research on the attitude-behavior connection. Judgments of the importance of the size of a given relationship are subjective (Prentice & Miller, 1992). Many small effects have important consequences when they emerge across studies or they point to theoretical relationships worthy of further research attention. Whereas the relationship between attitudes and behavior appears to be consistent across studies, the lack of a controlled examination of the relationship prevents us from confidently concluding that attitudes in and of themselves make a meaningful difference.

Violence within the family is, as many before us have concluded, multiply determined, and those studying the link between attitudes and violence must assess this linkage in relation to the larger set of predictors that also have been identified as correlates of aggression. Thus, not only should we study attitudes about the use of violence in relation to other types of attitudes and beliefs (e.g., attitudes toward women, religious beliefs), but we must consider how attitudes interact with ecological circumstances (e.g., Garbarino, 1976; Kaufman & Zigler, 1989) and biological proclivities (e.g., Dabbs, 1992) to influence behavior. Greater attention to the multiplicity of factors that influence the manifestation of violence will lead us to understand the conditions that strengthen and weaken the connection between aggressive cognition and aggressive actions and should lead to better interventions.

The existing body of research also fails largely to test the *predictive* utility of the relationship between attitudes and behavior. Researchers usually find groups of people who have engaged in violence or not and then assess their attitudes. These studies do not inform us about whether assessment of attitudes might lead to predictions about violence in a general population, about whether attitudes are a precursor or a consequence of violence, or indeed whether attitudes have any causal connection to violent behavior. Future investigations should address these important questions.

Finally, researchers must attend more carefully to the validity of the measures used to as-sess attitudes. As noted earlier, although the ATA appears to be reliable and valid, more testing is needed. The same is true for other measures that have been used for research on attitudes about violence (see especially Burt, 1980, and Smith, 1990). Attempts to study the explanatory power of attitudes will falter without well-validated measures on which to base assessment.

References

Boldizar, J. P., Perry, D. G., & Perry, L. C. (1989). Outcome values and aggression. *Child Development, 60,* 571-579.

Burt, M. R. (1980). Cultural myths and supports for rape. *Journal of Personality and Social Psychology, 38,* 217-230.

Crowne, D. P., & Marlowe, D. (1964). *The approval motive: Studies in evaluative dependence.* New York: John Wiley.

Dabbs, J. M. (1992). Testosterone measurements in social and clinical psychology. *Journal of Social and Clinical Psychology, 11,* 302-321.

Dibble, U., & Straus, M. A. (1980). Some social structure determinants of inconsistency between attitudes and behavior: The case of family violence. *Journal of Marriage and the Family, 42,* 71-80.

Eagly, A. H., & Chaiken, S. (1993). *The psychology of attitudes.* Fort Worth, TX: Harcourt Brace Jovanovich.

Eisikovits, Z. C., Edleson, J. L., Guttmann, E., & Sela-Amit, M. (1991). Cognitive styles and socialized attitudes of men who batter: Where should we intervene? *Family Relations, 40,* 72-77.

Garbarino, J. (1976). A preliminary study of some ecological correlates of child abuse: The impact of socioeconomic stress on mothers. *Child Development, 47,* 178-185.

Greenblat, C. S. (1985). "Don't hit your wife . . . unless . . .": Preliminary findings on normative support for the use of physical force by husbands. *Victimology, 10,* 221-241.

Herzberger, S. D., & Tennen, H. (1985). The effect of self-relevance on judgments of moderate and severe disciplinary encounters. *Journal of Marriage and the Family, 47,* 311-318.

Holden, G. W., Coleman, S. M., & Schmidt, K. L. (1995). Why 3-year-old children get spanked: Parent and child determinants as reported by college-educated mothers. *Merrill-Palmer Quarterly, 41,* 431-452.

Jennings, J. L. (1987). History and issues in the treatment of battering men: A case for unstructured group therapy. *Journal of Family Violence, 2,* 193-213.

Kaufman, J., & Zigler, E. (1989). The intergenerational transmission of child abuse. In D. Cicchetti & V. Carlson (Eds.), *Child maltreatment: Theory and research on the causes and consequences of child abuse and neglect* (pp. 129-150). Cambridge: Cambridge University Press.

Kelder, L. R., McNamara, J. R., Carlson, B., & Lynn, S. J. (1991). Perceptions of physical punishment: The relation to childhood and adolescent experiences. *Journal of Interpersonal Violence, 6,* 432-445.

Koski, P. R., & Mangold, W. D. (1988). Gender effects in attitudes about family violence. *Journal of Family Violence, 3,* 225-237.

Murphy, W. D., Coleman, E. M., & Haynes, M. R. (1986). Factors related to coercive sexual behavior in a nonclinical sample of males. *Violence and Victims, 1,* 255-298.

Prentice, D. A., & Miller, D. T. (1992). When small effects are impressive. *Psychological Bulletin, 112,* 160-164.

Saunders, D. G., Lynch, A. B., Grayson, M., & Linz, D. (1987). The Inventory of Beliefs about Wife Beating: The construction and initial validation of a measure of beliefs and attitudes. *Violence and Victims, 2,* 39-55.

Saunders, D. G., & Size, P. B. (1986). Attitudes about woman abuse among police officers, victims, and victim advocates. *Journal of Interpersonal Violence, 1,* 25-42.

Smith, M. D. (1990). Patriarchal ideology and wife beating: A test of a feminist hypothesis. *Violence and Victims, 5,* 257-273.

Stith, S. M., & Farley, S. C. (1993). A predictive model of male spousal violence. *Journal of Family Violence, 8,* 183-201.

Straus, M. A. (1989). *Manual for the Conflict Tactics Scales.* Durham: University of New Hampshire, Family Research Laboratory.

Sugarman, D. B., & Cohn, E. S. (1986). Origin and solution attributions of responsibility for wife abuse: Effects of outcome severity, prior history, and sex of subject. *Violence and Victims, 1,* 291-303.

Sugarman, D. B., & Frankel, S. L. (1996). Patriarchal ideology and wife-assault: A meta-analytic review. *Journal of Interpersonal Violence, 11,* 13-40.

Walker, L. E. (1984). *The battered woman syndrome.* New York: Springer.

Wolf, F. M. (1986). *Meta-analysis: Quantitative methods for research synthesis.* Beverly Hills, CA: Sage.

CHAPTER 13

Woman Battering

A Comparative Analysis of Black and White Women

Janice Joseph

Woman battering, also known as wife abuse, spousal violence, and domestic violence, is a well-established tradition in our society. Throughout most of history, woman battering was accepted as a legitimate act in relationships between intimates. In fact, only in the past hundred years have American men lost the right to use physical violence to control their wives or other intimates. It is estimated that one in six American women is abused by the man with whom she lives (Straus & Gelles, 1990). It is evident that violence against women by their husbands, once thought to be rare, is in reality a major problem. The purpose of the study was twofold: first, to examine the nature and extent of woman battering among White and Black women and, second, to consider whether social services are used differently by White and Black women.

Literature Review

Racial Differences

Several studies focus on racial and ethnic differences in woman battering. Findings from these studies, however, have been inconsistent because they use different types of samples of women. For example, Hampton and Gelles's (1994) analysis of the 1985 National Family Violence Survey found that Black wives were 1.23 times more likely than White wives to experience minor violence, and more than 2.36 times more likely to experience severe violence. They also reported that when they controlled for income, wife abuse was still higher among Blacks than Whites. Neff, Holamon, and Schluter's (1995) study also found that Black females were more likely than White females to report being beaten by a spouse.

Stark (1990) reported that although there seems to be little difference between African American and Caucasian women in terms of the incidence of partner violence, African American families had higher levels of lethal violence. Gondolf, Fisher, and McFerron's (1988) analysis of shelter residents found that there were no differences in the frequency of abuse among Hispanic, African American, and Caucasian women who were assaulted by their abusive mates. Harvey (1986) argued that for some Black females, the increased risk of violence may be in part a "scapegoat effect, in which the Black female becomes the repository of the anger and frustration of the Black male" (p. 167).

Social Services Use Among Black Women

Several studies have shown that Black women are less likely than Whites to use social agencies. Sorenson (1996) reported that African American women are hesitant to call the police even if there is extreme violence, for fear of how the Black batterer will be treated by the police. Gondolf, Fisher, and McFerron (1991) found that battered women from Black, White, and Hispanic backgrounds sought the same amount of assistance before entering a shelter. Hispanic American women, however, were least likely to contact a friend, minister, or social service. A greater number of White women contacted or visited a social agency, whereas more Black women contacted a minister or the police.

Asbury (1993) has suggested that African Americans are likely to be suspicious and distrustful of outsiders given the oppression they had to endure in American society. They, therefore, would use the services of social agencies only in extreme cases. Likewise, Peterson-Lewis, Turner, and Adams (1988) argue that African American women may attribute the causes of their abuse to the larger society. Consequently, they may be reluctant to involve police because

of their belief that African American males are more likely to be arrested and to be the victims of police abuse than White males. Asbury (1987) also argued that the availability of shelters and the support system of friends and family, the isolation African American women may feel in a shelter that is dominated by Euro-Americans, and reluctance to expose an African American man as a batterer because of his vulnerability in society are all barriers to help-seeking behavior by African American battered women.

The Criminal Justice Response to Woman Battering

In the past, battering by a domestic partner was considered a private matter rather than a "real" crime of assault (Buzawa & Buzawa, 1990; Dobash & Dobash, 1979). Consequently, the criminal justice system often trivialized the seriousness of woman battering. Police departments have traditionally favored an arrest-avoidance policy, and battered women were ignored unless they required a substantial number of stitches under the "stitch-rule" policy. Such cases constituted felonies so police felt obligated to arrest the batterer (Tong, 1986). Largely through the efforts of many community groups and lawsuits initiated by battered women, police departments have changed their policies toward woman battering. Many departments have adopted a "pro-arrest approach" in which police can arrest the batterer without a warrant if there is probable cause to believe that the battering did take place. Another reform in police practice is crisis intervention in which police officers attempt to resolve the dispute between the woman and her partner (Tong, 1986).

There have also been some improvements in the way prosecutors handle woman battering cases. Traditionally, prosecutors were unwilling to aggressively pursue criminal charges in many of these cases because they often viewed domestic violence against women as a private matter or they believed that some women precipitate the violence (Meier, 1987; Woods, 1981). Presently in some jurisdictions, prosecutors have taken woman battering seriously and have initiated procedures that allow them to prosecute batterers successfully. In other jurisdictions, however, prosecutors still view woman batter-ing as a minor offense (Ellis, 1984; Meier, 1987; Mickish & Schoen, 1988).

Social Services for Battered Women

Social services for battered women have im-proved over the years. There are a number of battered women shelters in the United States. Counseling is one feature of these shelters, of-fering advice on safety, independent living, per-sonal growth, advocacy, and options available to women. Other services include emergency hotlines that provide information and referrals for financial assistance, housing, medical ser-vices, and legal assistance. Community groups, including support groups, often consist of a net-work of abused women, treatment programs for battered women, outpatient mental health cen-ters, and crisis intervention units (Dutton-Douglas & Dionne, 1991).

The Importance of the Study

Although woman battering is considered a universal problem, the literature has failed to fo-cus comprehensively on the experiences of mi-nority women. The literature on battered women ignores the issue of race by using samples of only White women (Bowker, 1984) or by in-cluding some minority women in the samples, but not in proportions comparable to White women in the sample (Hofeller, 1982; Walker, 1984).

There is a general assumption, however, that the nature and extent of woman battering is uniquely different for White and Black women and these differences are the result of race and social class. In addition, the National Black Women's Health Project has identified woman battering as the number one health issue for Black women (Avery, 1990). However, few re-searchers have tested the above assertions em-pirically. One attempt at examining the racial differences in woman battering between Blacks and Whites was done by Lockhart (1991). She focused on the extent and causes of woman bat-tering, but failed to address the nature and the use of social agencies to deal with the abuse. The

present investigation intends to remedy these gaps in the literature. This study will fulfill the need for further research on woman battering, the need for more research on Black women, and the need for more rigorous research on woman battering among racial groups.

The importance of the study lies in its ability to enrich our understanding of the pattern of woman battering for White and Black women. This kind of study examines racial differences and can provide more powerful comparative evidence as opposed to racial inferences about Black and White abused women. Although the sample was small and nonrandom, making the results less generalizable, this study was de-signed to lay the foundation for further, and more elaborate, research on woman battering among Black and White women.

Research Design

Sample

The sample consisted of 204 women battered by the men they were legally married to or with whom they lived. Fifty-two percent (105) of the respondents were Black and 48% (99) were White. This was a nonrandom sample obtained through three sites: the family court, a battered women's shelter, and a homeless shelter. The in-vestigator and research assistants conducted personal interviews with each of the women us-ing an interview schedule designed to measure the nature, extent, and effects of the violence they experienced. In addition, information on the extent of the use of social services by these women was also collected. The first section of the interview schedule focused on the nature and duration of the violence. The second section col-lected data on factors associated with the vio-lence. The third section examined the use of so-cial agencies, such as police, courts, and shelters, and the fourth section collected data on demographics.

Nature of the Violence

The following question was used to measure the *frequency* of the violence: "How often does the violence occur?" (once a week, once a month, every six months, once a year, only once). To assess the *chronicity* of violence, the following question was asked: "How long has the violence been occurring?" (less than one month, 1-6 months, 7-12 months, 1-4 years, 5 years and over). The women were also asked about both *verbal and emotional abuse* they had experienced with the following questions: "Is he verbally abusive to you?" and "Is he emotionally abusive to you?" We also asked if the abuser had been *violent to others* in the family with the following question: "Is he violent to the children?"

Severity of Violence

Severity of violence was measured by the extent of the *injuries* sustained. Responses included slaps, bruises, and broken bones. Respondents were asked to explain any injuries that they had received as a result of the abuse and if they had ever been hospitalized or needed surgery for abuse related injuries. Respondents were asked what type of *weapon,* if any, was used against them.

Response to the Violence

Each woman was asked whether she had left her abuser, whether she fought back, and her perception of the effects of the violence. The following questions were used to measure the response to the abuse. "Did you ever leave him and return?" "After how many incidents did you decide to leave?" (1-3, 4-6, 7-9, 10 and over), "Did you ever injure the batterer?" "Are you still in the relationship?" and "How has the violence affected you?"

Substance Use

The use of drugs and alcohol at the time of the violence was measured using the following questions: "Is he often under the influence of substances at the time of the violence?" and "What kind of drugs does he use?"

TABLE 13.1 Social Characteristics by Race (in percentages)

	White (n = 99)	Black (n = 105)	χ^2
Age			
Under 25	21	34	
25-29	29	24	
30-34	35	42	
35 and over	15	0	7.22*
Religion			
Catholic	44	27	
Protestant	32	34	
Other	24	29	.45
Employment type			
Unskilled	56	74	
Semiskilled	29	13	
White collar	3	0	
Professional	12	13	4.29
Education			
Elementary	3	3	
High school	94	97	
College	3	0	.56
Number of children			
None	26	13	
One	27	50	
Two to four	27	37	4.64

*$p < .05$.

Results

■ Table 13.1 presents the social characteristics of the sample by racial group. Most women, both Black and White, were at least 25 years old when they were interviewed. However, more White women than Black women were over age 35 (15% vs. 0%). Age was the only social characteristic on which there was a statistically significant difference between Black and White women. White women in this sample were more likely than Black women to be Catholic; however, the difference was not statistically significant. The majority of women in this sample worked at unskilled or semiskilled occupations; however, Black women were somewhat more likely to be employed in unskilled occupations. Most women had a high school education. White women were more likely than Black women to have more than one child; however, the difference was not large enough to be significant.

TABLE 13.2 Nature of Last Incident by Race (in percentages)

	White (n = 99)	Black (n = 105)	χ^2
Time of last incident			
Less than 1 month	50	26	
1-6 months	44	55	
7-12 months	6	11	
1-4 years	0	8	6.28
Argument involved	82	92	1.46
Man intoxicated	53	66	1.23
Types of violence			
Slaps	26	34	
Bruises	53	50	
Broken bones	18	16	
Surgery	3	0	1.54
Used a weapon	59	79	3.42
Witnesses to incident			
Children	73	45	
Other relatives	12	19	
Friends	15	32	
Others	0	4	4.93
First incident	29	16	1.93

Nature of Last Incident

The women interviewed were asked to indicated how long ago the last violent incident that they experienced occurred (see Table 13.2). Half of the White women compared to just over one quarter of the Black women stated that it occurred less than one month prior to the interview; however, the difference was not statistically significant. The majority of both Black and White women reported that the violent incident also involved an argument. All the women claimed that they were not intoxicated at the time of the abuse, but just over half of the White women and two thirds of the Black women reported that the man was intoxicated during the incident. Among the types of violence experienced and resulting injuries were slaps, bruises, and broken bones. A small percentage (3%) of the White women required surgery. In addition, a large percentage of both Black and White women stated that the abusive incident involved a weapon. Almost half of the total sample of women (47%) indicated that there was a witness

to the last violent incident. Among the White women, most of these witnesses (73%) were children. For most women, regardless of race, this incident of violence was not the first they had experienced.

Nature of the General Violence

Table 13.3 looks at the characteristics of violence (nature, severity, and reaction) for White and Black women. There were no significant racial differences in either the nature or the severity of the violence; however, there were differences in the reaction to it. All of the Black women in the sample compared to almost three quarters of the White women indicated that they had left their abuser and then returned. In addition, Black women were more likely than White women to report experiencing a greater number of violent incidents before leaving their abuser. They were also significantly more likely than White women to have injured their abuser. Finally, Black women were significantly more likely to have remained in the relationship than their White counterparts.

Severity of the Violence

Fifty-one percent stated that they suffered bruises from the violence, 25% were slapped without bruises, 6% were punched without injuries, and 1% suffered broken bones. The man's limbs were most commonly used as the weapon (65%), followed by guns (35%). There were no racial differences regarding the severity of the violence.

Social Assistance

One of the other goals of this research was to look at racial differences in the use of social services. Table 13.4 presents the results of chi-square analyses looking at these differences. White victims were 1 ½ times more likely than their Black counterparts to call the police about their victimization. They were also more than twice as likely than Black women to have gone to court and almost 2 times more likely to have used the services of a family counselor. White

TABLE 13.3 Characteristics of the Violence by Race (in percentages)

	White (n = 99)	Black (n = 105)	χ^2
Nature of the violence			
Frequency			
First incident	9	3	
Once a week	47	42	
Once a month	29	34	
Every 6 months	6	16	
Once a year	9	5	3.38
Duration			
Less than 1 month	3	0	
1-6 months	32	13	
7-12 months	38	40	
1-4 years	18	29	
5 years and over	0	0	
Emotional abuse	68	76	.67
Verbal abuse	94	92	.11
Batterer violent to children	71	63	.44
Severity of abuse			
Injuries scale			
Slaps	20	26	
Bruises	23	29	
Broken bones	56	45	
Surgery	1	0	.89
Gun used	25	26	.01
Reaction to the violence			
Leave man and return	74	100	11.50***
Number of incidents before leaving			
1-3	18	2	
4-6	12	3	
7-9	38	37	
10 and over	32	58	8.89*
Injure batterer	27	55	6.12**
Still in relationship	18	45	6.01**

*$p < .05$, **$p < .01$; ***$p < .001$.

TABLE 13.4 Use of Social Services (in percentages)

Agencies	White (n = 99)	Black (n = 105)	χ^2
Police	59	39	4.38*
Court	38	16	4.65*
Counsel	47	24	4.34*
Shelter	21	5	3.85*
Request restraining order	76	39	10.02***
Ever hospitalized because of injuries	8	53	6.78**

*Significant at .05 level; **significant at .01 level; ***significant at .001 level.

women were also more than 4 times as likely as Black women to have gone to a shelter and almost 2 times more likely to have requested a restraining order against their abusive partner. Interestingly, Black women were 6 times more likely than White women to have been hospitalized as a result of injuries sustained.

One pretrial strategy to prevent violence is the issuing of an order of protection (restraining order) by a judge. Only 57% ever requested a restraining order, and 97% of those who did not request a restraining order stated that they did not do so because it does no good. One of the limitations of the protection order is the lack of enforcement. Sixty-three percent of women who requested a restraining order reported that the order was violated, and only 33% of the violators were punished.

A major problem with the issuing of a restraining order is the high rate of case attrition caused by the victim. It is not uncommon for battered women to withdraw restraining orders, and in this study, several of the women withdrew their request for a restraining order after making such a request. This researcher was astounded at the number of women who showed up before the family court judge stating that they no longer wanted an order of protection, although many of them were badly beaten when they made such a request. Interviews with family court personnel revealed that this was a common pattern for some "regulars," who request protection orders then withdraw those orders, many times and for many years. This situation was a very frustrating experience for family court personnel who were interviewed because of the time allocated to the cases and fear for the safety of the women.

Overall, significantly more Whites than Blacks reported the incidents to the police, brought charges against the batterer in court, requested a restraining order, sought counseling, and stayed in a shelter. This is perhaps due to the fact that many African Americans do not trust the criminal justice system. In addition, Black women may feel that they will experience cultural alienation when they seek assistance in these agencies. Moreover, Blacks are reluctant to discuss family and personal problems with strangers. They view this as "putting your business in the street" (Barbee, 1992).

Summary

■ In general, data from this research show that there were no significant differences in the nature and extent of the abuse between Black and White women. The major differences between the two groups was their response to the violence. Black women were more likely than White women to fight back, they were more likely to tolerate the abuse longer, and they were more likely to leave and return. Moreover, Black women were more reluctant than White women to use social services. At the same time, however, Black women were more likely to be hospitalized due to abuse-related injuries. One possible inference from these results is that fighting back for the Black woman is a coping response to the abuse, whereas White women seek the assistance of social service agencies. It is also quite possible that battered Black women distrust social agencies, such as the police, and rely on informal networks of support. Local communities and police departments, in particular, need to give greater attention and resources to battered women both in terms of the number and extent of their injuries.

Policy Implications

■ Many women expressed their dissatisfaction with the criminal justice system. More reforms are still needed in the system. All police officers should have special training on how to deal with domestic violence. More stringent laws regarding the violation of restraining orders are necessary. Such violations should be taken seriously and severe penalties should be given to violators. Unless law enforcement against the violation of restraining orders improves, these legal remedies will offer little protection to women.

There needs to be careful training for those who provide services for battered women. Research indicates that many professionals, including counselors, nurses, and physicians, may have negative, stereotypical, or inaccurate notions about battered women (Bowker, 1987; Kurz, 1987; Lavoie, Jacob, & Martin, 1989; Trute, Sarsfield, & MacKenzie, 1988). These attitudes can affect the quality of the services offered to battered women.

The services offered may be inappropriate for some women. This is particularly true for minority women, especially African Americans who may find the Eurocentric approach used in many service agencies inappropriate for their needs. Sorenson (1996) reported that many women of color state that if agencies were not respectful of their cultural backgrounds, they either did not use such services or they used them only briefly. Some researchers have argued that agencies' use of the Euro-American approach, which is based on materialism, individual autonomy, and segmentation of all aspects of reality, is antithetical and detrimental to African Americans whose culture emphasizes collectivity, interdependence, and interrelatedness of all things (Bell, 1986; Myers, 1987, 1988, 1990).

To successfully counsel Black battered women, professionals should dispel all negative myths, beliefs, and stereotypes of Black women, because the consequences of such perceptions can be disastrous. Professionals should also be knowledgeable about how Black women react to abuse, and the role racism plays in fostering violence against Black women. Finally, they need to provide culturally sensitive intervention strategies that are tailored to the specific needs of battered Black women. Such programs should use an Afrocentric approach that examines the sociocultural patterns and experiences of Blacks to explain behavior. Intervention should be based on the recognition that Black women have been socialized not to talk to strangers about their abuse, may be reluctant to seek help for their abuse, may be afraid to prosecute the man, and value the importance of friends and family networks. For example, given the importance of family and friends, professionals should endeavor to include family members and friends in counseling sessions with Black women.

More preventive programs are also needed. Society's response to woman battering is reactive, intervening after the assault has taken place. Reactive programs do not reach the core of the problem of woman abuse by men. Preventive programs should focus on the root causes of woman battering. It is necessary to identify women who are at risk for assault as well as those men who are likely to perpetrate violence against women. One approach to this problem is to focus on children who experience or witness violence in the home to prevent the "cycle of violence" in those children. It is also necessary to teach those at risk to adopt alternative coping skills and conflict resolution strategies instead of turning to violence.

Woman battering is a complex problem and requires complex and serious solutions. Too often, injured or threatened women are ignored. Too often, police see battering as a "family squabble" or "domestic disturbance." Although a great deal of progress has been made over the years, much more needs to be done to protect women. At present, there is still too much insensitivity among police officers and judges to the plight of battered women.

References

Asbury, J. (1987). African-American women in violent relationships: An exploration of cultural differences. In R. L. Harper (Ed.), *Violence and the Black family* (pp. 89-105). Lexington, MA: D. C. Heath.

Asbury, J. (1993). Violence in families of color in the United States. In R. C. Hampton, T. P. Gullotta, G. R. Adams, E. H. Potter, & R. P. Weissberg (Eds.), *Family violence: Prevention and treatment* (pp. 159-178). Newbury Park, CA: Sage.

Avery, B. (1990). Breathing life into ourselves: The evolution of the National Black Women's Project. In E. C. White (Ed.), *The Black woman's health book* (pp. 4-10). Seattle, WA: Seal.

Barbee, E. (1992). Ethnicity and woman abuse in United States. In M. Sampelle (Ed.), *Violence against women: Nursing research, education and practice* (pp. 153-166). New York: Hemisphere.

Bell, C. (1986). Impaired Black health professionals: Vulnerabilities and treatment approaches. *Journal of the American Medical Association, 78,* 1139-1141.

Bowker, L. H. (1984). Coping with wife abuse: Personal and social networks. In A. R. Roberts (Ed.), *Battered women and their families* (pp. 168-191). New York: Springer.

Bowker, L. H. (1987). Battered women as consumers of legal services: Report from a national survey. *Response, 10,* 10-17.

Buzawa, E. S., & Buzawa, C. G. (1990). *Domestic violence: The criminal justice response.* Newbury Park, CA: Sage.

Dobash, R. E., & Dobash, R. P. (1979). *Violence against wives: A case against the patriarchy.* New York: Free Press.

Dutton-Douglas, M. A., & Dionne, D. (1991). Counseling and shelter services for battered women. In M. Steinman (Ed.), *Woman battering: Policy response* (pp. 113-130). Cincinnati, OH: Anderson.

Ellis, J. (1984). Prosecutorial discretion to charge in cases of spouse assault: A dialogue. *Journal of Criminal Law and Criminology, 75,* 56-102.

Gondolf, E. W., Fisher, E., & McFerron, J. R. (1988). Racial differences among shelter residents: A comparison of Anglo, Black, and Hispanic battered women. *Journal of Family Violence, 3,* 39-51.

Gondolf, E. W., Fisher, E., & McFerron, J. R. (1991). Racial differences among shelter residents: A comparison of Anglo, Black, and Hispanic battered women. In R. Hampton (Ed.), *Black family violence: Current research and theory* (pp. 103-113). Lexington, MA: D. C. Heath.

Hampton, R. L., & Gelles, R. J. (1994). Violence toward Black women in a nationally representative sample of Black families. *Journal of Comparative Family Studies, 25,* 105-120.

Harvey, W. B. (1986). Homicide among young Black adults: Life in the subculture of exasperation. In D. F. Hawkins (Ed.), *Homicide among Black Americans* (pp. 153-171). Lanham, MD: University Press of America.

Hofeller, K. (1982). *Social, psychological and situational factors in wife abuse.* Palo Alto, CA: R & E Research Associates.

Kurz, D. (1987). Emergency department responses to battered women: Resistance to medicalization. *Social Problems, 34,* 69-81.

Lockhart, L. (1991). Spousal violence: A cross-racial perspective. In R. Hampton (Ed.), *Black family violence: Current research and theory* (pp. 85-102). Lexington, MA: D. C. Heath.

Lavoie, F., Jacob, M., & Martin, G. (1989). Police attitudes in assigning responsibility for wife abuse. *Journal of Family Violence, 4,* 369-388.

Meier, J. (1987). Battered justice. *Washington Monthly,* pp. 37-45.

Mickish, J., & Schoen, K. (1988). Domestic violence: Developing and maintaining an effective policy. *The Prosecutor,* pp. 15-20.

Myers, L. J. (1987). The deep structure of culture: Relevance of traditional culture in contemporary life. *Journal of Black Studies, 18,* 72-75.

Myers, L. J. (1988). *Understanding an Afrocentric world view: Introduction to an optimal psychology.* Dubuque, IA: Kendall/Hunt.

Myers, L. J. (1990). Understanding family violence: An Afrocentric analysis based upon optimal theory. In D. S.

Ruiz (Ed.), *Handbook of mental health and mental disorder among Black Americans* (pp. 183-189). New York: Greenwood.

Neff, J. A., Holamon, B., & Schluter, T. D. (1995). Spousal violence among Anglos, Blacks, and Mexican Americans: The role of demographic variables, psychosocial predictors, and alcohol consumption. *Journal of Family Violence, 10,* 1-21.

Peterson-Lewis, S., Turner, C. W., & Adams, A. M. (1988). Attributional processes in repeatedly abused women. In G. W. Russell (Ed.), *Violence in intimate relationships* (pp. 107-130). New York: Police Management Association.

Sorenson, S. A. (1996, April). Violence against women: Examining ethnic differences and commonalities. *Evaluation Review, 20,* 123-145.

Stark, E. (1990). Rethinking homicide: Violence, race, and the policies of gender. *International Journal of Health Sciences, 20,* 3-26.

Straus, M. A., & Gelles, R. J. (Eds.). (1990). *Physical violence in American families: Risk factors and adaptations to violence in 8,145 families.* New Brunswick, NJ: Transaction.

Tong, R. (1986). *Women, sex, and the law.* Totowa, NJ: Rowman & Allanheld.

Trute, B., Sarsfield, P., & MacKenzie, D. A. (1988). Medical response to wife abuse: A survey of physicians' attitudes and practices. *Canadian Journal of Community Mental Health, 7,* 61-71.

Walker, L. E. (1984). *The battered woman syndrome.* New York: Harper & Row.

Woods, L. (1981). Litigation on behalf of battered women. *Women's Rights Law Reporter, 7,* 39-45.

CHAPTER 14

Surviving Abusive Dating Relationships

Processes of Leaving, Healing, and Moving On

Karen H. Rosen
Sandra M. Stith

Interviews with battered women make it apparent that the experience of violence inflicted by partners in committed relationships is shocking and confusing. Battering is rarely perceived as an unambiguous assault demanding an end to the relationship to ensure future safety. Studies indicate that battered women frequently remain in abusive relationships for a considerable period of time after the abuse begins (Campbell, Miller, Cardwell, & Belknap, 1994; Ferraro & Johnson, 1983; Henton, Cate, Koval, Lloyd, & Christopher, 1983), and many battered women live their entire lives in abusive relationships. Although researchers have tried to explain why women remain in these relationships (Herbert, Silver, & Ellard, 1991; Johnson, 1992; Rosen, 1996), few studies have attempted to understand how women are able to disentangle themselves from abusive intimate relationships and to move ahead in their lives after leaving violent relationships. Furthermore, studies that have examined processes of leaving have focused primarily on the experience of battered wives. Although there are certainly similarities between marital abuse and premarital abuse, many of the barriers to leaving experienced by abused wives do not apply to women in premarital relationships. However, despite the fact that premarital relationships rarely have legal, financial, or familial ties that bind partners together as do marital relationships, disentangling from these relationships can be difficult (Rosen,

1996). Thus, we need to look specifically at abusive premarital relationships to understand how women leave these relationships once they become entrapped. This study examines the processes of disentangling from abusive premarital relationships and discusses how women are able to heal and to move on in their lives after leaving.

Review of the Literature

■ Studies have examined the differences between battered wives who are able to leave their partners and those who are not. For example, Herbert et al. (1991) conducted a study with 130 participants to determine differences between women who stayed with abusive partners (34%) and those who left (66%). In addition to family income, the variables that distinguished between the two groups most strongly reflected women's perceptions of their relationship and how their relationships compared to others. That is, women who were still with their abusive partners appraised their relationships more positively, saw little change in the frequency or severity of the abuse or the amount of love and affection expressed toward them, and appraised their relationship as being not as bad as it could be more often than those who chose to leave their abusive partners.

Ferraro and Johnson (1983) describe in more detail the forces that lead the formerly battered wife to begin to recognize that she is battered. These researchers were participant observers at a shelter for battered women for more than a year. In that time they observed and had conversations with 120 women and kept records of staff meetings and crisis phone conversations. They also taped interviews with 10 residents and five battered women who left their abusers without going to the shelter. Ferraro and Johnson concluded that changes in the relationship or the individual or changes in available resources were catalysts for redefining the violence. They identified six kinds of change: (a) in the level of violence, leading to the realization that battering could be fatal; (b) in resources, where the existence of a place to go becomes apparent; (c) in the relationship, such as the cessation or decrease in the level of remorse expressed by the

abuser for the abuse; (d) loss of hope that things will get better; (e) in the visibility of violence, where violence previously private begins to occur in public; and (f) in the level of concern or outrage expressed by friends or relatives. These researchers maintained that as the violence is reinterpreted as dangerous and unjustified, women begin a process of victimization, which is a period of turmoil where changes in their feelings about themselves, their spouses, and their situations lead to actively seeking alternatives. During this process "feelings of love and intimacy are gradually replaced with loneliness and pessimism" (p. 334).

Bowker and colleagues (Bowker, 1983, 1984; Donato & Bowker, 1984) studied women whose husbands stopped abusing them after violence had become a pattern in their relationship. These investigators used semistructured, in-depth interviews to collect data from 146 formerly battered women. When asked what enabled them to demand an end to the violence, participants reported two major factors: (a) feeling like they had no other choice but to end the abuse and (b) gaining information and confidence from participation in women's groups. In addition to these factors, they said that fear for children and confidence that developed as a result of counseling or the support of family members helped them demand an end to the violence. Bowker and colleagues concluded that these feelings of confidence gave the women the strength to insist that the violence stop. Thus, a combination of having the confidence to take a stand against violence and believing that the violence had to end seemed to be most significant in leading participants to demand the violence end in these marital relationships.

Several researchers examined the stages that abused women go through to get out of abusive relationships. For example, Landenburger (1989) used semistructured, open-ended interviews to understand the experiences of 30 women who were in or who had recently left an abusive relationship. She described disengagement as a complex process that began after the victim labeled herself as abused and after she recognized her partner's behavior was not normal. Landenburger indicated that a first step for the majority of women in her sample was to seek help. Participants frequently described a breaking point where they begin to believe that their lives were meaningless if they stayed in their relationships. This realization led to anger. Participants reported becoming angry with themselves and their partners and using this anger to move themselves out of the abusive relationship. After participants left their abusive relationships, they continued to struggle for survival and to grieve the loss.

Mills (1985) also examined stages battered women go through in leaving abusive marriages. She conducted 2-hour interviews with 10 women who sought help at a shelter after leaving their husbands. She found that these women experienced five stages: (a) entering the relationship, (b) managing the violence, (c) experiencing a loss of self, (d) reevaluating the relationship, and (e) restructuring the self. Mills found that the process of reevaluating the relationship for battered wives was the result of a slow process whereby women shifted from being compliant and feeling numb to being reflective actors who eventually decided to leave their husbands. This process included a series of fleeting insights questioning their husbands' assessment of the situation along with validation from others that helped them shake loose from old ways of seeing things. Sometimes the process resulted from a specific triggering event, such as an increased level of violence. For some, the decision to leave was sudden; for others, it was a result of challenging long-held perceptions that change was possible.

Graham and Rawlings (1991) present a theoretical model for viewing the responses of young women in abusive dating relationships as similar to the traumatic bonding experienced by war hostages. They describe intense, unconsciously driven "push-pull" dynamics as characteristic of the victim's orientation to the abuser. These dynamics involve powerful, survival-based feelings of being pulled toward the abuser (mutual bonding between the victim and abuser) and of being pushed away from him (because he threatens her survival).

These competing push-pull forces are described as opposite sides of a spiral by Kirkwood (1993), who used unstructured interviews to help her understand how women leave abusive

partners. She interviewed 30 women twice and allowed them to tell their own stories. Kirkwood described the process battered women go through in leaving abusive partners as a spiral, in which both inward and outward movement occurred. The women began to move outward when they recognized that their relationships were having significant negative effects on their lives. This recognition was a first step in the women's efforts to look at their relationships differently. A change in energy level brought on by either anger or fear was another important aspect of outward movement. This energy was vital to the woman's ability to go through the difficult process of disentangling from an abusive partner that sometimes included repeated leaving then returning. Kirkwood found that returning was part of the spiraling-out process.

> This progression of abuse may, on the surface, seem to mirror what she experienced before she left her partner. She may even feel that she has come full circle and blame herself for what seems like a repeat of the past. However, through the act of leaving, she has gained the knowledge that she can leave. . . . This knowledge, plus her past history with her partner, will give her a different perspective on the progression of abuse and, despite her return, she will not be as close to the center of the spiral as she was previously. (Kirkwood, 1993, p. 65)

Finally, NiCarthy (1987), in her study of women who left abusive relationships, constructs an image of these women as survivors rather than victims. She indicates that these women who left their abusers had not only survived the abuse but also survived the aftermath of abuse including depression, anxiety, and resurgence of romantic feelings for their partners. She suggests that their survival is an active, progressive effort.

Summary

Thus, previous studies have indicated that for battered wives to leave their abusive husbands, they seem first to need to reassess their relationship as abusive. Next, they seem to go through a push-pull or spiral process in which they struggle with competing demands to stay and to leave their abusive partners. Those who finally are able to leave seem to be actively involved in a progressive survival effort. The current study extends these efforts by examining the disengagement process that occurred in a group of women in violent dating relationships.

Method

Participants and Selection Process

Twenty-two women participated in this study. Participants were recruited through newspaper advertisements, flyers reaching the general public as well as university students, and referrals from clinical colleagues. Recruitment efforts were directed toward women who had been or were currently in serious dating relationships in which violence had been inflicted more than once. Participants ranged in age from 16 to 32 when they began their violent dating relationships (mean age is 21 years). Relationships lasted from 10 months to 9 years, the violence from 3 months to 8 years. All but 2 of the women had ended their relationships prior to participating in the study; 10 women had cohabited with their abusive partners; 2 married their abusive dating partners after violence had become a pattern in their relationships (both were divorced when they participated in the study); 1 gave birth to her abusive boyfriend's child.

The physical abuse ranged from moderate (e.g., pushing, shoving, holding down, grabbing, pinching) to severe (e.g., punching, choking, hitting with an object). All the women reported experiencing verbal and emotional abuse (e.g., constant criticism, name calling, yelling, destruction of property, and threats of harm). In addition to physical trauma (e.g., black eyes, bruises, permanent nerve damage, broken bones, cuts), the women reported a variety of psychological symptoms including anger and resentment, reduced academic and/or work productivity, nightmares, startle responses, distrust of men and intimate relationships, lowered self-esteem, feeling "crazy," and homicidal and/or suicidal ideations.

Participants' families of origin ranged from lower middle class to upper middle class. However, most participants saw themselves as growing up in middle-class families. One participant was African American; the remainder were White. Fifteen participants grew up in intact families; 3 were raised primarily by single mothers; 3 grew up in remarried families; and 1 was raised primarily by her grandparents. Seventeen women apparently neither witnessed nor received physical abuse during childhood, and 17 had not been physically abused in prior dating relationships.

Data Collection and Analysis

A grounded theory approach was taken in collecting and analyzing the data (Glaser & Strauss, 1967; Strauss & Corbin, 1990). Over the course of the project, data collection and analysis were carried out concurrently with new data serving to reshape our thinking for subsequent interviews. We sought to discover patterns and meaning in the data without prior hypotheses and to allow meaning to emerge through constantly comparing concepts identified within and across individuals. We validated our interpretations and enhanced our theoretical sensitivity throughout the process through the interplay of collecting and analyzing data, discussing interpretations, and reading pertinent literature (Strauss & Corbin, 1990).

Twelve women were interviewed once, and 10 women were selected to be interviewed in more depth (2-3 interviews each). Decisions about whom to select for in-depth study were made in part on the basis of their availability and in part according to the tenets of theoretical sampling outlined by Strauss and Corbin (1990). That is, women who were selected to interview more than once were those who seemed able to further our understanding of issues emerging as relevant or who appeared to be negative cases. Initial interviews varied from 1 to 3 hours; subsequent interviews tended to be more intense, varying from 2 to 4 hours. With the permission of participants, all interviews were audiotaped and transcribed. The interviewer asked questions about participants' expectations for their relationships, how their relationships began, circumstances surrounding violent incidents, how they responded to and made sense of the violence, and what role family and friends played throughout the process. Interviews were semi-structured to provide ample opportunity for a dialogue to develop between interviewer and participant.

Informants were given the opportunity to participate in the analysis process by reading and commenting on our initial interpretations of their stories (Thompson, 1992; Yin, 1989). Twelve participants provided feedback after reviewing their summary, which was incorporated into the results where appropriate. Other tactics for achieving trustworthiness included cross-coding transcript material (Yin, 1989) and regular discussions with colleagues to critically question analyses and to consider rival explanations (Marshall & Rossman, 1989). However, traditional ways of determining validity and reliability cannot be applied to qualitative research. Therefore, consumers must ultimately check the researcher's insights against what makes sense to them within their own set of values, experiences, and pragmatic concerns to decide its trustworthiness and its value (Atkinson, Heath, & Chenail, 1991).

Each transcript was read and reread. Then, through open coding, segments were named (coded) and placed in as many categories as possible. Higher-level categories—conceptualizations from a broader perspective—emerged as lower-level codes were grouped according to their similarities or differences from other codes. Finally, categories were related to each other to develop constructs that were grounded in the data. Theoretical insights that emerged during the data collection and analysis process or through discussions with colleagues were recorded into a written log. This log became a record of insights about interrelationships between various codes and categories and guided the iterative process of data collection and analysis. This log, composed of various levels of theoretical memos, was sorted and became the foundation for the final analysis and synthesis of the data.

Findings

■ This study confirms the notion hypothesized by others that becoming a battered woman and leaving a violent relationship is a process (Kirkwood, 1993; Mills, 1985). The women in this study became entrapped in abusive relationships where their needs (including safety and security) and self-interests became subsumed by and, to some degree, synonymous with their relationships. These relationships often became intense quickly and were fun and exciting at first with little conflict or unpleasantness. Soon conflict began to occur, often related to closeness and distance or power and control. Through an insidious process of entrapment (see Rosen, 1996), women remained committed to their relationships despite their boyfriends' use of emotional and physical abuse. Over time, women developed a readiness to leave their relationships and were able to loosen the emotional bonds tying them to their boyfriends.

Disentanglement Processes

There was no absolute point where entrapment processes clearly gave way to disentanglement processes. Instead, these processes were intertwined until the women made major shifts in perspective about themselves and their relationships. Disentanglement processes tended to move the women toward self-agency and empowerment. The process usually began with *seeds of doubt* and included various *turning points, reappraisals, objective reflections,* and *self-reclaiming actions* that were interrelated and part of a healthy cycle of building readiness to leave the relationship. It culminated for many of the women in what we labeled a *paradigmatic shift in perspective* about themselves and their relationship. They shifted from a position of "I need this relationship" to "I need to get out of this relationship." Paradigmatic shifts were usually accompanied by a *last straw event,* which provided the final impetus to leave the relationship. A more detailed description of each of the constructs that emerged as part of the disentanglement process follows.

Seeds of Doubt

What first alerted us to the notion of seeds of doubt was the women's use of words like "a part of me knew this would not work" or "a part of me knew things were not right" or "a small voice somewhere inside me saying, 'you don't deserve this'" and "little voices that you don't pay much attention to." Many of the women identified fleeting thoughts that their relationship would not work long before they consciously acknowledged that reality. These doubts did not seem to directly influence their behavior while they were focused on maintaining their relationships. Sometimes these seeds of doubt were sown after the first abusive incident although it may have been years before they germinated and bore fruit in the form of changes in thinking or action. This was the case for Tess, who clung to her relationship with her boyfriend, Matt, for 2 years after the first physically abusive incident. Although she admitted to herself that her relationship with Matt was troubled, she also had an overriding hope that things would get better. However, Tess felt that her relationship with Matt was never the same after he hit her for the first time, which to her meant that it was doomed to end, although neither realized it at the time.

> In a weird way it [the physical abuse] ended the relationship even though it didn't end directly after that. Even though we were both still clinging to it, it took a long time to break away. Once he did that, something was lost that could never be taken back.

For Cory, although she and her boyfriend were in love and becoming engaged, a part of her was having doubts because their arguments were getting more frequent and had escalated to mutual pushing and shoving. As Cory described it, one part of her was still committed to the relationship and another part had doubts. However, it took 2 months and two serious abusive events for Cory's seemingly silent partner to become active.

> It's like a two-stranded thing . . . the part that's actually there and goes through the motions and goes through the ritual and goes up and gets engaged, says I love you. . . . And there's the part that's very internalized and very factual. It's just kind of thinking and looking at things. . . . I was still showing up and I was still very loyal, but part of me was sitting back and checking things out

and making sure that I wasn't being real stupid by staying around.

Turning Points

Participants often identified turning points that had significant effects on the course of their relationships in the direction of change. Some turning points were intrapersonal events, such as small cognitive or emotional shifts. Some were interpersonal events, such as interactions with boyfriends, and some were critical life events such as high school graduation or pregnancy. However, unlike seeds of doubt, which were for the most part subconscious, turning points were recognized as having an overt role in the women's movement toward developing a readiness to leave. These events seemed to be part of a chain of events linking one disentanglement process to another.

For example, a turning point for Tess was a critical life event, her high school graduation. At this time in her life, she was so unhappy with her relationship with Matt that she began fantasizing about his or her own death. Graduation seemed to be a catalyst for Tess's change in perspective about herself and her future. She came to the realization that she was stagnating, that she was an adult and, as an adult, she needed to take control of her life.

> I was already starting to reach my point where I had come to the realization that if I was going to get away from him, I was going to have to do it on my own. I was thinking somehow, even though I had never told my parents what was going on, that they would bail me out of the situation.

The recognition that she needed to take action on her own behalf, and that she had hopes and dreams for herself that were not materializing, was the beginning of a series of steps where Tess slowly began to see her relationship differently and to take action.

A turning point for Alexandra was interpersonal. Although Fred had emotionally and physically abused her for several years, his abuse on learning that Alexandra was pregnant seemed to cross a line. Although she considered keeping the baby because she was financially stable and able to manage on her own, Fred was bitterly opposed to it. He pushed Alexandra down during the argument that ensued. For Alexandra, being pregnant was special. Fred's callousness, and the fact that he would throw her down when she was carrying his child, was unacceptable. Alexandra became depressed after this event, and it also marked the beginning of the end for her and Fred.

Going to see a counselor was a turning point for Sherrie. The counselor helped her reassess her relationship with Steve including identifying patterns and recognizing the likelihood that these patterns of behavior would continue. Therapy also helped Sherrie see the options that she had and develop a plan for leaving.

Objective Reflections and Reappraisals

Objective reflections and reappraisals are cognitive processes that often occurred together. *Objective reflection* is the term we use for the process of taking a psychological step back and thinking about what is happening from a more detached point of view. Objective reflection occurred when a woman pulled herself out of the emotional context to view, or sometimes review, her relationship and the consequences to her. This reflection sometimes enabled the woman to see patterns, allowed her to see contradictions, and sometimes led to reappraisals or self-reclaiming actions. Reappraisal is the process of reevaluating what is happening, what it means, and what can be done about it. Reappraisals were made on the basis of new information coming from the women's internal or external systems or were a reinterpretation of information they already had. Examples of reappraisals include recognizing that they were in real danger, that things would not change, that the violence was not their fault, that their boyfriends did not actually love them, that they had options, and/or labeling their boyfriends' aggression as abuse and themselves as abused women. Some reappraisals were implicit in the women's behavior and some were expressed directly. Sometimes reappraisals directly influenced subsequent coping efforts such as self-reclaiming actions (described in the next section).

When Tess left for college, the physical boundary between her and Matt and making new friends gave her the chance to view her relationship more objectively. She began to shed the belief that Matt's behavior was her fault and became more convinced that her relationship with Matt was a serious drain on her. Although she still could not tolerate the idea of living without him, Tess's readiness to leave was building.

Her engagement and the resulting change in status was a turning point for Cory that led her to reappraise her relationship with Carl. They were no longer boyfriend and girlfriend, but instead were future marital partners. Patterns that were developing (e.g., verbal abuse, minor violence) took on new meaning, and it became imperative to Cory to reflect objectively on what the long-term effects of these patterns might be. With this reflection, Cory reappraised how she was viewing his behavior and became more confrontive with Carl about changing. As part of this process, she began to come to terms with a dichotomy that many of the women in this study faced. Cory began to recognize that Carl could be sincere about his love for her and yet not change the behavior that was unacceptable to her.

> It was a very eye-opening thing. He could be so sincere, as much as he can be, as far as he's being truthful and feeling these things [his love for her]. . . . But at the same time, he can feel them to his heart's content and he can still drink like a fish and make an ass out of himself. And start turning on me and everything else.

A turning point for Mona occurred when her boyfriend, Pete, left her at the hospital and returned to a party rather than support her during the repair of the cut on her forehead that he had caused. After Mona was treated, she returned to the hospital waiting room to find that Pete had left, and she needed to take a taxi home. Until that moment, Mona had been able to excuse Pete's abusive behavior, because she believed that he loved her. For the first time, she questioned his love. Her reappraisal included the thought that if he could be that insensitive to her, he might be equally insensitive to children they might have in the future.

Self-Reclaiming Actions

Self-reclaiming actions are self-empowering steps taken by the women to gain more control over their lives. They were often taken following a turning point or a reappraisal. Sometimes these actions led to further reappraisals and, in turn, to further self-reclaiming actions. Some were efforts to set limits or construct boundaries. They had varying degrees of follow-through attached to them depending on where in the process of leaving the woman was at the time. They were a reflection of the woman's recognition of choices; of taking responsibility for making choices; and of shifts in focus from partner and relationship, to self. These actions seemed to emerge from the woman's awareness of herself and her worth as a person and were taken in an effort to assert herself in the relationship.

When Tess returned home after a semester in college, she again took steps to put distance between her and Matt. She found a job on the other side of town with a schedule that made it difficult to see him and a peer group who believed that the way Matt treated Tess was inappropriate. This step helped her with physical and emotional boundary setting, which eventually contributed to her decision to leave him.

> And I learned I had this new set of friends where this kind of action wasn't acceptable too well and that they didn't like Matt. . . . It definitely had something to do with it [her decision to leave him]. Not only was my schedule opposite his, but I was under a new influence of ideas and opinions.

After a number of abusive incidents, including rape, Sherrie found herself without support in a new country where she had moved to join Steve. Feeling depressed and desperate, she decided to seek counseling. The counselor helped her begin to take back her life.

> She started helping me realize that I could start breaking away in small pieces. I started breaking away emotionally just a little bit. Like not always being there when he came home. I went back to working out, which is something that I've always loved to do. I started planning in my mind how I was going to get back home, when will I buy my plane ticket.

When Pam was first beaten by Peter, her fiancee, it was an extension of the jealousy-based, verbal harangues that she had been suffering. After the first severe beating, the police were called by friends, and she left the house. Although they reconciled several times in the following months, Pam took small steps to regain her independence. For example, she never moved her things back into his home, she stopped accounting for her time when she was away from him, and she stopped trying to defend herself from his accusations of infidelity.

Paradigmatic Shifts and Last Straw Events

Paradigmatic shifts were shifts in perspective where the woman's agenda to maintain her relationship was discarded and replaced with an agenda to leave the relationship. The initial position that the relationship was a means to meet her needs was replaced with the position that the relationship must be dissolved to meet her needs. For some women, this shift was sudden and dramatic and led to almost immediate cessation of their relationships. For others, this shift was a result of an accumulation of small reappraisals and the exact point in time the shift was made was barely discernible. That a shift was made was only evident from the steps that were taken to leave a relationship that had before been so important to preserve. For three of the women there was no shift. Two women were still dating their boyfriends at the time of the interviews, and one woman, Debbie, was left by her boyfriend after she set a clear limit with him.

Last straw events were incidents that provided the impetus for the final decision to leave the abusive relationship. When the last straw event occurred, the women had reached a point of readiness and seemed poised at the brink of making a final move to leave. To use Phoebe's words, they were "sick and tired of being sick and tired." The last straw event was something that the women or their abusers did that was significant enough to trigger the final paradigmatic shift, or was an event that followed the shift and seemed to be the impetus for the final leave-taking steps.

For Tess, the last straw event was related to a critical life event—a pregnancy and resulting abortion. She had already come very close to the realization that she needed to end her relationship, but was stalled in actually taking the final steps, when Tess learned that she was 4 months pregnant. Matt's cold reaction to this news, in spite of his recent attempts to convince her that he had changed and was ready to be more respectful of her, was the last straw that made leaving him easier. His behavior snuffed out the last dregs of hope.

> I had no more hope that things were going to work out [between her and Matt]. I had no more hope that I was going to go back to school or that anything in my life was going to get better. And I saw Matt as the root of almost all my problems. And I think that's part of what pushed me over the edge to decide that I couldn't be with him anymore. It was like, on one hand I had Matt, on the other hand I had hope. It was like which one do I need more to survive? I needed the hope, so I had to get rid of him.

The last straw event for Alexandra was her own physical abuse of Fred. During their last months together, their relationship had deteriorated to mutual emotional and physical abuse. However, Alexandra had never totally lost control. She described herself as someone with a gentle nature who takes care not to hurt anyone or anything, not even insects. However, after suffering 5 years of abuse and after building her readiness to leave, Alexandra expressed her rage one day when Fred grabbed her. In fact, she became so enraged that she viciously tore at his face with her sharp fingernails. Because she seemed to be strengthened by years of accumulated anger, he could not stop her. This event seemed to push her to making a dramatic shift in the way she viewed herself and her relationship. Injuring Fred seemed to crystallize for Alexandra just how much of herself she had lost over the years.

> And at that point, I think that was it [the relationship was over]. . . . I think that was the clincher. I stayed with him the next day; I felt bad that I had done what I'd done, but I knew I had to get out. I

was disgusted with myself for doing what I did to his face. Because it just wasn't me. . . . I knew I was drowning. And that self-survival, it wasn't a conscious thing. . . . It was just a sense. I have to get out of here. I have to get out of here. This is not good for me.

For Cory, the last straw event was less of an existential crisis than it seemed to be for Tess and Alexandra. The last straw was the second time Carl was more than mildly physically abusive. The first time he choked her for a few seconds, and Cory had began to speculate whether it would happen again. A few days later, a second extreme incident occurred where Carl picked Cory up and threw her down on the hard floor. For Cory, Carl's taking an action that could have severely hurt her was crossing a line, and they could never go back. She left him.

> And that was it . . . this was what I needed . . . this was irrefutable, irrevocable, I am fully aware that this is definitely not cool. There is no excuse of why this might have happened. This just happened because you're a jerk. . . . I was aware of this feeling like, this is extremely serious. I could have been injured . . . it felt like, this heinous thing that had happened that you can't really speak . . . it's so horrible and you can't turn back.

Leave-taking, Healing, and Moving On

Although the shift in agenda from preserving the relationship to leaving the relationship had been made, leaving was often difficult and painful, and was managed in a variety of ways. Most women talked about having to deal with their anger about how they had been treated, some emphasized grief, some depression and loneliness, others shame. Many seemed to deal with all three to varying degrees. For some, particularly those who had been in their relationships for a long time, fear was one of the emotions they needed to deal with. For example, Alexandra felt that ending her relationship with Fred was almost like someone close to her had died. She was scared because she did not know what life would be like without her relationship with Fred and without the turmoil that went with it.

I can remember the night I finally knew that I made the decision. . . . I can remember gasping for breath. I was talking to my girlfriend saying, "I feel like I'm going to die. . . . I was really scared. . . . I didn't know who I was . . . I had no idea what life was outside all that craziness . . . I was scared what life offered, what was out there. . . . It was like I was in a big ocean and there was one little piece of wood out in the ocean. . . . I've got to get to the wood. . . . And I hung on to it and every day I wanted to go back. . . . It was like suffocating. It was awful. Especially with him bugging me everyday.

Tess reported that she was so used to being on an emotional roller coaster with Matt that she tended to make crises for herself after they broke up. She felt that a big part of her had been lost even though she realized that she could not survive and be with him.

I'd purposely put myself in a situation where I would have to see him, and I would have to talk to him. . . . I guess I was just so used to being in that for like, for a long time, I felt like a big part of me was missing because he wasn't there all the time. . . . I went through a big stage [after the breakup] where it didn't matter to me because I thrived on emotion and needed it. It was like how some people need alcohol or drugs. . . . To this day I'll still say I'm not in love with him, but I love him. I love him not because he is a good person, not because of anything he did for me. . . . It is purely because of everything we went through.

In almost all cases the women had to deal with boyfriends who continued to pursue them after the final breakup. They were resourceful about finding ways to protect themselves and to resist temptations to return. A few enlisted the help of the authorities, but most relied on family and friends to help put a buffer between them and their boyfriends. Some moved out of the area, usually back home to their families.

The process of healing and moving on took years for many of the women. A few women had the help of professionals, but most struggled through the process with less formal help, turning to friends or family for support and help in making sense of what had happened to them. For some, like Debbie, this meant reconnecting with

friends from whom she had become estranged while dating Dan. She found it particularly helpful to talk to a friend who had also survived an abusive relationship. Phoebe characterized her painful experience with Jack as a "nightmare and a blessing" because, although she was miserable for several years and suffered financially as well, she was forced to do "a great deal of introspection" that, in the end, made her a stronger person. Her tools for healing included reading self-help material, talking to her mother and sister, being alone with her thoughts, and participating in group and individual counseling. A major discovery Phoebe made during this healing process was that "I like myself just fine alone." She was really happy to build a life for herself where she was in control rather than devoting all her free time to an unhealthy partner. "Going to the movies by myself, taking a watercolor course by myself, biking by myself" were activities that she made count and that built her sense of strength and courage. "Learning to feel comfortable with myself" was a sign for Kathy that she was ready for another relationship. It took 2 years to reach this point. Her first healing step was finding a job that was satisfying and affirming; a second step was going back to school. Kathy also found that leading groups for battered women was therapeutic for her once she reached a certain level of stability. Tess talked about how her counselor helped her to reconnect with her mother and to establish goals for herself and to take steps to meet them.

Many women also found it helpful to rediscover hobbies they used to enjoy. For example, Phoebe took up gardening and hiking again; Pam began to write poetry. A couple of the women turned to new boyfriends. Cory was too embarrassed to tell her family or friends about being engaged to a man who beat her, but she was able to talk to her new boyfriend who listened and helped her process what had happened. However, most of the women were reluctant to begin new relationships. They either avoided dating altogether or sabotaged relationships they did start or found them boring.

Many of the women talked about what they had learned and how they planned to avoid becoming battered in the future. For example,

Sherrie talked about becoming "abuse proof" by learning to recognize relationship red flags and developing a clear idea of what she wanted in a relationship. Noreen talked about the importance of selecting trustworthy friends to whom she could turn for a "sanity check" should she have a question about normalcy in a relationship. Phoebe learned that it is important to keep a healthy balance between the affirmation she gets from a relationship and what she gets from other sources. She also talked about the importance of not losing sight of her own needs and wants. Eve is quick to recognize a man who cannot handle his anger appropriately and to leave the relationship immediately. It seemed that to some degree, participating in this study was part of the healing process for these women. Almost all of them talked about wanting to help other women avoid the pain they went through and many voiced an appreciation for having the opportunity to reprocess what had happened.

Discussion

■ This study confirms the notion hypothesized by others that leaving a violent relationship is a process (Kirkwood, 1993; Landenburger, 1989; Mills, 1985). In her book *Leaving Abusive Partners,* Kirkwood uses the metaphor of a spiral to describe the process of becoming entrapped and then disentangling from abusive relationships. Women "spiral in" as abusers gain control and the women lose their sense of agency; women "spiral out" as abusers lose control and the women regain self-agency. Spiraling inward and outward seems an appropriate metaphor for the experiences described by the women who participated in this study. The focus of this chapter was on how the women disentangled from their abusive relationships and regained control of their lives.

Through an interwoven series of turning points, objective reflections, reappraisals, and self-reclaiming actions, the abused women in this study slowly built their readiness to leave their abusive relationships. Last straw triggering events and paradigmatic shifts were the final impetus to their leaving. Interestingly, like the drug

addicts in Biernacki's (1986) study who self-initiated their recovery from drug addiction without treatment, the women in this study fell primarily into two groups: those who, after an accumulation of negative experiences coupled with a particularly disturbing event, thoughtfully decided to end a relationship to which they were significantly attached; and those whose decision to leave was sudden and dramatic and apparently connected to hitting a rock-bottom crisis point.

Whether decisions were dramatic or not, once they decided that they needed to end their relationships, the women were effective in marshaling the resources needed to make their resolve a reality. It seemed important to the healing process for women to process and make sense of what had happened to them. Reestablishing a relationship with themselves including taking control of their lives, establishing goals, and rediscovering what they needed and wanted were also important to their healing and moving on. Many of the women seemed to recognize a need to be vigilant about future relationships so they would not again become entrapped in relationships where their partners devalued and abused them.

Understanding how women break the ties that bind them to their abusive relationships has important implications for intervention and prevention. Clinicians who work with battered women can use their understanding of disentanglement processes in their work with clients. For example, a clinician can help a woman become aware of and give voice to her "seeds of doubt." Allowing a woman to give voice to her own doubts can be far more powerful than trying to tell her that the relationship is destructive and not workable (Rosen & Stith, 1993). In addition, a therapist is in a position to help a client gain a broader perspective about her relationship by challenging her belief that she must remain with her abusive partner and helping her to entertain other options. Furthermore, as her perspective begins to shift, the client can be helped to develop appropriate boundaries between herself and her partner, including boundaries between her partner's needs and her needs, as well as in reconnecting with support systems.

The women's stories also provide ideas for prevention. The social construction of gender roles where men are raised to be independent and dominant and women are raised to be dependent and subordinate are reflected even in dating relationships (Lloyd, 1991). In addition, young people in American culture have grown up with romantic images of close relationships portrayed in books, movies, soap operas, and love songs as based on mutual admiration, passion, and ecstasy and where love conquers all. This romanticism encourages young people to stay together despite extreme negative experiences. Furthermore, peer pressure can create a climate ripe for young women to think they need a boyfriend (or a husband) and to make their relationships work even if it means tolerating abuse. We saw the ramifications of some of this pressure in the stories of the women who participated in this study. Prevention can occur at many levels. A didactic support group approach is one avenue for dating violence prevention that could begin to neutralize some of these societal messages (Rosen & Bezold, 1996). Young women need to recognize that they are entitled to safe, healthy relationships where their needs, as well of the needs of their partners, are met. Young women also need to recognize warning signs of abuse, to learn conflict negotiation skills, and to be empowered to say no to relationships that are harmful to them emotionally or physically. Didactic support groups where young women learn from and support each other are ideal mediums for this growth to take place.

We were struck by how powerful the pull can be to remain in abusive dating relationships despite the fact that the women were free of legal, financial, or familial ties. The powerful effect that the shift in perspective from needing to maintain the relationship to needing to leave the relationship and the effect of leaving the relationship clearly illustrated the strength of abusive relationships. Yet despite the powerful pull to follow cultural messages to "stand by your man," these young women were able to break free and to reconnect with themselves and healthy support systems.

References

Atkinson, B., Heath, A., & Chenail, R. (1991). Qualitative research and the legitimization of knowledge. *Journal of Marital and Family Therapy, 17,* 175-180.

Biernacki, P. (1986). *Pathways from heroin addiction: Recovery without treatment.* Philadelphia: Temple University Press.

Bowker, L. H. (1983). *Beating wife beating.* Lexington, MA: Lexington Books.

Bowker, L. H. (1984). Coping with wife abuse: Personal and social networks. In A. R. Roberts (Ed.), *Battered women and their families: Intervention strategies and treatment programs.* New York: Springer.

Campbell, J. C., Miller, P., Cardwell, M., & Belknap, R. (1994). Relationship status of battered women over time. *Journal of Family Violence, 9,* 99-111.

Donato, K. M., & Bowker, L. H. (1984). Understanding the helpseeking behavior of battered women: A comparison of traditional service agencies and women's groups. *International Journal of Women's Studies, 7,* 99-109.

Ferraro, K. J., & Johnson, J. M. (1983). How women experience battering: The process of victimization. *Social Problems, 30,* 325-339.

Glaser, B. G., & Strauss, A. L. (1967). *The discovery of grounded theory: Strategies for qualitative research.* New York: Aldine de Gruyter.

Graham, D. L. R., & Rawlings, E. I. (1991). Bonding with abusive dating partners: Dynamics of Stockholm syndrome. In B. Levy (Ed.), *Dating violence: Young women in danger* (pp. 119-135). Seattle, WA: Seal.

Henton, J., Cate, R., Koval, J., Lloyd, S., & Christopher, S. (1983). Romance and violence in dating relationships. *Journal of Family Issues, 4,* 467-482.

Herbert, T. B., Silver, R. C., & Ellard, J. H. (1991). Coping with an abusive relationship: I. How and why do women stay? *Journal of Marriage and the Family, 5,* 311-325.

Johnson, I. M. (1992). Economic, situational, and psychological correlates of the decision-making process of battered women. *Families in Society: The Journal of Contemporary Human Services, 73,* 168-176.

Kirkwood, C. (1993). *Leaving abusive partners.* Newbury Park, CA: Sage.

Landenburger, K. (1989). A process of entrapment in and recovery from an abusive relationship. *Issues in Mental Health Nursing, 10,* 209-227.

Lloyd, S. A. (1991). The dark side of courtship: Violence and sexual exploitation. *Family Relations, 40,* 14-20.

Marshall, C., & Rossman, G. B. (1989). *Designing qualitative research.* Newbury Park, CA: Sage.

Mills, T. (1985). The assault on the self: Stages in coping with battering husbands. *Qualitative Sociology, 8,* 103-123.

NiCarthy, G. (1987). *The ones who got away: Women who left abusive partners.* Seattle, WA: Seal.

Rosen, K. H. (1996). The ties that bind women to violent premarital relationships: Processes of seduction and entrapment. In D. D. Cahn & S. A. Lloyd (Eds.), *Family violence from a communication perspective* (pp. 151-176). Thousand Oaks, CA: Sage.

Rosen, K. H., & Bezold, A. M. (1996). Dating violence prevention: A didactic support group model for young women. *Journal of Counseling and Development, 74,* 521-525.

Rosen, K. H., & Stith, S. M. (1993). Intervention strategies for treating women in violent dating relationships. *Family Relations, 42,* 427-433.

Strauss, A., & Corbin, J. (1990). *Basics of qualitative research.* Newbury Park, CA: Sage.

Thompson, L. (1992). Feminist methodology for family studies. *Journal of Marriage and the Family, 54,* 3-18.

Walker, L. E. (1979). *The battered woman.* New York: Harper & Row.

Yin, R. K. (1989). *Case study research.* Newbury Park, CA: Sage.

CHAPTER 15

Social Predictors of Wife Assault Cessation

Etiony Aldarondo
Glenda Kaufman Kantor

Much of the research on wife assault over the past three decades has been guided by the desire to identify men who batter their spouses and find ways to make them stop the violence. To fulfill this desire researchers have focused primarily on the characteristics of violent men and on the conditions under which men turn to violence. This line of research has led to the identification of multiple risk markers for wife assault and to the development of interventions to eliminate the violence. Perhaps one of the most important spin-offs of this process has been the recognition of diversity among the population of men who batter their female partners (Aldarondo, in press; Holtzworth-Munroe & Stuart, 1994; Johnson, 1995). Violent men have been found to differ in the severity of the violence (Johnson, 1995; Sugarman, Aldarondo, & Boney-McCoy, 1996), generality of the violence (Holtzworth-Munroe & Stuart, 1994), personality organization (Dutton, 1994, 1995a; Gondolf, 1988), physiological reactivity (Gottman et al., 1995; Jacobson, 1994), and psychopathology (Dutton, 1995b; Maiuro, Cahn, Vitaliano, Wagner, & Zegree, 1988). Variations in rates of violence and severity of violence may also reflect differ-

AUTHORS' NOTE: Glenda Kaufman Kantor's research reported here was supported by Research Grant RO1AA09070 from the National Institute on Alcohol Abuse and Alcoholism.

183

ences in study design and methodology, such as the population studied (e.g., clinical vs. community or national survey samples) or the particular risk markers for violence that are identified.

Yet another way in which men who batter differ from each other remains relatively unexplored. Violent men vary in their use of violence over time (Aldarondo, 1996; Follingstad, Laughlin, Polek, Rutledge, & Hause, 1991; O'Leary et al., 1989; Woffordt, Mihalic, & Menard, 1994). Some men are violent only once in a period of several years. Other men are violent occasionally over time. Another group of men repeatedly assault their female partners over the course of their relationships. Conceptualizing men's use of violence against their female partners in terms of continuity over time can help us refine our understanding of etiological factors and risk marker variables for violence. Moreover, this line of inquiry can help us tease out the specific contribution of social and psychological factors to the cessation of violence and the continued use of violence by men.

Recently, Aldarondo (1996) evaluated patterns of cessation and persistence of wife assault in the general population[1] and found that men who engage in relatively low levels of psychological aggression are more likely to cease or interrupt the violence than other violent men. Woffordt et al.'s (1994) analysis of the National Youth Survey longitudinal data indicated that men's history of "minor" physical violence against their partners and women's economic dependency were associated with an increased risk for the violence to continue. Aldarondo and Sugarman's (1996) study applied a factor analytic approach to data from the 3-year Panel Study on Deterrence Processes (Williams, 1992) to evaluate the characteristics of men who ceased or interrupted the use of violence against their spouse for 2 years, and men who persisted in the use of violence over a 3-year period. They found high levels of marital conflict and low socioeconomic status to be more important determinants of persistent violence against women than other risk markers, such as witnessing and experiencing violence in the family of origin. However, to date, few studies evaluate the relative contribution of important risk markers for

wife assault, such as alcohol use, drug use, and severity of violence, to the cessation and persistence of violence against women. Moreover, few studies consider how victims' histories might affect the likelihood that they will experience ongoing intimate violence.

The purpose of this study is to add to the existing body of knowledge about wife assault by assessing the adequacy of social risk markers and the history of wife assault to predict the cessation and persistence of violence against women. The proposed analysis differentiates persistent perpetrators of violence from men who interrupt the use of violence. We work with the assumption that violent men are all exposed to, and influenced by, the same social factors associated with an increased risk of wife assault. Consistent with Aldarondo and Sugarman (1996), we anticipate that some risk markers may be associated not only with the likelihood of any wife assault occurrence but also with the continuation of the violence. Thus, we expect the cessation of wife assault to be associated with higher levels of maturation factors such as age and the length of the relationship (Suitor, Pillemer, & Straus, 1990), and lower levels of situational variables such as substance abuse (Kaufman Kantor & Asdigian, 1996; Kaufman Kantor & Straus, 1987, 1989; Leonard & Senchak, 1993) or unemployment (Kaufman Kantor, Jasinski, & Aldarondo, 1994; McLaughlin, Leonard, & Senchak, 1992). A history of physical violence in the partners' families of origin is the most widely accepted risk marker for the occurrence of wife assault, and common to both clinical and general population samples where wife assault is identified (e.g., Kalmuss, 1984; Saunders, 1995; Straus, Gelles, & Steinmetz, 1980). However, it is not clear whether there is sufficient variability in violence history among the population of men who batter to discriminate who will stop or who will continue the abuse.

The present study uses data from the 1992 National Alcohol and Family Violence Survey (NAFVS) to identify a group of men who ceased or interrupted the violence and a group of persistent perpetrators of violence. These groups are compared on 15 risk markers both at the bivariate and multivariate levels. Data obtained from male and female respondents are analyzed separately. This strategy permits evaluation results from the perspective of both the victims and the perpetrators of violence.

Method

Sample

The data used for this chapter were obtained in 1992 as a part of the NAFVS (Kaufman Kantor et al., 1994). Face-to-face interviews were conducted with a national probability sample of 1,970 persons, including a Hispanic oversample, who were living as a couple with a member of the opposite sex. One member of each household, either the husband or the wife, was randomly selected and interviewed. Interviews lasted approximately an hour. The overall response rate for all eligible individuals was 75.4%.

Measures of Violence

Violence Group Membership

Membership in the cessation group or persistence group was determined by using the Conflict Tactics Scales (CTS; Straus, 1990). The CTS is the most widely used measure of physical violence among cohabiting and married couples. It has been used in three cross-sectional national surveys of family violence (Kaufman Kantor et al., 1994; Straus & Gelles, 1986; Straus et al., 1980), longitudinal studies of marital violence (O'Leary et al., 1989; Woffordt et al., 1994), clinical studies of violent men (e.g., Saunders, 1992), studies of battered women (e.g., Dutton & Painter, 1993), and studies of marital relationships in clinical settings (e.g., O'Leary, Vivian, & Malone, 1992). The scale has two stable factors, physical aggression and verbal aggression (Barling, O'Leary, Jouriles, Vivian, & MacEwen, 1987), and high internal reliability (Straus, 1990).

The scale asks respondents to indicate how many times in the past 12 months they, and their partner, have tried to "settle their differences" through the use of 19 specific tactics of conflict resolution. In addition, the CTS asks respon-

dents to indicate if any of these acts had "ever happened at any time in the past." Items are presented on a continuum from nonviolent to severely violent tactics. Examples of violence items are "threw something at partner," "slapped," "kicked, bit, or hit with a fist," and "used a knife or fired gun."

History of Adult Relationship Violence

Immediately following the administration of the CTS, respondents were asked a series of questions about the history of violence in their current relationship. Respondents were asked to indicate the first time the husband used physical violence against his spouse, the number of times over the course of their relationship he hit or got physical with her, and the last time that the husband hit or physically fought with his spouse.

The violence history questions and the CTS allowed for a more refined measure of wife assault than has been typically used in studies of wife assault. It provided the means to identify persistent perpetrators of violence and men who interrupted or ceased the use of violence in their current relationship. Persistent perpetrators of violence were violent at least once over the past 12 months, and also recorded acts of physical aggression in either the CTS "ever violence" questions or in the set of violence history questions. The cessation group included men with a past history of violence, either based on the CTS or in the violence history questions, and who were reportedly nonviolent toward their partner in the year prior to the study.

History of Violence in the Family of Origin

Child Abuse. Abuse during middle childhood (ages 6-12) was assessed by asking respondents whether their mothers and fathers perpetrated each of several acts of severe violence against them between the ages of 6 and 12. The acts of violence modified from the parent-to-child version of the CTS included "locked you in a closet or tied you up," "kicked or hit you with a fist," "hit you with an object," "threatened you with a knife or gun," "burned you," and "threatened to kill you." Separate indexes representing mother-to-child and father-to-child severe physical violence were created.

Witnessing Violence Between Parents. Parent-to-parent violence in the family of origin was measured with two items asking about the frequency with which the respondent's father "hit or threw something at" the respondent's mother and the frequency with which the respondent's mother "hit or threw something at" the respondent's father while the respondent was a teenager.

Measures of Substance Abuse

Problem Drinking Measures. Problem drinking was assessed by use of 12 of the 25 items in the Michigan Alcoholism Screening Test (MAST; Selzer, 1971). Shortened versions of the MAST (10 items) have been found to be as effective as the complete instrument in discriminating between alcoholics and nonalcoholics (Pokorny, Miller, & Kaplan, 1972). This inventory of alcohol-related drinking problems includes items such as "Have you ever attended a meeting of Alcoholics Anonymous, or A.A., for your own drinking problem?" "Have you ever gotten into fights when drinking?" and "Have you ever neglected your family or your work for 2 or more days in a row because of your drinking?" Respondents were asked the series of questions about their own drinking, and similar questions were asked for 12 of the 13 items regarding the partner's drinking. For reasons of possible limited reliability, partners were not asked if their spouse had "ever had delirium tremens, severe shaking, or seen things that weren't there after heavy drinking," and so this item was excluded in the analyses conducted for this chapter.

Illicit Drug Use. We used standard items measuring the type and frequency of illicit drug use in the past year or ever. The items are based on those used in the National Household Drug Survey (Miller et al., 1982) and by drug researchers (Elinson & Nurco, 1975). The "hard drug" designation refers to the use of illicit drugs other than marijuana (e.g., am-

phetamines, barbiturates, tranquilizers, cocaine, heroin). The "ever" items are used in this chapter to better encompass the period assessed for spousal violence.

Data Analytic Strategy

The analysis of data was done in two steps. First, bivariate analyses of 15 risk markers of theoretical importance were completed, including chi-square tests and *t* tests for independent samples, to evaluate the differences between the violence cessation and persistence groups. Second, multivariate logistic regression analyses (logits) were completed for male and female respondents separately to determine the relationship between a set of wife assault predictors and the probability of membership in the cessation group. Logit is the multivariate technique of choice when working with a dichotomous dependent variable, such as cessation or persistence of violence (Aldrich & Nelson, 1984; Hosmer & Lemeshow, 1989).

The first logit was based on data provided by male respondents. The second logit included information provided by female respondents. These separate analyses were necessary to evaluate the effect of important risk markers from the perspective of the male perpetrators and the female victims of violence. A blocking approach based on theoretical groupings (i.e., history of wife assault, family-of-origin violence, maturation factors, and situational factors) was used to enter the variables for the logit equations. A backward logistic regression strategy was then used to build the final regression models. In this strategy, the model starts with all predictors. The equation is then simplified by removing, one by one, those measures whose likelihood ratio statistic have the highest probability value and are greater than alpha ($p > .10$).

Results

Bivariate Analysis

History of Wife Assault. Table 15.1 presents chi-square tests and *t* tests for independent samples for all risk markers for male and fe-

TABLE 15.1 Bivariate Analysis on Risk Markers in Persistence and Cessation Groups by Gender

	Male Respondents (n = 152): Group Mean or Percentage		Female Respondents (n = 165): Group Mean or Percentage	
Risk Marker[a]	Persistence	Cessation	Persistence	Cessation
Part A: History of wife assault				
Years of physical fighting (mean)	3.7	1.5**	4.1	1.2**
Severe violence by husband (%)	26.9	4.4**	14.6	4.5
Part B: Physical violence in family of origin				
Paternal child abuse (%)	39.1	46.5	24.4	11.4
Maternal child abuse (%)	26.5	35.6	22.7	9.1
Witnessed mother hit father (%)	20.3	4.9*	35.4	15.4*
Witnessed father hit mother (%)	11.7	7.3	31.6	10.3*
Part C: Maturation factors				
Men age in years (mean)	36.4	44.4***	38.0	41.8
Women age in years (mean)	32.6	40.7***	36.2	41.7*
Length of relationship in years (mean)	10.1	17.8***	12.4	17.2*
Part D: Situational factors				
Marital status/cohabiting (%)	14.7	8.9	25.8	11.4*
Family income (mean)	6.2	8.1**	5.7	7.3*
Work less than full-time/unemployed (%)	20.0	14.3	22.9	17.5
Men MAST[b] (mean)	2.4	2.2	0.8	0.7
Men ever used hard drugs (%)	36.8	17.8*	11.4	6.8
Women ever used hard drugs (%)	14.7	4.4	14.6	6.8

a. All percentages represent the proportion of yes responses.
b. Michigan Alcoholism Screening Test (Selzer, 1971).
*$p < .05$; **$p < .01$; ***$p < .001$.

male respondents, separately. Part A in Table 15.1 shows that the continuity of wife assault is associated with the chronicity of physical aggression in the relationship. Persistent perpetrators of violence, $t(110) = -3.21$, $p < .01$, and female victims, $t(128) = -2.74$, reported significantly longer histories of physical fights in their intimate relationships than partners in the violence cessation group. Persistent perpetrators of violence reported 2 ½ times more years of physical fighting in their relationships than men in the cessation group. Female partners of persistent perpetrators of violence reported close to 3 ½ times more years of physical aggression in their relationships than female partners of men who ceased the violence.

In terms of violence severity, part A in Table 15.1 shows that according to male respondents the cessation and persistence groups were significantly different in their use of severe forms of violence, $\chi^2(1, 112) = 9.26$, $p < .01$. Persistent perpetrators of violence were 6 times more likely to severely assault their spouse than men

in the cessation group. Interestingly, male respondents categorized as persistent perpetrators reported using severe violence more than was reported by female victims. According to women respondents, persistent perpetrators were over 3 times more likely to use severe violence than men who ceased or interrupted the violence.

Family-of-Origin Violence. With respect to the history of physical violence in the family of origin, part B in Table 15.1 shows that a larger percentage of both men, $\chi^2(1, 100) = 4.80$, $p < .05$, and women, $\chi^2(1, 118) = 5.121$, $p < .05$, in the persistence group reported witnessing their mothers hit their fathers than partners in the cessation group. Female respondents also reported much more exposure to fathers' use of violence against their mothers than women in the cessation group, $\chi^2(1, 118) = 6.44$, $p < .05$. Men who ceased or interrupted the violence were 4 times less likely to report witnessing mother-to-father violence than men in the persistent violence

TABLE 15.2 Logistic Regression of Wife Assault Cessation for Male Respondents

Independent Variable	B	SE	Odds Ratio	p
Age of wife	0.07	0.03	1.07	.01
Family income	0.21	0.08	1.23	.01
Severe violence by husband	−2.91	1.12	0.05	.01
Witnessed mother hit father	−1.64	0.93	0.19	.08

−2 log likelihood = 92.49		Model χ^2 = 36.14, N = 95
df = 90		df = 4
p = .41		p = .00

Classification for persistence and cessation of wife assault

Observed	Predicted		
Correct	Persistence	Cessation	%
Persistence	44	12	78.57
Cessation	12	27	69.23
Overall			74.74

group. Female partners of men who ceased the use of violence were 2 ⅓ times less likely to report witnessing mother-to-father violence than female partners of men in the persistent violence group. In terms of father-to-mother violence, female partners of men who ceased the violence were 3 times less likely to report witnessing this form of parental violence than partners of persistent perpetrators of violence. Men in the violence cessation group also witnessed considerably less father-to-mother violence than persistent perpetrators of violence.

Part B in Table 15.1 also shows high rates of child abuse victimizations in the family of origin for both male and female respondents. Although the differences are not significant, fewer women in the cessation group experienced parental abuse as children. The high incidence (relative to the general population) of severe forms of child abuse in the history of men reporting wife abuse is notable. However, the history of child abuse, per se, was not associated with the continuity of violent behavior.

Maturation Factors. Part C in Table 15.1 shows the analyses of data on maturation factors. According to male respondents, partners in the cessation group were older, $t(111) = -3.91$, $p < .000$, for men's age, $t(111) = -4.20$, $p < .000$, for women's age, and had been together longer, $t(111) = -3.96$, $p < .01$, than partners

in the persistent group. Analysis for female respondents also found that the cessation and persistence groups were significantly different in the women's age, $t(131) = -2.50$, $p < .05$, and the length of the relationship, $t(131) = -2.50$, $p < .05$, but not in the men's age.

Situational Factors. With respect to situational factors, part D in Table 15.1 shows significant differences among the groups of men in their self-reported use of hard drugs. More than twice as many persistent perpetrators of violence reported using hard drugs at some point in their lives than men in the cessation group, χ^2 $(1, 113) = 4.72$, $p < .05$. Problem drinking histories were not significantly associated with the continuity of violent behavior. According to both men, $t(107) = -3.02$, $p < .01$, and women, $t(121) = -2.56$, $p < .05$, family income was significantly higher for couples in the cessation group than for couples in the persistence group. Although unemployment rates were higher among persistently violent men, compared to men who cease their assaults, the differences were not significant.

Logistic Regression Analyses

Tables 15.2 and 15.3 show the regression coefficients, standard error, the odds ratio, and the probabilities obtained in the final regression

TABLE 15.3 Logistic Regression of Wife Assault Cessation for Female Respondents

Independent Variable	B	SE	Odds Ratio	p
Age of wife	0.05	0.02	1.05	.02
Family income	0.21	0.08	1.23	.01
Paternal child abuse	−1.37	0.69	0.25	.05
Witnessed father hit mother	−1.92	0.71	0.15	.01
Years of physical fighting	−0.49	0.23	0.61	.03

-2 log likelihood $= 97.19$ Model $\chi^2 = 37.35$, $N = 108$
$df = 102$ $df = 5$
$p = .61$ $p = .00$

Classification for persistence and cessation of wife assault

Observed Correct	Predicted		%
	Persistence	Cessation	
Persistence	66	8	89.19
Cessation	20	14	41.18
Overall			74.07

equation for male and female respondents, respectively. The analysis for male respondents shows that family income and women's age have a significant positive association with the likelihood of wife assault cessation, suggesting that both the maturity of women and the acquisition of economic resources are associated with a greater likelihood that men will cease or interrupt the violence. On the other hand, men's use of severe forms of violence and witnessing mother-to-father physical aggression have a negative relationship with the probability of wife assault cessation.

Table 15.3 shows the final regression equation for female respondents. Consistent with the data provided by male respondents, the likelihood of wife assault cessation was positively associated with the women's age and the level of family income. The odds ratio for these factors also confirms the previous finding that as family income and women's age increases, violent men are more likely to cease the violence than to continue the abuse. In addition, for the women in this sample, experiencing both severe physical violence by their fathers during childhood and witnessing father-to-mother physical aggression were negatively associated with the possibility that their partners would stop the violence.

Although the regression models for female and male respondents correctly classified close to three fourths of the cases, they predicted the continuation of violence considerably better than wife assault cessation. Although the final model for female respondents accurately predicted close to 90% of all cases in the persistence group, it failed to predict more than half of the cases in the cessation group. Likewise, the regression model for male data predicted approximately 10% more cases of persistence than cases of wife assault cessation. Thus, neither model was particularly strong in predicting wife assault cessation.

Discussion

■ This study was designed to evaluate the usefulness of social risk markers for wife assault cessation in understanding the cessation and persistence of violence over time. A comparison was made between men who had ceased or interrupted the violence for at least 1 year and men with both past and current history of wife assault. We hypothesized that wife assault cessation would be associated with higher levels of maturation and lower levels of situational risk markers. We also anticipated that cessation would be negatively associated with a chronic and severe history of violence in the relationship. In addition, we were uncertain about the role of a history of physical violence in the partners' families of origin relative to the cessation or persistence of the violence. Although intergenerational violence has been a consistent risk marker for the presence of any current family spousal violence, its ability to predict violence persistence has been less well examined.

Bivariate analysis of data from male and female respondents provided partial support for our prediction about the cessation of violence against women by their male partners. Persistent perpetrators of violence were found to be older, were in their current relationship longer, had considerably more financial resources, and had experimented more with "hard core" illicit drugs than men in the cessation group. Persistent perpetrators also reported a more chronic and severe history of wife assault than men in the cessation group. In terms of family-of-origin violence, the bivariate analyses showed that a considerably higher proportion of men in the persistence group witnessed their mothers being physically violent toward their fathers compared to men in the cessation group.

Consistent with reports given by men, women in the persistence group reported experiencing a more chronic and severe history of wife assault, were older, had lived longer together with their partners (although they were more often cohabiting than married), had more financial resources, and had witnessed more mother-to-father violence than women in the cessation group. In addition, women in the persistence group were 3 times more likely to have witnessed parental victimizations than were women in the cessation group.

Logistic regression analyses of male and female respondent data yielded matching regression models. However, it should be noted that there are some limits to drawing firm conclusions about the results of our multivariate analyses due to small sample sizes in some of the cells. The final equations included risk markers associated with maturation, situational issues, history of violence in the relationship, and family-of-origin violence. In support of our prediction about wife assault cessation, maturation and situational variables were associated with the likelihood of wife assault cessation, whereas the history of violence in their intimate relationships

was associated with the continuation of the violence over time. Countering the inconsistencies in the literature, a history of violence in the family of origin was also found to increase the likelihood that the violence would continue. Moreover, both regression models predicted the continuation of the violence more correctly than the cessation or interruption of violence.

How Important Are Maturational and Situational Variables?

The regression equations for men and women included the same maturation and situational variables, that is, women's ages and family income, suggesting that women's youthfulness and lack of financial resources are associated with violent men's continued use of physical aggression over time. In accord with Aldarondo and Sugarman's (1996) analysis of risk markers, this study indicates that the likelihood of wife assault cessation is associated with the level of financial resources. Family income was the most powerful situational predictor of wife assault cessation in this study.

Does Family-of-Origin Violence Predict Wife Assault Persistence?

The final regression equations for male and female respondents included different items concerning the history of violence in both their families of origin and in their intimate relationships. For perpetrators of violence, having used severe forms of violence and having witnessed their mothers hit their fathers were associated with the continuation of the violence. For women, having experienced paternal physical abuse during childhood and having witnessed their fathers hit their mothers increased the likelihood that the violence would continue.

Does Severity or Chronicity Predict Violence Persistence?

These analyses suggest, on the one hand, that using the perspective of the perpetrators suggests that the severity of violence is a better predictor of the continuation of wife assault than is the chronicity of assault. On the other hand, the analyses of female respondent data suggest that chronicity of violence is a better predictor of continuation than severity. This difference is due in part to the fact that a considerably smaller percentage of women in the persistence group reported use of severe violence by their male partners than was reported by perpetrators of violence. It is, in fact, difficult to be certain about the meaning of this discrepancy. Several inferences are plausible. The difference may reflect the fact that women have greater tolerance for minor than severe violence (Kalmuss & Straus, 1990) and that use of severe violence by men often forecasts the termination of the relationship (McHugh, Frieze, & Browne, 1993). The results may also reflect the fears or reluctance of women to report the severity of the partner's violence for fear of the consequences to themselves or the batterer. Women may minimize their reports of severe victimizations due to shame, fear, or denial, or to rationalize their remaining in a violent relationship. Moreover, men who frankly acknowledge the nature of their abusive behavior might be more representative of the type of generally violent/antisocial type batterer described by Holtzworth-Munroe and Stuart (1995).

Contribution of Drug and Alcohol Abuse

We were surprised to find that clinical measures of alcoholism failed to discriminate among a violent sample of male spouse abusers. Alcohol has emerged as a consistent risk marker in virtually all of the wife abuse literature. The failure to find an effect of alcoholism history on the continuity of violence may be because there is little variability in the range of alcohol-related problems among the population of men who batter. However, we did find a significant effect of using hard drugs that have carried heavier penalties for usage by the law (e.g., heroin, cocaine). This latter finding is, in fact, consistent with clinical typologies of batterers showing the presence of more delinquent and criminally deviant histories among the most severely violent wife batterers (Gondolf, 1988; Gottman et al., 1995; Holtzworth-Munroe & Stuart, 1994). However, the unique contribution of this variable in the prediction of wife assault was greatly reduced when considered in relationship to other situational risk markers.

Does Aging Really Deter the Batterer?

Prior research suggests that there is a negative relationship between wife assault and men's age (e.g., O'Leary et al., 1989; Pan, Neidig, & O'Leary, 1994; Suitor et al., 1990). However, this is the second study that finds that men's age is not a powerful predictor of the continuity of violence when other maturation risk markers are taken into consideration (see also Aldarondo & Sugarman, 1996).

Implications for Practice

■ The results of this study highlight the need for practitioners to assess both the severity and chronicity of violence from the perspectives of both victims and perpetrators. Outreach and education provided to the public and to battered women need to emphasize that women experiencing the more severely violent victimizations (any kicking, biting, assaults with a fist, assaults with an object, beatings, choking, threats to kill, weapon use) are at the most risk of ongoing violence.

The results of this study are also important because they add to and parallel the developing literature suggesting varying typologies of batterers, and addressing the characteristics of victims that may contribute to initial and ongoing risk. Although further research is needed on the experiences and characteristics of victims, women were also more likely to be victimized on an ongoing basis when they had been severely abused by their father as a child, had witnessed abuse of their mothers, and had little in the way of family economic resources. Risks to women are further compounded when the husband is similarly handicapped by violent childhood experiences (in particular, witnessing violence by his mother) and admits to severe acts of violence against the wife. In addition, the results of this study suggest that we can benefit from studying wife assault not only in terms of the occurrence of the violence as is typically done but also in regard to the continuity of violence over time. Specifically, our findings show that exposure to violence in the family of origin and situational stressors combine to perpetuate the victimization of women by their male partners. It is important to improve our understanding of the interaction of distal and proximal risk markers of wife assault, and the contribution of these factors to the continuity of violence, so that appropriate prevention and intervention programs can be designed.

Note

1. This analysis used data from the 3-year Panel Study on Deterrence Processes (Williams, 1992) following a subsample of families first interviewed in the 1985 National Family Violence Survey (Straus & Gelles, 1986).

References

Aldarondo, E. (1996). Cessation and persistence of wife assault: A longitudinal analysis. *American Journal of Orthopsychiatry, 66,* 141-151.

Aldarondo, E. (in press). Perpetrators of domestic violence. In A. Bellack & M. Hersen (Eds.), *Comprehensive clinical psychology.* New York: Pergamon.

Aldarondo, E., & Sugarman, D. (1996). Risk markers analysis of cessation and persistence of wife assault. *Journal of Consulting and Clinical Psychology, 64,* 1010-1019.

Aldrich, J. H., & Nelson, F. D. (1984). *Linear probability, logit, and probit models.* Beverly Hills, CA: Sage.

Barling, J. N., O'Leary, K. D., Jouriles, E. V., Vivian, D., & MacEwen, C. (1987). Factor similarity of the Conflict Tactics Scales across samples, spouses, and sites: Issues and implications. *Journal of Family Violence, 2,* 37-53.

Dutton, D. G. (1994). The origin and structure of the abusive personality. *Journal of Personality Disorders, 8,* 181-191.

Dutton, D. G. (1995a). *The batterer: A psychological profile.* New York: Basic Books.

Dutton, D. G. (1995b). *The domestic assault of women: Psychological and criminal justice perspectives.* Vancouver: University of British Columbia Press.

Dutton, D. G., & Painter, S. (1993). The battered woman syndrome: Effects of severity and intermittency of abuse. *American Journal of Orthopsychiatry, 63,* 614-622.

Elinson, J., & Nurco, D. (1975). *Operational definitions in socio-behavioral drug research.* Rockville, MD: National Institute on Drug Abuse.

Follingstad D. R., Laughlin, J. E., Polek, D. S., Rutledge, L. L., & Hause. E. S. (1991). Identification of patterns of wife assault. *Journal of Interpersonal Violence, 6,* 187-204.

Gondolf, E. W. (1988). Who are those guys? Toward a behavioral typology of batterers. *Violence and Victims, 3,* 187-203.

Gottman, J. M., Jacobson, N. S., Rushe, R. H., Shortt, J. W., Babcock, J., La Taillade, J. J., & Waltz, J. (1995). The relationship between heart rate reactivity, emotionally aggressive behavior, and general violence in batterers. *Journal of Family Psychology, 9,* 227-248.

Holtzworth-Munroe, A., & Stuart, G. (1994). Typologies of male batterers: Three subtypes and the differences among them. *Psychological Bulletin, 116,* 476-497.

Hosmer, D. W., & Lemeshow, S. (1989). *Applied logistic regression.* New York: John Wiley.

Jacobson, N. S. (1994). Affect, verbal content and psychophysiology in the arguments of couples with a violent husband. *Journal of Consulting and Clinical Psychology, 62,* 982-988.

Johnson, M. P. (1995). Patriarchal terrorism and common couple violence: Two forms of violence against women. *Journal of Marriage and the Family, 57,* 283-294.

Kalmuss, D. (1984, February). The intergenerational transmission of marital aggression. *Journal of Marriage and the Family, 46,* 11-19.

Kalmuss, D. S., & Straus, M. A. (1990). Wife's marital dependency and wife abuse. In M. A. Straus & R. J. Gelles (Eds.), *Physical violence in American families: Risk factors and adaptations to violence in 8,145 families* (pp. 369-382). New Brunswick, NJ: Transaction.

Kaufman Kantor, G., & Asdigian, N. L. (1996). When women are under the influence: Does drinking or drug use by women provoke beatings by men? In M. Galanter (Ed.), *Recent developments in alcoholism: Vol. 13. Alcoholism and violence.* New York: Plenum.

Kaufman Kantor, G., Jasinski, J., & Aldarondo, E. (1994). Sociocultural status and incidence of marital violence in Hispanic families. *Violence and Victims, 9,* 207-222.

Kaufman Kantor, G., & Straus, M. A. (1987). The drunken bum theory of wife beating. *Social Problems, 34,* 213-230.

Kaufman Kantor, G., & Straus, M. A. (1989). Substance abuse as a precipitant of wife abuse victimizations. *American Journal of Drug and Alcohol Abuse, 15,* 173-189.

Leonard, K. E., & Senchak, M. (1993). Alcohol and premarital aggression among newly-wed couples. *Journal of Studies on Alcohol* (Suppl. 11), 96-108.

Maiuro, R. D., Cahn, T. S., Vitaliano, P. P., Wagner, B. C., & Zegree, J. B. (1988). Anger, hostility, and depression in domestically violent versus generally assaultive men and nonviolent control subjects. *Journal of Consulting and Clinical Psychology, 56,* 17-23.

McHugh, M. C., Frieze, I. H., & Browne, A. (1993). Research on battered women and their assailants. In F. L. Denmark & M. A. Paludi (Eds.), *Psychology of women: A handbook of issues and theories* (pp. 513-552). Westport, CT: Greenwood.

McLaughlin, I. G., Leonard, K. E., & Senchak, M. (1992). Prevalence and distribution of premarital aggression among couples applying for a marriage license. *Journal of Family Violence, 7,* 309-319.

Miller, Cisin, I. H., Gardner-Keaton, H., Harrell, A. V., Wirtz, W., Abelson, I., & Fishburne, P. M. (1982). *Na-*

tional survey on drug abuse: Main findings (DHHS Publication No. ADMO 84-1263) Washington, DC: U.S. Department of Health and Human Services, National Institute on Drug Abuse.

O'Leary, K. D., Barling, J., Arias, I., Rosenbaum, A., Malone, J., & Tyree, A. (1989). Prevalence and stability of physical aggression between spouses: A longitudinal analysis. *Journal of Consulting and Clinical Psychology, 57,* 263-268.

O'Leary, K. D., Vivian, D., & Malone, J. (1992). Assessment of physical aggression against women in marriage: The need for multimodal assessment. *Behavior Assessment, 14,* 5-14.

Pan, H. S., Neidig, P. H., & O'Leary, K. D. (1994). Predicting mild and severe husband-to-wife physical aggression. *Journal of Consulting and Clinical Psychology, 62,* 975-981.

Pokorny, A. D., Miller, B. A., & Kaplan, H. R. (1972). The brief MAST: A shortened version of the Michigan Alcoholism Screening Test. *American Journal of Psychiatry, 29,* 342-345.

Saunders, D. G. (1992). A typology of men who batter: Three types derived from cluster analysis. *American Journal of Orthopsychiatry, 62,* 264-275.

Saunders, D. G. (1995). Prediction of wife assault. In J. C. Campbell (Ed.), *Assessing dangerousness: Violence by sexual offenders, batterers, and child abusers* (pp. 68-95). Thousand Oaks, CA: Sage.

Selzer, M. (1971). The Michigan Alcoholism Screening Test: The quest for a new diagnostic instrument. *American Journal of Psychiatry, 127,* 1653-1658.

Straus, M. A. (1990). Measuring intrafamily conflict and violence: The Conflict Tactics Scales. In M. A. Straus & R. J. Gelles (Eds.), *Physical violence in American families: Risk factors and adaptations to violence in 8,145 families* (pp. 29-48). New Brunswick, NJ: Transaction.

Straus, M. A., & Gelles, R. J. (1986). Societal change and change in family violence from 1975 to 1985 as revealed by two national surveys. *Journal of Marriage and the Family, 48,* 465-480.

Straus, M. A., Gelles, R. J., & Steinmetz, S. K. (1980). *Behind closed doors: Violence in the American family.* New York: Doubleday.

Suitor, J. J., Pillemer, K., & Straus, M. A. (1990). Marital violence in a life course perspective. In M. A. Straus & R. J. Gelles (Eds.), *Physical violence in American families: Risk factors and adaptations to violence in 8,145 families* (pp. 305-317). New Brunswick, NJ: Transaction.

Sugarman, D. B., Aldarondo, E., & Boney-McCoy, S. (1996). Risk marker analysis of husband-to-wife violence: A continuum of aggression. *Journal of Applied Social Psychology, 26,* 313-337.

Williams, K. R. (1992). Social sources of marital violence and deterrence: Testing an integrated theory of assaults between spouses. *Journal of Marriage and the Family, 54,* 620-629.

Woffordt, S., Mihalic, D. E., & Menard, S. (1994). Continuities in marital violence. *Journal of Family Violence, 9,* 195-225.

CHAPTER 16

Wife Abuse in Intact Couples

A Review of Couples Treatment Programs

Pamela D. Brown
K. Daniel O'Leary

Despite considerable interest in the study of wife abuse for almost two decades, few published studies have examined couples treatment programs for husband-to-wife physical aggression. The failure to evaluate treatment programs for couples is particularly striking, especially considering that the majority of couples presenting for marital therapy report some level of husband-to-wife aggression in the past year (Cascardi, Langhinrichsen, & Vivian, 1992; Holtzworth-Munroe et al., 1992; O'Leary, Vivian, & Malone, 1992). Furthermore, without treatment, for some, the aggression continues (O'Leary et al., 1989) or escalates (Walker, 1979). With these notions in mind, it is important to develop systematic research of treatment

efficacy with intact and/or self-referring couples, a population often overlooked.

The majority of couples who seek marital treatment report mild to moderate levels of physical aggression, yet they frequently do not perceive physical aggression as a major relationship problem (Ehrensaft & Vivian, in press; O'Leary et al., 1992). Moreover, community survey data indicate that approximately 12% of the population at large report engaging in mild aggression in the past year, whereas only 4% report engaging in more severe aggression (Straus & Gelles, 1990). These data suggest that intact couples who report mild to moderate levels of aggression may constitute the largest percentage of physically aggressive couples seen by private

AUTHORS' NOTE: This chapter was supported by National Institute of Mental Health Grants MH 424-8804 and 5T MH 19107. Correspondence concerning this chapter should be addressed to K. Daniel O'Leary, Department of Psychology, the University at Stony Brook, Stony Brook, NY 11794-2500; e-mail: doleary@ccmail.sunysb.edu.

practitioners and community-based service providers. Therefore, research regarding intact and/or self-referring couples is necessary to maximally inform clinicians of what works and with whom.

Unfortunately, as stated previously, research on intact couples is sparse. The preponderance of spouse abuse research has been conducted with batterers who have been court mandated to treatment. Often these results are generalized to all physically aggressive couples. This is likely a mistaken tactic. In a comparison of batterers who were court mandated to treatment and those who were self-referred, significant differences between the two were found (Barrera, Palmer, Brown, & Kalaher, 1994). Court-involved batterers were more likely to be separated or divorced and had higher levels of anxiety, impulsivity, depressive symptomatology, social introversion, and alienation (Barrera et al., 1994). They also had less education, lower incomes, and were underemployed or unemployed. Furthermore, court-mandated treatment participants were more defensive and may well have had a higher rate or more severe level of physical aggression against their partners than self-referred populations in which the couple seeks treatment (A. Rosenbaum, personal communication, September 1996; Rosenfeld, 1992). Although much has been gained by studying the court-mandated batterer, research with this population regarding correlates, etiology, and treatment outcome may not be generalizable to self-referring couples who engage in lower levels of aggression (Okun, 1986) and display less denial regarding their aggressive behavior compared to their court-mandated counterparts (Barrera et al., 1994). There is increasing evidence that those who perpetrate violence at the two poles of the severity continuum may be dissimilar and reflect qualitatively and quantitatively distinct populations (Okun, 1986; O'Leary, 1993). With these notions in mind, it is likely that the perpetrator who is in an intact relationship and who seeks treatment with his partner may be more motivated to change his behavior.

Whereas only seven studies provided evaluations of treatment efficacy in intact and/or self-referring populations, more than 25 studies have evaluated treatment outcome for court-man-

dated participants (see reviews by Hamberger & Hastings, 1994; Rosenfeld, 1992). Both ideological and practical reasons appear to account for the dearth of literature evaluating the outcome of treatment programs for intact couples reporting physical aggression. First, many couples who experience aggression in their relationships do not seek treatment, much less for the violence. In fact, although 67% of couples presenting for couples counseling report some level of husband-to-wife aggression in the past year, only 6% of the women seeking marital therapy and reporting physical aggression identify the physical aggression as a major issue in their relationship (O'Leary et al., 1992). Another factor that may contribute to the paucity of literature evaluating efficacy of treatment programs for intact couples is an ideological one. That is, some argue that women and men should not be treated together either in an individual or group context (for debate on this issue, see O'Leary, 1996, and McMahon & Pence, 1996). A counter to this position regarding treatment format is that if the marital discord and mutual anger is not addressed, the woman may be facing increased risk of physical revictimization. This latter point is strengthened by the fact that marital discord is one of the strongest correlates of physical aggression (Pan, Neidig, & O'Leary, 1994a). Furthermore, some argue that a woman's participation in treatment might implicitly absolve the perpetrator of responsibility for his own violent behavior (e.g., Edleson & Tolman, 1992). However, our research on attribution of responsibility indicated, instead, that husbands showed increased responsibility for their own physical aggression at posttreatment (O'Leary, Heyman, & Neidig, 1996).

In reviewing the literature on treatment of husband-to-wife violence in intact, primarily self-referring couples, we will note the strengths and weaknesses of the literature, examine the efficacy of particular interventions, and suggest additions that can be made to improve treatment outcome and its study. First, we provide an overview of the programs, recruitment strategies, affiliations of the particular programs, demographics, treatment formats, and noteworthy pretreatment assessments. Next, the interventions themselves are reviewed, highlighting

TABLE 16.1 Descriptions of Program Participants and Content

Study	N	Site	Recruitment Strategies	Treatment Format	Data Source
Lindquist, Telch, and Taylor (1983)	8	Community	Self-referring	Couples group	Self-report
Deschner and McNeil (1986)	89	University	Self-referring	Combined gender-specific and couples groups	Self-report
Harris (1986)	40	Community	Self-referring	Combined individual and couples groups	Self-report
Shupe, Stacey, and Hazelwood (1987)	241	Community	Self-referring and court mandated	Individual couples, couples groups, and gender-specific groups	Partner report
Harris, Savage, Jones, and Brooke (1988)	81	Community	Self-referring	Individual and couples groups	Partner report
Brannen and Rubin (1996)	58	Community	Court mandated	Gender-specific and couples groups	Partner report
O'Leary, Heyman, and Neidig (1996)	70	University	Self-referring	Gender-specific and couples groups	Partner report

their targets, data sources, and the measures of assessment used. Finally, drop-out rates and actual outcomes are reported, followed by conclusions and future directions for researchers and clinicians.

The Studies

Program Overviews

The seven studies reviewed herein all had as their primary target the cessation of violence, primarily husband-to-wife violence. The interventions focused on anger management skills, communication training, and on misuse of power and control tactics. The samples of the studies ranged from 8 couples to 241 couples, the majority of whom were White, in their late 20s to early 30s, with children, and employed. The majority of program formats were couples groups, in contrast to gender-specific groups or individual couples therapy. With one exception (Harris, Savage, Jones, & Brooke, 1988), most programs lasted 10 to 16 weeks and consisted of weekly sessions that lasted 1.5 to 3 hours. (See Tables 16.1 and 16.2 for a listing of the studies reviewed herein.)

Recruitment

Five of the seven programs were for exclusively self-referring treatment participants. One was composed of three treatment programs, only one of which was for court-mandated batterers (Shupe, Stacey, & Hazelwood, 1987). Another was a treatment program for exclusively court-mandated batterers (Brannen & Rubin, 1996). The majority of couples may not have sought a program that specifically targeted partner violence initially; some of the programs emphasized other treatment foci including positive communication skills and stress management (Lindquist, Telch, & Taylor, 1983) and anger control (Deschner & McNeil, 1986). However, by the time of their actual treatment participation, couples in all the intervention programs knew that the counseling programs in which they had enrolled primarily targeted partner aggression.

Community Versus University Based

Of the seven studies, four were community based (Harris, 1986; Harris et al., 1988; Lindquist et al., 1983; Shupe et al., 1987). Two of the seven studies were conducted in univer-

TABLE 16.2 Descriptions of Program Outcomes

Study	Completers	Dropout (%)	Contacted at Follow-Up (%)	Follow-Up Period
Lindquist, Telch, and Taylor (1983)	8	40	50	6 months
Deschner and McNeil (1986)	82	39	54	6-8 months
Harris (1986)	40	No report	75	2 months-3 years
Shupe, Stacey, and Hazelwood (1987)[a]	102	41	61	1-3 years
Harris, Savage, Jones, and Brooke (1988)	32	35	65	6-12 months
Brannen and Rubin (1996)	42	14	62	6 months
O'Leary, Heyman, and Neidig (1996)	37	47	84	1 year

a. Follow-up was with all participants who could be located. As a result, 148 of 241 participants were contacted. Of the 148, 102 were completers and 42 were dropouts. Of the 102 completers, only 40 partners were located.

sity-based clinics that were affiliated with research programs (Deschner & McNeil, 1986; O'Leary et al., 1996). The remaining program was freestanding, developed as part of a dissertation project in cooperation with the criminal justice system in Austin, Texas (Brannen & Rubin, 1996). In community-based facilities, limited personnel may have potentially hindered comprehensive assessment, especially of the wives. Additionally, community-based clinics may have faced greater difficulty in conducting lengthy assessments and follow-ups.

Sample Size

The sample size of the studies ranged from 8 couples (Lindquist et al., 1983) to 148 couples (Shupe et al., 1987). In the Shupe et al. study, although 241 couples participated in treatment, only 148 were located at follow-up. Small sample sizes, like affiliation (i.e., community vs. university based), will limit the type and number of conclusions that can be drawn regarding treatment outcome.

Demographics

The demographic characteristics reported included marital status, age, number of children, income, employment status, race/ethnicity, and previous abuse history. As stated previously, the majority of the treatment participants were White married couples in their late 20s or early 30s with children. In addition, most had completed high school and were employed full time. More specifically, the percentage of married

couples ranged from 63% in the Harris (1986) program to 100% in the O'Leary et al. (1996) study. Furthermore, in one study, 70% had been married previously (Lindquist et al., 1983).

Only three of the seven studies reported information regarding ethnic/racial composition (Brannen & Rubin, 1996; Deschner & McNeil, 1986; O'Leary et al., 1996). In the Deschner and McNeil study, of a total of 134 clients, 4 participants were Black and 4 were Hispanic American. Of the 70 couples participating in the O'Leary et al. study, all but 4 participating couples were White. Of the 4 minority couples, 2 were Black and there were 2 couples in which 1 partner was Hispanic American and the other White. In the Brannen and Rubin study, in which only demographics for men were reported, the overall ethnic makeup was 50% Hispanic American. The remaining participants were White (36%), Black (9%), and Asian American (4.5%). Certainly, the paucity of data regarding minority populations leaves unanswered the question of whether results with respect to treatment dropout and success can be generalized to non-White samples.

Comorbidity

In two of the studies, participants reported problematic alcohol and drug use/abuse (Brannen & Rubin, 1996; Harris, 1986). Clearly, such substance problems may have had a deleterious effect on treatment outcome. In Harris (1986), 50% of participants reported drug or alcohol abuse. In the Brannen and Rubin study, 25% of the men who participated reported problematic alcohol use. Brannen and Rubin, unlike Harris, statistically controlled for alcohol's potential negative influence on treatment outcome and found that there were differential results based on alcohol use (to be documented later). In the O'Leary et al. (1996) study, men were excluded if they abused alcohol or drugs.

Intervention Formats

The majority of treatment programs used a group couples modality. Additionally, most of the studies compared two treatment formats. Only one study used a wait-list control (Harris et al., 1988), and although this study also included two treatment modalities, recidivism rates were reported for the two treatment groups but not for the wait-list group. The two treatment modalities were an integrated gender-specific and conjoint group format and an individual couples format. As stated previously, the study by Shupe and associates (1987) reported the results of three different treatment programs, all with different formats. Two were couples formats, one an individual couples program, the other a group couples program, and the third a gender-specific format (for the court-mandated participants), but that also provided marriage and alcohol counseling. Two of the seven treatment outcome studies compared the relative efficacy of gender-specific and conjoint formats (Brannen & Rubin, 1996; O'Leary et al., 1996). That is, both studies compared a gender-specific format in which men and women were in different groups with same gender therapists and a conjoint format in which both partners were present with male and female cotherapists. Two other treatment studies examined the overall efficacy of a conjoint group (Deschner & McNeil, 1986; Lindquist et al., 1983). In the Deschner and McNeil (1986) study, approximately half the participants also received individual counseling throughout the duration of the structured intervention. In the Harris (1986) study, couples also received individual counseling, although the provision of the individual sessions was stipulated by the protocol. Individual counseling was provided in the early sessions, and later sessions were primarily conjoint, with individual sessions interspersed throughout the treatment program (Harris, 1986).

Pretreatment Assessment/ Exclusionary Criteria

All treatment programs assessed aggression in some manner. Some screened for level of relationship discord/satisfaction, alcohol, substance abuse, and severe psychopathology. In several cases, the studies explicitly stated that special care was taken in the assessment phase to ensure the victim's safety. This often included providing the woman with shelter and hotline numbers, developing individualized safety plans, and instructing the couple in the use of time out. In other treatment programs, clear exclusionary criteria were used that served to protect the female partner from future acts of aggression, particularly those that might arise as a result of therapy. For instance, in the study by Harris and associates (1988), in addition to providing the woman with a safety plan in the pretreatment assessment phase, intake workers also assessed the degree of danger the aggressive spouse posed to the children as well as to his partner. Additionally, any couple in which the man was psychotic, had severe psychopathology, or had substance abuse that was not being treated concurrently was excluded from the program. Many of the programs explicitly stated that each partner was assessed separately (e.g., O'Leary et al., 1996). Moreover, O'Leary and associates (1996) excluded any couples in which the wife reported that she was fearful of her partner or had sought medical attention for injuries sustained as a result of her partner's aggression. It is important to note that only one couple was excluded on the basis of these criteria, suggesting that there is some self-selection occurring. That is, couples who are engaging in the most severe tactics are not very likely to seek conjoint treatment.

Interventions

All of the treatment programs targeted the elimination of partner violence. In most cases this included monitoring one's thoughts, using cool thoughts to lessen one's anger, recognizing one's anger cues, cognitive restructuring, and time out. In addition, most of the programs aimed to improve communication by teaching skills such as paraphrasing and reflection. Other targets of intervention included problem solving, stress management, relaxation training, assertiveness training, increasing positive exchanges, and focusing on issues of gender role stereotyping, power, control, and jealousy.

A noteworthy addition to the Brannen and Rubin (1996) study, conducted in Austin, Texas, was a 10-week stress management course. The criminal justice system in Austin requires those convicted of partner violence to enroll in the course. To minimize the differential effect that various therapists and locations might have on the stress management training, Brannen himself conducted the stress management module so as to make its effect more uniform. The stress management course was given after the aggression treatment program. This sequence functioned to minimize the potential confounding with the assessment of the pre- to posttreatment effect. On the other hand, the course may have influenced follow-up assessments. Although other individual treatment programs may have included a stress management component, it was probably considerably less than the 10-week component in Brannen and Rubin's study.

Data Sources

Whenever possible, all programs used wife's report as a corroborating source. In fact, both the Brannen and Rubin (1996) and Shupe and associates (1987) studies with court-mandated treatment participants used police reports as an additional corroborating source to minimize the likelihood that the partner might underreport the occurrence of violence. Only the study by Deschner and McNeil (1986) based the evaluation of treatment outcome solely on self-report. One study failed to report the source and measure of pre- or posttreatment level of aggression (Harris, 1986). In light of what we know regarding women's tendency to overreport and/or men's tendency to underreport incidence of partner aggression (Ganley, 1981), there is clearly some benefit from obtaining both part-

ners' reports (Barling, O'Leary, Jouriles, Vivian, & MacEwen, 1987; Heyman & Schlee, 1996; Malone, Tyree, & O'Leary, 1989; Strahan, 1980).

Measures of Aggression

In most cases, a standardized measure of aggression such as the Conflict Tactics Scale (CTS; Straus, 1979) was used. A number of the studies used a single measure such as this to assess both pretreatment, posttreatment, and follow-up level and frequency of aggression (O'Leary et al. 1996). Other studies used categorical variables such as presence versus absence (Brannen & Rubin, 1996; Harris et al., 1988) or increase, decrease, or no changes in the pattern of assaults (Shupe et al., 1987) to assess posttreatment level of aggression. Harris and associates (1988) based pretreatment assessment of aggression on the most violent CTS behavior. Thus, Harris and associates reported percentage rates of various tactics. Deschner and McNeil (1986) used yet another measure, relying on the number of people per week reporting physical aggression as the criterion of treatment success or failure. Although most studies used a standardized measure of aggression, the actual information (i.e., frequency, most severe tactic) provided by the studies limits meaningful comparisons across a number of the programs.

Dropout

The majority of studies reported drop-out rates, although two did not (Harris, 1986; Shupe et al., 1987), and though the definitions may have varied somewhat, the drop-out rates ranged from 14% (Brannen & Rubin, 1996) to 47% (O'Leary et al., 1996). One factor that may account for the low drop-out rate reported by Brannen and Rubin is the close affiliation of their program with the criminal justice system and the potential threat of incarceration that noncompliance (i.e., failure to attend treatment sessions) posed. Regarding the variability in definition of dropouts, a 60% attendance rate was equated with completing treatment in the Deschner and McNeil (1986) study, whereas a 70% attendance rate was used in the O'Leary and associates (1996) study. Additionally, some of the studies reported drop-out rates both prior to and during treatment. For example, 35% dropped out of the Harris and associates (1988) program before treatment even began. In addition, a differential drop-out rate was also reported for the two treatment modalities evaluated in the Harris and associates study. More specifically, once treatment began, 16% of those in the group couples format dropped out compared with 67% of those in the individual couples format.

Only two of the studies examined predictors of dropout (Harris et al., 1988; O'Leary et al., 1996). In the Harris and associates study, unemployment, increased external social support, and lower pretreatment levels of aggression were all positively associated with treatment dropout. In a separate study by Brown, O'Leary, and Feldbau (in press), based on the data set used to evaluate treatment success, husbands' severe psychological aggression and wives' mild psychological aggression were positively correlated with treatment dropout. Additionally, qualitative data based on dropouts' own reasons for terminating treatment indicated that although clients gained insight and acquired useful skills (e.g., improved communication, anger management), they felt that the group format did not provide adequate attention to individual couple issues.

The drop-out rates reported from treatment programs for self-referring intact couples are not inconsistent with rates reported from court-mandated treatment programs. A recent review by Hamberger and Hastings (1994) found that the drop-out rate averaged 42% across studies. This rate is considerably higher than rates reported in the general marital therapy literature. Although many marital therapy outcome studies do not even report drop-out rates (Hahlweg & Markman, 1988; Shadish et al., 1993), those that do, find attrition ranges from 0% to 25% (see reviews by Dunn & Schwebel, 1995; Hahlweg & Markman, 1988; Shadish et al., 1993). The modal rate of attrition reported in these reviews was closer to 5%. In light of the fact that participants in the studies reviewed herein were being treated for aggression and that denial characterizes many who engage in violent behavior (Barrera et al., 1994), drop-out rates would be expected to be as high or higher in treatment for wife/partner abuse than in standard marital therapy.

Treatment Outcome

Most of the studies reported success rates ranging from 50% to 90% based on follow-up data gathered 6 months after the treatment program had ended. Success rates reported were based on treatment completers. As mentioned earlier, the drop-out rates ranged from 14% to 47%. In addition, the various treatment programs defined success in a nonuniform manner.

Couples Groups. Lindquist et al. (1983) conducted a 6-week and 6-month follow-up, but reported that due to the small sample size (fewer than eight couples), and the absence of a control group, no meaningful analyses could be conducted. Pre-post comparisons suggested that treated couples were significantly less angry, less verbally and physically aggressive, less jealous, and more assertive. At posttreatment none of the women reported any recurrence of the abuse. At the 6-week follow-up, 50% reported no physical aggression, 30% reported one incident, and 20% reported two to four acts since treatment completion. At the 6-month follow-up, only four of the eight couples could be contacted, all of whom reported one to four incidents of partner violence since treatment ended. This study suggests that the greater the time since treatment, the more likely that there will be some recidivism.

Individual Couples Versus Group Couples. In one of the studies that compared the two treatment formats, Harris and associates (1988) reported that of the total sample, 89% of group counseling participants were located in contrast to 41% of those who participated in the individual couples counseling program. Thus, it appears that the group format was better able to retain clients. Although most couples remained together, of those who had separated or divorced, approximately 63% left the relationship because of continued abuse. Of those who remained with their partner, no differences were reported across the two treatment modalities in the levels of psychological and physical aggression. Regarding the physical aggression, 54% reported that it had ceased since treatment terminated, 14% reported that the aggression had decreased, and one participant reported that there was no change in the level or frequency of abuse. Regarding the psychological aggression, 21% reported no verbal or emotional abuse posttreatment, 36% reported that the verbal and emotional abuse had decreased, and 14% reported that there was no change in the level of psychological abuse. Overall, there was a 64% success rate. Although close to 4 times as many couples dropped out of the individual format as compared to the group approach, it is important to note that no differential treatment effects were observed. Because the focus of all intervention programs was cessation of husbands' aggression, it could be that the group format, at least initially, provided the man with some security. It may have been easier to disengage from the therapeutic process and deny one's behavior in the group format, whereas in the individual couples format this may have been more difficult.

Couples Versus Gender-Specific Groups. In the O'Leary and associates (1996) study, both psychological and physical aggression were significantly reduced at posttreatment and at 1-year follow-up in the gender-specific and conjoint formats, based on husbands' and wives' reports. There were no significant differences between group formats and cessation rates associated with each treatment. Regarding psychological aggression, there were significant reductions at both posttreatment and at 1-year follow-up. Regarding physical aggression, based on wives' reports, there was a 56% cessation rate of mild and severe physical aggression during treatment. At 1-year follow-up, 23% reported no physical aggression. Sixty-nine percent reported no severe physical aggression, whereas at pretreatment only 19% had reported no severe physical aggression. In sum, in the majority of cases, both mild and severe aggression ceased to occur. More detailed information regarding this study can be found in O'Leary et al. (1996). Also, wives

decreased in taking responsibility for their partner's aggression and husbands decreased in blaming their wives for their own aggressive behavior. Other beneficial effects of treatment included wives' decreased depressive symptomatology. No differential effects were observed between the gender-specific and conjoint modalities. In summary, both treatment modalities appeared to be successful in reducing physical and psychological aggression, as well as improving couples' marital satisfaction.

Results of the Brannen and Rubin (1996) study also indicated that both the gender-specific and couple treatments were effective. Postintervention data supplied by the probationer's partner were available for 42 of the 60 participants. No significant differences were found between couples groups and gender-specific group participants with respect to the psychological and physical aggression. Both couples and gender-specific groups showed a significant reduction in mild and severe physical aggression. Although there was a significant reduction of mild aggression for those assigned to the couples and gender-specific groups, those assigned to the couples group showed greater posttreatment reduction in mild physical aggression than those in the gender-specific group. Those assigned to gender-specific groups, and without a history of alcohol abuse, reported lower levels of physical aggression postintervention than their alcohol-abusing counterparts. In the couples groups, there was no effect of alcohol abuse on reductions in aggression. In sum, for those with a history of alcohol abuse, those in the couples format fared better than those in the gender-specific format. For those with no history of alcohol abuse, the two treatment modalities worked equally well. No significant differences postintervention were found for communication and marital satisfaction between the two treatment modalities.

Hybrid Treatments. Harris (1986) evaluated a treatment program that combined individual counseling with couples therapy. A 2-month to 3-year follow-up was conducted in which 40 participants out of 200 were contacted. Only 30 of the 40 participants who were contacted provided follow-up data. Respondents differed from nonrespondents in that they had attended more sessions. With this sampling limitation in mind, a 73% success rate (cessation of violence according to the wife) was observed for those who participated in the follow-up. Factors positively associated with treatment success were treatment continuance, later onset of aggression, older ages, and higher income.

Another hybrid program was reported by Shupe and associates (1987). One of the three programs reported on, the Austin program, serviced court-mandated men and included a unique treatment component. The last phase of intervention was tailored to the individual and included treatment for marital discord or drug or alcohol problems. All three treatment programs evaluated (i.e., Austin Family Violence Diversion Network, Tyler Family Preservation Project, and Arlington Anger Control Program) showed reduction in physical aggression, but there were no differential effects across the three treatment programs. Unfortunately, there was not random assignment to treatments, the interventions took place in different towns, and differed with regard to type of referral. Finally, only a subsample of the participants could be contacted after treatment, making firm conclusions about the results impossible.

Control Groups

Only one study (Harris et al., 1988) included a control group, although no comparison was made between it and the two treatment formats regarding recidivism rates. The failure to include control groups in the reviewed studies weakens the researchers' conclusions that treatment is effective in decreasing or eliminating partner violence. Indeed, some might argue that many of the couples who participated in the programs reviewed herein would have stopped their aggressive behavior regardless of whether they received treatment. However, in a sample of physically abusive couples, N. S. Jacobson found only 5% of the men ceased their physical aggression across a 2-year period (personal communication, November 17, 1995). Moreover, in a community sample of 272 newlyweds,

research on the stability of aggression indicated considerable stability of aggression among individuals who engaged in repeated acts of mild or a single act of severe aggression when followed up 1 year later (Malone & O'Leary, 1995). More specifically, if a man engaged in multiple acts of mild aggression 18 months after marriage, the likelihood of engaging in an act of physical aggression against a wife a year later was 84%. If a man engaged in multiple acts of severe aggression 18 months after marriage, the likelihood of engaging in some act of physical aggression against the wife a year later was 82%.

Summary

■ Having reviewed the available literature, several conclusions follow. First, given that approximately two thirds of couples seeking marital treatment also report physical aggression in their relationship, it is necessary that we know what treatments work with this population as well as how they work. This is particularly crucial, because these couples seeking marital therapy may represent the largest population of couples experiencing physical aggression. In addition, these couples are potentially the most tractable clients and least resistant to change. Second, posttreatment success rates defined as cessation of violence ranged from 56% (O'Leary et al., 1996) to 90% (Brannen & Rubin, 1996). In the latter study, the cessation rates were maintained at approximately 92% of the posttreatment rates at 6 months although only 62% of the sample could be contacted for follow-up assessment. Third, the finding that treatment programs that lasted approximately 4 months appeared to substantially reduce or eliminate the level of partner aggression is noteworthy, especially considering the heterogeneity among these intact couples. Two of the programs reported substantial levels of alcohol and/or substance abuse, ranging from 25% (Brannen & Rubin, 1996) to 50% (Harris, 1986). One study included spouses who not only aggressed on their partner but against their children as well (Deschner & McNeil, 1986). In addition, one study reported that 40% of participants had experienced partner violence in prior relationships

(Harris, 1986) and 70% had been previously married (Lindquist et al., 1983). Finally, drop-out rates in the aforementioned studies vary considerably ranging from 14% (Brannen & Rubin, 1996) to 47% (O'Leary et al., 1996). It is noteworthy that attrition rates are being addressed as a major issue in the spouse abuse area as they are considerably higher than in standard marital therapy or in therapy for anxiety and depression (Brown et al., in press; Cadsky, Hanson, Crawford, & Lalonde, 1996). The relatively high drop-out rate only highlights the necessity of our examining systematically predictors of dropout, especially those over which service providers may have some control (e.g., client-therapist interactions).

Control and Comparison Groups

Clearly, future treatment research should use comparison and/or control groups. With more severe types of violence, a no-intervention group would be seen by many, if not most, as unethical. Probably most palatable would be a comparison of different types of treatment or legal interventions (Fagan, 1996). At least two factors might guide the choice of a control group: the potential negative effect (e.g., injury) of continued violence and the marital distress these couples typically experience. It is likely that if these couples are distressed enough to seek treatment, they may be unwilling to wait several months before receiving any treatment. One solution that takes these factors into account is to provide limited treatment on demand in cases of emergency needs, a variant of the wait-list control.

Providing participants with standard behavioral marital treatment is another alternative that takes into consideration the practical and ethical concerns involved in assigning physically aggressive couples to a wait-list control condition. By placing participants in a treatment for marital discord, couples would be provided with the treatment they initially often seek. Moreover, standard behavioral marital treatment has been shown to be effective in improving marital satisfaction in approximately two thirds of cases (Jacobson & Addis, 1993; Jacobson et al., 1984). As we noted in the introduction to this

chapter, couples often do not seek treatment for marital violence per se, and few identify the marital violence as a primary relationship problem.

Another alternative to standard control groups would be to ascertain continuance rates of aggression in a nontreated sample with features that are similar to the one being treated. If continuance rates could be reliably established, it would make the task of demonstrating an intervention's usefulness without a control group less difficult. For example, if as noted earlier only 16%-18% of repeatedly physically aggressive men cease their aggressive behavior toward their partners over a year, a treatment that would significantly exceed that rate would be judged to have considerable promise and could be a candidate for a full-scale clinical trial.

Measurement Issues

In addition to the inclusion of a control group, more precise measurement and comprehensive assessment of aggression is also advised. Specifically, if aggression were assessed with a standardized measure, cross-study comparisons could be made more easily. Furthermore, if assessment were conducted with a continuous measure in contrast to a dichotomous one, practitioners and researchers could make a more adequate assessment of whether improvements were made, especially because total cessation of physical aggression may not be achieved in a significant percentage of cases. It is also recommended that because aggression can take any number of forms, practitioners and researchers assess verbal, psychological, physical, and sexual forms of aggression (e.g., Pan, Neidig, & O'Leary, 1994b); moreover, the context of aggression might be assessed because impact and meaning may differ for men and women. A measure that taps impact and injury might also be useful. One such measure is the adapted version of the CTS (cf. Cascardi et al., 1992).

Because there may be more than one representative population of partner-violent men, several etiological models may exist, suggesting alternative intervention strategies. Thus, the treatment one chooses to assess should be designed with a particular population in mind. An etiological model should account for partner violence in this population of interest. Then, the efficacy of a treatment whose design is guided by our knowledge regarding the etiology of partner violence could be established. Next, researchers might examine components of these strategies. To what extent is a particular intervention component critical to the eventual treatment outcome? Are there components whose addition to the treatment package might augment treatment success? For example, is anger management sufficient for change, or are the additional treatment components that target problem-solving necessary?

Subject Characteristics

Several researchers in the marital violence field have suggested that all partner-violent men are not alike (Okun, 1986; O'Leary, 1993). In fact, Holtzworth-Munroe and Stuart (1994), in their review of the batterer typology literature, find that batterers differ along several dimensions. Moreover, categorizing batterers according to these dimensions may effectively guide our assignment of partner-violent men to treatment in a manner that would maximize the likelihood that an individual would be helped by a given intervention. Establishing a batterer typology may go far in elucidating why a man who abuses his partner may be more or less appropriate for a particular treatment. However, it may also be important to consider other subject variables that may be less salient, may be more difficult to manipulate, may interact with typology, and may affect the likelihood of treatment success. Such factors might include demographic (e.g., age, education, income, race/ethnicity) and personality variables.

Therapist Characteristics

Yet another set of factors may also influence treatment outcome. Just as aspects of a client's functioning may interact with treatment and affect outcome, so may characteristics of the therapist and his or her functioning. In fact, it has been demonstrated that therapists' expectations regarding a client's capacity to change (Brucato, 1980), along with their gender, age, ethnicity, and personality style, may play a sig-

nificant role in treatment outcome (Garfield, 1986). We may gain meaningful and useful knowledge by examining what actually occurs in treatment. More specifically, researchers might consider interactions between therapist and client and how these interactions might facilitate change. Given the nature of husband-to-wife violence, the resistance often encountered on the part of the perpetrator, the increased difficulty encountered engaging two persons rather than one in therapy, and the greater frequency of dropout in this client population, the alliance between therapist and client(s) may merit investigation.

Dropout

Beyond the factors relating to treatment outcome such as client, therapist, and treatment characteristics, the issue of dropout needs to be considered. Dropout is an issue of considerable concern among spouse abuse researchers, and it should be a focus of treatment outcome research. Moreover, it is an area for further investigation, as dropout is plainly a measure of the utility of an intervention program. Clearly, it is financially impractical to contract therapists to run a treatment program if clients drop out at very high rates.

Regarding the prediction of dropout, the focus in both the spouse abuse and general psychotherapy literatures has been on demographic variables as predictors. However, demographics appear to account for little variance in dropout (Wierzbicki & Pekarik, 1993). Moreover, findings regarding the association between demographics and dropout yield few meaningful results in terms of modifications to treatment that would lower attrition rates. A finding in the court-mandated literature regarding treatment withdrawal indicates that treatment dropouts often fare as well as treatment completers in terms of recidivism rates (Edleson & Grusznski, 1988; Hamberger & Hastings, 1988), thus raising the possibility that treatment does not work. Alternatively, it might be that the dropouts to whom the completers are compared represent the most functional of the dropouts, "the cream of the attritters." In fact, as Shupe and associates (1987) have suggested, there may be some dropouts for whom even a little treatment is helpful. There may be others who will benefit little from treatments like those described above. Aggressive pursuit of dropouts may reveal that all dropouts are not treatment failures.

Predictors of Treatment Success and Follow-Up

To further increase our knowledge regarding the potential efficacy of couples treatment programs for male partner violence, in addition to a given intervention's overall effectiveness, predictors of treatment success should also be examined. This would bring us one step closer to determining for whom treatment works, as well as for whom it might not work. Finally, in keeping with what appears to be normative in this small literature, the maintenance of change at some follow-up period should be assessed. Recidivism status at some predetermined time after which treatment has ended might constitute a more comprehensive appraisal of a particular intervention than posttreatment status alone.

Conclusions

■ The treatment programs reviewed herein were only a first step in elucidating the potential efficacy of such interventions for the treatment of partner violence. However, several controversies remain. How should we conceptualize outcome? Should immediate and total cessation of aggression be the aim of treatment and the criterion by which its success is judged, as many studies currently do? Or should we, as some have suggested (Dutton, 1995; Jennings, 1990; Prochaska & DiClemente, 1986), view relapse as the rule, not the exception? Is it, in fact, realistic to expect the total elimination of a particular behavior after a brief intervention program? Should we necessarily throw out the baby with the bath water if the overwhelming majority of participants report that the aggression has significantly decreased after only a few months, but not ceased completely? This would seem foolish—particularly given what we know regarding the continuance of aggression. Parallel arguments have been made regarding the

evaluations of treatment programs for alcoholism in which cessation was originally the only dependent measure of interest and more recently, change in amount of drinking as well as a host of other measures have been included in assessing the outcome (Sobell, Sobell, & Gavin, 1995).

This review of treatment programs for intact couples suggests that intervention may be able to bring about desirable changes in maritally violent men, decreasing or eliminating their aggressive behavior in many cases. Although these programs yield promising results, we have yet to answer questions that concern many researchers and practitioners. Clearly, more studies are needed. Our recommendation for improving future research in this area can be broken down into two tiers, first and second order. First-order recommendations are those that we believe are critical to adequate treatment evaluation. First-order modifications should include standardized (i.e., with the CTS) and comprehensive assessment of aggression (i.e., psychological, physical, sexual) with a continuous, as opposed to a categorical, measure. The impact and injury associated with partner violence should also be assessed. To further tease apart the existing confusion regarding treatment efficacy, aggressive follow-up with dropouts is advised. Second-order recommendations would only serve to enhance the minimal standards of research established by the suggested first-order modifications. These would include searching for predictors of continuance and success (i.e., recidivism rates), perhaps even looking toward contributions that both the therapist and client make to the eventual outcome.

References

Barling, J., O'Leary, K. D., Jouriles, E. N., Vivian, D., & MacEwen, K. E. (1987). Factor similarity of the Conflict Tactics Scale across samples, spouse, and sites: Issues and implications. *Journal of Family Violence, 2,* 37-54.

Barrera, M., Palmer, S., Brown, R., & Kalaher, S. (1994). Characteristics of court-involved men and non court-involved men who abuse their wives. *Journal of Family Violence, 9,* 333-345.

Brannen, S. J., & Rubin, A. (1996). Comparing the effectiveness of gender-specific and couples groups in a court-mandated spouse abuse treatment program. *Research on Social Work Practice, 6,* 405-424.

Brown, P. D., O'Leary, K. D., & Feldbau, S. (in press). Drop-out in a treatment program for self-referring wife abusing men. *Journal of Family Violence.*

Brucato, L. L. (1980). Therapist and client expectancies: Educated guesses or causal agents? *Dissertation Abstracts International, 41,* 1493-1494.

Cadsky, O., Hanson, R. K., Crawford, M., & Lalonde, C. (1996). Attrition from a male batterer treatment program: Client-treatment congruence and lifestyle instability. *Violence and Victims, 11,* 51-64.

Cascardi, M., Langhinrichsen, J., & Vivian, D. (1992). Marital aggression, impact, injury, and health correlates for husbands and wives. *Archives of Internal Medicine, 152,* 1178-1184.

Deschner, J. P., & McNeil, J. S. (1986). Results of anger control training for battering couples. *Journal of Family Violence, 1,* 111-120.

Dunn, R. L., & Schwebel, A. I. (1995). Meta-analytic review of marital therapy outcome research. *Journal of Family Psychology, 9,* 58-68.

Dutton, D. G. (1995). *Domestic assault of women: Psychological and criminal justice perspective.* Vancouver: University of British Columbia Press.

Edleson, J. L., & Grusznski, R. J. (1988). Treating men who batter: Four years of outcome data from the Domestic Abuse Project. *Journal of Social Service Research, 12,* 3-22.

Edleson, J. L., & Tolman, R. M. (1992). *Intervention for men who batter.* Newbury Park, CA: Sage.

Ehrensaft, M. K., & Vivian, D. (in press). Spouses' reasons for not reporting existing physical aggression as a marital problem. *Journal of Family Psychology, 10,* 443-453.

Fagan, J. (1996). *The criminalization of domestic violence: Promises and limits.* Washington, DC: National Institute of Justice Research.

Ganley, A. L. (1981). *Court-mandated counseling for men who batter.* Manual available from the Center for Women's Policy Studies, Washington, DC.

Garfield, S. L. (1986). Research on client variables in psychotherapy. In S. L. Garfield & A. E. Bergin (Eds.), *Handbook of psychotherapy and behavior change* (3rd ed., pp. 213-256). New York: John Wiley.

Hahlweg, K., & Markman, H. J. (1988). Effectiveness of behavioral marital therapy: Empirical status of behavioral techniques in preventing and alleviating marital distress. *Journal of Consulting and Clinical Psychology, 56,* 440-447.

Hamberger, L. K., & Hastings, J. E. (1988). Characteristics of male spouse abusers consistent with personality disorders. *Hospital and Community Psychiatry, 39,* 763-770.

Hamberger, L. K., & Hastings, J. E. (1994). Court-mandated treatment of men who batter their partners: Issues, controversies and outcomes. In Z. Hilton (Ed.), *Legal responses to wife assault.* Newbury Park, CA: Sage.

Harris, J. (1986). Counseling violent couples using Walker's model. *Psychotherapy, 23,* 613-621.

Harris, R., Savage, S., Jones, T., & Brooke, W. (1988). A comparison of treatments for abusive men and their partners within a family-service agency. *Canadian Journal of Community Mental Health, 7,* 147-155.

Heyman, R. E., & Schlee, K. (1996). *Estimating the true level of wife abuse: Adjusting rates based on sensitivity of the Conflict Tactics Scale.* Manuscript submitted for publication.

Holtzworth-Munroe, A., & Stuart, G. L. (1994). Typologies of male batterers: Three subtypes and the differences among them. *Psychological Bulletin, 116,* 476-497.

Holtzworth-Munroe, A., Waltz, J., Jacobson, N. S., Monaco, V., Fehrenbach, P. A., & Gottman, J. M. (1992). Recruiting non-violent men as control subjects for research on marital violence: How easily can it be done? *Violence and Victims, 7,* 79-88.

Jacobson, N. S., & Addis, M. E. (1993). Research on couples and couples therapy: What do we know? Where are we going? *Journal of Consulting and Clinical Psychology, 61,* 85-93.

Jacobson, N. S., Follette, W. C., Revenstorf, D., Baucom, D., Hahlweg, K., & Margolin, G. (1984). Variability in outcome and clinical significance in behavioral marital therapy. *Journal of Consulting and Clinical Psychology, 53,* 419-421.

Jennings, J. L. (1990). Preventing relapse versus "stopping" domestic violence: Do we expect too much too soon from battering men? *Journal of Family Violence, 5,* 43-60.

Lindquist, C. U., Telch, C. F., & Taylor, J. (1983). Evaluation of a conjugal violence treatment program: A pilot study. *Behavioral Counseling and Community Intervention, 3*(1), 76-90.

Malone, J., & O'Leary, K. D. (1995, April). *Continuation and cessation of violence in young married couples.* Paper presented at the meetings of the Southern Sociological Society, Atlanta, GA.

Malone, J., Tyree, A., & O'Leary, K. D. (1989). Generalization and containment: Different effects of past aggression for wives and husbands. *Journal of Marriage and the Family, 51,* 687-697.

McMahon, M., & Pence, E. (1996). Replying to Dan O'Leary. *Journal of Interpersonal Violence, 11,* 452-455.

Okun, L. E. (1986). *Woman abuse: Facts replacing myths.* Albany: State University of New York Press.

O'Leary, K. D. (1993). Through a psychological lens: Personality traits, personality disorders, and levels of violence. In R. J. Gelles & D. R. Loseke (Eds.), *Current controversies on family violence* (pp. 7-30). Newbury Park, CA: Sage.

O'Leary, K. D. (1996). Physical aggression in intimate relationships can be treated within a marital context under certain circumstances. *Journal of Interpersonal Violence, 11,* 450-452.

O'Leary, K. D., Barling, J., Arias, I., Rosenbaum, A., Malone, J., & Tyree, A. (1989). Prevalence and stability of physical aggression between spouses: A longitudinal analysis. *Journal of Consulting and Clinical Psychology, 57,* 263-268.

O'Leary, K. D., Heyman, R. E., & Neidig, P. H. (1996). *Treatment of wife abuse: A comparison of gender-specific and couples approaches.* Manuscript submitted for publication.

O'Leary, K. D., Neidig, P. H., & Heyman, R. E. (1995). Assessment and treatment of partner abuse: A synopsis for the legal profession. *Albany Law Review, 58,* 1215-1234.

O'Leary, K. D., Vivian, D., & Malone, J. (1992). Assessment of physical aggression in marriage: The need for a multimodal method. *Behavioral Assessment, 14,* 5-14.

Pan, H. S., Neidig, P. H., & O'Leary, K. D. (1994a). Male-female and aggressor-victim differences in the factor structure of the modified Conflict Tactics Scale. *Journal of Interpersonal Violence, 9,* 366-382.

Pan, H., Neidig, P. H., & O'Leary, K. D. (1994b). Predicting mild and severe husband-to-wife physical aggression. *Journal of Consulting and Clinical Psychology, 62,* 975-981.

Prochaska, J. O., & DiClemente, C. C. (1986). Toward a comprehensive model of change. In W. Miller & N. Heather (Eds.), *Treating addictive behaviors* (pp. 3-27). New York: Plenum.

Rosenfeld, B. D. (1992). Court-ordered treatment of spouse abuse. *Clinical Psychology Review, 12,* 205-226.

Shadish, W. R., Montgomery, L. M., Wilson, P., Wilson, M. R., Bright, I., & Okwumabua, T. (1993). Effects of family and marital psychotherapies: A meta-analysis. *Journal of Consulting and Clinical Psychology, 61,* 992-1002.

Shupe, A., Stacey, W. A., & Hazelwood, L. R. (1987). *Violent men, violent couples.* Lexington, MA: Lexington Books.

Sobell, M. B., Sobell, L. C., & Gavin, D. R. (1995). Portraying alcohol treatment outcomes: Different yardsticks of success. *Behavior Therapy, 26,* 643-669.

Strahan, R. F. (1980). More on averaging judges' ratings: Determining the most reliable composite. *Journal of Consulting and Clinical Psychology, 48,* 587-589.

Straus, M. A. (1979). Measuring intrafamily conflict and violence: The Conflict Tactics (CT) Scales. *Journal of Marriage and the Family, 41,* 75-88.

Straus, M. A., & Gelles, R. J. (Eds.). (1990). *Physical violence in American families: Risk factors and adaptations to violence in 8,145 families.* New Brunswick, NJ: Transaction.

Walker, L. E. (1979). *The battered woman.* New York: Harper & Row.

Wierzbicki, M., & Pekarik, G. (1993). A meta-analysis of psychotherapy dropout. *Professional Psychology: Research and Practice, 24,* 190-195.

CHAPTER 17

Expanding Batterer Program Evaluation

Edward W. Gondolf

The advent of court-mandated batterer counseling in the mid-1980s prompted a dramatic expansion of batterer programs over the past 5 years (Finn, 1987). This expansion has not been without question, however. Battered women advocates, court officials, and mental health professionals are increasingly asking about the effectiveness of these programs. Do batterer programs really stop men from abusing women? Are they worth the time and money? Are arrest and separation in themselves a better bet?

The effectiveness of batterer programs admittedly remains an open question despite the evolution of batterer programs over the past 15 years. There have been approximately 30 published program evaluations and a few ambitious evaluations that have yet to be published. The bottom line is that these evaluations, critiqued in four major narrative reviews of the literature, offer very limited results (Eisikovits & Edleson, 1989; Gondolf, 1991; Rosenfeld, 1992; Tolman & Bennett, 1990), as do many of the program evaluations in other fields (Longabaugh & Lewis, 1988; Quinsey, Harris, Rice, & Lalumiere, 1993; Wilner, Freeman, Surber, & Goldstein, 1985). In a social science "court," most of the batterer program evaluations would be dismissed on technicalities or as circumstantial evidence (see Quinsey et al., 1993).

The inconclusive evaluations raise some crucial issues and opportunities. It may be that the conventional input-output evaluation design

AUTHOR'S NOTE: A version of this chapter was presented at the Third National Conference for Professionals Working With Men Who Batter, Minneapolis, Minnesota, April 1993. Barbara Hart, Pennsylvania Coalition Against Domestic Violence, and Paul Bukovec, Project RAP, Philadelphia, contributed to the conference presentation and development of the chapter. Preparation was supported by a grant from the Centers for Disease Control and Prevention (CDC) (Grant R49/CCR310525-01). The contents do not, however, necessarily represent the official views of the CDC.

cannot answer the scope of the questions about batterer programs (Rossi & Freeman, 1989). Most batterer program evaluations focus on the state of the batterers as they enter the program—"the input"—and on fixed behavior when they come out—"the output." This sort of evaluation is an expedient but rather simple representation of a complicated psychological and social process. An expansion of the evaluation process may be necessary to understand the role and contribution of batterer programs. We propose that a broader conception of batterer programs, including their specific role in the cessation of abuse, their relationship to other interventions, and their contribution to the community at large, needs to be weighed to more meaningfully evaluate batterer programs.

The discussion that follows argues for such an expansion of batterer program evaluations. I begin with a brief review of the prevailing findings of the existing batterer program evaluations and the methodological shortcomings that continue to compromise them. I pose methodological innovations that may improve conventional program evaluations (e.g., tracking systems, process outcome measures, record verifications, capture-recapture analysis) and additional considerations that may help revise their designs (e.g., patient matching, program implementation, and community collaborations). Finally, I raise some alternatives to conventional program evaluation drawing on evaluation approaches in other fields (e.g., consumer-based assessment, community and systems analysis, social impact assessment, and ethical decision making). This array of alternatives may not only help to address the questions and reservations about batterer programs but also offer new directions and possibilities for these programs.

Prevailing Findings

■ Batterer programs and program staff are often sustained by the noticeable changes and moving testimonials of some of the batterers in their programs (see Gondolf & Russell, 1987). These observations offer hope and encouragement in a difficult and challenging undertaking. More systematic program evaluations, however,

do not necessarily support the level of their hope. Program evaluations suggest a modicum of success relative to the number of men who enter a program and those who might stop their violence without a program (Rosenfeld, 1992). Moreover, the success may be attributable less to the program modality and "treatment," and more to program structure, implementation, and context (Edleson & Tolman, 1993; Gondolf, 1991).

Reviews of the batterer program evaluations show 50%-80% of the program completers to be nonviolent at the end of a 6-month to 1-year period, as verified by their partners (Tolman & Bennett, 1990). The reduction of other forms of abuse is less clear, but one study showed that only about 40%-50% of the participants were free of terroristic threats at a 6-month follow-up (Edleson & Syers, 1990). It may be that some men displace their physical abuse to heightened verbal and psychological abuse.

As with program evaluations in other fields (Hubbard et al., 1989; Wilner et al., 1985), the batterer program outcomes do not appear to vary substantially across modalities. However, the comparison of batterer program modalities has only been made across contrasting single-site evaluations, and not yet confirmed in a scientifically controlled comparison of batterer program modalities. The batterer program "success rates," although compromised by high dropouts and incomplete follow-ups, are comparable to those in drunk driving programs, drug and alcohol programs, sex offender programs, and check forging programs (see Furby, Blackshaw, & Weinrott, 1989; Hubbard et al., 1989; Kassebaum & Ward, 1991; Schare, 1992). Overall, the evaluations show the range of batterer program effectiveness to be about the same as in other fields.

The few batterer program evaluations that have managed a quasi-control group of dropouts, or a formal control group of men with no program contact, report relatively small differences in effectiveness based on victim reports (Tolman & Bennett, 1990). The most elaborate of these was a clinical trial sponsored by the National Institute of Justice in which batterers were randomly assigned to a 3-month batterer program, to probation, or to suspended prosecution without a batterer program (Harrell, 1991). An elaborate set of outcome measures revealed no significant differences between the batterer program and nonprogram groups. There remains some question whether the crucial independent variable—the batterer program intervention—was compromised in this particular study. The short duration, therapeutic approach, and implementation problems of the batterer program are suspect.

Some batterer program specialists (Adams, 1988; Pence, 1989) assert that a more confrontational format is appropriate and effective with batterers in court-mandated programs, who tend to have compounding alcohol and drug problems, criminal histories, and personality disorders, as is shown to be the case in juvenile rehabilitation programs (Izzo & Ross, 1990). Moreover, exploratory evaluations in Washington, Florida, and Arizona suggest that long-term treatment of 1 year has substantially higher success rates (Culter & Fueyo, 1991; Smith, 1991). In brief, a different kind of batterer program lasting for a year instead of 3 months may produce more positive results.

Methodological Problems

■ Several methodological problems make batterer programs especially difficult to evaluate and evaluation findings difficult to interpret (Gondolf, 1987b). Many evaluations are initiated by programs themselves under pressure to justify their program's existence and the venture of batterer programming in general. Consequently, some evaluations may be influenced by researcher bias and the need for expedience. Impartiality is certainly attempted, but the biases of program staff and local researchers can very subtly work their way into the evaluation (Rossi & Freeman, 1989). To save money and time, control or comparison groups may not be used and data may be collected by the same program staff who deliver the services; a positive face is put on the analysis by overlooking program dropouts, sample bias caused by low response rates, and the lack of opportunity to reoffend (the batterer's spouse may be unavailable). These issues of "poor design" are, of course, related to limited research funds, personnel, and exper-

tise—all of which are at a premium amid dwindling social service dollars.

The greatest methodological problem is probably with sampling procedures. Batterer program evaluations tend to be based on program completers and not account for the substantial portion of program dropouts (DeMaris, 1989; Gondolf & Foster, 1991). According to a survey of program directors, nearly half of the programs faced drop-out rates of over 50% of the men accepted at intake (Gondolf, 1990). One program documented that less than 5% of 200 men who contacted a batterer program completed the 6-month program (Gondolf & Foster, 1991). In some quasi-control evaluations, dropouts have been used as control groups, but the dropouts tend not to match or be directly comparable to program completers (e.g., Hamberger & Hastings, 1988).

Moreover, as few as 20%-40% of the completers are found after a follow-up period of 6-12 months (DeMaris & Jackson, 1987; Tolman & Bennett, 1990). Collecting a variety of phone numbers and addresses from a client, consulting police and social service records for client information, and periodic contact (every 2-3 months) with a client can substantially raise the follow-up response rate (Mulvey & Lidz, 1993). It is, however, tremendously costly and time-consuming to implement these practices with batterers, who tend to be a transient group. A statistical procedure known as ascertainment corrected rates (ACR), based on capture-recapture techniques developed in wildlife management, offers a means to adjust for missing cases or sample dropouts (McCarty, Tull, Moy, Kwoh, & LaPorte, 1993). ACR requires, however, several data sources to compute (i.e., self-report, police records, medical records, etc.).

Finally, few of the available batterer program evaluations control for background variables or external factors. Meta-analysis of drug program evaluations suggests that the percentage of successful cases is relatively constant across modalities when background factors are controlled (Hubbard et al., 1989), and evaluations of alcohol treatment programs identify the contribution of external social support to program outcome (Cocozzelli & Hudson, 1989). A clinical trial, which is commonplace in medical treatment evaluations, is the ideal research design to control for moderating (background) and mediating (other interventions and external factors) variables, but it is often too difficult and costly to implement in social service settings (Rosenfeld, 1992). A multisite clinical trial would employ highly regimented and supervised treatments to control for regional or local peculiarities, and randomly assign or match participants to the treatments and a "placebo" treatment. These design requirements are likely to impinge on current batterer program procedures and raise ethical concerns among battered women advocates. Moreover, a respectable clinical trial would take 3 to 5 years to complete and need a budget approaching a million dollars.

Even when a clinical trial is accomplished, the findings may still be unclear. Statistically significant differences may not be clinically significant (Rossi & Freeman, 1989). One program may, for example, produce a lower average score on an anger test, but the few points difference may not mean much in "real life." Another problem is that even verified outcome differences in terms of violence may be misinterpreted. For example, the men in a "get tough" confrontational program (e.g., Adams, 1988; Pence, 1989) could become hypersensitive to their abuses and violence and report more abuse during the follow-up than would those men who participated in a "feel good" program addressing shame, trauma, or personal pain (e.g., Waldo, 1987). Moreover, the effects of a particular test program could be the result of the enthusiasm of the "true believer" promoting it, rather than the result of some unique components of the program (Valliant, 1982). In fact, we would not know exactly why some men appeared to do better and others did not.

Nearly all of the batterer program evaluations follow an input-output design that does not examine the components within the program that account for the outcome. Several studies on program components in the field of psychotherapy have more recently been corroborated by research on recovering alcoholics and on people who have lost substantial amounts of weight (e.g., Luborsky, Crits-Christoph, Mintz, & Auerbach, 1988). So-called successful programs appear to have several things in common:

a decisive rationale for change and consequences for not changing, a clear and consistent message or credo of change, positive role models in the form of group leaders and changing participants, and ongoing surveillance and social support for the group members (Adams, 1988; Fagan, 1989; Wilner et al., 1985). An "evangelical ideology," in which the possibility of change is enthusiastically conveyed, as in Alcoholics Anonymous, may not only assure the presence of these components but also make sure that they are felt (Valliant, 1982). Success cases who have not attended a program or dropped out of one are likely to have encountered these components of change elsewhere.

The components associated with "success" suggest the importance of a social dimension to the change process in men who batter. When the social reinforcements for battering are countered and replaced, a cessation of violence appears to be more likely, as is the case with alcoholism treatment (Cocozzelli & Hudson, 1989). As proponents of social exchange theory have argued, "Men batter primarily because they can" (Gelles, 1983) and tend to reduce their battering when the costs outweigh the benefits. The components also suggest that some of the preoccupation with program modality and curriculum may be misplaced. More attention to community linkages, sanctions, and responsiveness may more substantially contribute to program outcome.

Conceptualizing Effectiveness

■ Perhaps the most fundamental aspect of program evaluations is determining what is meant by effectiveness. When asked what they are most trying to accomplish, program staff raise a wide range of possibilities. Battered women and battered women's advocates add even further considerations (see Hart, 1992). They include not only stopping the man's physical violence, verbal abuse, and psychological maltreatment but also promoting the woman's safety, autonomy, and well-being—all of which are extremely difficulty to operationalize—that is, define in concrete, measurable terms. Despite this range of possible program outcomes, effectiveness in program evaluations is generally considered to be a program participant's being nonviolent for an extended period of time (see Tolman & Bennett, 1990). As straightforward as this definition may appear, it not only leaves much out but also raises further issues.

The first issue regards what constitutes "nonviolent" behavior, and whether this is a sufficient program outcome (Morrison, 1988; Mulvey & Lidz, 1993). What if a man does not push or strike his partner but increases his verbal abuse and control? What if a participant is nonviolent, but his wife remains deadly fearful of him? What if a participant pushes and shoves his wife, but no longer punches and kicks her? What if a man is nonviolent because his wife has left him and is totally inaccessible? In part because of the range of contingencies and difficulty in giving them a weight or value, measurement experts question the validity of current composite scales for violence in its various forms and impacts (Morrison, 1988; Mulvey & Lidz, 1993). Such a measurement requires much more development and analysis than has currently been accomplished.

A second definitional issue is in determining the period of time for this nonviolence to count. If the period is too short, the outcome could be the aftereffect of simply being caught. If it is too long, intervening factors may account for the effect, and a majority of the participants will be difficult to find. What if a participant has a few periodic outbursts during the 3 months after the program and then becomes nonviolent? What if a participant is nonviolent for a year and then kills his wife in a sudden outburst? It is possible to account for these time-based contingencies in event-history analysis (Blossfeld, Hamerle, & Mayer, 1989), but such an analysis becomes extremely complex and difficult for many practitioners and policymakers to interpret.

Another issue related to defining batterer program effectiveness has to do with the focus on success. Whereas batterer program evaluations tend to focus on "successful" outcomes, much of the medical field tends to focus on the "failure" outcomes—that is, the severity of the risks or possible side effects of a new treatment. A new medication may be taken off the market or have highly restricted use because of harmful effects on as few as 5% of potential patients. In batterer programs, the degree to which a particular modality or format actually increases the severity of violence in some "failures" may be just as important as the percentage of men who are nonviolent. It may only take one brutal murder by a program participant to close down a program. Therefore, some measure of the severity and consequence of "failures," beyond just the category of "recidivism," needs to be considered. Borrowing inventories and instruments from injury control research may help address this issue. Injury research, for instance, employs extensive lists of kinds of injuries, diagrams indicating where injuries occurred, and listings of treatment received for the purposes of concretizing self-report and coding medical records.

There is an additional defining issue that relates to the conception of effectiveness itself. The focus on acts of violence or tactics of abuse presents the program outcome as an "event" to be counted rather than a contextualized process. Measurements such as the widely used Conflict Tactics Scales (Straus, 1979), for instance, reduce the violence to discrete actions; however, the violence may be experienced as a composite of anger, fright, humiliation, degradation, control, desperation, pain, and hurt within a prevailing "reign of terror" (Walker, 1983).

Naturalistic and longitudinal studies of the so-called cessation of violence, alcohol abuse, and other destructive behaviors suggest, moreover, a process of change that can easily elude evaluation efforts (Fagan, 1989; Gondolf, 1987a; Valliant, 1982). Cessation usually involves a mixture of some progress and some regressions. Many theorists, in fact, identify stages of change that constitute disruptive and dramatic transitions between long periods of constancy. A constellation of interventions and circumstances appears to contribute to the change process in batterers (Bowker, 1983). A batterer program may be more a reinforcement for a variety of interventions and circumstances than the instigator of change. This sort of process is seldom represented or considered in conventional batterer program evaluations, but could be addressed through more descriptive qualitative accounts and narratives of couple relations, arguments, and violent incidents.

Additional Considerations

■ Several additional considerations regarding the scope of programs have recently emerged. Borrowing from evaluations and program development in other fields, researchers are increasingly examining the role of patient matching, program implementation, and community collaboration in batterer programs.

Patient matching is the effort to match different types of individuals with different interventions. A variety of studies in the alcohol and drug fields, for instance, have attempted to sort dual-diagnosed patients into more intensive and comprehensive treatments (Mattson & Allen, 1991; Project MATCH, 1993). There is some preliminary evidence in the woman battering field, as well, that different types of batterers could account for some of the inconclusive and contradictory results of previous program evaluations. Batterers who are younger, less educated, and of minority status are less likely to complete court-mandated programs (Saunders & Parker, 1989). In studies of dropouts, those with alcohol and drug abuse backgrounds, long woman-battering histories, and previous criminal records are more likely not to complete programs with court-mandated and other referred participants (Grusznski & Carrillo, 1988; Hamberger & Hastings, 1989). There are also a few studies based on clinical observations and at least three formal empirical studies that suggest a typology of batterers that may warrant different kinds and intensities of treatments (Gondolf, 1988; Gottman et al., 1995; Hamberger & Hastings, 1991; Saunders, 1992). A significant portion of the court-ordered batterers may have generally antisocial or psychopathic tendencies, according to personality and psychopathy tests (Hamberger & Hastings, 1991; Hart, Dutton, & Newlove, 1993). Such men tend to be unresponsive to the structure and approach of conventional batterer programs and may require more intensive and extensive forms of intervention.

The most prominent and widely replicated batterer programs devote substantial attention to the issue of program implementation—in particular to the program's relationship to the criminal justice system in obtaining referrals and the action it takes in the case of noncompliant referrals (Edleson & Tolman, 1993; Pence & Paymar, 1993). Although program implementation is difficult to test empirically, a few studies have examined the impact of combined or coordinated criminal justice interventions (Edleson, 1991; Gamache, Edleson, & Schock, 1988; Steinman, 1988). These program-related studies show that combined interventions of arrest, legal advocates, victim services, and the court's action contribute to the reduction of recidivism. A program's relationship to the court, in particular, is crucial in reducing dropouts and violence. The court's criteria for court-mandated batterer counseling and response to noncompliant participants, for instance, contributes to a batterer program's effectiveness (Kaci & Tarrant, 1988).

Additionally, collaboration with drug and alcohol programs, mental health programs, and parenting programs, along with the courts and victim services, is also likely to increase the effectiveness of batterer programs (Eisikovits & Edleson, 1989; Gondolf, 1991, 1995). The kind of collaboration, however, may be important to consider. Formal agency linkages and combined programs, as opposed to informal referrals, may be crucial to effectiveness, as they have been with the criminal justice system. Although it has not been formally researched, case management, in which program staff coordinate a variety of interventions around a particular batterer, may more appropriately match batterers with the constellation of interventions they need and thus improve outcomes (Gondolf, 1991).

Broadening Evaluations

■ The focus of batterer program evaluations ultimately may need to be broadened to obtain more meaningful findings. Several alternative means developed in other fields might be considered in evaluating batterer programs: consumer-based assessment, community or systems analysis, social impact assessment, and ethical decision making. These approaches range from lesser to greater scope and abstraction, and from lesser to greater difficulty in implementation. Each remains, nevertheless, more likely to approximate the realities of program operation and outcome than do the prevailing program evaluations.

Consumer-based assessment, sometimes referred to as total quality management, has become fashionable in education circles as a way to refocus and redefine outcomes in a more meaningful way (Coleman, 1993). Consumer-based assessment differs from prevailing program evaluations in its broader range of outcomes that are set and observed by all those related to a particular program. In education, this refers to teachers, parents, communities, businesses, and social services—not only to researchers and administrators. In batterer programs, a consumer-based assessment would involve especially the battered women and battered women's advocates, but also potential "consumers" of batterer programs (see Sirles, Lipchik, & Kowalski, 1993). It would establish a more inclusive set of outcomes relevant to victims and potential victims and their goal of safety and autonomy. The objective of the evaluation in this process becomes: how might the batterer program better contribute to these needs?

Some of the needs that might be established in a consumer-based assessment of batterer programs are as follows: Battered women appear to need some "time out" from the abusive relationship to assess their needs and heal their emotional and physical wounds, rather than experience the heightened control or manipulation of their batterers who are claiming to be cured. Battered women want to be free of intimidation, threats, and stalking, especially if they attempt to leave or get help. Battered women desperately want more decisive responses from the police and courts, as opposed to greater delays, complications, and permissiveness. Because they may regard batterer counseling programs as being "soft" on offenders, battered women also want more surveillance of or restraints on their batterer from these programs. To what degree, then, do batterer programs contribute to this set of consumer-based needs?

Systems analysis is another alternative worth applying to batterer programs. Systems analysis was developed primarily to improve production within corporations, but has increasingly been applied to communities to assist with community development and planning (Harrison, 1991; Poplin, 1979). Systems analysis aims to examine the interrelationship of various organizational components and their contribution to the desired outcome. The question becomes: What combination of modality, format, duration, criminal justice sanctions, mental health and drug and alcohol treatments, follow-up and support groups, and victim's services is most effective and with what kind of batterers? Do additional components, such as the following, increase program effectiveness and impact: counseling as part of a court sentence (rather than as a diversion procedure), a series of didactic orientation sessions, a reparation stipulation in which the batterer pays for the victim's suffering, a year of monthly follow-up meetings for batterers, and complementary support groups for battered women and their children?

Different intervention systems might also be compared and tested. For instance, a multisite study comparing various systems while controlling for uniform background, system contact and use, and follow-up data could expose the relative effectiveness of different intervention systems. Some semblance of this approach with regard to batterer programs is already evident in the preliminary attempts to assess combined and coordinated criminal justice interventions (e.g., Edleson, 1991). Moreover, a cross-cultural study revealed a unique set of traditional sanctions and sanctuaries (e.g., protection of victims by kin or women neighbors, and banishment of batterers from the village) present in communities with lower levels of battering (Counts, Brown, & Campbell, 1992). It could be that batterer programs linked to community-based organizations, churches, and housing projects in the inner city are more appropriate and effective with minority populations than are criminal justice and therapeutic-based intervention systems. Community-based programs for Native Americans, such as White Bison, employ traditional symbols and myths to convey the means of spiritual healing and wholeness and address family, kin, and tribal relationships in the process of confronting alcohol abuse and woman battering.

How does this sort of system compare with conventional interventions and batterer programs?

An additional alternative to conventional program evaluation is *social impact assessment.* Social impact assessment was developed in the 1970s primarily to determine the effects of technological changes and development projects on the social environment (Wolf, 1983). The essential issue in social impact assessment is determination of the effect on the community at large. In the case of batterer programs, we would want to know how the program contributes to changes in public attitude, institutional response, involvement in other services, cultural norms and values, and to the overall reduction of violence. Does the batterer program contribute to public awareness about woman battering, or does the presence of a program allow the public to dismiss the problem as taken care of? We might also expect that the presence of a batterer program would stimulate more financial support for victim services and prevention programs, rather than less. Does the batterer program contribute to institutional reform? Because there is a batterer program in a community, we may expect that the police would be more likely to arrest and the courts more likely to prosecute batterers. Similarly, drug and alcohol programs may be more likely to screen for woman battering and make more appropriate referrals.

Most important, do the batterer programs provide any "symbolic deterrence"? That is, do they communicate a message to other men in the community that violence against women is not tolerated? Are more men seeking help from a variety of sources and is their violence in general being reduced? Finally, is the culture of the community at large changing toward one of opposition and outrage toward violence, as opposed to condoning or accepting violence against women? Are workplaces checking and challenging harassment? Are there more men's organizations speaking out against violence against women?

Ethical Decision Making

■ Ethical decision making, an approach employed in assessing many medical practices,

transcends immediate effectiveness but still suggests a kind of evaluative process (Beauchamp & Childress, 1990). In many cases, it is impossible to know the effectiveness of new or experimental treatments. It is also difficult to know the long-term social impact of these treatments. In these cases, we appeal, therefore, to a set of principles or assumptions to justify the treatment. Certain kinds of organ transplants, for instance, may be largely unsuccessful at this stage, but may be continued to help develop a future cure for several terminal diseases.

Ethical decision making is usually based on absolute or situational assessments. In absolute ethics, prevailing moral, philosophical, or ideological principles are applied to the treatment. Programs are evaluated on the basis of what makes the most sense from a particular point of view. In the woman battering field, couples counseling has been addressed primarily in this way. The opposition to couples counseling is based largely on principles and assumptions about victim safety (Bograd, 1984).

Situational ethics is more inductive, in contrast to the deductive nature of absolute ethics. The decision is based on what makes the most sense under the circumstances. Is a certain experimental treatment justified given the limited options and the nature of the problem? Many new medical practices, for instance, appear to be better than doing nothing when all else has failed, and they offer the opportunity for doctors to learn about a particular case and the problem in general. This is not to say that there are not severe abuses of ethical decision making, and especially situational ethics. High-risk medical operations are often conducted at extremely high costs despite previous ineffectiveness. However, ethical decision making may need to be improved rather than dismissed. Cases need to be reviewed by a board of citizens, former patients, and social workers, as well as medical experts, and the criteria for decision making need to be more extensively debated and concretely defined.

In the case of batterer programs, we might begin to weigh ethics in what cases to refuse from the courts. In what cases do we avoid partner contact, warn the potential victim of dangerousness, or terminate batterer counseling? Our current evaluations do not, and perhaps cannot, answer these sorts of important questions. We are left making decisions on the basis of absolute or situational ethics, or on an ad hoc basis or as part of crisis management. More needs to be done, therefore, to establish ethical standards and processes with regard to batterer programs, much as is being done in the field of medical ethics (see Jaggar, 1991). Some of the emerging state standards for batterer programs offer guiding principles and assumptions that could approximate an ethical foundation (see Hart, 1992).

The experimental nature of batterer programs and limitations of program evaluations may, in fact, necessitate a shift toward batterer program ethics. Such a shift might alleviate the increased pressure to prove the "unprovable" in effectiveness evaluations and reduce the misinformation that the confounded "success rates" convey. An ethical basis of evaluation might, furthermore, contribute to a more accurate portrayal of the experimental nature of batterer programs and prompt a more thoughtful consideration of their use. At the very least, this and other alternative approaches to evaluation can offer complementary information to the growing body of conventional batterer program evaluations.

Conclusions

■ The prevailing batterer program evaluations leave questions regarding the effectiveness of batterer programs. A majority of program completers do stop their violence for a period, but we do not know exactly why and how. Quasi-control and matching control groups are needed to assess the relative contribution of batterer interventions in interrupting and stopping violence. Moreover, the preliminary studies on program implementation suggest that the combination and coordination of interventions may be important to reducing violence and therefore need to be expanded. Related studies point, furthermore, to the need to consider patient matching—or types of batterers—in developing and evaluating batterer programs.

Because of numerous methodological limitations and the complexity of the cessation process, batterer program evaluations show mixed and, to some extent, contradictory results. Several methodological innovations are likely to improve the validity and reliability of batterer evaluations (e.g., periodic follow-up, tracking systems, broadened outcome measures, victim self-report verification with police or hospital records, capture-recapture and survival analysis). Even less "scientific" batterer program evaluations should continue as a means to obtain feedback for program staff and administrators. The more conventional evaluation designs are, however, unlikely in themselves to answer the difficult policy questions that persist.

The role of batterer programs in stopping woman battering may be better understood through broadening program evaluation. A broader focus that addresses a program's context is likely to produce a more accurate portrayal of the program's role in the change process and also a better understanding of how to improve that role. The alternative approaches outlined above (consumer-based assessment, community and systems analysis, social impact assessment, and ethical decision making) offer such a possibility. Programs that develop social impact assessments and ethical principles of their own, however preliminary, might do much to improve their effectiveness and ease some of the public's resistance to batterer programs.

The severest critics of batterer programs have pointed out that such programs are premised on an individualistic and therapeutic notion of change that is naive about the nature and reinforcements of woman battering (Dobash & Dobash, 1992; Thorne-Finch, 1992). The limitations of criminal justice and therapeutic interventions are, moreover, well documented (National Research Council, 1993). It may be that batterer programs as part of a larger community and social response are more effective in reducing violence among individual batterers, as well as deterring it in the community at large. Such a broader approach, however, will require an expanded conception of program evaluation to determine the impact of this view and to help identify its particulars. Amid the increasing demands for program evaluation and accountability, it may therefore be important to broaden our program evaluation, as well as address the limitations of more conventional evaluations.

References

Adams, D. (1988). Treatment models of men who batter: A pro-feminist analysis. In K. Yllö & M. Bograd (Eds.), *Feminist perspectives on wife abuse* (pp. 176-199). Newbury Park, CA: Sage.

Beauchamp, T., & Childress, J. (1990). *Principles of biomedical ethics.* New York: Oxford University Press.

Blossfeld, H., Hamerle, A., & Mayer, K. (1989). *Event history analysis.* New York: Lawrence Erlbaum.

Bograd, M. (1984). Family systems approaches to wife battering: A feminist critique. *American Journal of Psychiatry, 31,* 129-137.

Bowker, L. (1983). *Beating wife beating.* Lexington, MA: Lexington Books.

Cocozzelli, C., & Hudson, C. (1989). Recent advances in alcoholism diagnosis and treatment assessment research: Implications for practice. *Social Service Review, 37,* 533-552.

Coleman, J. (1993). The design of organizations and the right to act. *Sociological Forum, 8,* 527-546.

Counts, D., Brown, J., & Campbell, J. (1992). *Sanctions and sanctuary: Cultural perspectives on the beating of wives.* Boulder, CO: Westview.

Culter, M., & Fueyo, J. (1991). Evaluation of the Family Violence Intervention Program (Tampa, FL). Tampa: University of South Florida, College of Public Health.

DeMaris, A. (1989). Attrition in batterers counseling: The role of social and demographic factors. *Social Service Review, 63,* 142-154.

DeMaris, A., & Jackson, J. (1987). Batterers' reports of recidivism after counseling. *Social Casework, 68,* 142-154.

Dobash, R. E., & Dobash, R. P. (1992). *Women, violence, and social change.* New York: Routledge.

Edleson, J. (1991). Coordinated community responses to woman battering. In M. Steinman (Ed.), *Woman battering: Policy responses* (pp. 203-220). Cincinnati, OH: Anderson.

Edleson, J., & Syers, M. (1990). The relative effectiveness of group treatments for men who batter. *Social Work Research and Abstracts, 26,* 10-17.

Edleson, J., & Tolman, R. (1993). *Intervention for men who batter: An ecological approach.* Newbury Park, CA: Sage.

Eisikovits, Z. C., & Edleson, J. L. (1989). Intervening with men who batter: A critical review of the literature. *Social Service Review, 37,* 385-414.

Fagan, J. (1989). Cessation of family violence: Deterrence and dissuasion. In L. Ohlin & M. Tonry (Eds.), *Family violence* (pp. 377-425). Chicago: University of Chicago Press.

Finn, J. (1987). Men's domestic violence treatment: The court referral component. *Journal of Interpersonal Violence, 2,* 154-165.

Furby, L., Blackshaw, L., & Weinrott, M. (1989). Sex offender recidivism: A review. *Psychological Bulletin, 105,* 3-30.

Gamache, D. J., Edleson, J. L., & Schock, M. D. (1988). Coordinated police, judicial and social service response to woman battering: A multi-baseline evaluation across three communities. In G. T. Hotaling, D. Finkelhor, J. T. Kirkpatrick, & M. A. Straus (Eds.), *Coping with family violence: Research and policy perspectives* (pp. 193-209). Newbury Park, CA: Sage.

Gelles, R. J. (1983). An exchange/social control theory. In D. Finkelhor, R. J. Gelles, G. T. Hotaling, & M. A. Straus (Eds.), *The dark side of families: Current family violence research* (pp. 151-165). Beverly Hills, CA: Sage.

Gondolf, E. W. (1987a). Changing men who batter: A developmental model of integrated interventions. *Journal of Family Violence, 2,* 345-369.

Gondolf, E. W. (1987b). Seeing through smoke and mirrors: A guide to batterer program evaluations. *Response, 10,* 16-19.

Gondolf, E. W. (1988). Who are those guys? Towards a behavioral typology of men who batter. *Violence and Victims, 3,* 187-203.

Gondolf, E. W. (1990). An exploratory survey of court-mandated batterer programs. *Response, 13*(3), 7-11.

Gondolf, E. W. (1991). A victim-based assessment of court-mandated counseling for batterers. *Criminal Justice Review, 16,* 214-226.

Gondolf, E. W. (1995). Alcohol abuse, wife assault, and power needs. *Social Service Review, 69,* 274-284.

Gondolf, E. W., & Foster, R. A. (1991). Preprogram attrition in batterer programs. *Journal of Family Violence, 6,* 337-350.

Gondolf, E. W., & Russell, D. (1987). *Man to man: A guide for men in abusive relationships.* Bradenton, FL: Human Services Institute.

Grusznski, R. J., & Carrillo, T. P. (1988). Who completes batterer's treatment groups? An empirical investigation. *Journal of Family Violence, 3,* 141-150.

Gottman, J., Jacobson, N., Rushe, R., Short, J., Short, J., Babcock, J., La Taillade, J., & Waltz, J. (1995). The relationship between heart rate reactivity, emotionally aggressive behavior and general violence in batterers. *Journal of Family Psychology, 9,* 103-127.

Hamberger, L. K., & Hastings, J. E. (1988). Skills training for treatment of spouse abusers: An outcome study. *Journal of Family Violence, 3,* 121-130.

Hamberger, L. K., & Hastings, J. E. (1989). Counseling male spouse abusers: Characteristics of treatment completers and dropouts. *Violence and Victims, 4,* 275-286.

Hamberger, L. K., & Hastings, J. E. (1991). Personality correlates of men who batter and nonviolent men: Some continuities and discontinuities. *Journal of Family Violence, 6,* 131-148.

Harrell, A. (1991). *Evaluation of court-ordered treatment for domestic offenders.* Washington, DC: Urban Institute.

Harrison, M. (1991). Invitation to organizational diagnosis. *Sociological Practice Review, 2,* 169-179.

Hart, B. (Ed.). (1992). *Accountability: Program standards for batterer intervention services.* Reading: Pennsylvania Coalition Against Domestic Violence.

Hart, S., Dutton, D., & Newlove, T. (1993). The prevalence of personality disorders among wife assaulters. *Journal of Personality Disorders, 7,* 329-341.

Hubbard, R., Marsden, M. E., Rachal, J. V., Harwood, H., Cavanaugh, E., & Ginzburg, H. (1989). *Drug abuse treatment: A national survey of effectiveness.* Chapel Hill: University of North Carolina Press.

Izzo, R., & Ross, R. (1990). Meta-analysis of rehabilitation programs for juvenile delinquents. *Criminal Justice and Behavior, 17,* 135-142.

Jaggar, A. (1991). Feminist ethics: Projects, problems, prospects. In C. Card (Ed.), *Feminist ethics* (pp. 79-101). Lawrence: University Press of Kansas.

Kaci, J. H., & Tarrant, S. (1988). Attitudes of prosecutors and probation departments toward diversion in domestic violence cases in California. *Journal of Contemporary Criminal Justice, 4,* 187-200.

Kassebaum, G., & Ward, D. (1991). Analysis, reanalysis and mental analysis of correctional treatment effectiveness: Is the question what works or who works? *Sociological Practice Review, 2,* 159-168.

Longabaugh, R., & Lewis, D. (1988). Key issues in treatment outcome studies. *Alcohol Health & Research World, 12,* 168-175.

Luborsky, L., Crits-Christoph, P., Mintz, J., & Auerback, A. (1988). *Who will benefit from psychotherapy: Predicting therapeutic outcomes.* New York: Basic Books.

Mattson, M., & Allen, J. (1991). Research on matching alcoholic patients to treatments: Findings, issues, and implications. *Journal of Addictive Diseases, 11,* 33-49.

McCarty, D., Tull, E., Moy, C., Kwoh, C., & LaPorte, R. (1993). Ascertainment corrected rates: Applications of capture-recapture methods. *International Journal of Epidemiology, 22,* 559-565.

Morrison, E. (1988). Instrumentation issues in the measurement of violence in psychiatric in patients. *Issues in Mental Health Nursing, 9,* 9-16.

Mulvey, E. P., & Lidz, C. W. (1993). Measuring patient violence in dangerousness research. *Law and Human Behavior, 17,* 277-278.

National Research Council. (1993). *Understanding and preventing violence.* Washington, DC: National Academy Press.

Pence, E. (1989). Batterer programs: Shifting from community collusion to community confrontation. In P. L. Caesar & L. K. Hamberger (Eds.), *Treating men who batter: Theory, practice, and programs* (pp. 24-50). New York: Springer.

Pence, E., & Paymar, M. (1993). *Education groups for men who batter: The Duluth model.* New York: Springer.

Poplin, D. (1979). *Communities: A survey of theories and methods of research.* New York: Macmillan.

Project MATCH. (1993). Project MATCH: Rationale and methods for a multisite clinical trial matching patients to alcoholism treatment. *Alcoholism: Clinical and Experimental Research, 17,* 1130-1145.

Quinsey, V., Harris, G., Rice, M., & Lalumiere, M. (1993). Assessing treatment efficacy in outcome studies of sex offenders. *Journal of Interpersonal Violence, 8,* 512-523.

Rosenfeld, B. (1992). Court-ordered treatment of spouse abuse. *Clinical Psychology Review, 12,* 205-226.

Rossi, P., & Freeman, H. (1989). *Evaluation: A systematic approach.* Newbury Park, CA: Sage.

Saunders, D. G. (1992). A typology of men who batter: Three types derived from cluster analysis. *American Journal of Orthopsychiatry, 62,* 264-275.

Saunders, D. G., & Parker, J. C. (1989). Legal sanctions and treatment follow-through among men who batter: A multivariate analysis. *Social Work Research and Abstracts, 25,* 21-29.

Schare, M. (1992, June). *Needed directions in the psychotherapeutic treatment of drunk drivers.* Paper presented at International Perspectives on Crime, Justice, and Public Order, St. Petersburg, Russia.

Sirles, E., Lipchik, E., & Kowalski, K. (1993). A consumer's perspective on domestic violence interventions. *Journal of Family Violence, 8,* 267-276.

Smith, J. (1991). *A community approach to domestic violence: The Bellevue (WA) stipulated order of continuance program.* Bellevue, WA: Bellevue Police Department.

Steinman, M. (1988). Evaluating a system-wide response to domestic violence: Some initial findings. *Journal of Contemporary Criminal Justice, 4,* 172-186.

Straus, M. A. (1979). Measuring intrafamily conflict and violence: The Conflict Tactics (CT) Scales. *Journal of Marriage and the Family, 41,* 75-88.

Thorne-Finch, R. (1992). *Ending the silence: The origins and treatment of male violence against women.* Toronto: University of Toronto Press.

Tolman, R. M., & Bennett, L. W. (1990). A review of quantitative research on men who batter. *Journal of Interpersonal Violence, 5,* 87-118.

Valliant, G. (1982). *The natural history of alcoholism.* Cambridge, MA: Harvard University Press.

Waldo, M. (1987). Also victims: Understanding and treating men arrested for spouse abuse. *Journal of Counseling and Development, 65,* 385-388.

Walker, L. E. (1983). *The battered woman syndrome.* New York: Springer.

Wilner, D. M., Freeman, H. E., Surber, M., & Goldstein, M. S. (1985). Success in mental health treatment interventions: A review of 211 random assignment studies. *Journal of Social Service Research, 8,* 1-21.

Wolf, C. (1983). Social impact assessment: A methodological overview. In K. Finsterbusch (Ed.), *Social impact methods* (pp. 15-35). Beverly Hills, CA: Sage.

CHAPTER 18

Feminist Therapy for Battered Women

An Assessment

Maryse Rinfret-Raynor
Solange Cantin

For centuries, domestic violence was viewed as an accepted part of the relationship between men and women and was sanctioned by the social, political, economic, and religious structures of Western society. Only recently has wife abuse moved from the realm of personal problem to social problem, largely due to consciousness raising by the feminist movement.

According to Statistics Canada's (1993) national survey on violence against women, 30% of women currently or previously married in Canada have experienced at least one incident of physical or sexual violence at the hands of a spouse.

Domestic violence in all of its forms (physical, psychological, verbal, and sexual) cuts across social classes, age groups, races, and nationalities, and its drastic repercussions no longer need to be proven. The physical sequelae are the most visible, but the social and psychological consequences are far more serious: loss of self-esteem, anxiety, depression, social isolation, and children who witness violence and are often themselves abused, to mention only the most severe.

AUTHORS' NOTE: This chapter was originally presented as a paper at the 4th International Family Violence Research Conference, Durham, New Hampshire, July 1995.

Several studies in both Canada and the United States show that until the 1980s, the phenomenon of the battered woman remained largely ignored by social service agencies (Hilberman & Munson, 1978; Hodgins & Larouche, 1982). Practitioners did not understand this form of violence, felt incapable of working with it (Court, 1978), and received little information on it (Horley, 1989; Roy, 1977). Consequently there were shortcomings in the approaches taken to treating this clientele (Hodgins & Larouche, 1982; Martin, 1976).

In response to these shortcomings, Quebec social worker Ginette Larouche developed an alternative model for therapy based on feminist ideology. Two complementary research projects were undertaken: an action-research project to systematize the model and improve training, and a study to assess its effectiveness. This chapter presents some of the results of this longitudinal study, assessing the relative effectiveness of approaches based on the Larouche model and the approach usually taken in social service agencies.

Method

■ Although a pure experimental research design had been the original intention, the researchers had difficulty recruiting battered women who were using the social service network at the time of the study. The quasi-experimental design adopted in the end compared the effects of different types of therapy among three groups of 60 women who had been abused by their spouses: One experimental group was in group therapy based on the feminist model with practitioners trained as part of the action research done prior to the study, a second experimental group had individual therapy with the same practitioners according to the same model, and a comparison group had the standard therapy provided by social service agencies.

Data for the study were collected through interviews at four stages. The first interview (pretest) took place at the start of therapy; the second interview (posttest) 1 month after treatment had ended, or at the latest, 6 months after the pretest; and two follow-up interviews were conducted,

one 6 months later and one a year later. The design can be summarized as follows:

$$0_1\ X_1\ 0_2\ 0_3\ 0_4 \quad \text{where } X_1 = \text{feminist group therapy}$$

$$0'_1\ X_2\ 0'_2\ 0'_3\ 0'_4 X_2 = \text{feminist individual therapy}$$

$$0''_1\ X_3\ 0''_2\ 0''_3\ 0''_4 X_3 = \text{individual therapy using other approaches}$$

and 0 = research interviews at different stages of treatment.

The following three hypotheses were tested:

Hypothesis 1. All three types of treatment would produce improvement in the variables studied between the beginning and end of therapy and these changes would be maintained over time.

Hypothesis 2. The experimental feminist group therapy would produce results superior to those seen in participants receiving feminist individual therapy.

Hypothesis 3. The experimental feminist individual therapy would produce results superior to those seen in participants receiving individual therapy in the comparison group.

Variables and Instruments

A feminist analysis of the problem of domestic violence places responsibility for abuse with the batterer, and the objective of feminist therapy is to put an end to this abuse. The dependent variables and instruments listed in Table 18.1 were therefore chosen to measure the reduction of violence within the couple. Other characteristics measured had to do with improvements in participants' self-esteem and assertiveness. Data were gathered through structured interviews using scales, multiple-choice questionnaires completed by participants themselves, and questionnaires administered by a researcher. The choice of instruments was limited by practical considerations, including the requirement that they be methodologically acceptable and already validated in Quebec.

TABLE 18.1 Variables Observed and Instruments Used

Variable	Instrument
Independent variables	
Type of therapy	For experimental groups: Description of model Chart to be completed by practitioner For comparison group: Questionnaire for the practitioner to identify the principal characteristics of therapy Chart to be completed by practitioner
Dependent variables	
Characteristics of violence experienced	Conflict Tactics Scales (Straus, 1979, translated into French and adapted for study) Questionnaire on history of violence
Means of resolving conflicts within couple	Conflict Tactics Scales (Straus, 1979, translated and adapted for study)
General assertiveness	Rathus Assertiveness Schedule (Rathus, 1973, translated into French by Bouchard, Valiquette, & Nantel, 1975)
Assertiveness in couple	Marital Assertion Scale (Klostermann, 1980, translated into French and adapted for study)
Marital adjustment	Dyadic Adjustment Scale (Spanier, 1976, translated into French and adapted by Baillargeon, Dubois, & Marineau, 1986)
Social adjustment	Social Adjustment Scale—self-report (Weissman & Bothwell, 1976, translated and adapted for study)
Self-esteem	Tennessee Self-Concept Scale (Fitts, 1964-1965, translated into French and validated by Toulouse, 1971)
Intervening variables related to participants	
Clinical diagnosis (somatization, depression, anxiety, psychosis)	SCL-90-R (Derogatis, 1977, translated and validated by Fortin and Coutu-Wakulczyk, 1985)
Social support and characteristics of request for help	Questionnaire developed for the study
Attitudes toward feminine roles	Sex Role Ideology Scale (Kalin & Tilby, 1978, translated into French by Hardy, 1981)
Perception of quality of treatment and therapeutic relationship	Client Satisfaction Questionnaire (Larsen, Attkinson, Hargreaves, & Nguyen, 1979, translated into French) Relationship Inventory (Barrett-Lennard, 1962)
Scores on dependent variables in pretest	See instruments in section on dependent variables
Intervening variables related to practitioners	
Expectations as to the result of the intervention	Therapist Expectancy Inventory (Bernstein, Lecomte, & Desharnais, 1979)
Attitude toward battered women	Scale of Attitudes Toward Battered Women (Lavoie, Martin, & Valiquette, 1988, Laval University)

Therapy Models

The model for feminist therapy is based on a feminist analysis of the problem of spousal violence against women. According to Larouche (1982, 1985, 1986, 1987), the roots of wife abuse lie in a male-dominated society where love and intimacy within the couple create a favorable ground for the development and expression of possessiveness, jealousy, and oppression. Larouche identified three factors that explain women's tolerance of abuse: society's normalization of this behavior, women's internalization of related stereotypes, and personal factors.

Following from this analysis, she developed a therapeutic model along three lines: a feminist perspective, the importance of concrete help, and special consideration of each woman's personal experience. The feminist perspective denounces spousal violence, shifts responsibility for violence from the victim to the abuser, and situates the problem within patriarchal society to free women of their guilt and relieve their immediate tension.

Psychological, verbal, physical, and sexual violence escalates in a three-stage cycle of tension, aggression, and remission (Hofeller, 1982; Pagelow, 1984; Paltiel, 1981; Walker, 1979). Feminist therapy therefore has three components: crisis counseling, short-term therapy, and medium- or long-term therapy. Its goals are to eliminate violence and counteract the effects of the violence on the woman by increasing her self-esteem, general assertiveness, social adjustment, assertiveness toward her partner, and adjustment within the couple. It moves progressively from reducing tension and supporting the woman's decision, to eliminating victim behavior while reestablishing independence. The need for physical and psychological protection is addressed by informing the woman of her rights and the resources available and helping her demand these rights and make use of resources. Strategies may include individual therapy or group meetings.

The comparison group received the type of treatment usually provided by social service agencies. We analyzed practitioners' responses to questions about their theoretical framework, the implementation of this approach in work with referred clients, techniques used, how they related to clients, and their perception of responsibility for domestic violence. Sixty percent identified more than one school of thought, including psychosocial and systemic approaches; crisis counseling; structural, rational, psy-chodynamic, and feminist approaches; a task-oriented model; transactional analysis; and gestalt and reality therapy. Those most commonly mentioned were the psychosocial approach (60%), systemic approach (40%), and crisis counseling (26.6%), and these are the ones most widely used in social work practice (Rinfret-Raynor, Pâquet-Deehy, Larouche, & Cantin, 1989). The psychosocial approach favors active listening, support, clarification, and encouraging the client's independence to help her regain her self-confidence in a supportive setting.

It became clear that many of the individual techniques used by the practitioners in the comparison group were similar to those used in the experimental groups, except that in the comparison group, the feminist model was not followed in its entirety. This can be explained by the fact that public awareness campaigns in Quebec in the social and legal spheres between 1984 and 1989 led many social workers to incorporate aspects of feminist ideology into their work. Most of them believed in the premises of the Larouche model and attributed domestic violence to social conditioning, the patriarchal system, sex roles and stereotypes, values transmitted by the educational system, and the social silence that stifles victims of abuse.

The vast majority of the practitioners in the comparison group had received additional training since their last degree, a fact that eliminates any suspicion that the possible superior effectiveness of the feminist model would be due merely to additional training.

Sample

Study Participants. Participants eligible for the study had experienced physical violence or threats within the past 2 years. At the time of the violence, they were living with their partners or had been separated from them for less than 2 years.

Clients were referred to the study by social service centers. Most treatment took place in three social service centers and 15 community health centers, and to round out the sample, a program was run outside an institutional setting

TABLE 18.2 Principal Socioeconomic Characteristics of Research Participants ($N = 181$)

	n	%		n	%
Age			**Schooling**		
Less than 25 years	16	8.9	6 years or less	13	7.2
25-29 years	39	21.5	7-11 years	112	61.9
30-34 years	47	26.0	12-14 years	42	23.2
35-39 years	35	19.3	15 years or more	14	7.7
40-44 years	27	14.9	Mean = 10.5 years		
45-49 years	9	5.0			
50 years and over	8	4.4			
Mean = 34 years					
Principal occupation			**Number of children**		
Homemaker	82	45.3	None	23	12.7
Employed	58	32.0	1	49	27.1
Unemployed	16	8.9	2	61	33.7
Disabled	4	2.2	3	26	14.4
Student	18	9.9	4	14	7.7
Other	3	1.7	5	6	3.3
			More than 5	2	1.1
			Mean = 2.22		
			Mean living with mother = 1.79		
Marital status			**Income**		
Married	38	21.0	Less than $5,000/year	17	9.4
Living common-law	31	17.1	$5,000-$9,999	77	42.5
Separated	36	19.9	$10,000-$14,999	43	23.8
Divorced	35	19.3	$15,000-$19,999	15	8.3
Separated from			$20,000-$29,999	13	7.2
common-law husband	38	21.0	$30,000-$39,999	2	1.1
Widowed	3	1.7	$40,000-$49,999	2	1.1
Lives with partner	69	38.1	$50,000 and more	1	0.5
Does not live with partner	112	61.9	No information	11	6.1
			Mean = $11,016		

as part of the study. Approximately equal numbers of women were treated in each of the three types of facility.

Participants came from all over the province of Quebec. Close to two thirds of the women in the sample were from cities with a population of 25,000 or more. The remainder were equally divided between towns (5,000-25,000 inhabitants) and rural areas (fewer than 5,000 inhabitants).

Data collection took place over a period of 42 months, from January 1987 to June 1990. Fifty eight of the 181 participants (32%) dropped out of the project, mostly because they dropped out of therapy; this left 123 participants at the second follow-up interview, which was the end of the study period. The drop-out rate was

roughly the same in all three groups. Participants were paid $15 for each of the first two interviews and $10 for each follow-up interview. All 123 who finished received a $20 bonus.

Sample Profile. Ninety-six percent of participants were French speaking, and 95.6% were born in Quebec. As is shown in Table 18.2, they ranged in age from 19 to 60, with a mean of 34 years; two thirds were between 25 and 39 years of age. The sample was older than the population of battered women usually reported in the literature, but younger than the mean age of Quebec women.

Participants had a mean of 10.5 years of schooling: Close to two thirds had attended or finished high school, and almost a quarter had gone to college. The women were therefore better educated than has been reported in other Canadian studies of battered women. They were similar to Quebec women as a whole in regard to high school level, but had less postsecondary education.

Most were homemakers (45%). A third were in the workforce, 10% were unemployed, and 10% were students. Statistics Canada reports that, in 1986, 51.3% of Quebec women were working or looking for work. Our sample therefore had a smaller than average percentage of women in the workforce, but a greater percentage of working women than other Canadian studies of battered women.

Close to 90% were mothers, and they had on average 2.2 children, but only 75% had children living with them when the study began. The mean number of children residing with their mothers was slightly less than 2.

The main source of income for more than 40% of the women was welfare, whereas 30% relied mainly on their earnings, and 10% lived on unemployment insurance. Mean annual income was $11,016, and 75% of participants had an annual income of less than $15,000. In other words, these women were poor.

At the time of the first interview, the women had been married or living common-law for a mean of 10.9 years, but only 38% ($n = 69$) of participants were still living with their partners. Of these 69 women, slightly over half were married, and the rest were living in common-law relationships; half had been separated at least once. Separated women had been married a mean of 7.3 years and had been separated about a year; two thirds were still in touch with their partners.

A closer look at the groups shows that natural selection of participants resulted in some statistically significant differences in socioeconomic status between the three groups. In general, women in the comparison group were best off, and those in feminist group therapy were the worst off, specifically for the variables of occupation, marital status, income, and length of time married or living with their partners. There were also significant differences between those in feminist group therapy and those in the comparison group with regard to the level of education and number of children.

Results and Discussion

Socioeconomic Characteristics

The socioeconomic status of participants underwent changes over the course of this study. By the end of treatment, the number of women working had increased from 32.0% to 43.3%, and the number of homemakers decreased. With more than 50% of respondents working, on unemployment, or seeking work, the proportion of women in the workforce at the end of treatment approaches the Quebec norm (Statistics Canada, 1986). On the other hand, new arrivals on the labor market are in a vulnerable position, and many women were enrolled in income supplementation programs for welfare recipients. By the end of therapy, wages surpassed welfare as principal source of income. Even though this greater financial independence translated into an increase in mean income, approaching Quebec norms (Statistics Canada, 1986), most of the women in the sample were below the poverty line established by the Canadian Council on Social Development (Ross & Shillington, 1989). Long-term studies are needed to determine whether the women who entered the labor force or went back to school remained there, and whether their changes in status were accompanied by higher incomes that would raise them above the poverty line.

Among women who left their husbands, fewer than 30% resumed life with partners (slightly more than half of them with their ex-partners) and fewer than 20% were still with the same partners at the end of the study. This is far from a morbid dependence on their ex-partners. As well, at the pretest, many respondents reported having tried numerous separations during their married life. Thus, breakups became final and may be considered developmental (Larouche, 1985; Pfouts, 1978). The low number of relationships with new partners indicate that there were few "rescue" relationships, that is, for protection from violent ex-partners or to

TABLE 18.3 Behavior of Partner or Ex-Partner in Conflicts During Couple's Life Together, as Perceived by the Woman at Beginning of Therapy

| Behavior of Partner or Ex-Partner | All Respondents | | Experimental Groups | | | | Comparison Group | |
| | | | Group Therapy | | Individual Therapy | | | |
	n	%	n	%	n	%	n	%
Reasoning								
a. He discussed the issue calmly	23	12.7	5	8.3	8	13.1	10	16.7
b. He got information to back up his side of things	37	20.4	11	18.3	13	21.3	13	21.7
c. He brought in or tried to bring in someone to help settle things	34	18.8	13	21.7	8	13.1	13	21.7
Verbal Aggression								
d. He insulted or swore at you	179	98.9	60	100.0	59	96.7	60	100.0
e. He sulked or refused to talk about it	153	84.5	52	86.7	53	86.9	48	80.0
f. He stomped out of the room or the house, or the yard	130	71.8	49	81.7	44	72.1	37	61.7
h.[a] He did or said something to spite you	176	97.2	59	98.3	58	95.1	59	98.3
i. He threatened to hit or throw something at you	145	80.1	48	80.0	52	85.3	45	75.0
j. He threw or smashed or hit or kicked something	140	77.4	46	76.7	48	78.7	46	76.7
Physical Aggression								
k. He threw something at you	74	40.9	27	45.0	22	36.1	25	41.7
l. He pushed, grabbed, or shoved you	176	97.2	57	95.0	60	98.4	59	98.3
m. He slapped you	113	62.4	34	56.7	43	70.5	36	60.0
n. He kicked, bit, or hit you with a fist	107	59.1	32	53.3	35	57.4	40	66.7
o. He hit, or tried to hit you with something	33	18.2	9	15.0	15	24.6	9	15.0
p. He beat you up	93	51.4	27	45.0	35	57.4	31	51.7
q. He threatened you with a knife or gun	52	28.7	21	35.0	18	29.5	13	21.7
r. He used a knife or gun	25	13.8	12	20.0	5	8.2	8	13.3

SOURCE: Conflict Tactics Scales (Straus, 1979).

a. Item g (He cried) was omitted, as calculations do not take this item into account.

prevent an eventual reunion with them (Hofeller, 1982).

Characteristics of Violence Experienced Before Therapy

A French version of the Conflict Tactics Scales (CTS; Straus, 1979) was used to determine the frequency and severity of violence. The three scales measure the use of reasoning (see Table 18.3, Items a to c), verbal abuse (Items d to j), and physical abuse (Items k to r). Table 18.3 shows the men's behavior as perceived by the women at the time of the first research interview, when the women were asked two questions to enable us to detect changes over 6-month periods:

1. Had their husbands or ex-husbands done any of the things on the list during their relationship?

2. If so, had they done any of them within the last 6 months (or last 6 months they were living together, if separated)?

There was a very low frequency of reasoning behavior, with individual scores ranging from 0 to 14 out of a possible 18, and a mean of 1.71; group means ranged from 1.53 to 1.85. Only 12.7% of respondents reported that they had discussed the issue calmly when they had a disagreement, 18.8% reported that their partners had brought in or tried to bring in someone to help settle the conflict, and 20.4% reported that their partners had got information to back up their side of things.

The frequency of behavior on the verbal aggression scale was noticeably higher, with a mean score of 22.95 out of a possible 36. As many as 71.8% of men had stomped out of the room or house, and 98.9% had insulted or sworn at their partners.

Most women had experienced half of the eight behaviors on the physical aggression scale, and 14% to 40% had been subjected to other behaviors on the scale. The most common violent acts experienced were having been pushed, grabbed, or shoved; having been slapped; having been kicked, bitten, hit, or punched; or having been beaten up. A total of 28.7% of the women had been threatened with a knife or gun, and their partners had actually used a knife or gun against 13.8% of the 181 women interviewed.

Participants had been verbally abused by their partners by a mean of 7.7 years, with a minimum duration of 2 months and a maximum of 34 years. Physical violence had lasted a mean of 6.1 years, with a minimum duration of 2 weeks and a maximum of 30 years.

The women generally responded openly to the questions regarding sexual abuse by their partners. More than two thirds (68.5%) admitted having had sexual relations with their partners to "buy peace." About half the women (51.9%) stated that they generally had, or previously had, sexual relations with their husbands or ex-husbands after they had been verbally abused.

Close to a third (31.5%) reported that sexual relations had generally taken place immediately after or within hours of an episode of physical aggression.

The separated women had suffered more severe or more frequent violence during the past 6 months of their lives with their partners than had the women who were living with their partners during the 6 months preceding the data collection. The latter may have underestimated the frequency and severity of acts of violence, whereas the separated women may have overestimated them or simply have been more capable of acknowledging them without feeling that their ability to function was in question. A more realistic explanation for the difference might be the fact that it was the increase in physical violence that motivated them to leave their husbands (Gelles, 1976).

A third of mothers (56 of 158) stated that their children had been abused by one or more members of the family. The father was most often named as the abuser (41 of 56), but 17 mothers admitted having physically mistreated their children.

Analysis of the results concerning the violence experienced by the women before the first therapy session indicated that the 181 women studied had experienced all forms of domestic violence (verbal, psychological, physical, and sexual), confirming other observations that they occur together (Walker, 1979). In our study, as in others, the humiliation and degradation involved were very often perceived as being just as destructive as the blows, or even more so (Larouche, 1987; MacLeod, 1987). Our study also confirmed Walker's (1979) findings that verbal and physical violence in a couple are often accompanied by sexual violence.

Effectiveness of Therapy as Measured by Changes in Dependent Variables

Changes in Violence Experienced. At the pretest, participants were asked if their partners or ex-partners had displayed the behaviors listed in the CTS during the last 6 months (the last 6 months together in the case of separated women). At the posttest and both follow-up interviews, which were 6 months apart, we

TABLE 18.4 Analysis of Variance Results (repeated measures) of Conflict Tactics Scales for Women Who Completed Therapy and Living With Partner or in Contact With Ex-Partner, for Each Group

Scale Results at Each Stage	Experimental Group				Control Group	
	Group Therapy		Individual Therapy			
	Mean	n	Mean	n	Mean	n
Reasoning						
A. Pretest	1.79	34	1.27	33	1.31	29
Posttest	4.53	34	3.36	33	5.41	29
ANOVA	$F = 21.826$,	$p = .000*$	$F = 15.880$,	$p = .000*$	$F = 23.791$,	$p = .000*$
B. Pretest	1.25	28	1.08	25	1.58	24
Posttest	4.11	28	3.48	25	6.00	24
Follow-up interview	6.07	28	4.16	25	7.63	24
ANOVA	$F = 16.638$,	$p = .000*$[a]	$F = 6.996$,	$p = .002*$[a]	$F = 19.152$,	$p = .000*$[a]
Verbal Aggression						
A. Pretest	22.65	37	22.82	38	22.03	31
Posttest	13.49	37	13.13	38	11.94	31
ANOVA	$F = 39.664$,	$p = .000*$	$F = 27.231$,	$p = .000*$	$F = 34.268$,	$p = .000*$
B. Pretest	23.03	32	21.63	30	21.57	28
Posttest	13.84	32	13.30	30	11.36	28
Follow-up interview	11.47	32	11.40	30	8.93	28
ANOVA	$F = 29.066$,	$p = .000*$[a]	$F = 16.972$,	$p = .000*$[a]	$F = 31.813$,	$p = .000*$[a]
Physical Aggression						
A. Pretest	7.24	37	9.68	38	9.39	31
Posttest	1.62	37	1.63	38	1.74	31
ANOVA	$F = 25.782$,	$p = .000*$	$F = 28.96$,	$p = .000*$	$F = 31.256$,	$p = .000*$
B. Pretest	7.00	32	8.53	30	8.96	28
Posttest	1.13	32	1.17	30	1.75	28
Follow-up interview	1.31	32	0.73	30	0.57	28
ANOVA	$F = 20.054$,	$p = .000*$[a]	$F = 26.292$,	$p = .000*$[a]	$F = 26.488$,	$p = .000*$[a]

a. Differences between the pretest and each subsequent measurement are significant.
$*p \leq .005$.

asked about the husbands' (and, if there was contact, the ex-husbands') behavior since the last interview.

At the posttest, 21.7% (35/161) of the women who were not living with, and without any contact with, their partners were no longer being abused. The proportion was 24% (30/124) at the first follow-up interview, and 11.4% (14/123) at the second.

For the women who continued to live with their violent partner or who had contact with a violent ex-partner during the period studied, Table 18.4 presents the results of analysis of variance (repeated measures) applied to the CTS. In part A, pretest and posttest results are compared for each participant; in part B, results are analyzed for each participant for the pretest, posttest, and second follow-up interview.

Reasoning scale scores increased significantly ($p < .005$) in each of the groups between the beginning and the end of therapy, demonstrating increased use of reasoning behaviors, but this increase was more marked among partners than ex-partners. The changes continued over time, as shown by the ANOVA applied to the three periods. Verbal abuse scale scores also decreased significantly between the pretest and the posttest in each of the three groups, indicating a reduction in verbal abuse, especially by ex-partners, which persisted over time. The same tendency can be seen in physical abuse scale scores, except for a very slight increase from the posttest to the second follow-up interview for women in group therapy. The decrease in verbal and physical abuse and increase in use of reasoning by husbands and ex-husbands confirm both parts of Hypothesis 1.

According to the cycle of abuse theory, verbal abuse begins first and stops last, and this is what we found with the women in our study. In-

TABLE 18.5 Analysis of Variance Results (repeated measures) for Each Group: (A) Between Pretest and Posttest and (B) Between the Four Stages

Scale Results at Each Stage	Experimental Group				Control Group	
	Group Therapy		Individual Therapy			
	Mean	n	Mean	n	Mean	n
Self-esteem (Tennessee Self-Concept Scale; Fitts, 1964-1965, translated into French by Toulouse, 1971)						
A. Pretest	318.79	42	317.43	47	331.64	42
Posttest	331.83	42	331.06	47	346.31	42
ANOVA	$F = 8.051,$	$p = .007*$	$F = 6.209,$	$p = .016*$	$F = 15.542,$	$p = .000**$
B. Pretest	317.97	37	318.20	41	334.08	37
Posttest	332.84	37	332.15	41	350.32	37
First follow-up interview	342.30	37	345.12	41	360.95	37
Second follow-up interview	346.73	37	350.34	41	368.70	37
ANOVA	$F = 9.066,$	$p = .000*$[c]	$F = 13.457,$	$p = .000$[d]	$F = 25.193,$	$p = .000**$[b]
Assertiveness (Rathus Assertiveness Schedule; Rathus, 1973, translated into French by Bouchard, Valiquette, & Nantel, 1975)						
A. Pretest	−12.10	41	−10.23	43	0.70	37
Posttest	2.93	41	3.77	43	10.68	37
ANOVA	$F = 17.383,$	$p = .000**$	$F = 13.854,$	$p = .001**$	$F = 11.688,$	$p = .002**$
B. Pretest	−12.35	37	−9.83	41	0.88	33
Posttest	3.62	37	4.07	41	11.33	33
First follow-up interview	9.33	37	9.34	41	17.55	33
Second follow-up interview	10.62	37	13.37	41	24.12	33
ANOVA	$F = 13.450,$	$p = .000**$[a]	$F = 15.987,$	$p = .000**$[a]	$F = 17.1780,$	$p = .000**$[b]
Social Adjustment Scale (Weissman & Bothwell, 1976, translated for study)						
A. Pretest	2.25	43	2.35	47	2.13	44
Posttest	2.07	43	2.16	47	1.87	44
ANOVA	$F = 6.677,$	$p = .013*$	$F = 4.498,$	$p = .039*$	$F = 18.077,$	$p = .000*$
B. Pretest	2.23	40	2.32	44	2.09	39
Posttest	2.08	40	2.11	44	1.82	39
First follow-up interview	1.96	40	2.02	44	1.82	39
Second follow-up interview	1.86	40	1.93	44	1.67	39
ANOVA	$F = 9.361,$	$p = .000**$[d]	$F = 8.787,$	$p = .000**$[a]	$F = 17.237,$	$p = .000**$[a]

a. Differences are significant between the pretest and each of the three subsequent measurements.

b. Differences are significant between the pretest and each of the three subsequent measurements, and between measurements of the posttest and the last follow-up interview.

c. Differences are significant between the pretest and each of the two follow-up interviews.

d. Differences are significant between the pretest and each of the two follow-up interviews, and between measurements of the posttest and the last follow-up interview.

$*p \leq .05; **p \leq .005.$

cidents of verbal abuse were also closer together than those of physical abuse, which confirms observations made by practitioners and victims alike. Research on the development of domestic violence indicates that verbal abuse may continue when physical abuse has stopped (Tolman, Beeman, & Mendoza, 1987; Edleson & Grusznski, 1987, as cited in Werk, 1989). That is why it is just as important to take into account verbal abuse and threats, as physical abuse, in determining whether violence has ceased and the quality of life has improved (Werk, 1989).

Changes in Self-Esteem, Assertiveness, and Social Adjustment. Table 18.5 shows that statistically significant improvements in self-esteem, assertiveness, and social adjustment occurred between the pretest and the posttest in all three groups. Analysis of variance (repeated measures) applied to the results of participants who completed the questionnaires at all four stages of the study shows that these changes were maintained throughout the research period. Improvements seen at the end of therapy were also noted at both follow-up interviews, although the changes continued at a slower rate. (Only total scores were used in computing results; all but the Rathus Behavioral Assertion Schedule have subscales.)

At the beginning of the study, participants showed levels of self-esteem significantly lower than the Quebec norms on the Tennessee Self-Concept Scale (Toulouse, 1971). Taking into account that the norms might be somewhat dated, given the women's movement in the past 20 years, these data confirm the low level of self-esteem of the women at the start of therapy. By the end of treatment, the situation had improved to such an extent that the women in the study caught up with the 1971 norms for global self-esteem scores. Six months and 1 year later, self-esteem continued to improve, though more slowly.

Assertiveness also changed in a parallel fashion. The women initially showed little assertiveness, in keeping with other observations of battered women (Rosenbaum & O'Leary, 1981), but it had increased greatly by the end of treatment, and higher scores were seen at both follow-up interviews, although the increases were not as sharp.

Similar results were found with regard to social adjustment. Although weaknesses in our translation of the scale may make comparison somewhat difficult, initial scores for our group (2.16 to 2.37 out of 5) were higher than those obtained using the original scale with a sample of American women (mean of 1.61). Weissman and Bothwell (1976) obtained a mean score of 2.53 with a sample of severely depressed women. At the end of therapy, we saw a general lowering of mean scores on all subscales as well as on total scores, indicating a reduction in social

problems. Six months and 1 year later the situation was stable or slightly better.

These results concerning the individual characteristics of the women led us to conclude that Hypothesis 1 was confirmed regarding the three variables studied.

Changes in Marital Assertion and Dyadic Adjustment. Table 18.6 shows changes in the variables applicable solely to women living with their husbands.

The mean global marital assertion score obtained at the pretest was moderate and showed that at the beginning of the study, women living with their partners were not very assertive with them. This is backed up by other researchers' findings (Jakubowski, 1977; Rosenbaum & O'Leary, 1981). There are, however, some methodological weaknesses in the scale we used, which was translated for the purposes of our study (Rinfret-Raynor et al., 1989). Comparative data from a representative sample of Quebec wives would be needed to make a valid interpretation. At each follow-up interview, we observed a slight increase in the women's assertiveness toward their partners, but it was mainly their nonassertive behavior that decreased, confirming that it is easier to reduce nonassertive behavior than it is to increase assertive behavior (Beaudry, 1981). It is also possible that in living with an aggressive partner, avoidance of assertive behavior is a survival strategy to minimize the risk of abuse.

Global pretest scores on the Dyadic Adjustment Scale (Spanier, 1976) of women living with their husbands were also very low, particularly among comparison group participants and group therapy participants, indicating a poor quality of marital life. Differences between the three groups are not statistically significant. The number of women in each group living with their husbands at all four stages of the study was too small to permit statistically valid testing of the hypothesis. Generally speaking, marital relationships in the three groups changed over the course of the treatment period, with the women becoming increasingly assertive with their husbands, and this change tended to be maintained over time. Initial scores on the Dyadic Adjustment Scale and subscales indicated that respon-

TABLE 18.6 Women's Scores on Marital Assertion Scale and Dyadic Adjustment Scale

| | Experimental Group | | | | Comparison Group | |
| | Group Therapy | | Individual Therapy | | | |
	Mean	n	Mean	n	Mean	n
Marital Assertion Scale[a]						
A. Pretest	91.29	17	92.93	14	84.89	9
Posttest	80.41	17	81.43	14	76.11	9
B. Pretest	90.36	11	88.11	9	87.71	7
Posttest	76.64	11	78.33	9	77.29	7
First follow-up interview	74.91	11	81.56	9	67.00	7
Second follow-up interview	74.27	11	77.33	9	64.43	7
Dyadic Adjustment Scale[b]						
A. Pretest	61.00	14	80.08	12	62.00	11
Posttest	80.71	14	69.92	12	70.46	11
B. Pretest	58.20	10	87.88	8	56.86	7
Posttest	76.40	10	79.25	8	64.86	7
First follow-up interview	74.00	10	73.63	8	94.43	7
Second follow-up interview	79.80	10	82.38	8	105.14	7

a. Klostermann (1980, translated for study).

b. Spanier (1976, translated into French by Baillargeon, Dubois, & Marineau, 1986).

dents living with partners perceived their marital life as poor. All the scores in our sample were lower than those of a sample of Quebec women (Baillargeon, Dubois, & Marineau, 1986), with satisfaction and cohesion scores only half as high. After treatment, scores increased overall, except among participants in feminist individual therapy, who started out with a more positive perception of how their couples functioned. The fact that they had experienced more abuse could explain why their outlook might darken as their awareness of the violence increased.

These findings support Hypothesis 1 concerning the effectiveness of each type of therapy.

Comparative Effectiveness of Types of Therapy

Hypotheses 2 and 3, which compared the effectiveness of the three types of therapy, were tested using analysis of covariance. The contribution of each type of treatment to changes in the dependent variable was determined, taking into account the means for each group of participants at the start of the study. This analysis

was necessary because the participants were not randomly assigned to the three groups and because differences in dependent variables were observed in the three groups at the start of treatment. These differences were not statistically significant, except for a few items (assertiveness, physical aspect of self-concept, and financial aspect of social adjustment).

The analysis involved the data presented in part B of Tables 18.4, 18.5, and 18.6, and the results are shown in Table 18.7. They indicate that Hypothesis 2, that feminist group therapy is superior to feminist individual therapy, must be rejected for each of the dependent variables analyzed.

Hypothesis 2 is based on (a) the greater correspondence between the group approach and the theoretical basis of the model, and (b) the practitioners' perception that in a group, change is more rapid, or at least more apparent. The practitioners believed that the confrontations battered women are faced with are more apparent in a group setting and that therefore group therapy must be more effective. Lewis (1983) sums up the elements that would make group

TABLE 18.7 Analysis of Covariance

	(A) Hypothesis 2			(B) Hypothesis 3		
	n	F	p	n	F	p
Conflict Tactics Scales (Straus)						
Reasoning	53	2.216	.143	49	4.728	.035*
Verbal Aggression	62	0.025	.874	58	0.787	.379
Physical Aggression	62	0.969	.329	58	0.185	.669[a]
Self-esteem (Fitts)	78	0.057	.812	78	1.418	.238
General assertiveness (Rathus)	78	0.480	.490	74	1.053	.308
Social adjustment (Weissman)	84	0.104	.748	83	1.075	.303
Marital Assertion Scale (Klostermann) Women living with partners	20	0.259	.618	16	0.006	.938
Dyadic Adjustment Scale (Spanier) Women living with partners	18	0.545	.711	15	0.452	.517

ANCOVA: Measured at the last follow-up interview (dependent variable); measured at the pretest, posttest, and first follow-up interview (concomitant variables).[b]

NOTE: Analysis of covariance expresses the differences (A) between the two types of feminist therapy (see Hypothesis 2) and (B) between individual feminist therapy and therapies in the comparison group (see Hypothesis 3), regarding their contribution to change over the course of the study, for each of the dependent variables defining the effectiveness of treatment.

a. A significant interactive effect ($F = 7.844$; $p = .007$) is observed between the mode of treatment and the results of concomitant variables.

b. For the CTS, only pretest and posttest variables were kept as concomitant variables.

*Difference in each type of therapy's contribution to change is significant ($p \leq .05$).

therapy superior to individual therapy with abused women as follows: The realization that her situation is fairly common reduces the woman's embarrassment and negative self-concept, and the group itself reduces the social isolation that leads to depression and a feeling of powerless.

The lack of observable differences between the feminist group and individual therapy in terms of their effects on the variables studied may be interpreted in different ways (Rinfret-Raynor, Pâquet-Deehy, Larouche, & Cantin, 1991). First, the assumptions behind the perceived superiority of the group approach could be examined. It is also possible that the group may make a specific contribution that was not considered in our research design. Finally, the differences observed at the start of treatment between women in group therapy and those in individual therapy may explain, at least in part, the lack of difference in the effectiveness of the two approaches.

Hypothesis 3, that feminist individual therapy is superior to other individual approaches studied, must also be rejected. The women in the comparison group reported a greater increase than the others in the use of reasoning by partners and ex-partners, whereas those in the feminist individual therapy experienced a greater decrease in physical violence than the comparison group.

Conclusions

■ This evaluative study demonstrated the effectiveness of the approaches studied for working with battered women. Our findings are encouraging for them as well as for the practitioners who worked with them. Given adequate help, these women were able to draw on personal resources and those of their social network to eliminate or diminish the violence they experienced. They were able to rebuild their personal and social lives, as can be seen in their improved socioeconomic conditions, self-esteem, assertiveness, social adjustment, and general state of mental health.

It is clear that social work with abused women, when it has certain basic features, can truly help this type of client regain control of her life and decrease the level of violence she suffers. We believe that these are the features common to comparison and experimental group practitioners:

- A feminist analysis of the problem and the resulting choice of therapy
- Work centered on the woman rather than the couple or family
- Emphasis on restoring self-esteem, growth, and independence
- Openness to emotions
- Importance of concrete assistance

These features are key to an integrated approach in which treatment is tailored to the type of violence within the family and the client's position as victim or batterer, and the dynamics of family violence are analyzed in terms of power and dependency that may increase the vulnerability of the victims (Larouche, 1990; Larouche & Gagné, 1990). Our findings show that a woman-centered approach with the other characteristics listed above can simultaneously reduce the level of violence experienced and increase the woman's self-esteem and independence and improve her mental health.

These encouraging findings also challenge earlier claims that the helping professions, and social work in particular, demonstrate little effectiveness (Eysenck, 1952, 1961, 1966; Fischer, 1982). On the contrary, since the 1970s, it has been generally recognized that some types of psychotherapy, used by certain therapists with some clients, produce results superior to those seen in battered women who receive no help (Garske & Lynn, 1985). Although our research did not look at battered women who did not receive assistance, it does tend to confirm that a certain type of therapy is useful with some types of clients. This does not mean that the types of therapy we assessed do not share with other ef-

fective forms of intervention the active ingredients that make them instruments of change (Garske & Lynn, 1985), but a deeper analysis of these ingredients was beyond the scope of our study. We will simply point out that feminist therapy and the approach taken by the comparison group practitioners incorporate techniques borrowed from a variety of theories, and according to some authors, this is typical of the most effective and most frequently used approaches (Garfield & Kurtz, 1976; Goldfried, 1980).

In addition to the positive effect it may have on practice, this evaluative study is an interesting example of how operational links can be forged between practice and research; such links are actively sought in the social services, but difficult to achieve. The feminist model of therapy was itself developed and implemented in close contact with the researchers and practitioners who were essential partners in assessing it, just as they were in applying and systematizing it (Larouche, 1987; Pâquet-Deehy, Rinfret-Raynor, & Larouche, 1989; Rinfret-Raynor et al., 1989). This exercise in complementarity between research and practice was not without difficulties, but all the practitioners and researchers came out of it more sensitive to the needs, problems, and constraints imposed on both practice and research, and enriched by the process.

Despite this special cooperation between researchers and practitioners, we had a number of problems in recruiting participants for the study (see Rinfret-Raynor et al., 1989, 1991), forcing us to alter our original research plan several times. Many researchers have emphasized that evaluative research must adapt to situations encountered in practice. Controlling experimental situations to meet the needs of a study would significantly modify the therapeutic process, thus limiting the value of the results obtained.

Evaluative research must keep pace with action. In this study, the changing social context had a major impact on changes in attitudes, and that meant that the initial research plan had to be revised as we went along. These changes limit the validity of generalization of our findings, largely due to the particular characteristics of the practitioners and clients who voluntarily took part in the study, but they did enable us to uncover certain characteristics of effective intervention that can guide the organization and distribution of services. As Gauthier (1982) says, evaluative research is not effective unless it is conscious of its framework of action, and our research went hand in hand with a process of transformation of social work practice.

In conclusion, it is important to point out that feminist therapy with battered women does not attempt to change the behavior of batterers, but rather to minimize the violence suffered by the client. When the woman demonstrates, one way or another, that she intends to stop or diminish the violence against her, the batterer is left with the responsibility to choose whether to stop or continue his violent behavior. By seeking help, a woman increases her strength and power relative to her abuser. The changes that occurred in study participants between the beginning and end of therapy were very impressive in two highly important areas: the degree of violence experienced and the psychological variables affected by the violence.

References

Baillargeon, J., Dubois, G., & Marineau, R. (1986). Traduction française de l'échelle d'ajustement dyadique. *Canadian Journal of Behavioural Science/Revue canadienne de la science du comportement, 18,* 25-34.

Barrett-Lennard, G. T. (1962). Dimensions of therapist response as causal factors in therapeutic change. *Psychological Monographs, 76*(43).

Beaudry, M. (1981). La femme et les difficultés d'affirmation de soi. *Service Social, 30*(1-2), 61-69.

Bernstein, B. L., Lecomte, C., & Desharnais, G. (1983). Therapist expectancy inventory: Development and preliminary validation. *Psychological Reports, 52,* 479-487.

Bouchard, M. A., Valiquette, C., & Nantel, M. (1975) *Etude psychometrique de la traduction française du Rathus Assertiveness Schedule. Revue de modification du comportement, 5,* 89-103.

Court, J. (1978). Violence in the home. *Social Work Today, 9,* 27.

Derogatis, L. R. (1977). *SCL-90-R (revised version): Administration, scoring and procedures. Manual I.* Baltimore: Johns Hopkins University School of Medicine.

Eysenck, H. J. (1952). The effects of psychotherapy: An evaluation. *Journal of Consulting Psychology 16,* 319-324.

Eysenck, H. J. (1961). The effects of psychotherapy. In H. J. Eysenck (Ed.), *Handbook of abnormal psychology: An experimental approach* (pp. 697-725). New York: Basic Books.

Eysenck, H. J. (1966). *The effects of psychotherapy.* New York: International Science Press.

Fischer, J. (1982). Does anything work? *Journal of Social Service Research, 1,* 215-243.

Fitts, W. (1964-1965). *Manual: Tennessee Self-Concept Scale.* Nashville, TN: Counselor Recordings and Tests.

Fortin, F., & Coutu-Wakulczyk, G. (1985). *Validation et normalisation d'une mesure de santé mentale, le SCL-90-R.* Montreal: Université de Montréal, Faculté des sciences infirmières.

Garfield, S. L., & Kurtz, R. (1976). Clinical psychologists in the 1970s. *American Psychologist, 31,* 1-9.

Garske, J. P., & Lynn, S. J. (1985). Toward a general scheme for psychotherapy: Effectiveness, common factors, and integration. In J. P. Garske & S. J. Lynn (Eds.), *Contemporary psychotherapy: Models and methods* (pp. 497-516). Toronto: Merrill.

Gauthier, B. (1982). *Méta-évaluation en affaires sociales: Analyse de 100 cas de recherches évaluatives.* Hull, Quebec: Secrétariat à la coordination de la recherche and Conseil québécois de la recherche sociale.

Gelles, R. J. (1976). Abused wives: Why do they stay? *Journal of Marriage and the Family, 38,* 659-668.

Goldfried, M. R. (1980). Toward a delineation of therapeutic change principles. *American Psychologist, 35,* 991-999.

Hardy, J. (1981). *Le sexisme chez des étudiantes(ts) sous-graduees(es) en service social.* Master's thesis, Laval University, Quebec.

Hilberman, E., & Munson, K. (1978). Sixty battered women. *Victimology, 2,* 460-470.

Hodgins, S., & Larouche, G. (1982). La femme violentée et les services qui lui sont offerts. *Intervention, 63,* 7-14.

Hofeller, K. (1982). *Social psychological situational factors in wife abuse.* Palo Alto, CA: R & E Research Associates.

Horley, S. (1989, January). Woman abuse and training. *Social Work Today,* p. 22.

Jakubowski, P. A. (1977). Self-assertion training procedures for women. In E. I. Rawlings & D. K. Carter (Eds.), *Psychotherapy for women: Treatment towards equality* (pp. 168-190). Springfield, IL: Charles C Thomas.

Kalin, R., & Tilby, P. J. (1978). Development and validation of a sex-role ideology scale. *Psychology Reports, 42,* 731-738.

Klostermann, L. A. R. (1980). *A reliability and validity study of the Marital Assertion Scale.* Ph.D. dissertation, St. Louis University.

Larouche, G. (1982). *Protocole d'intervention en service social auprès de la clientèle des femmes battues.* Montreal: Corporation professionnelle des travailleurs sociaux du Québec.

Larouche, G. (1985). *Guide d'intervention auprès des femmes violentées.* Montreal: Corporation professionnelle des travailleurs sociaux du Québec.

Larouche, G. (1986). *A guide to intervention with battered women.* Montreal: Corporation professionnelle des travailleurs sociaux du Québec.

Larouche, G. (1987). *Agir contre la violence: Une option féministe à l'intervention auprès des femmes battues.* Montreal: La pleine lune.

234 OUT OF THE DARKNESS

Larouche, G. (1990). Une intervention coordonnée. *Vis-à-vis, 8*(3), 4-5.

Larouche, G., & Gagné, L. (1990). Où en est la situation de la violence envers les femmes dans le milieu familial, dix ans après les colloques sur la violence? *Criminologie, 23*(2), 23-45.

Larsen, D. L., Attkinson, C. C., Hargreaves, W. A., & Nguyen, T. D. (1979). Assessment of client/patient satisfaction: Development of a general scale. *Evaluation and Program Planning, 2,* 197-207.

Lavoie, F., Martin, G., & Valiquette, L. (1988). Le développement d'une échelle d'attitude envers les femmes violentées par leur conjoint. *Canadian Journal of Community Mental Health/Revue canadienne de santé mentale communautaire, 7*(1), 17-29.

Lewis, E. (1983). The group treatment of battered women. *Women and Therapy, 2*(1), 51-58.

MacLeod, L. (1987). *Wife battering in Canada: The vicious circle.* Ottawa: Canadian Advisory Council on the Status of Women.

Martin, D. (1976). *Battered wives.* San Francisco: Glide.

Pagelow, M. D. (1984). *Family violence.* New York: Praeger.

Paltiel, F. L. (1981). Shaping futures for women. *Women's Studies International Quarterly, 4,* 13-25.

Pâquet-Deehy, A., Rinfret-Raynor, M., & Larouche, G. (1989). *Apprendre à intervenir auprès des femmes violentées: Une perspective féministe* (Research report). Montreal: University of Montreal.

Pfouts, J. H. (1978). Violent families: Coping responses of abused wives. *Child Welfare, 57,* 101-111.

Rathus, S. A. (1973). A 30-item schedule for assessing behavior. *Behavior Therapy, 4,* 398-406.

Rinfret-Raynor, M., Pâquet-Deehy, A., Larouche, G., & Cantin, S. (1989). *Intervenir auprès des femmes violentées: Évaluation de l'efficacité d'un modèle féministe. Rapport de recherche no 1. Méthodologie de la recherche et caractéristiques des participantes.* Montréal: École de service social, Université de Montréal.

Rinfret-Raynor, M., Pâquet-Deehy, A., Larouche, G., & Cantin, S. (1991). *Intervenir auprès des femmes violentées: Évaluation de l'efficacité d'un modèle féministe. Rapport de recherche no 2. Présentation et discussion des résultats.* Montreal: École de service social, Université de Montréal.

Rosenbaum, A., & O'Leary, K. D. (1981). Marital violence: Characteristics of abusive couples. *Journal of Consulting and Clinical Psychology, 49,* 63-71.

Ross, D. P., & Shillington, R. (1989). *The Canadian fact book on poverty, 1989.* Ottawa and Montreal: Canadian Council on Social Development.

Roy, M. (1977). *Battered women.* New York: Van Nostrand.

Spanier, G. B. (1976). Measuring dyadic adjustment: New scales for assessing the quality of marriage and similar dyads. *Journal of Marriage and the Family, 38,* 15-28.

Statistics Canada. (1986). *Census of Canada, 1986.* Publications 93-101, 93-102, 93-106, 93-109, 94-109, 94-110. Ottawa: Author.

Statistics Canada. (1993). *Violence Against Women Survey.* Catalogue 11-001E, ISSN 0380-6103. Ottawa: Author.

Straus, M. A. (1979). Measuring intrafamily conflict and violence: The Conflict Tactics (CT) Scales. *Journal of Marriage and the Family, 41,* 75-88.

Tolman, R. M., Beeman, S., & Mendoza, C. (1987). *The effectiveness of a shelter-sponsored program for men who batter: Preliminary results.* Paper presented at the Third Family Violence Conference for Researchers, Durham, NH.

Toulouse, J. M. (1971). *Mesure du concept de soi—TSSC manuel* (Photocopy). Montreal: University of Montreal.

Walker, L. E. (1979). *The battered woman.* New York: Harper & Row.

Weissman, M. M., & Bothwell, S. (1976). The assessment of social adjustment by patient self-report. *Archives of General Psychiatry, 33,* 1111-1115.

Werk, A. (1989). Les conditions de l'efficacité. In J. Broué & C. Guévremont (Eds.), *Quand l'amour fait mal* (pp. 143-151). Montreal: Éditions Saint-Martin.

CHAPTER 19

Controlling Domestic Violence

Victim Resources and Police Intervention

JoAnn L. Miller
Amy C. Krull

Based on the once famous, and now some-what infamous, Minneapolis domestic violence experiment (Sherman & Berk, 1984), the National Institute of Justice (NIJ) funded seven enhanced replication studies[1] conducted between 1986 and 1989. Social scientists ap-plauded NIJ, convinced that a single experiment should not be the basis for police policy across U.S. cities. After all, each city in the United States is unique, with its own culture, its own "personality," its own sociodemographic pro-file, its own crime problem. Surely, these and other urban features would permit two reason-able inferences: (a) Domestic violence (and other forms of family violence) is *different* across cities, and (b) police response can have *different* consequences on different types of per-sons, living in different urban environments.

Nonetheless, the Minneapolis experiment, published and thoroughly publicized (Lempert, 1989) had been widely cited by policymakers and feminist groups to justify mandatory, mis-demeanor domestic violence arrest policies in most cities across the United States. By 1988, 90% of cities across the United States had im-plemented mandatory or preferred arrest poli-cies (Sherman, 1992).

The Minneapolis experiment found that ar-rest (compared to separation or advice condi-tions) resulted in the lowest percentage of cases

AUTHORS' NOTE: We are very grateful to William Stroup and John Wybraniec, who prepared the Omaha and Colorado Springs data for analysis. Jonathan Miller made significant contributions to this project.

in which recidivistic violence occurred within 6 months following police intervention. The Minneapolis experiment was an extremely well-designed and a relatively well-implemented social experiment. Thus, relying on its major finding (that is, that arrest has a general deterrent effect) to make policy, would be a wise decision. What could be problematic?

Besides relying on one study, conducted in one urban setting, its heavy reliance on offender behavior data,[2] especially police data, to claim that arrest "works best" to deter recidivistic domestic violence is indeed problematic. At least since 1980 we have understood clearly that domestic violence occurs *Behind Closed Doors* (Straus, Gelles, & Steinmetz, 1980). Only a small percentage of any type of offender ends up in official police data. That percentage is substantially reduced for family violence offenders. If we want to know what happens following police intervention, we must *ask the victims*. If we want to make policy that can have a positive result for victims, we must examine the victims' experiences and attitudes.

In this research, we examine victim-reported behaviors, perceptions, and experiences. We compare findings from three of the NIJ-funded domestic violence replication experiments—Milwaukee, Colorado Springs, and Omaha. This is not a meta-analysis, similar to what Richard Berk and his colleagues (Berk, Campbell, Klap, & Western, 1992a, 1992b) have conducted to explain the effects of arrest on offender behavior across research sites. Rather, it is a comparative study of victims of domestic violence across three cities.

Our research focus is to explain variation in levels of domestic violence as a function of victim resources. We construct a measure of repeated or recidivistic violence that incorporates four types of violence: threats, property damage, physical violence, and restricting behaviors. We mirror the analyses of police intervention and arrest studies in two central ways. First, we examine police behavior, as the arrest studies do. In this research, however, we consider the police as a potential resource (and a potential liability) for the victim. Second, we examine how the victim's resources, especially those representing her ties to conventional society, affect the likelihood of experiencing repeated acts of violence. The domestic violence arrest studies find consistently, in support of a social control perspective (Agnew, 1993; Gagné, 1992; Lemert, 1993), that the offender's ties to conventional society—especially his employment status and his marital status—interact and affect the probability of the offender's recidivistic violence. Offender race is also a personal characteristic found to be associated with recidivistic violence. We attempt to mirror these findings by examining how the victim's employment status, marital and familial status, and race influence the violence or the lack of violence a victim experiences subsequent to police intervention. Overall, we attempt to summarize what victims from three cities tell us about the resources they have, and the resources they use—personal resources and police resources—to control the violence directed against them by their cohabiting partners.

Throughout this chapter we use the terms *victims* and *suspects* to distinguish the social actors efficiently. We recognize the unfortunate connotations associated with each term. Nonetheless, we choose the terms because each case in the data files we analyzed contains information about domestic violence victims and suspects.

Victims and Suspects in Three Cities

Milwaukee Victims and Suspects:
A Sociodemographic Profile

From a total of 1,200 cases eligible for the 1987-1989 Milwaukee domestic violence experiment, 705 individual victims (59%) were interviewed initially. They reported on the domestic violence incident that initiated police contact, their backgrounds, the suspect's background, and events and perceptions subsequent to police intervention.

Sex, Age, and Socioeconomic Indicators of Social Status. As Table 19.1 shows, the majority of victims (70.8%) and suspects (75.8%) are Black. Victims range in age from 17 to 69.

TABLE 19.1 Victim and Suspect Demographic
Profile, Milwaukee (N = 705)

	Victims	Suspects
Sex		
Female (%)	90.5	9.0
Male (%)	9.5	91.0
Race		
Black (%)	70.8	75.8
White (%)	25.3	19.8
Hispanic (%)	2.8	3.8
Asian or Native		
American (%)	1.1	0.6
Age ($\bar{x}$)	28.9	31.3
Education		
< High school		
diploma (%)	44.0	43.0
High school		
diploma (%)	29.0	35.5
Some college (%)	23.0	19.0
College degree (%)	4.0	2.5
Working (%)	31.8	50.0
Unemployment		
in months ($\bar{x}$)	34.7	21.9
	(42.4)	(28.2)

As a group, they are younger than the suspects.
Their average age is 28.94 (SD = 8.17).

Fewer victims, compared to suspects, have
completed high school, but more victims, compared to suspects, have earned a college degree.
Forty-four percent of the victims have not
earned a high school diploma.

A Milwaukee victim is less likely than a suspect to have been working outside the home at
the time of the domestic violence incident. Only
31.8% of the victims were employed. Moreover,
only 14.1% of the victims report that they
worked steadily during the past year. Among the
unemployed victims, the average length of unemployment is 34.74 months. Nearly 46% have
been unemployed for 1 year or less, but 22.8%
are chronically unemployed, that is, unemployed for 5 or more years.

Milwaukee's victims, like the suspects, tend
to work at factory and fast food jobs. In addition,
many report working at other, female-dominated,
blue-collar type jobs, such as housekeeper,

cleaner, waitress, and nurse's aide. Like the suspects, an occasional victim holds a white-collar
job. One is a writer, one is an academic, and one
is a bookkeeper. Victims also hold pink-collar
jobs, such as cashier and clerical and secretarial
positions.

Household Composition. Most (86.8%) of the
victims report living with at least one other
person in addition to the suspect. Most are the
victim's child or stepchild and most (54.6%)
are 4 years old or younger (mean age = 7.8).[3]

Only the larger households tend to contain
grandparents and grandchildren as well as
nieces, nephews, and unrelated persons, such as
"sister's boyfriend."

Colorado Springs Victims and Suspects:
A Sociodemographic Profile

From a total of 1,202 cases that received a
randomly assigned treatment for the 1987-1989
Colorado Springs spouse assault experiment,
1,078 individual victims (70%) were interviewed within 6 months of the incident that resulted in a police call. The victims reported on
the incident, their fears, the violence prior to and
subsequent to the incident, their backgrounds,
the suspects' backgrounds, and the behavior of
the police who responded to the call.

*Sex, Age, and Socioeconomic Indicators of
Social Status.* Table 19.2 shows that the majority of victims and suspects in Colorado Springs
are White. Fewer victims than suspects are
Black, Hispanic, or Native American. Victims
are, on average, 1 year younger than the suspects (mean age = 29.7).

Colorado Springs is home to a U.S. Air Force
base. Nearly 8% of the victims and 21.2% of the
suspects are in the military. Unlike the Milwaukee sample, the majority of victims (62.6%)
were employed in the civilian labor force or in
the military at the time of the domestic violence
incident that resulted in the police call. More
suspects than victims have professional, mana-
gerial, or skilled work occupations. Conversely,
more victims (43.4%) than suspects (35.1%)
either hold unskilled labor occupations or fall

TABLE 19.2 Victim and Suspect Characteristics, Colorado Springs ($N = 1,078$)

	Victims	Suspects
Sex		
Female (%)	88.6	11.5
Male (%)	11.3	88.4
Race		
Black (%)	22.9	28.7
White (%)	60.3	54.5
Hispanic or Native American (%)	13.6	14.9
Asian (%)	2.4	0.9
Age	28.7	29.7
Working (%)	62.6	71.2
Occupation		
In military (%)	7.6	21.2
Professional (%)	4.8	3.2
Skilled (%)	17.6	21.2
Unskilled (%)	21.9	21.5
Housewife, student, retired, disabled (%)	21.5	13.6

TABLE 19.3 Victim and Suspect Demographic Profile, Omaha ($N = 470$)

	Victims	Suspects
Sex		
Female (%)	95.8	4.2
Male (%)	4.2	95.8
Race		
Black (%)	38.7	45.9
White (%)	54.1	47.8
Hispanic or Native American (%)	2.9	3.6
Asian (%)	2.9	3.6
Age ($\bar{x}$)	29.7	30.7
Education		
< High school diploma (%)	33.6	32.8
High school diploma (%)	44.7	44.0
Some college (%)	17.2	11.5
Four years of college (%)	4.5	11.7
Highest grade completed	11.9 (2.2)	12.5 (3.5)
Working (%)	48.7	64.9
Occupational prestige		
Hollingshead scale (1-9)	4.5 (1.8)	3.9 (1.8)
Duncan SES) index (0-96)	34.6 (19.7)	27.2 (18.8)
On public assistance (%)	31.5	34.9

NOTE: Standard deviations are in parentheses.

into the category of housewife, student, retired, or disabled.

Household Composition. The typical Colorado Springs victim is married to the suspect. She has either one or two children. The average age of the child in a one-child household is 3.42 years. In a two-child household, the second child is, on average, 1.75 years old.

Omaha Victims and Suspects: A Sociodemographic Profile

The Omaha experiment was conducted between 1986 and 1987. It is the oldest of the three studies we analyzed. It is also the smallest with a total of 577 cases eligible for the experiment. Initial interviews were completed with 470 victims, yielding the highest response rate (76%) of the three studies.

Sex, Age, and Socioeconomic Indicators of Social Status. Unlike the Milwaukee and Colorado Springs samples, Omaha victims (Table 19.3) are almost all women (95.8%).

Nearly 39% of the victims and 45.9% of the suspects are Black. More than half the victims, but less than half the suspects, are White.

The typical victim in Omaha is almost 30 years old and the suspect is 1 year older. Approximately the same percentages of victims and suspects either have not completed high school or have a high school diploma. More victims than suspects have completed some college, but more suspects compared to victims have completed at least 4 years of college.

Nearly two thirds of the Omaha suspects were working outside the home at the time of the domestic violence incident that resulted in a

TABLE 19.4 Overrepresentation of Blacks and Hispanics in Victim Samples

	GP 1990, % Black (A)	*Overrepresentation*		GP 1990, % Hispanic (D)	*Overrepresentation*	
		Victims, % Black (B)	Factor (C) (B)/.5(A)		Victims, % Hispanic (E)	Factor (F) (E)/.5(D)
Milwaukee	13.3	70.8	10.6	3.6	2.8	1.6
Colorado Springs	7.1	22.9	6.5	9.2	13.6	3.0
Omaha	8.3	38.7	9.3	3.0	2.9	1.9

NOTE: GP 1990 = general population census. Overrepresentation factor = % Black suspects /.5 of % of Blacks in general population.

police call. This was not the case for the victims. Only 48.7% were working. Approximately one third of the victims report that they were on some form of public assistance at the time of the violent incident.

Researchers measured occupational prestige on two scales, the 9-point Hollingshead scale and the 0- to 96-point Duncan SES index. Victims' occupations, on average, are higher than suspects' occupations on both measures of prestige (4.5 compared to 3.9 points on the Hollingshead scale and 34.6 compared to 27.2 on the Duncan SES index).

Household Composition. Thirty-three percent of the victims are married. Not all, but most, are married to the suspects, and 20.3% of the victims have at least one child living with them. The average number of children per victim is 1.3.

A Comparison of the Three Cities

■ In all three cities, there are more White victims than White suspects, and there are more Black suspects than Black victims. In Omaha, occupational prestige is higher for victims than it is for suspects. In Colorado Springs, more victims than suspects have professional positions.

How They Are Alike. National prevalence and incidence studies find that domestic violence affects families, and individuals within families, of both sexes, from all social classes and all racial, ethnic, and cultural groups. Research on the criminal justice, public health, and social welfare response to violent families

or to episodes of domestic violence, however, consistently shows that not all segments of U.S. society are equally represented in criminal case files or social science data files (Buzawa & Buzawa, 1993). It is the working-class family that elicits the police response to an episode of family violence. It is the poor family, the unemployed spouse, the cohabiting couple living in an apartment with "thin walls" that is disproportionately likely to face a formal agent of social control—the police—in response to social deviance. All three studies examined here illustrate this point clearly. The victims who experienced a police response to incidents of domestic violence are, with few exceptions, likely to work in low-prestige jobs and are highly unlikely to have had completed college.

How They Are Different. There are, however, three ways in which these cities differ from each other—along the dimensions of victim sex, race, and employment status—that warrant careful attention. First, the largest percentage of male victims (11.3%) is in Colorado Springs. In Omaha, we see the smallest percentage of male victims (4.2%). Second, the overrepresentation of Blacks in the victim samples varies across the three cities. Table 19.4 summarizes this finding. In Milwaukee, Blacks are overrepresented in the victim sample, relative to their representation in the general population, by a factor of 10.6[4] and Hispanics are overrepresented by a factor of 1.6. In Colorado Springs, Blacks are overrepresented in the victim sample by a factor of 6.5 and Hispanics are overrepresented by a factor of 3.0. Omaha overrepresents Blacks in the

TABLE 19.5 Top Five Reasons for Argument (in percentages)

Provocation: Reasons for Fight or Argument				Provocation: Suspect's Reasons/Explanations for Domestic Violence, Colorado Springs (N = 1,078)	
Milwaukee (N = 705)		Omaha (N = 469)			
Suspect's jealousy	27.5	Suspect's alcohol use	32.1	Lost temper	30.4
Suspect's drinking	27.5	Money	23.6	Self-defense	13.0
Money	16.0	Children	21.3	Intoxicated or high	12.6
Friends (suspect's or victim's)	14.5	Jealousy	13.0	Get victim to behave	5.2
Treatment of children	11.0	In-laws	11.9	Teach victim a lesson	1.7

victim sample by a factor of 9.3 and Hispanics by a factor of 1.9. Colorado Springs is most extreme in the overrepresentation of Hispanics, and Milwaukee in the overrepresentation of Blacks,[5] in samples of domestic violence victims.

Third, the percentage of victims employed varies widely across the three cities. In round numbers, only one third of the victims are working in Milwaukee. In Colorado Springs, two thirds are working. Between the extremes, we find that less than one half of the victims were working outside the home in Omaha at the time of the domestic violence incident that resulted in a police call. Unemployed suspects and Black suspects, according to researchers who have analyzed these data by focusing on offender behavior (Berk et al., 1992a, 1992b; Sherman, 1992), are at greater risk than employed or White suspects for recidivistic domestic violence. Therefore, the victim's race and employment differences observed across the three cities must be considered carefully when interpreting and comparing findings of recidivistic domestic violence from the victim's perspective.

Provocations and Consequences of Domestic Violence

■ What, according to victims, provokes an incident of familial violence that leads to police intervention? Milwaukee and Omaha victims told interviewers that arguments or fights typically preceded the incident.[6] Moreover, many

suspects and/or victims were drinking or using illicit drugs at the time of the incident.

Arguments

More than 93% of the Milwaukee victims report an argument that lasted, on average, for 1 hour led to the incident that resulted in police intervention. The top five reasons for the arguments are shown in Table 19.5. (Respondents reported more than one reason.) The suspect's jealously is what most victims perceive they and the suspect fought about, followed by the suspect's drinking, money, friends, and the treatment of children.

In Omaha, 86.6% of the victims told interviewers that a verbal argument preceded the fight that led to police intervention. Although the majority of those victims (64.3%) claim that the suspect alone was responsible for starting the argument, 23.6% claim that both the suspect and the victim were responsible. In addition, 12.2% of the victims claim that they alone were primarily responsible for initiating the verbal argument that led to an incident of physical, domestic violence.

What did they argue about? The top five list from Omaha looks remarkably similar to the Milwaukee list. Victims report that they argued most about alcohol, money, children, jealousy, and in-laws.

Interviewers in Omaha asked victims, "Who was the most aggressive, i.e., who shouted the most, who was the maddest, who pushed the argument the most?" Most victims (72.2%) said that the suspect was the most aggressive. How-

TABLE 19.6 Alcohol and Drug Use at Time of Violent Incident (in percentages)

| | *Provocation: Alcohol and Drugs, Milwaukee* | | | |
	Drinking Alcohol	*Using Drugs*	*Using Alcohol or Drugs*	*Using Alcohol and Drugs*
Suspect (*n* = 703)	69.4	12.8	72.5	5.8
Victim (*n* = 701)	36.2	1.6	36.6	0.7

	Provocation: Alcohol or Drugs *(reported by suspect),* *Colorado Springs (N = 1,078)*
Suspect	58.3 (drinking or using drugs)
Victim	32.1 (drinking or using drugs)

| | *Provocation: Alcohol and Drug Use, Omaha (N = 447)* | | | |
	Alcohol	*Marijuana*	*Hard Drugs*	*Prescription Drugs*
Suspect (6-month frequency)	76.9	30.9	4.7	15.7
	(74.7)	(59.9)	(25.1)	(68.0)
Victim (6-month frequency)	26.2	6.5	NA	25.2
	(45.5)	(24.8)		(13.6)

NOTE: Standard deviations are in parentheses.

ever, 12.3% said the suspect and the victim were equally aggressive, and 15.5% of the victims report that they were the most aggressive.[7]

Alcohol and Drugs

Empirical studies that are too numerous to count report a connection between the excessive or abusive use of alcohol or illicit drugs and acts of violence that range in severity from fist fights to murder. Likewise, family violence researchers report an association between alcohol use and intimate violence (Kaufman Kantor & Straus, 1992). Although there is no adequate theory to explain the connection between alcohol and violence within the home or outside the home, one prevailing argument focuses on the disinhibiting effect of alcohol in a social context that encourages the emergence of a socially learned pattern of violent behavior (Stacey, Hazelwood, & Shupe, 1994).

Victims in all three of the cities we studied report drinking and/or the use of illicit drugs by most suspects of domestic violence, contributing to the growing evidence that establishes a link between alcohol or drug use and injurious behaviors.

Milwaukee victims report (Table 19.6) that most of the suspects were either drinking alcohol, using drugs, or drinking and using drugs at the time of the violent incident. They also report that fewer victims than suspects were drinking or using drugs. A similar pattern is found in Colorado Springs. Most suspects, according to the police, were either drinking or using drugs at the time of the domestic violence incident. Fewer victims, according to the police, were using alcohol or drugs.

Omaha victims were asked to estimate how frequently they and the suspects had used alcohol and drugs over the recent 6 months. According to the victims, suspects had consumed alcohol, on average, 76.9 times and the victims had consumed alcohol on 26.2 occasions. Victims report that they had used marijuana much less frequently than the suspects had. They report, however, that they used prescription drugs more frequently than the suspects had.

Consequences of Violence

Table 19.7 summarizes one consequence of domestic violence, that is, types of physical injury that result. Victims in Milwaukee and Omaha

TABLE 19.7 Some Consequences of Domestic Violence (in percentages)

Type of Experience/ Injury	Suspect	Victim
Milwaukee (N = 705)		
Damage property	11.1	70.1
Slap, hit, injure	45.4	94.9
Hit, kick, choke	35.7	87.9
Pain experienced	15.7	67.5
Internal injuries	0.6	4.3
Scratches, cuts, bruises	20.0	73.2
Concussion	0.0	0.1
Broken bones or teeth	0.1	3.4
Knife wound	0.6	0.9
No injury	19.7	12.1
Medical treatment received	7.8	14.2
Omaha (N = 469)		
Property damaged	4.3	43.2
Pushed, shoved	39.3	70.4
Hit with object	9.0	15.3
Hit with fist	20.3	43.5
Beat up	5.7	36.6
Threatened with gun	1.6	4.2
Cut or stabbed	0.9	4.0
Knocked unconscious	NA	4.5
Broken bones or teeth	NA	8.2
Scratches, cuts, bruises	NA	81.0
No injury	NA	19.6
Medical treatment received	NA	18.9

were asked what the suspects did to them as well as what they did to the suspects. The data clearly show that victims are more likely to be injured, and they are more likely to be seriously injured, than are the suspects as a consequence of an incident of misdemeanor domestic violence that results in a police call.

Milwaukee victims report that in 70.1% of the incidents, suspects damaged property. Almost all the victims (94.9%) were slapped, hit, or physically injured, and 67.5% report that they experienced of pain as a result. Of the victims, 73.2% report cuts, scratches or bruises, and the more severely injured, although few in number, experienced a knife wound, a concussion, or broken bones or teeth. More than 14% received medical treatment as a consequence of their injuries.

In Omaha, 70.4% of the victims were pushed or shoved, 58.8% were hit either by the suspect's

fist or by an object. Thirty-seven percent of the victims were beat up. As many victims received medical treatment as were uninjured.

According to these victims, they inflicted considerably less damage and injury on the suspects, disputing any violence symmetry hypothesis. The Milwaukee victims report that only 15.7% of the suspects experienced pain as a result of a domestic violence incident. Twenty percent of the suspects were scratched, cut, or bruised, and the same number (19.7%) were not injured at all. Nearly 8% of the Milwaukee suspects received medical treatment as a consequence of an incident of misdemeanor domestic violence. Omaha victims did not report on the medical treatment received by the suspects.[8]

The Police Response to Misdemeanor Domestic Violence

Who Called?

Only in Milwaukee were the majority of the calls to the police made by the victims. In Omaha, 41.6% of the calls were made by the victim, and in Colorado Springs, only 33.9% of the victims made the call. Suspects called only in a minority of the cases in any of the three cities. The remaining calls were made by children living within the household, by other family members, or by neighbors.

The police arrived quickly in most cases. On average, they arrived within 30 minutes although in a small minority of Milwaukee cases (5.0%), the police took more than an hour to respond. Typically, the police remained on the scene for an average of 30 minutes in Milwaukee or in Omaha.

What the Police Did

In Milwaukee, victims (59.9%) told interviewers that the police "calmed things down" once they arrived at the scene, usually a residence, of a domestic violence incident. However, one third of the victims report that the police were not successful in calming things down. Almost all the victims across the three cities said that the police talked to the victim alone, without the suspect, and to the suspect alone without the victim. In a small number of cases, the police talked to the victim and suspect together, either advising them on how to solve their problem or in an effort to dissipate the conflict and tension.

Most Milwaukee victims believed that the police officer listened to their side of the story, but only 22.3% believed that the police took their side. The majority of victims (58%) believed that the police remained neutral.

Many of the Omaha victims had had prior contact with the police. On average, victims report that the police had been called to their homes on four other occasions. Yet 66% of the Omaha victims told interviewers that there also had been times when they could or should have called the police and chose not to. Fear of injury by the suspect (15.4%), the belief that police intervention would make things worse (14.4%), and having no access to a telephone (14.4%) are the three most common reasons given by victims who had not called the police in response to earlier acts of domestic violence perpetrated against them.

Types of Help Given by Police

The police officer, responding to a call of domestic violence, is acting as a formal social control agent responsible for stopping the violence and for arresting, warning, or threatening to arrest the offender. The police officer also is a service provider and a referral agent for the victim of domestic violence. Said differently, police intervention can be studied as a victim resource or liability (Ford, 1991; Teichman & Teichman, 1989) when attempting to explain how victims use various resources to control domestic violence.

In these experiments, the officer imposed a randomly assigned disposition on the offender.[9] The officer exercised discretion, however, when offering several types of help to the victim.

Separate types of help and referral were measured across the cities.[10] We classify them as "information," "advice," "recommendations," "calling," and "transportation." Information includes information on legal rights, information on women's shelters, a pamphlet of

TABLE 19.8 Types of Help Given by Police (in percentages)

Type of Help	Milwaukee	Colorado Springs
Information	51.9 (n = 700)	67.3 (n = 932)
Advice	47.4 (n = 702)	46.8 (n = 932)
Recommendations	52.6 (n = 701)	36.5 (n = 896)
Made call	25.8 (n = 703)	11.2 (n = 838)
Transport to hospital or shelter	3.4 (n = 702)	2.7 (n = 819)

information of various resources for battered women, and information on how to press charges against the suspect. Police officers offered advice on how to get along, on counseling, and on obtaining legal assistance. They could offer a recommendation to a shelter, a recommendation to family counseling, and a recommendation to a witness advocacy program. In addition, the officer, in 44% of the cases in Milwaukee, and in 25% of the cases in Colorado Springs, called a woman's shelter and put the victim on the phone. In a small minority of cases in each of the three cities, the police helped the victim by transporting her to a hospital or to a shelter.

Table 19.8 compares the help offered to victims by police officers in Milwaukee and Colorado Springs. More Colorado Springs victims received the "information" type of help, and more Milwaukee victims received "recommendations" and help calling a women's shelter.

Problems Caused by Police Intervention

Although most victims report receiving numerous types of help from the police, many victims also report that they experienced problems as a consequence of police intervention. Said differently, the police can be a liability, as well as a resource, for the individual who has been victimized by domestic violence.

TABLE 19.9 Problems Caused by Police, Milwaukee (in percentages)

Type of Problem	Victims Who Report Problem
Any problem	42.6
Harassment by suspect	22.9
Violence by suspect	15.8
Family problems	14.5
Financial problems	14.1
Child visitation problems	10.4
Marital problems	9.2
Legal problems	8.7
Average number of problems reported = 1.058	
$SD = 1.679$	
$n = 704$	

TABLE 19.10 "After the Police Left, How Safe Did You Feel?" Milwaukee

	β	T Value
Problems caused by police (0-8 point scale)	−.059	−1.513
Information given by police (0-4 point scale)	.146	3.440*
Advice given by police (0-2 point scale)	−.125	−2.992*
Police made call to shelter	.041	1.080
Male victim	−.011	−.298
Ex-spouse suspect	−.012	−.307
Injury experienced	−.012	.800
Intercept	1.368	
$SE = .189$		
Adjusted $R^2 = .035*$		
Mean = 1.598, $SD = 1.351$		
$n = 698$		

*$p < .001$.

Table 19.9 shows that 42.6% of the Milwaukee victims perceive the police caused at least one type of problem as a result of their response to an incident of domestic violence. Nearly 23% report that the suspects harassed them, and nearly 16% report an episode of violence by the suspect as a consequence of police intervention. Victims also report that family problems, financial problems, child visitation problems, marital problems, and legal problems were experienced because the police responded to a domestic violence call at their homes.

How Safe Do Victims Feel After Police Intervention?

Milwaukee interviewers asked victims, "After the police left, how safe did you feel?" Responses include "very safe," "not sure," and "not at all safe." A single-equation multiple regression model was specified to explain variation in feelings of safety as a function of the help provided by the police and the problems caused by the police. The findings, summarized in Table 19.10, show that although victims perceive that police intervention causes interpersonal and familial problems, those problems do not affect perceptions of safety. The information given to victims by police increases their feeling of safety, but the advice given by police decreases victims' perceptions of safety after the police leave the scene of domestic conflict. It is possible that victims perceive "advice" as "warn-

ings"—warnings that can diminish perceptions of safety.

Six Months Later[11]

■ Three- or 6-month follow-up interviews were conducted with 1,078 victims in Colorado Springs, and 6-month follow-up interviews were conducted with 921 victims in Milwaukee and 357 victims in Omaha. All of the victims were asked to report on changes in their personal relationships, including the relationship with the suspect, their work status, and acts of domestic violence that they experienced subsequent to police intervention.

Milwaukee

Forty-one percent of the Milwaukee victims reported that they were living with the suspect at the time of the follow-up interview. On average they had lived together for only 6 months ($SD = 4.1$ months). Most victims (64%) report that as a consequence of police action, they would be more willing nowadays to call the police in response to a domestic violence incident. Most victims (68.7%) also report that the suspects are

TABLE 19.11 Levels of Recidivistic Domestic Violence: Victim Perceptions

	Milwaukee Raw Scores	Milwaukee Z Scores	Omaha Raw Scores	Omaha Z Scores	Colorado Springs Raw Scores	Colorado Springs Z Scores
	2.61	0	3.51	0	4.24	0
SD	2.86	1	3.52	1	3.45	1
Minimum	0 (49.6%)	−.78	0 (35.9%)	−1.00	0 (25.9%)	−1.23
Maximum	11 (2.1%)	2.84	11 (6.7%)	2.13	11 (6.7%)	1.96
n	921		357		1,078	

more afraid of being arrested and jailed as a consequence of earlier police action.

Colorado Springs

In Colorado Springs, 57.1% of the victims report that they lived with the suspect continuously since the domestic violence incident that resulted in police intervention. An additional 9.5% of the victims had lived with the suspect "from time to time." Most victims (82.1%) believed that the police wanted to help. They also tend to perceive that the suspect is less likely to hurt them again, and they are now better able to protect themselves, because of police intervention.

Omaha

More victims in Omaha (62.1%) compared to victims in Milwaukee or Colorado Springs had lived with the suspects continuously since the domestic violence incident. Most victims (71.9%) report a change in their relationship with the victim as a consequence of police intervention. Among those who report changes, 27% told interviewers that their relationship had ended. Others report that their relationship was better, or that the suspect's behaviors and attitudes had improved. Nearly one quarter of the individuals victimized in Omaha perceived, 6 months later, that the fighting and the violence had either decreased or stopped, as a function of police intervention.

In all three cities, we find that victims perceive the police are indeed a resource that can assist them in their ability to control or prevent recidivistic domestic violence.

Levels of Recidivistic Domestic Violence

We switch focus now from victim perceptions to victim experiences. How did police intervention affect experiences of repeated or recidivistic domestic violence? To compare data across the three cities, we constructed a 12-point level of recidivistic domestic violence scale by weighing and combining responses to four types of questions. Interviewers asked if the suspect (a) had threatened the victim, (b) had damaged property, (c) had hit or injured the victim, and (d) attempted to restrict the victim's behavior following the incident that resulted in the police call.

We treated damaging property to be twice as severe as a threat, and we treated hitting and restrictions to be twice as severe as damaging property. We assigned numerical codes (1,2,4) to the 16 unique combinations of experiences, based on victims' responses to the interviewer's four types of questions. If none of the four types of events had occurred, the resulting level of recidivistic violence score is 0. If all four occurred, the resulting score is 11.[12]

The Milwaukee victims (see Table 19.11) experienced, on average, recidivistic violence at the level of 2.6 points ($SD = 2.5$). Nearly one half (49.6%) of the victims were not revictimized. Two percent were revictimized at the highest level captured by this measure. Although Milwaukee cases were all initiated with acts of physical violence, Milwaukee victims, compared to victims in the other two cities, report the lowest level of recidivistic violence.

At the other extreme is Colorado Springs. In this city, 54% of the cases were initiated with harassment charges, in which there were no reports of physical violence. Yet Colorado Springs victims, on average, experienced the highest level (mean = 4.2 points) of recidivistic domestic violence following police intervention. Only 25.9% of the Colorado Springs victims did not report acts of recidivistic violence, whereas 6.7% of the sample reported that they experienced the highest level of violence captured by the composite measure.

Between the two extremes are the Omaha victims, who, on average, experienced recidivistic violence at the level of 3.5 points on the 0- to 11-point scale that we constructed for comparative purposes. Only 35.6% of the victims did not experience recidivistic domestic violence, whereas 6.7% of the sample (the same percentage as Colorado Springs) experienced the highest level. What accounts for variation in victims' experiences? Table 19.12 compares bivariate-level associations between recidivistic domestic violence experiences and either victim or suspect characteristics, or police intervention across the three cities. Levels of recidivistic violence are expressed as z scores to enable comparisons.

To mirror the domestic violence arrest studies (Sherman, 1992), we first focus on victim race, employment status, and marital status. Second, instead of examining the influence of arrest on offender behavior (including rearrest), we analyze the association between police intervention and the level of recidivistic violence experienced by victims. (The data summarized in Table 19.12 are a series of ANOVA findings.)

Race. At the bivariate level of analysis, we find a race association only in Colorado Springs. White victims experience a higher level of recidivistic violence than Blacks, Asians, or Hispanics. Furthermore, a White couple, compared to a mixed-race or -ethnicity couple and compared to a Black couple, experiences a higher level of recidivistic violence. A Black couple, compared to other types of couples, experiences a lower level of recidivistic violence. The Colorado Springs findings, coupled with the lack of a race and violence association in Milwaukee and Omaha, refute the conten-

tion that Blacks perpetrate more domestic violence than other racial or ethnic groups.

Suspect and Victim Unemployment. Analyses of rearrest data from these experiments find that unemployed suspects, having a lesser stake in conformity and conventional society, are at risk for recidivistic violence (Sherman, 1992). We mirror those analyses by examining the empirical association between victim unemployment or suspect unemployment and revictimization. In Milwaukee we observe no significant connection between either victim or suspect unemployment[13] status and recidivistic domestic violence at the bivariate level of analysis. In Colorado Springs and Omaha, we find that suspect unemployment status does not matter. Victim unemployment status, however, does make a difference. The unemployed victim experiences a higher level of recidivistic violence in Omaha and Colorado Springs. (The relationship does not achieve statistical significance at the .05 level in Colorado Springs.)

Marital Status. Another indicator of ties to conformity and conventional society, according to social control perspectives, is being married. Sherman (1992) argues that marital status is, therefore, related to the effectiveness of police intervention to deter recidivistic violence. He argues that married suspects are more deterred by arrest than unmarried suspects.

What happens to married victims? We find that in Colorado Springs, the victim married to the suspect experiences a higher level of recidivistic domestic violence than the victim not married to the suspect. This finding does not support a social control hypothesis. Rather, it corresponds more closely to Stets and Straus's (1992) observation that the marriage license is a "hitting license."

In Omaha, we find that married victims are revictimized at a lower level than victims not married to the suspects. The Omaha finding more closely reflects Sherman's perspective. We can only claim that we have no definitive finding about marital status when we compare revictimization levels across three cities.

TABLE 19.12 Levels of Recidivistic Domestic
Violence: Victim Perceptions/
Victim and Suspect Characteristics

	Milwaukee Z Scores[a]	Colorado Spring Z Scores[a]	Omaha Z Scores[a]
Victim sex			
Female	.05	.02	.00
Male	−.01	−.11	−.02
	($F = .25$)	($F = 1.76$)	($F = .003$)
Victim race			
White	.08	.08	−.06
Black	−.03	−.15	−.11
Hispanic	−.07	−.05	.00
Asian	.21	−.19	.03
	($F = .72$)	($F = 3.04$)*	($F = .361$)
White couple			
Yes	.05	.10	.03
No	−.03	−.10	−.06
	($F = .70$)	($F = 9.85$)*	($F = .637$)
Black couple			
Yes	−.03	−.17	−.06
No	.04	.05	.03
	($F = .78$)	($F = 8.50$)*	($F = .381$)
Suspect unemployed			
Yes	.03	.00	.12
No	.03	.00	−.05
	($F = .001$)	($F = .001$)	($F = 2.17$)
Victim unemployed			
Yes	.02	.19	.17
No	.04	−.01	−.16
	($F = .04$)	($F = 2.18$)	($F = 10.24$)*
Offender spouse			
Yes	.02	.23	−.16
No	.04	−.19	.09
	($F = .09$)	($F = 48.15$)***	($F = 5.01$)*
No. of children			
1	.02	.10	−.06
2	−.15	.07	.01
3	.54	−.14	−.01
4-5	.21	−.32	.27
	($F = .64$)	($F = 2.78$)*	($F = .450$)

TABLE 19.12 *Continued*

	Milwaukee Z Scores[a]	Colorado Spring Z Scores[a]	Omaha Z Scores[a]
Victim alcohol			
Yes	.43	−.05	−.27
No	−.05	.02	.07
	($F = 18.64$)***	($F = 1.27$)	($F = 7.33$)*
Suspect alcohol			
Yes	.26	−.05	.09
No	−.38	.06	−.05
	($F = 99.78$)***	($F = 3.21$)	($F = 1.73$)
Injury/medical treatment			
No	.05	−.13	−.05
Minor/ at scene	−.04	.12	.00
Severe/at hospital	−.14	.80	.13
	($F = .39$)	($F = 8.88$)***	($F = 2.01$)
Police advice			
Yes	.03	.03	NA
No	−.01	.01	NA
	($F = .85$)	($F = .05$)	
Police recommendations			
Yes	.08	.03	NA
No	−.02	.01	NA
	($F = 1.36$)	($F = .10$)	
Police contact shelter			
Yes	.07	−.04	NA
No	.00	.04	NA
	($F = .87$)	($F = .49$)	
Police transport			
Yes	.46	−.09	NA
No	.02	.03	NA
	($F = 4.35$)*	($F = .35$)	
n	701	1,078	357

a. $(F) \times p < .05$; **$p < .001$.
*$p < .05$; **$p < .01$; ***$p < .001$.

Police Intervention. In two cities, similar questions were asked about types of police intervention. The data shown in Table 19.12 indicate that police advice, police recommendations, and the police contacting a women's shelter for the victim are not significantly related to revictimization experiences. Although we cannot conclude that police intervention per se helped victims prevent revictimization, we can conclude that police intervention did not intensify revictimization, as labeling perspectives would argue.

In Milwaukee, victims transported by the police to a shelter or to a medical facility experienced a higher level of recidivistic domestic violence than those not transported. This finding does not indicate that police transport increases the likelihood of violence. From this finding, we infer that police transport is more likely for the more chronic or severe case of domestic violence.

The comparison across the three cities suggests overall that victim and offender characteristics and police intervention affect recidivistic domestic violence in nonuniform ways. Race matters in one city. Being married is associated with a higher level of revictimization in one city and a lower level in another. Police intervention has different consequences for different types of victims. From comparisons of the experiments that examined rearrest data, we learned that arresting suspects can deter or escalate subsequent violence. Sherman (1992) summarizes the dilemma:

> Imagine a drug that cures patients in some cities but makes them sicker in others. . . . Imagine a drug that works well in hospitals with mostly white and Hispanic women patients, but does not work at all in hospitals with mostly black women patients. Suppose that doctors could predict who among us is going to get sick, but they were forbidden to do anything about it. (p. 1)

We address the dilemma from the victim's perspective by estimating unique, multivariate models to explain variance in revictimization levels in Milwaukee, Colorado Springs, and Omaha.

The Milwaukee Victims

A single-equation multiple regression model was specified to explain variance in levels of recidivistic domestic violence as a function of victim characteristics, suspect characteristics, victim perceptions of the police response to the initial incident, and the severity of the initial incident, measured only indirectly by the medical treatment given in response to the incident that resulted in the police call. Table 19.13 summarizes the Milwaukee model.

We find that whether the suspect and victim are married, whether they continued cohabiting after police intervention, and the number of children in the household do not affect the level of

TABLE 19.13 Levels of Recidivistic Violence: Victim and Suspect Characteristics/Police and Medical Response, Milwaukee

	β (T Value)
Victim and suspect characteristics	
Victim and suspect living together	−.037 (−1.335)
No. of children (log$_e$)	−.013 (−.480)
Suspect is ex-spouse	−.023 (−.846)
Suspect has alcohol problem	.228 (7.996)***
Victim has alcohol problem	.069 (2.479)*
Victim months of unemployment (log$_e$)	.086 (3.091)**
Suspect months of unemployment (log$_e$)	−.029 (−.941)
Police and medical response	
Medical treatment	−.025 (−.912)
Police caused problems	.165 (5.968)***
Police recommendation help	.060 (2.194)*

Intercept = 1.175
SE = .429
Adjusted R^2 = 121***
Mean = 2.609, SD = 2.502
n = 678

*$p < .05$; **$p < .01$; ***$p < .001$.

recidivistic domestic violence experienced by victims in Milwaukee. A key measure of the victim's resources—duration of unemployment—does, however, significantly influence the level at which she experiences recidivistic violence. Although we found, at the bivariate level of analysis, no relationship between unemployment status and revictimization, we find that the longer the victim is unemployed, the higher the level of recidivistic violence she experiences. Perhaps this victim unemployment finding indicates that unemployed victims spend more time in their homes; thus, suspects encounter increased opportunities to inflict acts or threats of violence.

For the Milwaukee victim who reports having an alcohol problem, the level of recidivistic violence is higher than it is for those victims who do not perceive they have a problem with alcohol. For persons victimized by suspects with drinking problems, the level of recidivistic domestic violence again increases. Alcohol apparently has a twofold effect on recidivistic domestic violence in Milwaukee.

The medical treatment received by the victim in response to the initial act of domestic violence (measured on a 3-point scale) does not affect the level of recidivistic violence experienced. Offenders who hurt their victims severely enough to warrant medical treatment are apparently not more or less likely to stop or to continue the violence. Those victims who perceived that the police, when responding to the initial incident of domestic violence, caused problems (family problems, financial problems, harassment, violence, etc.) are more likely than those who did not perceive problems to experience a higher level of recidivistic violence. If the police provided help in the form of recommendations (recommended a shelter, a counseling program, and/or a witness advocacy program), the victim is likely to have experienced a higher level of recidivistic violence. We contend this indicates that the police, exercising discretion, made recommendations to those couples who can be accurately characterized as *violent couples* (Stacey et al., 1994), rather than couples who experienced an isolated episode of domestic violence.

The Colorado Springs Victims

Contrary to the Milwaukee model, we find that family composition and race do indeed explain variance in levels of recidivistic domestic violence experienced by victims in Colorado Springs (see Table 19.14). The children who live with the victim seem to provide a protective or insulating influence. As the number of children increases, the level of recidivistic domestic violence decreases. The individuals who are victimized by their spouses, however, experience an increased level of recidivistic violence, relative to those victims who are not married to the suspects.

Perhaps in a way that counterbalances the spouse effect, we find that the victim who lives

TABLE 19.14 Levels of Recidivistic Violence: Personal Resources/Police Response, Colorado Springs

	β (T *Value*)
No. of children	−.059 (−2.122)*
White suspect	.079 (2.849)**
Victim and suspect live together after incident	−.070 (−2.454)*
Suspect is spouse	.092 (3.075)**
Suspect alcohol use	−.058 (−2.108)*
Victim alcohol use	−.006 (−.212)
Victim unemployed	.050 (1.712)
Police issued protective order	.185 (6.141)***
Police wanted to help	.203 (6.200)***
Victim better able to protect self	.084 (2.757)**
Injury experienced from initial incident	.125 (4.554)***

Intercept = 1.692
SE = .279
Adjusted R^2 = .191***
Mean = 4.238, SD = 3.450
n = 626

NOTE: Scale = 0-11 points.
*p < .05; **p < .01; ***p < .001.

with the suspect after the initial incident experiences a lower level of recidivistic violence, compared to the victim who was violated by an individual with whom she did not live following the incident that resulted in police intervention.

Also contrary to the Milwaukee model, we find that victim alcohol use (at the time of the incident) and victim unemployment do not affect the levels of recidivistic domestic violence experienced by Colorado Springs victims.[14]

Moreover, the victim assaulted or harassed by a suspect who was drinking at the time of the initial incident is revictimized at a *lower* level than the victim assaulted or harassed by a suspect who was not drinking when the police were called.

What the police did explains variance in levels of recidivistic violence. If the police issued an emergency protective order, if the victim perceived that the police "wanted to help," or if the victim believes that as a consequence of police intervention she is better able to protect herself against the suspect, the victim, relative to other victims, experienced a *higher* level of recidivistic violence. Again, this does not mean that police intervention escalates violence. We infer that the more extreme police responses are associated with the more severe or chronic cases of domestic violence in Colorado Springs. To support this argument we also find that victims injured more seriously during the initial incident are more likely than others to experience higher levels of recidivistic violence.

The Omaha Victims

The Omaha model yields a third set of findings regarding family composition (see Table 19.15). A large number of children living with the victim does not protect her against recidivistic violence. Whereas the victim violated by her spouse in Colorado Springs experienced an increased level of recidivistic violence, the victim violated by her spouse in Omaha experienced a decreased level of recidivistic violence.

The alcohol question was measured in three different ways in these cities. In Milwaukee, victims reported their perceptions regarding their own alcohol problems or the suspects' alcohol problems. In Colorado Springs, police reported whether the victim and/or the suspect were consuming alcohol at the time of domestic violence incident that resulted in their intervention. In Omaha, victims reported on the frequency of alcohol and drug use, over the recent 6 months, by the victim and by the offender. We coded cases above and below the mean on alcohol use and find that the suspect's use of alcohol has no influence on levels of recidivistic violence. However, *victims* who drink more frequently than the average victim experienced relatively higher levels of revictimization.

Similar to what we found in Milwaukee, we find that in Omaha, suspect unemployment does not matter, but victim unemployment does. Un-

TABLE 19.15 Levels of Recidivistic Violence: Personal Resources/Police Response, Omaha

	β (T *Value*)
No. of children	−.018 (−.466)
Black suspect	−.070 (−1.750)
Suspect is spouse	−.111 (−2.743)**
Suspect alcohol use	−.020 (−.482)
Victim alcohol use	.096 (2.395)*
Suspect unemployed	.048 (1.202)
Victim unemployed	.157 (3.853)***
Victim or both initiated argument	−.124 (−3.134)**
Victim witnessed physical violence by parents	.082 (2.104)*
Police action helped reduce violence	−.174 (−4.417)***
Police action caused problems with suspect	.189 (4.837)***

Intercept = .792
SE = .121
Adjusted R^2 = .158***
SD = .718
n = 357

NOTE: Scale = 0-11 points, log_e.
*$p < .05$; **$p < .01$; ***$p < .001$.

employment status (and not duration of unemployment) was measured. Unemployed victims face a higher level of recidivistic violence than employed victims.

In Omaha, victim interviews contained questions that were, unfortunately, not asked in the other cities. These questions are critically important for any adequate understanding of domestic violence. Some writers (Sherman, 1992) claim that NIJ was somewhat reluctant to fund the "add-on" victim interviews in their Minneapolis replications. Unfortunately, only in Omaha were some of the more insightful questions raised.

Omaha victims told interviewers who was responsible for starting the arguments that preceded the violent incidents that led to police intervention: the suspect, the victim, or both. We find that victims who perceive that either the victim or both parties were responsible experienced a lower level of recidivistic violence, compared to those women who perceive the suspect alone was responsible for initiating the argument. What does this imply? Perhaps that victims who are in control or who perceive control—even control over starting fights—have a personal resource that helps prevent recidivistic violence. This contradicts Campbell's (1993) proposition that women do not use violence instrumentally, as men do.

Omaha victims were also asked if they had ever witnessed acts of physical violence by their parents or any parental figure. The victims from families that were also victimized by domestic violence experience higher levels of recidivistic violence compared to victims who had not witnessed their parents' acts of domestic violence. This finding supports a social learning hypothesis for explaining domestic violence (Bandura & Walters, 1963; Boyce-Beaman, Leonard, & Senchak, 1995; Tedeschi & Felson, 1994; Williams, 1989). It does not, however, support an intergenerational transmission of violence thesis (Muller, Hunter, & Stollak, 1995): Most of the Omaha victims had not witnessed violence, yet they were all victimized themselves.

Finally, we observe that Omaha victims who perceive that police intervention helped reduce violence were revictimized less than others, but victims who perceive that the police caused problems with the suspect experienced a higher level of recidivistic domestic violence than others.

Conclusions and Future Research

■ Three types of conclusions are justified, based on this empirical and comparative study: (a) The police matter, (b) the victim's resources matter, and (c) differences across cities matter when explaining variance in recidivistic domestic violence. Analogously, three sets of future research questions are raised by this study.

The Police

In all of the cities we studied, we find clear and convincing evidence that police intervention influences victim perceptions and recidivistic domestic violence (Dunford, Huizinga, & Elliott, 1990; Gartin, 1991; Hirschel, Hutchison, & Dean, 1992; Stark, 1993). The police can be a helpful resource or a liability.

Police intervention can positively affect victim perceptions and emotions. The victim is likely to feel better about herself and her ability to protect herself following police intervention. She is likely to believe that the police are concerned and is therefore more willing to call on the police in the future. The victim is also likely to believe that the suspect, on account of police intervention, is less likely to injure her in the future. This perception can be dangerous. Thus, we contend that how the police influence victim perceptions and emotions warrants careful and thorough research.

We also found that police intervention can influence what the victim experiences after the police leave the scene. The actions a police officer takes, in the form of issuing protective orders or providing recommendations or transportation, explain variance in levels of recidivistic violence. These forms of police action are discretionary. Ordinances and police policy can mandate official, legalistic responses to domestic violence; the behaviors of a formal social control agent cannot be mandated. What a police officer does, how a police officer behaves, can affect what a victim experiences subsequent to police intervention. Thus, the discretionary behavior of police officers who respond to a domestic violence call warrants careful and systematic research.

Finally, we acknowledge that it is indeed possible that police intervention, at the aggregate level, can escalate violence. In Colorado Springs, police responded mostly to incidents characterized as harassing and menacing. Only a minority of cases were initiated with battery, that is, physical violence. Yet Colorado Springs victims experienced the highest level of recidivistic violence in our study. Does this imply that police intervention in certain types of domestic violence cases—harassment cases—can worsen the violence experienced by a victim subsequent to police work? We will address this question in our future research that incorporates the studies conducted in Minneapolis, Dade County, and Charlotte.

The Victim

The victim's marital status, her household and family composition, her employment, and to a lesser extent, her race affect what she will experience following a police call in response to an incident of domestic violence. What we do not fully comprehend is how these factors interact. Nor do we understand how occupational prestige, income, and other measures of socioeconomic status influence recidivistic domestic violence. Our future research will examine the role of socioeconomic status, and like the arrest studies already have, we will examine interactions among those factors that summarize the individual's stake in conventional society. This study examined police actions that were directed at the victim. Our future research will examine how offender disposition influences the victims' perceptions of recidivistic violence, her fear, and her perceptions of safety.

Differences Across Cities

This comparative study shows that the police response to domestic violence in different cities affects victims differently. These observed differences suggest that a social structural explanation of domestic violence and recidivistic violence is necessary. Our future research will attempt to document, at an urban level of analysis, a social structural explanation for variation across cities. Based on what we observed in three cities, we will focus on sociodemographic profiles, socioeconomic status, race and ethnic composition, and employment and occupational factors.

Differences at the Individual and Interpersonal Levels

The domestic violence arrest studies, in part, were designed to reflect social control, labeling,

and victim empowerment perspectives. Our future research will contribute to these perspectives, based on what we observed in this comparative study. It will examine, at an interpersonal level of analysis, how social control, labeling, and victim empowerment explain recidivistic violence or the lack of it.

In this study, we see that victims with a greater stake in conventional society—married victims, victims with children, or employed victims—are more likely to act as agents of social control to prevent recidivistic violence than are those women initially victimized who have fewer ties to conformity and conventional society. Women with fewer ties rely more on formal social control agents—the police—to control conflict.

We also see that some victims face an increased likelihood of revictimization as a consequence of police intervention. We must better understand the dynamic. Do victims experience a labeling process, a process of stigmatization, whereby they become increasingly vulnerable to recidivistic violence?

Finally, at the interpersonal level, our future research will examine victim empowerment from two angles: how the criminal justice process empowers the victim to control revictimization, and how the victim's human capital—her educational attainment, her work history, and her occupational status relative to the suspect's—empowers her to control recidivistic violence.

Notes

1. Studies were conducted in Minneapolis, Omaha, Charlotte, Milwaukee, Colorado Springs, Miami, and Atlanta. At least early research reports have been published or distributed from all but the Atlanta study.

2. Victims in the 1980 Minneapolis experiment were interviewed, and they reported the lowest prevalence of physical violence, by the same suspect, was in the arrest group. However, the victim interviews show the highest prevalence of recidivistic physical violence in the advice group. Moreover, many acts of violence occurred, including verbal violence and property damage, that were not considered official acts of recidivistic, physical violence.

3. An inspection of the age distributions shows that the median age of each additional person increases as the household size increases. In households with one additional

person, the median age is 4. It is 6 for the second additional person, 9 for the third, 10 for the fourth, 12 for the fifth, and 14 for the sixth.

4. To compute an overrepresentation factor, the distribution of Blacks or Hispanics in the general population, according to 1990 census data, is divided by 2 (to account for the distribution of males and females in the population) and is divided into the percentage of Blacks or Hispanics in the victim samples.

5. Milwaukee is reportedly among the most racially segregated cities in the nation with 63% of its Black citizens living in census tracts that are at least 75% Black (Sherman, 1992). Colorado Springs population includes its military population. This implies that Blacks and Hispanics come to the city, for a limited number of years, from all over the United States.

6. In Colorado Springs, suspects told interviewers their reasons or explanations for domestic violence.

7. In Colorado Springs, interviewers asked suspects why they engaged in the behavior that resulted in police action. Approximately 30% of the suspects said they lost their temper, whereas 13.0% explained their domestic violence as self-defense. Nearly 13% report they were drunk or high on illicit drugs. A small percentage (5.2% and 1.7%, respectively) claimed that they engaged in an act of domestic violence to get the victim to behave or to teach the victim a lesson.

8. We do not compare victim and suspect experiences and injuries in Colorado to the other cities here because battery was committed in only 38% of the cases. Most cases that resulted in police intervention were harassment cases (54%). In Omaha and Milwaukee, a case was not eligible for the experiment unless there was probable cause that battery had occurred.

9. In Milwaukee, 98% of the cases received the treatment randomly assigned. The other experiments did not achieve this level of design compliance.

10. In Omaha, interviewers asked victims about different forms or types of help received from the police that varied as a function of the experimental treatment. Therefore, they are not compared here to the types of help offered by police in Milwaukee and Colorado Springs.

11. In Colorado Springs, victims were interviewed either within 3 or 6 months following the incident that resulted in the police call. In Milwaukee and Omaha, the follow-up interviews are at 6 months. Omaha victims were also followed up at 12 months but we do not study those interviews here.

12. This measure is best for comparing levels of recidivistic violence across three cities because it summarizes similar measures of recidivistic violence. It is not, however, an ideal measure for any particular city. Different behaviors were measured in each city. Sexual assault, for example, was not measured in Omaha. But the frequency of each type of violence experienced was only measured in Omaha. In future research, we will examine more completely the unique data obtained from victims in each of the cities that conducted experiments.

13. These are measured in the follow-up interview. That is, we are examining victim and suspect unemployment sub-

sequent to the initial incident that resulted in police intervention.

14. Most Colorado Springs victims were employed, and duration of unemployment was not measured. Statistically speaking, we could argue that the relative lack of variance in unemployment precludes an unemployment finding. What troubles us, however, is the observation that Colorado Springs victims are revictimized at a high level, even though most are employed outside the home

References

Agnew, R. (1993). Why do they do it? An examination of the intervening mechanisms between "social control" variables and delinquency. *Journal of Research in Crime and Delinquency, 30,* 245-266.

Bandura, A., & Walters, R. H. (1963). *Social learning and personality development.* New York: Holt, Rinehart & Winston.

Berk, R. A., Campbell, A., Klap, R., & Western, B. (1992a). Bayesian analysis of the Colorado Springs spouse abuse experiment. *Journal of Criminal Law and Criminology, 83,* 170-200.

Berk, R. A., Campbell, A., Klap, R., & Western, B. (1992b). The deterrent effect of arrest in incidents of domestic violence: A Bayesian analysis of four field experiments. *American Sociological Review, 57,* 698-708.

Boyce-Beaman, J. M., Leonard, K., & Senchak, M. (1995, August). *The intergenerational transmission of physical aggression: Testing a path model.* Paper presented at the annual meeting of the American Sociological Association, Washington, DC.

Buzawa, E. S., & Buzawa, C. G. (1993). The impact of arrest on domestic violence: Introduction. *American Behavioral Scientist, 36,* 558-574.

Campbell, A. (1993). *Men, women, and aggression: From rage in marriage to violence in the streets—How gender affects the way we act.* New York: Basic Books.

Dunford, F. W., Huizinga, D., & Elliott, D. S. (1990). The role of arrest in domestic assault: The Omaha police experiment. *Criminology, 28,* 183-206.

Ford, D. (1991). Prosecution as a victim power resource: A note on empowering women in violent conjugal relationships. *Law and Society Review, 25,* 313-334.

Gagné, P. (1992). Appalachian women: Violence and social control. *Journal of Contemporary Ethnography, 20,* 387-415.

Gartin, P. (1991). *The individual effects of arrest in domestic violence cases: A reanalysis of the Minneapolis domestic violence experiment.* Final report submitted to the National Institute of Justice. Washington, DC: National Institute of Justice.

Hirschel, J. D., Hutchison, I. W., III, & Dean, C. W. (1992). The failure of arrest to deter spouse abuse. *Journal of Research in Crime and Delinquency, 29,* 7-33.

Kaufman Kantor, G., & Straus, M. A. (1992). The "drunken bum" theory of wife beating. In M. A. Straus & R. J. Gelles (Eds.), *Physical violence in American families:*

Risk factors and adaptations to violence in 8,145 families (pp. 203-219). New Brunswick, NJ: Transaction.

Lemert, E. M. (1993). Visions of social control. *Crime & Delinquency, 39,* 447-461.

Lempert, R. (1989). Humility is a virtue: On the publicization of policy-relevant research. *Law and Society Review, 23,* 145-161.

Muller, R. T., Hunter, J. E., & Stollak, G. (1995). The intergenerational transmission of corporal punishment: A comparison of social learning and temperament models. *Child Abuse & Neglect, 19,* 1323-1335.

Sherman, L. W. (1992). *Policing domestic violence: Experiments and dilemmas.* New York: Free Press.

Sherman, L. W., & Berk, R. A. (1984). The specific deterrent effects of arrest for domestic assault. *American Sociological Review, 49,* 261-272.

Stacey, W. A., Hazelwood, L. R., & Shupe, A. (1994). *The violent couple.* Westport, CT: Praeger.

Stark, E. (1993). Mandatory arrest of batterers: A reply to its critics. *American Behavioral Scientist, 36,* 651-680.

Stets, J. E., & Straus, M. A. (1992). The marriage license as a hitting license: A comparison of dating, cohabitating, and married couples. In M. A. Straus & R. J. Gelles (Eds.), *Physical violence in American families: Risk factors and adaptations to violence in 8,145 families* (pp. 227-244). New Brunswick, NJ: Transaction.

Straus, M. A., Gelles, R. J., & Steinmetz, S. K. (1980). *Behind closed doors: Violence in the American family.* New York: Anchor.

Tedeschi, J. T., & Felson, R. B. (1994). *Violence, aggression, and coercive actions.* Washington, DC: American Psychological Association.

Teichman, M., & Teichman, Y. (1989). Violence in the family: An analysis in terms of interpersonal resource-exchange. *Journal of Family Violence, 4,* 127-142.

Williams, O. (1989). Spouse abuse: Social learning, attribution, and interventions. *Journal of Health and Social Policy, 1,* 91-107.

CHAPTER 20

Collaboration Between Researchers and Advocates

Edward W. Gondolf
Kersti Yllö
Jacquelyn Campbell

Collaboration has long been a watchword in applied research. Textbooks on program evaluation especially address the need for researchers to accommodate so-called stake holders, interest groups, and gatekeepers (e.g., Rossi & Freeman, 1989), and action research designs incorporate agency practitioners as informants who provide a source of feedback and retesting (Weiss, 1972). Community development research has been built around technical assistance and planning that requires researchers to act as "brokers" or counselors among community groups and leaders (Gondolf & Wells, 1985). Collaboration ultimately implies working together toward some common goal. It goes beyond cooperation in accessing participants or discussing research implications. It implies some sense of shared conception, decision making, and implementation. The question is, how do we accomplish this level of exchange in a way that accommodates the demands of social science and the needs of social services or social action groups?

In the domestic violence field, collaboration has been a particularly essential part of research but without clear guidelines or expectations. In fact, confusion and conflict between researchers and advocates have frequently marked the field (Yllö, 1988). There have been sharp differences in perspective, terminology, methods, interpretations, and concerns. Similar conflicts have beset the alcohol and mental health fields and certainly face AIDS and environmental research as well. The way of collaboration remains, moreover, somewhat vague in the domestic violence field. Collaboration may entail everything from obtaining a last-minute letter of support from a cooperating agency to having an agency solicit a researcher in a consulting capacity.

The call for collaboration in domestic violence research has dramatically increased recently as the result of several policy initiatives prompted in a large part by advocates. Several federal funding agencies, including the Centers for Disease Control, National Institute of Justice, and National Institute of Alcohol Abuse and Alcoholism, specify collaboration as a necessary part of current research proposals on domestic violence. Collaboration is a prerequisite for the wave of evaluation research prompted by the Violence Against Women Act and related violence-against-women initiatives. It is seen as a means to enhance research design, improve research implementation, gain access to program clients, ensure safety and well-being of clients, obtain the best information to enhance the quality of programs, and increase the relevance and utility of the research. Consequently, models of collaboration are emerging that might be further explored and developed to increase constructive collaborative efforts.

In this chapter, we offer a sampling of researcher-advocate collaborations to illustrate the issues and possibilities of collaboration in the domestic violence field. We pose a range of roles for researchers seeking collaboration and in the process identify some common ingredients for successful collaboration and some of the issues collaborations face. We describe the domestic violence researcher acting as a translator, in partnership with advocates, and as an advocacy researcher to achieve collaboration. The researcher roles and collaboration modes outlined here, of course, are not exhaustive or necessarily representative. However, they do serve to raise considerations that must be addressed if collaboration is to be achieved: the need to build trust and cooperation, to develop a self-awareness of the researcher "culture," and to establish agreements about ethical procedures, funding allocations, and publication rights.

Advocates for battered women have openly criticized domestic violence researchers in the past for a number of reasons. They feel that researchers may not be sufficiently sensitive to the ethical and safety issues of their participants. Probing questions about domestic violence may reactivate emotional hurts, prompt retaliation or threats from a batterer, or promote self-blame by focusing on the woman's behavior. Some advocates also claim that much of the research does not make sense to them. Much of the research has addressed esoteric notions in highly technical ways, rather than relating to the life-and-death crises advocates face on a daily basis (Yllö, 1988). The agenda and concerns of advocates seem lost or trivialized in contrived experimental designs, complex statistical analyses, and self-contained theorization.

Researchers, on the other hand, are confronted with stiff competition in the pursuit of research funds. Rigorous scientific and methodological standards are usually essential for a positive review of a research proposal or a research report. Researchers may also perceive advocates' multiplicity of needs, wants, questions, and issues as unfocused and problematic. Advocates tend to pose a series of obstacles to a scientific research design: elaborate safety checks for clients, limits to records and tracking of clients, evolving treatment and intervention approaches, and staff and administrative priorities. Clinical concerns often usurp the need for more objective instrumentation, and the instability of social services may undo fixed research protocol.

Researcher as Translator

Feminist Researchers' Role

Perhaps the most immediate and direct way to foster collaboration between advocates and researchers is through a kind of conflict resolution approach in which a domestic violence researcher acts as a mediator between differing perspectives and positions. Domestic violence researchers often occupy a gray area between those who see themselves as doing "objective" research and those committed to political activism. They are frequently part of a larger research team or a funding review committee that includes both battered women's advocates and mainstream researchers. The domestic violence researcher in this position may have to help identify the various contributions of team members and integrate them into a position that addresses the range of scientific, ethical, and intervention concerns that surround domestic violence research. He or she may need to assume a translator role in which assumptions of one position are articulated in a way that has meaning and relevance to those of another position.

It might be argued that "feminist researchers" are particularly well suited for the translator role required to bring about such integration. *Feminist researcher* refers here to someone who holds the lived experience of women as the fundamental starting point for formulating social interpretations that further social justice, especially for women (Reinharz, 1992; Yllö, 1993). Although trained in the principles of social science, the feminist researcher also has a concern for doing research that supports social change. Feminist research can be the nexus of systematic investigation and political activism. It can often serve as a middle ground or bridge between social science and activism. The feminist researcher is likely to be conversant with both positions and able to grasp their languages and intents.

Because feminist researchers, themselves, struggle with the conflicting demands of science and politics, they can be empathetic mediators between groups who are deeply committed to one or the other. A classic article by Marcia Westkott (1979), titled *Feminist Criticism of the Social Sciences,* addresses the critical dialogues feminist scholars create within traditional disciplines:

These dialogues are not debates between outsiders and insiders; they are, rather, critical confrontations among those who have been educated and trained within particular disciplines. The feminist debate arises because some of these insiders, who are women, are also outsiders. . . . We as critics also oppose ourselves. (p. 422)

A Clinic Team Project

The experience of one of the authors as a research associate at the Family Development Clinic at Boston Children's Hospital illustrates the translator role of a domestic violence researcher. The clinic included physicians, nurses, social workers, psychologists, epidemiologists, and a psychiatrist, as well as several feminist battered women's advocates and one feminist researcher. Different training, assumptions, methods, values, goals, and social statuses created what might be thought of, metaphorically, as different "cultures"—each with its own terminology or language (Jacobson, 1994). As with societal cultures, the various clinic members tended to be ethnocentric, meaning that they judged others by the standards of their own group or, in this case, their own profession (Theodorson, 1969). Such a setting can be very rich and stimulating, but it also holds tremendous potential for misunderstanding, charges of bias, and even ill will.

The clinic at Children's Hospital was developing a study of battering during pregnancy and adverse birth outcomes. An interdisciplinary team—including a neonatologist, an obstetrician, and a pediatrician (all of whom were also trained as epidemiologists), two feminist activists (also trained as social workers), and a feminist researcher—came together to develop a grant proposal and a pilot research project. The team decided to study women who had given birth to babies with some sort of adverse outcome, meaning low birth weight, congenital defects, and other injuries. It hypothesized that the rate of battering of these women would be significantly higher than in a matched control group of new mothers whose babies had no adverse outcomes (Newberger et al., 1992).

Such a domestic violence study is fraught with scientific, political, and ethical challenges, which are exacerbated by the different cultures of science and advocacy. The different perspectives and priorities make for different interpretations of what should be done in terms of recruiting women as research participants, data collection procedures with women at an especially vulnerable period, and assuring the women's safety in risky situations. Nevertheless, integrating the two approaches can also strengthen such a project immeasurably. A close look at one particular disagreement and its resolution helps to make this point.

Interviewing Battered Women

The project research team met to discuss the proposed procedure for interviewing the research participants. As mentioned, these participants were to be women who had just experienced adverse birth outcomes and who, according to the hypothesis, had also experienced higher rates of abuse. In other words, the team wanted to interview (within hours of childbirth) battered women who had newborns with serious problems. The issue at hand was who would conduct the interviews and under what circumstances.

The epidemiologists proposed that the interviews be done in the patients' rooms by interviewers who knew nothing of the purpose of the research, arguing that these interviewers would be able to obtain the most efficient, objective, scientific data. They also suggested that the interviews could be conducted using a tape recorder to mechanically ask the questions and record the responses. The supposed advantage of the tape recorders was that they would pose prerecorded questions in a consistent way, not respond to any answers, and therefore not bias the results.

The feminist advocates insisted that the interviewers be advocates who were formerly battered women. They argued that the interviewers needed to be well aware of the purpose of the study and should, in fact, be specially trained to inquire about, *and intervene in,* battering situations. Furthermore, the interviews would have to be conducted in secluded rooms, rather than in the patients' rooms, where women felt safe from their violent partners and anyone overhearing them. The advocacy approach was presented as the only ethical way to do interviews.

The feminist researcher felt she could have argued either position quite clearly, but neither with full-fledged conviction. From the advocates' perspective, the scientific approach was cold and unethical and amounted to further exploitation of battered women. From the epidemiologists' point of view, the advocates were not talking about a study at all; rather, their political bias was turning research into intervention. Assuming the role as translator, the feminist researcher on the team tried to highlight the strengths and weaknesses of both sides.

There was, on one hand, good reason to be concerned about conducting unbiased interviews. There is, for instance, a history of blind experiments that have contributed enormously to medical advances (Meinert, 1986). On the other hand, an approach that is very powerful for comparing the efficacy of drugs is not necessarily the best for obtaining information from battered women who have just given birth. It is likely to put off women who have been abused. They are likely to be suspicious and even fearful of the interviewer. As a result, a tape recorder (or a person impersonating a tape recorder) would not get less biased data; in fact, it would probably not get any useful data at all. Furthermore, it is likely that blind interviewers would be so shocked by the stories they heard that their unintended responses would bias the data. The advocates, by contrast, had a deep understanding of battered women, their needs, and what they would respond to. Interviewers with that sort of empathy would elicit much more data and more valid information than purportedly objective interviewers (Reinharz, 1992).

The feminist researcher helped to reach a resolution through representing the various issues and advantages to those more inclined to science and those committed to activism. The team came to the shared position that the valid, scientific demands for objective, reliable data could best be met by employing advocate interviewers, who were trained by mainstream researchers and followed a structured interview, but who could also empathetically elicit the painful stories needed for the study. At the same time, the women participants could get intervention support from the advocates, if they so chose—thus addressing an ethical issue raised by the data collection, namely, what to do about reported violence, abuse, and injury.

In this case, science, ethics, and political advocacy came together in an uneasy, but strong alliance. That alliance was facilitated by a domestic violence researcher who could discern, appreciate, represent, and ultimately translate the varying positions and orientations of the team members. This kind of translator or mediating role seems to be at least one way to achieve collaboration on domestic violence research in complex practice settings.

Collaboration as Partnership

Building Partnerships

Another way to view collaboration is as a partnership in which researchers and advocates join together as equals, in their specialized roles, to develop and implement a research project. Fundamental to a sense of partnership is that everyone involved feels as if he or she gains from the relationship. To achieve such a sense of partnership, valuing of and respect for the work on all sides is essential. Too often in the past, advocates have felt that researchers have been patronizing toward them, and researchers have felt advocates were unduly suspicious of their motives and commitment (Hoff, 1988; Schechter, 1988). Consequently, there needs to be frank discussion of these past tendencies against the possible gains of a partnership for all parties. All the fears as well as hopes for collaboration need to be put on the table. Researchers and advocates also need to visit and observe each other's domains to better realize the constraints and risks on both sides.

Genuine partnerships in the domestic violence field also include battered women, the recipients of the service, at every step of the evaluation process (Schechter, 1988). They need to be valued planners of the research enterprise as well as validators of the results. Survivors of domestic violence can often suggest useful outcome variables and identify the contextual factors that will modify those outcomes. Thus, they are important specifiers of the theory as well as facilitators of the pragmatics of the evaluation process. Battered women, along with program staff, will often be able to suggest the strategies that will maximize response rates and minimize attrition. They can help especially with identifi-

cation of the safety risks of the investigation, as well as the potential benefits of the research.

In a research partnership, there will need to be up front agreements about the scope of the research budget and program operation costs, the allocation of indirect costs or administrative costs, and strategies for seeking multiple funding sources. There can be agreements to carry out some aspects of the project even if not externally funded. Additionally, the status of the principal investigator (PI) versus other partners and immediate contributions of the research endeavor to the program need to be promptly considered. For instance, is there training that can be provided to the program staff and/or can the researcher provide materials, such as books, manuals, computers, or phones to the program?

A researcher-advocate partnership should also include discussions of the conceptual framework informing the research. This process is not only useful in identifying appropriate intermediate and outcome measures but also in exposing and reconciling underlying assumptions, beliefs, and values (Connell, Kubisch, Schorr, & Weiss, 1995). The theoretical brainstorming sessions among researchers and advocates can be constructive and also incredibly revealing. It forces academics to talk in "real life" terms and for advocates to substantiate their causal assumptions and claims. The outcomes are creative and instructive.

The ideal is for the initial discussions to evolve slowly, with a formal commitment from both sides before seeking funding opportunities. There are, however, often serious time constraints in establishing such a partnership, especially if the researchers face an immediate submission deadline for request for proposals (RFP). In fact, an RFP or evaluation mandate often initiates meetings and planning among potential collaborators. Hasty meetings themselves can nonetheless offer an excellent means for testing the potential for a partnership. They can reveal the tangible benefits of the research to the program, the likely decision-making process, the balance of power among the parties, and the diversity of assumptions and beliefs. If an RFP is involved, regular meetings after the proposal is submitted may continue to develop agreements, make revisions that will help with the probable resubmission, and continue the process of building a relationship.

The research and evaluation process is best conceptualized as a long-term process, investigating and testing many aspects of the program rather than a short-term single study with an end-point pronouncement that the program works or does not. Such an evaluative process is reiterative with the program, providing information on which to improve service, and design innovations, which, in turn, are further evaluated (Connell et al., 1995).

Design Obstacles

The greatest obstacles to building a researcher-advocate partnership lie in the research design (Hoff, 1988; Schechter, 1988). The prevailing experimental and quasi-experimental design of program evaluation research raises several barriers to collaboration in general. The design tends to put researchers in a detached, external position manipulating persons' participation and often the program structure itself. Program staff often feel like they themselves are being "put under the microscope." Staff may be asked to administer an experimental treatment not fully in line with their training, common practice, or clinical instincts. Their work and worth is often being tested in the terms of some discrete outcome they are supposed to be producing. In a fiscally conservative environment, the evaluation results may affect funding and ultimately the jobs of the staff participating in the program and the survival of the program itself.

One way to ease some of this contrivance is to employ accompanying or alternative process evaluation. Using program observations and in-depth interviewing to examine the process allows for a broader conception of outcome. It helps identify secondary effects and the paths of change that are often obscured in conventional dichotomous (success-failure) outcome studies. It also helps to identify the multifaceted contributions of staff and program activity that tend to be missed in a controlled experimental design. In-depth interviews with random or purposive (e.g., one ethnic group for which the intervention was not originally designed) subsam-

ples can also increase the contribution and concerns of underrepresented staff. The importance of interviewing staff both in terms of process information gained and for increased inclusion cannot be overestimated.

The use of control groups raises especially difficult issues with ongoing interventions that try to serve all comers. A program may, for instance, not be willing to compromise the safety of clients in a no-treatment control group. Possible solutions include using triage to identify those most in danger and providing full services for them while randomly assigning those in lesser crisis. When there is already a waiting list for services, a wait-list control group (or step) design can be used. Other possible approaches that still give valid results include (a) contrasting standard care or minimal services with an innovative design when an agency is expanding services, and (b) comparing general model programs with a less extensive program approximating a control group (e.g., Gondolf, 1994).

Most conventional evaluations, also, use carefully developed and specific manuals of the "experimental treatment" to control what is being tested and to assist in replicating the treatment. However, most community-based interventions are responsive to individual needs rather than using a uniform protocol because of the great variation in individual experiences, problems, and needs. For instance, safety planning for battered women varies tremendously depending on whether the woman is planning to stay in the relationship, is in the (often prolonged) process of leaving, or has left. One remedy to this issue is for program staff, program participants, and researchers to formulate multiple protocols for the contingencies of the program and account for them in the analysis of the data.

Outcome Measures

One of the primary concerns program staff have had about conventional evaluation research is that they often appear to measure program "success" in terms of global outcomes. For instance, the reduction of repeat violence is often the focus of evaluations of battered women's shelters, but the eventuality of the violence is usually out of the victim's and the shelter's control. Repeat violence tends to reflect community sanctions and protections, the extent of complementary resources and supports, and the characteristics of the batterer himself (Gamache, Edleson, & Schock, 1988; Steinman, 1988).

The efficacy of any domestic violence intervention is to a great extent dependent on the other structural processes and supports available in the community. For instance, the success of batterer treatment (and of the evaluation in terms of attrition) is often dependent on the ability of the criminal justice system to keep the perpetrator in attendance (Shepard, 1992). Widespread unemployment and affordable housing shortages may undermine both violence prevention efforts and women's ability to maintain independent living situations after shelter stays. Therefore, the evaluation outcomes need to be analyzed in light of data collected about the community realities in which they are embedded.

Another issue is that outcomes often get worse before they get better. For instance, health care costs may increase in the short term with better identification and assessment of battered women, or shelter use may increase as more women see the services as useful. An important research strategy, therefore, is to measure many different outcomes, immediate and long term, over multiple time periods, using both self-report and observational measures (e.g., arrests, hospital records, and social service records) and different levels of outcomes (e.g., individual, institutional, and community).

One trend in addressing many of these concerns is to employ multiple methods in research. Gathering both qualitative and quantitative data about the same processes for validation, and complementing quantitative data with qualitative data about other issues not amenable to traditional measurement, is increasingly recommended and even expected in evaluation research (Connell et al., 1995). The use of a variety of methods can help disarm the concerns and resistance of program staff and further the spirit of researcher-advocate collaboration. The most persuasive case in policy and public arenas

is usually made with a combination of qualitative and quantitative data. Both kinds of analysis have their strengths and shortcomings, and a combination best answers both the complaints of neglecting the program and individual context and the demands for controlling for competing explanations for any changes seen. Either evaluators with expertise in both types of analyses or teams of evaluators having both skills can be used (Ford-Gilboe, Campbell, & Berman, 1995). University researchers can often provide students to complement the main evaluation plan with other small studies using complementary methods and/or measures (e.g., Sullivan, Tan, Basta, Rumptz, & Davidson, 1992).

Additional Issues

Another issue that can obstruct collaboration is how to assure the safety of women involved in domestic violence research. Research confidentiality often conflicts with program requirements to report threats of suicide, cases of child abuse, or impending violence or potential harm. Therefore, collaboration among the research team, program staff, and representatives of related agencies (e.g., child or adult protective services) is essential in developing specific procedures and strategies for reporting and safety. Program staff especially need to pose the range of problems that arise and guide the development of a review and response system. The solutions to the issues raised are specific to the agency and evaluation being planned and will need several partnership discussion sessions and probably a prolonged institutional review board review process. Additionally, the Traumatic Stress Section of the National Institute of Mental Health Violence has prepared a document identifying issues involved in each type of family violence research (e.g., child, wife, and elder abuse). This document can help guide and contain the discussions among researchers and advocates about safety concerns.

An additional issue facing many conventional evaluation designs is misrepresentation of minority populations that result from not addressing a fuller context. Minority cultural groups are often overrepresented in urban battered women shelters, generally because of the limited options as a result of their economic status and the demographics of American cities today. The proportion of minorities in batterer programs often reflects the heavy policing and arrest practices in minority neighborhoods. In many cases, programs have not developed sufficient sensitivity and support for minority groups; consequently, they appear in outcomes to be unresponsive or resistant to intervention. Cultural competence and representation is therefore needed in the research process to help detect cultural and racial factors at play. Advocacy for empowerment for disenfranchised cultural groups may even be warranted in some cases. The programs match with the cultural background of their participants, and the community resources available for various minority groups need to be considered in making sense of program and participant performance (Williams & Becker, 1994).

Finally, there are reporting issues to be addressed. Publications in academic journals are helpful and often essential for the researchers in establishing the record needed to obtain large-scale funding, and the dissemination of findings in local practitioner newsletters and in publications of national advocacy organizations (e.g., National Coalition Against Domestic Violence and National Resource Center on Domestic Violence) are helpful to advancing and promoting a program. The kind and placement of publications need to be mutually decided, along with the authorship, editing responsibilities, and time frames. Several other related issues need to be discussed at the outset of an evaluation: how to handle the publication of findings that may adversely affect agency funding; who has the "final say" on what actually gets submitted to different outlets (e.g., the research funding agency, the programs' funders, local press, academic journals); and how findings will be used to improve services as opposed to contribute to theory or broader policy development. Ideally, the research team and program staff will develop a long-term relationship that goes beyond a single evaluation study. Researchers and advocates might in fact plan at the beginning how a proposed evaluation will contribute to a larger objective of continuous collaboration. For in-

stance, graduate students may be involved with the program to conduct additional smaller projects and assist with program development.

Collaborating for Advocacy

Advocacy Research

Another, more involved model of collaboration in the domestic violence field is advocacy research. Critics have suggested that some of the research in the domestic violence field borders on a kind of advocacy research that results in biased and distorted results. They argue that the findings are inflammatory and alarmist (Gilbert, 1992; Sommers, 1994). Advocacy research, on the other hand, can offer more valid, relevant, and insightful findings and be less distorted and misleading than some of the so-called value-neutral research. It depends on the format, structure, and checks built into the collaboration. Advocacy research can certainly maximize collaboration by putting the research in the service of battered women rather than making it subservient to a rarefied research or academic agenda.

Advocacy research can be defined as research that attempts to empirically document the assertions and elaborate the concerns of battered women's advocates. It contributes to programmatic development, institutional reform, and social change. An advocacy researcher, therefore, serves much as a lawyer who represents a defendant in a court of law. The researcher collects evidence on behalf of advocates to present to an academic or policy "court of law"—that is, to journal reviewers, academic conference audiences, and policy-making groups. He or she does help present a point of view or "plea" to these "jurors," but usually in the face of countering evidence or charges. The decision of the most appropriate truth or "verdict" lies in the hands of those weighing the larger body of evidence and information.

The Advocacy Process

The process of advocacy research accommodates many of the researcher roles suggested in other collaborative models, but perhaps more consciously attempts to identify and advance advocates' concerns. The advocate researcher begins much as an anthropologist entering the field (Johnson, 1983). The researcher attempts to bracket personal, professional, or academic interests to more openly hear and observe the experience of advocates and the battered women they represent. Ideally, there is a phase of "immersion" in which the researcher experiences the perspective and culture of advocacy. The researcher, in the process, listens for emerging questions and issues. These may appear at first entangled or complicated, and they therefore need to be sifted and sorted against the context of observed experience and research precedent.

Advocacy researchers next work with advocates to refine their emerging questions and translate them into research hypotheses and designs. They formulate measures with advocates' input, review, and refinement and negotiate between practical realities and research designs. The researcher becomes, at this point, a kind of negotiator enumerating the trade-offs of different research designs and methods. Finally, the advocate researcher discusses findings with advocates to develop interpretations and implications. The researcher may attempt to put findings in a context of previous theory and research, whereas advocates may see them more for their implications to service, institutional, and social change. Researchers' conclusions tend to be more tentative posing qualifications and limitations; advocates appreciate decisive implications for action and policy. A negotiation of sorts again may be in order to balance these two orientations and formulate a mutually acceptable conclusion.

Advocacy Structure

The most neglected aspect of advocacy research, and probably of collaborative efforts in general, is the structural arrangements between researchers and advocates. The decision-making steps, authority line, responsibilities and duties, and meeting protocol need to be made as explicit as possible at the outset. Frequently, they are implicitly projected and left to varying interpretations by different parties. The challenge is to set forth a structure that does not inadvertently re-

inforce the status researchers generally bring to a research project. Advocates can easily feel intimidated by the technical language and design demands of the research, and frustrated by the funds and authority that researchers tend to possess relative to the advocates. How do we establish a structure that reduces the power differentials, yet remains focused on the research task and objective—despite inevitable compromises and limitations of research?

Although there is no fixed blueprint for the structural dimensions of collaboration, there are some fundamental considerations. One is to identify and enlist coalition organizations that have the authority of a variety of domestic violence services and have a range of experience from programmatic to policy levels. Several state and national coalitions of battered women services have sophisticated expertise, contacts, and legislative influence that are essential not only in formulating research questions but also in having them implemented. A second consideration is to employ consultants from a variety of agencies serving a cross section of populations. Adequate funds to ensure adequate compensation and commitment, an explicit schedule of periodic meeting times, and designated responsibilities and input need to be set forth at the outset. Rather than acting like a token review committee, the consultants may pretest and revise instruments, devise protocols for participant recruitment, and lead interpretation of the findings (Rumptz, Sullivan, Davidson, & Basta, 1991).

A third structural aspect is establishing a shared system of case review for ethical and safety issues. An explicit protocol might include regular meetings with advocates for case review and a protocol that has researchers confer with them when certain issues arise (Monahan, Appelbaum, Mulvey, Robbins, & Lidz, 1993). Advocates might also be enlisted to develop protocol for data collection and to conduct some of the data collection. There are some clear advantages to this. Advocates have an understanding of the program operations and participant resistance that must be addressed to successfully recruit participants. Their role in data collection also increases the investment of advocates in the research process, and consequently raises their empathy for the researchers. There are, of course, some constraints to having advocates and clinicians collecting their own data, but most of these can be neutralized through training, supervision, and monitoring from researchers.

Finally, a conferencing system needs to be established to review and interpret findings. One of most contentious areas between researchers and advocates is not so much the data themselves, but what they mean. The different perspectives and experiences of advocates often pose a different context to otherwise decontextualized data. The preliminary findings might be presented to coalition representatives, advocate consultants, and program staff for discussion, and drafts of the conclusions might be circulated among these parties for comment. Some ground rules regarding review time, extent of revisions, scope of implications, and decision-making procedures can help contain what might otherwise be an exhausting process. This conferencing and review system might approach the peer review process of an academic journal with its procedures, timetables, and editorial decision making.

Impact Assessment

An area that has been neglected in domestic violence research in general is the impact of the research on program staff, program funding, institutional response, government policies, and even public sentiment. The effects cannot, of course, be fully anticipated, but advocates often have a keen sense of how the field will respond to information and to the secondary consequences of the research, and the misuses of research that may result. For instance, police studies have contributed to policies that have increased the arrests of battered women along with batterers (Sherman, 1992). Court studies have contributed to prosecutions that limit women's self-determination and sometimes neglect their personal needs (Ford & Regoli, 1993). It is not a matter of censoring findings that have negative effects, but qualifying them with potential repercussions and consequences. Outlining potential effects can help advocates

prepare for them in a manner that reduces harmful or disrupting effects.

Advocacy researchers might in fact set forth a social impact statement as part of the proposal, much as construction developers have been required to do for construction projects (Wolf, 1983). A substantial set of methods and procedures has already been developed in the field of social impact assessment that could be adapted to assessing potential research impacts. Researchers might project the contributions of their research not only to participants but also to programs, institutions, and social change. What is the practical worth of the research, so to speak? This practice would most obviously be a help to advocates attempting to weigh the extent of their participation with the potential contribution of the research. It would make researchers more accountable to the eventual consumers of researchers as well. Impact assessment need not be seen as an imposition on researchers but a step that extends their contribution to, and their collaboration with, the field.

Curbing Bias

One of the principal criticisms of advocacy research is that it is openly biased toward the viewpoint, philosophy, and ideology of battered women advocates. Some advocacy researchers, of course, would counter that so-called value-free research also promotes a viewpoint or position: behaviorist, psychoanalytic of family systems perspectives (Yllö, 1988). They might also argue that in the postmodern academic climate, as opposed to fundamentally positivist one, a variety of "truths" warrant consideration (Guba & Lincoln, 1989). The issue becomes how subjectivity is to be minimized and various truths sorted out.

Several features of the research process assist in this regard. Advocacy research, as described here, still employs scientific research designs that attempt to heighten the validity and reliability of the findings. Second, advocacy research should also enlist coinvestigators from other disciplines and perspectives. These coinvestigators can assert scientific rigor and alternative viewpoints to balance the more subjective concerns of advocates. The advocacy researcher, as suggested in a previous section, may serve as a translator or mediator between these two groupings in a way that promotes a synthesis or at least an integration of various viewpoints. The advocacy researcher acts as a "co-learner rather than expert, a conveyor of information rather than deliverer of truth," and "enabling partner, helping the initiative's participants articulate and form their goals in ways that can be assessed over time" (Brown, 1995, p. 203). Finally, the journal peer review, to which most research reports are subject, offers another check on the "biases" inherent in advocacy research. Advocacy researchers are left to clarify, justify, and defend their research just as other researchers. In the process, they must establish the merit and utility of their work and the positions it represents.

Advocacy Evaluation

The development of a multisite evaluation of batterer programs illustrates some of these points about advocacy research (Gondolf, 1994). Representatives from two state advocacy coalitions raised the research questions that the researcher in turn shaped into a research proposal. Advocate consultants critiqued the implementation of the research and posed revisions in measures and human subject procedures. In fact, they promoted the development of a measure not originally considered in the proposal: an assessment of the women's "quality of life" beyond the customary domestic violence measures of controlling, threatening, and violent behavior. Program staff at the research sites were trained to assist with participant recruitment and data collection, and in the process established protocol responsive to the idiosyncrasies of each program's intake protocols and curriculum. Similarly, program staff helped to develop human subject procedures and were consulted in case of reported child abuse, suicide threats, threats of violence, and impending violence. Three coinvestigators brought a balance of perspectives, as well as scientific expertise, to research design, data collection procedures, statistical analysis, and interpretation of findings: a physician researcher, a health sciences re-

searcher, and an epidemiologist, none of whom had previous experience in the domestic violence field. The result was truly a collaborative effort meshing battered women advocacy with scientific research procedures, and in the process making a substantial case for some longstanding concerns among battered women advocates.

Conclusion

■ The researcher roles, collaboration models, and advocacy issues raised here suggest a range of responses to the call for collaboration in domestic violence research. They also point to several common considerations that may contribute to successful collaboration. One of the most elusive may be the building of trust, empathy, and cooperation. The mechanics are not as clear in this regard, however fundamental a certain "attitude" may be to collaboration. The researcher roles of translator, partner, and advocacy researcher, discussed above, suggest the importance of some authentic "reflective listening" in which researchers listen long and hard to advocates. They also suggest the importance of immersion in the research settings to better appreciate the issues, priorities, and demands of advocates—where they are coming from, so to speak. Researchers also need to be sensitive to their own "culture" and how that might encumber collaboration efforts. As researchers, we are often trained to debate, counter, defend, and argue the importance of our "science" and as a consequence may inadvertently act defensively or presumptuously among advocates. As mentioned, we also usually assume status, authority, or power as a result of academic credentials, research funds, and recognized expertise that may complicate interactions with advocates. Researchers need to openly acknowledge and discuss the differences in cultures, perspectives, and agenda to identify the limits and intersections among them.

Researchers at this juncture often need to act as translators and negotiators. They can help explain the relevance of scientific procedures to advocacy work. They offer a means of verification, clarification, and refinement of so-called clinical observations and grounded theories. The researchers are also in a position to translate advocacy concerns, issues, and questions into testable hypothesis with support of previous research and corroborating experience of advocates. Negotiation is often essential in weighing the compromises and trade-offs of different research designs, data collection procedures, and varying interpretations.

The demands of collaboration minimally call for more explicit structuring of the collaboration process. Grant proposals might outline a specific collaboration process and structure. This outline can serve as a kind of contract and guide in the course of the actual collaboration efforts. Researchers might also establish a social impact assessment of their research, much as they construct a human subjects statement in proposals. The impact assessment would help advocates anticipate and plan for possible consequences and repercussions to the research (including potential misinterpretations and misuses) and help researchers to appreciate more fully the context and implications of their work.

The examples of collaboration also imply that these features are not accomplished on an impromptu basis. The kind of collaboration outlined here emerges from long-standing partnerships with advocates and program staff. It takes time, give-and-take, and consideration—as it does in any relationship—to achieve the necessary trust and understanding that allow for constructive disagreements and satisfying compromises. From our observation, such partnership building continues to increase in the wake of previous contentions and divisions in the field. An increasing number of advocates have become researchers in their own right, and researchers have become further involved in advocacy work. Some "pure" researchers have argued that their contextual perspective on social interactions and human behavior in general is openly compatible with even the feminist perspective of many advocates (Jacobson, 1994). The field itself may be maturing toward greater convergence as researchers and advocates realize their need for one another. The result should be a more grounded, practical, relevant, and influential knowledge about domestic violence.

References

Brown, P. (1995). The role of the evaluator in comprehensive community initiatives. In J. Connell, A. Kubisch, L. Schorr, & C. H. Weiss (Eds.), *New approaches to evaluating community initiatives* (pp. 201-225). Washington, DC: Aspen Institute.

Connell, J. P., Kubisch, A. C., Schorr, L. B., & Weiss, C. H. (Eds.). (1995). *New approaches to evaluating community initiatives.* Washington, DC: Aspen Institute.

Ford, D., & Regoli, M. (1993). The criminal prosecution of wife assaulters: Process, problems and effects. In N. Hilton (Ed.), *Legal responses to wife assault* (pp. 127-164). Newbury Park, CA: Sage.

Ford-Gilboe, M., Campbell, J. C., & Berman, H. (1995). Stories and numbers: Coexistence without compromise. *Advances in Nursing Science, 18,*(1) 14-26.

Gamache, D., Edleson, J., & Schock, M. (1988). Coordinated police, judicial and social service response to woman battering: A multi-baseline evaluation across three communities. In G. Hotaling, D. Finkelhor, J. Kirkpatrick, & M. Straus (Eds.), *Coping with family violence: Research and policy perspectives* (pp. 193-209). Newbury Park, CA: Sage.

Gilbert, N. (1992, May/June). Realities and mythologies of rape. *Society,* pp. 4-10.

Gondolf, E., & Wells, S. (1985). Community research as community counseling. *Rural Sociologist, 5,* 23-30.

Gondolf, E. W. (1994). *Multi-site evaluation of batterer intervention systems* (Grant proposal). Washington, DC: U.S. Department of Health and Human Services, Centers for Disease Control and Prevention, Injury Prevention for Violence Against Women Program.

Guba, E., & Lincoln, Y. (1989). *Fourth generation evaluation.* Newbury Park, CA: Sage.

Hoff, L. A. (1988). Collaborative feminist research and the myth of objectivity. In K. Yllö & M. Bograd (Eds.), *Feminist perspectives on wife abuse* (pp. 269-281). Newbury Park, CA: Sage.

Jacobson, N. (1994). Rewards and dangers in researching domestic violence. *Family Process, 33,* 81-85.

Johnson, J. (1993). Trust and personal involvements in fieldwork. In R. Emerson (Ed.), *Contemporary field research* (pp. 203-215). Prospects Heights, IL: Wayland.

Meinert, C. L. (1986). *Clinical trials: Design, conduct, and analysis.* New York: Oxford University Press.

Monahan, J., Appelbaum, P., Mulvey, E., Robbins, P. C., & Lidz, C. (1993). Ethical and legal duties in conducting research on violence: Lessons from the MacArthur Risk Assessment Study. *Violence and Victims, 8,* 387-396.

Newberger, E., Barkan, S., Leiberman, E., McCormick, M., Yllö, K., Garey, L., & Schecter, S. (1992). Abuse of pregnant women and adverse birth outcomes: Current knowledge and implications for practice. *Journal of the American Medical Association, 67,* 2370-2372.

Reinharz, S. (1992). *Feminist methods in social science.* New York: Oxford University Press.

Rossi, P., & Freeman, H. (1989). *Evaluation: A systematic approach.* Newbury Park, CA: Sage.

Rumptz, M., Sullivan, C., Davidson, W., & Basta, J. (1991). An ecological approach to tracking battered women over time. *Violence and Victims, 6,* 237-244.

Schechter, S. (1988). Building bridges between activists, professionals, and researchers. In K. Ylló & M. Bograd (Eds.), *Feminist perspectives on wife abuse* (pp. 299-312). Newbury Park, CA: Sage.

Shepard, M. (1992). Predicting batterer recidivism five years after community intervention. *Journal of Family Violence, 7,* 167-178.

Sherman, L. W. (1992). *Policing domestic violence: Experiments and dilemmas.* New York: Free Press.

Sommers, C. (1994). *Who stole feminism? How women have been betrayed.* New York: Simon & Schuster.

Steinman, M. (1988). Evaluating a system-wide response to domestic violence: Some initial findings. *Journal of Contemporary Criminal Justice, 4,* 172-186.

Sullivan, C., Tan, C., Basta, J., Rumptz, M., & Davidson, W. (1992). An advocacy intervention program for women with abusive partners: Initial evaluation. *American Journal of Community Psychology, 20,* 309-331.

Theodorson, G. (1969). *A modern dictionary of sociology.* New York: Barnes & Noble.

Weiss, C. H. (1972). The politicization of evaluation research. In C. H. Weiss (Ed.), *Evaluative action programs: Readings in social action and education* (pp. 3-28). Boston: Allyn & Bacon.

Westkott, M. (1979). Feminist criticism of the social sciences. *Harvard Educational Review, 49,* 422-430.

Williams, O. J., & Becker, R. L. (1994). Domestic partner abuse treatment programs and cultural competence: The results of a national survey. *Violence and Victims, 9,* 287-296.

Wolf, C. (1983). Social impact assessment: A methodological overview. In K. Finsterbusch (Ed.), *Social impact methods* (pp. 15-35). Beverly Hills, CA: Sage.

Ylló, K. (1988). Political and methodological debates in wife abuse research. In K. Ylló & M. Bograd (Eds.), *Feminist perspective on wife abuse* (pp. 28-51). Newbury Park, CA: Sage.

Ylló, K. (1993). Through a feminist lens: Gender, power, and violence. In R. J. Gelles & D. R. Loseke (Eds.), *Current controversies on family violence* (pp. 47-62) Newbury Park, CA: Sage.

PART IV

ETHICAL AND CULTURAL ISSUES IN FAMILY VIOLENCE

CHAPTER 21

Ethical Issues in Trauma Research

The Evolution of an Empirical Model for Decision Making

Elana Newman
Danny G. Kaloupek
Terence M. Keane
Susan F. Folstein

Over the past two decades, research that examines family violence and traumatic stress has rapidly expanded our understanding of the psychological impact of these experiences and both the treatment and prevention of such problems subsequent to traumatic exposure. The majority of these research designs require that trauma-exposed research participants re- flect on and discuss traumatic experiences and their impact. Most often, research interviews and surveys require trauma survivors to answer questions about the nature of their trauma expo- sure and trauma-related symptoms. In addition, behavioral, physiological, and biological chal- lenge tasks are used to examine trauma-related reactions firsthand. For example, in studies of

AUTHORS' NOTE: This chapter is an expanded version of a talk delivered at the 4th International Family Violence Research Conference, Durham, New Hampshire, July 1995. We would like to acknowledge the contributions of Marshall Folstein, Leslie Goldman, Stephen Robinson, Howard Spivak, and Melanie Vielhauer. For correspondence, please contact Elana Newman, Ph.D., University of Tulsa, Department of Psychology, Lorton Hall, 600 South College Ave., Tulsa, OK 74104-3189.

marital violence, violent couples are asked to role-play instances of marital conflict in front of a camera. In physiological and biological assessments, trauma survivors' physiological reactions (e.g., heart rate, blood pressure, catecholamines) are measured while they are exposed to visual or auditory reminders of their traumatic experiences. Although these paradigms have received favorable evaluation from individual ethics boards, each method carries relative risks and benefits that need to be carefully considered. What are the psychological costs and benefits of such research participation? Is asking detailed information about trauma invasive? What do you tell people about the risk of participation? Often researchers identify children and adults as trauma exposed from medical and legal records, and then proceed to recruit them for participation in various protocols. What should these individuals be told about the basis for their selection? It is important to resolve these ethical issues in ways that minimize risk and enable us to learn more about the impact, treatment, and prevention of violence.

Understanding such issues becomes extremely complex because the study of traumatic stress and family violence evokes strong attitudes and emotions that make it difficult for individuals to consider rationally the complex issues (e.g., Sieber, 1993). Emotions and attitudes, even when subtle, can influence the most rational of scientists in evaluating sensitive or controversial research topics (e.g., Ceci, Peters, & Plotkin, 1985). In studies of traumatic stress, these strong emotions may interfere with an ability to evaluate scientifically the ethical dilemmas. There is a need for informed scientific and rational discussion regarding these ethical issues among clinicians and researchers specializing in trauma research.

The purpose of this chapter is to focus on ethical dilemmas that can arise in research protocols that explicitly ask adult research participants to think about or report their exposure to potentially traumatic events (e.g., disaster, assault, childhood maltreatment) and the subsequent impact of these events on their mental health (e.g., post-traumatic stress disorder [PTSD], depression, dissociative disorder, social stigma). There are many critical issues to

examine. Can encouraging people to think about reminders of a trauma cause or heighten psychological distress? Are trauma survivors particularly vulnerable to decompensation? Does the shame and stigma associated with trauma increase the risk of psychological problems subsequent to research participation? We identify several such ethical dilemmas and offer an empirically based approach to clarifying the issues they entail. As we discuss each dilemma, we offer (a) current bodies of evidence to consider in relationship to particular dilemmas, (b) ways to address concerns in ongoing research in a cost-effective manner, and (c) future studies that may provide useful answers to extant questions.

The chapter is organized into seven sections. The first section provides pertinent background information and introduces our approach toward clarifying ethical dilemmas. The next three sections illustrate our approach as applied to key issues concerning participant vulnerability, risk-benefit determination, and informed consent. The fifth section highlights the major challenges for researchers to overcome in examining ethical dilemmas. We conclude by outlining future research policy directions.

To frame this presentation, we will assume that researchers are well-intentioned, moral, and competent individuals who have the best interests of research participants, society, and science at heart. Although we will be focusing on adult research participants to streamline this presentation, many of the issues, arguments, and approaches can be extended to child research participants (e.g., Urquiza, 1991). To further narrow the presentation, we will not address the safeguards and precautions that are necessary when research involves those deemed legally incompetent to give informed consent (for a through discussion of these issues, see Levine, 1981).

Ethical Decision Making in Research

■ The principles underlying contemporary ethical decision making can be traced to the Nuremberg Code (1949) although they were not incorporated into policy by government and professional bodies in the United States until nearly three decades later (American Psychological Association, 1981; Department of Health and Human Services, 1981; National Commission for the Protection of Human Subjects of Biomedical and Behavioral Research, 1978). The three basic principles that underlie such decision making are (a) beneficence, (b) respect/autonomy, and (c) justice (National Commission for the Protection of Human Subjects of Biomedical and Behavioral Research, 1978). Beneficence refers to the obligation to conduct research in a manner that does not harm anyone and that is aimed at creating benefits to society. It is the principle dedicated to maximizing benefit while minimizing harm. Autonomy refers to respecting the deliberate choices of those who are able to competently make choices, and protecting those with impaired autonomy. In addition to respecting individuals' decisions, the principle of autonomy is generally interpreted as a commitment to treating individuals with respect and dignity in all matters. The principle of justice is concerned with ensuring that reasonable nonexploitative protocols are in place and that the burdens of research do not fall on one sector of society to benefit another.

Unfortunately, the relative balancing of these principles is difficult, especially so in cases where they conflict with one another. Often these dilemmas are most pronounced while working with samples that are perceived to be vulnerable in some respect or when using a procedure judged as risky. Protecting against the possibility of psychological, social, or physical harm is of paramount importance, especially when dealing with individuals who are at heightened risk of harm. On the other hand, rigid application of extreme protection is not advisable because it can constitute a form of disrespect to persons (Levine, 1981, p. 47), which is discriminatory in denying someone the right to research participation (Bayer, 1990). The alternative is a balanced, flexible approach that carefully examines and weighs ethical considerations in relation to one another.

Typically, in cases that pose difficult dilemmas, professionals rely on multiple methods of decision making such as (a) prior experience, (b) common sense, (c) clinical knowledge, (d) imagining personal substitution with the research participant, and (e) multidisciplinary consultation. For example, in the multisite MacArthur Risk Assessment Study, a study of violent behaviors among the mentally ill, the staff struggled to create protocols that balanced the risk of harm to the research participant, research staff, and others with the obligation to maintain confidentiality (Monahan, Appelbaum, Mulvey, Robbins, & Lidz, 1993). These investigators openly discussed the ways their staff at different sites approached the dilemmas and derived different protocols that were each ethical and legally sound. Although this study provides a good model for approaching dilemmas and opens the dialogue regarding research ethics, it does maintain an emphasis on traditional ethical problem solving.

We contend that researchers have failed to depend on the very tool with which they are most experienced—empirical evidence. The scientific community, at large, has failed to be self-reflective and examine the impact of research on participants. The merit of using such scientific data is the ability to distinguish unsubstantiated claims, impressions, and biases from those concerns with documented merit. By distinguishing facts from prejudices, decisions about the ethics of studies may be derived in rational and informed ways. In controversial areas of research, those where politics, moral stances, attitudes, and emotions merge, scientific data can be an important way to filter the varying agendas, distinguishing the true concerns.

In general we advocate a multistep process of ethical decision making that integrates scientific knowledge into ethical decision making. The first step is to identify the ethical concerns and assumptions, and then to pose each concern as an empirical hypothesis. The second step requires the evaluation of any existing evidence that might address each hypothesis. In addition to conducting a comprehensive literature review, consultation with colleagues who have experience in the field may offer provisional data and advice. On completing these two steps, certain concerns may be eliminated, others may be supported, and new hypotheses may emerge that require evaluation. Carefully enumerating the dilemmas and clarifying the risks and benefits enhance the utility of applying other elements of ethical decision making. It also makes it easier to generate options that might increase benefit and reduce risks.

An empirically grounded approach to ethical decisions in studies of traumatic stress seems advantageous because beliefs about the relative resilience or fragility of trauma-exposed individuals appear to strongly influence perceptions about the types of experimental procedures warranted for use with them. Decision makers who believe that traumatized populations are relatively resilient and capable of managing anxiety-provoking inquiries without injury are inclined to allow the use of procedures that their counterparts who view trauma survivors as vulnerable and fragile would never consider. Clearly, the impact of belief systems on ethical decisions regarding research is not unique to studies of trauma survivors; research with children (Keith-Spiegel, 1976; Keith-Spiegel & Koocher, 1985, p. 388) and laboratory paradigms that require alcohol consumption (Lisman & Brandon, 1995) have raised similar issues. Our empirical approach could apply to each of these research topics.

We will now use the issues of participant vulnerability, risk-benefit, and informed consent to illustrate this approach among trauma-related studies. First, we will describe some of the ethical objections, questions, and issues that arise in each area. Then we will describe some of the major challenges for researchers in using a scientific approach. We conclude by suggesting future research and policy directions.

The Relative Vulnerability of Trauma Survivors

■ Discussion of research procedures employed in studies of violence and traumatic stress often turn to analyzing the potential to "retraumatize" research participants. Caution about the potential impact that any study may have on participants is a reasonable and responsible approach and will result in protocols to minimize risks. However, we contend that retraumatization is a concept that when used in the context of certain research studies creates more problems than it

solves. A distinction needs to be made between *talking about* the experience of violence, neglect, or life threat and having the experience occur. It is essentially a distinction between distress that emanates from recall and, for example, the "intense fear, helplessness, or horror" (American Psychiatric Association, 1994, p. 424) that emanates from direct experience. Failure to maintain this distinction undermines all efforts to understand the risks and benefits of such research. The question needs to be restated as an examination of the extent to which trauma survivors are a particularly vulnerable or otherwise unique psychiatric research population.

To examine potential vulnerabilities of trauma survivors, we have identified some of the key questions and assumptions underlying ethical concerns in the following section. We provide a brief overview of each question and a discussion of ways to examine this issue.

Vulnerability Question 1:
Are individuals with trauma
more vulnerable to psychological
harm than other individuals?

There appears to be an unsubstantiated claim that trauma exposure poses lasting and unique problems to survivors that result in greater psychological risk during research participation. This issue can be approached from several empirical vantage points. First, it may be useful to examine the extent and nature of harm from studies. Bergen (1993), for example, reported that in a study she conducted on marital rape, "several women had negative reactions, such as flashbacks and nightmares after the interview" (p. 208). However, the lack of specificity about the number of women affected, duration of distress, and method of determining this relationship lessened her effectiveness in explaining the extent of the potential problem. Other scientists have kept records on the number of participants who used free therapy or took referral cards (e.g., C. S. Widom, personal communication, September 8, 1995; L. M. Williams, personal communication, May 9, 1995). Such methods can be enhanced by evaluating distress in the context of baseline functioning and conducting between-group comparisons based on diagnostic status and trauma exposure. In this manner, evidence regarding the relative risks for trauma survivors and other comparable subjects for distress and psychological decompensation under interview conditions could be ascertained.

Second, it may be fruitful to examine whether individuals with PTSD symptoms are vulnerable to risks in research contexts in ways that differ from individuals with other disorders (e.g., depression, schizophrenia, and medical illnesses). In studies of depression, for example, tasks or questions that tap depressive symptoms are implemented and not considered to put depressed individuals at greater psychological risk. Do particular PTSD symptoms (e.g., re-experiencing) make trauma-exposed individuals more at psychological risk when discussing symptoms in the research context? Studies comparing such relative risks across disorders would be a meaningful contribution.

Vulnerability Question 2:
Is research with trauma survivors
a re-creation of abusive dynamics?

Feminist theorists have argued that the hierarchical nature of the relationship between researcher and participant creates a power differential that can be problematic in all research (e.g., Reinharz & Davidman, 1992). Specifically with respect to research on incest, Castor-Lewis (1988) argues that a power inequality between investigator and research participant exists that may be reminiscent of the power inequity between abuser and victim, and that may evoke painful feelings on behalf of the volunteer. By extension, she argues that the mere request for information from incest survivors may be perceived by the survivor as a boundary violation. Consequently, evidence evaluating if there are indeed particular aspects of the research process that systematically pose specific risks to survivors of interpersonal violence is necessary. Evaluating if trauma survivors are more likely to experience the research process as especially intrusive, or whether this is a prejudice applied to trauma-exposed individuals would be worthwhile. In addition, the extent of participants' powerlessness may be assessed by examining the frequency with which questions

are skipped and participants' perceived ability to refuse to answer certain questions. Finally, research on trauma survivors' relative sensitivity and response to hierarchical interpersonal cues may provide a sufficient database specifying relative risks in interview protocols.

Vulnerability Question 3:
Do public attitudes toward violence
and disaster make the discussion of
this area more distressing for participants
than discussion of other topics?

Research regarding trauma exposure, especially interpersonal violence, is embedded in a cultural context of disbelief, fear, and blame (e.g., Bloom, 1995; Burt, 1980; Field, 1978; Lebowitz & Roth, 1994). Moreover, the social context may foster a fear or distrust among trauma-exposed participants about the objectives and intentions of the research or research team members. This concern again suggests the possibility that trauma-exposed individuals might be more ready to anticipate or interpret certain questions or procedures as insulting or offensive. Understanding differences between participants' perceptions of, and expectations about, researchers' intent, empathy, and trustworthiness across participants in research studies could clarify whether this is a substantial concern. Similarly, consulting the clinical literature (e.g., on shame and trauma) and the experimental literature (e.g., shame) might help us understand the parameters of risk and ways to reduce shame-inducing procedures.

Vulnerability Question 4:
Does participation in research
on traumatic stress result in
greater physical risk?

Contrary to popular notions and fears, the physical hazards of being a research subject are minimal, even among medical procedures (Levine, 1981, p. 25). Obviously, each study needs to be carefully evaluated for potential physical risks, and trauma studies are no exception. For example, might certain research procedures elicit long-lasting and/or intense reactions (e.g., dissociative flashbacks) such that a research participant could experience immediate homicidal or suicidal urges? It might be useful to understand if any particular group of research participants is at risk for this occurrence. Additionally, follow-up studies might evaluate if research participation escalates ongoing violence and maltreatment among those research participants who are experiencing ongoing intrafamilial interpersonal violence. Evaluation of the prevalence and potential risk of such occurrences may help us to appreciate the relative risks and produce methods that prevent or minimize such problems.

Rewards of Research

■ The same empirical method of analysis can be applied to the hypothesized rewards and benefits of research on violence and trauma. Although the actual benefits as opposed to the intended benefits of a research project are often difficult to estimate prior to conducting a particular study (Keith-Spiegel & Koocher, 1985, p. 395), both the intended and actual rewards may be examined prospectively and retrospectively as part of any study. We briefly review some potential rewards of research and project possible directions for additional research. Although researchers' enthusiasm may tend to produce optimistic predictions regarding the intended benefits of research (Levine, 1981, p. 37), the collection of empirical data, over time, helps scientists develop realistic estimations of benefits.

Benefit Question 1:
Can talking and reflecting on trauma exposure and its impact be beneficial to health?

Pennebaker's substantial compendium of work suggests that writing about or talking about stressful life events results in increased positive mood states, health gains, and reduced use of health services (Pennebaker, 1993; Pennebaker, Barger, & Tiebout, 1989; Pennebaker & Beall, 1986; Pennebaker, Colder, & Sharp, 1990; Pennebaker, Kiecolt-Glaser, & Glaser,

1988; Pennebaker & Susman, 1988). Follow-up research to examine long-term beneficial health outcomes of study participation would also be useful. In addition, it may be possible that research participation is a safe way for individuals to begin engaging in help-seeking behaviors from mental health professionals. It may be useful to see how many people report research participation as an initial means of accessing health care.

Benefit Question 2:
Do research participants derive satisfaction from volunteering time to participate in such research?

Altruistic behavior and volunteer work have been hypothesized to enhance self-esteem and improve mood (e.g., Simmons, 1991). Research volunteers, regardless of trauma-exposure status, may experience these benefits following research participation. In addition, the satisfaction derived from making a valuable contribution to others or having an opportunity to express one's opinion can result in positive outcomes for certain individuals. Also, research participation may be a welcome diversion for people experiencing emotional pain. Understanding the motivation associated with research participation among trauma-exposed and non-trauma-exposed groups could provide a basis to understand intended benefits of research. Actual benefits could be assessed by having research participants rate the degree to which anticipated benefits were met. Between-group comparisons based on diagnostic and trauma-exposure status (PTSD vs. non-PTSD) could provide one line of evidence on the relative benefits of participation for trauma survivors.

Benefit Question 3:
Do trauma survivors feel empowered by transforming painful experiences into potentially helpful experiences for other people?

Some trauma survivors may experience the opportunity to contribute to science in a meaningful way to transform a negative, disruptive experience into one that could be potentially helpful to others. Systematically collecting data on the meaning of research participation to individuals would be advantageous. For example, it may be fruitful to establish to what degree research participants experience a sense of affiliation in relation to the intended beneficiaries of the research.

Informed Consent

■ In concordance with the principle of self-determination and autonomy, informed consent fulfills the researcher's obligation to provide a fair, respectful, and clear agreement between the research participant and the research staff. Informed consent requires that individuals feel free from coercive influences, are given all relevant information, comprehend the information, and are competent to consent. Although an extensive discussion of informed consent is beyond the scope of this chapter, we will briefly discuss three salient and controversial issues regarding studies of traumatic stress.

Informed Consent Issue 1:
Do you inform participants in a trauma study that they were selected on the basis of their status as trauma survivors?

Typically, prospective participants for a study are notified by phone or letter why they have been selected to participate in a particular study. One of the most controversial issues in studies of traumatic stress is whether to tell potential participants that they or some portion of the sample have been selected on the basis of suspicion or reports of family violence. Such information might make all respondents (targeted subjects and controls) less likely to participate and/or more likely to avoid revealing certain behaviors or emotions. Alternatively, such procedures might evoke emotional distress and mistrust or threaten confidentiality if others inadvertently read the recruitment letter or informed consent form. Is failure to provide this information a form of concealment or deception, or might it be viewed as legitimate protection of

the experimental validity of the protocol? Kinard (1985) argues that full disclosure about selection criteria when the research concerns sensitive information might result in harm because it could evoke distress, panic, or suspicion among participants and their families. Also, such a disclosure could compromise the confidentiality of participants among their fellow participants by suggesting that other participants are likely to be a member of social stigmatized group (Kinard, 1985). It may be useful to conduct surveys or focus groups with survivors and nonsurvivors about the best ways to preserve participants' faith in research while attending to the well-being of the public (e.g., Fisher, Higgens, Rau, Kuther-Qubeck, & Belanger, 1995).

Informed Consent Issue 2:
How do you tell people your interview asks about traumatic life events?

Whether or not a researcher chooses to tell potential participants about selection criteria, it is essential that they are informed about the nature of their participation in ways they can understand. Although most research on ethics has addressed the problem of establishing informed consent, we are unaware of research that concentrates on how best to establish informed consent in studies of traumatic stress. For example, although most investigators warn potential participants about possible aftereffects of research participation it is unknown how effective and understandable such information might be. Similarly, it is unknown how best to word consent forms to maximize understanding among potential participants about the nature of questions to be asked. One potential area of evidence to rely on may be research on phrasing questions in epidemiological studies of traumatic stress. For example, self-definitions of terms such as *abuse, rape,* and *neglect* have been found unreliable because people may have experienced or perpetrated events that are operationally defined as such but not perceived as such by the respondent (Koss, 1992; Lisak & Roth, 1990; Widom, 1988). Consultation on this research may be advisable in creating clearer consent forms.

Similarly, research examining the effects of wording on readability, participation rates, and satisfaction of respondents that specifically focuses on trauma survivors is needed. Ongoing studies might include a question in debriefing to assess if participants felt sufficiently prepared about the nature of the questions asked in the protocol. In addition, many researchers routinely rely on focus groups to help inform them about the needs, fears, and concerns of targeted samples for research. More systematic discussion of the lessons learned from focus groups would contribute valuable new knowledge to this research area.

Informed Consent Issue 3:
Do you tell prospective participants about the conditions under which you would break confidentiality?

Overdisclosure and underdisclosure each carries distinct risks and benefits (Levine, 1981, p. 76). Balancing the need for all information to be clear so that faith in the research process may be preserved without supplying so much information as to overwhelm potential participants can be difficult. This is most difficult in addressing issues of confidentiality. If a research team plans to break confidentiality in the case of emergencies when the participant or others are at risk of harm, research teams must decide how explicitly to state this in the consent form. Furthermore, research teams may vary in how detailed an example they provide the participant (e.g., emergencies, child or elder abuse, homicidal or suicidal plans, confidentiality is assured within confines of the law), and this in turn may affect participation rates and the type of data subsequently collected. Research on the impact of such disclosure on participation rates, reports of violence, and response bias indexes may provide important evidence to guide researchers in this area.

Although concerns about the need to violate confidentiality are substantial, we actually know very little about the frequency of risk involved in studies of mental health in general and, in particular, studies of trauma. Lidz, Mulvey, and Gardner (1993) provide a useful model of

how to ascertain such risks in their study of violence; they only needed to compromise confidentiality on 12 occasions (0.3%) over the course of the 4,000 interviews conducted with released psychiatric inpatients (Monahan et al., 1993). Similar studies regarding the parameters of confidentiality violations in studies of traumatic stress are clearly needed to conduct an accurate risk assessment in this field.

Major Challenges

■ Clearly, collecting and evaluating scientific evidence allows us to discriminate unsubstantiated claims from those with merit. As we have suggested, one of the major problems in the trauma field is the assumption that trauma survivors differ significantly from nonsurvivors in terms of research vulnerability and benefits. Importantly, it is unclear if concerns about risk apply to all individuals who were exposed to traumatic events or if the concern is limited to those individuals who became symptomatic in response to the events. Similarly, there is a claim that questions about trauma exposure substantially differ from questions about other significant life events. Unfortunately, no research has examined these issues using a comparison group of individuals. In fact, much to our surprise, little research is available to inform ethical decision making about the parameters of risk among most samples of research participants. Thus, although important concerns have been raised in relation to trauma research, it is our contention that most of the ethical concerns are equally applicable to studies outside the field of traumatic stress.

This lack of research evidence may be due to several methodological challenges. One major obstacle facing researchers is determining whether the research context elicits unique reactions that are not part of the person's symptomatic condition. This question appears reminiscent to concerns once raised over whether asking individuals about suicidal and homicidal ideation might foster such experiences. Specifically in relation to traumatic stress, we need to understand more fully if research that focuses on traumatic life events elicits symptoms, or if the symptoms that occur in trauma-exposed people's lives are expressed or experienced in the interview (e.g., Cook, 1995). With little understanding of the phasic and longitudinal course of most mental disorders, including PTSD, this may be a difficult but worthy issue to examine.

Second, when trying to assess the potential risk and benefits of research participation, it becomes difficult to separate the degree to which changes in a person are a direct result of research participation as opposed to the timing of participation. For example, research participation might coincide with, foster, or mitigate a course of decline in someone's disorder. Conversely, an increase in self-interest and help-seeking may simultaneously occur with an invitation to participate in research. Therefore, specifying with accuracy the relative benefits and risks becomes a difficult task. Methodological creativity needs to address this problem. In the meantime, integrating the participants' subjective appraisal of the meaning and impact of research participation may add worthwhile information in understanding this complex relationship.

Future Research

■ Throughout this chapter we have emphasized that studies of ethics can be easily incorporated in a cost-effective manner into ongoing projects by systematically collecting data on the research participants' perceived distress, benefit, and cost of participation. For example, as part of debriefing procedures, investigators can collect systematic data on participants' experiences (e.g., E. B. Carlson, personal communication, June 8, 1995; Parkes, 1995) and comprehension of informed consent. Similarly, follow-up studies regarding the impact of participating in such research can be readily conducted (e.g., Cook & Bosley, 1995). Such data will allow us to know, given the heterogeneity of trauma survivors, which particular trauma-exposed group may be at greatest risk for problems attendant to participation in research protocols. Eventually, such work can be integrated into manuals for consul-

tation by investigators and institutional review boards.

Second, information gathered in the course of a study can be used dynamically to direct the protocol in ways that might increase benefit or reduce harm as the study is conducted. For example, measures of participant distress, perceived harm, and benefit could be collected and examined at regular intervals to guide data gathering. These data could provide feedback to the investigator regarding the effects of each component within a protocol. For example, if subjective units of distress scores (SUDS) ratings were especially high for one or more tasks they could be discontinued early.

In addition, experimental designs that address ethical questions can be readily embedded into ongoing research protocols. For example, it might be useful for trauma researchers to insert two different recruitment strategies or different versions of consent forms into a particular study design. This would allow for the examination of participation rates, completion rates, and number of questions refused across groups thereby increasing our understanding of the impact of certain research recruitment or consent procedures.

Finally, as we have suggested, research that specifically addresses ethical concerns in relation to traumatic stress is needed. Primary research might address consent issues related to asking about traumatic life events, the benefits and harms of violating confidentiality under certain conditions (e.g., protective services), or participant's appraisal of the benefits and costs of the research process. For example, one study might examine content (potentially traumatic events, divorce, bereavement) by format (surveys, interviews, computerized format) to determine the emotional reactions across different samples. Another might consist of a survey comparing the experiences of trauma researchers with those who conduct similar studies in other specialty areas. Clearly, as our factual knowledge regarding ethics grows, we can better identify groups that incur injury, procedures that provoke strong emotional reactions, and the types of specific risks involved in various protocols. With this knowledge, trauma researchers will be in a substantially better position to conduct meaningful research in the safest possible research environment.

Research Policy Directions

■ Over time, procedures that inform ethical concerns can be routinely incorporated into research studies. Findings can then be included in formal reports of these studies. For example, researchers might routinely summarize information on refusal rates and no-shows as part of the Method section on recruitment. Similarly, reporting instances in which confidentiality needed to be violated might become an important part of the Method section of a research report. In the Results sections, authors might offer the mean number of items left unanswered by content area or group. Eventually, we imagine that such practices could evolve more fully into a requisite Ethics section that addresses the nature of informed consent, confidentiality, and the types of problems encountered during the conduct of the study.

In addition, it would be useful to create a professional forum to share critical incidents and negative outcomes of research. This could be accomplished via an electronic forum medium such as the Internet, ethics journals, or a national clearinghouse. The exchange of such information could be instrumental in pinpointing potential dilemmas and avoiding errors previously made. Such work will allow us to define and convey the relative risks and benefits in trauma research and help us to identify ways of minimizing risk. Furthermore, it would provide a basis on which to train emerging researchers about recent developments in the ethical practice of psychological sciences.

Summary

■ In this review, we have illustrated how assumptions about the nature of research with trauma survivors and perpetrators can be addressed, and in some cases resolved, by reviewing the extant empirical research. Although in many cases, judgments about a protocol may ul-

timately rely on value judgments, the integration of evidence from research can remove speculations and bias in arriving at decisions of the relative merits of a particular study on trauma.

Our goal has been to urge the scientific community to reflect on ethical choices and patterns of decision making and integrate empirical evidence into this process. We encourage researchers to be proactive in gathering empirical evidence to delineate both the relative vulnerabilities of their research participants and the relative costs and benefits to participants of research protocols on trauma. By such rational approaches, we hope that researchers may anticipate potential problems and use advance planning to minimize any potential ethical problems that might emerge during a protocol, thereby facilitating positive outcomes for all involved.

References

American Psychiatric Association. (1994). *Diagnostic and statistical manual of mental disorders* (4th ed.). Washington, DC: Author.

American Psychological Association. (1981). Ethical principles of psychologists. *American Psychologist, 36,*, 633-638.

Bayer, R. (1990). Beyond the burdens of protection: AIDS and the ethics of research. *Evaluation Review, 14,* 443-446.

Bergen, R. K. (1993). Interviewing survivors of marital rape: Doing feminist research on sensitive topics. In C. M. Renzetti & R. M. Lee (Eds.), *Researching sensitive topics* (pp. 197-211). Newbury Park, CA: Sage.

Bloom, S. L. (1995). When good people do bad things: Meditations on the "backlash." *Journal of Psychohistory, 22,* 274-305.

Burt, M. R. (1980). Cultural myths and supports for rape. *Journal of Personality and Social Psychology, 38,* 217-230.

Castor-Lewis, C. (1988). On doing research with adult incest survivors: Some initial thoughts and considerations. *Women & Therapy, 7,* 73-80.

Ceci, S. J., Peters, D., & Plotkin, J. (1985). Human subjects review, personal values, and regulation of social science research. *American Psychologist, 40,* 994-1002.

Cook, A. S. (1995). Ethical issues in bereavement research: An overview. *Death Studies, 19,* 103-122.

Cook, A. S., & Bosley, G. (1995). The experience of participating in bereavement research: Stressful or therapeutic. *Death Studies, 19,* 157-170.

Department of Health and Human Services. (1981). Final regulations amending basic HHS policy for the protection of human research subjects. *Federal Register, 46,* 8366-8391. (Codified as 45 C.F.R. pt. 46)

Field, H. S. (1978). Attitudes toward rape: A comparative analysis of police, rapists, crisis counselors, and citizens. *Journal of Personality and Social Psychology, 36,* 156-179.

Fisher, C. B., Higgens, A., Rau, M. B., Kuther-Qubeck, T. L., & Belanger, S. (1995, August). *Referring and reporting research participants: A view from urban adolescents.* Poster presented at the 103rd annual American Psychological Association, New York.

Keith-Spiegel, P. (1976). Children's rights as participants in research. In G. P. Koocher (Ed.), *Children's rights and the mental health professions* (pp. 53-82). New York: John Wiley.

Keith-Spiegel, P., & Koocher, G. P. (1985). *Ethics in psychology: Professional standards and cases.* New York: Random House.

Kinard, M. (1985). Ethical issues in research with abused children. *Child Abuse & Neglect, 9,* 301-311.

Koss, M. P. (1992). The underdetection of rape: Methodological choices influence incidence estimates. *Journal of Social Issues, 48,* 61-75.

Lebowitz, L., & Roth, S. (1994). I felt like a slut: The cultural context and women's response to being raped. *Journal of Traumatic Stress, 7,* 363-390.

Levine, M. (1981). *Ethics and regulation of clinical research.* Baltimore: Urban & Schwarsenberg.

Lidz, C., Mulvey, E., & Gardner, W. (1993). The accuracy of predictions of violence to others. *Journal of the American Medical Association, 269,* 1007-1011.

Lisak, D., & Roth, S. (1990). Motives and psychodynamics of self-reported unincarcerated rapists. *American Journal of Orthopsychiatry, 60,* 268-280.

Lisman, S. A., & Brandon, T. H. (1995). Alcohol, ethics, and research: Implications for science and practice. *Division 50 Newsletter, 2,* 10.

Monahan, J., Appelbaum, P. S., Mulvey, E. P., Robbins, P. C., & Lidz, C. W. (1993). Ethical and legal duties in conducting research on violence. *Violence and Victims, 8,* 387-396.

National Commission for the Protection of Human Subjects of Biomedical and Behavioral Research. (1978). *The Belmont Report: Ethical principles and guidelines for the protection of human subjects of research* (DHEW Publication No. OS 78-0012). Washington, DC: Department of Health, Education, and Welfare.

Nuremberg Code. (1949). *Trials of war criminals before the Nuremberg Military tribunals under control council law no. 10, 2,* p. 181. Washington, DC: Government Printing Office.

Parkes, C. M. (1995). Guidelines for conducting ethical bereavement research. *Death Studies, 19* 171-181.

Pennebaker, J. W. (1993). Putting stress into words: Health, linguistic and therapeutic implications. *Behavior Research and Therapy, 31,* 539-548.

Pennebaker, J. W., Barger, S. D., & Tiebout, J. (1989). Disclosure of traumas and health among Holocaust survivors. *Psychosomatic Medicine, 51,* 577-589.

Pennebaker, J. W., & Beall, S. K. (1986). Confronting a traumatic event: Toward an understanding of inhibition and disease. *Journal of Abnormal Psychology, 95,* 274-281.

Pennebaker, J. W., Colder, M., & Sharp, L. K. (1990). Accelerating the coping process. *Journal of Personality and Social Psychology, 58,* 528-537.

Pennebaker, J. W., Kiecolt-Glaser, J. K., & Glaser, R. (1988). Disclosure of traumas and immune function: Health implications for psychotherapy. *Journal of Consulting and Clinical Psychology, 56,* 239-245.

Pennebaker, J. W., & Susman, J. R. (1988). Disclosure of traumas and psychosomatic processes. *Social Science and Medicine, 26,* 327-332. [Special issue: Stress and coping in relation to health and disease]

Reinharz, S., & Davidman, L. (1992). *Feminist methods in social research.* New York: Oxford University Press.

Sieber, J. E. (1993). The ethics and politics of sensitive research. In C. M. Renzetti & R. M. Lee (Eds.), *Researching sensitive topics* (pp. 14-26). Newbury Park, CA: Sage.

Simmons, R. G. (1991). Altruism and sociology. *Sociological Quarterly, 32,* 1-22.

Urquiza, A. J. (1991). Retrospective methodology in family violence research. *Journal of Interpersonal Violence, 6,* 119-126.

Widom, C. (1988). Sampling biases and implications for child abuse research. *American Journal of Orthopsychiatry, 5,* 260-270.

CHAPTER 22

Ethical Dimensions of Intervention With Violent Partners

Priorities in the Values and Beliefs of Practitioners

Gilles Rondeau
Jocelyn Lindsay
Ginette Beaudoin
Normand Brodeur

☐ This chapter is about an exploratory research project conducted in collaboration with the Quebec Association of Resources Working With Violent Partners (ARIHV[1]) on the ethical dimensions involved in direct practice with violent partners. The research is both qualitative and quantitative in its nature, and we hope to establish an inventory of the principal ethical dilemmas that confront the practitioners and to identify their means of resolution. This chapter

AUTHORS' NOTE: This chapter was originally presented as a paper at the 4th International Family Violence Research Conference, Durham, New Hampshire, July 1995. For information, contact Gilles Rondeau at École de service social, Université de Montreal, C.P. 6128, Succ.Centre-Ville, Montreal, Quebec H3C 3J7 Canada, e-mail: rondeaug@ere.umontreal.ca; or Jocelyn Lindsay at École de service social, Université Laval, Ste-Foy, Quebec, G1K 7P4 Canada, e-mail: jocelyn.lindsay@svs.ulaval.ca.

will present mainly the results of one aspect of the research, that of identifying the principal values of practitioners with regard to their ethical preoccupation.

Context and Objectives of the Research

■ Intervention with violent partners constitutes a new form of practice that in the past 10 years was established and developed quickly. Across Quebec, there are now more than 25 organizations offering programs to violent partners designed to help them put an end to their violent behavior. These organizations are, for the most part (more than 20 of them), members of the ARIHV, which constitutes on the provincial level the principal spokesman for them. The ARIHV also organizes meetings and debates and encourages reflection about this field of practice. In other respects, in the context of the current reform, the Ministry of Health and Social Services (MSSS) adopted in 1992, following an in-depth consultation with organizations concerned with conjugal violence, a document that defines the preferred orientations with regard to violent partners (Gouvernement du Québec, 1992).

If most of the energy of the member organizations of the ARIHV has to date been mobilized essentially by questions relative to the establishment, maintenance, and survival of programs, the recent agreements with MSSS have provided relative stability for organizations and consequently for newly arising considerations. Among these are the problems and ethical dilemmas experienced daily by frontline workers.

Practitioners working with violent partners are confronted with difficult problems and ethical dilemmas. Their situation is relatively similar to that experienced by other practitioners in related fields, but seems more acute because of many factors such as the nature of the clientele, the type of problems they present, and the societal and ideological debates that mark this type of intervention. These problems and dilemmas create malaise, tension, and hesitation in relations with clients, and with other people and or-

ganizations working in partnership. They are thus serious obstacles to establishing a productive alliance with the client and to developing a real collaborative approach with other resources in the community.

If the theoretical literature on ethics and professional values is relatively abundant, there is little actual field research. For example, in social work, Holland and Kilpatrick (1991) underline the lack of systematic studies concerning ethical questions in current practice. They mention that we know very little about how social workers come to terms with ethical and moral questions, how they understand them and integrate them into different aspects of their work or what resources are used and are necessary to ameliorate this regard for professional ethics and the decision making that follows from it. Their study of 27 social workers brought to light the fact that none of the respondents mentioned his or her professional code of ethics as a resource to negotiate complex ethical problems. Each one expressed a sense of solitude and isolation when having to cope with questions of a moral nature.

Cossom (1992) cites Congress, who comes to the same conclusions "that while social work has written much about its ethics and values, there is a paucity of study of practitioners' values, ethical knowledge, perceptions, attitudes and practice, or the basis for these" (Congress, 1986, p. 18).

The objectives of this research project are as follows:

1. Establish an inventory of major problems and ethical dilemmas with which practitioners working with violent partners are confronted

2. Identify solutions and strategies used by practitioners when they are confronted with ethical dilemmas related to violence

3. List the most important values identified by practitioners with regard to their ethical preoccupations

4. Develop a helpful strategy for practitioners and propose a plan for its application.

In this chapter, the data presented relate to the third objective.

Underlying Factors of Ethical Questioning

■ The interest in ethics by organizations working with violent partners should be seen primarily in a larger social context where moral questions have become central. In the past several years, governments, scientists, and members of different professions showed a renewed interest in ethics. This interest followed profound changes in values associated with sweeping social transformations. Among these, one notes, for example, the disintegrating of religious convictions, the composition of an increasingly multiethnic and multicultural society, the growing influence of charters of rights or rights acts that have been passed, the crisis of the welfare state, and the influences of technological advances.

Ethical questioning on the part of organizations should also be viewed in light of problems that confront the helping professions in general. These face skepticism by the public that, informed about numerous cases of abuse by professionals, questions "the capacity of professions to monitor and deal with unethical behaviour of their members, and to protect the public they serve" (Cossom, 1992, p. 165).

In addition, since the coming into force of modifications to the Health and Social Services Law in 1993, community organizations are now officially recognized in Quebec as partners in the network of public social services (Gouvernement du Québec, 1994). These changes in the governmental policies prompt organizations to adjust their practice norms to those of the public sector.

Interest for ethical issues on the part of community organizations working with violent partners can also be seen as part of a process to better establish the credibility of their services and to increase their prestige and attain a higher social status because of their subscribing to highly ethical principles.

In other respects, one must also consider the criticism to which organizations working with violent partners are subjected to understand the meaning of this move. Because of limited results and the risk of violence to the victims, intervention with violent partners has been and remains a practice whose results are closely scrutinized and continues to be viewed by many with suspicion.

Also, the complementarity of helping services to victims raises many questions, particularly with regard to the degree of loyalty that is due to the victims, the respect for the confidential nature of the revelations of the men, and the theoretical approaches to be adopted to guide intervention.

Judicial intervention and therapeutic intervention with men follow a common objective, to foster a sense of responsibility. In all cases, the function of "helping" exercised by organizations and that of "social control" exercised by the judicial system are perceived by some practitioners as being incompatible (Bélanger, 1994). One recognizes the complementary nature and the legitimacy of each of these interventions taken independently. But it is much more difficult to define how the systems of help and of control can intervene together. The problem becomes particularly evident when determining the nature and the content of communications that must be established between the partner organizations for them to collaborate effectively.

Therapeutic intervention with partners who are in the justice system also presents problems regarding help under constraint. At the time of referral, the client in the justice system is rarely suffering or motivated to change.

Major Ethical Dilemmas Reviewed in the Literature

■ Overall, this research project chooses to emphasize the perceptions and points of view of practitioners facing different ethical dilemmas in their practice. By *ethical dilemma,* we refer to a situation in which two or more ethical principles in the code of ethics are in conflict, and where a response is required that must honor one or more principles at the expense of one or more other principles (Kugelman-Jaffee, cited by Cossom, 1992). As this definition suggests, solving ethical dilemmas requires considering values and beliefs with regard to professional practice with violent partners. Here we will clarify the issues associated with the most significant dilemmas confronting practitioners in organizations for violent partners. These dilemmas are subdivided into three areas, those of loyalty, confidentiality, and conflicting values.

Loyalty

In the field of conjugal violence, one observes that a certain number of ideas form the basis for a large consensus. For example, one can easily recognize that violence is unacceptable in the context of intimate relationships and is seen as a criminal act like any other violent aggression. One agrees also to the necessity of protecting the victim and to the fact that a concurrent intervention with the aggressor is legitimate. On the other hand, there are numerous differences of opinion. These can be attributed to divergent explanations of the causes of the violence, the socioeconomic position of the people involved in the debate, the professional affiliations (e.g., social work, psychology, criminology) of the people involved, and differences in the particular roles of each organization.

The difficulty in defining who is the client for organizations working with violent partners illustrates the multiple points of view, the fragile nature of the consensus on matters of conjugal violence, and the resulting ethical dilemmas. Indeed, whom should the organization consider to be its client? Is it essentially the man who is in treatment, or is it more accurately the woman and children victims of the violence who are the clients? Would it be appropriate to consider the family unit in its totality as the actual client? Finally, some say that the client is the person or organization that referred the man for help. Thus, one can ask, up to what point are organizations for violent partners indebted to the justice system that refers them clients? The responses to these questions have an important impact on practice. They help to determine to whom the practitioner should be loyal in the event of a divergence of interests between the parties concerned. Because settling this debate once and for all is impossible, the practitioner must, at the very least, be capable of setting priorities among the people or groups vying for his or her loyalty. The next section of this chapter explores the elements of this dilemma in greater detail.

From a strictly professional point of view, the client is usually the person or the group to whom the practitioner renders services. If the members of the family or the couple are not seen together by the practitioner, the individual must be considered to be the client. It is to him and him alone that the professional must be loyal. This concept stems from a long psychotherapeutic tradition in which the individual and the therapist are the principal actors. It depends principally on the idea that a therapeutic alliance is an essential condition for the help provided to be effective. For this alliance to develop, the person who comes for help must be assured of the complete support of the therapist and have the conviction that the therapist is working for the client's interests.

The feminist perspective takes an opposing stance. Instead of putting emphasis on individual ethics, this model is built on a social ethic in which violence is understood as an act of domination of men over women. Consequently, the intervention must first of all serve the interests of the victim, who belongs to the dominated group. The objectives of intervention with violent men should therefore be designed in such a way as to increase the freedom of women and their sense of security. To meet these objectives, the man must become conscious of the control that he exercises over his partner, and then concentrate on satisfying her needs (Dankwort, 1988).

The family is considered by many as bearing a very important social value that must be preserved. In this perspective, its integrity must be maintained, notably with the purpose of providing the children with a stable environment. Those who are in a relationship where there is conjugal violence often hold these values. Even the victims who use the services designed to help them are imbued with the value of maintaining the family, even when it poses a threat to their security (Martin & Lavoie, 1986). For the men who ask for services from violent partners programs, the maintenance of the nuclear family and of the conjugal relationship is often the primary source of motivation to participate in treatment. They agree to go for consultation in the hope that their partner will return home or that she will not go through with her threat to leave. Consequently, professionals are under the pressure of individuals who demand their intervention with the goal of preserving the integrity of the family and helping the family to regain its harmony.

Organizations for violent partners can consider one last group as their clients: the institutions of the justice or correctional system that refer men to treatment programs. In probation, suspended sentence, or parole situations, it is these institutions that judge the behavior of the man to be unacceptable and who ultimately demand change from the individual who comes for treatment. In addition, they often have rules and demands that organizations for violent partners must respect (Broué & Guèvremont, 1994). It may seem strange to label these institutions as clients, because they do not benefit directly from the intervention. Nevertheless, they exert a sufficiently noteworthy influence that one must examine the degree of loyalty given to them by the organizations and their practitioners.

Confidentiality

In the context of a therapeutic relationship, confidentiality refers to the obligation incumbent on the professional to keep secret the information divulged by the client (Gosselin, 1991). In general, confidentiality of information obtained in the context of the relationship with the client must be maintained apart from any person outside of the client-worker relationship.

Respect for confidentiality constitutes an indispensable ingredient in the construction of an effective therapeutic relationship, because it permits the establishment and maintenance of confidence between the therapist and the client. In effect, the confidential character of communications allows the latter to consult without fear of being stigmatized or punished because of his problems. Knowing that the exchange occurs under a veil of secrecy, the client is encouraged to reveal all information that is pertinent to the resolution of his difficulties (McWhinney, Haskins-Herkenham, & Hare, 1992). Confidentiality also allows the client to develop the conviction that the practitioner is concerned with him,

that he or she will not judge the client, and that he or she believes in the client's capacity to change (Sonkin & Allison, 1986), which facilitates effective change.

When confidentiality comes into conflict with other values, it can be considered from two differing philosophical perspectives. It is seen as an absolute by those who believe that action must be guided by principles evaluated as intrinsically good (Goldberg, 1989). In this perspective, confidentiality must come before all other considerations, given the value with which it is recognized. For others, confidentiality is relative. This point of view is based in the utilitarian tradition that is more concerned with the consequences expected to result from actions (Goldberg, 1989). What counts is not the intrinsic value of the principle but the consequences of its application for the individual and for society. It seems therefore to be legitimate to breach confidentiality if the benefits to society surpass the damage caused to the relationship.

The question of the absolute or relative nature of confidentiality becomes truly meaningful when it is juxtaposed with the principle of the moral obligation to protect persons in danger. One can think of three possible scenarios: those where a potentially violent client represents a threat to an adult victim, where the behavior of the client compromises the security and the development of a child, and where the individual is a threat to himself.

In the United States, the need to protect has received a great deal of attention in the literature in the past 20 years, following an affirmation of the principle in a number of judicial decisions that became jurisprudence. These decisions had an effect on the therapeutic community, which has had to adjust to new norms. The 1976 *Tarasoff* case introduced the notion of the duty to protect whereby the therapist must directly inform the potential victim of the danger (Sonkin, 1986).

Most American states and Canadian provinces have adopted laws that delineate in a much stricter fashion the need to protect children. In fact, according to the Youth Protection Act of Quebec, "Any person, even someone bound by professional secret, who has a reasonable motive to believe that the security or the development of a child is endangered, . . . has the obligation to report without delay the situation to the director [of youth protection]" (Gouvernement du Québec, 1991, Loi sur la protection de la jeunesse, Article 39, our translation).

The law gives professionals immunity against any legal action taken by those involved in the reporting of the case (Gouvernement du Québec, 1991, Loi sur la protection de la jeunesse, Article 43). This creates a breach in the principle of confidentiality because the professional is relieved from the obligation of secrecy and is obliged to report to an outside authority some of the confidences or facts that he or she learned of in the context of the relationship with the client. The obligatory nature of reporting has given rise to many types of criticism: about its impact on the client-worker relationship, about the perverse effects stemming from the obligatory nature of alerting the authorities, and about the effectiveness of the organizations mandated to help child victims and their families.

A final type of situation exists in cases where the duty to protect could supersede the respect for confidentiality, for example, where the client constitutes a threat to himself (Corey, Corey, & Callanan, 1988).

The protection of the client who is a threat to himself raises less controversy than the situations previously discussed, because the ethical dilemma is not of the same nature. In fact, protection of third parties forces the professional to weigh the rights of his or her client against those of others and of society as a whole. In contrast, the protection of the client from himself reflects a paternalistic approach (Leong, Silva, & Weinstock, 1988) The dilemma consists of determining to what extent it is legitimate to act in the interest of the individual despite his opposition to the actions taken.

Conflicting Values

In addition to questions of loyalty and of confidentiality, we examine the possible value conflicts between the practitioner and the client. In this respect, three principles can be seen as difficult to apply: neutrality, self-determination, and informed consent. The practitioner and the client confront their values in the course of their exchanges. Such a confrontation is even more complex in the context of a group intervention, because of the number of individuals taking part in the interaction. In addition, the value issues cannot be reduced to personal values, because each person carries also the values of the social group to which he or she belongs. The values expressed by the client can, for example, reflect his or her belonging to a social class, a religion, or a particular ethnic group. In other respects, the practitioner expresses with more or less conviction the values of his or her profession and of the organization for which he or she works.

The interventions that touch on family life potentially comprise a number of value conflicts, because the clients, the professionals, and the institutions can have very different ideas regarding how to maintain family unity, extramarital relations, or gender roles (Margolin, 1982). Intervention with aggressors raises conflicts of values from the beginning as the aggressive behavior, a priori, is judged unacceptable, and the objective of treatment is to end it (Rondeau, 1993).

For many, the role of professionals is to help the clients to find solutions to their problems. The professionals do not have the mandate to crusade for their own personal values, nor do they have the right to judge those of their clients in terms of what is right or wrong (Wendorf & Wendorf, 1985). Solutions to problems must be found that respect the values of the clients. In this perspective, neutrality—meaning abstaining from taking the side of one or the other party—is in order.

On the other hand, abstaining from making judgments in these situations engenders confusion, considering the impact of actions against the victims. The silence of the practitioner about his or her own values with regard to violence can itself be interpreted as an indication of complicity with the aggressor (Bograd, 1992). For this reason, the capacity to make a moral judgment in situations of violence is an important therapeutic tool (Willbach, 1989).

Other situations raise the issue of neutrality of the practitioners, such as the attribution of the source of family problems to dysfunctional family interactions as well as the social control function played by the programs.

The egalitarian ideal implies that the client is considered to be a responsible, rational, and competent person who has the right to self-determination and respect for his or her individuality. Despite his or her vulnerability, the client is free to make choices. The practitioner is not authorized to make decisions in the client's place, or to impose his or her own values on the client. The antithesis of the right for self-determination is paternalism, in which the individual in a position of authority intervenes to protect a person from the consequences of his or her own actions (Huston, 1984). Paternalism can be justified in situations where the competence of the individual is limited.

In a context of authority, the obligatory nature of treatment sends a message that the values the individual has acted on are unacceptable and that he must acquire other values, which he will learn in the course of treatment. By putting in place an apparatus designed to control the behavior of the client and/or in obliging him to undergo a process of rehabilitation, social institutions are judging him to be incompetent. The right to self-determination is therefore put to severe test.

There is a clear consensus that consent of the client must be obtained before proceeding with treatment. For the consensus to be valid, the client must receive all of the pertinent information. This can touch on, among other things, the objectives and the content of the intervention, the length of time and expected costs, and the elements of confidentiality. The objective in requiring the consent of the client is to increase his level of understanding of the therapeutic process. In this sense, a clear consent can be defined as a continuous process of information that is carried throughout the therapy. Some factual information can be given to the client in a routine way. In contrast, the discussion of the limits of treatment programs with clients requires more tact, especially at the beginning of the program. Practitioners therefore find themselves in a delicate position, where they wish to provide objective information about the effectiveness of their services and, at the same time, raise the hope of change and the confidence in their ability to help (Sonkin, 1986).

Values and Beliefs of the Practitioners

■ A questionnaire was mailed in December 1994 to all practitioners who had a minimum of 6 months of experience ($N = 81$) and were employed by 1 of the 30 resources operating in Quebec that specialized in working with violent partners. Of these resources, 21 were members of the ARIHV. Two resources from the public sector and two others from the private sector were added as well as five community resources not members of ARIHV. Altogether this list included all identified organizations working with violent partners in Quebec except one that declined the invitation to take part in the research. The purpose of the survey was to (a) establish an inventory of the major problems and ethical dilemmas the practitioners were confronted with, (b) identify the solutions and strategies they used in these instances, and (c) list the most important values they identified with regard to their ethical preoccupations.

In total, 45 practitioners of 81 responded to the mailed questionnaire (response rate: 55%). The questionnaire is composed of five sections: personal characteristics, organizational characteristics of the resources, principal values selected, actual dilemmas and the difficulties they represent, and resolution of ethical dilemmas. In this chapter, we present a summary profile of the respondents, and the results from the third section of the questionnaire, which deals with the principal values selected by the practitioners.

Of those who responded, 80.0% were men and 20.0% were women, and were on average 39 years old. A total of 51.1% of practitioners hold a bachelor's degree and 33.3% have a master's degree. The disciplines studied were mainly social work (36.1%) and psychology (25.0%). Almost half of the respondents (46.6%) had between 6 months and 3 years of experience in intervention with violent partners. The others had more.

Section 3 of the questionnaire consisted of 33 statements about values and beliefs associated with the professional practice with violent partners. For each statement, the respondent had to indicate the degree to which he or she agreed

TABLE 22.1 Statements Dealing With the Philosophy of Intervention

Statement	Agree		Disagree		Total	
	%	n	%	n	%	n
3. It is correct for a practitioner to influence his or her clients so that they will adopt healthier values with regard to the problem of violence	76.8	33	23.2	10	100.0	43
7. It is important to distinguish between the person and his behavior	95.5	43	4.4	2	100.0	45
11. Challenging the way of life of the client is a role of the practitioner	35.5	16	64.4	29	100.0	45
14. The practitioner should remain neutral regardless of the values of the client	36.4	16	63.6	28	100.0	45
23. The therapeutic alliance with the client is essential to change	88.8	40	11.1	5	100.0	45
27. The practitioner cannot remain neutral when faced with certain attitudes or comments by the client that, according to him, are related to the problem of violence	91.1	41	8.8	4	100.0	45
28. The practitioner must subtly bring the client around to reconsidering his values	75.6	34	24.4	11	100.0	45
31. The practitioner can express his or her values, but should not impose them on the clients	91.1	41	8.9	4	100.0	45

or disagreed. The statements covered the following dimensions: the philosophy of intervention, intervention, confidentiality in the context of intervention and in collaboration with other organizations or professionals, codes of ethics, loyalty, the analysis of violence, confidentiality and the duty to protect, and the roles of organizations or of programs for violent partners.

Table 22.1[2] shows that the majority of practitioners agree with most of the statements dealing with the philosophical dimension of intervention (Statements 7, 23, 27, and 31). The most divergent opinions on the part of the practitioners are with regard to Statements 11 and 14. More than one third of the respondents believe that challenging the way of life of the clients is a part of the role of the professional (Statement 11); however, the majority (64.4%) estimate that this is not a part of their role. Two thirds (63.6%) responded elsewhere that the practitioner should remain neutral with regard to the values of the client (Statement 14), compared to 36.4% who disagreed with this approach. In general, then, the practitioners seem to be saying that one cannot be neutral but should, with subtlety, bring the client to reconsider his values, without ever imposing one's own, and without going as far as challenging the way of life of the clients.

The practitioners are unanimously in agreement, or very largely in agreement, with the statements presented about "intervention" (Table 22.2). All the respondents (100.0%) believe that the practitioner should inform the client in such a way that he can make informed choices (Statement 18). One can see that 97.8% of the respondents agreed that practitioners should always underline the responsibility of the client for his violent actions (Statement 30). It is with regard to Statement 19 that one can see less of a convergence in the responses. However, almost 90% of the practitioners believe that the violent partners have a greater need for therapy than for a controlling environment to bring about change.

There are certain oppositions in the responses to statements regarding confidentiality in the context of intervention and in collaboration with other organizations or other professionals (Table 22.3). Although 95.6% of the practitioners believe that to combat violence, there must be direct collaboration between all the organizations involved (Statement 21),

TABLE 22.2 Statements Dealing With the Dimension of Intervention

Statement	Agree		Disagree		Total	
	%	n	%	n	%	n
17. Before commencing a group intervention, the practitioner must inform the clients of the goals, rules, techniques, and procedures employed	95.6	43	4.4	2	100.0	45
18. The practitioner must inform the client in such a way that he can make informed decisions	100.0	45	—	—	100.0	45
19. Violent partners have a greater need for therapy than for a controlling environment in order to bring about change	88.9	40	11.1	5	100.0	45
29. In working with the client, the practitioner must actively and systematically denounce all forms of violence	93.4	42	6.6	3	100.0	45
30. The practitioner must always underline the responsibility of the client for his violent actions	97.8	44	2.2	1	100.0	45

64.5% of the respondents also agreed with the statement that the practitioner need not communicate with the women's shelter information about the client (Statement 20). In addition, 77.8% of respondents do not believe that the practitioner should communicate as much information as possible to the probation officer (Statement 12). This does not mean, however, that the practitioner does not pass on some information.

For those statements referring to codes of ethics, one can see in Table 22.4 that the practitioners agree almost unanimously with the fact that they must respect and be familiar with the codes of ethics of their professions and of their organization.

The question of loyalty, that is, to determine who indeed is the client, is another area mentioned in the literature. One can see in Table 22.5 how the responses of the practitioners are not unanimous on the statements dealing with this question. Although 95.5% of respondents believe that the practitioner must first and foremost be loyal to the consulting client (Statement 2), almost 40% indicated that the practitioner must be loyal primarily to the organization that referred the consulting client (Statement 10), and 36.3% responded that the practitioner should be loyal primarily to the victim of the consulting client (Statement 16). The contradiction in the given responses to Statements 10 and 16 com-

TABLE 22.3 Statements Dealing With the Dimension of Confidentiality in the Context of Intervention and in Collaboration With Other Organizations and Professionals

Statement	Agree		Disagree		Total	
	%	n	%	n	%	n
1. In a therapeutic relationship, confidentiality must be absolute	90.9	40	9.1	4	100.0	44
9. Clients must be informed at the beginning of the intervention of the limits of confidentiality	97.7	44	2.2	1	100.0	45
12. The practitioner should communicate as much information as possible to the probation officer	22.2	16	77.8	35	100.0	45
20. The practitioner need not communicate with the women's shelter information about the client	64.5	29	35.5	16	100.0	45
21. In order to combat violence, there must be close collaboration between all the organizations involved	95.6	43	4.4	2	100.0	45

TABLE 22.4 Statements Dealing With Codes of Ethics

Statement	Agree		Disagree		Total	
	%	n	%	n	%	n
8. The practitioner must familiarize him- or herself with the code of ethics of his or her profession	100.0	45	—	—	100.0	45
25. The practitioner must respect the code of ethics of his or her profession at all times	100.0	45	—	—	100.0	45
22. The practitioner must familiarize him- or herself with the code of ethics of his or her organization	100.0	45	—	—	100.0	45
33. The practitioner must respect the code of ethics of his or her organization at all times	97.8	44	2.2	1	100.0	45

pared with Statement 2 illustrates this dilemma of loyalty.

Using Table 22.6, let us now look at how practitioners respond to the statements dealing with confidentiality and the duty to protect. Respondents agree unanimously that the practitioner must take action to protect a person threatened by a dangerous client (Statement 15) and must respect the laws that oblige professionals to report all situations abusive to a minor (Statement 24). For the obligation to take action to protect a client who demonstrates suicidal tendencies (Statement 4), 97.7% are in agreement with this statement.

It is with regard to the statements dealing with the analysis of violence (Table 22.7) that one encounters the most divergent opinions among the respondents. Statement 32, "Violence is a relational process in which man and woman share responsibility to some degree," divides the respondents into two camps (50.0% agree, 50.0% disagree). On the other hand, almost 40% of respondents believe that male violence toward women is mainly attributable to in-

dividual factors (Statement 13). At the same time, almost 90.0% of respondents indicated a belief that in analyzing situations of violence, the practitioner should put forward that it is an act of male domination over the woman (Statement 5). Therefore, even though there is a certain consensus for this last statement, the same cannot be said for the other responses dealing specifically with the issue of responsibility for violence.

When one examines the beliefs of practitioners with regard to the roles of organizations or of programs for violent partners (Table 22.8), one observes that almost all of the practitioners (97.8%) believe that the function of the programs for violent partners is not to control but instead to help the clients to change their behavior (Statement 26). One would expect to find as great a proportion of respondents disagreeing with Statement 6 because it can be seen as being to some degree the opposite of Statement 26, but this is not the case. Even though the majority of respondents (84.4%) do not believe in the role of the organizations for violent partners as one

TABLE 22.5 Statements Dealing With the Dimension of Loyalty

Statement	Agree		Disagree		Total	
	%	n	%	n	%	n
2. The practitioner must first and foremost be loyal to the consulting client	95.5	43	4.4	2	100.0	44
10. The practitioner must first and foremost be loyal to the organization that referred the consulting client	38.7	17	61.3	27	100.0	45
16. The practitioner must first and foremost be loyal to the victim of the consulting client	36.3	16	63.6	28	100.0	45

TABLE 22.6 Statements Dealing With the Dimension of Confidentiality and the Need to Protect

Statement	Agree		Disagree		Total	
	%	n	%	n	%	n
4. It is the duty of the practitioner to take action to protect a client who demonstrates suicidal tendencies	97.7	43	2.3	1	100.0	44
15. The practitioner must take action to protect a person threatened by a dangerous client	100.0	45	—	—	100.0	45
24. The practitioner must respect the laws that oblige professionals to report all situations abusive to a minor	100.0	45	—	—	100.0	45

of control over the men to prevent all new forms of violence toward the victims (Statement 6), one still finds 15.6% of practitioners who believe it is.

In an exploratory fashion, many cross-tabulations were made. We hoped to determine if practitioners responded differently to statements regarding values and to those regarding the nature of dilemmas experienced, according to individual characteristics, or to characteristics related to their workplace. Because we had a relatively limited number of participants, the chi-square for most of these cross-tabulations are effectively not valid. Regardless, we found some statistically significant relationships, which we will present.

One observes in Table 22.9 that the responses to the statement are not the same for the practitioners who identified themselves and those who did not identify themselves as having been victims of conjugal or family violence. Slightly more than half (52.6%) of those who identified themselves as having been victims of violence stated that controlling the way of life of the client is part of the role of the professional. Among

respondents who claimed not to have been victims of violence, the proportion drops to 23.0%. Therefore, the majority of these respondents do not feel that challenging the way of life of clients is a part of their work.

Finally, one can see in Table 22.10 that the respondents can also have different perceptions based on the environment of the organization in which they are employed. A large majority of the respondents working in a heavily urban environment (81.8%) do not believe that the practitioner should be primarily loyal to the victim of the consulting client. In the semiurban or rural setting, there seems to be more importance placed on the victim of the client: More than half of these respondents (54.5%) stated that the practitioner must first of all be loyal to the victim of the consulting client. A possible explanation for this result is that the urban setting allows for more anonymity, the practitioner having less risk of knowing the victim of the consulting client.

In summary, one finds a great deal of consensus regarding all of the statements dealing with codes of ethics, confidentiality, and the

TABLE 22.7 Statements Dealing With the Dimension of Analysis of Violence

Statement	Agree		Disagree		Total	
	%	n	%	n	%	n
5. In analyzing situations of violence, the practitioner should put forward that it is an act of male domination over the woman	86.7	39	13.3	6	100.0	45
13. Male violence toward women is mainly attributable to individual factors	37.8	17	62.2	28	100.0	45
32. Violence is a relational process in which man and woman share responsibility to some degree	50.0	22	50.0	22	100.0	44

TABLE 22.8 Statements Dealing With the Dimension of Roles of Organizations or Programs for Violent Partners

Statement	Agree		Disagree		Total	
	%	n	%	n	%	n
6. The role of the organizations for violent partners is to control these men in order to prevent all new forms of violence toward the victims	15.6	7	84.4	38	100.0	45
26. The function of the programs for violent partners is not to control but to help the clients to change their behavior	97.8	44	2.2	1	100.0	45

duty to protect. Respondents agreed unanimously or almost unanimously that practitioners must respect and familiarize themselves with the ethics codes of their professions and their organizations and that it is their duty to protect the client who shows suicidal tendencies, or the person who is threatened by a dangerous client, or the minor who is a victim of abuse.

It is in connection with one of the statements dealing with responsibility for violence (dimension of analysis of violence) that one observes the greatest divergence of opinions. In fact, the statement "Violence is a relational process in which man and woman share responsibility to some degree" divides the respondents into two camps (50.0% agree, 50.0% disagree). We also noted some contradictions in answers to statements about loyalty and about confidentiality when collaborating with other organizations or professionals. Finally, we have seen that the majority of respondents who identified themselves as having been victims of family or conjugal violence state that challenging the way of life of

the client is part of the work of the practitioner (a statistically significant relationship). On the other hand, practitioners working in semiurban and rural settings, compared to those who work in a heavily urban environment, are more likely to say that the practitioner should be loyal first and foremost to the victim of the consulting client (a statistically significant relationship).

Conclusion

■ This chapter has put forward the values and beliefs of practitioners with regard to professional practice with violent partners. The data presented should be considered in conjunction with other quantitative data on the characteristics of practitioners and organizations and on the dilemmas and the difficulties faced by practitioners as well as the resolution of ethical dilemmas. The qualitative part we are now completing will allow for a more in-depth exploration of the experience of practitioners, their re-

TABLE 22.9 Proportion of Practitioners Who Agree or Disagree With the Statement According to Whether They Had Themselves Been Victims of Conjugal or Family Violence

Statement	Agree		Disagree		Total	
	%	n	%	n	%	n
11. Challenging the way of life of the client is part of the practitioner's work						
Having been victim of conjugal or family violence	52.6	10	47.4	9	100.0	19
	22.2		20.0		42.2	
Not having been victim of conjugal or family violence	23.0	6	76.9	20	100.0	26
	13.3		44.4		57.7	
Total	35.5	16	64.4	29	100.0	45

$\chi^2 = 4.185$; $p = .041$ (smaller than .05 therefore significant).

TABLE 22.10 Proportion of Practitioners Who Agree or Disagree With the Statement According to Type of Setting of the Specialized Resource

Statement	Agree		Disagree		Total	
	%	n	%	n	%	n
16. The practitioner must first of all be loyal to the victim of the consulting client	18.1	4	81.8	18	100.0	22
Heavily urban setting	9.1		40.9		50.0	
	54.5	12	45.4	10	100.0	22
Semiurban and rural settings	27.2		22.7		50.0	
Total	36.3	16	63.6	28	100.0	44

$\chi^2 = 6.286$; $p = .012$ (smaller than .05, therefore significant).

flections on this subject, the strategies they use to resolve problems, and the values implied therein. Finally, giving these data as feedback to the practitioners shall provide in return better information regarding the possible options available to those who try to resolve complex ethical questions in the field of violence.

Notes

1. l'Association des ressources intervenant auprès des conjoints violents.

2. Note that in all the tables presented, the percentages for agreement include the sum of the frequency for categories "agree fully" and "agree somewhat." The percentages for disagreement include the sum of the frequency for categories "disagree fully" and "disagree somewhat."

References

Bélanger, S. (1994). L'épineuse et litigieuse question des rôles distincts et complémentaires du socio-judiciaire et du clinique dans le processus de "responsibilisation" des conjoints violents. In *Les aspects cliniques et judiciaires de la responsibilisation des hommes violents en contexte de socio-judiciarisation de la violence conjugal Actes du séminaire provincial sur l'intervention auprès des hommes violents* (pp. 20-37). Montreal: Association des Ressources Intervenant auprès des Hommes Violents.

Bograd, M. (1992). Values in conflict: Challenges for family therapists' thinking. *Journal of Marital and Family Therapy, 18*, 245-256.

Broué, J., & Guèvremont, C. (1994). L'aide contrainte ou comment ne pas se tirer dans les pieds. In *Les aspets cliniques et judiciaires de la responsibilisation des hommes violents en contexte de socio-judiciarisation de la violence conjugal Actes du séminaire provincial sur l'intervention auprès des hommes violents* (pp. 10-18). Montreal: Association des Ressources Intervenant auprès des Hommes Violents.

Congress, E. P. (1986). *An analysis of ethical practice among field instructors in social work education.* Unpublished doctoral dissertation, City University of New York, New York.

Corey, G., Corey, M. S., & Callanan, P. (1988). *Issues and ethics in the helping professions* (3rd ed.). Monterey, CA: Brooks/Cole.

Cossom, J. (1992). What do we know about social workers' ethics? *The Social Worker (Le Travailleur Social), 60,* 165-171.

Dankwort, J. (1988). Une conception alternative de la violence conjugale: Vers une intervention efficace auprès des hommes violents. *Service Social, 37*(1-2), 85-115.

Goldberg, J. E. (1989). AIDS: Confidentiality and the social worker. *Social Thought, 15,* 116-127.

Gosselin, J. (1991). Le respect du secret: Esquisse d'une grille d'analyse. *Service Social, 40*(1), 53-70.

Gouvernement du Québec. (1991). *Loi sur la protection de la jeunesse.* Quebec: Éditeur officiel du Québec.

Gouvernement du Québec. (1992). *Intervention auprès des conjoints violents orientations.* Quebec: Ministère de la Santé et des Services Sociaux.

Gouvernement du Québec. (1994). *Loi sur l'accès aux documents publics et sur la protection des renseignements personnels.* Quebec: Éditeur officiel du Québec.

Holland, T. P., & Kilpatrick, A. (1991). Ethical issues in social work: Toward a grounded theory of professional ethics. *Social Work, 6,* 138-144.

Huston, K. (1984). Ethical decisions in treating battered women. *Professional Psychology Research and Practice, 15,* 822-832.

Leong, G. B., Silva, J. A., & Weinstock, R. (1988). Ethical considerations of clinical use of Miranda-like warnings. *Psychiatric Quarterly, 59,* 293-305

Margolin, G. (1982). Ethical and legal considerations in marital and family therapy. *American Psychologist, 37,* 788-801.

Martin, G., & Lavoie, F. (1986). Dilemmes et interventions dans le contexte de la violence conjugale. *Intervention, 75,* 37-47.

McWhinney, M., Haskins-Herkenham, D., & Hare, I. (1992). NASW commission on education position statement: The school social worker and confidentiality. *School Social Work Journal, 17*(1), 38-46.

Rondeau, G. (1993). *Dimensions sociales et professionnelles associées à la mise en place d'un code d'éthique pour les organismes membres de l'ARIHV.* Paper presented at the Association of Resources Working With Violent Partners Conference, Quebec City, Canada.

Sonkin, D. J. (1986). Clairvoyance versus common sense: Therapist's duty to warn and protect. *Violence and Victims, 1,* 7-22.

Sonkin, D. J., & Allison, J. E. (1986). The therapist's duty to protect victims of domestic violence: Where we have been and where we are going. *Violence and Victims, 1,* 205-214.

Wendorf, J. D., & Wendorf, R. J. (1985). A systemic view of family therapy ethics. *Family Process, 4,* 443-452.

Willbach, D. (1989). Ethics and family therapy: The case management of family violence. *Journal of Marital and Family Therapy, 15*(1), 43-52.

CHAPTER 23

Conducting Ethical Cross-Cultural Research on Family Violence

Lisa Aronson Fontes

Cross-cultural research on family violence can be fraught with ethical dilemmas. Unfortunately, good intentions alone will not prevent researchers from abusing their power and inflicting harm. This chapter is meant to offer ideas and impetus for researchers to conduct their inquiries in ways that are respectful, relevant, helpful, and in synch with the people studied, as well as meaningful to the research community. With careful attention to their use of power, researchers can build sound bodies of knowledge that will contribute to the reduction of violence in families from a variety of cultures.

Ethics

■ Research ethics are often considered in the narrowest of frames, as referring to the prescriptions and proscriptions of professional organizations. In this chapter, I consider as "ethics" broader moral questions, such as "whose interests are served by research, and how can the subjectivity and authority of research participants be preserved" (Thompson, 1992) or enhanced? An additional question considered here is: "How can researchers best understand, interpret, and present findings about culture and vio-

AUTHOR'S NOTE: Correspondence should be sent to Lisa Fontes, 359 Montague Road, Shutesbury, MA 01072; e-mail: lfontes@javanet.com. I would like to thank Pam Choice, Michael Morgan, and Carlos Fontes for their helpful comments on an earlier version of this chapter.

lence in the family?" I believe this is an ethical question because misunderstandings and the uninformed use of research results can result in distorted theory and public policy. And, finally, "How can family violence researchers avoid abusing their power in cross-cultural studies?" Although questions of power and abuse of power are important in all research, they gain particular salience in cross-cultural and family violence research because contact between cultures and family violence—as separate phenomena—often include elements of exploitation. When family violence is considered in a cross-cultural context, the potential for abusing power increases dramatically.

Cross-Cultural Research

■ Most research on family violence has been monocultural, and what determines legitimate knowledge has been thought to be "plain common sense without class, gender or cultural influences" (L. T. Smith, 1992, p. 3). Cross-cultural research in family violence is rare but sorely needed if we are to understand phenomena such as battering and child abuse in all their complexity.

I am using the term *cross-cultural research* to refer to investigations in which the researcher is studying members of a group to which he or she does not belong (investigator-different research), and to investigations in which two or more groups are compared (comparative cross-cultural research).

Investigator-Different Research

The difference between the researchers and the participants in investigator-different cross-cultural research could be due to one or more of the following characteristics, among others: race, ethnicity, religion, social class, gender, age, nationality, educational background, sexual orientation, or profession. By providing this rather long list, I do not mean to say that racial and professional differences are of the same order of importance, for instance, but rather to assert that when a researcher studies a group of people who are part of a community and share

a major characteristic that the researcher does not possess, this is cross-cultural research, and should be regarded as such.

When there is an obvious difference between researchers and participants such as race, researchers are more apt to recognize the cross-cultural nature of their undertaking. However, researchers frequently conduct studies across gender or social class lines, for instance, without recognizing the background differences between themselves and the participants, or compensating for the ways these differences may affect their ability to understand, interpret, and convey that which they encounter. The lack of explicit attention to issues of crossing cultures in research may be most problematic where the researchers are "the same" as some of the participants in a given variable and different from others of the participants in the same variable and yet fail to recognize how this may distort their perspective (the most typical example may be the male ethnographers who study tribes in developing countries and document men's lives in great detail while ignoring or marginalizing women's experiences). According to this definition, then, a European American psychologist studying African American families is conducting cross-cultural research, as is an upper-middle-class Puerto Rican sociologist studying Puerto Rican ghetto children, as well as a European American gay male studying European American lesbians. Although each researcher may share certain characteristics with the participants, and the degree and kind of difference varies in each case, I believe the research will be improved by awareness of the cross-cultural nature of the research and the special attention to ethics that this requires.

Comparative Cross-Cultural Research

The second type of research included in my definition of cross-cultural involves the risky business of comparing two or more groups of people on a given variable. Comparative cross-cultural investigators often seek to determine the relative rates of prevalence or reported effects of a certain type of family violence with members of two or more groups (e.g., Russell, Schurman, & Trocki, 1988; Wyatt, 1985). Qualitative comparative cross-cultural research is apt to offer descriptions of a given problem for members of two or more groups (e.g., Richie, 1996).

The two most common types of errors in conducting comparative cross-cultural research may be called "alpha" and "beta" prejudice (from Hare-Mustin, 1987). The former involves overstating intergroup differences, and the latter involves ignoring them. Because comparative cross-cultural research seeks to identify differences among groups, it is apt to be designed and results reported in such a way that even small intergroup differences are found and highlighted (alpha error). All the many ways in which the groups may be similar tend to slip into the background as "insignificant difference." Also, when comparative cross-cultural research looks for differences in prevalence or severity, for instance, and uses quantitative methods to document these differences, the results tend to be presented with limited or no information on the contexts (Lockhart, 1985). In these cases "culture" and "race" become mere demographic variables, and the complex circumstances that might lead to these apparent differences (including, e.g., true differences in prevalence, or differences in willingness to disclose) are masked.

Beta error is also endemic to the field of family violence. Until recently, members of all ethnic and cultural groups were treated as if the manifestations, effects, prevention, and recovery from various types of family violence would follow from models and research developed for the most part by and with White Americans (Fontes, 1993a). Fortunately, a recent spate of research has challenged the notion that sexual child abuse (e.g., Fontes, 1993b), wife battering (e.g., Gondolf, Fisher, & McFerron, 1988; Richie, 1996), and child maltreatment (e.g., Deyoung & Zigler, 1994; Ima & Hohm, 1991) are the same (i.e., manifest as they do with White people) among people from a variety of groups. Acknowledging the possibility of intergroup differences has facilitated a small growth spurt of literature on intervention geared toward members of specific groups (e.g., Agtuca, 1992; Fontes, 1995; Wilson, 1994).

Regardless of the content of the inquiry, cross-cultural researchers share basic assumptions that are likely to be hidden but that are worth examining. Cross-cultural researchers generally assume the following:

1. Social phenomena will differ by group.
2. Their choice of cultural group and the boundary they set around it make sense (e.g., Asian Americans or Chinese Americans or first-generation Chinese Americans in Los Angeles).
3. They will be able to release themselves from their own cultural biases and backgrounds sufficiently to be able to "uncover" a differing social reality and understand its limits and the context in which it occurs.
4. They will be able to present this social reality in a way that reflects the viewpoints of the participants from the target culture(s) as well as their own theories and viewpoints.
5. They will be able to disseminate their findings in a "helpful" way.

Although philosophers of the social sciences in general and qualitative researchers in particular have become simultaneously more sophisticated and more humble in their claims about their ability to "uncover the truth" or "speak for" research participants (e.g., Fine, 1992; Hubbard, 1988), the special issues facing family violence researchers who hope to span cultural gulfs remain largely unexplored (see Lockhart, 1985, and Ruback & Weiner, 1993, for notable exceptions).

Problems with the current limited cross-cultural research on family violence include overemphasizing differences and neglecting similarities between groups; denying diversity within groups; defining the groups poorly (see later discussion of ethnic lumping); ignoring the immediate and wider structural contexts; and masking power, inequality, conflict, and change (see Thompson, 1992, on gender).

Addressing Ethical Issues at Each Phase of Research

■ Certain ethical concerns arise at expected moments in cross-cultural research, along a developmental pathway through the following four stages: designing research, gathering data, analyzing data, and disseminating findings.

Designing Research

How can researchers design cross-cultural studies on family violence that are ethical? Here I will discuss the following subphases of research design for their importance in terms of the ethical issues that emerge: choosing the research question, defining the sample, and choosing the instrument.

Choosing the Research Question

Deciding on a research question is a highly idiosyncratic process, usually determined by some combination of researcher curiosity, funding availability, gaps in the literature, a practical problem, and chance. Factors influencing the investigator's choice of research questions include colleagues, tenure and promotion concerns, human subjects review boards, journal editors, personal and professional histories, funding agencies, politics, "real world" dilemmas, and scholarly trends. Although these pragmatic demands cannot be ignored, they need to be counterbalanced with a sense of obligation to engage in work that will make a difference in the lives of people affected by violence. The decision to invest time, energy, and funding in a specific area may be seen as an ethical decision due to many ways in which conducting research can affect the people and settings being studied.

Research is often used to shape funding priorities, boosting or diminishing support for policy initiatives, an important real-world consequence. Research sets into motion social processes in the settings where the research occurs, above and beyond the activities directly linked to the investigation (Bogdan & Biklen, 1992). Asking clients to engage in an outcome survey or interview after a clinical intervention, for instance, can motivate changes in the content of the intervention program.

How, then, can researchers increase the ethicality of their choice of a question for study? Many cross-cultural researchers (e.g., Darou, Hum, & Kurtness, 1993), advocates of participatory research (e.g., Maguire, 1987), and feminist researchers (e.g., Thompson, 1992) suggest that the groups that provide the research information should have some say in the questions

addressed. Researchers who are contemplating cross-cultural investigations are advised to contact the community they wish to study and ask, "What issues are you facing now?" Sometimes local needs can be determined by reading local publications, sitting in on school board and other meetings, and contacting local leaders.

At times, decisions about the general area of investigation (e.g., battering of women) will be predetermined by the researcher based on some of the constraints described above. In these cases, the researcher might still do well to run focus groups with potential participants, and/or leaders of the community that will be studied, and ask, "What would you like to know about the battering of women in your community?" This would be followed by the question, "What do you think is the best way to find this out?" Although most researchers will have a more sophisticated understanding of the options in terms of research methods, potential participants are apt to convey information about the context, which can be key in research design.

Defining the Sample

Defining the research sample with care is central to ethical and useful research. Singling out people, objects, and events to study alters their meanings. For example, investigating the racial composition of people served by shelters for battered women can lead shelter directors and staff to perceive their clients and their mission differently (Donnelly & Cook, 1995). Choice of data sources can affect the findings in unintended ways. For example, relying on data from shelters, public hospitals, and police to assess rates of family violence can reinforce racist and classist assumptions about family violence (Greaves et al., 1995).

Cross-cultural family violence research is a welcome relief from the beta error of monocultural research that assumes that all families are the same (e.g., like White families), often "controlling for ethnicity" by using all-White samples (e.g., Herman, 1981), failing to report the ethnicity of the people studied (e.g., Ligezinska et al., 1996), or reporting on the ethnic mix in the description of the sample but failing to assess for differences among groups in reporting the results (e.g., Barnett, Martinez, & Keyson, 1996). However, simply conducting research that compares groups is no panacea. Cross-cultural family violence research is fraught with problems of sample selection and definition, which often leads to methodological and theoretical errors or misinterpretation and overgeneralization.

Lockhart (1985) describes the danger of labeling as racial differences, findings that may be partially due to social class differences among groups. This is most likely to occur when researchers conduct post hoc racial comparisons based on a diverse sample or a nationally representative sample as if the groups studied were equivalent, rather than checking for differences in education, occupation, and family income among the groups.

Overgeneralizations generally stem from two types of "ethnic lumping":

> In the first, one subgroup is considered representative of a collection of diverse peoples, as when Mexican-Americans are [studied] and labeled "Hispanics" (e.g., Kercher & McShane, 1984; Russell, 1986), implying that the findings will be relevant to Cubans, Dominicans, Puerto Ricans and other Latinos. In the second type of "ethnic lumping," diverse groups are collapsed into large categories. People of Japanese, Chinese, Korean, Filipino, Pacific Island, Vietnamese, Cambodian, East Indian, and other origins who speak different languages, practice different religions, and have differing degrees of acculturation are usually classified as "Asians" and conclusions are drawn about people from this category without establishing whether "Asians" is a valid construct in regard to social phenomena (Shon & Ja, 1982). Ethnic lumping obscures the differences among the widely varied groups that fall under these general names. (Fontes, 1993a, p. 34)

Cross-cultural research often assumes homogeneity in the group that is "other," or within each group that is being compared. Hardy (1989) terms this "the theoretical myth of sameness." Ethnic groups tend to be described as if they were monolithic. Using the typical line of thinking of comparative cross-cultural researchers, a report states:

> In this analysis, each group was treated as an aggregate sample, rather than as a collection of individuals, in order to establish overall behavioral frequencies. A basic assumption here was that within-group differences would be minimal. (Callaghan, 1981, pp. 115-131)

How can researchers avoid ethnic lumping? Only rarely will researchers be able to use a sample that is truly representative of the ethnic composition of the group being studied (e.g., "Hispanics" would have a certain mix of Puerto Ricans, Cubans, etc., from certain social classes and with representative degrees of acculturation. Even in this design, the differences among the subcategories of Hispanics would need to be explored). A more common solution would be for researchers to limit their claims to the reality studied and provide ample information about the sample so readers can draw their own conclusions about the transferability of the findings. In other words, if the sample consisted of Mexican Americans from Texas, the study would be described as relevant to this group, not "Latinos."

The "myth of sameness" can pose problems in studies of family violence among Whites as well. For example, Busby, Glenn, Steggell, and Adamson (1993) describe the sample in their study on victims of physical and sexual abuse as 95% White, composed of people who sought therapy at a center at Brigham Young University. The authors fail to mention the religious background of the participants. Given that the study takes place at a Mormon university in Utah, it would be important to know if most of the participants were Mormon, and how this might influence the results. Without this important piece of contextual information, the readers are led to assume the results would apply to all Whites. Because they are the racially dominant group, Whites are often seen as culture free or without ethnicity. When studied in greater depth, specific groups of White people are found to be highly influenced by cultural and systemic factors (e.g., for discussions of sexual abuse and Anglo-Americans and Jews, respectively, see Schmidt, 1995, and Featherman, 1995).

I have developed personal guidelines for resolving some of ethical dilemmas that emerge in selecting and recruiting participants for cross-cultural research. I ask myself, "Whose voice do I hope to amplify through my research?" and "Whose predicament needs to be more widely known?" I try to give voice to those who have a unique perspective, are currently ignored in the literature, and may have limited access to resources. In many cases this means those who are disenfranchised due to their gender, national origin, economic status, race, or other characteristics. Even so, my research is constrained by the limits of cross-cultural research outlined in this chapter.

Using an entirely different line of thinking, Galliher (1983) and others suggest that we study superordinates, so readers can learn more about the government, courts, large corporations, police, and other major institutions that affect their lives. What would this look like in cross-cultural family violence research? It would lead to studies of the ways courts, police, media, and social service agencies handle family violence depending on the ethnicity of the alleged perpetrators; it would lead to studies of why men from different groups choose to hurt the women they love, in addition to studying why women stay in abusive relationships; it would lead to studies of how the ethnic, economic, and gender backgrounds of the powerful affect their decisions; and so on. Researching those who are powerful in terms of family violence would require an investigation of those who are violent as well as the judges, policymakers, producers of violent media, and others who may have a role in the maintenance of a social order in which poor women and children are most often victimized. We have studied the psychology of victims ad infinitum, but we know little about the psychology of politicians who cut the funds provided under the Aid to Families With Dependent Children Act with apparent disregard for the women and children who may be forced to remain in violent homes because of such cuts. We know little about the culture of the judicial system wherein children are repeatedly returned to the homes of parents who have abused them. And we know little about the political incentives for politicians to support legislation like "Megan's Law," designed to make convicted sex offenders publicly identifiable on release, while supporting legislation that puts children at greater risk for abuse and neglect, in the package of "parental rights."

Choosing the Instrument

Once researchers have defined the question and group(s) they wish to study, they must choose an instrument that will be able to address the questions with this particular group. The better the method fits the group under study, the more accurate the findings are apt to be. Frequently, researchers take instruments and procedures that have been developed with White populations in North America and use these inappropriately in other contexts. People are asked to use instruments or engage in procedures that are alien and may be alienating to them.

If the researcher has chosen an instrument that does not fit naturally, she or he should consider choosing another instrument. Where this is not possible, researchers must compensate in every way possible to make sure the instrument or procedures do not offend people, and are valid. To determine whether the instrument or procedures fit with the culture(s) studied, researchers will need to include members of the culture(s) in the design, implementation, and analysis of the research, as will be discussed below.

In a monograph on research on the Maori (Hohepa & Smith, 1992), New Zealand researchers from European (Pakeha) and Maori backgrounds repeatedly decry the way Pakeha researchers believe they have a "divine right" to investigate the topic of their choice with the Maori. They describe Maori research participants who "provide answers (if they cooperate at all), which they think the researcher wants, out of politeness and hospitality; or may even occasionally deliberately distort responses according to a Maori logic not perceived or understood by the researcher" (Stokes, 1992, p. 6). They describe a spiritual dimension toward knowledge that is different from the knowledge-worship of Western researchers. The Maori may assume that knowledge should be imparted to selected individuals only after an apprenticeship that includes being able to prove oneself worthy of receiving such knowledge. It should be clear from this example that the answers given in an anonymous survey on the Maori are not apt to portray Maori life accurately!

Comparative cross-cultural studies of family violence using standard quantitative instruments may suffer from these methodological problems. At the 4th International Family Violence Research Conference in 1995, prominent and groundbreaking leaders in the field of family violence from the Family Research Laboratory at the University of New Hampshire advocated the implementation of a multinational survey of family violence to enable cross-national comparisons of prevalence. Although the 60 or so researchers from all over the world who were present were generally intrigued by the idea of gathering such data, serious concerns were raised about the legitimacy of using the same methodology from country to country. Surely, the meaning of completing a survey would vary from rural Indonesia to urban Kenya to suburban Ohio, and using the same instrument would in no way guarantee the validity of the results. (Additional concerns expressed about the possible political implications of the use of findings from such a study will not be discussed here.)

Traditional empirical approaches using standardized quantitative methods may not be sufficient for some cross-cultural research on family violence. Research methods are sorely needed that take the cultural contexts of all participants and researchers into account. Written and telephone surveys are not likely to be the instrument of choice for assessing violence among members of low-income, immigrant, or oppressed groups, who feel alienated from professionals and authorities. It is ironic that these same anonymous surveys may be the method most likely to gain approval from human subjects review boards (Berg, 1995).

The importance of methodological variety can be seen in Johnson's (1995) refutation of the family violence versus feminist theory debate on couple violence. He suggests that family violence theorists rely on data gathered in large-sample surveys, whereas feminists tend to rely on qualitative and quantitative data gathered from women's shelters. He suggests that neither perspective is incorrect; rather, each has studied and described a population with a different kind of couple violence, which he calls common couple violence and patriarchal terrorism, respectively. If each side can recognize that it is measuring a different aspect of the problem, rather than arguing that the other is wrong, then the two perspectives can enhance each other. Without this methodological variety, only one type of battering would be known to researchers.

With the directness typical of so much of her writing, Audre Lorde (1993) asks, "What does it mean when the tools of a racist patriarchy are used to examine the fruits of that same patriarchy?" Although such language is not common in discussions of scholarly inquiry, cross-cultural researchers are advised to examine the assumptions behind the instruments and procedures they use, and create new ones, where indicated.

Simply translating instruments is not enough. Even when instruments are well translated, back-translated for accuracy, and pre-tested, undoubtedly the meaning of answering the questions, the definitions of the violent acts, and the meaning of responding to researchers vary with the cultural context of the participants. Ample information on the cultural contexts of the study and of the participants' lives will help render the research meaningful. Some of the potential dangers of poor cross-cultural research in family violence will be discussed later in this chapter.

Gathering Data:
Understanding Benefit and Harm

How can data be gathered in a way that benefits and does not harm participants?

Research is based on human interaction and always includes a human relationship. Although this relationship is most obvious in the intimate setting of an in-depth interview, even anonymous telephone or written surveys create and emerge from a relationship. Researchers need to ask themselves, "What kind of relationship do I have with the participants? What kind of relationship do I want to construct with them through the research?"

Graham Hingangaroa Smith (1992) suggests four models for culturally appropriate research on the Maori that can be used to increase the cultural appropriateness of research on/with members of other groups as well: (a) the mentor model, where authoritative Maori people guide and mediate the research; (b) the adoption model, "where researchers become adopted by the community . . . to the extent that they are considered as one of the [community] who happen[s] to be doing research and therefore can be trusted to do it right"; (c) the power sharing model, where researchers seek meaningful community assistance in supporting the development of the research; and (d) the empowering outcomes model, where the research benefits the Maori and the findings "relate to the original research questions and provide information that Maori themselves want to know" (pp. 8-9).

Feminists frequently discuss the power dynamics of gathering data. For example, Baber (1994) wonders how much she should guide the discussion of focus groups on sexuality and whether she should introduce information about AIDS:

In this project we want women to determine the topics important to them and the direction in which the discussion moves. However, we believe that some critical issues need to be addressed in the groups. At what point do we exert our "expertness" regarding factual information or move the discussion toward a subject not yet considered? (p. 69)

Concerns over the use and abuse of power in data gathering become highlighted in cross-cultural research. Researchers must ask themselves how their knowledge or lack of knowledge of members of the group(s) in the study influences the research process. For cross-cultural researchers to understand the people they are studying and empower them in the process of the research and in handling the results, they must work to become more familiar with the participants' culture(s) (Fontes, in press). Reading about history and culture, enjoying the arts, and making friends with people from the group(s) are effective means of beginning to have insight into the lives and meaning systems of the people who are being studied. Familiarity with the culture can help researchers guard against mistakes of misunderstanding in all phases of the research, from using alienating or offensive instruments to misinterpreting the results to disseminating results in a way that may be harmful to the participants' group. Familiarity with the culture can also help researchers guard against mistakes of power, such as using authority in a way that harms the participants. Although researchers will not be able to become members of cultural groups that are not their own, all efforts toward greater cultural understanding strengthen the foundation on which they can subsequently build the cross-cultural research.

The process of conducting research tends to reinforce the power imbalances of society. Researchers usually study down the societal power hierarchy, studying people who are poorer, less educated, more discriminated against, and in a variety of ways less socially powerful than themselves (Keith-Spiegel & Koocher, 1985). This may be seen as a glaring problem in family violence research because power and abuses of power are key to the violence under study. If family violence researchers favor the reduction of violence, it behooves us to adopt nonviolent (nonexploitative) methods of research.

In the research setting, the researcher is always more powerful than the participant. Although this is most obviously true for experimental research conducted in a laboratory, where the participants are manipulated in some way, even the most collaborative methods—such as participant observation—do not erase this imbalance. Researchers always have the option of leaving the setting; they know they have a life and identity other than the one that they are trying on (like a coat) for the duration of the study. It has been argued that one cannot really know what it is like to be a crack addict or mental hospital resident or homeless person, for instance, by doing fieldwork in this area, no matter how long the researcher stays in the field and no matter how thoroughly he or she adopts local customs. A key part of being in any of these positions is the knowledge that one may not be able to get out (Wieder, 1983). If a researcher promises not to interrupt violent episodes for the sake of observation or recording, this poses a new ethical dilemma.

Potential Benefits of Participation

To what extent will the research participants benefit directly from the research? Human subjects review boards usually concern themselves with issues of benefit to the field. Here I am not referring to some theoretical benefit down the road, but rather to the extent to which the participants will be changed (beneficially) by their participation. If the research has low direct benefit, the participants and their circumstances will be much the same after participating. For instance, archival research offers no direct benefit to those who provided the original data.

Depending on the content and processes of data collection, both qualitative and quantitative methods can provide high or low benefit to participants. In survey research, for example, a question can be phrased in a way that gives participants insight into their lives. Interviewing people alone or in groups can break isolation and offer avenues to recovery from family violence, or can retraumatize, depending on the participants, the methods, and the intentions and ability of the interviewer. Research can help participants recognize resources within themselves and within their communities and can teach participants new skills. These may be primary goals of the research (as in action research) or planned in as "side benefits."

Research is always an intervention of some kind. Especially when investigating a dangerous phenomenon like family violence, one might ask, "Is it ethical to leave participants as vulnerable when they complete the study as before they participated?"

Risk of Harm to Participants

Collecting cross-cultural data on family violence, whether through interviews, questionnaires, experiments, observations, or other means, has a high potential for inflicting harm on participants. Echoes from traumatic historic events may influence the context of the research and the relationship between the researcher and the participants (e.g., a Cambodian being inter-

viewed about family violence may remember the interrogations she faced in resettlement camps). Considering risk is particularly important when conducting cross-cultural inquiry because researchers and human subjects review boards may not be aware of all the potential harm that might befall participants in their specific contexts. The potential harm to participants may be of a psychological, physical, social, or political nature.

Psychological Harm. Research on sensitive topics can provoke a powerful emotional response in participants. Lee and Renzetti (1993) describe a sensitive research topic as "one that potentially poses for those involved a substantial threat, the emergence of which renders problematic for the researcher and/or the researched the collection, holding, and/or dissemination of research data" (p. 5). Lee and Renzetti assert that research is more likely to be threatening when it involves private or deeply personal material, concerns deviance and social control, "impinges on the vested interests of powerful persons or the exercise of coercion or domination," and where it touches on material that is considered sacred (p. 6). Family violence research would seem to meet all these criteria for being sensitive and threatening.

Given that family violence is a sensitive topic, researchers must become highly familiar with the phenomena they are studying and the people who have been affected by it. All the personnel who have contact with the participants must be well versed in the topic under study and well trained in the social skills necessary to conduct quality research, not just research methods. Featherman (1989) describes her decision to conduct all the interviews and administer all the tests in her study of survivors of sexual abuse herself:

This decision was made in order to avoid the kind of interviewer bias resulting from only a cursory knowledge of sexual abuse. Victims of sexual abuse have by definition been intruded upon and have already had their privacy violated in a damaging and insensitive manner. . . . A well-meaning yet naive interviewer, due either to ignorance or to widespread misconceptions about sexual abuse (i.e., that seductive children invite abuse, that memories of sexual abuse are likely to be simply Oedipal fantasies, etc.), may unintentionally discourage full disclosures and leave the subject feeling further victimized. (pp. 29-30)

What kind of obligation for participants' psychological well-being do researchers have to participants once a study has been completed? Gerrard (1995) coined the term *research abuse* to describe

the practice of researchers parachuting into people's lives, interfering, raising painful old feelings, and then vanishing—leaving the participants to deal with unresolved feelings alone and isolated. There is often a sense of "us" and "them" perpetrated by researchers so that the subjects feel "examined," sometimes exposed and judged. (p. 59)

There are two elements here: not only the reawakening of old feelings but also the sense gained by participants that they have been used by the researchers for their own purposes and then abandoned, which in some cases may replicate the original abusive relationship. Researchers have handled this dilemma by achieving different degrees of postresearch proximity with participants, including staying in touch (Matocha, 1992); holding a party for participants and their families in which the research results are presented (Julia Paley, personal communication, September 1996); facilitating access to health, legal, and social services for participants in need (Richie, 1996); and more typically, mailing a copy of the research reports to those participants who have requested it.

Family violence researchers can reduce the likelihood of psychological harm through careful choice of their research sample and questions. In one study (Fontes, 1993b), for example, I decided to interview only those victims of sexual abuse who had been in therapy. That, of course, limited the findings to a clinical sample and therefore partially shaped the research questions. Like many researchers before me, I made this decision so the participants would have had some initial processing of the abuse and would be less likely to be thrown into a crisis by the research process (Castor-Lewis, 1988). This choice enabled me to focus on issues in therapy for Puerto Ricans who had been abused sexually, but limited my ability to study people who had not sought therapy.

Retraumatization and misunderstanding are more apt to occur in cross-cultural contexts, where researchers are not fully aware of the cultural meanings around asking certain questions, or asking them in certain ways. Questions may be biased by the researchers' assumptions that all respondents will be similarly motivated (e.g., to provide the maximum number of answers possible, to guess when uncertain, and to provide the truth rather than save face). Research questions are often phrased in ways that are syntactically complex, and language is used that may not be comfortable for some participants, introducing bias against less educated and nonnative speakers (see Canino & Spurlock, 1994, p. 97).

In their applications to human subjects committees, researchers routinely say they will offer to stop the interview or refer participants to therapists if the participants become emotionally upset, but these measures are not always adequate. Researchers may not be able to recognize when they are retraumatizing research participants who are from other cultures, because cultural norms around expression of distress vary widely. Investigators should offer a variety of alternatives for participants who may be upset by the research including consultations with trained clergy, self-help materials, support groups, and referrals to anonymous telephone hotlines. Offering mental health referrals as the only option to people from groups who are less likely to use mental health services may constitute unequal protection of the participants from these groups.

The potential for research to be emotionally upsetting is not limited to interviews, and errors of omission can feel as upsetting as errors of commission. For example, victims of rape and sexual abuse have described to me being upset by survey instruments on sexuality that do not give them an opportunity to tell that their first sexual experience was an assault. People of mixed racial or ethnic background are sometimes offended by having to choose only one category in the demographic sections of research instruments.

Physical, Social, and Political Harm. Physical harm to participants can result from attacks by offenders who are angry about having their secrets told, and by others who feel threatened by the research. It may be difficult for researchers unfamiliar with the participants' social context to assess this threat accurately. For instance, a researcher from India described to me the difficulty in conducting research with women who had been attacked by their husbands or husbands' families for the perceived lack of an adequate dowry (Shobha Pais, personal communication, October 1994). She feared that merely approaching these women about the possibility of participating would put them in increased physical danger.

Crossing cultures in research on sensitive topics increases the potential for unrecognized social harm to individual participants and their communities. Darou et al. (1993) describe ignoring local systems of authority as the most egregious error in conducting research with Native Canadian populations. They provide the following example:

> A research assistant arrived in a remote Cree village. On the first day, he asked the chief for access to subjects. He was refused. He then asked the local school principal. He was again refused. He next asked the minister. The minister agreed. The next day, the principal, chief, and minister met for their regular weekly lunch to discuss community issues. They felt that the research assistant's actions had caused the potential for conflict among them. The research assistant was then told to "take the next airplane out of the village or sleep in a snow bank." . . . From the chief's point of view, an undersupervised and arrogant stranger had come to his village and endangered the social peace. (p. 327)

Cross-cultural researchers need to be acutely aware of their personal and institutional power. Although they themselves may feel and try to present themselves as "regular people," their (usually) high levels of education, university or government affiliations, access to media and to powerful people, and relationship to the research setting often distinguish them from the researched. In another role—as friends or teachers, neighbors or co-workers—perhaps the investigators would not have increased power over the participants. But in the relationship of researcher to researched—regardless of the degree of disclosure that has been used—researchers must be acutely aware of their heightened power, and use it wisely.

Differing definitions of family and notions of ownership of information can complicate issues of consent for researchers in cross-cultural settings. Lipson (1994) writes about being caught between her own Euro-American ethical values and the Afghan worldview:

> Afghans do not think of themselves as individuals who have their own rights or autonomy, but as members of families. When considering protection of human subjects, I have to think in terms of family privacy or risks to the family. This notion is not easy for an individually oriented researcher. (p. 342)

How can the notion of harm be measured, then, when an individual consents to participate in a study but that individual may reveal sensitive information about another person who has not given consent? These revelations can affect nonparticipants' privacy and all aspects of their future, as when participants reveal information about children who are currently at risk for abuse that requires reporting to authorities. Other than assuring confidentiality and anonymity to the extent afforded by the law, and informing participants of the exceptions to confidentiality, it is hard to know how to handle these dilemmas.

In conducting research in Third World situations of extreme poverty and few structural resources for victims of family violence, the implications of raising awareness of family violence may be serious, indeed. If a disclosure leads to an abusive man who is the monetary provider leaving the home, for instance, his family could be pushed over the edge from the brink of hunger. I conduct myself with the general motto that "knowledge is power," but this truism does not relieve me of my sense of moral responsibility to participants and their families and communities.

Participating in research may also expose participants to political risk. Simply speaking with a researcher may brand a participant as a collaborator with an enemy group (whether that group is seen as "the establishment," "the feminists," "the communists," or whomever). Participants in my focus group study on sexual abuse in Chilean shanty towns (Fontes, 1996) described how the dictatorship influenced their experiences of family violence. Some described their courageous involvement in activities intended to overthrow or resist the Pinochet dictatorship. It is clear that if a brutal dictatorship ever returns to Chile, the mere fact that they participated in the focus groups could put them at risk. They would not be identifiable through my publications, but secret police and informers were rampant under previous regimes in Chile, and could emerge again. My presence as a facilitator of the focus groups gave the appearance of safety to them. For now there is no problem, but the political winds are fickle, and this is a real source of concern.

Other kinds of potential harm to participants in cross-cultural family violence research are harder to categorize. For instance, through their studies researchers may influence the thinking or create a category of harm that will have implications for the participants and their communities. In Chile, for example, I asked focus group participants if a sexual relationship between a 30-year-old male and his 12-year-old female neighbor would be considered sexual abuse. With some qualifications, there was general agreement that it would. I then asked if a sexual relationship between a 30-year-old female and her 12-year-old male neighbor would be considered abuse. There was considerably more debate on this point. By juxtaposing these questions, I made an intervention that could be described in two ways: I created awareness of the sexual abuse of boys by women (that is the description using my lens on the world) or I created a category of harm and victimization that did not previously exist. To date, I have no sense of the long-term implications of this intervention.

Analyzing Data

Data do not simply present themselves neutrally so that all who find them would report them similarly. Rather, researchers work like tailors, selecting, cutting, shaping, and sewing together bits of data into a piece that then bears evidence of their own design. Investigators make decisions regularly about which results to highlight and which to allow to fall into the background. We also make decisions about how to contextualize our results. Because of the potential power of research, these may be seen as ethical decisions.

How can data be analyzed in a way that is respectful of the participants and reflects both the participants' and the researchers' views of reality? And what happens when there are differences in interpretation, such as when researchers regard aspects of participants' lives as oppressive or in need of intervention, and the participants themselves interpret their experiences in a different way? Fine (1992) has eloquently described this dilemma in a number of articles collected in *Disruptive Voices: The Possibilities of Feminist Research*. In one, she describes efforts to motivate a rape victim she is interviewing to "take control" and report the rape to the police, when the victim would rather wash, forget, and get on with her life. In another, she describes researchers' efforts to "empower" participants, when the participants would rather be "represented" by the researchers at school meetings.

Here I will discuss two ways researchers can increase the ethicality of their data analysis and presentation procedures: by using integrated research teams and by choosing a stance that makes their biases clear in their data analysis and presentation.

Integrated Research Teams

One way to improve the likelihood that cross-cultural research will be respectful of those it studies is to include people from the culture or cultures being studied in the planning, implementation, interpretation, and dissemination of the research. The more they are present, the more likely it is that the research will be designed, implemented, and used in an ethical way. Having people from the culture(s) being studied on the team, but only in the lowest positions without a real voice, does not help, however, and may serve to legitimize research that is exploitative. (I am reminded of an African American colleague who conducted interviews in a home-based study of abusive families, but then was excluded by the White senior researcher from the data analysis, write-up, and conference presentations and was not acknowledged when the results were published. Her work as an interviewer probably led participants to believe their viewpoints were being handled by a culturally sensitive team, but my colleague believes that—ultimately—they were not.)

Our teams must be structured in such a way that members of the culture being studied have a powerful hand in shaping the research. When we make sure our research teams include people from the culture being studied, it is important to ask ourselves what we mean by "from the culture." What combinations of race, native language, gender, economic class, geographic origin, religion, level of education, and other variables are most important here? When I was writing my dissertation on issues of disclosure around sexual abuse for low-income Puerto Ricans in the United States (Fontes, 1993b), I was fortunate to have had colleagues from low-income Puerto Rican families as members of a collaborative dissertation research group. The fact that we were on equal footing structurally— we were all graduate students—helped them feel free to critique me and my work. They helped me check for bias, oversight, and lack of understanding due to cultural and background differences at every step of the design and conduct of the research.

The actual processes of data analysis vary, of course, with the research methods and questions. However, in all types of research, qualitative and quantitative, experimental and naturalistic, there are a variety of ways to include members of the group being studied in the interpretation of the findings. Some of these include member checks (Bloor, 1983) where researchers return to the people studied for confirmation, elaboration, or correction of the findings; integrated research teams where members of the group studied are active and empowered members of the actual research teams (Fontes, in press); and the use of consultants who are professionals from the cultural group in question who are paid for their services in helping the researchers plan effective and culturally sensitive studies and understand the results (e.g., G. H. Smith, 1992).

No results speak for themselves. Whether the data obtained are numbers or words, researchers engaging in cross-cultural inquiry who wish to analyze their data in an ethical way will break out of the Lone Ranger model of intellectual success and collaborate, collaborate, collaborate.

Disseminating Findings

The ultimate phase of research, that of disseminating the findings, is given the least attention in the methodological literature. It is almost as if researchers believe that their decisions about how and where to inform others about their results are neutral and unimportant, or are in some way beyond their control. Social scientists are often seen as taking a great deal and giving little in return. Carefully attending to the ways in which we disseminate our findings is an important final step in conducting ethical research.

The first step in disseminating findings is deciding who will be part of the conversation. In other words, who are the researchers as they present the findings (are they speaking or writing primarily as scientists, academics, activists, advocates, or members of a certain group?), and who is the intended audience for the findings? The answers to these questions will determine the voice used and the intended vehicle for dissemination, respectively.

Choosing a Voice for Presenting the Data

Fine (1992) describes three stances that researchers can adopt in analyzing and presenting their research: ventriloquy, voices, and activism. Ventriloquy, the typical, "scientific," objective stance, describ[es] behaviors, attitudes, and preferences as if these descriptions were static and immutable, "out there," and unconnected to political contexts. . . . Such texts render oblique the ways in which we, as researchers, construct our analyses and narratives. Indeed, these texts are written as if researchers were simply vehicles for transmission, with no voices of their own. (p. 211)

This stance is easily recognizable as the most common. Family violence researchers often fail to discuss the intense emotional reactions that we may experience at various points during the research process. Researchers are also apt to hide their passionate commitment to the issues for fear this will tarnish the perceived objectivity of their findings. When writing from the ventriloquist's position, researchers write in the third person and "treat subjects as objects while calling them subjects" (Fine, 1992, p. 214).

In the "voices" position, which applies most clearly to qualitative research, quotes are selected, edited, and used to advance the researchers' ideas, generally camouflaging the "delicate tailoring" (Fine, 1992, p. 218) that researchers do to transform stacks of transcripts into an article. According to Fine, "The problem is not that we tailor but that so few researchers reveal *how* we do this work" (p. 218).

The voices position is commonly used in the popular literature on family violence, where testimonials of "women who got away" from battering relationships (NiCarthy, 1987), survivors of incest (Bass & Davis, 1988), and victims of all kinds of abuse are quoted about their experiences, advancing the ideas and often bolstering the theories, reputations, and lecture tour fees of the book editors. Research reports from this position are not as common but do exist, including some of the most vivid and compelling snippets of testimony that I have ever read (e.g., Berliner & Conte, 1990; Conte, Wolf, & Smith, 1989).

I adopted the voices stance in my first formal report on research (Fontes, 1993b) where I reported solely on the methods and findings, neglecting my personhood and the intense ethical issues that I faced as a White therapist conducting research on Puerto Rican clients who had been abused sexually. I reported the words of

the participants and portrayed their dilemmas as competently as I could but I hid my self, thinking that was how "real" researchers gained authority in their study reports. I also assumed that by using the disembodied voice of the scientist, I might be able to ease some of the suspicions of qualitative research that are endemic to the social sciences.

The risks of the voices position are that researchers' motives, actions, and opinions are disguised; the richness, diversity, and inherent contradictions of members of the group studied may be collapsed into "representative quotes"; and the people whose voices are quoted are often "romanticized" (Fine, 1992, pp. 218-219).

The final stance described by Fine is "activist," in which researchers engage in self-conscious, critical, and participatory inquiry and analysis, engaging with the participants but also maintaining and explicitly describing their distinct position. The goals of activist research clearly extend beyond simple hypothesis testing:

Activist research projects seek to unearth, interrupt, and open new frames for intellectual and political theory and change. Researchers critique what seems natural, spin images of what's possible, and engage in questions of how to move from here to there. (Fine, 1992, p. 220)

Fine further suggests "that knowledge is best gathered in the midst of social change projects" (p. 227). A rich, exciting, and international literature on action research describes a wide range of projects in schools, community organizations, battered women's shelters, prisons, and a variety of other settings geared toward understanding and changing the perspectives and material conditions of the participants.

Without entering into discussions that fall beyond the scope of this chapter, I would like to suggest that people who conduct cross-cultural research on family violence consider their own position and choose a voice with care; that they attend to and record their decisions throughout the research process and especially in data analysis; and that they present their own positions in their research reports to enhance understanding of the research. I am not suggesting that all cross-cultural research in family violence should be of an activist nature (although wouldn't it be interesting if it all were, for a couple of years!), but rather that a wider space be opened in the traditional journals and conferences for research of an activist bent. This would relieve some of the historic tensions between the researchers and the activists.

Where to Publish

Investigators who are academics are pressured to publish in those journals with the greatest prestige and visibility to improve their standing in the field. Those who believe they have an urgent message may also write for popular publications to reach the largest number of people. Other options available to researchers include disseminating findings through television, radio, and the Internet; using varying levels of complexity depending on the intended audience; developing practical workshops for professionals (e.g., therapists, shelter workers) or laypeople based on the findings; developing relevant brochures to be distributed to a variety of audiences through community organizations; making presentations to organizations of survivors or victims; writing for survivor or victim publications; and serving as consultants to public service organizations on the topic of their research. Research results can be disseminated through articles, comic books, soap operas, videos, songs, murals, handouts, theater, dance, and a variety of other means. The ethical issue involved here is the response to Fals-Borda's (1996, p. 78) question, "Knowledge for what? Knowledge for whom?"

Linda Tuhiwai Smith (1992), a Maori researcher, writes that although the Maori people have been studied extensively by Pakeha researchers and this research may have added to the knowledge base of the European New Zealanders, "it has done little for Maori people and in many cases simply confirmed what was obvious. . . . Researchers appeared to be willing bedfellows of assimilationist, victim-blaming policies" (p. 7). One might similarly ask what the decades of cross-cultural research into every aspect of society have done to benefit people from disempowered groups in the United States.

Guilty Knowledge

Researchers may be tempted to hide some results so they cannot be used against the participants. Steinberg (cited in Gottfried, 1996) calls this "guilty knowledge," that is, knowledge gained in a study that potentially compromises the interests of the individual or group under study. For example, one researcher on woman battering described her dilemma when she found small but statistically significant differences between racial groups in reported levels of battering, but was unsure as to the meaning of this finding and uncomfortable with the ways in which this result could be misinterpreted and misused:

> On the one hand, if Black men are more likely to beat their wives, then the research and clinical community needs this information so that intervention programs can be developed that specifically target this "at-risk" population (Black men). That is where the money and efforts should be spent. On the other hand, when I think about how the lay community may interpret this "racial differences" information, it makes me sick and very cautious. You and I know that family violence cuts across racial and class lines. (Pam Choice, personal communication, May 16, 1996)

Researchers who devise questions or uncover findings that are not politically palatable may find themselves in the awkward position of having to choose between suppressing the questions or the findings, or publishing findings that may then be used to damage the community studied. Although careful social scientists include cautions in their published work (e.g., that what appears to be a racial difference may stem from a social class difference), these works are often distorted by the press or presented out of context by subsequent writers.

When researchers ponder their motives for conducting research, they may have a clearer idea of where and what to publish. Are they conducting research *on family violence* only, or are they conducting research *for the elimination of family violence*? Is the purpose to discover truth or to displace dominant knowledge and ideologies that oppress people (Gavey, 1989)? Undoubtedly, there will be much variation among researchers in relation to these questions. I believe a dynamic and vibrant field will benefit from inquiry conducted from several of these positions. The important point here is that ethical researchers must examine their options and choose their stances explicitly.

Conclusion

■ I hope this chapter will help investigators engage in more and better cross-cultural research on family violence. Although the potential for ethical problems in this kind of research is great, so is the potential for tremendous rewards. Quality cross-cultural research on family violence not only can contribute to improved theory but will also lead to changes in public policy and interventions that will make family life safer for people from a variety of groups. Through intensive reflection, analysis, evaluation of current practices, and planning for the future, the good intentions held by researchers "can be reflected in good practice and not just good rhetoric," (L. T. Smith, 1992, p. 2).

References

Agtuca, J. R. (1992). *A community secret: For the Filipina in an abusive relationship.* Seattle, WA: Seal.

Baber, K. A. (1994). Studying women's sexualities: Feminist transformations. In D. L. Sollie & L. A. Leslie (Eds.), *Gender, families, and close relationships: Feminist research journeys* (pp. 50-73). Newbury Park, CA: Sage.

Barnett, O. L., Martinez, T. E., & Keyson, M. (1996). The relationship between violence, social support, and self-blame in battered women. *Journal of Interpersonal Violence, 11,* 221-233.

Bass, E., & Davis, L. (1988). *The courage to heal: A guide for women survivors of child sexual abuse.* New York: Harper & Row.

Berg, B. L. (1995). *Qualitative research methods for the social sciences* (2nd ed.). Boston: Allyn & Bacon.

Berliner, L., & Conte, J. (1990). The process of victimization: The victims' perspective. *Child Abuse & Neglect, 14,* 29-40.

Bloor, M. J. (1983). Notes on member validation. In R. M. Emerson (Ed.), *Contemporary field research* (pp. 156-172). Prospect Heights, IL: Waveland.

Bogdan, R. C., & Biklen, S. K. (1992). *Qualitative research for education.* Boston: Allyn & Bacon.

Busby, D. M., Glenn, E., Steggell, G. L., & Adamson, D. W. (1993). Treatment issues for survivors of physical and sexual abuse. *Journal of Marital and Family Therapy, 19,* 377-392.

Callaghan, J. W. (1981). A comparison of Anglo, Hopi, and Navajo mothers and infants. In T. M. Field, A. M. Sostek, P. Vietze, & P. H. Leiderman (Eds.), *Culture and early interactions* (pp. 115-131). Hillsdale, NJ: Lawrence Erlbaum.

Canino, I. A., & Spurlock, J. (1994). *Culturally diverse children and adolescents: Assessment and treatment.* New York: Guilford.

Castor-Lewis, C. (1988). On doing research with adult incest survivors: Some initial thoughts and consideration. *Women and Therapy, 7*(1), 73-80.

Conte, J., Wolf, S., & Smith, T. (1989). What sexual offenders tell us about prevention strategies. *Child Abuse & Neglect, 13,* 293-301.

Darou, W. G., Hum, A., & Kurtness, J. (1993). An investigation of the impact of psychosocial research on a native population. *Professional Psychology: Research and Practice, 24,* 325-329.

Deyoung, Y., & Zigler, E. F. (1994). Machismo in two cultures: Relation to punitive child-rearing practices. *American Journal of Orthopsychiatry, 64,* 386-395.

Donnelly, D., & Cook, K. (1995, July). *Racial differences in shelter utilization in the deep south.* Paper presented at the 4th International Family Violence Research Conference, Durham, NH.

Fals-Borda, O. (1996). A North-South convergence on the quest for meaning. *Qualitative Inquiry, 2*(1), 76-87.

Featherman, J. (1989). *Factors relating to the quality of adult adjustment in female victims of child sexual abuse.* Doctoral dissertation, University of Massachusetts, Amherst.

Featherman, J. (1995). Jews and sexual child abuse. In L. A. Fontes (Ed.), *Sexual abuse in nine North American cultures: Treatment and prevention* (pp. 128-155). Thousand Oaks, CA: Sage.

Fine, M. (1992). Passions, politics, and power: Feminist research possibilities. In M. Fine (Ed.), *Disruptive voices: The possibilities of feminist research* (pp. 205-231). Ann Arbor: University of Michigan Press.

Fontes, L. (1993a). Considering culture and oppression: Steps toward an ecology of sexual child abuse. *Journal of Feminist Family Therapy, 5*(1), 25-54.

Fontes, L. (1993b). Disclosures of sexual abuse for Puerto Rican children: Oppression and cultural barriers. *Journal of Child Sexual Abuse, 2*(1), 21-35.

Fontes, L. (in press). Ethics in family violence research: Cross-cultural issues.

Fontes, L. (Ed.). (1995). *Sexual abuse in nine North American cultures: Treatment and prevention.* Thousand Oaks, CA: Sage.

Fontes, L. (1996). Sexual abuse in Chile: Preliminary reflections. *The Link, 51* (newsletter of the International Society for the Prevention of Child Abuse and Neglect), p. 2.

Galliher, J. F. (1983). Social scientists' ethical responsibilities to superordinates: Looking upward meekly. In R. M.

Emerson (Ed.), *Contemporary field research* (pp. 300-311). Prospect Heights, IL: Waveland.

Gavey, N. (1989). Feminist poststructuralism and discourse analysis: Contributions to a feminist psychology. *Psychology of Women Quarterly, 13,* 459-475.

Gerrard, N. (1995). Some painful experiences of White feminist therapists doing research with women of colour. In J. Adelman & G. Enguidanos (Eds.), *Racism in the lives of women* (pp. 55-63). New York: Haworth.

Gondolf, E. W., Fisher, E., & McFerron, R. J. (1988). Racial differences among shelter residents: A comparison of Anglo, Black, and Hispanic battered women. *Journal of Family Violence, 3*(1), 39-51.

Gottfried, H. (1996). Engaging women's communities: Dilemmas and contradictions in feminist research. In H. Gottfried (Ed.), *Feminism and social change: Bridging theory and practice* (pp. 1-20). Chicago: University of Illinois Press.

Greaves, L., Wylie, A., Champagne, C., Karch, L., Lapp, R., Lee, J., & Osthoff, B. (1995). Women and violence: Feminist practice and quantitative method. In S. Burt & L. Code (Eds.), *Changing methods: Feminists transforming practice* (pp. 301-325). Peterborough, Ontario: Broadview.

Hardy, K. V. (1989). The theoretical myth of sameness: A critical issue in family therapy training and treatment. In G. W. Saba, B. M. Karrer, & K. V. Hardy (Eds.), *Minorities and family therapy* (pp. 17-33). New York: Haworth.

Hare-Mustin, R. (1987). The problem of gender in family therapy. *Family Process, 26,* 15-27.

Herman, J. L. (1981). *Father-daughter incest.* Cambridge, MA: Harvard University Press.

Hohepa, M. K., & Smith, G. H. (Eds.). (1992). *The issue of research and Maori* (Monograph No. 9). Auckland: University of Auckland, Research Unit for Maori Education.

Hubbard, R. (1988). Some thoughts about the masculinity of the natural sciences. In M. M. Gergen (Ed.), *Feminist thought and the structure of knowledge* (pp. 1-15). New York: New York University Press.

Ima, K., & Hohm, C. F. (1991). Child maltreatment among Asian and Pacific Islander refugees and immigrants: The San Diego case. *Journal of Interpersonal Violence, 6,* 267-285.

Johnson, M. (1995). Patriarchal terrorism and common couple violence: Two forms of violence against women. *Journal of Marriage and the Family, 57,* 283-294.

Keith-Spiegel, P., & Koocher, G. P. (1985). *Ethics in psychology.* New York: Random House.

Lee, R. M., & Renzetti, C. M. (1993). The problems of researching sensitive topics: An overview and introduction. In C. M. Renzetti & R. M. Lee (Eds.), *Researching sensitive topics* (pp. 3-13). Newbury Park, CA: Sage.

Ligezinska, M., Firestone, P., Manion, I. G., McIntyre, J., Ensom, R., & Wells, G. (1996). Children's emotional and behavioral reactions following the disclosure of extrafamilial sexual abuse: Initial effects. *Child Abuse & Neglect, 20,* 111-125.

Lipson, J. G. (1994). Ethical issues in ethnography. In J. M. Morse (Ed.), *Critical issues in qualitative research methods,* pp. 333-355. Newbury Park, CA: Sage.

Lockhart, L. L. (1985). Methodological issues in comparative racial analyses: The case of wife abuse. *Social Work Research and Abstracts, 21,* 35-41.

Lorde, A. (1993). The master's tools will never dismantle the master's house. In L. Richardson & V. Taylor (Eds.), *Feminist frontiers III* (pp. 98-101). New York: McGraw-Hill.

Maguire, P. (1987). *Doing participatory research: A feminist approach.* Amherst: University of Massachusetts, Center for International Education.

Matocha, L. K. (1992). Case study interviews: Caring for persons with AIDS. In J. F. Gilgun, K. Daly, & G. Handel (Eds.), *Qualitative methods in family research* (pp. 66-84). Newbury Park, CA: Sage.

NiCarthy, G. (1987). *The ones who got away: Women who left abusive partners.* Seattle, WA: Seal.

Richie, B. E. (1996). *Compelled to crime: The gender entrapment of battered Black women.* New York: Routledge.

Ruback, R. B., & Weiner, N. A. (Eds.). (1993). Cross-culture research on violence [Special issue]. *Violence and Victims, 8*(3).

Russell, D. E. H., Schurman, R. A., & Trocki, K. (1988). The long-term effects of incestuous abuse: A comparison of Afro-American and White American victims. In G. E. Wyatt & G. J. Powell (Eds.), *Lasting effects of child sexual abuse* (pp. 119-134). Newbury Park, CA: Sage.

Schmidt, M. (1995). Anglo Americans and sexual child abuse. In L. A. Fontes (Ed.), *Sexual abuse in nine North American cultures: Treatment and prevention* (pp. 156-175). Thousand Oaks, CA: Sage.

Smith, G. H. (1992). Research issues related to Maori education. In M. K. Hohepa & G. H. Smith (Eds.), *The issue of research and Maori* (Monograph No. 9). Auckland: University of Auckland, Research Unit for Maori Education.

Smith, L. T. (1992). Te raapunga I te ao maarama: The search for the world of light. In M. K. Hohepa & G. H. Smith (Eds.), *The issue of research and Maori* (Monograph No. 9). Auckland: University of Auckland, Research Unit for Maori Education.

Stokes, E. (1992). Maori research and development. In M. K. Hohepa & G. H. Smith (Eds.), *The issue of research and Maori* (Monograph No. 9). Auckland: University of Auckland, Research Unit for Maori Education.

Thompson, L. (1992). Feminist methodology for family studies. *Journal of Marriage and the Family, 54,* 3-18.

Wieder, D. L. (1983). Telling the convict code. In R. M. Emerson (Ed.), *Contemporary field research* (pp. 78-90). Prospect Heights, IL: Waveland.

Wilson, M. (1994). *Crossing the boundary: Black women survive incest.* Seattle, WA: Seal.

Wyatt, G. E. (1985). The sexual abuse of Afro-American and White-American women in childhood. *Child Abuse & Neglect, 9,* 507-519.

Name Index

Abbott, D. A., 121, 134
Abel, G. G., 73, 77
Abelson, I., 186, 192
Abney, V. D., 80, 82, 88
Abramson, L. Y., 50, 56
Achenbach, T. M., 50, 56, 141, 146
Adams, A. M., 162, 169
Adams, D., 210, 211, 217
Adams, S. L., 121, 134
Adamson, D. W., 300, 311
Addis, M. E., 203, 206
Agnew, R., 236, 253
Agtuca, J. R., 298, 311
Aldarondo, E., 5, 15, 125, 134, 183,
    184, 185, 190, 191, 192
Alder, T., 95, 103
Alfaro, J. D., 25, 33
Allan, E., 13, 15, 61, 71, 77
Allen, J., 213, 218
Allison, J. E., 286, 295
Alloy, L. B., 50, 56
Alrich, J. H., 186, 192
Amari, M., 23, 29, 33
Amato, P. R., 125, 133
American Psychiatric Association,
    123, 133, 273, 274, 280
Amick-McMullan, A., 37, 45
Amir, M., 4, 15
Ammerman, R. T., 137, 146
Anderson, G., 93, 103
Anzinger, N. K., 23, 29, 33
Appelbaum, P. S., 263, 266, 273,
    281

Arias, I., 6, 14, 15, 126, 133, 184,
    185, 191, 193, 194, 206
Arny, L., 137, 146
Asbury, J., 162, 168
Asdigian, N. L., 14, 15, 17, 184, 192
Astin, M. C., 35, 37, 44, 45
Atkinson, B., 174, 181
Attkinson, D. L., 221, 234
Auback, A., 211, 218
Avery, B., 163, 168

Babcock, J., 183, 191, 192, 213, 217
Bachman, R., 4, 15, 43, 45
Baillargeon, J., 221, 230, 233
Baird, M., 62, 72, 78
Baldwin, M., 61, 63, 69, 71, 77
Baldwin, M. A., 62, 77
Bandura, A., 251, 253
Barbee, E., 167, 168
Barber, K. A., 303, 311
Barger, S. D., 276, 281
Barkan, S., 257, 266
Barling, J. N., 184, 185, 191, 192,
    193, 194, 199, 205, 206
Barnett, D., 136, 137, 139, 143,
    145, 146
Barnett, O. L., 300, 311
Barn, R., 86, 88
Baron, L., 4, 15, 26, 33
Baron, R. M., 91, 101, 103
Barrera, M., 195, 200, 205
Barret-Lennard, G. T., 221, 233

Barry, K., 61, 77
Bass, E., 309, 311
Basta, J., 261, 263, 267
Bates, J. E., 55, 56
Baucom, D., 203, 206
Bavolek, S. J., 129, 133
Baxter, M., 60, 63, 77
Bayer, R., 273, 280
Beach, S. R. H., 126, 133
Beall, S. K., 276, 281
Beattie, M., 52, 56
Beauchamp, T., 215, 217
Beaudoin, G., 282
Beaudry, M., 229, 233
Becerra, R. M., 122, 133
Beck, A. T., 54, 56
Becker, J. V., 73, 77
Becker, R. L., 262, 267
Becker-Lausen, E., 49, 50, 51, 54,
    56, 57
Beddington, A., 86, 88
Beeman, S., 228, 234
Belanger, S., 277, 281, 284, 294
Belknap, R., 170, 181
Bell, C., 167, 168
Bell, C. C., 91, 103
Bell, R. Q., 102, 103
Belsky, J., 101, 103
Bennett, L. W., 208, 209, 210, 212,
    218
Bentovim, A., 74, 78
Berg, B. L., 302, 311
Bergen, R. K., 274, 280

Bergman, B., 36, 45
Berk, R. A., 235, 236, 240, 253, 254
Berliner, L., 309, 311
Berman, H., 261, 264, 266
Bernard, C., 80, 81-82, 83, 88
Bernstein, B. L., 221, 233
Bernstein, E. M., 54, 56
Berry, E., 121, 127, 133
Besharov, D., 32, 33
Best, C. L., 35, 38, 43, 45, 46
Biernacki, P., 180, 181
Bilinkoff, J., 102, 103
Blackshaw, L., 209, 217
Blau, J. R., 4, 15
Blau, P. M., 4, 15
Block, J., 91, 103
Block, J. H., 91, 103
Bloom, S. L., 275, 280
Bloor, M. J., 308, 311
Blossfeld, H., 212, 217
Bogdan, R. C., 299, 311
Bograd, M., 215, 217, 287, 294
Boldizar, J. P., 151, 159
Booney-McCoy, S., 119, 135, 183, 193
Bosley, G., 279, 280
Bothwell, S., 221, 228, 229, 234
Bouchard, M. A., 221, 228, 233
Boucher, R. J., 61, 71, 77
Bowker, L., 212, 217
Bowker, L. H., 163, 167, 168, 171, 181
Boyce-Beaman, J. M., 251, 253
Brandon, T. H., 274, 281
Brannen, S. J., 196, 197, 198, 199, 201, 202, 203
Brennan, A., 37, 45
Briere, J., 50, 51, 52, 55, 56, 71, 77
Bright, I., 200, 207
Brismar, B., 36, 45
Broadhurst, D. D., 129, 134
Brodeur, N., 282
Brongersma, E., 73, 77
Brooke, W., 196, 198, 199, 200, 202, 206
Broue, J., 286, 294
Brown, J., 217
Brown, P. D., 194, 200, 203, 206, 265, 266
Brown, R., 195, 200, 205
Browne, A., 49, 50, 56, 72, 74, 78, 191, 192
Brucato, L. L., 204, 206
Bukovec, P., 208
Burgess, A. W., 60, 62, 71, 72, 77
Burhrmester, D., 95, 103
Burman, B., 91, 103
Burt, M. R., 157, 159, 275, 280
Burton, S., 60, 78

Busby, D. M., 300, 311
Buzawa, C. G., 162, 168, 239, 253
Buzawa, E. S., 162, 168, 239, 253

Cadsky, O., 203, 206
Cahn, T. S., 183, 192
Callanan, P., 287, 294
Calvert, R., 4, 15
Campbell, A., 236, 240, 251, 253
Campbell, D. T., 24, 34
Campbell, J., 170, 181, 214, 217, 255, 261, 264, 266
Canino, I. A., 305, 311
Cantin, S., 219
Cantrell, P. J., 121, 133
Cardarelli, A. P., 81, 88
Cardwell, M., 170, 181
Carey, M., 95, 104
Carlson, B., 151, 160
Carnie, J., 59, 79
Carnochan, J., 136, 137, 146
Carpenter, M. M., 23, 34
Carrico, M. F., 121, 133
Carrillo, T. P., 213, 217
Carter, D. L., 61, 71, 77
Cascardi, M., 194, 203, 206
Castor-Lewis, C., 275, 280, 305, 311
Cate, R., 170, 181
Cavanaugh, E., 209, 210, 218
Ceci, S. J., 272, 280
Chaiken, S., 155, 159
Champagne, C., 299, 311
Channer, Y., 86, 88
Check, J. V. P., 53, 56
Chenail, R., 174, 181
Chiaramonte, J., 22, 33
Childress, J., 215, 217
Chinsky, J. M., 50, 54, 56
Choice, P., 296
Christensen, A., 100, 102, 104
Christoffel, K. K., 17, 22, 23, 25, 29, 33
Christopher, S., 170, 181
Cicchetti, D., 90, 92, 104, 136, 137, 139, 143, 145, 146, 147
Cisin, I. H., 192
Cleaver, H., 73, 77
Clingempeel, W. G., 96, 104
Clum, G. A., 35, 36, 44, 46
Cocozzelli, C., 210, 211, 217
Cohn, E. S., 152, 160
Colbus, D., 95, 104
Colder, M., 276, 281
Coleman, E. M., 35, 37, 44, 45, 51, 52, 53, 55, 56, 73, 77, 157, 158, 160
Coleman, J., 214, 217
Coleman, L., 81, 89

Coleman, S. M., 156, 159
Collins, P., 105
Compaan, C., 25, 34
Congress, E. P., 283, 294
Connell, J. P., 259, 260, 261, 266
Conte, J., 309, 311
Cook, A., 137, 146
Cook, A. S., 279, 280
Cook, K., 299, 311
Copeland, A. R., 25, 33
Corbin, J., 173, 182
Corey, G., 287, 294
Corey, M. S., 287, 294
Cortes, R. M., 90, 92, 104
Corzine, J., 4, 15
Cossom, J., 283, 284, 294
Counts, D., 214, 217
Court, J., 220, 233
Courtois, C. A., 49, 56
Coutu-Wakulczyk, G., 221, 233
Cowan, C. P., 96, 104
Cowan, P. A., 96, 104
Craig, S. E., 29, 33
Crawford, M., 203, 206
Creighton, S. J., 62, 78
Crisafulli, A., 101, 104
Crits-Christoph, P., 211, 218
Crittenden, P. A., 29, 33
Crowne, D. P., 152, 159
Culter, M., 210, 217
Cummingham-Rathner, J., 73, 77
Cummings, E. M., 91, 101, 103
Cyr Carmody, D., 119

Dabbs, J. M., 159
Danica, E., 63, 69, 70, 78
Dankwort, J., 285, 294
Dansky, B., 38, 46
Daro, D., 23, 24, 25, 32, 34
Darou, W. G., 299, 306, 311
Davidman, L., 275, 281
Davidson, W., 261, 263, 267
Davis, L., 309, 311
Davis, N., 63, 69, 70, 71, 78
Davis, P. T., 101, 103
Dawd, S., 90.92.104
Dawes, R. M., 120, 133
Day, B., 126, 134
Dean, C. W., 251, 253
Deblinger, E., 81, 88
DeCamp, J. W., 63, 70, 78
DeMaris, A., 210, 217
Dembo, R., 121, 127, 133
Dempster, H., 81, 88
DePaola, L. M., 93, 103
Department of Health and Human Services, 273, 280
Derogatis, L. R., 221, 233

Deschner, J. P., 196, 197, 198, 199, 202, 206
Desharnais, G., 221, 233
Dey, C., 81, 89
Deyoung, Y., 298, 311
Dibble, U., 157, 159
Dickstein, S., 91, 103
DiClemente, C. C., 205, 207
Dionne, D., 163, 168
Dobash, R., 3, 15, 59, 79, 216, 217
Dobash, R. E., 3, 15, 162, 168, 216, 217
Dodge, K., 50, 51, 53, 55, 56
Donato, K. M., 171, 181
Donnelly, D., 299, 311
Dornfeld, M., 126, 134
Doumas, D., 93, 103
Downs, W. R., 121, 127, 133
Driver, E., 82, 88
Droegemueller, W., 130, 134
Droisen, A., 82, 88
Dubois, G., 221, 230, 233
Dubrow, N., 91, 103
Duncan, L., 17
Dunford, F. W., 251, 253
Dunn, R. L., 200, 206
Durfee, M., 17, 22, 33
Dutton, D. G., 183, 185, 192, 205, 206, 213, 218
Dutton, M., 37, 45
Dutton-Douglas, M. A., 163, 168
Dutt, R., 87, 89
Dziuba-Leatherman, J., 29, 34, 56

Eagly, A. H., 9, 13, 15, 155, 159
Eblen, C. N., 121, 127, 133
Eckenrode, John, 105
Edelbrock, C., 50, 56
Edfeldt, A. W., 120, 133
Edleson, J. L., 157, 158, 159, 195, 204, 206, 208, 209, 213, 214, 217, 261, 266
Ehrensaft, M. K., 194, 206
Eisikovits, Z. C., 157, 158, 159, 208, 213, 217
Eldridge, H. J., 73, 78
Elinson, J., 186, 192
Ellard, J. H., 170, 171, 181
Elliott, D. M., 49, 51, 54, 56
Elliott, D. S., 251, 253
Ellis, J., 163, 168
Emerick, S. J., 24, 34
Emery, R. E., 91, 101, 103
Engfer, A., 100, 103
Ennew, J., 60, 61, 62, 71, 78
Ensom, R., 299, 312
Erel, O., 91, 103
Erooga, M., 81, 88

European Forum on Child Welfare (EFCW), 62, 78
Ewigman, B., 23, 32, 34
Ewigman, B. G., 23, 34
Eysenck, H. J., 232, 233

Fagan, J., 44, 45, 71, 78, 203, 206, 211, 212, 217
Falk, R. F., 91, 94, 96, 103
Fallon, B. C., 43, 45
Fals-Borda, O., 310, 311
Fantuzzo, J. W., 93, 103
Farley, S. C., 157, 158, 160
Farrington, D. P., 92, 103
Farris, A. M., 101, 104
Fauber, R., 91, 103
Faust, D., 120, 133
Featherman, J., 300, 304, 311
Fehrenbach, P. A., 194, 206
Feldbau, S., 200, 203, 206
Feld, S. L., 13, 15
Felson, R. B., 251, 254
Ferraro, K. J., 170, 171, 181
Fiala, R., 25, 26, 31, 34
Fichman, L., 50, 56
Field, H. S., 275, 281
Figueredo, A. S., 92, 104, 126, 134
Finch, A. J., 95, 104
Fincham, F. D., 91, 101, 103
Fine, M., 298, 307, 308, 309, 311
Fink, A., 120, 133
Finkel, M., 81, 88
Finkelhor, D., 17, 29, 34, 49, 50, 51, 56, 59, 72, 74, 78, 81, 88, 119, 120, 125, 126, 128, 129, 135, 136, 145, 146, 184, 192
Finn, J., 208, 217
Firestone, P., 299, 312
Fishburne, P. M., 186, 192
Fisher, C. B., 277, 281
Fisher, E., 162, 168, 298, 312
Fisher, J., 232, 233
Fitts, W., 221, 228
Follette, W. C., 203, 206
Follingstad, D., 37, 45
Folstein, S. F., 271
Fontes, C., 296
Fontes, L. A., 296, 298, 303, 305, 307, 308, 309, 311
Foo, L., 93, 104
Ford, D., 243, 253
Ford-Gilboe, M., 261, 264, 266
Forehand, R., 91, 103
Fortin, F., 221, 233
Foster, L. R., 24, 34
Foster, R. A., 209, 210, 217
Fox, J. A., 22, 34
Foy, D. W., 35, 37, 44, 45

Frankel, S. L., 155, 156, 157, 160
Franklin, J. N., 121, 133
Freedy, J., 45
Freeman, H., 209, 210, 211, 218, 255, 267
Freeman, H. E., 208, 209, 211
Freeman, P., 73, 77
Frieze, I. H., 191, 192
Froehlke, R. G., 23, 34
Frongillo, E., 105
Fueyo, J., 210, 217
Furby, L., 209, 217
Furman, W., 95, 103

Gabrielsen, D. L., 49, 51, 54, 56
Gagné, L., 232, 234
Gagné, P., 236, 253
Gallagher, B., 63, 78
Galliher, J. F., 301, 311
Gamache, D. J., 213, 266; 217.261
Ganley, A. L., 199, 206
Garbarino, J., 91, 103, 122, 133, 159
Gardner, K. H., 186, 192
Gardner, W., 276, 278, 281
Garey, L., 257, 266
Garfield, S. L., 204, 206, 232, 233
Garmezy, N., 102, 103
Garske, J. P., 232, 233
Gartin, P., 251, 253
Garvin, D. R., 205, 207
Gauthier, B., 233
Gavey, N., 310, 312
Gellert, G., 22, 33
Gelles, R. J., 3, 4, 5, 13, 15, 16, 32, 34, 36, 42, 46, 49, 50, 56, 57, 120, 121, 122, 125, 126, 127, 129, 132, 133, 135, 161, 168, 169, 184, 185, 193, 211, 217, 223, 233, 236, 254
Gerrard, N., 305, 312
Getreu, A., 121, 127, 133
Ghosh, C., 91, 104
Gibbon, M., 39, 46
Gilbert, N., 262, 266
Giles-Sims, J., 121, 133
Ginzburg, H., 209, 210, 218
Giovannoni, J. M., 122, 133
Glaser, B. G., 173, 181
Glaser, R., 276, 281
Glenn, E., 300, 311
Goldberg, J. E., 286, 294
Goldfriend, M. R., 232, 233
Goldman, L., 281
Goldstein, M. S., 208, 209, 211, 218
Gomes-Schwartz, B., 81, 88
Gondolf, E. W., 162, 168, 183, 191, 192, 208, 209, 210, 212, 213,

217, 255, 260, 265, 266, 298, 312
Goodman, M. S., 43, 45
Gordis, E., 91, 104
Gosselin, J., 286, 294
Gottfried, H., 310, 312
Gottman, J., 213, 217
Gottman, J. M., 183, 191, 192, 194
Gouvernement du Québec, 283, 284, 287, 294
Graham, D. L. R., 172, 181
Grayson, M., 151, 152, 157, 158, 160
Greaves, L., 299, 311
Green, B., 35, 37, 45
Greenbaum, C., 90, 92, 104
Greenblat, C. S., 6, 9, 13, 14, 15, 152, 159
Groner, L., 60, 62, 78
Groth, A. N., 72, 77
Grubb, H. J., 121, 133
Gruscznski, R. J., 204, 206, 213, 217
Grych, J. H., 101, 103
Guba, E., 264, 266
Guévremont, C., 286, 294
Gunn, M., 85, 88
Guttmann, E., 157, 158, 159

Hahlweg, K., 200, 203, 206
Hamberger, L. K., 195, 200, 204, 206, 210, 213, 217
Hamby, S. L., 17, 119, 120, 125, 126, 128, 129, 135
Hamerle, A., 212, 217
Hames, M., 60, 78
Hammond, M., 50, 57
Hampton, R. L., 120, 133, 161, 168
Hansen, D. J., 43, 44, 45
Hanson, R., 203, 206
Hanusa, D., 126, 134
Hardy, J., 221, 233
Hardy, K. V., 300, 312
Hare, I., 286, 295
Hare-Mustin, R., 298, 312
Hargreaves, W. A., 221, 234
Hargrove, J., 54, 56
Harper, L. V., 102, 103
Harrell, A. V., 186, 192, 209, 217
Harris, G., 208, 218
Harris, J., 196, 197, 198, 199, 201, 203, 206
Harris, R., 196, 198, 199, 206
Harrison, M., 214, 218
Harrop, J. W., 50, 57, 120, 121, 122, 124, 127, 128, 133, 135
Hart, B., 208, 211, 216, 218
Hart, S., 213, 218
Hartman, C. R., 60, 62, 77
Harvey, W. B., 162, 168

Harwood, H., 209, 210, 218
Haskin-Herkenham, D., 286, 295
Hastings, J. E., 195, 200, 204, 206, 210, 213, 217
Hause, E., 37, 45
Hause, E. S., 184, 192
Haynes, M. R., 157, 158, 160
Hazelwood, L. R., 196, 197, 198, 199, 202, 204, 207, 241, 249, 254
Heath, A., 174, 181
Helfer, R. E., 129, 134
Henton, J., 170, 181
Herbert, T. B., 170, 171, 181
Herman, J. L., 55, 56, 299, 312
Herrenkohl, R. C., 137, 146
Hersen, M., 137, 146
Herzberger, S. D., 151, 159
Hetherington, E. M., 96, 104
Heyman, R. E., 195, 197, 198, 199, 200, 201, 202, 203, 206, 207
Higgens, A., 277, 281
Hilberman, E., 220, 233
Hill, R. H., 4, 15
Hinde, R. A., 100, 103
Hindelang, M. J., 4, 15
Hirschel, J. D., 251, 253
Hochstadt, N. J., 144, 146
Hodgins, S., 220, 233
Hofeller, K., 163, 168, 222, 225, 233
Hoff, L.A., 259, 260, 266
Hoffmeister, J. K., 129, 134
Hohepa, M. K., 301, 312
Holamon, B., 162, 169
Holden, G. W., 90, 91, 103, 156, 159
Holinger, D. P., 26, 34
Holinger, P. C., 26, 34
Holland, T. P., 283, 294
Holm, C. F., 298, 312
Holtzworth-Munroe, A., 128, 133, 183, 191, 192, 194, 204, 206
Hooper, C. A., 81, 86, 88
Horley, S., 220, 233
Horney, J., 4, 15
Horowitz, J. M., 81, 88
Hosmer, D. W., 186, 192
Hotaling, G. T., 49, 56, 121, 122, 124, 126, 127, 133, 134, 135
Houskamp, B., 37, 45
Hower, M. G., 54, 56
Howes, P., 91, 103
Howitt, D., 73, 74, 78
Hubbard, R., 209, 210, 218, 298, 312
Hudson, C., 210, 211, 217
Huff-Corzine, L., 4, 15
Hughes, B., 63, 78
Hughes, H. M., 92, 103
Huizinga, D., 251, 253
Hum, A., 299, 306, 311

Hunt, P., 62, 72, 78
Hunter, J. E., 251, 254
Huston, K., 288, 294
Hutchison, I. W., III, 251, 253

Ima, K., 298, 312
Ireland, K., 62, 78
Itzin, C., 58, 59, 60, 64, 78
Izzo, R., 210, 218

Jackson, J., 210, 217
Jacob, M., 167, 168
Jacobs, J. L., 81, 88
Jacobson, N., 213, 217, 257, 266
Jacobson, N. S., 183, 191, 192, 194, 203, 206
Jaffe, P. G., 14, 15, 93, 100, 103, 139, 146
Jaggar, A., 216, 218
Jakubowski, P. A., 229, 233
Janoff-Bulmann, R., 91, 104
Jasinski, J. L., 5, 15, 25, 34, 125, 134, 185, 192
Jason, J., 23, 34
Jaudes, P. K., 144, 146
Jenkins, E. J., 91, 103
Jenkins, J. M., 102, 104
Jennings, J. L., 151, 159, 205, 206
John, R. S., 90, 91, 93, 100, 102, 103, 104
Johnson, I. M., 170, 181
Johnson, J., 263, 266
Johnson, J.M., 170, 171, 181
Johnson, J.T., 81, 88
Johnson, M., 302, 312
Johnson, M. P., 13, 15, 183, 192
Johnson, M. R. D., 86, 88
Johnson, P., 6, 14, 15
Jones, A., 87, 88
Jones, B., 137, 146
Jones, T., 196, 198, 199, 200, 202, 206
Joseph, J., 161
Jouriles, E. N., 36, 45, 91, 100, 104, 121, 126, 127, 134, 185, 192, 199, 205
Julien, P., 54, 56

Kaci, J. H., 213, 218
Kaiser, H. F., 5, 15
Kalaher, S., 195, 200, 205
Kalmuss, D., 184, 191, 192
Kaloupek, D. G., 271
Kaplan, H. R., 186, 193
Karch, L., 299, 312
Karlin, R., 221, 233
Kassebaum, G., 209, 218

Kaufman, J., 49, 56, 137, 146, 155, 159
Kaufman Kantor, G., 3, 4, 5, 13, 14, 15, 25, 34, 121, 125, 127, 129, 134, 135, 183, 184, 185, 192, 241, 253
Kazdim, A. E., 95, 104, 126, 134
Keane, T. M., 271
Keith, A., 17
Keith-Spiegel, P., 274, 276, 281, 303, 312
Kelder, L. R., 151, 160
Kelly, L., 59, 60, 73, 74, 75, 78
Kemp, A., 35, 37, 45
Kempe, C. H., 130, 134
Kendall-Tackett, K. A., 105, 136, 145, 146
Kennedy, L. W., 23, 34
Kenney, D. A., 91, 101, 103
Keyson, M., 300, 311
Kiecolt-Glaser, J. K., 276, 281
Kilpatrick, A., 283, 294
Kilpatrick, D. G., 35, 37, 38, 39, 43, 44, 45, 46
Kinard, M., 17, 277, 281
Kirkwood, C., 172, 174, 180, 181
Kivlahan, C., 23, 24, 32, 34
Klang, M., 36, 45
Klap, R., 236, 240, 253
Klostermann, L. A. R., 221, 233
Knight, R., 61, 71, 73, 77
Knudsen, D. D., 120, 134
Kocher, G. P., 303, 312
Koestner, R., 50, 56
Kolko, D. J., 126, 134
Koocher, G. P., 274, 276, 281
Korbin, J. E., 122, 134
Koski, P. R., 152, 160
Koss, M. P., 92, 104, 277, 281
Kostelny, K., 91, 103
Kovac, M., 95, 104
Koval, J., 170, 181
Kowalski, K., 214, 218
Krispin, O., 90, 92, 104
Kroon, L., 63, 78
Krugman, R. D., 25, 34
Krull, A. C., 235
Kruttschnitt, C., 126, 134
Kruz, D., 167, 168
Kubisch, A. C., 259, 260, 261, 266
Kurtness, J., 299, 306, 311
Kurtz, R., 232, 233
Kuther-Qubeck, T. L., 277, 281
Kwoh, C., 210, 218

LaFontaine, J. S., 63, 69, 78
LaFree, G., 25, 26, 31, 34
Lalonde, C., 203, 206
Lalumiere, M., 208, 218

Lamb, M. E., 90, 92, 104
Lambert, L., 93, 103
Landenburger, K., 171, 180, 181
Land, G., 23, 24, 32, 34
Langevin, R., 59, 73, 78
Langhinrichsen, J., 194, 206
Lang, R. A., 59, 73, 78
LaPorte, R., 210, 218
Lapp, R., 299, 312
Larouche, G., 220, 221, 222, 224, 226, 229, 231, 232, 233, 234
Larsen, D. L., 221, 234
Larsson, G., 36, 45
La Taillade, J. J., 183, 191, 192, 213, 217
Laughlin, J. E., 184, 192
Lavoie, F., 167, 168, 221, 234, 285, 295
LaVoie, L., 121, 127, 133
Layne, C., 50, 56
Lebowitz, L., 275, 281
LeCompte, S. H., 91, 100, 104
Lecomte, C., 221, 233
Lee, J., 299, 312
Lee, R. M., 304, 312
Leiberman, E., 257, 266
Lemert, E. M., 236, 254
Lemeshow, S., 186, 192
Lempert, R., 235, 254
Leonard, K., 251, 253
Leonard, K. E., 184, 192
Leong, G. B., 287, 294
Levine, M., 25, 34, 272, 273, 275, 278, 281
Lewis, D., 208, 218
Lewis, E., 230, 234
Lewis, I. A., 49, 56
Lidz, C., 276, 278, 281
Lidz, C. W., 210, 212, 218, 273, 278, 281
Ligezinska, M., 299, 312
Light, R. J., 130, 134
Lincoln, A. J., 121, 122, 124, 133
Lincoln, Y., 264, 266
Lindquist, C. U., 196, 197, 198, 200, 206
Lindsay, J., 282
Lindsey, D., 32, 34
Linz, D., 151, 152, 157, 158, 160
Lipchik, E., 214, 218
Lippmann, J., 81, 88
Lipson, J. G., 3, 306, 312
Lisak, D., 277, 281
Lisman, S. A., 274, 281
Litrownik, Alan J., 136
Liu, K., 25, 33
Lloyd, S., 170, 181
Lockhart, L., 163, 168
Lockhart, L. L., 298, 300, 312

Lofberg, C. E., 81, 89
Loftin,C., 4, 15
Longbaugh, R., 208, 218
Long, N., 91, 103
Lorde, A., 302, 312
Lorey, R., 90, 92, 104
Luborsky, L., 211, 218
Lynch, A. B., 151, 152, 157, 158, 160
Lynch, M. A., 74, 78
Lynn, S. J., 151, 160, 232, 233

Maccoby, E. E., 92, 104
MacEwen, C., 185, 192, 199, 205
MacKellar, F. L., 27, 34
MacKenzie, D. A., 167, 169
MacLeod, L., 226, 234
MacLeod, M., 81, 82, 88
Maguire, P., 299, 312
Maiuro, R. D., 183, 192
Malamuth, N. M, 53, 56
Malinosky-Rummell, R., 43, 44, 45
Mallon-Kraft, S., 49
Malone, J., 184, 185, 191, 193, 194, 195, 199, 202, 206, 207
Mama, A., 85, 89
Mangold, W. D., 152, 160
Manion, I. G., 299, 311
Manly, J. T., 137, 139, 143, 145, 146, 147
Marcus, P., 121, 134
Margolin, G., 90, 91, 92, 93, 100, 102, 103, 104, 203, 206, 287, 294
Margolin, L., 25, 34
Marineau, R., 221, 230, 233
Markman, H. J., 200, 206
Markman, J. J., 91, 103
Marlowe, D., 152, 159
Marsden, M. E., 209, 210, 218
Marshall, C., 174, 181
Marshall, W. L., 51, 52, 53, 54, 56, 61, 78
Martin, D., 220, 234
Martin, G., 167, 168, 221, 234, 285, 295
Martin, J. A., 92, 104
Martinez, P., 91, 104, 126, 128, 134
Martinez, T. E., 300, 311
Martino, T., 93, 103
Masson, H., 81, 88
Matocha, L. K., 305, 312
Matthews, D. J., 102, 104
Mattson, M., 213, 218
Mayer, K., 212, 217
McCarty, D., 210, 218
McCausland, M. P., 72, 77
McClain, P. W., 23, 24, 34
McCloskey, L., 120, 126, 133, 134

McCloskey, L. A., 92, 104
McCormick, M., 257, 266
McCurdy, K., 23, 34
McDonald, R., 101, 104
McEvoy, J., III, 4, 5, 15
McFerron, J. R., 162, 168
McFerron, R. J., 298, 312
McGee, R. A., 136, 137, 146
McHugh, M. C., 191, 192
McIntyre, J., 299, 312
McLaughlin, I. G., 184, 192
McMahon, M., 195, 206
McNamara, J. R., 151, 160
McNeil, J. S., 196, 197, 198, 199, 202, 206
McWhinney, M., 286, 295
Meehl, P. E., 120, 133
Meier, J., 163, 168
Meinert, C. L., 258, 266
Mendoza, C., 228, 234
Menard, S., 184, 185, 193
Meredith, W. H., 121, 134
Meyer, M., 81, 89
Mickish, J., 163, 168
Mihalic, D. E., 184, 185, 193
Miles, J., 86, 88
Milkulincer, M., 53, 56
Miller, B. A., 121, 127, 133, 186, 193
Miller, D. T., 157, 159, 160
Miller, J., 235
Miller, N. B., 91, 94, 96, 103
Miller, P., 170, 181
Mills, T., 172, 174, 180, 181
Milner, J., 81, 84, 89
Milner, J. S., 129, 134
Minneapolis Hearings (1988), 63
Mintz, J., 211, 218
Mittelman, M., 73, 77
Monaco, V., 194, 206
Monahan, J., 263, 266, 273, 278, 281
Montgomery, L. M., 200, 207
Moore, D. W., 3, 119, 120, 125, 126, 128, 129, 135
Morash, M., 120, 134
Morgan, M., 296
Morrison, A., 91, 103
Morrison, E., 212, 218
Moy, C., 210, 218
Mrazek, P., 74, 78
Mtezuka, M., 80, 82, 89
Muller, R., 251, 254
Mulvey, E., 210, 212, 218, 263, 266, 273, 276, 278, 281
Munson, K., 220, 233
Muntarbhorn, V., 62, 78
Murphy, W. D., 157, 158, 160
Myers, L. J., 162, 167, 168

Nantel, M., 221, 228, 233
National Center on Child Abuse and Neglect, 125, 129, 134, 138, 147
National Commission on the Causes and Prevention of Violence, 4, 5, 15
National Commission for the Protection of Human Subjects of Biomedical and Behavioral Research, 273, 281
National Committee for Prevention of Child Abuse, 121, 134
National Research Council, 216, 218
Neckerman, A., 37, 45
Neff, J. A., 162, 169
Neidig, P. H., 36, 45, 191, 193, 195, 197, 198, 199, 200, 201, 202, 203, 207
Nelson, C., 4, 15
Nelson, F. D., 186, 192
Nelson, W. M., 95, 104
Newberger, C., 126, 134
Newberger, E., 257, 266
New Hampshire v. Johnson, 123, 134
Newlove, T., 213, 217
Newman, Elana, 271
Nguyen, T. D., 221, 234
NiCarthy, G., 172, 181, 309, 312
Norwood, W. D., 121, 126, 127, 134
Nurco, D., 186, 192
Nuremberg Code, 272, 281

Ogland-Hand, S. M., 35, 37, 44, 45
Ohenaba-Sakyi, Y., 121, 134
O'Keefe, M., 91, 93, 104, 121, 126, 127, 134
Okun, L. E., 195, 204, 206
Okwumabua, T., 200, 207
O'Leary, K. D., 36, 42, 43, 44, 45, 91, 104, 184, 185, 191, 192, 193, 194, 195, 197, 198, 199, 200, 201, 202, 203, 204, 205, 206, 207, 229, 234
Osborne, L. H., 101, 103
Osthoff, B., 299, 312
Owens, D., 5, 15

Pagelow, M. D., 222, 234
Painter, S., 185, 192
Palmer, S., 195, 200, 205
Paltiel, F. L., 222, 234
Pan, H. S., 36, 45, 191, 193, 195, 203, 207
Panek, D. D., 121, 127, 133
Pâquet-Deehy, A., 222, 229, 231, 232, 234

Pardo, C., 91, 103
Parke, R., 91.103
Parke, R. D., 92, 104
Parker, H., 63, 78
Parker, J. C., 213, 218
Parker, R. N., 4, 15
Parkes, C. M., 279, 281
Parkinson, D., 92, 103
Parton, N., 86, 88
Patterson, G. R., 92, 104
Paymar, M., 213, 218
Pekarik, G., 204, 207
Pelcovitz, D., 45
Pence, E., 195, 206, 210, 211, 213, 218
Pennebaker, J. W., 276, 281
Perlman, D., 53, 56
Perry, L. C., 151, 159
Peters, D., 272, 280
Peterson-Lewis, S., 162, 169
Pettit, G. S., 55, 56
Pfiffner, L. J., 91, 104
Pfouts, J. H., 223, 234
Phillips, M., 82, 83, 87, 89
Pillemer, K., 4, 16, 184, 191, 193
Pines, A., 61, 71, 79
Pittinsky, T., 137, 146
Pless, I. B., 130, 134
Plotkin, J., 272, 280
Pokorny, A. D., 186, 193
Polek, D., 37, 45
Polek, D. S., 184, 192
Politano, M., 95, 104
Prentice, D. A., 157, 159
Prentky, R. A., 61, 71, 77, 78
Price, H., 151
Print, B., 81, 89
Pritchard, C., 32, 34
Prochaska, J. O., 205, 207
Project MATCH, 213, 218
Putnam, F. W., 54, 56

Quinsey, V., 208, 218

Rachal, J. V., 209, 210, 218
Radbill, S. X., 122, 134
Random House Webster's College Dictionary, 51, 55, 56
Rathus, S. A., 221, 228, 234
Rau, M. B., 277, 281
Rawlings, E., 35, 37, 45
Rawlings, E. I., 172, 181
Reed, J. S., 4, 15
Regan, L., 60, 78
Reid, W. J., 101, 104
Reinharz, S., 257, 258, 266, 275, 281

Renzetti, C. M., 304, 312
Resick, P., 45
Resnick, H. S., 35, 38, 43, 44, 45, 46
Resnick, P. J., 27, 34, 39, 45
Revenstorf, D., 203, 206
Rice, M., 208, 218
Richie, B. E., 298, 305, 312
Richie, K. L., 90, 91, 103
Richters, J. E., 91, 104, 126, 128, 134
Rickel, A. U., 49, 57
Riggs, D., 37, 44, 46
Rinfret-Raynor, M., 219, 222, 229, 231, 232, 234
Robbins, P. C., 263, 266, 273, 278, 281
Robinson, S., 271
Rodgers, A., 95, 104
Rollins, B. C., 121, 134
Rondeau, G., 282, 287, 295
Roosa, M., 93, 104
Rosen, K. H., 170-171, 174, 180, 181, 182
Rosenbaum, A., 181, 184, 185, 193, 194, 206, 229, 234
Rosenfeld, B. D., 195, 207, 208, 209, 211, 218
Ross, D. P., 224, 234
Ross, R., 210, 218
Rossi, P., 209, 210, 211, 218, 255, 267
Rossman, G. B., 174, 181
Roth, S., 45, 275, 277, 281
Rothbaum, F., 92, 104
Rotter, J. B., 53, 55, 56, 57
Rouleau, J. L., 73, 77
Rowe, E., 105
Roy, M., 223, 234
Ruback, R. B., 298, 312
Rubin, A., 196, 197, 198, 199, 201, 202, 203, 205
Rueckert, Quentin H., 151
Rumptz, M., 261, 263, 267
Runtz, M., 50, 56, 71, 77
Runyan, D., 120, 125, 126, 128, 129, 135
Rushe, R. H., 183, 191, 192, 213, 217
Russell, D., 209, 217
Russell, D. E. H., 59, 61, 74, 79, 81, 89, 297, 312
Russell, M. D., 130, 134
Russell Hathaway, C., 81, 88
Rutledge, L. L., 37, 45, 184, 192
Ryan, R. M., 137, 147

Sacks, J. J., 23, 34
Salt, P., 81, 89
Salter, A. C., 73, 79

Sampson, R. J., 20, 31, 34
Sandler, I. N., 93, 104
Sandlow, J., 26, 34
Sarga, E., 81, 82, 88, 89
Sariola, H., 62, 79
Sarsfield, P., 167, 169
Saunders, B. E., 35, 37, 38, 43, 45, 46, 50, 54, 56, 57
Saunders, D. G., 126, 134, 151, 152, 156, 157, 158, 160, 184, 185, 193, 213, 218
Sauzier, M., 81, 89
Savage, S., 196, 198, 199, 200, 202, 206
Saylor, M., 73, 79
Schacter, J., 144, 146
Schaef, A. W., 52, 57
Schare, M., 209, 218
Schechter, S., 4, 15, 257, 259, 260, 266, 267
Schlee, K., 199, 206
Schluter, T. D., 162, 169
Schmeidler, J., 121, 127, 133
Schmidt, K. L., 156, 159
Schmidt, M., 300, 312
Schneider, C., 129, 134
Schock, M., 261, 266
Schock, M. D., 213, 217
Schoen, K., 163, 168
Schorr, L. B., 259, 260, 261, 266
Schurman, R. A., 297, 312
Schwebel, A. I., 200, 206
Sedlak, A. J., 129, 134
Segal, J., 53, 56
Seghorn, T. K., 71, 78
Sela-Amit, M., 157, 158, 159
Selzer, M., 186, 193
Senchak, M., 184, 192, 251, 253
Seng, M. J., 59, 71, 73, 79
Shadish, W. R., 200, 207
Sharpe, L. K., 276, 281
Sheley, J. F., 20, 34
Shepard, M., 261, 267
Sherman, L. W., 4, 15, 235, 246, 250, 254, 258, 264, 267
Shields, A. M., 137, 147
Shillington, R., 224, 234
Short, J., 213, 217
Shortt, J. W., 183, 191, 192
Shupe, A., 196, 197, 198, 199, 202, 204, 207, 241, 249, 254
Sibald, A. D., 130, 134
Sieber, J. E., 272, 281
Siegel, T., 95, 104
Silbert, M., 61, 71, 79
Silva, J. A., 287, 294
Silver, H. K., 130, 134
Silver, R. C., 170, 171, 181
Silverman, F. H., 134, 1130
Silverman, R. A., 23, 34

Simmons, R. G., 276, 281
Simon, L. M. L., 36, 44, 46
Simonetti, R. M., 20, 34
Sirles, E. A., 81, 89, 214, 218
Size, P. B., 156, 160
Slaby, R. G., 92, 104
Smith, C., 49, 56, 119
Smith, G., 81, 89
Smith, G. H., 301, 303, 308, 312
Smith, J., 210, 218
Smith, L. T., 297, 310, 311, 312
Smith, M. A., 102, 104, 130, 134
Smith, M. D., 157, 158, 159, 160
Smith, S. M., 157, 158, 160
Smith, T., 309, 311
Sobel, L. C., 205, 207
Sobell, M. B., 205, 207
Sommers, C., 262, 267
Sonkin, D. J., 286, 288, 295
Sorenson, S. A., 162, 167, 169
Spaccarelli, S., 93, 104
Spanier, G. B., 221, 229, 234
Spielberger, C., 95, 104
Spitzer, R., 39, 46
Spivak, H., 271
Spohn, C., 4, 15
Spurlock, J., 305, 311
Stacey, W. A., 196, 197, 198, 199, 202, 204, 207, 241, 249, 254
Stark, E., 162, 169, 251, 254
Stark, R., 4, 5, 15
Statistics Canada, 224, 234
Stauffer, J., 81, 88
Steele, B. F., 130, 134
Steer, R., 81, 88
Steffen, V. J., 9, 13, 15
Steffensmeir, D., 13, 15
Steggell, G. L., 300, 311
Steinman, M., 213, 218, 261, 267
Steinmetz, S. K., 4, 16, 36, 42, 46, 120, 125, 127, 132, 135, 184, 193, 236, 254
Sternberg, K. J., 90, 92, 104
Stets, J. E., 4, 15, 122, 134, 246, 254
Stevenson-Hinde, J., 100, 103
Stith, S. M., 170, 180, 182
Stokes, E., 301, 312
Stollak, G., 251, 254
Stouthamer-Loeber, M., 92, 104
Straham, R. F., 199, 207
Strand, V. C., 81, 89
Straus, M. A., 3, 4, 5, 13, 14, 15, 16, 17, 25, 31, 34, 36, 42, 46, 50, 57, 94, 104, 119, 120, 121, 122, 123, 124, 125, 126, 127, 128, 129, 132, 133, 134, 135, 154, 157, 159, 160, 161, 169, 184, 185, 191, 192, 193, 194, 199, 207, 212, 218, 221, 225, 234, 236, 246, 254

Strauss, A. L., 173, 181, 182
Streifel, C., 241, 254
Stroup, W., 235
Stuart, G. L., 128, 133, 183, 191, 192, 204, 206
Sugarman, D. B., 119, 126, 127, 134, 135, 152, 155, 156, 157, 160, 183, 184, 190, 191, 192
Suitor, J. J., 4, 16, 184, 191, 193
Sullivan, C., 261, 263, 267
Surber, M., 208, 209, 211, 218
Susman, J. R., 276, 281
Sutton, S., 93, 103
Syers, M., 209, 217

Tan, C., 261, 267
Tarasoff v. Regents of the University of California, California Supreme Court 529 T2d 553.
Tarrant, S., 213, 218
Tate, T., 60, 79
Taussig, H. N., 136
Taylor, J., 196, 197, 198, 200, 206
Tedeschi, J. T., 251, 254
Teichman, M., 243, 254
Teichman, Y., 243, 254
Telch, C. U., 196, 197, 198, 200, 206
Tennen, H., 151, 159
Theodorson, G., 257, 267
Thomas, A. M., 91, 126, 134
Thomas, J., 151
Thompson, L., 174, 182, 296, 298, 299, 312
Thorne-Finch, R., 216, 218
Tiebout, J., 276, 281
Tilby, P. J., 221, 233
Tilton Durfee, D., 22, 33
Tolman, R. M., 195, 206, 208, 209, 210, 212, 213, 217, 218, 228, 234
Tong, R., 162, 169
Toth, S. L., 139, 143, 145, 147
Toulouse, J. M., 221, 228, 229, 234
Trocki, K., 297, 312
Trocme, N., 32, 34
Trute, B., 167, 169
Tull, E., 210, 218
Turner, C. W., 162, 169
Tyler, C. W., 23, 34
Tyree, A., 184, 185, 191, 193, 194, 199, 206

United States Advisory Board, 22, 23, 24, 25, 33, 34

United States Department of Justice, 121-122, 135
Urquiza, A. J., 272, 281

Valliant, G., 211, 212, 218
Van der Kolk, B., 45
Vanderveer, P. L., 61, 71, 77
Vargo, M., 92, 103
Veronen, L., 37, 45
Vilehauer, M., 271
Viliquette, C., 221, 228, 233, 234
Vissing, Y. M., 50, 57, 121, 122, 124, 127, 128, 135
Vitaliano, P. P., 183, 192
Vivian, D., 185, 192, 194, 195, 199, 205, 206, 207
Vormbrock, J., 37, 45

Wagner, B. C., 183, 192
Walbash, M., 121, 127, 133
Waldo, M., 211, 218
Walker, L. E., 156-157, 160, 163, 169, 194, 207, 212, 218, 222, 226, 234
Walters, R. H., 251, 253
Waltz, J., 183, 191, 194, 206, 213, 217
Ward, D., 209, 218
Waterhouse, L., 59, 72, 74, 79
Wauchope, B., 119, 120, 134
Weaver, T. L., 35, 36, 43, 44, 46
Webster-Stratton, C., 50, 57
Weiner, N. A., 298, 312
Weinrott, M. R., 73, 79, 209, 217
Weinstock, R., 287, 294
Weise, D., 23, 24, 25, 32, 34
Weiss, B., 95, 104
Weiss, C. H., 172, 259, 260, 261, 266, 267
Weiss, R. S., 53, 57
Weissman, M. M., 221, 228, 229, 234
Weisz, J. R., 92, 95, 104
Wells, G., 299, 312
Wells, S., 255, 266
Wendorf, J. D., 287, 295
Wendorf, R. J., 287, 295
Werk, A., 228, 234
West, C., 17
Western, B., 236, 240, 253
Westkott, M., 257, 267
Wexler, S., 71, 78
White, K. M., 126, 134
Widom, C. S., 50, 51, 57, 92, 104, 274, 277, 281

Wieder, D. L., 303, 312
Wierson, M., 91, 103
Wierzbicki, M., 204, 207
Wild, N. J., 62, 63, 72, 79
Willback, D., 287, 295
Williams, J., 39, 46
Williams, K. R., 184, 193
Williams, L., 25, 34
Williams, L. M., 136, 145, 146
Williams, O. J., 251, 254, 262, 267
Williams, W., 121, 127, 133
Wilner, D. M., 208, 209, 211, 218
Wilson, M. R., 80, 82, 83, 85, 86, 89, 200, 207, 298, 312
Wilson, P., 200, 207
Wilson, S., 139, 146
Wilson, S. K., 14, 15, 93, 100, 103, 136, 137, 146
Wingfield, R., 60, 78
Wirtz, W., 186, 192
Wish, E. D., 121, 127, 133
Woffardt, S., 184, 185, 193
Wolak, J., 17
Wolf, C., 215, 218
Wolf, S., 309, 311
Wolfe, C., 264, 267
Wolfe, D., 139, 146
Wolfe, D. A., 14, 15, 93, 104, 136, 137, 146
Wolfe, F. M., 157, 160
Wolfgang, M. E., 4, 16
Woods, L., 162, 169
World Health Organization, 17, 34
Wright, J. D., 20, 34
Wyatt, G. E., 81, 89, 297, 312
Wybraniecm, J., 235
Wylie, A., 299, 312
Wyre, R., 61, 72, 73, 79

Yanagishita, M., 27, 34
Yin, R. K., 174, 182
Yllö, K., 255, 256, 257, 264, 266, 267
Yuen, S. A., 136, 137, 146

Zak, L., 93, 103, 139, 146
Zdep, S. M., 126, 135
Zegree, J. B., 183, 192
Zieserl, E. J., 22, 33
Zigler, E. F., 49, 56, 155, 159, 298, 311
Zimo, D. A., 144, 146
Zuroff, D. C., 50, 56

Subject Index

Academic performance, child neglect and, 105-111
Adult-Adolescent Parenting Inventory (ASPI), 129
Adults, sexual abuse. *See* Sexual abuse (of adults)
Advocacy, collaborating for, 262-265
African Americans:
  child homicide and, 18, 21-22
  marital violence surveys, 5, 10
  mothers' responses to children's sexual abuse, 80-88
  spousal violence, 161-168, 236-252
Age:
  child homicide and, 29, 30
  marital violence and, 4, 10-11, 191
  romantic partner assault, 39
Aggression:
  attitudes, towards in families, 151-159
  psychological aggression scale, 125, 128
Alcohol, romantic partner abuse and, 44-45, 165, 186, 191, 241
Arrest, of violent husbands, 4, 162-163, 235-252
Assault. *See* Physical assault; Romantic partner assault; Wife abuse
Attitudes Towards Aggression Scale (ATA), 152-159

Battered women. *See* Romantic partner assault; Wife abuse
Batterer programs, 208-217
Beck Depression Inventory, 54
Black population. *See* African Americans

CAP Inventory, 129, 130
CAT (Child Abuse and Trauma) scale, 50, 54
Child abuse:
  academic achievement and disciplinary problems, 105-111
  approval won through, 67-68, 70
  by family members, 63-67
  by rapists, 73
  characteristics of, 76
  Child Abuse Act (1974), 121
  classifying maltreatment, 113-117, 119-133, 136-146
  coercion through violence in, 70
  cognitive development affected by, 50
  defined, 59, 69
  denial characteristics of, 72
  emotional abuse and, 54, 65, 70
  externalized aggressive behavior from, 50, 51
  factors for decrease, 27
  fatalities, 24-26
  group sex as, 66, 67
  intergenerational nature of, 49, 65, 66, 69, 71, 76

  internalized behavior from, 50, 51
  interpersonal difficulties and, 49-51
  intimacy problems following, 49-56
  measuring maltreatment, 122-133
  national incidence studies, 59, 129, 136-146
  officially reported cases, 129
  as organized abuse, 76
  organized crime and, 62
  pandemic outcomes, 49-56
  pornography and, 60-77
  prostitution and, 71-72
  research. *See* Research
  revictimization in, 43, 71
  romantic partner abuse and, 43-44
  treatment programs, 27
  trust and, 54-55
  types of abusers, 72-74
  verbal aggression, 50
  See also Child homicide; Child neglect; Child sexual abuse
Child Abuse Act (1974), 121
Child Abuse Potential (CAP) Inventory, 129, 130
Child Abuse and Trauma (CAT) scale, 50, 54
Child homicide, 17-34
  accidental deaths, 22
  development perspective, 29-31
  gender and, 18, 19, 26, 29-31
  infanticide, 23-24
  informational sources for, 32

of middle childhood, 26-29
statistics, 17-19, 23, 31-33
teen homicides, 19-22
young children, 22-23
Child molestation, 59, 71
See also Child sexual abuse
Child neglect:
academic achievement and disciplinary problems, 105-111
defined, 24
interpersonal difficulties and, 49
maltreatment as, 105
school performance and, 106
statistics, 24
See also Child abuse
Child pornography. See Pornography
Children:
academic achievements, 105-111
disciplinary problems, 108-111
Traumatic Events Screening Inventory (TESI), 111-117
witnessing marital violence, 91-100
Children's Impact of Traumatic Events Scale, 114
Child sexual abuse:
battered women, history of, 36-37
Black mothers' response to, 80-88
child molesters, 59
denial and, 72
extrafamilial abuse, 59, 66, 69, 73, 75
group sex, 66, 67
incest, 59, 68, 69, 73, 74
intergenerational, 71
intrafamilial abuse, 59, 65-66, 75, 76, 84
organized abuse, 62, 63-67, 76
pedophiles, 27, 59, 62, 72-74
perpetrator networks, 67, 70, 71
pornography and, 60-61
prostitution, 59, 61-62
sexualized children, 68, 72, 74
statistics, 59
violence, 66
of women, 38, 43-44, 59
Chronicity, 122, 132
Circle of victimization, 36
Class differences, marital violence, 4
Codependency, 52
Colorado Springs (CO), domestic violence and police intervention, 236-253
Common law rule, 4
Confidentiality, in therapeutic intervention, 286-287
Conflict Tactics Scale (CTS), 119-133, 185-186, 199

Attitude Towards Aggression correlation, 154-156
chronicity, 132
limitations, 127-128
physical maltreatment measures, 123-125
psychological maltreatment measures, 125
relevance rates, 132
reliability, 126-127
validity, 126-127
Counseling:
batterer programs, 208-218
for Black battered women, 168-169
couples treatment programs, 194-205
feminist therapy for battered women, 219-233
wife abuse victims, 167-168, 219-233
Criminal justice system, spousal abuse of women, 4, 36, 162-163, 166-167, 235-252
Cross-cultural research, 296-311
Cultural norms, marital violence, 3-14
Cycle of victimization, 36
Cycle of violence, 44

Dating, abusive relationships, 170-181
Death. See Child homicide
Death certificates, as source of statistics, 32
Decision making:
included in batterer treatment program, 215-216
in research, 271-280
Depression, child abuse and, 50
Developmental victimology, 29-31
Disciplinary problems, child neglect and, 105-111
Dissociative Experiences Scale, 54
"Domestic disturbance," arrest following, 4, 162-163, 167-168, 235-252
Domestic violence. See Child abuse; Husband abuse; Marital abuse; Romantic partner assault; Wife abuse
Drinking, romantic partner abuse and, 44-45, 165, 186, 191, 241
Drug use:
child homicide and, 20
pornography and prostitution and, 69-70
wife abuse and, 186, 191, 241

Education, marital violence and, 11-12, 13
Emotional abuse, 54, 65, 70
Emotional loneliness, 53-56
Ethical cross-cultural research:
cross-cultural defined, 297
implementing ethical issues in, 298-311
need for, 296-297
research types of, 297-298
Ethical decision making, 215-216
Ethics:
cross-cultural research, 296-311
decision making, in research protocol, 271-280
intervention with violent partners, 282-294
Ethnic lumping, 300
Ethnic minorities:
child homicide, 18
cross-cultural research, 296-311
marital violence and, 5, 10
romantic partner assault, 43
social services appropriateness for, 167
teens, 20
treatment programs and, 197
Extrafamilial child sexual abuse, 59, 66, 69, 73, 75

Family Research Laboratory, 119
Family violence:
advocacy, 262-265
aggression, attitudes toward, 151-159
causes for, 151-152
collaboration between researchers and advocates, 255-266
discussion of research results on, 157-159
family of origin, 185, 187-188
research. See Research
suicide-homicide, 27
See also Child abuse; Marital abuse; Romantic partner assault
FBI (Federal Bureau of Investigation) Uniform Crime Report, 23, 24, 27, 29, 32, 121
Feminist research, 256-257, 303
Feminist therapy, 219-233

Gallup Survey (1994), 5
Gangs, child homicide and, 20, 27
Gender:

attitudes toward aggression, 151-159
Black families and child abuse, 80, 86, 87
child homicide, 18, 19, 26, 29-31
children witnessing marital aggression, 93
child sexual abuse and, 69
marital violence and, 4, 7, 9, 10, 12
pornography and child abuse, 69
Gender roles, 181
Group sex, 66, 67
Guilty knowledge, 310
Guns, child homicides and, 20, 26, 27

Hispanic Americans:
child homicide, 18
marital violence surveys, 5, 10
Homicide, children. *See* Child homicide
Husband abuse:
intervention, ethical issues in, 282-294
slapping surveys, 6, 7, 10, 13

Incest, 59, 64-65
as abuse of power, 69
by abused adults, 71
defined, 69
emotional abuse and, 65
intergenerational nature of, 65, 66, 69, 71
obedience in, 67-68
Infanticide, 23-24
Informed consent, for research, 277-278
Interpersonal discomfort (ID), 54
Interpersonal sensitivity (IS), 54
Intervention:
confidentiality and, 286-287
ethical issues in, 282-294
loyalty and, 285-286
practitioner values and beliefs, 288-293
Intimacy:
defined, 51, 55
model for, 51-56
Intimacy dysfunctions, defined, 52-53, 55, 56
Intrafamilial child sexual abuse, 59, 65-66, 75, 76, 84

Journal of Traumatic Stress, 113
Juvenile homicide. *See* Child homicide

Klaas, Polly, 17

Loneliness, 53
Loyalty, in therapeutic intervention, 285-286

Maltreatment, classifying, 113-117, 119-133, 136-146
See also Child abuse
Marital abuse:
advocacy, 262-265
age and, 4, 10-11, 191
aggression, attitudes toward, 151-159
approval of, 7, 9, 12-13
arrest for, 4, 162-163, 235-252
child outcomes affected by, 91-93, 101-102
child's perspective of, 92-93, 100
collaboration between researchers and advocates, 255-266
counseling for victims, 167-168
depression in children of, 95, 99, 100-102
education and, 11-12, 13
ethnic minorities, 5, 10
Gallup Survey (1994), 5
gender and, 4, 7, 9, 10, 12, 93, 96-100, 100-102
hostility in children of, 95, 99, 100-102
intervention, ethical issues in, 282-294
National Alcohol and Family Violence Survey (1992), 5
National Commission on Cause and Prevention of Violence studies (1968), 4
National Family Violence Survey (1985), 5
National Violence Survey (1968), 5
parenting and, 91, 96-100
police intervention and, 4, 36, 162-163, 166-167, 235-252
research. *See* Research
slapping surveys, 4-14
treatment. *See* Counseling; Treatment programs
See also Husband abuse; Romantic partner assault; Wife abuse
Marital counseling, intact couples, 194-205
Men. *See* Husband abuse
Men of power:
abuse against not believed, 65, 71

feminist view of, 73-74
participate in child pornography, 67
Michigan Alcoholism Screening Test (MAST), 186
Milwaukee (WI), domestic violence and police intervention, 236-253
Minorities. *See* Ethnic minorities
Murder. *See* Child homicide

National Alcohol and Family Violence Survey (1992), 5
National Commission on the Cause and Prevention of Violence Survey, 4-5
National Family Violence Survey (1985), 5
National Society for the Prevention of Cruelty to Children survey (1993), 62
National Violence Survey (1968), 5
National Women's Study, romantic partner abuse, 37-45

Objective reflection, 176
Object Relations Scale (ORS), 54
Omaha (NE), domestic violence and police intervention, 236-253
Order of protection, 4, 166-167
Organized abuse, 72, 75
Organized crime, 62, 63

Parenting, marital violence and, 91-100
Pedophilia, 27, 59, 70
characteristics of, 72, 73, 76
defined, 59, 73
feminist concern over, 73-74
as income source, 62
Physical assault:
CTS Physical Assault scale, 123
of women, 45-56, 161-168
See also Romantic partner assault; Wife abuse
Police response, spousal abuse of women, 4, 36, 162-163, 166-167, 235-252
Pornography, 58-59
adult networks for, 67, 70
availability of, 77
blackmail use of, 61
bondage, 69
by family member, 65-69
child sexual abuse and, 59-77
coercion through violence, 70
drug addiction induced, 70

incest and, 64-65, 73, 74
organized abuse, 63-67
organized crime and, 62
physical abuse in, 70
poverty induced, 70
prostitution and, 61, 67, 69-70
pseudo child pornography, 77
rape in, 70
sex rings and, 62-63
sexual assaults and, 71
victims not believed, 71
Positive parenting, 92, 94-100
Post-traumatic stress disorder
   (PTSD):
   childhood trauma and, 113, 114,
      115
   in women, 38-39, 44-45
Poverty, pornography and
   prostitution and, 69-70
Power assertive parenting, 92,
   94-100
Premarital abuse. See Romantic
   partner assault
Prevalence, 122, 132
Prostitution:
   by family members, 66, 69
   child abuse victims and, 71-72
   child sexual abuse induced,
      69-70, 71
   coercion, 70
   drug addiction induced, 70
   group prostitution and, 67
   international trafficking for, 62
   organized abuse and, 63
   pornography and, 61, 69-70
   poverty induced, 64, 70
Protective issues, classifying
   maltreatment of children,
   136-146
Pseudo child pornography, 77
Psychological aggression scale,
   125, 128
PTSD. See Post-traumatic stress
   disorder

Racism, Black families, and child
   abuse, 80-88
Research:
   advocacy, 262-265
   collaboration in, 255-266
   cross cultural, 296-311
   data gathering, 302-308
   ethical decision making in,
      271-280
   feminist research, 256-257, 303
   informed consent, 277-278

Restraining order, 4, 166-167
Risk markers, wife assault
   cessation, 183-192
Romantic partner assault:
   abusive dating relationships,
      170-181
   child victimization and, 35-45
   leaving and healing, 178-180
   See also Marital abuse; Wife
      abuse

School performance, child neglect
   and, 105-111
Sex rings, 62-63, 72
Sexual abuse (of adults)
   child sexual abuse and, 36-37
   international trafficking of
      women for, 62
   intimacy and, 54
   Third World women and, 62
Sexual abuse (of children). See
   Child sexual abuse
Sexual exploitation of children, 59
   See also Child sexual abuse
Sexualized children, 68, 72, 74
Sexual tourism, 62, 74
Sexual violence. See Child sexual
   abuse; Sexual abuse (of adults)
SIDS. See Sudden infant death
   syndrome
Slapping surveys, 4-14
Smith, Susan, 17
Snuff pornography, 70
Social loneliness, 53
Spousal abuse. See Husband abuse;
   Wife abuse
Steinberg, Joel, 17
Sudden infant death syndrome
   (SIDS), 22, 27, 33

Teen homicide, 19-22
Therapeutic intervention, ethical
   issues in, 282-294
Trauma screening, in children,
   113-115, 117
Traumatic Events Screening
   Inventory (TESI), 114-117
Treatment programs:
   for batterers, 208-217
   child abusers, 27
   for couples, 194-205
   feminist therapy for battered
      women, 219-233
   intervention, ethical issues in,
      282-294

Trust, 54, 55

Verbal abuse, of children, 50
Victimization, etiological role in, 36
Violence. See Child abuse; Family
   violence; Marital abuse;
   Romantic partner assault
Vital records, as source of statistics,
   32

Wife abuse, 3-4
   advocacy, 262-265
   arrest of violent men, 4, 162-163,
      235-252
   batterer programs, 208-217
   batterer's attitude toward,
      151-152
   cessation, 184, 190, 191
   characteristics of batterers, 91
   collaboration between
      researchers and advocates,
      255-266
   counseling of victims, 167-168
   couples treatment programs,
      194-205
   criminal justice and, 4, 162-163,
      167, 235-242
   cultural norms, 3-14, 161
   feminist therapy for battered
      women, 219-233
   intervention, ethical issues in,
      282-294
   police intervention and, 4, 36,
      162-163, 166-167, 235-252
   premarital assault, 171-180
   preventive programs, 168
   racial differences in, 161-162,
      163
   research. See Research
   restraining orders in, 4, 166-167
   self-referring couples for therapy
      of, 195
   slapping survey, 4-14
   social predictors of cessation,
      183-192
   social services for, 4, 162, 163
   therapy decreases violence in,
      205
   treatment. See Counseling;
      Treatment programs
   See also Romantic partner assault
Women:
   childhood victimization of, 36, 38
   physical abuse of, 35-45
   prostitution, 62, 63-67

About the Editors

Glenda Kaufman Kantor has been a Research Professor at the University of New Hampshire, Family Research Laboratory for several years. Her major research interests are related to the etiology and prevention of intimate violence and fatal child abuse; the criminal justice system response to family violence; the linkages between substance abuse and family violence, and structural and cultural influences on alcohol and wife abuse. Her recent federally (NIAAA) funded research projects include a longitudinal analysis of family members' alcohol use, marital conflict and violence, and a national study of alcohol and intra-family violence in Latino and Anglo-American families.

Jana L. Jasinski, Ph.D., is a National Institute of Mental Health postdoctoral Research Fellow at the Family Research Laboratory at the University of New Hampshire. Her research interests are in the area of interpersonal violence, in particular partner violence among Latinos, the response of the criminal justice system to violence, and substance abuse as a negative consequence of child sexual assault. In addition, she has research interests in criminology, research methodology, and social policy development. She has presented her research at numerous conferences and has published several articles.

About the Contributors

Etiony Aldarondo, Ph.D., is Assistant Professor of Counseling Psychology at Boston College, where he conducts research on risk markers for wife assault, the resolution of violence in intimate relationships, and the treatment of men who batter. Academic awards include Phi Beta Kappa, the Ford Foundation Minority Dissertation Fellowship, and the American Psychological Association Dissertation Award.

Ginette Beaudoin, M.S., is Research Assistant at Laval University in Quebec. She currently works with researchers of the Interdisciplinary Research Center on Family Violence and Violence Against Women on different aspects of domestic violence.

Evvie Becker-Lausen, Ph.D., Assistant Professor of Clinical Psychology at the University of Connecticut, was a 1993-1994 Fellow at Boston Children's Hospital and Harvard University and the recipient of a National Research Service Award for research in family violence. Prior to that, she was a 1992-1993 Congressional Science Fellow sponsored by the American Psychological Association (APA).

Claudia Bernard teaches in the Department of Applied Human Sciences at Goldsmith's College, University of London. She has previously worked with children and families as a social worker and counselor. She has worked on issues of violence against women and children for a number of years. Her research focuses on the interplay between race, gender, social class, and social welfare.

Connie L. Best is a clinical psychologist and Associate Professor of Clinical Psychology in the Department of Psychiatry and Behavioral Sciences of the Medical University of South Carolina in Charleston. She is Director of Adult Services at the National Crime Victims Research and Treatment Center. She is well published in professional journals and has made presentations to local, national, and international groups.

Normand Brodeur, M.S., is Research Assistant at the University of Montreal, Quebec. He has worked as a therapist with batterers and participated in research projects in this field.

Pamela D. Brown received her B.A. from Wheaton College and an M.S. in experimental psychology from Howard University. She is completing her Ph.D. in clinical psychology at the University at Stony Brook. Her dissertation examines the therapeutic alliance and its relationship to both treatment dropout and treatment outcome (i.e., increased marital satisfaction and decreased psychological and physical aggression).

Jacquelyn Campbell, Ph.D., R.N., FAAN, is currently the Anna D. Wolf Endowed Professor and Director of the doctoral programs at Johns Hopkins University School of Nursing with a joint appointment in the School of Hygiene and Public Health. She is principal investigator of five NIH, DOD, or CDC major funded research studies on battering and author or coauthor of more than 50 publications.

Solange Cantin, M.A., is a professional social worker and Coordinator of the research team on conjugal violence at the Interdisciplinary Research Center on Family Violence and Violence Against Women. She has also participated in many research projects on conjugal violence and has published many reports and articles dealing with this subject.

John Eckenrode is Professor in the Department of Human Development and Family Studies at Cornell University and Associate Director of the Family Life Development Center. His research concerns child abuse and neglect, and stress and coping processes. He is a social psychologist and has directed federally funded projects. He has authored of over 30 journal articles and chapters and edited two books, *Stress Between Work and Family* and *The Social Context of Coping.*

Jason H. Edwards, Ph.D., is Assistant Professor of Psychology and Coordinator of the Marital and Family Therapy Concentration in the Department of Psychology at Assumption College. His teaching, research, and clinical interests are in the area of clinical child and family psychology.

David Finkelhor, Ph.D., is Codirector of the Family Research Laboratory at the University of New Hampshire. He has studied the problem of family violence since 1977 and has published numerous books, including *Sourcebook on Child Sexual Abuse, Nursery Crimes, Stopping Family Violence, License to Rape,* and *Child Sexual Abuse: New Theory and Research.* He is coeditor of *Dark Side of Families* and *New Directions in Family Violence and Abuse Research.*

Susan F. Folstein, M.D., is Director of Child and Adolescent Psychiatry at Tufts University School of Medicine/New England Medical Center. She has published extensively on topics regarding psychiatric genetics and child and adolescent psychiatry. She is interested in the ethical issues regarding genetic testing, especially the implications of presymptomatic genetic testing.

Lisa Aronson Fontes, Ph.D., has written and presented extensively on issues of culture in family violence, particularly child sexual abuse. She has conducted research in Santiago, Chile, in rural Indiana, and with Puerto Ricans in Massachusetts. She has worked as a clinical supervisor and a family, individual, and group therapist in a variety of settings. She is editor of *Sexual Abuse in Nine North American Cultures: Treatment and Prevention.*

Edward W. Gondolf, Ed.D., M.P.H., is Associate Director of Research for the Mid-Atlantic Addiction Training Institute, where he conducts research on the response of the courts, mental health practitioners, alcohol treatment clinicians, and batterer treatment programs. He is also Professor of Sociology at Indiana University of Pennsylvania and a faculty associate of the Center for Injury Research and Control at the University of Pittsburgh Medical Center.

Sherry L. Hamby, Ph.D., has been involved in the research and treatment of domestic violence for over 10 years. She received her Ph.D. in clinical psychology from the University of North Carolina. She was Research Fellow at the Family Research Laboratory in 1994-1996, where she helped revise the Conflict Tactics Scales, among other projects. She is currently a clinical and research psychologist for the San Carlos

Apache Tribe in Arizona. In addition to her research and clinical work, she is active in community education efforts.

Sharon D. Herzberger is Professor of Psychology at Trinity College in Hartford, CT. She received her B.A. from Pennsylvania State University and her M.A. and Ph.D. from the University of Illinois. She taught at Northwestern University before coming to Trinity in 1980. She teaches courses in social psychology, aggression, and socialization within the family. Her book, *Violence Within the Family: Social Psychological Perspectives,* was published in 1996.

Catherine Itzin, Ph.D., is Research Professor in Social Work and Social Policy in the School of Social and International Studies at the University of Sunderland, U.K. She is editor and coauthor of *Pornography: Women, Violence, and Civil Liberties* and author of "Pornographic and Violent Videos" in *Video Violence and Young Offenders* and "Pornography, Harm and Human Rights: The European Context" in *Sexual Politics and the European Union.*

Richard S. John, Ph.D., is Associate Professor of Psychology at the University of Southern California. He received his Ph.D. in qualitative psychology from the University of Southern California. His research has focused on the dynamics of family systems.

Janice Joseph is Associate Professor in the Criminal Justice Program at Richard Stockton College of New Jersey. Her research interests include violence against women, women and criminal justice youth violence, juvenile delinquency, gangs, and minorities and criminal justice.

Danny G. Kaloupek, Ph.D., is a clinical psychologist, Deputy Director of the Behavioral Science Division of the National Center for PTSD at the Boston VA Medical Center, and Clinical Associate Professor of Psychiatry (Psychology) at Tufts University School of Medicine. His recent work addresses the use of psychophysiological measures to assess PTSD and the iden-

tification of trauma-related problems among individuals in primary care medical clinics.

Terence M. Keane, Ph.D., is Director of the National Center for PTSD–Behavioral Sciences Division, Professor of Psychiatry at Boston University School of Medicine, and Chief of the Psychology Service at the Boston VA Medical Center. Currently President of the International Society for Traumatic Stress Studies, Keane has published extensively on the topics of assessment, diagnosis, and treatment of PTSD.

Kathleen A. Kendall-Tackett, Ph.D., is a developmental psychologist, a consulting psychologist with the Perinatal Education Group of Henniker, New Hampshire, and Research Associate at the Family Research Laboratory, University of New Hampshire. Her research interests include child maltreatment, perinatal health, maternal depression, and breast-feeding.

Dean G. Kilpatrick is Professor of Clinical Psychology and Director of the National Crime Victims Research and Treatment Center at the Medical University of South Carolina in Charleston. He and his colleagues have received several grants from the National Institute of Mental Health, National Institute of Justice, and the National Institute on Drug Abuse supporting their research on the scope of violent crime and its psychological effect on victims. He has over 100 journal publications and has made numerous presentations.

Amy C. Krull is a Ph.D. candidate in sociology at Purdue University. She teaches a sociology course on child abuse and neglect. Her Ph.D. research examines caretakers' responsibilities for elder family members.

Jocelyn Lindsay, Ph.D., is a faculty member of the School of Social Work at Laval University in Quebec, teaching group work. Lindsay is also affiliated with the Interdisciplinary Research Center on Family Violence and Violence Against Women and has conducted research on the effectiveness of treatment programs for men who batter and on psychological violence.

Alan J. Litrownik is Professor and former Chair of the Psychology Department at San Diego State University. He is one of the founders of the San Diego State University/University of California, San Diego Joint Doctoral Program in Clinical Psychology, and he is currently a member of its faculty. In addition, he is currently Codirector of the Interdisciplinary Child Abuse Training Program initially funded by NCCAN, and Associate Director of NIMH's Child and Adolescent Mental Health Services Research Center.

Sharon Mallon-Kraft is a doctoral candidate in clinical psychology at the University of Connecticut, where her research focuses on the relationship between childhood trauma and the capacity for intimate relationships in young adulthood. She received a B.S. with honors in psychology from Trinity College and is a member of Phi Beta Kappa and Pi Gamma Mu Honor Societies. At Trinity, she conducted research on children's perceptions of gender stereotyping in storybooks. Prior to entering graduate school, she was an elementary school teacher.

Gayla Margolin is Professor of Psychology at the University of Southern California. She received her Ph.D. in clinical psychology from the University of Oregon. She received a Guggenheim Career Development Award and the 1993 Award for Distinguished Contribution to Family Research from the American Family Therapy Academy. Her research and writings have focused on marital therapy, family interaction, and marital violence and its effects on children.

JoAnn L. Miller is Associate Professor of Sociology at Purdue University. Her research and teaching are in the sociology of law field, especially family law and domestic violence. Her scholarship is largely influenced by her mentor, Dean D. Knudsen, who works on behalf of all victims of family violence.

David W. Moore is currently a vice president at the Gallup Organization and Managing Editor of the Gallup Poll. Previously, he was Professor of Political Science at the University of New Hampshire and Research Associate at the Family Research Laboratory, University of New Hampshire, where he participated in studies that focused on child abuse and on elder abuse in nursing homes. At the Gallup Organization, he has participated in the design of national surveys that measure people's attitudes about disciplining children.

Elana Newman, Ph.D., is a clinical psychologist and Assistant Professor of Psychology at the University of Tulsa. She conducts research on the assessment, diagnosis, and treatment of trauma-related disorders with children and adults. Her current endeavors include a study of trauma exposure and sex role egalitarian beliefs among college students, an empirical investigation on the impact of being a participant in trauma-related studies, and a study of the relationship of previous trauma exposure and sexual risk-taking behaviors.

K. Daniel O'Leary is Distinguished Professor of Psychology at the University at Stony Brook. He was president of the American Association for Advancement of Behavior Therapy and received the Distinguished Scientist Award from the Clinical Division of the American Psychological Association. He holds an NIMH Research Training Grant for pre- and postdoctoral fellows who study wife abuse. Most recently, he wrote the *DSM-IV Diagnosis for Relationship Problems With Partner Abuse* and the corresponding source book chapter on partner abuse.

Heidi S. Resnick, Ph.D., is Associate Professor of Clinical Psychology at the National Crime Victims Research and Treatment Center at the Medical University of South Carolina. Her major research interest is the study of factors involved in the development of posttraumatic stress following civilian trauma. In addition, she is studying rape victims' concerns about their physical health following rape, and development of appropriate medical care and health care counseling for rape victims, including information about HIV and risk reduction.

Maryse Rinfret-Raynor, Ph.D., is Professor in the School of Social Work and Vice-Dean of Academics in the Faculty of Arts and Sciences at the University of Montreal, Quebec. She is Codirector of the Interdisciplinary Research Center on Family Violence and Violence Against Women. As a specialist in evaluation research, she has directed many research projects on conjugal violence and is well published on the subject.

Karen C. Rogers is a psychologist who works in community mental health and is Adjunct Research Associate at Dartmouth Medical School. Her research interests include the prevalence and impact of trauma and stress in childhood.

Gilles Rondeau, Ph.D., teaches social work at the University of Montreal, Quebec. Over the past decade, he has been involved in the development of treatment programs for men who batter, in policy development to stop family violence, and in research in this field. He is currently affiliated with the Interdisciplinary Research Center on Family Violence Against Women.

Karen H. Rosen, Ed.D., is Assistant Professor in the Department of Family and Child Development at Virginia Tech. She is also licensed as a professional counselor in Virginia and a Clinical Member and Approved Supervisor of the American Association for Marriage and Family Therapy. Domestic violence is her major research focus. She has coedited a book on this topic with Sandra Stith, *Violence Hits Home,* and has published numerous book chapters and journal articles relating to the etiology, prevention, and treatment of domestic violence.

Quentin H. Rueckert is Primary Counselor at The Blue Ridge Center in Bloomfield, CT. He received his B.S. in psychology from Trinity College. Since 1990, he has been working with chemically dependent people and their families. He is currently pursuing doctoral studies in clinical psychology.

Benjamin E. Saunders is Associate Professor in the Department of Psychiatry and Behavioral Sciences at the Medical University of South Carolina. He directs the Family and Child Program of the National Crime Victims Research

and Treatment Center. He has published numerous scientific papers and made many scientific and training presentations concerning criminal victimization, child sexual assault, sexual offenders, and marital and family relationships. He also maintains an active clinical and consulting practice.

Sandra M. Stith is Associate Professor in the Department of Family and Child Development and Director of Virginia Tech's Marriage and Family Therapy program. She is an AAMFT Clinical Member and Approved Supervisor and a licensed professional counselor in Virginia. Her primary research interests are in partner violence and adolescent sexual offending. She is principal editor of *Understanding Partner Violence: Prevalence, Causes, Consequences and Solutions,* coedited with Murray Straus, and *Violence Hits Home,* coedited with Karen Rosen and Mary Beth Williams.

Murray A. Straus is Professor of Sociology and founder and Codirector of the Family Research Laboratory at the University of New Hampshire. He is author or coauthor of over 200 articles on the family, research methods, and South Asia, and 15 books, including *Stress, Culture, and Aggression, Beating the Devil Out of Them: Corporal Punishment in American Families, Physical Violence in American Families, Four Theories of Rape, Intimate Violence, Social Stress in the United States, The Dark Side of Families,* and *Behind Closed Doors: Violence in the American Family.*

Heather N. Taussig is a fourth-year doctoral student in the San Diego State University/ University of California, San Diego Joint Doctoral Program in Clinical Psychology. She has been conducting research with the Child and Family Research Group in San Diego for several years, and she plans to pursue an academic career after her predoctoral clinical internship at Stanford.

Terri L. Weaver, Ph.D., is Assistant Research Professor of Psychology at the University of Missouri–St. Louis, Center for Trauma Recovery. She received her Ph.D. in clinical psychology from Virginia Polytechnic Institute and State University. She completed an NIMH-funded fellowship at the National Crime Victims Research and Treatment Center. Currently, research and clinical interests include assessment and treatment of victims of rape and domestic violence, etiological factors related to the development of PTSD, and examination of the impact of trauma on health and physical functioning.

Kersti Yllö is Professor of Sociology at Wheaton College in Massachusetts. She received her

Ph.D. from the University of New Hampshire where she was Research Associate with the Family Research Laboratory. She has written on the status of women and wife abuse, cohabitation, marital rape, battering during pregnancy, and feminist methodology. Her publications include *Feminist Perspectives on Wife Abuse* (with M. Bograd) and *License to Rape* (with D. Finkelhor). She is currently working on projects with the AWAKE program at Boston Children's Hospital and the U.S. Marine Corps.